D1713759

# The Sand Creek Massacre

## A DOCUMENTARY HISTORY

*With an Introduction by*
John M. Carroll

## Amereon
## House

First published as a report of the Joint Committee
on the Conduct of the War, Massacre of the
Cheyenne Indians, 38th Congress, Second Session,
Washington, 1965; and report of the Secretary
of War, 39th Congress, Second Session, Senate
Executive Document No. 26, Washington, 1867

The edition includes the reply of Governor Evans
of the Territory of Colorado, 1865


Reprinted 1973 in a one-volume Limited Edition
of 500 copies by Sol Lewis

*Special Contents 1973 © by Sol Lewis*

Library of Congress Catalogue Card Number 73-85602
International Standard Book Number 0-914074-03-2



MANUFACTURED IN THE UNITED STATES OF AMERICA




SOL LEWIS, New York 10003

# INTRODUCTION

There is an old favorite folk-song in this country which goes like this:
The toe-bone is connected to the foot-bone,
The foot-bone is connected to the ankle-bone,
The ankle-bone is connected to the leg-bone,
Now hear the words of the Lord.
It continues until the whole skeleton of man is accounted for as an entity. Now, this song can be translated into:
The Lt. Grattan massacre is connected to the
  Sioux War of 1862,
The Sioux War of 1862 is connected to the
  Sand Creek Massacre of 1864,
The Sand Creek Massacre of 1864 is connected to
  the Battle of the Washita in 1868,
Now hear the words of the Lord.
Of course, the rhythm of the song has been disturbed by the introduction of new words but the final product, the interrelation of all the Indian wars, massacres and battles, is the same. When totalled, their sum is equal to the general policy of elimination of the Indian in the west. Only no one ever seemed to listen to the words of the Lord.

In 1864, toward the end of the Civil War, Governor John Evans of the Territory of Colorado attempted to get help in the form of Federal troops to put down what he implied was a large scale Indian uprising. In effect, there were isolated instances of Indian raids, theft and other depredations, but they were not part of a large and organized effort by the Indians; instead, they were little pockets of resistance much like that found anywhere in the world at anytime when change is inevitable but not necessarily accepted by all. But the Governor, for reasons never fully explained, had advocated war with the Indians from the time he took office. Perhaps it was part of a grand scheme of a movement toward statehood, and the end of hostilities would bring the settlers into Colorado

i

Territory in the necessary numbers to assure a voting balance in favor of statehood. But there has never been any official evidence of his motives in print or a matter of record.

When he believed the time was ripe—or necessary—to seek national recognition of his unpublished plan, he wired Washington: "Extensive Indian depredations, with murder of families, occurred yesterday thirty miles south of Denver. Our lines of communication are cut . . . Large bodies of Indians are undoubtedly near Denver, and we are in danger of destruction both from attacks of Indians and from starvation." There was never any shred of proof to verify these extraordinary claims of his, and fortunately cooler heads prevailed in Washington and they refused to send troops. Besides, a war was going on back East and no large number of military could be spared. Instead, they gave official Federal sanction to the creation of a volunteer regiment—the 3rd Colorado Volunteers—for a specified period of time to take care of the "problems" faced by the Territory and the Governor, real or imaginary. It was the 3rd. Colorado Volunteers lead by Colonel Chivington—more for political purposes than any other—and guided by the famous black mountain man, James Beckwourth, who were directly responsible for the infamous Sand Creek Massacre exposed here in print and found in official documents published in Washington.

There was ample evidence of various kinds of frontier problems and dangers, but they were on a minor scale and isolated and performed by malcontents within the ranks of the Indian tribes who were friendly and some not so friendly. This, however, is an over-all observation and not one based on personal or individual cases which tend to slant opinions and attitudes. Certainly there were immediate problems to look after such as kidnappings and the like. The following statement of Mrs. Ewbanks is but one example:

*Statement of Mrs. Ewbanks, giving an account of her captivity among the Indians. She was taken by the* CHEYENNES, *and was one of the prisoners proposed to be given up by Black Kettle, White Antelope and others, in the Council at Denver.*

Mrs. Lucinda Ewbanks states that she was born in Pennsylvania; is 24 years of age; she resided on the Little Blue, at or near the Narrows. She says that on the 8th day of August, 1864, the house was attacked, robbed, burned, and herself and two children, with her nephew and Miss Roper, were captured by the Cheyenne Indians. Her eldest child, at the time, was three years old; her youngest was one year old; her nephew was six years old. When taken from her home, was, by the Indians, taken south across the Republican, and west to a creek the name of which she does not remember. Here, for a short time, was their village or camping place. They were traveling all winter. When first taken by the Cheyennes, she was taken to the lodge of an old chief whose name she does [not] recollect. He forced me, by the most terrible threats and menaces, to yield my person to him. He treated me as his wife. He then traded me to Two Face, a Sioux, who did not treat me as a wife, but forced me to do all menial labor done by squaws, and he beat me terribly. Two Face traded me to Black Foot (Sioux) who treated me as his wife, and because I resisted him his squaws abused and ill-used me. Black Foot also beat me unmercifully, and the Indians generally treated me as though I was a dog, on account of my showing so much detestation towards Black Foot. Two Face traded for me again. I then received a little better treatment. I was better treated among the Sioux than the Cheyennes, that is, the Sioux gave me more to eat. When with the Cheyennes, I was often hungry. Her purchase from the Cheyennes was made early last Fall, and she remained with them until May, 1865. During the winter the Cheyennes came to buy me and the child, for the purpose of burning us, but Two Face would not let them have me. During the winter we were on the North Platte, the Indians were killing the whites all the time and running off their stock. They would bring in the scalps of the whites and show them to me and laugh about it. They ordered me frequently to wean my baby, but I always refused: for I felt convinced if he was weaned they would take him from me and I should never see him again. They took my daughter from me just after we were captured, and I never saw her after. I have seen the man to-day who had her—his name is Davenport. He lives in Denver. He received her from a Dr. Smith. She was given up by the Cheyennes to Major Wynkoop, but from injuries received while with the Indians, she died last February. My nephew also was given up to Major Wynkoop, but he, too, died at Denver. The Doctor said it was caused by bad treatment from the Indians. Whilst encamped on the North Platte, Elston came to the village, and I went with him and Two Face to Fort Laramie.

I have heard it stated that a story had been told by me, to the effect that Two Face's son had saved my life. I never made any such statement, as I have no knowledge of any such thing, and I think if my life had been in danger he would not have troubled himself about it.

    (Signed)                                                      LUCINDA EWBANKS.

Witness: J. H. Triggs, 1st Lt. Comd'g Co. D, 7th Iowa Cavalry; E. B. Zabriskie, Capt. 1st Cav. Nev. Volunteers, Judge Advocate, Dist. of the Plains.

JULESBURG, C. T., June 22, 1865.

However, these problems were best handled by the responsible agents and most certainly not by hysterical telegrams to Washington containing fraudulant exaggerations.

Major Wynkoop even attempted a peace maneuver by bringing several of the Indian chiefs to Denver for a parley with Governor Evans and other officials of the Territory. A copy of the report of this council is included here:

# REPORT

Of Council with Cheyenne and Arapahoe Chiefs and Warriors, brought to Denver by Major Wynkoop; taken down by U. S. Indian Agent Simeon Whiteley as it Progressed.

CAMP WELD, DENVER, Wednesday, Sept. 28, 1864.

PRESENT—Gov. John Evans, Col. Chivington, Comd'g Dist. Colorado, Col. Geo. L. Shoup, Third Colorado Volunteer Cavalry, Maj. E. Wynkoop, Colorado First, S. Whiteley, U. S. Ind. Agt.

Black Kettle, leading Cheyenne Chief.
White Antelope, Chief central Cheyenne band.
Bull Bear, leader of Dog Soldiers, [Cheyenne.)
Neva, sub-Arapahoe Chief, (who was in Washington.)
Bosse, sub-Arapahoe Chief.
Heap of Buffalo, Arapahoe Chief.
Na-ta-nee, Arapahoe Chief

The Arapahoes are all relatives of Left Hand, Chief of the Arapahoes, and are sent by him in his stead.

John Smith, Interpreter to the Upper Arkansas Agency, and many other citizens and officers.

His Excellency Gov. Evans asked the Indians what they had to say.

Black Kettle then said: On sight of your circular of June 27th, 1864, I took hold of the matter, and have now come to talk to you about it. I told Mr. Bent, who brought it, that I accepted it, but it would take some time to get all my people together—many of my young men being absent—and I have done everything in my power, since then, to keep peace with the whites. As soon as I could get my people together, we held a council, and got a half-breed who was with them, to write a letter to inform Major Wynkoop, or other military officer nearest to them, of their intention to comply with the terms of the circular. Major Wynkoop was kind enough to receive the letter, and visited them in camp, to whom they delivered four white prisoners—one other (Mrs. Snyder,) having killed herself; that there are two women and one child yet in their camp, whom they will deliver up as soon as they can get them in: Laura Roper, 16 or 17 years; Ambrose Asher, 7 or 8 years; Daniel Marble, 7 or 8 years, Isabel Ubanks, 4 or 5 years. The prisoners still with them [are] Mrs. Ubanks and babe, and a Mrs. Morton, who was taken on the Platte. Mrs. Snyder is the name of the woman who hung herself. The boys were taken between Fort Kearney and the Blue.

I followed Maj. Wynkoop to Fort Lyon, and Major Wynkoop proposed that we come up to see you. We have come with our eyes shut, following his handful of men, like coming through the fire. All we ask is that we may have peace with the whites. We want to hold you by the hand. You are our father. We have been traveling through a cloud. The sky has been dark ever since the war began. These braves who are with me are all willing to do what I say. We want to take good tidings home to our people, that they may sleep in peace. I want you to give all these chiefs of the soldiers here to understand that we are for peace, and that we have made peace, that we may not be mistaken by them for enemies. I have not come here with a little wolf bark, but have come to talk plain with you. We must live near the buffalo, or starve. When we came here we came free, without any apprehension, to see you, and when I go home and tell my people that I have taken your hand, and the hands of all the chiefs here in Denver, they will feel well, and so will all the different tribes of Indians on the plains, after we have eaten and drank with them.

Gov. Evans replied: I am sorry you did not respond to my appeal at once. You have gone into an alliance with the Sioux, who were at war with us. You have done a great deal of damage—have stolen stock, and now have possession of it. However much a few individuals may have tried to keep the peace, as a nation you have gone to war. While we have been spending thousands of dollars in opening farms for you, and making preparations to feed, protect, and make you comfortable, you have joined our enemies and gone to war. Hearing, last fall, that they were dissatisfied, the Great Father at Washington sent me out on the plains to talk with you and make it all right. I sent messengers out to tell you that I had presents, and would make you a feast, but you sent word to me that you did not want to have anything to do with me, and to the Great Father at Washington that you could get along without him. Bull Bear wanted to come in to see me, at the head of the Republican, but his people held a council and would not let him come.

*Black Kettle*—That is true.

*Gov. Evans*—I was under the necessity, after all my trouble, and all the expense I was at, of returning home without seeing them. Instead of this, your people went away and smoked the war pipe with our enemies.

*Black Kettle*—I don't know who could have told you this.

*Gov. Evans*—No matter who said this, but your conduct has proved to my satisfaction that was the case.

*Several Indians*—This is a mistake. We have made no alliance with the Sioux or any one else.

*Gov.* Evans explained that smoking the war pipe was a figurative term, but their conduct had been such as to show they had an understanding with other tribes.

*Several Indians*—We acknowledge that our actions have given you reason to believe this.

*Gov. Evans*—So far as making a treaty now, is concerned, we are in no condition to do it. Your young men are on the war path. My soldiers are preparing for the fight. You, so far, have had the advantage; but the time is near at hand when the plains will swarm with United States soldiers. I understand that these men who have come to see me now, have been opposed to the war all the time, but that their people have controlled them and they could not help themselves. Is this so?

*All the Indians*—It has been so.

*Gov. Evans*—The fact that they have not been able to prevent their people from going to war in the past spring, when there was plenty of grass and game, makes me believe that they will not be able to make a peace which will last longer than until winter is past.

*White Antelope*—I will answer that after a time.

*Gov. Evans*—The time when you can make war best, is in the summer time; when I can make war best, is in the winter. You, so far, have had the advantage; my time is just coming. I have learned that you understand that as the whites are at war among themselves, you think you can now drive the whites from this country. But this reliance is false. The Great Father at Washington has men enough to drive all the Indians off the plains, and whip the rebels at the same time. Now the war with the whites is nearly through, and the Great Father will not know what to do with all his soldiers, except to send them after the Indians on the plains. My proposition to the friendly Indians has gone out; I shall be glad to have them all come in, under it. I have no new propositions to make. Another reason that I am not in a condition to make a treaty, is, that war is begun, and the power to make a treaty of peace has passed from me to the great War Chief. My advice to you, is, to turn on the side of the government, and show, by your acts, that friendly disposition you profess to me. It is utterly out of the question for you to be at peace with us, while living with our enemies, and being on friendly terms with them.

*Inquiry made by one Indian*—What was meant by being on the side of the government?

Explanation being made, all gave assent, saying "All right."

*Gov. Evans*—The only way you can show this friendship is by making some arrangement with the soldiers to help them.

*Black Kettle*—We will return with Major Wynkoop to Fort Lyon; we will then proceed to our village, and take back word to my young men, every word you say. I cannot answer for all of them, but think there will be but little difficulty in getting them to assent to help the soldiers.

*Major Wynkoop*—Did not the Dog Soldiers agree, when I had my council with you, to do whatever you said, after you had been here?

*Black Kettle*—Yes.

*Gov.* Evans explained that if the Indians did not keep with the U. S. soldiers, or have an arrangement with them, they would be all treated as enemies. You understand, if you are at peace with us it is necessary to keep away from our enemies. But I hand you over to the military, one of the chiefs of which is here to-day, and can speak for himself, to them, if he chooses.

*White Antelope*—I understand every word you have said, and will hold on to it. I will give you an answer directly. The Cheyennes, all of them, have their eyes open this way, and they will hear what you say. He is proud to have seen the chief of all the whites in this country. He will tell his people. Ever since he went to Washington and received this medal, I have called all white men as my brothers. But other Indians have since been to Washington, and got medals, and now the soldiers do not shake hands, but seek to kill me. What do you mean by us fighting your enemies? Who are they?

*Gov. Evans*—All Indians who are fighting us.

*White Antelope*—How can we be protected from the soldiers on the plains?

*Gov. Evans*—You must make that arrangement with the Military Chief.

*White Antelope*—I fear that these new soldiers who have gone out, may kill some of my people while I am here.

*Gov. Evans*—There is great danger of it.

*White Antelope*—When we sent our letter to Major Wynkoop, it was like going through a strong fire or blast, for Major Wynkoop's men to come to our camp; it was the same for us to come to see you. We have our doubts whether the Indians south of the Arkansas, or those north of the Platte, will do as you say. A large number of Sioux have crossed the Platte, in the vicinity of the Junction, into their country. When Major Wynkoop came, we proposed to make peace. He said he had no power to make a peace, except to bring them here and return them safe.

*Gov. Evans*— Again, whatever peace they make, must be with the soldiers, and not with me.

*Gov. Evans*—Are the Apaches at war with the whites?

*White Antelope*—Yes, and the Camanches and Kiowas as well: also a tribe of Indians from Texas, whose names we do not know. There are thirteen different bands of Sioux who have crossed the Platte and are in alliance with the others named.

*Gov. Evans*—How many warriors with the Apaches, Kiowas and Camanches?

*White Antelope*—A good many. Don't know.

*Gov. Evans*—How many of the Sioux?

*White Antelope*—Don't know, but many more than of the southern tribes.

*Gov. Evans*—Who committed the depredation on the trains near the Junction, about the 1st of August?

*White Antelope*—Do not know—did not know any was committed. Have taken you by the hand, and will tell the truth, keeping back nothing.

*Gov. Evans*—Who committed the murder of the Hungate family, on Running Creek?

*Neva*—The Arapahoes; a party of the northern band who were passing north. It was Medicine Man, or Roman Nose, and three others. I am satisfied from the time he left a certain camp for the north, that it was this party of four persons.

*Agent Whiteley*—That cannot be true.

*Gov. Evans*—Where is Roman Nose?

*Neva*—You ought to know better than me. You have been nearer to him.

*Gov. Evans*—Who killed the man and boy at the head of Cherry Creek?

*Neva*—(After consultation)—Kiowas and Camanches.

*Gov. Evans*—Who stole soldier's horses and mules from Jimmy's Camp, twenty-seven days ago?

*Neva*—Fourteen Cheyennes and Arapahoes, together.

*Gov. Evans*—What were their names?

*Neva*—Powder Face and Whirlwind, who are now in our camp, were the leaders.

*Col. Shoup*—I counted twenty Indians, on that occasion.

*Gov. Evans*—Who stole Charley Autobee's horses?

*Neva*—Raven's son.

*Gov. Evans*—Who took the stock from Fremont's Orchard, and had the first fight with the soldiers this spring, north of there?

*White Antelope*—Before answering this question I would like for you to know that this was the beginning of war, and I should like to know what it was for, a soldier fired first.

*Gov. Evans*—The Indians had stolen about forty horses, the soldiers went to recover them, and the Indians fired a volley into their ranks.

*White Antelope*—This is all a mistake. They were coming down the Bijou, and found one horse and one mule. They returned one horse before they got to Geary's, to a man, then went to Geary's, expecting to turn the other one over to some one. They then heard that the soldiers and Indians were fighting, somewhere down the Platte; then they took fright and all fled.

*Gov. Evans*—Who were the Indians who had the fight?

*White Antelope*—They were headed by the Fool Badger's son, a young man, one of the greatest of the Cheyenne warriors, who was wounded, and though still alive he will never recover.

*Neva*—I want to say something. It makes me feel bad to be talking about these things and opening old sores.

*Gov. Evans*—Let him speak.

*Neva*—Mr. Smith has known me ever since I was a child. Has he ever known me commit depredations on the whites? I went to Washington last year—received good council. I hold on to it. I determined to always keep peace with the whites. Now, when I shake hands with them they seem to pull away. I came here to seek peace and nothing else.

*Gov. Evans*—We feel that they have, by their stealing and murdering, done us great damage. They come here and say they will tell me all, and that is what I am trying to get.

*Neva*—The Camanches, Kiowas and Sioux have done much more injury than we have. We will tell what we know, but cannot speak for others.

*Gov. Evans*—I suppose you acknowledge the depredations on the Little Blue, as you have the prisoners then taken, in your possession.

*White Antelope*—We (the Cheyennes) took two prisoners, west of Fort Kearney, and destroyed the trains.

*Gov. Evans*—Who committed depredations at Cottonwood?

*White Antelope*—The Sioux. What band, we do not know.

*Gov. Evans*—What are the Sioux going to do next?

*Bull Bear*—Their plan is to clean out all this country. They are angry, and will do all the damage to the whites they can. I am with you and the troops to fight all those who have no ears to listen to what you say. Who are they? Show them to me. I am not yet old—I am young. I have never hurt a white man. I am pushing for something good. I am always going to be friends with the whites—they can do me good.

*Gov. Evans*— Where are the Sioux?

*Bull Bear*—Down on the Republican, where it opens out.

*Gov. Evans*—Do you know that they intend to attack the trains this week?

*Bull Bear*—Yes. About one-half of all the Missouri River Sioux and Yanktons, who were driven from Minnesota, are those who have crossed the Platte I am young and can fight. I have given my word to fight with the whites. My brother (Lean Bear) died in trying to keep peace with the whites. I am willing to die in the same way, and expect to do so.

*Neva*—I know the value of the presents which we receive from Washington. We cannot live without them. That is why I try so hard to keep peace with the whites.

*Gov. Evans*—I cannot say anything about those things, now.

*Neva*—I can speak for all the Arapahoes under Left Hand. Raven has sent no one here to speak for him. Raven has fought the whites.

*Gov. Evans*—Are there any white men among your people?

*Neva*—There are none except Keith, who is now in the store at Fort Larned.

*Col. Chivington*—I am not a big war chief, but all the soldiers in this country are at my command. My rule of fighting white men or Indians is to fight them until they lay down their arms and submit to military authority. They are nearer Major Wynkoop than any one else, and they can go to him when they get ready to do that.

The Council then adjourned.

---

I CERTIFY that this report is correct and complete; that I took down the talk of the Indians in the exact words of the Interpreter, and of the other parties as given to him, without change of phraseology, or correction of any kind whatever.      SIMEON WHITELEY.

It is noteworthy to observe at this time the embarrassment experienced by Governor Evans by this turn of events. If the Indians were to "turn friendly" or to "become peaceful" then he would be made to look the total fool. How could he explain away the fears expressed in his telegram to Washington? What would he do with the volunteer regiment already formed? The regiment was "raised to kill Indians and they must kill Indians," was his rationalization for their continuance. Because Major Wynkoop had "jeopordized" his "grand plan," he was replaced by order of the Governor by Major Scott J. Anthony who shared, somewhat, Wynkoop's humanistic feelings toward his Indian wards, but he took orders regardless of their objectives or consequences. In this way Governor Evans eliminated his constant reminder of the dangerous and brutal path he had elected to follow. The rest is history; and not one of the major antagonists in this horrendous moment in our history ever reaped the anticipated rewards for his participation.

The total weight of the media was shifted against Governor Evans and Colonel Chivington. The Conduct of the War documents clearly exposed the disgusting behavior of the volunteer regiment and its leaders at Sand Creek as well as the physical horrors perpetrated by them against the Indians. Because of the uproar across the country by concerned citizens, Governor Evans felt it incumbent upon him to try to justify his official position and the regiment's actions at Sand Creek. The following document, his reply to the massacre of Cheyenne Indians, is one of the rarest documents at rest in any institution today; in fact, according to Howes (E-224), there are only four known copies in existence. In it, the Governor attempts to argue the findings of the Committee on the Conduct of the War, and in each point he presents what can best be described as an argument based on semantics and omissions, but let the record speak for itself:

# REPLY

OF

# GOVERNOR EVANS,

OF THE

## TERRITORY OF COLORADO.

TO THAT PART REFERRING TO HIM, OF THE REPORT OF "THE
COMMITTEE ON THE CONDUCT OF THE WAR," HEADED

## "MASSACRE OF CHEYENNE INDIANS."

EXECUTIVE DEPARTMENT,
AND SUPERINTENDENCY OF INDIAN AFFAIRS, C. T.
DENVER, Aug. 6th, 1865.

To THE PUBLIC:

I have just seen, for the first time, a copy of the Report of the Committee
on the Conduct of the War, headed "Massacre of Cheyenne Indians."

As it does me great injustice, and by its partial, unfair, and erroneous
statements, will mislead the public, I respectfully ask a suspension of opinion
in my case until I shall have time to present the facts to said committee, or
some equally high authority, and ask a correction.

In the meantime, I desire to lay a few facts before the public.

The Committee on the Conduct of the War, as shown by the resolution
of the House of Representatives heading the Report, had power "to enquire
into and report all the facts connected with the late attack, by the Third
Regiment Colorado Volunteers, under Col. Chivington, on a village of the
Cheyenne tribe of Indians, near Fort Lyon."

They had no power to enquire into my management of Indian affairs,
except in so far as it related to this battle; and the Chairman of the Committee assured me that they would *not* enquire into such general management.
Having no connection whatever with the battle, and, at the time, knowing
nothing of the immediate facts connected therewith, I so stated to the Committee, and relying upon the above assurance of the Chairman, addressed myself to another committee which had been appointed to investigate the management of Indian affairs generally, in the United States. Of this committee,
Senator Doolittle was Chairman, and to it, I believe, I have rendered a satisfactory account of my stewardship.

The Committee on the Conduct of the War, however, have seen fit to go beyond the scope of their powers, and to enter into a hasty and general investigation of Indian affairs in this Superintendency, and in their report attack matters occurring at remote periods from, and entirely disconnected with, the subject matter of investigation.

Under these circumstances, having been censured unheard, I claim the privilege of presenting proof of the falsity of their charges, in order that, so far as it can be done, the Committee, or equally high authority, may repair the great injury done me. And I pledge myself to prove, by official correspondence and accredited testimony, to their satisfaction, and that of all fair-minded men, the truth and justice of my complaint.

I do not propose to discuss the merits or demerits of the Sand Creek battle, but simply to meet the attempt, on the part of the Committee, to connect my name with it, and to throw discredit on my testimony. I shall not ask the public to take my assertions, except so far as I shall sustain them by undoubted authority, a large part of which is published in Government documents, by the authority of the honorable body of which the Committee are members. The Report begins:

"In the summer of 1864, Gov. Evans, of Colorado Territory, as acting Superintendent of Indian Affairs, sent notice to the various bands and tribes of Indians within his jurisdiction, that such as desired to be considered friendly to the whites should repair to the nearest military post, in order to be protected from the soldiers who were to take the field against the hostile Indians."

This statement is true as to such notice having been sent, but conveys the false impression that it was at the beginning of hostilities, and the declaration of war. The truth is, it was issued, by authority of the Indian Department, months after the war had become general, for the purpose of inducing the Indians to cease hostilities, and to protect those who had been, or would become friendly, from the inevitable dangers to which they were exposed. This "Notice" may be found published in the Report of the Commissioner of Indian Affairs, for 1864, page 218.

The report continues:

"About the close of the summer, some Cheyenne Indians in the neighborhood of the Smoky Hill, sent word to Major Wynkoop, commanding at Fort Lyon, that they had in their possession, and were willing to deliver up, some white captives they had purchased of other Indians. Major Wynkoop, with a force of over one hundred met those Indians and recovered the white captives. On his return, he was accompanied by a number of the chiefs and leading men of the Indians, whom he had brought to visit Denver, for the purpose of conferring with the authorities there in regard to keeping the peace. Among them, were Black Kettle and White Antelope, of the Cheyennes, and some chiefs of the Arapahoes. The council was held, and these chiefs stated that they were friendly to the whites and had always been."

Again they say:

"All the testimony goes to show that the Indians under the immediate control of Black Kettle and White Antelope, of the Cheyennes, and Left Hand, of the Arapahoes, were and had been friendly to the whites, and had not been guilty of any acts of hostility or depredations."

This word which the Committee say was sent to Major Wynkoop, was a letter to U. S. Indian Agent Major Colley, which is published in the Report of the Commissioner of Indian Affairs, for 1864, page 233, and is as follows:

CHEYENNE VILLAGE, August 29th, 1864.

"TO MAJOR COLLEY:

"We received a letter from Bent, wishing us to make peace. We held a council in regard to it. All come to the conclusion to make peace with you, providing you make peace with the Kiowas, Camanches, Arapahoes, Apaches and Sioux. We are going to send a messenger to the Kiowas, and to the other nations, about our going to make peace with you. We heard that you have some [prisoners] in Denver. We have seven prisoners of yours which we are willing to give up, providing you give up yours. There are three war parties out yet, and two of Arapahoes. They have been out some time and expected in soon. When we held this council there were few Arapahoes and Sioux present. We want true news from you in return. That is a letter. BLACK KETTLE, *And other Chiefs.*"

Compare the above extract from the report of the Committee, with this published letter of Black Kettle, and the admission of the Indians in the council at Denver.

The Committee say, the prisoners proposed to be delivered up *were purchased of other Indians.* Black Kettle, in his letter, says: "We have seven prisoners of yours, which we are willing to give up, providing you give up yours."

They say nothing about prisoners whom they had *purchased.* On the other hand, in the council held in Denver, Black Kettle said:

"Major Wynkoop was kind enough to receive the letter, and visited them in camp, to whom they delivered four white prisoners—one other (Mrs. Snyder,) having killed herself: that there are two women and one child yet in their camp, whom they will deliver up as soon as they can get them in; Laura Roper, 16 or 17 years; Ambrose Asher, 7 or 8 years; Daniel Marble, 7 or 8 years; Isabel Ubanks, 4 or 5 years. The prisoners still with them [are] Mrs. Ubanks and babe, and a Mrs. Norton, who was taken on the Platte. Mrs. Snyder is the name of the woman who hung herself. The boys were taken between Fort Kearney and the Blue."

Again, they did not deny having captured the prisoners, when I told them that having the prisoners in their possession was evidence of their having committed the depredations when they were taken. But White Antelope said: "We (the Cheyennes) took two prisoners west of Kearney, and destroyed the trains." Had they *purchased* the prisoners, they would not have been slow to make it known in this council.

The Committee say the chiefs went to Denver to confer with the authorities about *keeping the peace.* Black Kettle says: "All come to the conclusion to *make peace* with you, providing you will *make peace* with the Kiowas, Camanches, Arapahoes, Apaches and Sioux."

Again, the Committee say:

"All the testimony goes to show that the Indians under the immediate control of Black Kettle and White Antelope, of the Cheyennes, and Left Hand, of the Arapahoes, *were, and had been, friendly to the whites, and had not been guilty of any acts of hostility or depredations.*"

Black Kettle says, in his letter: "We received a letter from Bent, wishing us to make peace." Why did Bent send a letter to *friendly* Indians, and want to make peace with Indians "*who had always been friendly?*" Again, they say, "we have held a council in regard to it." Why did they hold a council in regard to making peace, when they were already peaceable? Again, they say, "all come to the conclusion to *make peace* with you, *providing* you make peace with the Kiowas, Camanches, Arapahoes, Apaches and Sioux. We have seven prisoners of yours, which we are willing to give up, providing you give up yours. There are three *war* (not *peace*) *parties* out yet, and two of Arapahoes."

Every line of this letter shows that they were and had been at war. I desire to throw additional light upon this assertion of the Committee that these Indians "were and had been friendly to the whites, and had not been guilty of any acts of hostility or depredations;" for it is upon this point that the Committee accuse me of prevarication.

In the council held at Denver, White Antelope said: "We (the Cheyennes) took two prisoners, west of Kearney, and destroyed the trains." This was one of the most destructive and bloody raids of the war. Again, Neva (Left Hand's brother) said: "The Camanches, Kiowas and Sioux have done much more harm than we have."

The entire report of this council, which is hereunto attached, shows that the Indians had been at war, and had been "guilty of acts of hostility and depredations."

As showing more fully the status and disposition of these Indians, I call attention to the following extract from the report of Major Wynkoop, published in the report of the Commissioner of Indian Affairs, for 1864, page 234, and a letter from Major Colley, their agent; same Report, page 230. Also statement of Robert North; same report, page 224.

FORT LYON, C. T., September 18th, 1864.

SIR:—

•      •      •      •      •      •      •      •      •      •      •      •

"Taking with me, under strict guard, the Indians I had in my possession, I reached my destination, and was confronted by from six to eight hundred Indian warriors, drawn up in line of battle, and prepared to fight.

"Putting on as bold a front as I could, under the circumstances, I formed my command in as good order as possible for the purpose of acting on the offensive or defensive, as might be necessary, and advanced towards them, at the same time sending forward one of the Indians I had with me, as an emissary, to state that I had come for the purpose of holding a consultation with the chiefs of the Arapahoes and Cheyennes, to come to an understanding which might result in mutual benefit; that I had not come desiring strife, but was prepared for it if necessary, and I advised them to listen to what I had to say, previous to making any more warlike demonstrations.

"They consented to meet me in council, and I then proposed to them that if they desired peace, to give me palpable evidence of their sincerity by delivering into my hands their white prisoners. I told them that I was not authorized to conclude terms of peace with them, but if they acceded to my protection, I would take what chiefs they might choose to select, to the Governor of Colorado Territory, state the circumstances to him, and that I believed it would result in what it was their desire to accomplish— 'peace with their white brothers.' I had reference, particularly, to the Arapahoe and Cheyenne tribes.

"The council was divided—*undecided*—and could not come to an understanding among themselves. I told them that I would march to a certain locality, distant twelve miles, and await a given time for their action in the matter. I took a strong position in the locality named, and remained three days. In the interval, they brought in and turned over four white prisoners, all that was possible for them at the time being to turn over, the balance of the seven being (as they stated) with another band far to the northward.

•      •      •      •      •      •      •      •      •      •      •      •

"I have the principal chiefs of the two tribes with me, and propose starting immediately to Denver, to put into effect the aforementioned proposition made by me to them.

"They agree to deliver up the balance of the prisoners as soon as it is possible to procure them which can be done better from Denver City than from this point. I have the honor, Governor, to be

"Your Obedient Servant,

"E. W. WYNKOOP,

"*Major First Cav. Col., Comd'g Fort Lyon, C. T.*

"His Excellency JOHN EVANS, Governor of Colorado, Denver, C. T."

"Fort Lyon, Colorado Territory, July 26th, 1864.

"Sir:—

"When I last wrote you I was in hopes that our Indian troubles were at an end. Col. Chivington has just arrived from Larned, and gives a sad account of affairs at that Post. They have killed some ten men from a train, and run off all the stock from the Post.

"As near as they can learn, all tribes were engaged in it. The Colonel will give you the particulars. There is no dependence to be put in any of them. I have done everything in my power to keep the peace; I now think a little powder and lead is the best food for them.

"Respectfully, Your Ob't Serv't,

"S. G. Colley,
"United States Indian Agent.

Hon. John Evans, Governor and Superintendent Indian Affairs.

The following statement by Robert North, was made to me:

November 10th, 1863.

"Having recovered an Arapahoe prisoner (a squaw) from the Utes, I obtained the confidence of the Indians completely. I have lived with them from a boy, and my wife is an Arapahoe.

In honor of my exploit in recovering the prisoner, the Indians recently gave me a "big Medicine Dance," about fifty miles below Fort Lyon, on the Arkansas River, at which the leading chiefs and warriors of several of the tribes of the plains met.

"The Camanches, Apaches, Kiowas, the northern band of Arapahoes, and all of the Cheyennes, with the Sioux, have pledged one another to go to war with the whites as soon as they can procure ammunition in the spring. I heard them discuss the matter often, and the few of them who opposed it were forced to be quiet, and were really in danger of their lives. I saw the principal chiefs pledge to each other that they would be friendly and shake hands with the whites until they procured ammunition and guns so as to be ready when they strike. Plundering, to get means, has already commenced; and the plan is to commence the war at several points in the sparse settlements early in the spring. They wanted me to join them in the war, saying that they would take a great many white women and children prisoners, and get a heap of property, blankets &c.; but while I am connected with them by marriage, and live with them, I am yet a white man, and wish to avoid bloodshed. There are many Mexicans with the Camanche and Apache Indians, all of whom urge on the war, promising to help the Indians themselves, and that a great many more Mexicans would come up from New Mexico for the purpose in the spring."

In addition to the statement showing that all the Cheyennes were in the alliance, I desire to add the following frank admission from the Indians in the council:

Gov. Evans explained that smoking the war pipe was a figurative term, but their conduct had been such as to show they had an understanding with other tribes.

"Several Indians—We acknowledge that our actions have given you reason to believe this."

In addition to all this, I refer to the appended statement of Mrs. Ewbanks. She is one of the prisoners that Black Kettle, in the council, said they had. Instead of purchasing her, it will be observed that they first captured her on the Little Blue, and then sold her to the Sioux.

Mrs. Martin, another rescued prisoner, was captured by the Cheyennes on Plum Creek, west of Kearney, with a boy nine years old. These were the prisoners of which White Antelope said, in the council, "We took two prisoners west of Kearney, and destroyed the trains." In her published statement, she says, the party who captured her and the boy, killed eleven men and destroyed the trains, and were mostly Cheyennes.

Thus I have proved by the Indian chiefs named in the Report, by Agent Colley and Major Wynkoop, to whom they refer to sustain their assertion to the contrary, that these Indians had "been at war, and had committed acts of hostility and depredations."

This documentary evidence could be extended much farther, but enough has been produced to show the utter recklessness of their statements, and because I would not admit, in the face of these published facts, that these Indians "were, and always had been friendly, and had not been guilty of any acts of hostility or depredations," the Committee accuse me of "prevarication." They say that I prevaricated "for the evident purpose of avoiding the admission that he was fully aware that the Indians massacred so brutally at Sand Creek, were then, *and had been, actuated by the most friendly feelings towards the whites.*"

I had left the Indians in the hands of the military authorities, as I shall presently show—there were many conflicting rumors as to the disposition made of them. I was absent from the Territory, and could state nothing positive in regard to their status after the council.

In regard to their status prior to the council at Denver, the foregoing public documents which I have cited, show how utterly devoid of truth or foundation is the assertion that these Indians "had been friendly to the whites, and had not been guilty of any acts of hostility or depredations." Ignorance of the facts contained in the Report of the Commissioner of Indian Affairs, for 1864, is inexcusable on the part of the Committee, for I particularly referred them to it.

I am obliged to the Committee, however, for stating wherein I prevaricated, for I am thus enabled to repel their gross attack on my character as a witness, by showing that they were *mistaken* and I was *correct* in my testimony.

The next paragraph of the report is as follows:

"A northern band of the Cheyennes, known as the 'Dog Soldiers, had been guilty of acts of hostility; but all the testimony goes to prove that they had no connection with Black Kettle's band, and acted in spite of his authority and influence. Black Kettle and his band denied all connection with, or responsibility for, the Dog Soldiers, and Left Hand and his band were equally friendly."

The Committee and the public will be surprised to learn the fact that these Dog Soldiers, on which the Committee throw the *slight* blame of acts of hostility, were really among Black Kettle's and White Antelope's own warriors, in the "*friendly*" camp to which Major Wynkoop made his expedition, and their head man, Bull Bear, was one of the prominent men of the deputation brought in to see me at Denver. By reference to the accompanying report of the council with the chiefs, to which I referred the Committee, it will be observed that Black Kettle and all present, based their propositions to *make peace* upon the assent of *their bands,* and that these Dog Soldiers were especially referred to.

The Report continues:

"These Indians, at the suggestion of Governor Evans and Col. Chivington, repaired to Fort Lyon and placed themselves under the protection of Major Wynkoop," &c.

The connection of my name in this, is again wrong. As will be seen by the accompanying report of the council, to which I referred in my testimony, I simply left them in the hands of the military authorities, where I found them, and my action was approved by the Indian Bureau.

The following extracts from the accompanying report of the council will prove this, conclusively. I stated to the Indians:

  °   °   °   "Another reason that I am not in a condition to make a treaty, is, that the war is begun, and the power to make a treaty of peace has passed from me to the great War Chief."

I also said: "Again, whatever peace they make must be with the soldiers, and not with me."

And again, in reply to White Antelope's enquiry, "How can we be protected from the soldiers on the plains?" I said: "You must make that arrangement with the military chief."

The morning after this council I addressed the following letter to the agent of these Indians, which is published in the Report of the Commissioner of Indian Affairs for 1864, page 220:

COLORADO SUPERINTENDENCY INDIAN AFFAIRS,
DENVER, September 29th, 1864.

SIR:—

The chiefs brought in by Major Wynkoop have been heard. I have declined to make any peace with them, lest it might embarrass the military operations against the hostile Indians of the plains. The Arapahoe and Cheyenne Indians being now at war with the United States government, must make peace with the military authorities. Of course this arrangement relieves the Indian Bureau of their care until peace is declared with them; and as these tribes are yet scattered, and all except Friday's band are at war, it is not probable that it will be done immediately. You will be particular to impress upon these chiefs the fact that my talk with them was for the purpose of ascertaining their views, and not to offer them anything whatever. They must deal with the military authorities until peace, in which case, alone, they will be in proper position to treat with the government in relation to the future.

I have the honor to be,

Very Respectfully, Your Obedient Servant,

JOHN EVANS.
*Governor C. T., and ex officio Supt. Indian Affairs.*

Major S. G. COLLEY, *U.S. Indian Agent, Upper Arkansas.*

That this course accorded with the policy of the military authorities, was confirmed by a telegram from the Department Commander, sent from Headquarters at Leavenworth, to the District Commander, on the day of the council, in which he said: "I fear Agent of Interior Department will be ready to make presents too soon. It is better to chastise, before giving anything but a little tobacco to talk over. No peace must be made without my directions."

It will thus be seen that I had with the approval of the Indian Bureau, turned the adjustment of difficulties with hostile Indians entirely over to the military authorities: that I had instructed Agent Colley, at Fort Lyon, that this would relieve the Bureau of further care of the Arapahoes and Cheyennes, until peace was made, and having had no notice of such peace, or instructions to change the arrangement, the status of these Indians was in no respect within my jurisdiction or under my official inspection.

In the face of all these facts—matters of public record—the Committee attempt to make me responsible for the care of these Indians at the time of the battle.

It may be proper for me to say, further, that it will appear in evidence that I had no intimation of the direction in which the campaign against the hostile Indians was to move, or against what bands it was to be made, when I left the Territory last fall, and that I was absent from Colorado when the Sand Creek battle occurred.

The report continues:

"It is true that there seems to have been excited among the people inhabiting that region of country, a hostile feeling towards the Indians. Some had committed acts of hostility towards the whites, but no effort seems to have been made, by the authorities there, to prevent these hostilities, other than by the commission of even worse acts."

"*The people inhabiting that region of country!*" A form of expression of frequent occurrence in the reports of exploring expeditions, when speaking of avages and unknown tribes, but scarcely a respectful mode of mention of the people of Colorado.

"*Some* had committed acts of hostility towards the whites!" Hear the facts: In the fall of 1863, a general alliance of the Indians of the plains was affected with the Sioux, and in the language of Bull Bear, in the report of the council, appended, "Their plan is to clean out all this country."

The war opened early in the spring of 1864. The people of the East, absorbed in the greater interest of the Rebellion, know but little of its history. Stock was stolen, ranches destroyed, houses burned, freight trains plundered and their contents carried away or scattered upon the plains; settlers in the frontier counties murdered, or forced to seek safety for themselves and families in block-houses and interior towns; emigrants to our Territory were surprised in their camps, children were slain, and wives taken prisoners; our trade and travel with the States was cut off; the necessaries of life were at starvation prices; the interests of the Territory were being damaged to the extent of millions; every species of atrocity and barbarity which characterizes savage warfare was committed. This is no fancy sketch, but a plain statement of facts of which the Committee seem to have had no proper realization. All this history of war and blood—all this history of rapine and ruin—all this story of outrage and suffering on the part of our people—is summed up by the Committee, and given to the public, in the one mild sentence, "*Some* had committed acts of hostility against the whites."

The Committee not only ignore the general and terrible character of our Indian war, and the great sufferings of our people, but make the grave charge that "no effort seems to have been made by the authorities there to prevent all these hostilities."

Had the Committee taken the trouble, as they certainly should have done before making so grave a charge, to have read the public documents of the Government, examined the record and files of the Indian Bureau, of the War Department and of this Superintendency, instead of adopting the language of some hostile and irresponsible witness, as they appear to have done, they would have found that the most earnest and persistent efforts had been made, on my part, to prevent hostilities. The records show that early in the spring of 1863, U. S. Indian Agent Loree, of the Upper Platte Agency, reported to me in person that the Sioux under his agency and the Arapahoes and Cheyennes, were negotiating an alliance for war on the whites. I immediately wrote an urgent appeal for authority to avert the danger, and sent Agent Loree as special messenger with the dispatch to Washington. In response, authority was given, and an earnest effort was made to collect the Indians in council. The following admission, in the appended report of the council, explains the result:

"*Gov. Evans*— ° ° ° Hearing, last fall, that they were dissatisfied, the Great Father at Washington sent me out on the plains to talk with you and make it all right. I sent messengers out to tell you that I had presents, and would make you a feast, but you sent word to me that you did not want to have anything to do with me, and to the Great Father at Washington that you could get along without him. Bull Bear wanted to come in to see me, at the head of the Republican, but his people held a council and would not let him come.

"*Black Kettle*—That is true.

"*Gov. Evans*—I was under the necessity, after all my trouble, and all the expense I was at, of returning home without seeing them. Instead of this, your people went away and smoked the war pipe with our enemies."

Notwithstanding these unsuccessful efforts, I still hoped to preserve peace.

The records of these offices also show that in the autumn of 1863, I was reliably advised from various sources, that nearly all the Indians of the plains had formed an alliance for the purpose of going to war in the spring, and I immediately commenced my efforts to avert the imminent danger. From that time forward, by letter, by telegram, and personal representation to the Commissioner of Indian Affairs, the Secretary of War, the commanders of the Department and District; by traveling for weeks in the wilderness of the plains; by distribution of annuities and presents; by sending notice to the Indians to leave the hostile alliance, by every means within my power, I endeavored to preserve peace and protect the interests of the people of the Territory. And in the face of all this, which the records abundantly show, the Committee say: "No effort seems to have been made by the authorities there to prevent these hostilities, other than by the commission of even worse acts."

They do not point out any of these acts, unless the continuation of the paragraph is intended to do so. It proceeds:

"The hatred of the whites to the Indians would seem to have been inflamed and excited to the utmost. The bodies of persons killed at a distance—whether by Indians or not is not certain—were brought to the capital of the Territory and exposed to the public gaze, for the purpose of inflaming still more the already excited feeling of the people."

There is no mention in this of anything that was done by authority, but it is so full of misrepresentation, in apology for Indians, and unjust reflection on a people who have a right, from their birth, education, and ties of sympathy with the people they so recently left behind them, to have at least a just consideration. The bodies referred to were those of the Hungate family, who were brutally murdered by the Indians, within twenty-five miles of Denver. No one here ever doubted that the Indians did it, and it was admitted by the Indians in the council. This was early in the summer, and before the notice, sent in June, to the friendly Indians. Their mangled bodies were brought to Denver for decent burial. Many of our people went to see them, as any people would have done. It did produce excitement and consternation, and where are the people who could have witnessed it without emotion? Would the Committee have the people shut their eyes to such scenes at their very doors?

The next sentence, equally unjust and unfair, refers to my proclamation, issued two months after this occurrence, and four months before the "attack" they were investigating, and having no connection with it or with the troops engaged in it. It is as follows:

"The cupidity was appealed to, for the Governor, in a proclamation, calls upon all, either individually, or in such parties as they may organize, to kill and destroy, as enemies of the country, wherever they may be found, all such hostile Indians; authorizing them to hold, to their own use and benefit, all the property of said hostile Indians they may capture. What Indians he would ever term friendly, it is impossible to tell."

I offer the following statement of the circumstances under which this proclamation was issued, by the Hon. D. A. Chever.

It is as follows:

EXECUTIVE DEPARTMENT, COLORADO TERRITORY, }
August 21st, 1865. }

I, David A. Chever, clerk in the office of the Governor of the Territory of Colorado, do solemnly swear, that the people of said Territory, from the Purgatoire to the Cache la Poudre rivers—a distance of over two hundred miles—and for a like distance along the Platte River, being the whole of our settlements on the Plains, were thrown into the greatest alarm and consternation, by numerous and almost simultaneous attacks and depredations by hostile Indians, early last Summer; that they left their unreaped crops, and collecting into communities, built block houses and stockades, for protection, at central points throughout the long line of settlements; that those living in the vicinity of Denver City fled to it, and that the people of said city were in great fear of sharing the fate of New Ulm. Minnesota; that the threatened loss of crops, and the interruption of communication with the States, by the combined hostilities, threatened the very existence of the whole people; that this feeling of danger was universal: that a flood of petitions and deputations poured into this office, from the people of all parts of the Territory, praying for protection and for arms and authority to protect themselves; that the defects of the milria law and the want of means to provide for defence, was proved by the failure of this Department, after the utmost endeavors, to secure an effective organization under it; that reliable reports of the presence of a large body of hostile warriors at no great distance east of this place, were received, which reports were afterwards proved to be true, by the statement of Elbridge Gerry, page 232, Report of Commissioner of Indian Affairs for 1864; that repeated and urgent applications to the War Department, for protection and the authority to raise troops for the purpose, had failed; that urgent applications to Department and District commanders had failed to bring any prospect of relief, and that in the midst of this terrible consternation, and apparently defenceless condition, it had been announced to this office, from District Headquarters, that all the Colorado troops in the service of the United States had been peremptorily ordered away, and nearly all of them had marched to the Arkansas River, to be in position to repel the threatened invasion of the rebels into Kansas and Missouri; that reliable reports of depredations and murders by the Indians, from all parts of our extended lines of exposed settlements, became daily more numerous, until the simultaneous attacks on trains along the Overland Stage Line was reported by telegraph, on the 8th of August, described in the letter of George K. Otis, Superintendent of Overland Stage Line, published on page 254, of Report of Commissioner of Indian Affairs for 1864. Under these circumstances, on the 11th of August, the Governor issued his proclamation to the people, calling upon them to defend their homes and families from the savage foe; that it prevented anarchy; that several militia companies immediately organized under it, and aided in inspiring confidence; that under its authority, no act of impropriety has been reported, and I do not believe that any occurred; that it had no reference to, or connection with, the Third Regiment, one hundred days men, that was subsequently raised by authority of the War Department, under a different proclamation, calling for volunteers, or with any of the troops engaged in the "Sand Creek Affair," and that the reference to it in such connection, in the report of the Committee on the Conduct of the War, is a perversion of the history and facts in the case.

DAVID A. CHEVER

TERRITORY OF COLORADO, ⎫
    ARAPAHOE COUNTY,     ⎬  ss.
        CITY OF DENVER.   ⎭


Subscribed and sworn to before me, this 21st day of August, A. D. 1865.
                                                ELI M. ASHLEY, *Notary Public.*


    I had appealed by telegraph, June 14th, to the War Department, for authority to call the militia into the United States service or to raise one hundred troops—also had written to our Delegate in Congress to see why I got no response, and had received his reply to the effect that he could learn nothing about it; had received a notice, from the Department Commander, declining to take the responsibility of asking the militia for United States service—throwing the people entirely on the necessity of taking care of themselves.
    It was under these circumstances of trial, suffering and danger on the

If my statement did not agree with what they supposed to be the truth, my position was such as to demand that they should at least go to the trouble of investigating the public documents to which I called their attention, before publishing a report containing charges of so grave a character.

That the Committee on the Conduct of the War should have published a report containing so many errors, is to be regretted. It is composed of honorable gentlemen—members of the Congress of the United States—to whom have been entrusted duties of the gravest character, and from whom is expected, first, *thorough investigation*, and then *careful statement*, so that their reports may be relied upon as *truth*, so far as truth is ascertainable by human means.

This report, so full of mistakes which ordinary investigation would have avoided; so full of slander, which ordinary care of the character of men would have prevented, is to be regretted, for the reason that it throws doubt upon the reliability of all reports which have emanated from the same source, during the last four years of war.

I am confident that the public will see, from the facts herein set forth, the great injustice done me; and I am further confident that the Committee, when they know these and other facts I shall lay before them, will also see this injustice, and, as far as possible, repair it.

Very Respectfully Your Obedient Servant,

JOHN EVANS,
*Governor of the Territory of Colorado, and ex-officio Supt. Ind. Affairs.*

But how does this dreadful incident fit into the folksong already cited? Well, for one thing, Chief Black Kettle lost his life in yet another massacre; this time he died at the Washita in Custer's triumphant display of total callousness, even though it was a brilliant military strategy. This was four years after Sand Creek. Eight years later Custer lost his life in the Sioux Campaign of 1876 at the Little Big Horn. And still no one listened to the words of the Lord. Nor, apparently, do they listen today.

JOHN M. CARROLL
New Brunswick, New Jersey

would have been awkward. Had they not suppressed it, its appearance in its proper connection would have answered one of their most serious charges against me.

Why is this? Does it not look like a persistent determination on their part to place me before the public in an improper and unjust position? If such a thing *is possible*, from so high a source, where is there any safety for the character of public men?

Before closing this reply, it is perhaps just that I should say that when I testified before the Committee, the chairman and all its members except three were absent, and I think when the truth becomes known, this report will trace its parentage to a single member of the Committee.

I have thus noticed such portions of the report as refer to myself, and shown conclusively that the Committee in every mention they have made of me, have been, to say the least, *mistaken.*

*First*—The Committee, for the evident purpose of maintaining their position that these Indians had not been engaged in the war, say the prisoners they held were *purchased*. The testimony is to the effect that they *captured* them.

*Second*—The Committee say that these Indians were and always had been friendly and had committed no acts of hostility or depredations. The public documents to which I refer, show conclusively that they had been hostile, and had committed many acts of hostility and depredations.

*Third*—They say that I joined in sending these Indians to Fort Lyon. The published report of the Commissioner of Indian Affairs, and of the Indian council, show that I left them entirely in the hands of the military authorities.

*Fourth*—They say nothing seems to have been done by the authorities to prevent hostilities. The public documents and files of the Indian Bureau and of my Superintendency show constant and unremitting diligence and effort on my part to prevent hostilities and protect the people.

*Fifth*—They say that I prevaricated for the purpose of avoiding the admission that these Indians "were and had been actuated by the most friendly feelings towards the whites." Public documents cited show conclusively that the admission they desired me to make was *false*, and that my statement, instead of being a *prevarication*, was *true*, although not in accordance with the preconceived and mistaken opinions of the Committee.

Those who read this will be curious for some explanation of this slanderous report. To me it is plain. I am Governor of Colorado, and as is usual with men in public position, have enemies. Many of these gentlemen were in the City of Washington, last winter, endeavoring to effect my removal, and were not particular as to the character of the means they employed, so that the desired result was accomplished. For this purpose, they conspired to connect my name with the Sand Creek battle, although they knew that I was in no way connected with it. A friend in that city, writing to me in regard to this attempt, and mentioning the names of certain of these gentlemen, said: "They are much in communication with —— a member of the committee charged with the investigation of the Chivington Affair." These gentlemen, by their false and unscrupulous representations, have misled the Committee.

I do not charge the Committee with any *intentional* wrong. My charge against the Committee is that they have been *culpably negligent* and *culpably hasty*. Culpably negligent in not examining the public documents to which I called their attention, and which would have exonerated me, and saved them from many serious, unjust and mistaken representations. *Culpably hasty*, in concluding that I had prevaricated, because my statement did not agree with the falsehoods they had embraced.

part of the people, and of fruitless appeal upon my part to the general government for aid, that I issued my proclamation of the 11th August, 1864, of which the Committee complain.

Without means to mount or pay militia—and failing to get government authority to raise forces—and under the withdrawal of the few troops in the Territory—could any other course be pursued?

The people were asked to fight on their own account—at their own expense—and in lieu of the protection the government failed to render. They were authorized to kill only the Indians that were murdering and robbing them in hostility, and to keep the property captured from them. How the Committee would have them fight these savages, and what other disposition they would make of the property captured, the public will be curious to know. Would they fight without killing? Would they have the captured property turned over to the government, as if captured by United States troops? Would they forbid such captures? Would they restore it to the hostile tribes?

The absurdity of the Committee's saying that this was an "appeal to the cupidity," is too palpable to require much comment. Would men leave high wages, mount and equip themselves at enormous expense,—as some patriotically did,—for the poor chance of capturing property, as a mere speculation, from the prowling bands of Indians that infested the settlements and were murdering their families? The thing is preposterous.

For this proclamation I have no apology. It had its origin and has its justification in the imperative necessities of the case. A merciless foe surrounded us. Without means to mount or pay militia,—unable to secure government authority to raise forces, and our own troops ordered away, again I ask, could any other course be pursued?

Capain Tyler's and other companies organized under it, at enormous expense, left their lucrative business, high wages and profitable employment, and served without other pay than the consciousness of having done noble and patriotic service; and no act of impropriety has ever been laid to the charge of any party acting under this proclamation. They had all been disbanded months before the "attack" was made that the committee were investigating.

The Third Regiment was organized under authority from the War Department subsequently received by telegraph, and under a subsequent proclamation issued on the 13th of August, and were regularly mustered into the service of the United States about three months before the battle the Committee were investigating occurred.

Before leaving this subject, I desire to call attention to the following significant fact; the part of my proclamation from which the Committee quote reads as follows:

"Now, therefore, I, John Evans, Governor of Colorado Territory, do issue this, my proclamation, authorizing all citizens of Colorado, either individually or in such parties as they may organize, to go in pursuit of all hostile Indians on the Plains, *scrupulously avoiding those who have responded to my call to rendezvous at the points indicated.* Also to kill and destroy, as enemies of the country, wherever they may be found, all such hostile Indians."

The language which I have italicised, in the foregoing quotation shows that I forbade, in this proclamation, the disturbance of the friendly Indians and only authorized killing the hostile.

The Committee, in their censorious mention of the proclamation, omit this sentence which I have italicised, although they quote the language immediately in connection with it, and add the exclamation, "what Indians he would ever term friendly it is impossible to tell." Had they not suppressed this sentence their exclamation

## PUBLISHER'S NOTE

The Introduction includes several reports extracted from the testimony contained in the Appendix (38th Congress, Second Session, 1865). This has been repeated intentionally because of its relevancy in introducing this combined documentary history.

This volume is a compilation of several documents. The original pagination has been retained. The publisher has added sequential page numbers at the bottom of each page to maintain continuity.

# MASSACRE OF CHEYENNE INDIANS
38th Congress, Second Session
Washington, D.C., 1865

# MASSACRE OF CHEYENNE INDIANS.

## THIRTY-EIGHTH CONGRESS, SECOND SESSION.

### CONGRESS OF THE UNITED STATES.

#### IN THE HOUSE OF REPRESENTATIVES, *January* 10, 1865.

On motion of Mr. Orth,

*Resolved*, That the Committee on the Conduct of the War be required to inquire into and report all the facts connected with the late attack of the third regiment of Colorado volunteers, under Colonel Chivington, on a village of the Cheyenne tribe of Indians, near Fort Lyon.

Attest: ———— ————, *Clerk.*

---

The Joint Committee on the Conduct of the War submit the following report :

In the summer of 1864 Governor Evans, of Colorado Territory, as acting superintendent of Indian affairs, sent notice to the various bands and tribes of Indians within his jurisdiction that such as desired to be considered friendly to the whites should at once repair to the nearest military post in order to be protected from the soldiers who were to take the field against the hostile Indians.

About the close of the summer, some Cheyenne Indians, in the neighborhood of the Smoke Hills, sent word to Major Wynkoop, the commandant of the post of Fort Lyon, that they had in their possession, and were willing to deliver up, some white captives they had purchased of other Indians. Major Wynkoop, with a force of over 100 men, visited those Indians and received the white captives. On his return he was accompanied by a number of the chiefs and leading men of the Indians, whom he had invited to visit Denver for the purpose of conferring with the authorities there in regard to keeping peace. Among them were Black Kettle and White Antelope of the Cheyennes, and some chiefs of the Arapahoes. The council was held, and these chiefs stated that they were friendly to the whites, and always had been, and that they desired peace. Governor Evans and Colonel Chivington, the commander of that military district, advised them to repair to Fort Lyon and submit to whatever terms the military commander there should impose. This was done by the Indians, who were treated somewhat as prisoners of war, receiving rations, and being obliged to remain within certain bounds.

3

All the testimony goes to show that the Indians, under the immediate control of Black Kettle and White Antelope of the Cheyennes, and Left Hand of the Arapahoes, were and had been friendly to the whites, and had not been guilty of any acts of hostility or depredation. The Indian agents, the Indian interpreter and others examined by your committee, all testify to the good character of those Indians. Even Governor Evans and Major Anthony, though evidently willing to convey to your committee a false impression of the character of those Indians, were forced, in spite of their prevarication, to admit that they knew of nothing they had done which rendered them deserving of punishment.

A northern band of the Cheyennes, known as the Dog Soldiers, had been guilty of acts of hostility ; but all the testimony goes to prove that they had no connexion with Black Kettle's band, but acted in despite of his authority and influence. Black Kettle and his band denied all connexion with or responsibility for the Dog Soldiers, and Left Hand and his band of Arapahoes were equally friendly.

These Indians, at the suggestion of Governor Evans and Colonel Chivington, repaired to Fort Lyon and placed themselves under the protection of Major Wynkoop. They were led to believe that they were regarded in the light of friendly Indians, and would be treated as such so long as they conducted themselves quietly.

The treatment extended to those Indians by Major Wynkoop does not seem to have satisfied those in authority there, and for some cause, which does not appear, he was removed, and Major Scott J. Anthony was assigned to the command of Fort Lyon ; but even Major Anthony seems to have found it difficult at first to pursue any different course towards the Indians he found there. They were entirely within the power of the military. Major Anthony having demanded their arms, which they surrendered to him, they conducted themselves quietly, and in every way manifested a disposition to remain at peace with the whites. For a time even he continued issuing rations to them as Major Wynkoop had done ; but it was determined by Major Anthony (whether upon his own motion or at the suggestion of others does not appear) to pursue a different course towards these friendly Indians. They were called together and told that rations could no longer be issued to them, and they had better go where they could obtain subsistence by hunting. At the suggestion of Major Anthony (and from one in his position a suggestion was equivalent to a command) these Indians went to a place on Sand creek, about thirty-five miles from Fort Lyon, and there established their camp, their arms being restored to them. He told them that he then had no authority to make peace with them ; but in case he received such authority he would inform them of it. In his testimony he says :

"I told them they might go back on Sand creek, or between there and the headwaters of the Smoky Hill, and remain there until I received instructions from the department headquarters, from General Curtis : and that in case I did receive any authority to make peace with them I would go right over and let them know it. *I did not state to them that I would give them notice in case we intended to attack them.* They went away with that understanding, that in case I received instructions from department headquarters I was to let them know it."

And in order, as it were, to render these Indians less apprehensive of any danger, One Eye, a Cheyenne chief, was allowed to remain with them to obtain information for the use of the military authorities. He was employed at $125 a month, and several times brought to Major Anthony, at Fort Lyon, information of proposed movements of other and hostile bands. Jack Smith, a half-breed son of John S. Smith, an Indian interpreter, employed by the government, was also there for the same purpose. A United States soldier was allowed to remain there, and two days before the massacre Mr. Smith, the interpreter, was permitted to go there with goods to trade with the Indians. Everything seems to have been done to remove from the minds of these Indians any fear of approaching danger ; and when Colonel Chivington commenced his movement he took all the precautions in his power to prevent these Indians learning of his approach. For some days all travel on that route was forcibly stopped by him, not even the mail being allowed to pass. On the morning of the 28th of November he appeared at Fort Lyon with over 700 mounted men and two pieces of artillery. One of his first acts was to throw a guard around the post to prevent any one leaving it. At this place Major Anthony joined him with 125 men and two pieces of artillery.

On the night of the 28th the entire party started from Fort Lyon, and, by a forced march, arrived at the Indian camp, on Sand creek, shortly after daybreak. This Indian camp consisted of about 100 lodges of Cheyennes, under Black Kettle, and from 8 to 10 lodges of Arapahoes under Left Hand. It is estimated that each lodge contained five or more persons, and that more than one-half were women and children.

Upon observing the approach of the soldiers, Black-Kettle, the head chief, ran up to the top of his lodge an American flag, which had been presented to him some years before by Commissioner Greenwood, with a small white flag under it, as he had been advised to do in case he met with any troops on the prairies. Mr. Smith, the interpreter, supposing they might be strange troops, unaware of the character of the Indians encamped there, advanced from his lodge to meet them, but was fired upon, and returned to his lodge.

And then the scene of murder and barbarity began—men, women, and children were indiscriminately slaughtered. In a few minutes all the Indians were flying over the plain in terror and confusion. A few who endeavored to hide themselves under the bank of the creek were surrounded and shot down in cold blood, offering but feeble resistance. From the sucking babe to the old warrior, all who were overtaken were deliberately murdered. Not content with killing women and children, who were incapable of offering any resistance, the soldiers indulged in acts of barbarity of the most revolting char-

5

acter; such, it is to be hoped, as never before disgraced the acts of men claiming to be civilized. No attempt was made by the officers to restrain the savage cruelty of the men under their command, but they stood by and witnessed these acts without one word of reproof, if they did not incite their commission. For more than two hours the work of murder and barbarity was continued, until more than one hundred dead bodies, three-fourths of them of women and children, lay on the plain as evidences of the fiendish malignity and cruelty of the officers who had so sedulously and carefully plotted the massacre, and of the soldiers who had so faithfully acted out the spirit of their officers.

It is difficult to believe that beings in the form of men, and disgracing the uniform of United States soldiers and officers, could commit or countenance the commission of such acts of cruelty and barbarity as are detailed in the testimony, but which your committee will not specify in their report. It is true that there seems to have existed among the people inhabiting that region of country a hostile feeling towards the Indians. Some of the Indians had committed acts of hostility towards the whites ; but no effort seems to have been made by the authorities there to prevent these hostilities, other than by the commission of even worse acts. The hatred of the whites to the Indians would seem to have been inflamed and excited to the utmost; the bodies of persons killed at a great distance—whether by Indians or not, is not certain—were brought to the capital of the Territory and exposed to the public gaze for the purpose of inflaming still more the already excited feeling of the people. Their cupidity was appealed to, for the governor in a proclamation calls upon all, "either individually or in such parties as they may organize," "to kill and destroy as enemies of the country, wherever they may be found, all such hostile Indians," authorizing them to "hold to their own private use and benefit all the property of said hostile Indians that they may capture." What Indians he would ever term friendly it is impossible to tell. His testimony before your committee was characterized by such prevarication and shuffling as has been shown by no witness they have examined during the four years they have been engaged in their investigations; and for the evident purpose of avoiding the admission that he was fully aware that the Indians massacred so brutally at Sand creek, were then, and had been, actuated by the most friendly feelings towards the whites, and had done all in their power to restrain those less friendly disposed.

The testimony of Major Anthony, who succeeded an officer disposed to treat these Indians with justice and humanity, is sufficient of itself to show how unprovoked and unwarranted was this massacre. He testifies that he found these Indians in the neighborhood of Fort Lyon when he assumed command of that post; that they professed their friendliness to the whites, and their willingness to do whatever he demanded of them; that they delivered their arms up to him; that they went to and encamped upon the place designated by him; that they gave him information from time to time of acts of hostility which were meditated by other and hostile bands, and in every way conducted themselves properly and peaceably, and yet he says it was fear and not principle which prevented his killing them while they were completely in his power. And when Colonel Chivington appeared at Fort Lyon, on his mission of murder and barbarity, Major Anthony made haste to accompany him with men and artillery, although Colonel Chivington had no authority whatever over him.

As to Colonel Chivington, your committee can hardly find fitting terms to describe his conduct. Wearing the uniform of the United States, which should be the emblem of justice and humanity; holding the important position of commander of a military district, and therefore having the honor of the government to that extent in his keeping, he deliberately planned and executed a foul and dastardly massacre which would have disgraced the veriest savage among those who were the victims of his cruelty. Having full knowledge of their friendly character, having himself been instrumental to some extent in placing them in their position of fancied security, he took advantage of their inapprehension and defenceless condition to gratify the worst passions that ever cursed the heart of man. It is thought by some that desire for political preferment prompted him to this cowardly act; that he supposed that by pandering to the inflamed passions of an excited population he could recommend himself to their regard and consideration. Others think it was to avoid the being sent where there was more of danger and hard service to be performed; that he was willing to get up a show of hostility on the part of the Indians by committing himself acts which savages themselves would never premeditate. Whatever may have been his motive, it is to be hoped that the authority of this government will never again be disgraced by acts such as he and those acting with him have been guilty of committing.

There were *hostile* Indians not far distant, against which Colonel Chivington could have led the force under his command. Major Anthony testifies that but three or four days' march from his post were several hundreds of Indians, generally believed to be engaged in acts of hostility towards the whites. And he deliberately testifies that only the fear of them prevented him from killing those who were friendly and entirely within his reach and control. It is true that to reach them required some days of hard marching. It was not to be expected that they could be surprised as easily as those on Sand creek; and the warriors among them were almost, if not quite, as numerous as the soldiers under the control of Colonel Chivington. Whatever influence this may have had upon Colonel Chivington, the truth is that he surprised and murdered, in cold blood, the unsuspecting men, women, and children on Sand creek, who had every reason to believe they were under the protection of the United States authorities, and then returned to Denver and boasted of the brave deeds he and the men under his command had performed.

The Congress of the United States, at its last session, authorized the appointment of a commission to investigate all matters relating to the administration of Indian affairs within the limits of the United States. Your committee most sincerely trust that the result of their

7

inquiry will be the adoption of measures which will render impossible the employment of officers, civil and military, such as have heretofore made the administration of Indian affairs in this country a byword and reproach.

In conclusion, your committee are of the opinion that for the purpose of vindicating the cause of justice and upholding the honor of the nation, prompt and energetic measures should be at once taken to remove from office those who have thus disgraced the government by whom they are employed, and to punish, as their crimes deserve, those who have been guilty of these brutal and cowardly acts.

Respectfully submitted.

B. F. WADE, *Chairman.*

NOTE.—See journal of committee, May 4, 1865.

# MASSACRE OF CHEYENNE INDIANS.

*Testimony of Mr. Jesse H. Leavenworth.*

WASHINGTON, *March* 13, 1865.

Mr. JESSE H. LEAVENWORTH sworn and examined,

By the chairman:

Question. Where do you reside?

Answer. My home is in the city of Milwaukee, Wisconsin; but I am the Indian agent of the Kiowas, Camanches, and Apache Indians, who roam over the plains between Fort Larned, on the Sante Fé road, and the borders of Mexico, through the western part of Texas.

Question. What do you know about the band of Indians said to have been massacred by a force of troops under Colonel Chivington, of Colorado?

Answer. I am perfectly acquainted with them. I have known them intimately since 1862. Being in command of that southwestern frontier, I have constantly had occasion to come in contact with them.

Question. What is that band called?

Answer. That band is called the Cheyennes; but there were also ten lodges of Arapahoes with them. Their reservation is on the Arkansas river, commencing at the Big Timbers and extending up the river ninety miles, and bounded on the north by the Big Sandy. Fort Lyon is situated upon their reservation.

Question. Is this in the Territory of Colorado?

Answer. Yes, sir. Fort Lyon was my headquarters for nearly two years, and I had occasion to meet these Indians almost daily. The chiefs Black Kettle, White Antelope, and Big Jake have travelled with me hundreds and hundreds of miles. Left Hand, the second chief of the Arapahoes, and Little Raven, the first chief of the Arapahoes, have been with me on scouts and in my camps for months together. Left Hand was killed by Chivington; so I am told by the agent and by others. His lodge happened to be one of the ten. A year ago Little Raven requested me to try and get the military removed from his reservation, which I did, through Mr. H. P. Bennet. You will see the correspondence in the report of the Commissioner of Indian Affairs for 1864. I can say that they were always friendly. They have often stated to me that they would not fight the whites under any circumstances. Left Hand particularly has said that the whites might murder their men and do anything they pleased to them, but they would never fight the whites.

Question. What caused our troops to make this attack upon them?

Answer. I do not know the immediate cause of Colonel Chivington attacking this village. I know that a year ago this spring Major Waller, of the regular army, crossed the plains and passed the reservation of the Cheyennes and Arapahoes; and he communicated to the Indian department that if Colonel Chivington was not stopped in his course of hunting down these Indians it would get us into a war that would cost us millions of dollars. I also saw from the reports in the papers that Lieutenant Ayres was hunting these Indians from camp to camp. Knowing their disposition, and knowing Lieutenant Ayres, having

9

appointed him myself as a lieutenant, I stated to the Indian department that if Colonel Chivington was not stopped in his course of sending Lieutenant Ayres after these Indians we should get into a general Indian war on the frontier.

Question. What was their object in hunting these Indians? what cause was there for it?

Answer. I could tell you the ostensible cause, but the real cause is beyond my knowledge. Colonel Chivington was ordered by General Curtis to rendezvous his forces last spring in the southeast part of Colorado for the ostensible purpose of making a raid into Texas. But, as they claimed, the Indian difficulties prevented him from doing so, and he kept his troops there hunting these Indians.

Question. You say that these Indians were of a remarkably friendly disposition?

Answer. Yes, sir.

Question. And inoffensive towards our people?

Answer. There never were two bands of Indians more friendly to the whites than Black Kettle's band and White Antelope's band, and One Eye, who was also killed in this massacre.

Question. Where were you when this massacre took place?

Answer. I was between Fort Leavenworth and the Camanche country, trying to meet the wild tribes of which I was appointed the agent. I found it very difficult to get to them. Little Raven had escaped from the massacre and got into the Camanche country. He was half a Camanche himself, speaking their language well, and is now with the Camanches with his band, and is one of the best men there. I am begging protection for him, if I can get to him.

Question. Can you state anything more in regard to this massacre?

Answer. I do not know anything positively, because I was not there; but I have my information from persons who were present. One of them, Captain Smith, is in this city now. He was there trading under the authority of Major Anthony; and I think Major Anthony is also in this city. He was second in command in that expedition. From them you can get more reliable information than I can give you, for mine is hearsay. I only know that these Indians were of a most friendly disposition. Mr. D. D. Colley is also here; he has been a trader in their camp for two years. His father, Major Colley, is their agent, and knows them intimately; better, if anything, than I do.

Question. Do you know whether these Indians had ever committed any depredations upon the whites?

Answer. I was not aware that they had; not this particular band.

---

*Testimony of Mr. John S. Smith.*

WASHINGTON, *March* 14, 1865.

Mr. JOHN S. SMITH sworn and examined.

By Mr. Gooch:

Question. Where is your place of residence?

Answer. Fort Lyon, Colorado.

Question. What is your occupation?

Answer. United States Indian interpreter and special Indian agent.

Question. Will you state to the committee all that you know in relation to the attack of Colonel Chivington upon the Cheyenne and Arapahoe Indians in November last?

10

Answer. Major Anthony was in command at Fort Lyon at the time. Those Indians had been induced to remain in the vicinity of Fort Lyon, and were promised protection by the commanding officer at Fort Lyon. The commanding officer saw proper to keep them some thirty or forty miles distant from the fort, for fear of some conflict between them and the soldiers or the travelling population, for Fort Lyon is on a great thoroughfare. He advised them to go out on what is called Sand creek, about forty miles, a little east of north from Fort Lyon. Some days after they had left Fort Lyon, when I had just recovered from a long spell of sickness, I was called on by Major S. G. Colley, who asked me if I was able and willing to go out and pay a visit to these Indians, ascertain their numbers, their general disposition toward the whites, and the points where other bands might be located in the interior.

Question. What was the necessity for obtaining that information?

Answer. Because there were different bands which were supposed to be at war; in fact, we knew at the time that they were at war with the white population in that country; but this band had been in and left the post perfectly satisfied. I left to go to this village of Indians on the 26th of November last. I arrived there on the 27th and remained there the 28th. On the morning of the 29th, between daylight and sunrise—nearer sunrise than daybreak—a large number of troops were discovered from three-quarters of a mile to a mile below the village. The Indians, who discovered them, ran to my camp, called me out, and wanted me to go and see what troops they were, and what they wanted. The head chief of the nation, Black Kettle, and head chief of the Cheyennes, was encamped there with us. Some years previous he had been presented with a fine American flag by Colonel Greenwood, a commissioner, who had been sent out there. Black Kettle ran this American flag up to the top of his lodge, with a small white flag tied right under it, as he had been advised to do in case he should meet with any troops out on the prairies. I then left my own camp and started for that portion of the troops that was nearest the village, supposing I could go up to them. I did not know but they might be strange troops, and thought my presence and explanations could reconcile matters. Lieutenant Wilson was in command of the detachment to which I tried to make my approach; but they fired several volleys at me, and I returned back to my camp and entered my lodge.

Question. Did these troops know you to be a white man?

Answer. Yes, sir; and the troops that went there knew I was in the village.

Question. Did you see Lieutenant Wilson, or were you seen by him?

Answer. I cannot say I was seen by him; but his troops were the first to fire at me.

Question. Did they know you to be a white man?

Answer. They could not help knowing it. I had on pants, a soldier's overcoat, and a hat such as I am wearing now. I was dressed differently from any Indian in the country. On my return I entered my lodge, not expecting to get out of it alive. I had two other men there with me : one was David Louderbach, a soldier, belonging to company G, 1st Colorado cavalry; the other, a man by the name of Watson, who was a hired hand of Mr. D. D. Colley, the son of Major Colley, the agent.

After I had left my lodge to go out and see what was going on, Colonel Chivington rode up to within fifty or sixty yards of where I was camped; he recognized me at once. They all call me Uncle John in that country. He said, "Run here, Uncle John; you are all right." I went to him as fast as I could. He told me to get in between him and his troops, who were then coming up very fast; I did so; directly another officer who knew me—Lieutenant Baldwin, in command of a battery—tried to assist me to get a horse; but there was no loose horse there at the time. He said, "Catch hold of the caisson, and keep up with us."

11

By this time the Indians had fled; had scattered in every direction. The troops were some on one side of the river and some on the other, following up the Indians. We had been encamped on the north side of the river; I followed along, holding on the caisson, sometimes running, sometimes walking. Finally, about a mile above the village, the troops had got a parcel of the Indians hemmed in under the bank of the river; as soon as the troops overtook them, they commenced firing on them; some troops had got above them, so that they were completely surrounded. There were probably a hundred Indians hemmed in there, men, women, and children; the most of the men in the village escaped.

By the time I got up with the battery to the place where these Indians were surrounded there had been some considerable firing. Four or five soldiers had been killed, some with arrows and some with bullets. The soldiers continued firing on these Indians, who numbered about a hundred, until they had almost completely destroyed them. I think I saw altogether some seventy dead bodies lying there; the greater portion women and children. There may have been thirty warriors, old and young; the rest were women and small children of different ages and sizes.

The troops at that time were very much scattered. There were not over two hundred troops in the main fight, engaged in killing this body of Indians under the bank. The balance of the troops were scattered in different directions, running after small parties of Indians who were trying to make their escape. I did not go to see how many they might have killed outside of this party under the bank of the river. Being still quite weak from my last sickness, I returned with the first body of troops that went back to the camp.

The Indians had left their lodges and property; everything they owned. I do not think more than one-half of the Indians left their lodges with their arms. I think there were between 800 and 1,000 men in this command of Un ted States troops. There was a part of three companies of the 1st Colorado, and the balance were what were called 100-days men of the 3d regiment. I am not able to say which party did the most execution on the Indians, because it was very much mixed up at the time.

We remained there that day after the fight. By 11 o'clock, I think, the entire number of soldiers had returned back to the camp where Colonel Chivington had returned. On their return he ordered the soldiers to destroy all the Indian property there, which they did, with the exception of what plunder they took away with them, which was considerable.

Question. How many Indians were there there?

Answer. There were 100 families of Cheyennes, and some six or eight lodges of Arapahoes.

Question. How many persons in all, should you say?

Answer. About 500; we estimate them at five to a lodge.

Question. 500 men, women, and children?

Answer. Yes, sir.

Question. Do you know the reason for that attack on the Indians?

Answer. I do not know any exact reason. I have heard a great many reasons given. I have heard that that whole Indian war had been brought on for selfish purposes. Colonel Chivington was running for Congress in Colorado, and there were other things of that kind; and last spring a year ago he was looking for an order to go to the front, and I understand he had this Indian war in view to retain himself and his troops in that country, to carry out his electioneering purposes.

Question. In what way did this attack on the Indians further the purpose of Colonel Chivington?

Answer. It was said—I did not hear him say it myself, but it was said that he would do something; he had this regiment of three-months men, and did not want them to go out without doing some service. Now he had been told repeatedly by different persons—by myself, as well as others—where he could find the hostile bands.

The same chiefs who were killed in this village of Cheyennes had been up to see Colonel Chivington in Denver but a short time previous to this attack. He himself told them that he had no power to treat with them; that he had received telegrams from General Curtis directing him to fight all Indians he met with in that country. Still he would advise them, if they wanted any assistance from the whites, to go to their nearest military post in their country, give up their arms and the stolen property, if they had any, and then they would receive directions in what way to act. This was told them by Colonel Chivington and by Governor Evans, of Colorado. I myself interpreted for them and for the Indians.

Question. Did Colonel Chivington hold any communication with these Indians, or any of them, before making the attack upon them?

Answer. No, sir, not then. He had some time previously held a council with them at Denver city. When we first recovered the white prisoners from the Indians, we invited some of the chiefs to go to Denver, inasmuch as they had sued for peace, and were willing to give up these white prisoners. We promised to take the chiefs to Denver, where they had an interview with men who had more power than Major Wynkoop had, who was the officer in command of the detachment that went out to recover these white prisoners. Governor Evans and Colonel Chivington were in Denver, and were present at this council. They told the Indians to return with Major Wynkoop, and whatever he agreed on doing with them would be recognized by them.

I returned with the Indians to Fort Lyon. There we let them go out to their villages to bring in their families, as they had been invited through the proclamation or circular of the governor during the month of June, I think. They were gone some twelve or fifteen days from Fort Lyon, and then they returned with their families. Major Wynkoop had made them one or two issues of provisions previous to the arrival of Major Anthony there to assume command. Then Major Wynkoop, who is now in command at Fort Lyon, was ordered to Fort Leavenworth on some business with General Curtis, I think.

Then Major Anthony, through me, told the Indians that he did not have it in his power to issue rations to them, as Major Wynkoop had done. He said that he had assumed command at Fort Lyon, and his orders were positive from headquarters to fight the Indians in the vicinity of Fort Lyon, or at any other point in the Territory where they could find them. He said that he had understood that they had been behaving very badly. But on seeing Major Wynkoop and others there at Fort Lyon, he was happy to say that things were not as had been represented, and he could not pursue any other course than that of Major Wynkoop, except the issuing rations to them. He then advised them to go out to some near point, where there was buffalo, not too far from Fort Lyon, or they might meet with troops from the Platte, who would not know them from the hostile bands. This was the southern band of Cheyennes; there is another band called the northern band. They had no apprehensions in the world of any trouble with the whites at the time this attack was made.

Question. Had there been, to your knowledge, any hostile act or demonstration on the part of these Indians, or any of them?

Answer. Not in this band. But the northern band, the band known by the name of Dog soldiers of Cheyennes, had committed many depredations on the Platte.

Question. Do you know whether or not Colonel Chivington knew the friendly character of these Indians before he made the attack upon them?

Answer. It is my opinion that he did.

Question. On what is that opinion based?

Answer. On this fact, that he stopped all persons from going on ahead of him.

He stopped the mail, and would not allow any person to go on ahead of him at the time he was on his way from Denver city to Fort Lyon. He placed a guard around old Colonel Bent, the former agent there; he stopped a Mr. Hagues and many men who were on their way to Fort Lyon. He took the fort by surprise, and as soon as he got there he posted pickets all around the fort, and then left at 8 o'clock that night for this Indian camp.

Question. Was that anything more than the exercise of ordinary precaution in following Indians?

Answer. Well, sir, he was told that there were no Indians in the vicinity of Fort Lyon, except Black Kettle's band of Cheyennes and Left Hand's band of Arapahoes.

Question. How do you know that?

Answer. I was told so.

By Mr. Buckalew:

Question. Do you know it of your own knowledge?

Answer. I cannot say I do.

Question. You did not talk with him about it before the attack?

Answer. No, sir.

By Mr. Gooch:

Question. When you went out to him, you had no opportunity to hold intercourse with him?

Answer. None whatever; he had just commenced his fire against the Indians.

Question. Did you have any communication with him at any time while there?

Answer. Yes, sir.

Question. What was it?

Answer. He asked me many questions about a son of mine, who was killed there afterwards. He asked me what Indians were there, what chiefs; and I told him as fully as I knew.

By Mr. Buckalew:

Question. When did you talk with him?

Answer. On the day of the attack. He asked me many questions about the chiefs who were there, and if I could recognize them if I saw them. I told him it was possible I might recollect the principal chiefs. They were terribly mutilated, lying there in the water and sand; most of them in the bed of the creek, dead and dying, making many struggles. They were so badly mutilated and covered with sand and water that it was very hard for me to tell one from another. However, I recognized some of them—among them the chief One Eye, who was employed by our government at $125 a month and rations to remain in the village as a spy. There was another called War Bonnet, who was here two years ago with me. There was another by the name of Standing-in-the-Water, and I supposed Black Kettle was among them, but it was not Black Kettle. There was one there of his size and dimensions in every way, but so tremendously mutilated that I was mistaken in him. I went out with Lieutenant Colonel Bowen, to see how many I could recognize.

By Mr. Gooch:

Question. Did you tell Colonel Chivington the character and disposition of these Indians at any time during your interviews on this day?

Answer. Yes, sir.

Question. What did he say in reply?

Answer. He said he could not help it; that his orders were positive to attack the Indians.

Question. From whom did he receive these orders?

Answer. I do not know; I presume from General Curtis.

Question. Did he tell you?

Answer. Not to my recollection.

Question. Were the women and children slaughtered indiscriminately, or only so far as they were with the warriors ?

Answer. Indiscriminately.

Question. Were there any acts of barbarity perpetrated there that came under your own observation ?

Answer. Yes, sir; I saw the bodies of those lying there cut all to pieces, worse mutilated than any I ever saw before; the women cut all to pieces.

By Mr. Buckalew:

Question. How cut ?

Answer. With knives; scalped; their brains knocked out; children two or three months old; all ages lying there, from sucking infants up to warriors.

By Mr. Gooch :

Question. Did you see it done ?

Answer. Yes, sir; I saw them fall.

Question. Fall when they were killed ?

Answer. Yes, sir.

Question. Did you see them when they were mutilated ?

Answer. Yes, sir.

Question. By whom were they mutilated ?

Answer. By the United States troops.

Question. Do you know whether or not it was done by the direction or consent of any of the officers ?

Answer. I do not; I hardly think it was.

By Mr. Buckalew :

Question. What was the date of that massacre ?

Answer. On the 29th of November last.

Question. Did you speak of these barbarities to Colonel Chivington ?

Answer. No, sir; I had nothing at all to say about it, because at that time they were hostile towards me, from the fact of my being there. They probably supposed that I might be compromised with them in some way or other.

Question. Who called on you to designate the bodies of those who were killed ?

Answer. Colonel Chivington himself asked me if I would ride out with Lieutenant Colonel Bowen, and see how many chiefs or principal men I could recognize.

Question. Can you state how many Indians were killed—how many women and how many children ?

Answer. Perhaps one-half were men, and the balance were women and children. I do not think that I saw more than 70 lying dead then, as far as I went. But I saw parties of men scattered in every direction, pursuing little bands of Indians.

Question. What time of day or night was this attack made ?

Answer. The attack commenced about sunrise, and lasted until between 10 and 11 o'clock.

Question. How large a body of troops ?

Answer. From 800 to 1,000 men.

By Mr. Gooch :

Question. What amount of resistance did the Indians make ?

Answer. I think that probably there may have been about 60 or 70 warriors who were armed and stood their ground and fought. Those that were unarmed got out of the way as they best could.

Question. How many of our troops were killed, and how many wounded ?

Answer. There were ten killed on the ground, and thirty-eight wounded; four of the wounded died at Fort Lyon before I came on east.

15

Question. Were there any other barbarities or atrocities committed there other than those you have mentioned, that you saw?

Answer. Yes, sir; I had a half-breed son there, who gave himself up. He started at the time the Indians fled; being a half-breed he had but little hope of being spared, and seeing them fire at me, he ran away with the Indians for the distance of about a mile. During the fight up there he walked back to my camp and went into the lodge. It was surrounded by soldiers at the time. He came in quietly and sat down; he remained there that day, that night, and the next day in the afternoon; about four o'clock in the evening, as I was sitting inside the camp, a soldier came up outside of the lodge and called me by name. I got up and went out; he took me by the arm and walked towards Colonel Chivington's camp, which was about sixty yards from my camp. Said he, "I am sorry to tell you, but they are going to kill your son Jack." I knew the feeling towards the whole camp of Indians, and that there was no use to make any resistance. I said, "I can't help it." I then walked on towards where Colonel Chivington was standing by his camp-fire; when I had got within a few feet of him I heard a gun fired, and saw a crowd run to my lodge, and they told me that Jack was dead.

Question. What action did Colonel Chivington take in regard to that matter?

Answer. Major Anthony, who was present, told Colonel Chivington that he had heard some remarks made, indicating that they were desirous of killing Jack; and that he (Colonel Chivington) had it in his power to save him, and that by saving him he might make him a very useful man, as he was well acquainted with all the Cheyenne and Arapahoe country, and he could be used as a guide or interpreter. Colonel Chivington replied to Major Anthony, as the Major himself told me, that he had no orders to receive and no advice to give. Major Anthony is now in this city.

By Mr. Buckalew:

Question. Did Chivington say anything to you, or you to him, about the firing?

Answer. Nothing directly; there were a number of officers sitting around the fire, with the most of whom I was acquainted.

Question. Was there any business to transact at Chivington's camp when you were brought there?

Answer. None with me; except that I was invited to go there and remain in that camp, as I might be considered in danger of losing my life if I was away from there.

By Mr. Gooch:

Question. Were there any other Indians or half-breeds there at that time?

Answer. Yes, sir; Mr. Bent had three sons there; one employed as a guide for these troops at the time, and two others living there in the village with the Indians; and a Mr. Gerry had a son there.

Question. Were there any other murders after the first day's massacre?

Answer. There was none, except of my son.

Question. Were there any other atrocities which you have not mentioned?

Answer. None that I saw myself. There were two women that white men had families by; they were saved from the fact of being in my lodge at the time. One ran to my lodge; the other was taken prisoner by a soldier who knew her and brought her to my lodge for safety. They both had children. There were some small children, six or seven years old, who were taken prisoners near the camp. I think there were three of them taken to Denver with these troops.

Question. Were the women and children that were killed, killed during the fight with the Indians?

Answer. During the fight, or during the time of the attack.

Question. Did you see any women or children killed after the fight was over?
Answer. None.
Question. Did you see any Indians killed after the fight was over?
Answer. No, sir.

By Mr. Buckalew:

Question. Were the warriors and women and children all huddled together when they were attacked?
Answer. They started and left the village altogether, in a body, trying to escape.

By Mr. Gooch:

Question. Do you know anything as to the amount of property that those Indians had there?
Answer. Nothing more than their horses. They were supposed to own ten horses and mules to a lodge; that would make about a thousand head of horses and mules in that camp. The soldiers drove off about six hundred head.
Question. Had they any money?
Answer. I understood that some of the soldiers found some money, but I did not see it. Mr. D. D. Colley had some provisions and goods in the village at the time, and Mr. Louderback and Mr. Watson were employed by him to trade there. I was to interpret for them, direct them, and see that they were cared for in the village. They had traded for one hundred and four buffalo robes, one fine mule, and two horses. This was all taken away from them. Colonel Chivington came to me and told me I might rest assured that he would see the goods paid for. He had confiscated these buffalo robes for the dead and wounded; and there was also some sugar and coffee and tea taken for the same purpose.

I would state that in his report Colonel Chivington states that after this raid on Sand creek against the Cheyenne and Arapahoe Indians he travelled northeast some eighty miles in the direction of some hostile bands of Sioux Indians. Now that is very incorrect, according to my knowledge of matters; I remained with Colonel Chivington's camp, and returned on his trail towards Fort Lyon from the camp where he made this raid. I went down with him to what is called the forks of the Sandy. He then took a due south course for the Arkansas river, and I went to Fort Lyon with the killed and wounded, and an escort to take us in. Colonel Chivington proceeded down the Arkansas river, and got within eleven miles of another band of Arapahoe Indians, but did not succeed in overtaking them. He then returned to Fort Lyon, re-equipped, and started immediately for Denver.

Question. Have you spent any considerable portion of your life with the Indians?
Answer. The most of it.
Question. How many years have you been with the Indians?
Answer. I have been twenty seven successive years with the Cheyennes and Arapahoes. Before that I was in the country as a trapper and hunter in the Rocky mountains.
Question. For how long time have you acted as Indian interpreter?
Answer. For some fifteen or eighteen years.
Question. By whom have you been so employed?
Answer. By Major Fitzpatrick, Colonel Bent, Major Colley, Colonel J. W. Whitfield, and a great deal of the time for the military as guide and interpreter?

By Mr. Buckalew:

Question. How many warriors were estimated in Colonel Chivington's report as having been in this Indian camp?
Answer. About nine hundred.

17

Question. How many were there?
Answer. About two hundred warriors; they average about two warriors to a lodge, and there were about one hundred lodges.

---

### Testimony of Captain S. M. Robbins.

WASHINGTON, *March* 14, 1865.

Captain S. M. ROBBINS sworn and examined.

By Mr. Gooch:

Question. What is your position in the army?
Answer. I am a captain of the 1st Colorado cavalry.
Question. Were you with Colonel Chivington at the time of the attack on the Cheyenne Indians, in November last?
Answer. I was not.
Question. Have you any knowledge relating to that attack?
Answer. I have no personal knowlege of anything that transpired at Sand creek.
Question. Have you any knowledge in relation to matters connected with that massacre?
Answer. I know about the Indian difficulties in that country, but nothing with regard to that particular difficulty.
Question. What do you know about that campaign?
Answer. I only know that a campaign was organized against the Indians.

By Mr. Loan:

Question. What Indians?
Answer. The Cheyennes and Arapahoes, and all others that were hostile, or were supposed to be hostile.

By Mr. Gooch:

Question. Do you know under what orders Colonel Chivington was acting?
Answer. No, sir. I never saw any orders. I suppose that he acted under the authority of the department commander, General Curtis; but I know nothing positively about that.
Question. Where were you at the time of this attack?
Answer. In the city of Denver, Colorado.

By Mr. Loan:

Question. Who was the district commander at Denver?
Answer. Colonel Chivington was.
Question. You were on his staff?
Answer. Yes, sir.
Question. In what capacity?
Answer. Chief of cavalry.
Question. What was the character of these Cheyenne Indians on Sand creek?
Answer. I do not know.
Question. Do you know whether they were hostile or friendly?
Answer. I saw a portion of their chiefs in the city of Denver, some two months before this action, or massacre, or assault took place. They came there under an escort furnished by Major Wynkoop. They came for the purpose of holding a consultation with the governor, who I believe is acting superintendent of Indian affairs there. They were all the tribe I ever saw.

Question. What bands were killed there?

Answer. The Cheyennes and Arapahoes?

Question. What particular bands of these Indians?

Answer. I merely know from hearsay the names of those chiefs.

Question. As chief of cavalry, on Colonel Chivington's staff, do you know anything of the orders General Curtis sent him in regard to this matter?

Answer. No, sir.

Question. Do you know anything about the organization of the force that went out under Colonel Chivington?

Answer. I do.

Question. State it.

Answer. It was organized by direction of the Secretary of War, for the purpose of operating in that country against the Indians. It was a hundred-days regiment.

Question. Was Colonel Chivington the colonel of it?

Answer. No, sir; Colonel George H. Shoup was the colonel of it. There was great difficulty in furnishing the horses and ordnance stores necessary to mount and equip the regiment. Two months of their time had expired before they were ready to move. They moved from that point about the first of November. And on the 29th of November, I think, this action was fought, or this massacre was made, at Sand creek.

Question. At what time did Colonel Chivington join this command, and what other troops had he with him?

Answer. He joined the command in person, I should think about the 15th of November, and had with him part of six companies of the 1st regiment of Colorado volunteers.

Question. What was his whole force?

Answer. I should judge about 700 men.

Question. The regiment of hundred-days men, and the battalion of 1st Colorado volunteers?

Answer. The whole of the hundred-days regiment were not there. They were not all mounted.

Question. Will you state a little further about the Indians that came into Denver with Major Wynkoop? What was the object of their coming in?

Answer. For some time previous there had been massacres of whites, in the vicinity of Denver, by Indians, as we supposed, and prisoners were taken. Some time in August or September Major Wynkoop, commanding at Fort Lyon, received information from the Indians in the vicinity of Smoky Hill that they had some white prisoners whom they were anxious to give up, or exchange for two Indians that were with one of our companies as scouts. At all events, this communication from the Indians induced Major Wynkoop to take 150 men and two or three pieces of artillery and go out there. He went out there, and, as I understood, when he came back he brought the white prisoners the Indians had held, and a number of their principal chiefs came with him to Denver—out of the district in which Major Wynkoop was serving into the district of Colorado. There they had a consultation with Governor Evans, of Colorado, Colonel Chivington, and other prominent and leading men. The Indians made statements, which I heard interpreted by Mr. Smith, in regard to their friendly feelings towards the whites. Whether their acts justified them or not was rather an open question. They stated their desire for peace. My recollection is that the governor told them they had levied war against the United States, or what amounts to that, and that soon the white soldiers would cover the plains. He said that if they were friendly, as they had said, they must seek the protection of the military posts, for the whites could not discriminate between Indians on the plains. That their going on the military reservations would afford the best evidence of their friendly feelings towards the whites; and my understanding is that a portion of those Indians, if not all of them, sought the military reservation at Fort Lyon with that understanding.

By Mr. Gooch :

Question. Were they on that military reservation when this attack was made on them ?

Answer. No, sir. I suppose it was found inconvenient to have so many of them in the vicinity of the post, on account of their natural thieving propensities, and they were ordered off on this Sand creek, about thirty-five miles from the fort, on their own reservation, where they could hunt.

Question. They were where they had been directed, by the military authorities, to go ?

Answer. So I understand. Major Anthony, who is here, was a portion of the time in command at Fort Lyon, and he could tell about that.

For the information of the committee, I should like to say a friendly word, under the circumstances, in the Chivington interest. For a year and a half past there has been a state of war existing between the Indians and the whites, as far as the opinion of the Indians was concerned ; whether by the authority of the head chiefs or not we cannot tell. At all events, the interruption of communication on the Arkansas route and on the Platte route raised the price of everything consumed by the people out here. And the people emphatically demanded that something should be done. The point I wish to make is, that perhaps Colonel Chivington might have been forced into this by the sentiment of the people.

Question. Would the sentiment of the people lead a man to attack Indians who were known to be friendly, and who were known to be trying to avert hostilities ?

Answer. I should say it would. They wanted some Indians killed ; whether friendly or not they did not stop long to inquire.

---

*Testimony of Mr. D. D. Colley.*

WASHINGTON, *March* 14, 1865.

Mr. D. D. COLLEY sworn and examined.

By Mr. Gooch :

Question. Where is your place of residence ?
Answer. At Fort Lyon.

Question. What is your occupation ?
Answer. I have been trading with the Indians more or less for the last three years.

Question. Will you state what you know in relation to the attack on the Cheyenne Indians by Colonel Chivington, on the 29th of November last?

Answer. I was in St. Louis at that time. But I was at Fort Lyon when two Indians came in and told Major Wynkoop that they had some white prisoners. They rode in and rode up to the major's headquarters. The major, as well as the balance of us, felt like using them a little rough, for we were all feeling a little hard towards the Indians. I went out and saw they were two Indians with whom I was well acquainted, and who I knew had been trying to keep peace between the Indians and the whites. Just as I went up to them the major came up and spoke very harsh to them, and told them to get down off their horses. I told the major that I knew them, and that they were both friendly. They then got down off their horses and went into the major's room, and told him that they had some white prisoners, and that he could get them by going after them.

The major took his command of 125 or 150 men, and was gone about two weeks, and brought the white prisoners. Some Indians, I do not know how many, 20 or 30 of them, came back with him, and went to Denver with him. I went there also. There they had a council with Colonel Chivington and Governor Evans, and promises were made to them. There was also a council held with them by Major Wynkoop. Major Anthony, after he took command at Fort Lyon, also held a council with them. It was thought best to have them come in at Fort Lyon. Major Wynkoop promised them protection if they would come in, and they came in on the strength of those promises. I talked with them several times after they had brought their families in. The major promised them protection until he could hear from General Curtis. Then if they proposed to make a treaty, all right; if not, he would let them go in time to get out of the country.

Shortly after that, Major Anthony took command of Fort Lyon by order of General Curtis. He said he was ordered to kill these Indians and drive them away. I told him what promises had been made them. They were called together, and they told him that they considered themselves prisoners of war, and that they would not fight under any circumstances. I know that a number of the chiefs present there had been laboring over a year to keep peace between the Indians and whites. They told Major Anthony that he could take them out and kill them if he saw fit. He told them he was sent there to fight Indians. But he would ask them to give up their arms, and some stock they had which belonged to the government; and if they did so he would issue to them prisoners' rations until such time as he had other orders. And they were living there and getting these rations until I left Fort Lyon to come to St. Louis.

Question. Did they comply with the terms proposed by Major Anthony?

Answer. Yes, sir.

Question. Do you know whether Colonel Chivington was informed of this arrangement?

Answer. I know that he was.

Question. How do you know that?

Answer. Because the Indian agent told me he had informed him.

Question. Informed him before he made his attack?

Answer. Yes, sir. When he came down there to make the attack he was told that the Indians were out there under promise of protection. They had been at the post until a short time before, when they had moved out on the Big Sandy at the request of Major Anthony. The Sioux, and a party of Cheyennes called the Dog soldiers, were at war with the whites. And these Indians on the Big Sandy would come in occasionally and report what the other Indians were doing.

Question. Do you know what induced Colonel Chivington to attack these Indians?

Answer. I do not know; I have my opinion.

Question. Can you think of any reason which induced him to make the attack?

Answer. I have thought for more than a year that he was determined to have a war with these Indians. That has been the general belief of men in our part of the country. I was acquainted with all the chiefs who were there, and I know they had all tried hard to keep peace between the Indians and whites. I was with a portion of this same village a year ago last winter, when the first talk of an outbreak commenced. All the chiefs who were killed by Colonel Chivington have labored as hard as men could to keep peace between the whites and Indians. They could not control the band called Dog soldiers, who had undoubtedly committed depredations.

21

Question. Do you know anything else in connexion with this matter that is important, which you have not stated?

Answer. I do not know that I do.

By Mr. Loan:

Question. What is the distinguishing name of this band of Indians upon which the attack was made?

Answer. They were known as Black Kettle's band. Black Kettle was the chief of the whole Cheyenne nation; but this was the band that was always with him. The other chiefs that were there were also with him.

Question. There must have been a chief to have led the hostile Indians?

Answer. Yes, sir. But this band was the one always with Black Kettle.

Question. About what number do you suppose were killed on Sand creek?

Answer. I should judge there were between 100 and 150. What I judge from is this: the inspector of the district went with me to Fort Lyon, and he went out to the battle-field. The bodies were lying there then. They spent half a day on the battle-field, and found 69 bodies.

Question. Were there any women and children killed?

Answer. The inspector told me that about three-fourths of them were women and children.

---

*Testimony of Major Scott J. Anthony.*

WASHINGTON, *March* 14, 1865.

Major SCOTT J. ANTHONY sworn and examined.

By Mr. Loan:

Question. What is your place of residence?

Answer. Fort Lyon, Colorado Territory.

Question. Do you hold any position in the military or civil service of the government?

Answer. None at present.

Question. Have you held any at any time?

Answer. I was major of the 1st Colorado cavalry from the 1st of November, 1862, until the 21st of January, 1865.

Question. Were you present at the killing of the Cheyenne Indians, on their reserve, not far from Fort Lyon, on Sand creek?

Answer. It was not an Indian reserve. I was present at the time.

Question. State what force was organized, under what orders it acted, under whose command it was, and what was done.

Answer. The command reached Fort Lyon on the morning of the 28th of November last, under command of Colonel Chivington. It consisted of a portion of the 1st regiment of Colorado cavalry, and about 600 men of the 3d regiment of Colorado cavalry; numbering in all in the neighborhood of 700 men, with two pieces of artillery. I joined them there with 125 men and two pieces of artillery. We left on the night of the 28th, for Sand creek, and reached there on the morning of the 29th at daybreak. We found an Indian camp of about 130 lodges, consisting mostly of Cheyennes; there were a small band of Arapahoe Indians with them. The Indians were attacked by us, under command of Colonel Chivington, about sunrise in the morning. Detachments from the command took position on two sides of their camp. There had been a little firing before that. When I first came up with my command, the Indians, men, women, and children, were in a group together, and there was firing from our command upon them. The Indians attempted to escape, the women and children, and our artillery opened on them while they were running. Quite a party of Indians took position under the bank, in the bed of the creek, and returned fire upon us. We fought them about seven hours, I should think, there being firing on both sides. The loss on our side was 49 men killed and wounded; on theirs I suppose it was about 125.

Question. Under what chief was that band of Indians?

Answer. Black Kettle, I think, was the principal chief. There were several chiefs in the camp, but Black Kettle, I think, was the head chief.

Question. Were there any warriors in that camp?

Answer. There were.

Question. What number, do you suppose?

Answer. I would not be able to tell very accurately. There were a great many men who fought us; I should think there were in the neighborhood of a hundred men who were fighting us while we were there. Perhaps there were not quite so many as that, but as near as I could judge there were from 75 to 100 Indians returning our fire. I was in command at Fort Lyon, and had held a council with these Indians before; had talked with them, and had recognized Black Kettle as their head chief.

Question. What was the result of the conference you had with them?

Answer. The circumstances were about these : I was in command at Fort Larned, 240 miles east of Fort Lyon, which place the Indians had attacked in the spring, stealing all the stock at the post, burning the bridges, and damaging the post considerably. Major Wynkoop, who had been in command at Fort Lyon, had had some difficulty with the Indians at that point. He had proposed terms of peace with the Indians, which action was not approved at the head-quarters of the department or district.

Question. Were there any military orders issued disapproving his arrangements?

Answer. There were.

Question. Can you give the numbers of these orders, and by whom issued?

Answer. I have copies of them, I think. One was Special Order No. 4, paragraph No. 7, from headquarters of the district of Upper Kansas. There were several orders in regard to the same matter.

Question. What I want is the order of department headquarters disapproving of what Major Wynkoop had done, and also the order of district headquarters.

Answer. I do not think I have those orders in the city.

Question. Do you know who has them?

Answer. I do not. General Curtis was the commander of the department at the time this difficulty took place between Major Wynkoop and the Indians at Smoky Hill, and Major General Blunt was in command of the district. I was out with Major General Blunt in a campaign against the Indians.

Question. Did you ever see those orders from the department headquarters disapproving of Major Wynkoop's action in regard to that matter?

Answer. Only so far as it related to his unmilitary conduct.

Question. I mean his attempt to pacify the Indians?

Answer. I have never seen those orders; I have heard of them.

Question. Now, to return to the point when you were in command at Fort Lyon.

Answer. I took command there on the second day of November.

Question. You say you held a conference with the Indians? State what occurred.

Answer. At the time I took command at the post there was a band of Arapahoe Indians encamped about a mile from the post, numbering, in men, women, and children, 652. They were visiting the post almost every day. I met them and had a talk with them. Among them was Left Hand, who was a chief among the Arapahoes. He with his band was with the party at that time. I talked with them, and they proposed to do whatever I said; whatever

Part VI——2

23

I said for them to do they would do. I told them that I could not feed them; that I could not give them anything to eat; that there were positive orders forbidding that; and that I could not permit them to come within the limits of the post. At the same time they might remain where they were, and I would treat them as prisoners of war if they remained; that they would have to surrender to me all their arms and turn over to me all stolen property they had taken from the government or citizens. These terms they accepted. They turned over to me some twenty head of stock, mules, and horses, and a few arms, but not a quarter of the arms that report stated they had in their possession. The arms they turned over to me were almost useless. I fed them for some ten days. At the end of that time I told them I could not feed them any more; that they better go out to the buffalo country where they could kill game to subsist upon. I returned their arms to them, and they left the post. But before leaving they sent word out to the Cheyennes that I was not very friendly towards them.

Question. How do you know that?

Answer. Through several of their chiefs; Neva, an Arapahoe chief; Left Hand, of the Arapahoes; then Black Kettle and War Bonnet, of the Cheyennes. A delegation of the Cheyennes, numbering, I suppose, fifty or sixty men, came in just before the Arapahoes left the post. I met them outside of the post and talked with them. They said they wanted to make peace; that they had no desire to fight against us any longer; that there had been difficulty between the whites and Indians there, and they had no desire to fight any longer. I told them I had no authority from department headquarters to make peace with them; that I could not permit them to visit the post and come within the lines; that when they had been permitted to do so at Fort Larned, while the squaws and children of the different tribes that visited that post were dancing in front of the officers' quarters and on the parade ground, the Indians had made an attack on the post, fired on the guard, and run off the stock, and I was afraid the same thing might occur at Fort Lyon. I would not permit them to visit the post at all. I told them I could make no offers of peace to them until I heard from district headquarters. I told them, however, that they might go out and camp on Sand creek, and remain there if they chose to do so; but they should not camp in the vicinity of the post; and if I had authority to make peace with them I would go out and let them know of it.

In the mean time I was writing to district headquarters constantly, stating to them that there was a band of Indians within forty miles of the post—a small band—while a very large band was about 100 miles from the post. That I was strong enough with the force I had with me to fight the Indians on Sand creek, but not strong enough to fight the main band. That I should try to keep the Indians quiet until such time as I received re-enforcements; and that as soon as re-enforcements did arrive we should go further and find the main party.

But before the re-enforcements came from district headquarters, Colonel Chivington came to Fort Lyon with his command, and I joined him and went out on that expedition to Sand creek. I never made any offer to the Indians. It was the understanding that I was not in favor of peace with them. They so understood me, I suppose; at least I intended they should. In fact, I often heard of it through their interpreters that they did not suppose we were friendly towards them.

Question. What number of men did you have at Fort Lyon?

Answer. I had about 280 men.

Question. What was the number of Indians around Fort Lyon at any one time when you were talking to them?

Answer. I do not think there were over 725 Indians—men, women and children—within the vicinity of the post.

24

Question. At the time you held the conference with the Arapahoes, Left Hand, and others, how many men were present above the age of eighteen?

Answer. I should suppose from 80 to 100.

Question. Why did you not capture those Indians at that time?

Answer. I might say I did. I did not take them because I had instructions from district headquarters, as I construed them, to go and fight them wherever I met them. While they were there at the post I did intend to open fire upon them, in accordance with my instructions.

Question. Why did you not do it?

Answer. They were willing to accede to any request I might make. They turned over to me their arms and the property they had stolen from the government and citizens.

Question. What property did they turn over?

Answer. Fourteen head of mules and six head of horses.

Question. Was it property purporting to have been stolen by them?

Answer. Yes, sir.

Question. From whom?

Answer. They did not say. Yet some of it was recognized; some of it was branded " U. S." Some was recognized as being stock that belonged to citizens. It was generally understood afterwards—I did not know it at that time—that the son of the head chief of the Arapahoes, Little Raven, and I think another, had attacked a small government train and killed one man.

Question. What had Little Raven to do with Black Kettle's band?

Answer. He was not with them at the time; Left Hand was.

Question. These Indians surrendered to you, and you took their arms from them?

Answer. Yes, sir.

Question. Did you issue rations to them?

Answer. I did.

Question. What authority had you for returning their arms to them and ordering them off?

Answer. I had no orders in the matter. My instructions were to act upon my own judgment. At the same time there were orders issued that they should not be fed or clothed at the post.

Question. Who issued those orders?

Answer. General Curtis.

Question. Were those orders issued after you had received the arms of the Indians?

Answer. Before that.

Question. Then why did you receive those arms, and feed those Indians in violation of General Curtis's orders?

Answer. I received the arms and told the Indians I could only issue them rations as prisoners. I fed them while there as prisoners, but afterwards released them.

Question. That is what I want to get at. Where did you get authority for releasing the prisoners that were captured?

Answer. I had no written authority for it.

Question. You did it upon your own judgment.

Answer. Yes, sir. That was my instructions, to act upon my own judgment in the matter. I thought we could not afford to feed them at the post; and they were in the buffalo country where they could subsist themselves.

Question. If they were dangerous to the government, why did you release them?

Answer. I did not so consider them then. They were most all women and children, this Arapahoe band.

Question. Who was the chief of that band?

25

Answer. Little Raven was the chief of those I held as prisoners.

Question. Was Black Kettle with his band at the fort at any time you were in command?

Answer. No, sir, not at the fort; they passed by it.

Question. Did you ever hold any conference with them?

Answer. I did.

Question. At what place?

Answer. At the commissary building, about a half a mile from the fort.

Question. What number of men were with Black Kettle at that time?

Answer. I should think not far from sixty.

Question. State what passed at that conference, so far as you can remember.

Answer. They came in and inquired of me whether I had any authority to make peace with them. They said that they had heard through the Arapahoes that "things looked dark"—that was the term they used—that we were at war with them; that they had come in to ascertain whether these bad reports they had received were correct or not. I stated to them that I had no authority to make peace with them. That their young men were then out in the field fighting against us, and that I had no authority and no instructions to make any peace with them. I told them they might go back on Sand creek, or between there and the headquarters of the Smoky Hills, and remain there until I received instructions from the department headquarters, from General Curtis; and that in case I did receive any authority to make peace with them I would go right over and let them know it. I did not state to them that I would give them notice in case we intended to attack them. They went away with that understanding, that in case I received instructions from department headquarters I was to let them know it. But before I did receive any such instructions Colonel Chivington arrived there, and this affair on Sand creek took place.

Question. Why did you not arrest Black Kettle and his band there, or attack them when you had them at your mercy?

Answer. I did not do it, because I did not consider it a matter of policy to do it.

Question. Why not?

Answer. Because within 100 miles of us was a party of 2,500 or 3,000 Indians. Black Kettle's band belonged to the same tribe of Indians, and I believed that so soon as I made any attack upon Black Kettle's party, this whole tribe of Indians would rise and cut off our communication on both routes.

Question. How did you know that that party of 3,000 Indians were within 100 miles?

Answer. Black Kettle told me so himself. Jack Smith, the son of the Indian interpreter there, a half-breed, told me the same. One Eye, a Cheyenne chief, told me the same. On two different occasions One Eye told me when small raiding parties were going to start out from the main Sioux and Cheyenne camp to commit depredations on the road, and depredations were committed just about the time they said they would be, yet too soon for us to prevent it. I was satisfied in my own mind that if I had attacked Black Kettle there, although I might have taken his entire camp at any time, it would be the cause of opening up a general Indian war, and I was not strong enough to defend the settlements in case they commenced again.

Question. I understood you to say that the Indians were already at war with the whites.

Answer. Yes, sir. That is, they were sending out their raiding parties. Their men came there on Smoke Hill, and every little while a raiding party would make an attack on some train or some ranch, yet there was no large party at that particular time.

Question. Were there any other Indians at Sand creek, except Black Kettle's band and the Arapahoes of whom you have spoken?

Answer. There were none but Black Kettle's band, and, as I have since ascertained, a few lodges of Arapahoes, under Left Hand.

Question. Little Raven's band was not there?

Answer. No, sir. There was but a small portion of Black Kettle's band there. He was the chief of all the Cheyennes.

Question. There was a particular band that went with him, of which he was the immediate chief, notwithstanding he was also the chief of the whole nation?

Answer. Yes, sir.

Question. And it was the subordinate chiefs who were at war with the whites.

Answer. Yes, sir.

Question. Black Kettle had a band which were always with him?

Answer. Yes, sir.

Question. Now, what I want to know is, what other Indians were at Sand creek when you advised Black Kettle and his band to go over there?

Answer. I think there were only a very few Arapahoes under Left Hand.

Question. Did they have their women and children with them?

Answer. Yes, sir.

Question. How long were they at Sand creek before Colonel Chivington came along with his force?

Answer. I should think about twelve days.

Question. Did you receive any communication from those Indians on Sand creek during those twelve days? Did they furnish you with information of any kind?

Answer. I received some information; I do not know that it came from that band. I had employed at that time, on a salary of $125 a month and a ration, One Eye, who was a chief of the Cheyennes. He was to remain in this Cheyenne camp as a spy, and give me information from time to time of the movements of this particular band, and also to go over to the head of the Smoke Hill to the Sioux and Cheyenne camp there, and notify me whenever any movement was made by those Indians; but he had gone only as far as Sand creek when Colonel Chivington made this attack on the Indians at Sand creek, and he was killed there.

Question. Then you cannot tell whether you had any communications during those twelve days from the Indians on Sand creek?

Answer. They would send in to the post frequently. General Curtis had issued an order that no Indian should be permitted to visit the post. I had ordered them away, and the guard had fired upon them when they refused to obey that order—fired upon them several times. I told them they could not come in, and that if they had any communication to make with me I would meet them outside of the post and talk with them. They sent to me several times, but they were always begging parties.

Question. Did they give you any information whatever of the movements of any of the hostile Indians?

Answer. Yes, sir; One Eye did, and I think Jack Smith did. He came in at one time and stated that a party of Indians were going to make an attack on the settlements down in the vicinity of the mouth of Walnut creek. I reported the matter to the district headquarters, stating that there would be an attack made about such a day. The attack was made at about that time, so that the information he gave was correct.

Question. Were the women and children of this band of Black Kettle in camp with him?

Answer. Yes, sir.

Question. About what number of souls were in that camp when you attacked it?

Answer. I thought at the time there were a thousand or more; but, from in-

27

formation I have received since, I am satisfied that there were not so many as that; probably in the neighborhood of 700 men, women, and children.

Question. Did you send any word to Black Kettle that you intended to attack him or his band at any time?

Answer. None, whatever. It was a surprise, made without any notice whatever to them.

Question. What number of women and children were killed there?

Answer. I do not know. I made a report to Colonel Chivington the next day. I made it partly upon information I had received through the men who were with me, and partly from observation. I stated to him that there were 300 Indians killed, including women and children. I have ascertained since that there were not so many killed; at least I am satisfied that there were not over 125 killed. At one time I sent out a scouting party and told them to look over the ground. They came back and reported to me that they had counted 69 dead bodies there. About two-thirds of those were women and children.

Question. Was your command a mounted command?

Answer. Yes, sir.

Question. How did the remainder of the Indians escape?

Answer. On foot.

Question. What kind of country was it?

Answer. Prairie country, slightly rolling; grass very short.

Question. Do you say that Colonel Chivington's command of 700 mounted men allowed 500 of these Indians to escape?

Answer. Yes, sir; and we ourselves lost 49 in killed and wounded.

Question. Why did you not pursue the flying Indians and kill them?

Answer. I do not know; that was the fault I found with Colonel Chivington at the time.

Question. Did he call off the troops?

Answer. No, sir. The Indians took a position in the bed of the creek, which was from 200 to 500 yards wide. The banks upon the side of the creek were two or three feet high, in some places as high as ten feet; the bed of the creek was of sand, and perfectly level. The Indian warriors took their position right along the bank, dug holes in the sand in which to secrete themselves, and fired upon our men in that way. We fought them there. While the women and children were escaping, the men stood under the bank and fought us all day.

Question. How many pieces of artillery did you have?

Answer. We had four pieces.

Question. And the Indians held you in check there for seven hours?

Answer. I think fully seven hours. I was ordered back eighteen miles on the road before the firing ceased.

Question. Did you capture any prisoners?

Answer. Before I left I saw two prisoners in the Indian lodges, in their camp, where our men were quartered.

Question. Did you ever see those prisoners after Colonel Chivington returned?

Answer. Only one of them, Charles Bent.

Question. What became of the other?

Answer. I only ascertained from common report. I went to Colonel Chivington and told him that Jack Smith was a man he might make very useful to him; that he could be made a good guide or scout for us; "but," said I to him, "unless you give your men to understand that you want the man saved, he is going to be killed. He will be killed before to-morrow morning, unless you give your men to understand that you don't want him killed." Colonel Chivington replied, "I have given my instructions; have told my men not to take any prisoners. I have no further instructions to give." I replied to him that he could make that man very useful, and I thought that perhaps

28

he had better give the men to understand that he did not want him killed. The colonel replied again, "I said at the start that I did not want any prisoners taken, and I have no further instructions to give." I then left him. I learned afterwards that Jack Smith was killed in the camp, in an Indian lodge.

Question. Jack Smith was a half-breed?

Answer. Yes, sir.

Question. And an interpreter?

Answer. I had never met him but once. He spoke English and Indian.

Question. Where was Jack Smith's father at that time?

Answer. He was in the Indian camp, trading with the Indians by my permission; and at the same time I had sent him there partly as a spy upon the camp. I wanted to know what movements they were going to make. When I was about to send him out there he said he wanted to take some goods out there to trade with the Indians, and I gave my permission.

Question. What property was captured there?

Answer. About 700 horses, I should think; quite a large number of buffalo robes. I do not know how many, though I think I saw 150 buffalo robes. There were a great many lodges, which were all burned. There were a great many blankets; some few bows and arrows, and I saw some few guns. However, outside of horses, the value to the white man of the whole would be very little.

By Mr. Buckalew:

Question. Were there any mules?

Answer. Yes, sir, there were some mules; I saw a few mules branded " U. S.," that were being driven away.

By Mr. Loan:

Question. What was done with that property?

Answer. I have never learned since.

Question. Did you have possession or control of any of that property?

Answer. Colonel Chivington instructed me to order my quartermaster to receive the stock, and feed them full rations of corn and hay while they remained at Fort Lyon. But there were only 407 head received at Fort Lyon, as I afterwards ascertained. As to the balance, I received information that led me to believe that 225 head of the stock was run off into New Mexico by a portion of Colonel Chivington's command; 60 more driven up the river nearly 100 miles, were there met by an officer who was coming down, and he brought them back to Fort Lyon. When Colonel Chivington's command left Fort Lyon he took away all of this stock that was there, and I have never heard of it since.

Question. Who issued the order to your quartermaster directing him to deliver this property over to Colonel Chivington?

Answer. There was no written order. A verbal order was given me by Colonel Chivington, which I turned over to the quartermaster.

Question. To whom was that stock delivered?

Answer. To Colonel Shoup.

Question. What position did he hold as an accounting officer?

Answer. There was no quartermaster, I think, that ever had it in charge, with the exception of the acting assistant quartermaster at Fort Lyon, who took it in charge for a few days, by verbal order from Colonel Chivington, and turned it over again in the same manner.

Question. Do you know of any acts of hostility committed by Black Kettle or any of his band that were encamped on Sand creek?

Answer. I do not, except this: I was out with Major General Blunt in an engagement with the Indians on Pawnee fork. There was one man there at that time whom I afterwards recognized as being of Black Kettle's party, and who fought us at Pawnee fork; that was War Bonnet. He was at Pawnee fork, and was very active there. He apparently had charge of a small band of Indians. It was on the 26th of August that we fought them there.

29

Question. How long had you been acquainted with War Bonnet?

Answer. I had met him but twice, with the exception of that fight I had with him on Pawnee fork.

Question. You had met him twice previous to that?

Answer. Since that.

Question. Where did you first meet him after that?

Answer. At Fort Lyon.

Question. Why did you not then arrest him and punish him for fighting at Pawnee fork?

Answer. I thought if I did so it would enrage the balance of the Indians, who were then encamped at Smoke Hill, and I was trying to keep them quiet, until such time as a sufficient number of troops had arrived to enable us to go out and fight the whole party.

Question. If you had reason to think that Black Kettle, or any of his party, intended to fight against the United States, or the whites, state what that reason was.

Answer. I had no reason to suppose it further than my general knowledge of the Indian character. I have been there for upwards of two years, and during that time it has been the constant complaint of travellers upon the road that the Indians were annoying their trains, even when they did not profess to be at war at all. It had always been a source of constant annoyance to us there. Trains came into the post and complained that the Indians were taking their property from them.

Question. How far from Fort Lyon were Black Kettle and his people encamped when you made the attack?

Answer. Between 30 and 40 miles.

Question. Why was not Mr. Smith, the trader, also killed?

Answer. As I came up with my command, my men formed in line very close to the Indian camp; among the first persons I saw was John Smith. I had not given any instructions to my men to fire. Firing was going on on both sides of me, a portion of Colonel Chivington's command on the right and another portion on the left were firing. I did not give any instructions to my men to fire. I saw John Smith, who appeared to be frightened, and I rode out in front of my men and called out to him to come to me. I held up my hands, called him by name, and swung my hat at him. He started towards me, and as he started, I supposed he imagined some one was firing at him. Whether they were or not I do not know; I did not see any shots fired at him. I am sure no man of mine fired. At that time all the command, with the exception of my men, were firing. As I was calling out to him to come to me, he turned and started to run the other way. Just at that time one of my men rode out and said, "Major, let me bring him out." The man rode past me, and as he rode around Smith, to take hold of him and lead him out of the Indian camp, he was shot; at least I thought so from his motions in the saddle. He passed on by again, and his horse was shot down. After his horse was shot down he attempted to get up. and some Indian ran up to him, snatched his gun from him, and beat him over the head and killed him. That was the first man of our command I saw killed. The Indians at that time commenced firing upon me, and then my men commenced firing.

By Mr. Buckalew:

Question. What became of Smith?

Answer. I did not know what became of him; I did not see him for three or four hours afterwards. The next I saw of him he was coming down the bank of the river, with some of our soldiers.

By Mr. Loan:

Question. What became of the buffalo robes that were taken there?

Answer. I do not know. I had some buffalo robes, my own bedding, which went at the same time, and we have never been able to ascertain what became of them. I went to Colonel Chivington and reported to him that John Smith had lost all his buffalo robes; I wanted them recovered. He said to me, "You go to John Smith and tell him that he need have no fear at all about the matter; I will give an order confiscating that property for the use of the hospital." I afterwards ascertained that I had lost all my own bedding and buffalo robes, and also provision for ten men for thirty days, that I had taken out there. The colonel said, "Well, we will give you an order confiscating that for the use of the hospital, and you can be reimbursed; you shall not lose a cent." However, the order never was issued, confiscating the property.

Question. Do you know by what authority the 225 head of stock were taken off to New Mexico?

Answer. I do not. Captain Cook told me he knew how many men there were, and he knew who had them in charge; but he never gave me the names.

This is the way in which we have been situated out there. I have been in command of a body of troops at Fort Larned or Fort Lyon for upwards of two years. About two years ago in September the Indians were professing to be perfectly friendly. These were the Cheyennes, the Camanches, the Apaches, the Arapahoes, the Kiowas, encamped at different points on the Arkansas river between Fort Larned and Fort Lyon. Trains were going up to Fort Lyon frequently. and scarcely a train came in but had some complaint to make about the Indians. I recollect that one particular day three trains came in to the post and reported to me that the Indians had robbed them of their provisions. We at the post had to issue provisions to them constantly. Trains that were carrying government freight to New Mexico would stop there and get their supplies replenished on account of the Indians having taken theirs on the road.

At one time I took two pieces of artillery and 125 men, and went down to meet the Indians. As soon as I got there they were apparently friendly. A Kiowa chief perhaps would say to me that his men were perfectly friendly, and felt all right towards the whites, but the Arapahoes were very bad Indians. Go to the Arapahoe camp, they would perhaps charge everything upon the Camanches, while the Camanches would charge it upon the Cheyennes; yet each band there was professing friendship towards us.

These troubles have been going on for some time, until the settlers in that part of the country, and all through western Kansas and Colorado do not think they can bear it. When these troubles commenced upwards of a year ago I received information that led me to believe that the Indians were going to make a general war this last spring. I supposed so at the time. They were endeavoring by every means to purchase arms and ammunition. They would offer the best horse they had for a revolver, or a musket, or a little ammunition.

This last spring it seemed to have commenced; I do not know how. I know, however, that at the different posts they were professing friendship. They were encamped in pretty large numbers in the vicinity of the posts, and while their women and children were dancing right alongside the officers' quarters, the Indians secreted themselves in a ravine in the neighborhood of the post, and at a signal jumped out and run off the stock, firing at the guards; at the same time the women and children jumped on their ponies, and away they went. They burned down the bridges, and almost held the post under their control for three or four days. About the same time they commenced depredations on the road. The mails could not pass without a pretty large escort. At least, whenever we sent them without an escort the Indians attacked them, and the people considered it very unsafe to travel the roads.

When the Indians took their prisoners (in fact, however, they generally took no prisoners) near Simmering spring, they killed ten men. I was told by Captain Davis, of the California volunteers, that the Indians cut off the heads of the men after they had scalped them, and piled them in a pile on the ground, and danced around them, and kicked their bodies around over the ground, &c. It is the general impression among the people of that country that the only way to fight Indians is to fight them as they fight us ; if they scalp and mutilate the bodies we must do the same.

I recollect one occasion, when I had a fight on Pawnee fork with the Indians there, I had fifty-nine men with me, and the Indians numbered several hundred. I was retreating, and they had followed me then about five miles. I had eleven men of my party shot at that time. I had with my party then a few Delaware Indians, and one Captain Fall-Leaf, of the Delaware tribe, had his horse shot; we had to stop every few minutes, dismount and fire upon the Indians to keep them off. They formed a circle right around us. Finally we shot down one Indian very close to us. I saw Fall-Leaf make a movement as though he wanted to scalp the Indian. I asked him if he wanted that Indian's scalp, and he said he did. We kept up a fire to keep the Indians off, while he went down and took off his scalp, and gave his Delaware war-whoop. That seemed to strike more terror into those Indians than anything else we had done that day. And I do think, that if it had not been for that one thing, we should have lost a great many more of my men. I think it struck a terror to them, so that they kept away from us.

It is the general impression of the people of that country that the only way to fight them is to fight as they fight; kill their women and children and kill them. At the same time, of course, we consider it a barbarous practice.

Question. Did the troops mutilate the Indians killed at Sand creek ?

Answer. They did in some instances that I know of; but I saw nothing to the extent I have since heard stated.

Question. State what you saw.

Answer. I saw one man dismount from his horse; he was standing by the side of Colonel Chivington. There was a dead squaw there who had apparently been killed some little time before. The man got down off his horse, took hold of the squaw, took out his knife and tried to cut off her scalp. I thought the squaw had been scalped before ; a spot on the side of the head had evidently been cut off before with a knife; it might possibly have been done by a grape-shot, or something of that kind. I saw a great many Indians and squaws that had been scalped; I do not know how many, but several. There have been different reports about these matters. I heard a report some twenty days after the fight—I saw a notice in Colonel Chivington's report—that a scalp three days old, a white woman's scalp, was found in the Cheyenne camp. I did not hear anything about that until after Colonel Chivington had reached Denver. I was with him for ten days after the fight, and never heard a word about a white woman's scalp being found in the camp until afterwards.

On the other hand, on the day I left Fort Lyon to come east, on the 30th of January, I saw an official report from Major Wynkoop, together with affidavits from different men ; among them was one man who was my adjutant at that time ; he speaks in his affidavit about the bodies of the Indians having been so badly mutilated, their privates cut off, and all that kind of thing. I never saw anything of that ; and I never heard it until I saw it in those affidavits at Fort Lyon, two months after the fight. Yet it was a matter of daily conversation between us at the posts. I, however, did myself see some bodies on the ground that were mutilated.

Question. Anything further than you have stated?

Answer. No, sir. I saw what convinced me that, in attempting to escape with two children, one squaw had been mortally wounded, and had drawn her knife, gathered her two children near her, and cut both of their throats. That was not done by our men. I did not see any one mutilating any Indian, with the exception of the one man I have spoken of, while Colonel Chivington was standing by the side of him.

I saw one instance, however. There was one little child, probably three years old, just big enough to walk through the sand. The Indians had gone ahead, and this little child was behind following after them. The little fellow was perfectly naked, travelling on the sand. I saw one man get off his horse, at a distance of about seventy-five yards, and draw up his rifle and fire—he missed the child. Another man came up and said, "Let me try the son of a bitch; I can hit him." He got down off his horse, kneeled down and fired at the little child, but he missed him. A third man came up and made a similar remark, and fired, and the little fellow dropped.

By Mr. Buckalew:

Question. Those were men of your command?
Answer. Of Colonel Chivington's command.

By Mr. Loan:

Question. Had the officers control of their men at that time?
Answer. There did not seem to be any control.
Question. Could the officers have controlled their men, or were the men acting in defiance of the orders of their officers?
Answer. I did not hear any orders given but what were obeyed. As a general thing the officers and men were doing just what they saw fit to do.

By Mr. Gooch:

Question. Did you communicate to Colonel Chivington, when he came to Fort Lyon, the relations you had had with those Indians?
Answer. Yes, sir.
Question. Did you, under the circumstances, approve of this attack upon those Indians?
Answer. I did not.
Question. Did you not feel that you were bound in good faith not to attack those Indians after they had surrendered to you, and after they had taken up a position which you yourself had indicated?
Answer. I did not consider that they had surrendered to me; I never would consent that they should surrender to me. My instructions were such that I felt in duty bound to fight them wherever I found them; provided I considered it good policy to do so. I did not consider it good policy to attack this party of Indians on Sand creek unless I was strong enough to go on and fight the main band at the Smoke Hills, some seventy miles further. If I had had that force I should have gone out and fought this band on Sand creek.
Question. The Arapahoes had surrendered to you?
Answer. I considered them differently from the Cheyennes.
Question. They were with the Cheyennes, or a part of them were?
Answer. I understood afterwards that some six or eight or ten lodges of the Arapahoes were there.
Question. Did you not know at the time you made this attack that those Arapahoes were there with the Cheyennes?
Answer. I did not. A part of the Cheyennes had left; a part of them said they did not believe we at the post felt friendly towards them; and I have since learned that a part of them had left.
Question. These very Indians had come in and held communication with you, and had taken up the position you had directed them to take?
Answer. No, sir; I told them they should not remain on the road, but they might go back on Sand creek, or some place where they could kill game.

33

Question. You advised them to go there?

Answer. Yes, sir.

Question. Did you not suppose that they understood from you that if they went there and behaved themselves they would not be attacked by you?

Answer. I do not think they thought so. I think they were afraid I was going to attack them. I judge so from words that came to me like this: "That they did not like that red-eyed chief; that they believed he wanted to fight them."

Question. You say you did not approve of the attack upon them by Colonel Chivington. Did you remonstrate with Colonel Chivington against making that attack?

Answer. I did.

Question. You felt that you ought not to make the attack under the circumstances?

Answer. I did. I made a great many harsh remarks in regard to it. At the same time I did not so much object to the killing of the Indians, as a matter of principle—merely as a matter of policy. I considered it a very bad policy, as it would open up the war in that whole country again, which was quiet for the time. I am very well satisfied the Indians intended a general outbreak as soon as the weather would permit.

Question. You think the attack made upon those Indians there, in addition to the other characteristics which it possesses, was impolitic?

Answer. I do, very much so. I think it was the occasion of what has occurred on the Platte since that time. I have so stated in my report to the headquarters of the district and of the department. I stated before Colonel Chivington arrived there that the Indians were encamped at this point; that I had a force with me sufficiently strong to go out and fight them; but I did not think it policy to do so, for I was not strong enough to fight the main band. If I fought this band, the main band would immediately strike the settlements. But so soon as the party should be strong enough to fight the main band, I should be in favor of making the war general against the Indians. I stated to them also that I did not believe we could fight one band without fighting them all; that in case we fought one party of Indians and whipped them, those that escaped would go into another band that was apparently friendly, and that band would secrete those who had been committing depredations before. As it was with Little Raven's band; his own sons attacked a train a short distance above Fort Lyon, killed one soldier, took a government wagon and mules, some horses, and took some women prisoners. One woman they afterwards outraged, and she hung herself; the other one, I think, they still hold. Some of the Indians have married her, as they call it, and she is still held in their camp, as I have understood; not now in the camp of those who took her prisoner, but she has been sold to the Sioux and Cheyennes. The instructions we constantly received from the headquarters, both of the district and the department, were that we should show as little mercy to the Indians as possible.

By Mr. Loan:

Question. Could you furnish us copies of those instructions?

Answer. I have in the city some private letters, and I think I have also some confidential communications, that go to show something of that nature.

Question. I should be glad to have copies of some of them.

Answer. I think I have some of them. I have copies of some letters I wrote to department and district headquarters. My reports were always approved; they sent back word every time that my reports were approved. I stated that I would hold on to those Indians; let them remain dormant until such time as troops enough arrived to fight the main band. They always approved my action in the matter. When Colonel Chivington arrived there with his command, I immediately reported to headquarters that he had arrived.

34

Question. Who was the district commander?

Answer. Major Henning.

Question. How did a major command a colonel?

Answer. Colonel Chivington was in entirely another district. The district I was in was in upper Arkansas, and was commanded by Major Henning. Colonel Chivington commanded the district of Colorado.

Question. Then Fort Lyon was not in Colonel Chivington's district?

Answer. No, sir.

Question. By what authority did you act in concert with Colonel Chivington?

Answer. By the authority of the instructions I had received from my own district commander, that I should fight the Indians wherever I met them. When Colonel Chivington came down I talked with him; he told me where he was going, and asked me if I wanted to go with him. I told him if he was going to make a general war with the Indians I did. He gave me to understand that he was going to make it general.

Question. Can you furnish us a copy of those instructions that authorized you to go under Colonel Chivington when he was out of his district?

Answer. I had no instructions to go under him at all. I have, however, some papers to show the feeling in regard to the district. I told Colonel Chivington, several times on that march to Sand creek, that One Eye was there, employed by me; that Black Kettle was there, and that I considered Black Kettle friendly towards us; that Left Hand was there; that, probably, John Smith was there by my permission; that there was a soldier there with Smith whom I had sent off as a sort of spy, too; and that I wanted, if he did fight those Indians, by all means to save those parties; that if he did fight them he should give notice beforehand in order to get them out. I advised him to surround the camp, and not let one escape, and then push right forward and fight the main band; that he was strong enough for them. I believed at the time that if we should attack the main band, it would put an end to all our Indian troubles there. And I supposed he was going to do it; that was the understanding at the time we left Fort Lyon. I took twenty-three days' rations for my men, with the understanding that we were to be gone at least that length of time.

---

*Testimony of Major S. G. Colley.*

WASHINGTON, *March* 14, 1865.

Major S. G. COLLEY sworn and examined.

By Mr. Loan:

Question. Where do you reside?

Answer. At Fort Lyon.

Question. Do you hold any official position, civil or military?

Answer. I am an Indian agent.

Question. Will you state what you know of the Indians out there, their disposition towards the whites, &c., and what you know about the massacre at Sand creek?

Answer. I was not present at that fight.

Question. How long have you been agent for those Indians?

Answer. My appointment was in July, 1861.

Question. Were you intimately acquainted with the character and conduct of Black Kettle and his band of Indians?

Answer. I think I was.

Question. What do you know about Left Hand's band of the Arapahoes?

*Answer.* I know nothing bad about them. I have been with them hundreds of times.

*Question.* What has been their general character for peace and good conduct towards the whites? Have they been guilty of any acts of hostility, theft, or anything of the kind?

*Answer.* Nearly a year ago I heard of some troubles on the Platte with some Cheyenne Indians. When the treaty was made with those Indians in 1860, before I went out there, there was claimed to be two bands of Cheyennes and Arapahoes; the one of the North Platte, and the one of the South Platte. This North Platte band was not a party to that treaty, and were dissatisfied with it. There was an effort made to get those Indians to join the southern band, as it was called, but the effort was never successful. The governor, myself, and another man met the northern Indians to see if we could not get them to unite with the southern Indians, and all go on a reservation. But we failed in that. Early in the spring of last year I understood from Denver, perhaps from Governor Evans himself, that there had been a collision between the soldiers and Indians. I did not know what effect it would have upon our Indians below. I immediately went out and found all the Indians I could, and communicated with them, and told them there had been trouble on the Platte, and asked them if they knew anything about it. They said they had heard of it, but supposed it was some of the Dog Soldiers over there, as this northern band is called. They said they themselves did not want to have any trouble, but if the soldiers followed them up they supposed they would have to fight. I told them I wished they would come in on the Arkansas as close as they could and stay there, and be out of trouble. Previous to this, for two years, we have been satisfied that there was an effort being made by the Sioux Indians to induce these Indians to join them and make war upon the whites. We have labored for two years to keep it down. The Sioux Indians, many of them from Minnesota, are there in that country, and have been endeavoring to unite these Indians for the purpose of making a general war upon the whites. These Indians said the Sioux had been there with the war-pipe, but they did not mean to go to war with the whites.

There were a great many depredations committed below our place, at Larned, by some Indians. It was sometimes reported that all the bands were engaged in them; then it was reported that they were committed by the Sioux. It was impossible to ascertain what Indians were engaged. But so far as I met the Cheyennes and the Arapahoes on the Arkansas, they disclaimed it, and pretended to be friendly.

In June last I received a circular from Governor Evans, requesting me to invite any of the Indians that had not been at war with the whites to Fort Lyon; the Cheyennes and Arapahoes of the North Platte to Fort Collins; the Cheyennes and Arapahoes of the Arkansas at Fort Lyon; the Kiowas and Camanches at Larned, and tell them if they would come in and behave themselves, they should be fed and cared for. I immediately sent Mr. Smith, Jack Smith, who was killed, and Colonel Bent, to all these Indians to carry them this information. During this time occurred this trouble at Fort Larned, by the Kiowas running off the stock. Orders were then issued that no Indians should come to that post, as I understood it. After One Eye had come back and said he had seen Black Kettle, who said he would bring in his Indians, I sent him out again to see what was going on.

During this time orders were issued, I understood from General Curtis, that no Indians should visit a military post; but it was a long while before One Eye got in; he did not get in until the 4th day of September, and he got in then by accident. If he had been met by a soldier he would have been shot; but he happened to meet some other soldiers, who took him prisoner and brought him in then. Major Wynkoop took him and kept him in the guard-house that day.

36

He told us that there were some white prisoners with the Cheyennes whom they had brought, and whom they were willing to deliver up, if we would go out for them. Major Wynkoop went out with one hundred men, had a conversation with the Indians, and brought in four prisoners, one girl and three children.

Black Kettle and his principal men, some twenty or thirty of them, came in with Major Wynkoop, and went to Denver and had a conference with Governor Evans. The governor declined to make any peace with them, but turned them over to the military. Black Kettle went out and brought in quite a number of lodges, and the young men came in to the post.

Before this time, General Curtis, through representations from some quarter, was apparently led to believe that the Indians were behaving very badly at Fort Lyon; and Major Wynkoop was relieved of his command by Major Anthony. At that time the Arapahoes were there, being fed by Major Wynkoop. When Major Anthony came, he said he was ordered to fight those Indians; but he found things different from what he expected, and he did not think it policy then to fight them; that there was no danger from those Indians; they could be kept there, and killed at any time it was necessary. He told them that he did not feel authorized to give them any rations, and that they better go out a piece where they could kill buffalo.

After Major Wynkoop had brought those Indians in, and until after this fight, I do not know of any depredations having been committed in our country. There may have been some committed below in the vicinity of Fort Larned; but during that time, two months or over, the Indians in our country did not commit any depredations.

Question. Have you any means of knowing the number of Indians in that camp on Sand creek?

Answer. I have no personal knowledge of the number of lodges there. But there were about one hundred lodges of the Arapahoes at the post at the time Major Anthony took the command there. Left Hand's band had gone out to Sand creek, and Black Kettle's band of the Cheyennes.

Question. How many were in Left Hand's band?

Answer. About eight lodges.

Question. How many to a lodge?

Answer. About five.

Question. About how strong was Black Kettle's band?

Answer. I do not know of my own knowledge. I only know from what men told me who had counted them. At one time when One Eye was out, we did suppose, from what we had heard, that the Indians were all going to unite against us.

Question. Judging from all your information as Indian agent, have you any reason to believe that Black Kettle or Left Hand had been guilty of or intended any hostility towards us?

Answer. I have no reason to believe that of either of them.

Question. Have you any reason to know that they desired to remain at peace, and were opposed to fighting the people of the United States?

Answer. Left Hand, who speaks English, told me that he never would fight the whites. He said that some of his boys got mad after he was fired at at Fort Larned. Left Hand had come in there and offered to assist in the recovery of some stock that had been stampeded there. He was fired on by the soldiers at Fort Larned. He said, "I was not much mad; but my boys were mad, and I could not control them. But as for me, I will not fight the whites, and you cannot make me do it. You may imprison me or kill me; but I will not fight the whites."

Question. What was the feeling of Black Kettle?

Answer. He himself always appeared to be friendly.

37

Question. Did you ever know of his committing any act of hostility towards the whites, or sanctioning it in others ?
Answer. I never did.
Question. What relation did he bear to the Cheyenne tribe of Indians ?
Answer. He was acknowledged as the head chief of the southern bands of Cheyennes. There were subordinate chiefs who were heads of bands.

By Mr. Buckalew :

Question. What has become of Black Kettle ?
Answer. I have seen a half-breed who was there with Mr. Smith, and could not get back to the soldiers, and ran off with the Indians, and was with them for fourteen days after they got over to the Sioux Indians. From what he told me—and I could rely upon it—Black Kettle was not killed, but Left Hand was wounded, and died after he got over there.
Question. Of the fight itself you know nothing ?
Answer. No, sir; I was not there ; I was at Fort Lyon at the time.
Question. The Jack Smith who was killed there was the son of a white man?
Answer. Yes, sir; of John Smith.
Question. He was an interpreter ?
Answer. He interpreted for me ; he spoke both English and Indian.
Question. Had you any reason to think that Mr. Smith or his son entertained any hostility to the whites ?
Answer. The old gentleman was always our main man there, communicating with the Indians, for he had lived with them so long. Nobody doubted his fidelity to the government.
Question. Was there any reason to doubt that of the son ?
Answer. Captain Hardee informed me, when he went out there on the stage, that he thought Jack Smith was one of the party that attacked the stage. When Jack came I told him what I had heard. He said he had rode up to the stage and wanted to know if his father was in the coach ; and he wanted to know what the trouble was that he had heard of in the east; that they then fired upon them, and then the Indians returned the fire.
Question. Was there any other act of Jack denoting hostility ?
Answer. I never heard of any. He was at Fort Lyon at work haying there for some men. In July last, I think, Colonel Chivington was at Fort Lyon. This One Eye was near about the fort, and wanted to go out and see the Indians, but was afraid of the soldiers. Colonel Chivington wrote out a certificate of his good character, stating that he was a friendly Indian, and then told him if he came across any soldiers to show that to them ; if they shot before he got to them to show a white flag, and that would protect him. He was an Indian we relied upon a great deal for information. He was killed at Sand creek. I asked Colonel Chivington if there was any way these Indians, Black Kettle, Left Hand, and some others, could be treated with. He said his orders from General Curtis were that it could be done on these conditions: that they must give up their stolen property, make restitution for any damage they had done, &c., and I supposed he was going to do that.

---

*Testimony of Governor John Evans.*

WASHINGTON, *March* 15, 1865.
Governor JOHN EVANS sworn and examined.
By Mr. Loan:

Question. What is your present official position ?
Answer. Governor of Colorado Territory, and superintendent of Indian affairs.

Question. Do you know anything of a band of Indians under the lead of a chief of the name of Black Kettle?

Answer. There is a band of Cheyenne Indians under a chief of that name, roaming over the plains.

Question. In what part of the country were they located, relative to the other bands of Indians?

Answer. The Indians that were with Black Kettle—I do not know that he was the leader of them entirely, but the Indians he went with, and was the chief among, were mainly roaming in the neighborhood of the Smoke Hill and Republican fork, and down on the south Arkansas. Sometimes they went up as far as the Platte.

Question. How many other bands were there?

Answer. There is a band up in the neighborhood of Fort Laramie, some of whose chiefs, the Shield and Spotted Horse, were with them.

Question. Was there any other band of the tribe of Cheyenne Indians than those on the Platte and those on the Arkansas?

Answer. Yes, sir; I think so. How far they were divided into bands it is rather difficult to say; and where each band is located is very difficult to say, because they range from away below the Arkansas to above Fort Laramie, or to Powder river. For years they have been in the habit of roaming back and forth over the plains.

Question. Will you give us the names of the head chiefs of the Cheyennes that you, as superintendent of Indian affairs, recognized?

Answer. There was Black Kettle, White Antelope, and Bull Bear among them.

Question. Having the supreme control of the Cheyenne nation?

Answer. No, sir; I do not think there was any such chief recognized. They had a party of about forty young men, called the Dog soldiers, who several years ago took the control of the tribe mainly out of the hands of the chiefs. They were clubbed together as a band of braves, and the chiefs could not control them.

Question. What part of the country did Black Kettle and the Indians with him occupy during last summer?

Answer. From information which I have received I think they were mainly on the head of the Smoke Hill.

Question. How far from Fort Lyon?

Answer. Sometimes nearer, sometimes farther off. As I stated before, they are entirely nomadic, and they pass from one part of the country to another. The most precise information I have of their precise locality, at any particular time, is the report of Major Wynkoop, who went out and saw their camp, in the latter part of August, or in the early part of September last.

Question. Where were they then?

Answer. At what is called Big Timbers, on the head of Smoke Hill.

Question. Have you any knowledge that they were north of Denver at any time during last summer? If so, state at what places they were.

Answer. I have the information from the chiefs that during the summer they were on the Platte, in the neighborhood of Plum creek, a little west of Fort Kearney; and on the Blue, east of Fort Kearney. They ranged away down into Kansas and Nebraska there during the summer.

Question. From whom did you derive this information?

Answer. It was either Black Kettle or White Antelope who told me so.

Question. At what time?

Answer. At the time of the depredations on the trains that were perpetrated in August last.

Question. I mean at what time did they tell you this?

Answer. They told me so on the 28th of September.

Part VI——3

Question. You say they were down on Plum creek at the time these depredations were committed?

Answer. They said the Cheyennes committed them.

Question. What I want to know is whether you have information that Black Kettle, or any of the band that travel with him, had been north of Denver last summer. Did Black Kettle tell you that either he himself, or any of the band under his immediate control, had been there?

Answer. I inferred they had from his saying that the Cheyennes had committed those depredations. As a matter of course I told him they had committed them, because they had some white prisoners who had been captured there, and whom they claimed as theirs. He did not answer to that proposition. He said the Cheyennes committed the depredations east of Kearney. He did not say directly that they had been on the Blue. They gave up to Major Wynkoop the prisoners that were captured on the Little Blue, and then he said that the Cheyennes committed the depredations.

Question. Did Black Kettle say that his band had done it?

Answer. He did not say which band of Cheyennes. I inferred that they were his band because they did not speak of any other bands. These Cheyennes that range on the head of the Smoke Hill and Republican seem all to band together.

Question. What is the distance from their location about Fort Lyon to Fort Kearney, and from there to Little Blue?

Answer. I should have to guess at the distance.

Question. You have travelled that country frequently, have you not?

Answer. Not across in that direction.

Question. You have a general knowledge of that country and the bearing of it, and can estimate it from the route you have travelled?

Answer. From the Big Timbers on the head of the Smoke Hill.

Question. Or about Fort Lyon?

Answer. It is at least from ninety to one hundred miles from Fort Lyon, and from Big Timbers to Fort Kearney would probably be 150 miles. I may be mistaken as to that.

Question. How far east of Denver is Fort Lyon?

Answer. It is southeast.

Question. How far east?

Answer. Something like 100 miles.

Question. What distance is Fort Lyon from Denver by a right line?

Answer. I suppose about 200 miles. It is about 250 miles the way they travel. It must be quite 200 miles on an air line.

Question. Where was it that Black Kettle was telling you about this?

Answer. At Denver.

Question. State the circumstances under which that conversation arose.

Answer. He with other chiefs and headmen——

Question. Please name them.

Answer. I cannot give all their names.

Question. State as many as you can remember.

Answer. Black Kettle, White Antelope, and Bull Bear, of the Cheyennes; Nevy and two or three others of the Arapahoes. They were brought to Denver for the purpose of council by Major Wynkoop, after he had been out to their camp, brought there for the purpose of making a treaty of peace.

Question. You were acting as superintendent of Indian affairs?

Answer. Yes, sir.

Question. What propositions did you make to them, and what was the conclusion of that conference?

Answer. Major Wynkoop's report is published in my report to the Commissioner of Indian Affairs.

40

Question. That may be; but you can state it?

Answer. In brief, he reported that he had been out to their camp, and found them drawn up in line of battle. He sent in an Indian he had with him to get them to council instead of to fight; and he held a council in the presence of their warriors with their bows and arrows drawn. They agreed to allow these men to come to see me in reference to making peace, with the assurance that he would see them safe back again to their camp, as he states in his report or letter to me in regard to it.

Question. When you saw the Indians, what occurred?

Answer. The Indians made their statement, that they had come in through great fear and tribulation to see me, and proposed that I should make peace with them; or they said to me that they desired me to make peace. To which I replied that I was not the proper authority, as they were at war and had been fighting, and had made an alliance with the Sioux, Kiowas, and Comanches to go to war; that they should make their terms of peace with the military authorities. I also told them that they should make such arrangements, or I advised them to make such arrangements as they could, and submit to whatever terms were imposed by the military authorities as their best course.

Question. What reply did they make to that?

Answer. They proposed that that would be satisfactory, and that they would make terms of peace. The next day I got a despatch from Major General Curtis, commanding the department, approving my course, although he did not know what it was. But the despatch contained an order that no peace should be made with the Indians without his assent and authority; dictating some terms for them to be governed by in making the peace.

Question. Have you a copy of that despatch with you?

Answer. It is published in my annual report.

Question. Did you communicate that fact to the Indians?

Answer. It was after the Indians had left that I received a despatch. The despatch came to the commander of the district; and a copy was sent to me for the purpose of giving me notice.

Question. Was anything further said in that conference with the Indians?

Answer. I took occasion to gather as much information as I could in regard to the extent of hostile feelings among the Indians, and especially in regard to what bands had been committing the depredations along the line and through the settlements, which had been very extensive.

Question. What did Black Kettle say in regard to his band; and what did the other Indians say in regard to their bands?

Answer. Black Kettle said he and White Antelope had been opposed all the time to going to war, but they could not control their young men—these Dog soldiers; they have been very bad.

Question. These Dog soldiers were on the Blue?

Answer. They were in his camp; they were his young men; Black Kettle was an old man.

Question. Where was his camp?

Answer. At the Big Timbers.

Question. Where Major Wynkoop found them?

Answer. Yes, sir.

Question. How do you know that fact?

Answer. By the statement that their warriors were there.

Question. Did Major Wynkoop make that statement to you?

Answer. Yes, sir; in his letter to me giving the circumstances under which he brought these Indians to me.

Question. Did Major Wynkoop report to you that the Dog soldiers, of the Cheyennes, were in Black Kettle's camp?

41

Answer. He did not mention the Dog soldiers; but the Dog soldiers are warriors of the Cheyenne tribe.

Question. I understand that; but you say there is no head chief that you recognized as such. I wanted to know if these Dog soldiers belonged to the band under the lead of Black Kettle?

Answer. The Dog soldiers belonged to the bands commanded by Black Kettle, White Antelope, and Bull Bear, which all run together. There is no known separation among them.

Question. Do I understand you, then, to say that the Indians indiscriminately occupy that country from below the Arkansas to the North Platte?

Answer. The Cheyenne Indians, the Sioux Indians, the Arapahoe Indians, roam indiscriminately through there.

Question. Then there was no particular band that made their homes about the head of the Smoky fork?

Answer. There were a number of bands and tribes that hunted through there indiscriminately.

Question. What I want to know is the usual locality of Black Kettle's band?

Answer. It was like all the rest. He goes where he thinks there is the best hunting; he ranges from one part of the country to the other.

Question. Do you know that the Indians known as Dog soldiers ever were in Black Kettle's camp; and if so, at what time, and how do you know the fact?

Answer. I will not name them as Dog soldiers.

Question. I mean the warriors known as the Dog soldiers of the Cheyennes Indians. Have they ever been in his camp at any time that you know of?

Answer. Bull Bear, who was to see me, was the head of the Dog soldiers himself, the head one of that band, a sub-chief. They said they left nearly all their warriors at this bunch of timbers.

Question. Where Black Kettle's camp was?

Answer. Black Kettle was in the camp. You have the idea that Black Kettle had some particular camp. The distinction between White Antelope and Black Kettle, as an authority among the tribes, has varied at different times. The government has never recognized either of them as head chief that I know of.

Question. You have omitted to answer the question whether you know of these Dog soldiers, at any time or at any place, being in Black Kettle's camp or under his control?

Answer. I know the answer that Bull Bear gave when he came to Denver. He was recognized as the leader of the Dog soldiers. He, with Black Kettle and White Antelope, said that they left their warriors down at the bunch of timbers; and Major Wynkoop reports the same thing.

Question. You inferred that the warriors referred to were the Dog soldiers?

Answer. I did.

Question. At this conference, when Bull Bear told you this, what did he say in regard to war and peace?

Answer. He said he was ready to make peace. They spoke of some of their warriors being out. Their war is a guerilla warfare. They go off in little bands of twenty or thirty together and commit these depredations, so that there is scarcely ever more than that many seen in any of these attacks. They reported that some of their young men were out upon the war-path, or had been out, and they did not know whether they were in at the time. That, I think, was stated at that time, or in a communication that came from them a short time before this. I got a letter from Black Kettle through Bent; it was sent up to me. Upon which Major Wynkoop went out to their camp, and either that or their statement at the conference gave me the information that a portion of their warriors were still out.

42

## MASSACRE OF CHEYENNE INDIANS.

Question. How did Major Wynkoop know in regard to this letter or its contents?

Answer. It was brought in to Major Colley, at Fort Lyon, where Major Wynkoop was in command, by two or three Indians; and immediately upon their coming in Major Wynkoop took these Indians, and went with them, as guides.

Question. That was before you saw the letter?

Answer. Yes, sir; and they immediately sent me a copy of the letter.

Question. Did these Indians propose to do anything that you, as their superintendent, directed them to do in this matter, for the purpose of keeping peace?

Answer. They did not suggest about keeping peace; they proposed to make peace. They acknowledged that they were at war, and had been at war during the spring. They expressed themselves as satisfied with the references I gave them to the military authorities; and they went back, as I understood, with the expectation of making peace with "the soldiers," as they termed them—with the military authorities.

Question. Why did you permit those Indians to go back, under the circumstances, when you knew they were at war with the whites?

Answer. Because they were under the control and authority of the military, over which I, as superintendent of Indian affairs, had no control.

Question. Did you make application to the district commander there to detain those Indians?

Answer. No, sir.

Question. Why did you not do it?

Answer. Because the military commander was at the council.

Question. What was his name?

Answer. Colonel Chivington. I told the Indians he was present and could speak in reference to those matters we had been speaking about.

Question. Were any orders given to Major Wynkoop, either by yourself or by Colonel Chivington, in regard to his action towards those Indians?

Answer. I gave no orders, because I had no authority to give any.

Question. Did Colonel Chivington give any?

Answer. He made these remarks in the presence of the council: that he was commander of the district; that his rule of fighting white men and Indians was to fight them until they laid down their arms; if they were ready to do that, then Major Wynkoop was nearer to them than he was, and they could go to him.

Question. Do you know whether he issued any orders to Major Wynkoop to govern his conduct in the matter?

Answer. I do not. Major Wynkoop was not under his command, however. I understood that Fort Lyon was not in the command that Colonel Chivington was exercising at the time. It was a separate command, under General Blunt, of the military district of the Arkansas, as I understood it.

Question. Were the Indian chiefs sent back to their homes in pursuance of any orders given to Major Wynkoop, that you know of?

Answer. No, sir. I will say further, in regard to my course, that it was reported to the Indian bureau, and approved by the Indian bureau as proper, not to interfere with the military, which will appear in my annual report. I have no official knowledge of what transpired after this council, so far as these Indians are concerned, except that I notified the agent that they were under the military authority, and I supposed they would be treated as prisoners.

Question. How long have you been superintendent of Indian affairs there?

Answer. Since the spring of 1862.

Question. Have you any knowledge of any acts committed by either of those chiefs, or by the bands immediately under their control—any personal knowledge?

Answer. In 1862, a party of these Dog soldiers——

43

Question. I am not asking about the Dog soldiers, but about Black Kettle's band.

Answer. They are the same Indians. The Dog soldiers were a sort of vigilance committee under those old chiefs.

Question. I understood you to say, a few minutes ago, that the Dog soldiers threw off the authority of the old chiefs, and were independent of them?

Answer. That they managed the tribe instead of the chiefs.

Question. What act of hostility was committed by the Dog soldiers, in pursuance of the authority of any of the chiefs of the nation?

Answer. That I could not say, for I have no way of ascertaining what authority they have—only what I gather from the agent, who was intimate with them.

Question. What is the name of that agent?

Answer. Colley. He is familiar with those Indians, and said that the Dog soldiers were to blame for their ugly conduct.

Question. That is what I understand; and I wanted you, as superintendent of Indian affairs, to tell us if these Dog soldiers were under the command of any chief that had control of them, and the name of that chief, if you know it.

Answer. The identification of the chief that commands them is what I am not able to do, because they have in that band, or tribe, the chiefs that I have mentioned. Which of them is superior in authority I am not advised.

Question. What was the general reputation of Black Kettle, as a hostile or a friendly Indian, during your control there as superintendent of Indian affairs?

Answer. Black Kettle has had the reputation of being himself a good Indian.

Question. Peaceably inclined, and well disposed towards the whites?

Answer. Yes, sir; and White Antelope more particularly. But I was going on to state in regard to their conduct. In the summer of 1862 a party of warriors of the Cheyennes came to Denver and called on me, and wanted something to eat.

Question. Can you designate what particular band they belonged to?

Answer. They were of the same band we are fighting about the Blue—Black Kettle, White Antelope, and Bull Bear's Indians, that range mainly down in the neighborhood of Smoke Hill. They came to Denver on a war expedition against the Utes. I advised them to cease their hostilities. When I went there I had an idea of trying to get everybody to live without fighting, the Indians among the rest. The Indians on the mountains and on the plains spent their time in chasing one another. I was in this delicate position : the Utes, who are a very warlike and dangerous tribe, had got a jealousy of the Indians on the plains, and the whites who live on the plains also. The whites were constantly giving presents to the begging portion of the plains Indians. The superintendency and the agency were constantly giving goods to them; and the Utes complained that the whites were fitting out the plains Indians in their war parties against the Utes, which was true to some extent. The Utes said that when they chased the Cheyennes and Arapahoes, which run together almost constantly, and the Sioux—there are parties of Sioux with the Arapahoes and Cheyennes in nearly all their war parties—when the Utes would chase them down into the plains, they had to stop because the whites interfered, and they did not dare to go down into the plains. They were of the opinion that the whites were taking the side of the Indians of the plains; and they were on the point of going to war with us.

I suggested to these Indians that it was better for them to make peace. I went with Colonel Leavenworth down to the camp of the Sioux, Arapahoes, and Cheyennes, at a subsequent period, and tried to arrange with them. I had a Ute agent with me to make the arrangement to quit fighting. When this party came, in 1862, I mentioned these things, showing the advantages, and they promised me they would go back; I gave them some bacon and flour, and other things, for subsistence. They started under a promise that they would go back, and not go up to the Utes, and jeopard our safety with them. Instead of that, they started for the South Park, the Ute battle-ground, where they usually fight, and the next day or two afterwards messengers came in from the settlers on the road, saying that the Indians were committing depredations; that they had cleaned out and outraged one landlord; had insulted a woman; had gone in and taken possession of several of these sparsely settled places; had made one woman cook for the whole party, and I think they had sent in for protection. Some six soldiers went up to protect the neighborhood; but when they got there, these Indians had gone back on the plains by another route.

Question. What was the name of the chief in command of that party?

Answer. I do not know; that was their first visit.

Question. Was it Black Kettle, or White Antelope, or Bull Bear?

Answer. I could not say it was not them, nor that it was. It was a party of warriors from the same party that Black Kettle, White Antelope and Bull Bear ranged with.

Question. Although you had a conversation with them, and furnished them with supplies, and induced them to return, you do not know the name of the chief?

Answer. There were several chiefs.

Question. Can you name any one of them?

Answer. I cannot give the name; I might get it if I were in my office.

Question. As governor of Colorado Territory, did you have any troops organized there last summer?

Answer. Yes, sir; I organized a regiment.

Question. For what term of service?

Answer. For one hundred days.

Question. Who was the colonel of that regiment?

Answer. George L. Shoup.

Question. Did you ever issue any orders to that regiment, or to any part of it?

Answer. No, sir.

Question. Were they organized as United States troops?

Answer. Yes, sir.

Question. Were they placed under the control of the district commander as soon as organized?

Answer. Before they were organized, for this reason: while the regiment was being raised, there was information come in of a camp of about 800 of these Indians; a report of which will be found in my annual report to the Commissioner of Indian Affairs. It came in in this way: Little Geary, a grandson of the signer of the Declaration of Independence, lives on the Platte, sixty miles south of Denver. In the night two Cheyenne chiefs came to him.

Question. What were their names?

Answer. It seems to me one of them was Crooked Neck. The statement I was going to make was this: these Indians came in and notified Geary to get out of the way. He was living on ranch with a large amount of stock, and with a Cheyenne wife. He had Spotted Horse there with him under protection. Spotted Horse, a Cheyenne Indian of Fort Laramie, had been friendly all the time, and was there under protection. These Indians made these statements to him, as you will see in the printed copy of my report to the Commissioner of Indian Affairs.

I think about 800 Indians were camped at the head of Beaver, at the Point of Rocks on the Beaver, which is about 120 miles east of Denver, composed of Arapahoes, Cheyennes, Sioux, Kiowas, Camanches and Apaches. They said that their plan was, in two or three nights, to divide into small parties of about 200, going in the neighborhood of ———, which was about 40 miles below Geary's; 100 going just above Geary's to Fort Lumpton; about 250 to the head of Cherry creek, which is 25 or 30 miles south of Denver; and the remainder of them to go to the Arkansas, at Fountaine que Bonille. That these parties were to be divided into little bands, and each take a farm-house, clean it out and steal the stock, and in this way commit the most wholesale and extensive massacre that has ever been known. I have no doubt it would have been so, but for the vigilance that was taken to prevent it.

Geary, who is an educated and sensible man, immediately took Spotted Horse, who heard these Indians give their account; it was done confidentially by them. Geary, who has been in my employ as a spy over the Indians, who has been out among them as a messenger, started the next morning—they got to his house about midnight, or 2 o'clock. Geary started immediately in the morning with Spotted Horse, and got to my house at 11 o'clock; riding between 60 and 70 miles during the day, for the purpose of giving me this information. I immediately notified the district commander, and put the recruits which were supposed to be subject to my command under his command, by an order; and any militia that might be organized was subject to his command for the purposes of defence. He sent express in every direction to notify the settlers. I telegraphed, and also sent messengers. It so happened that a militia company had gone down there, and were near that, and that a militia company had gone to Fort Lumpton, or near there.

The Indians came in at these different points on the second night, skulking along under the bluffs, where their trails were seen. They found the settlements all alarmed, and went back again, except at the head of Cherry creek, where they killed two or three and took quite a large number of cattle; and at Fort Lumpton they killed one man. And before Geary got back they stole some of his horses and the horses of one or two of his neighbors, and ran them off.

Question. At what time was this?

Answer. It must have been early in August.

Question. At what time was this hundred-days regiment organized?

Answer. Early in September.

Question. At what time was it mounted?

Answer. Some companies were mounted before the regiment was full; others were mounted subsequently, as they could get horses.

Question. How were horses obtained, and from whom?

Answer. The quartermaster of the department.

Question. Do you know anything further than you have stated in connexion with this attack upon Black Kettle and his band on Sand creek? Did you issue any orders, or take any part in any transaction having in view any such attack?

Answer. I did not know anything about it. After I got here, I got a letter from the secretary of the territory, saying it was rumored they were going there.

Question. Whom did "they" refer to?

Answer. Colonel Chivington and his force. I think he said it was surmised that they were going to Fort Lyon. It is proper for me to say that I understood they were going to make an expedition against the Indians. But I had no knowledge of where they were going.

Question. After Major Wynkoop left you in September, do you know what was done with these Indians?

Answer. I do not.

Question. Do you know what action the Indians took afterwards?

Answer. I do not.

Question. Do you know where they were encamped?

Answer. I accidentally heard—I had no official knowledge of the fact—that there were several hundred of them at Fort Lyon. The next day after this council I started for a place about 300 miles off, to hold a treaty with the Utes down on the Rio Grande, and was gone nearly a month.

Question. At what time did you start to come east?

Answer. I think I started on the 15th of November.

Question. Is Colonel Shoup yet in service?

Answer. No, sir; when I came away he was encamped at Bijou Basin, about 75 miles east of Denver, where they had been for a considerable length of time.

Question. How did he get out of the service?

Answer. His time expired, and he was regularly mustered out, so I understand.

Question. You have not been back since?

Answer. No, sir.

Question. Was there any property accounted for to you, or to any officer of the government, so far as you know, that was taken at Black Kettle's camp?

Answer. Not any. I would say, however, that any property the army captured they would not be likely to turn over to me.

I was asked if I knew of any depredations committed by these Indians, and I stated what was done in 1862. Before going further, I will say, that Black Kettle told me in that council that he and White Antelope had been opposed to depredations all the time, but could not control their tribes. They admitted that their tribes, that the Arapahoes and Sioux, had made a large number of attacks, and told me where each depredation I inquired about had been committed by the different tribes.

I gave to the committee of investigation on Indian affairs, the other day, a sketch of the minutes kept of that council. There was quite a large number of these depredations referred to and inquired of in that council, but not by any means all the depredations that were committed last summer.

The Cheyennes commenced their depredations early in the spring with the Arapahoes, Kiowas, Comanches, and Sioux. Agreeably to a previous treaty or council held by them in the winter of 1863 and 1864—which treaty was the consummation of an arrangement that the Sioux tried to make with our Indians in 1863, which I reported to the Indian bureau, and they sent me out authority to treat with them—I went to the head of the Republican, and spent about a month there trying to get them together, having my messengers out. Little Geary went to the camp of Bull Bear, Black Kettle, White Antelope, and a large number of others. The report of this attempt is published in my annual report for 1863.

The result of that failure was, that they told Mr. Geary, after agreeing first to come and see me, that they had made up their minds to have nothing more to do with us; that they did not want any more of our goods; that they might as well be killed as starved to death; that they were being driven out of their country by the whites; that they repudiated the treaty of Fort Wise, under which we were making preparations to settle them, as you will see by looking into my report, in which I give Geary's sworn statement.

After coming back a portion of these Indians ran together. You will observe that they made the treaty of 1861 together. A portion of them commenced committing depredations that fall. They stole a lot of horses, a portion of which we recovered in the autumn. A man who was present at their "big medicine" on the Arkansas, by the name of North, came to me privately and secretly from this band of Indians that committed depredations in November, 1863, within about twenty miles of Denver; he came to me from their camp, and made a statement which I forwarded to the War Department and to the Indian bureau, which is also in my annual report for this year.

47

North told me that the Kiowas, Comanches, Apaches, Cheyennes, a portion of the Arapahoes, and the Sioux, had held a council, at which he was present, and shook hands over it. That they would pretend to be friendly with the whites until they could get sufficient ammunition ; then in the spring they would divide into little parties and commence a war on the whites. Early last spring the first depredation they committed was to steal one hundred and seventy-five head of cattle, which was done by the Cheyennes, from Irwin & Jackman, government contractors, for transportation across the plains. Irwin & Jackman's men followed them about twenty miles down Sand creek, until they struck off to the head of the Republican. They then came to Denver and reported to the military commander, Colonel Chivington, and requested a force to go with them to recover their cattle. That force was sent out, and after being gone a week or two they returned, having recovered about a dozen of the cattle, one soldier having been wounded. He returned for the want of subsistence, and was sent again, and went through to Fort Larned on the route. That was Lieutenant Ayres, and during the time he was gone he had a battle with the Indians, in which they drove him. They attacked him as he was passing through with his battery to Fort Larned, which is in Kansas. At that battle one of the Indians, who was said to be a very friendly Indian to the whites, was killed. He was said to be in favor of making peace, and preventing the battle, and was in the act of trying to pacify the Indians when he was shot. But Lieutenant Ayres's report has never been furnished to me, and consequently I cannot give the details of it; but this was the statement the lieutenant made when he got back. He got away from the Indians without being captured. They were in very large force. He got away and got to Fort Larned. That is the end of the effort to get back these cattle. He and the rest of his battery—he had a section of a battery, I think, two guns—was at Fort Larned for some time. But the commander there, who was said to be an intemperate man, was not on the alert; and the Kiowas and some other Indians, mainly Kiowas, captured the whole of the battery's horses, one hundred and forty, and ran them off right from the fort. While Satant, the commander of the Indians, was talking with the officer in command, making great professions of friendship at the time, they made this raid upon the battery's horses and got away with them.

I would say still further, that to give a description of all the depredations that were committed during the summer, and fall, and this winter, would require a statement which would be very extensive. I would like this, as there is an impression in the minds of people here that the Indian war out there has not amounted to much—I would like this, that this committee, for the purpose of ascertaining, would deputize somebody to gather the reports of the attacks, the number of people killed, and the amount of property destroyed during the past year.

By Mr. Gooch:

Question. With all the knowledge you have in relation to these attacks and depredations by the Indians, do you think they afford any justification for the attack made by Colonel Chivington on these friendly Indians, under the circumstances under which it was made?

Answer. As a matter of course, no one could justify an attack on Indians while under the protection of the flag. If those Indians were there under the protection of the flag, it would be a question that would be scarcely worth asking, because nobody could say anything in favor of the attack. I have heard, however—that is only a report—that there was a statement on the part of Colonel Chivington and his friends that these Indians had assumed a hostile attitude before he attacked them. I do not know whether that is so or not    I have said all I have had to do with them. I supposed they were being treated as prisoners of war in some way or other.

I had a letter from General Curtis, after I got here, saying he was troubled to know what to do with so many nominal prisoners of war, as they were so expensive to feed there. The subsistence of the fort was short, and it was a long way to get subsistence, and through a hostile country, and he was troubled to know what to do with them.

Question. But from all the circumstances which you know, all the facts in relation to that matter, do you deem that Colonel Chivington had any justification for that attack?

Answer. So far as giving an opinion is concerned, I would say this: That the reports that have been made here, a great many of them, have come through persons whom I know to be personal enemies of Colonel Chivington for a long time. And I would rather not give an opinion on the subject until I have heard the other side of the question, which I have not heard yet.

Question. I do not ask for an opinion. Do you know of any circumstance which would justify that attack?

Answer. I do not know of any circumstance connected with it subsequent to the time those Indians left me and I started for another part of the country. It is proper for me to say, that these attacks during the summer, and up to the time I came away, were of very frequent occurrence. The destruction of property was very great. Our people suffered wonderfully, especially in their property, and in their loss of life. They murdered a family some twenty-odd miles east of Denver. The attacks by hostile Indians, about the time I came away, were very numerous along the Platte. There was an attack as I came in, about the month of November. It was in the evening, about sundown, and I passed over the ground in the night in the stage with my family, and a few days afterwards a party of emigrants, returning from Colorado, were murdered near the same ground, which was near Plum creek; and for a considerable length of time, immediately after I came in, the attacks were very numerous and very violent, until the stage was interrupted so that it has not been running since, until within a few days.

I started home and could not get there because there was no transportation. I came back here and shall return in a few days again. I mention this in order to do away with the impression that might exist that hostilities had ceased, and that this attack of Colonel Chivington had excited the recent hostilities.

These Indians told me, when they were there, that the Sioux were in large force on the head of the Republican, and would make an attack about the time I expected to come in. I delayed my coming in a short time on account of what they told me, and when I did come in I found some Indians commencing their depredations, which they continued about the month following, both before and after the attack made by Colonel Chivington. General Curtis wrote to me that he did not think Chivington's attack was the instigation of the hostilities perpetrated along the Platte.

---

*Testimony of Mr. A. C. Hunt.*

WASHINGTON, *March* 15, 1865.

Mr. A. C. HUNT sworn and examined.

By Mr. Loan:

Question. Where do you reside?

Answer. I reside at Denver, Colorado.

Question. What is your official position?

Answer. I am United States marshal for the district of Colorado. I have been in Denver since 1859.

Question. Do you know anything in connexion with the killing of the Indians at Sand creek, about the last of November, 1864?

Answer. I do not suppose I know anything that would be admissible as evidence. All I know is from general rumor, not being on the ground at all. I was in Denver when the regiment returned.

Question. Did you hear anything about it from Colonel Chivington, or any one of his command?

Answer. I heard an immense sight from soldiers in his command.

Question. State what they told you.

Answer. I also talked a long time with the guide, James Beckwith, after they returned.

Question. State anything that was said by any one connected with that transaction in regard to what was done.

Answer. I talked longer with Melrose, a private in Captain Baxtor's company, under Colonel Shoup. He gave me quite a history of the fight, and everything pertaining to it. He enlisted from the Arkansas. There is a general disposition, on the part of those who enlisted from that neighborhood, to cry down the whole transaction as being very badly managed, and very murderous. They made no secret of telling what had been done, but made no boast of it at all. They said they were heartily ashamed of it.

Question. State what they said was done.

Answer. According to their understanding, when they started out, they were enlisted for the purpose of fighting hostile Indians, there being any quantity of them on the plains. They knew nothing of their whereabouts. They went under the orders of Colonel Chivington, who led the command. They came within 80 miles of Fort Lyon, where they were halted for some days, and all communication stopped. No person, not even the United States mail, was permitted to go down the road for quite a length of time, until the forces which had been straggling back had all been collected together. When they did march to Fort Lyon they went very rapidly, taking every person about the fort by surprise, no person anticipating their coming at all. Their first movement was to throw a guard around the fort. That surprised the soldiers very much; they said they did not know the object of it. That night they were ordered to march again in a northeast direction. I think that and perhaps the next night they marched some 35 miles to fall upon this camp of Indians on Sand creek. None of the soldiers were posted as to what Indians they were fighting, or anything about it, until they got an explanation, after the attack was made, from various white men in the camp. Those white men told the soldiers that they were Black Kettle's band, who had been there for some time; a part of the time had been drawing rations from the fort—were, to all intents and purposes, friendly Indians. Beyond that I know that the colonel, as soon as the fight was over, came back to Denver. I met him the day he came in. The command afterwards returned in marching time. They had evidences of what they had been doing—among the rest, White Antelope's medal; I think they had about 20 of Black Kettle's scalps—quite that many, I think, were exhibited; they had White Antelope's commission, or something like that, from Commissioner Dole—something like a recommend; they had a thousand and one trophies in the way of finely worked buffalo robes, spurs, and bits, and things of that kind; all of which, I suppose, was contraband of war— they were taken on the field of battle.

Question. Did they say anything about how the attack was made, at what time, and under what circumstances?

Answer. I understood them to say it was made just at daylight. The Indians that were not armed almost all fled and escaped. The impression of the men I talked with was that they had killed over 100 of them; the impression of some others was that they had killed 400 or 500.

Question. Was anything said about killing women and children?

Answer. Yes, sir; they killed everything alive in the camp that they could get at. I believe that was part of the understanding, that none should be spared. I believe it is generally the understanding that you fight Indians in that way.

Question. What were those ornamented buffalo robes worth in the market?

Answer. They are very valuable—worth from $20 to $50 each.

Question. In whose possession did you see them?

Answer. They were mostly in private hands—in the hands of the men who were in the fight; by permission, I suppose. I do not suppose there was any demand made for them by any person. I suppose each man who had one of them thought he was entitled to it.

Question. Is that the rule out there, that the soldiers of the United States are entitled to all they capture?

Answer. That is the only battle they have ever had; so that I do not know as there is any particular rule about that matter.

Question. How long did they say the fight continued?

Answer. I am under the impression now that they said it continued some two or three hours. That is my impression from the representations made by the parties engaged in the fight.

Question. How many Indians did they say were engaged in the fight?

Answer. It has been estimated that there were from 500 to 3,000 there. I suppose the agent knows almost exactly how many there were of them. They judge from the lodges, and there are from five to six in a lodge, so far as my experience goes. From the best information I could get there were from 100 to 120 lodges there.

Question. Was there anything said about the number that escaped?

Answer. A large proportion of them escaped; that was the supposition of the soldiers I talked with.

Question. In what way, on horseback or on foot?

Answer. Those of the warriors who had horses that they could get hold of escaped on horseback. The women and young ones, who had no horses, went on foot.

Question. Did they take any prisoners in that fight?

Answer. I never heard of any prisoners being taken that were brought in.

Question. Do you know whether they captured any property from the Indians?

Answer. I think they were possessed of no property except what I have mentioned.

Question. Did they have no horses, ponies, and mules?

Answer. Yes, sir; I saw a great many ponies. A New Mexican company was mostly mounted on ponies that they had captured. I saw them come in on Indian horses; they were poor, thin horses.

Question. Did you hear Colonel Chivington himself say anything about that transaction?

Answer. No, sir, except in a public speech he made afterwards, and in that he did not say much about it.

Question. Did he assign any reason why, under the circumstances, he attacked that band of Indians?

Answer. He said all the time that they were hostile Indians, and was very wroth with any of the community who knew anything about the Indians, who had been in the country a long while, who knew something about Black Kettle and White Antelope, and who denominated them friendly Indians, and who differed with him as to the policy of bringing those Indians down upon us at that time. He was very wroth with me particularly, and one or two others; and I suppose that was what brought forth the remarks that he made.

Question. What was his policy?

51

Answer. To exterminate the Indians.

Question. To kill them all ?

Answer. Yes, sir, I should judge so ; and that seemed to be quite a popular notion too.

Question. Did you have any means of knowing the reputation of Black Kettle and White Antelope?

Answer. We have always regarded Black Kettle and White Antelope as the special friends of the white man ever since I have been in the country.

Question. Do you know of any acts of hostility committed by them, or with their consent?

Answer. No, sir; I do not.

Question. Did you ever hear any acts of hostility attributed to them by any one?

Answer. No, sir.

By Mr. Gooch:

Question. Is there a general feeling among the whites there in favor of the extermination of the Indians ?

Answer. That feeling prevails in all new countries where the Indians have committed any depredations. And most especially will people fly off the handle in that way when you exhibit the corpse of some one who has been murdered by the Indians. When they come to their sober senses they reflect that the Indians have feelings as well as we have, and are entitled to certain rights; which, by the by, they never get.

Question. Had there been any such acts committed by the Indians at that time ?

Answer. No, sir; not for months. But last summer there were exhibitions that were horrid to tell, and there were terrible imprudences in consequence. Persons killed thirty or forty miles off were brought into Denver and exhibited there.

Question. There had been nothing of that kind for some time previous to this attack by Colonel Chivington ?

Answer. No, sir.

Question. Do you know of any motive which actuated Colonel Chivington in making this attack ?

Answer. It may be invidious in me to give my idea of his motive. I was entirely satisfied that his motive was not a good and virtuous one—so much so, that when I was where he stopped his command I wrote a letter to Judge Bennett, giving him my views about the matter, and telling him what I thought was his object. We regarded those Indians on the reservation as safe, and ought not to be attacked. That opinion, perhaps, was not shared by the community, though I presume the great majority of the command were aware of the Indians they were going to kill.

Question. If you have no objection, I would like you to state what you think was his motive.

Answer. I think it was hope of promotion. He had read of Kit Carson, General Harney, and others, who had become noted for their Indian fighting. I have no objection to state that.

Mr. Gooch. The reason why I ask these questions is, that this attack seems to us to be of such a character that we are anxious to ascertain, if possible, what could have been the motive which actuated an officer to make such an attack under the circumstances.

The witness. I have no doubt that what I have stated was one motive.

*Papers submitted by Hon. H. P. Bennet, delegate in Congress from Colorado Territory.*

WASHINGTON CITY, *March* 20, 1865.

SIR: I am compelled to leave to-night for New York, to be gone several days, and it will likely be impossible for me to appear before the committee at all. But, as you requested, I will furnish the committee with such official and unofficial documents as I have touching upon the " Sand creek affair."

Herewith enclosed please find the official reports of all the principal officers engaged in the transaction; also, a copy of Governor Evans's proclamation, after which the one-hundred-day regiment was raised; also, some slips cut from the "Rocky Mountain News," the organ of Governor Evans, and edited by the postmaster at Denver; also, find an extract from Secretary Elbert's message made to the legislature and published in the "Rocky Mountain News." All the foregoing papers I believe to be genuine copies of what they purport to be.

Very respectfully,

H. P. BENNET.

Hon. Mr. GOOCH.

*Proclamation by Governor Evans, of Colorado Territory.*

PROCLAMATION.

Having sent special messengers to the Indians of the plains, directing the friendly to rendezvous at Fort Lyon, Fort Larned, Fort Laramie, and Camp Collins for safety and protection, warning them that all hostile Indians would be pursued and destroyed, and the last of said messengers having now returned, and the evidence being conclusive that most of the Indian tribes of the plains are at war and hostile to the whites, and having to the utmost of my ability endeavored to induce all of the Indians of the plains to come to said places of rendezvous, promising them subsistence and protection, which, with a few exceptions, they have refused to do:

Now, therefore, I, John Evans, governor of Colorado Territory, do issue this my proclamation, authorizing all citizens of Colorado, either individually or in such parties as they may organize, to go in pursuit of all hostile Indians on the plains, scrupulously avoiding those who have responded to my said call to rendezvous at the points indicated; also, to kill and destroy, as enemies of the country, wherever they may be found, all such hostile Indians. And further, as the only reward I am authorized to offer for such services, I hereby empower such citizens, or parties of citizens, to take captive, and hold to their own private use and benefit, all the property of said hostile Indians that they may capture, and to receive for all stolen property recovered from said Indians such reward as may be deemed proper and just therefor.

I further offer to all such parties as will organize under the militia law of the Territory for the purpose to furnish them arms and ammunition, and to present their accounts for pay as regular soldiers for themselves, their horses, their subsistence, and transportation, to Congress, under the assurance of the department commander that they will be paid.

The conflict is upon us, and all good citizens are called upon to do their duty for the defence of their homes and families.

In testimony whereof, I have hereunto set my hand and caused the great seal of the Territory of Colorado to be affixed this 11th day of August, A. D. 1864.

[SEAL.]　　　　　　　　　　　JOHN EVANS.

By the governor:

S. H. ELBERT, *Secretary of Colorado Territory.*

# MASSACRE OF CHEYENNE INDIANS.

OFFICIAL REPORTS OF OFFICERS ENGAGED IN THE AFFAIR OF SANDY CREEK, PUBLISHED IN THE ROCKY MOUNTAIN NEWS.

### First report of Colonel Chivington.

HEADQUARTERS DISTRICT OF COLORADO,
*In the field, on Big Bend of Sandy Creek, Col. Ter., Nov.* 29, 1864.

SIR: I have not the time to give you a detailed history of our engagement of to-day, or to mention those officers and men who distinguished themselves in one of the most bloody Indian battles ever fought on these plains. You will find enclosed the report of my surgeon in charge, which will bring to many anxious friends the sad fate of loved ones who are and have been risking everything to avenge the horrid deeds of those savages we have so severely handled. We made a forced march of forty miles, and surprised, at break of day, one of the most powerful villages of the Cheyenne nation, and captured over five hundred animals; killing the celebrated chiefs One Eye, White Antelope, Knock Kno, Black Kettle, and Little Robe, with about five hundred of their people, destroying all their lodges and equipage, making almost an annihilation of the entire tribe.

I shall leave here, as soon as I can see our wounded safely on the way to the hospital at Fort Lyon, for the villages of the Sioux, which are reported about eighty miles from here, on the Smoky Hill, and three thousand strong; so look out for more fighting. I will state, for the consideration of gentlemen who are opposed to fighting these red scoundrels, that I was shown, by my chief surgeon, the scalp of a white man taken from the lodge of one of the chiefs, which could not have been more than two or three days taken; and I could mention many more things to show how these Indians, who have been drawing government rations at Fort Lyon, are and have been acting.

Very respectfully, your obedient servant,
J. M. CHIVINGTON,
*Col. Comd'g Colorado Expedition against Indians on Plains.*
CHAS. WHEELER, A. A. A. G.,
*Headquarters District of Colorado, Denver.*

---

### Second report of Colonel Chivington.

HEADQUARTERS DISTRICT OF COLORADO,
*Denver, C. T., December* 16, 1864.

GENERAL: I have the honor to transmit the following report of operations of the Indian expedition under my command, of which brief notice was given you by my telegram of November 29, 1864:

Having ascertained that the hostile Indians had proceeded south from the Platte, and were almost within striking distance of Fort Lyon, I ordered Colonel Geo. L. Shoup, 3d regiment Colorado volunteer cavalry, (100-day service,) to proceed with the mounted men of his regiment in that direction.

On the 20th of November I left Denver and Booneville, C. T.; on the 24th of November joined and took command in person of the expedition which had been increased by a battalion of the 1st cavalry of Colorado, consisting of detachments of companies C, E and H. I proceeded with the utmost caution down the Arkansas river, and on the morning of the 28th instant arrived at Fort Lyon, to the surprise of the garrison of that post. On the same morning I resumed my march, being joined by Major Scott J. Anthony, 1st cavalry of Colorado, with one hundred and twenty-five men of said regiment, consisting of detachments of companies D G and H, with two howitzers. The command then proceeded in a northeasterly direction, travelling all night, and at daylight of the 29th November striking Sand creek about forty (40) miles from Fort Lyon.

Here was discovered an Indian village of one hundred and thirty (130) lodges, composed of Black Kettle's band of Cheyennes and eight (8) lodges of Arapahoes, with Left Hand. My line of battle was formed with Lieutenant Wilson's battalion of the 1st regiment, numbering about 125 men, on the right, Colonel Shoup's 3d regiment, numbering about 450 men, in the centre, and Major Anthony's battalion, numbering 125 men, 1st regiment, on the left.

The attack was immediately made upon the Indian's camp by Lieutenant Wilson, who dashed forward, cutting the enemy off from their herd, and driving them out of their camp, which was subsequently destroyed.

The Indians, numbering from 900 to 1,000, though taken by surprise, speedily rallied and formed a line of battle across the creek, about three-fourths of a mile above the village, stubbornly contesting every inch of ground.

The commands of Colonel Shoup and Major Anthony pressed rapidly forward and attacked the enemy sharply, and the engagement became general, we constantly driving the Indians, who fell back from one position to another for five miles, and finally abandoned resistance and dispersed in all directions and were pursued by my troops until nightfall.

It may, perhaps, be unnecessary for me to state that I captured no prisoners. Between five and six hundred Indians were left dead upon the field. About five hundred and fifty ponies, mules and horses were captured, and all their lodges were destroyed, the contents of which has served to supply the command with an abundance of trophies, comprising the paraphernalia of Indian warfare and life. My loss was eight (8) killed on the field and forty (40) wounded, of which two have since died. Of the conduct of the 3d regiment (100-day service) I have to say that they well sustained the reputation of our Colorado troops for bravery and effectiveness; were well commanded by their gallant young Colonel, Geo. L. Shoup, ably assisted by Lieutenant Colonel L. L. Bowen, Major Hal Sayr and Captain Theodore G. Cree, commanding 1st, 2d and 3d battalions of that regiment

Of the conduct of the two battalions of the 1st regiment I have but to remark that they sustained their reputation as second to none, and were ably handled by their commanders, Major Anthony, Lieutenant Wilson and Lieutenant Clark Dunn, upon whom the command devolved after the disability of Lieutenant Wilson from wounds received.

Night coming on, the pursuit of the flying Indians was of necessity abandoned, and my command encamped within sight of the field.

On the 1st instant, having sent the wounded and dead to Fort Lyon, the first to be cared for, and the latter to be buried upon our own soil. I resumed the pursuit in the direction of Camp Wynkoop on the Arkansas river, marching all night of the 3d and 4th instant, in hopes of overtaking a large encampment of Arapahoes and Cheyennes, under Little Raven, but the enemy had been apprized of my advance, and on the morning of the 5th instant, at 3 o'clock, precipitately broke camp and fled. My stock was exhausted. For one hundred miles the snow had been two feet deep, and for the previous fifteen days—excepting on November 29 and 30—the marches had been forced and incessant.

Under these circumstances, and the fact of the time of the 3d regiment being nearly out, I determined for the present to relinquish the pursuit.

Of the effect of the punishment sustained by the Indians you will be the judge. Their chiefs Black Kettle, White Antelope, One Eye, Knock Knee, and Little Robe, were numbered with the killed and their bands almost annihilated. I was shown the scalp of a white man, found in one of the lodges, which could not have been taken more than two or three days previous. For full particulars and reports of the several commanders I respectfully refer you to the following copies

Part VI——4

herewith enclosed, of Colonel George L. Shoup, 3d regiment, December 6, 1864; Colonel Shoup, 3d regiment, December 7, 1864; Colonel L. L. Bowen, 3d regiment, November 30, 1864; Major Hal Sayr, 3d regiment, December 6, 1864; Captain Theodore G. Cree, 3d regiment, December 6, 1864; Major Scott J. Anthony, 1st regiment, December 1, 1864; Lieutenant Clark Dunn, 1st regiment, November 30, 1864; Lieutenant J. J. Kennedy, November 30, 1864.

If all the companies of the 1st cavalry of Colorado and the 11th Ohio volunteer cavalry, stationed at camps and posts near here, were ordered to report to me, I could organize a campaign, which, in my judgment, would effectually rid the country between the Platte and Arkansas rivers of these red rebels.

I would respectfully request to be informed, if another campaign should be authorized from here, whether I could employ one or two hundred friendly Utes, (Indians,) furnishing them subsistence, arms and ammunition for the campaign.

\* \* \* \* \* \* \* \* \*

I am, general, very respectfully, your obedient servant,

J. M. CHIVINGTON,
*Col. 1st Cavalry of Colorado, Commanding District of Colorado.*

---

*First report of Colonel Shoup.*

HEADQUARTERS THIRD COLORADO CAVALRY,
*In field,* 100 *miles below Fort Lyon, December* 6, 1864.

CAPTAIN: In answer to your communication of this date, asking me to consult with the officers of my regiment, and report their opinion as to the propriety and willingness of themselves and the enlisted men under my command to continue this expedition against the Indians to the Smoky Hill and Republican, I have to say—

My "officers and men" will obey orders and go to the Smoky Hill and Republican, if the colonel commanding, after due deliberation, will so order. However, they are nearly all of the opinion, (the officers,) that an expedition to the above named streams at present must fail. This opinion is based upon the fact that their horses are worn out, and in an unserviceable condition; most of the animals would fail on the first forced march.

They are of the further opinion that many of these men will re-enlist to prosecute this campaign if we meet with no reverse and the men are not worn out and disheartened in a fruitless march just before the expiration of their term of enlistment.

All the above is fully indorsed by me; and while I am more than eager to duplicate the great victory of November 29, I think an expedition to the Smoky Hill and Republican, considering the worn-out condition of my horses, would prove more of a disaster than a success, at present; the failure of which would so dishearten my men, that no inducement could be held out that would cause them to re-enlist. All of which is most respectfully submitted.

GEORGE L. SHOUP,
*Colonel 3d Colorado Cavalry.*

Captain J. S. MAYNARD,
*A. A. A. General, District of Colorado, in the field.*

---

*Second report of Colonel Shoup.*

HEADQUARTERS DISTRICT OF COLORADO,
*In the field, December* 7, 1864.

DEAR SIR: I have the honor to report the part taken by my regiment, 3d Colorado cavalry, in the engagement with the Indians on Sand creek, forty (40) miles north of Fort Lyon, Colorado Territory, November 29, 1864.

I brought my regiment into action at sunrise. The first order given was to Captain John McCannon, company I, to cut off the Indians from their ponies on the south side of the village; this order was obeyed with great celerity and success. Captain McCannon captured about two hundred (200) ponies at the first dash, but being closely pressed by hundreds of Indians, sent the ponies to the rear, and opened a terrible and withering fire on the Indians, completely checking them, killing many, and causing them to retreat up Sand creek. Captain O. H. P. Baxter, with his company G, was sent to re-enforce Captain McCannon. The two companies then fought the Indians up the south side of the creek for about two (2) miles, and at this point many of the Indians took refuge in the banks of the creek, where they had prepared rifle-pits. Captain McCannon, with his company, remained at that place until late in the afternoon, and was the last to leave the field of battle. His brave company killed twenty-six (26) Indians in one pit, and must have killed fifty (50) or more during the engagement. Company G, led by Captain Baxter and Lieutenant Templeton, pursued the demoralized and flying savages to the south and west, killing upwards of twenty Indians. Lieutenant W. E. Grinnell, with a detachment of 21 men of company K, fought during part of the engagement on the southwest side of the battle-field. This brave little detachment deserve honorable mention for their gallant conduct on the field. They lost one-fifth of their number, killed and wounded. At the opening of the engagement I led about four hundred (400) of my men up the north side of the creek and engaged the main body of the Indians, who were retreating to the west. I dismounted my men and fought them for some time on foot.

At this point Captain Talbott, of company M, fell severely wounded, while bravely leading his men in a charge on a body of Indians who had taken refuge on the banks on the north side of the creek. Here a terrible hand-to-hand encounter ensued between the Indians and Captain Talbott's men and others who had rushed forward to their aid—the Indians trying to secure the scalp of Captain Talbott. I think the hardest fighting of the day occurred at that point, some of our men fighting with club muskets; the 1st and 3d Coloradoans fighting side by side, each trying to excel in bravery, and each ambitious to kill at least one Indian. Many valuable lives of officers and men were saved by the bravery of others just as the fatal knife was raised to perform its work of death. Early in the engagement, Captain Nickols, with his company D, pursued a band of Indians that were trying to escape to the northeast ; he overtook and punished them severely, killing twenty-five or thirty and captured some ponies.

Other companies of my regiment fought with zeal and bravery, but after 10 o'clock a. m. the battle became so general and covered so wide a field that it became necessary to divide my command into small detachments, sending them in all directions to pursue the flying Indians.

I am told by my officers and men that some of their comrades engaged the Indians in close combat. I am satisfied, from my own observation, that the historian will search in vain for braver deeds than were committed on that field of battle.

My loss is nine (9) men killed, one missing, supposed to be killed, and forty-four (44) wounded.

Captain Presley Talbott and Lieutenant C. H. Hawley are the only officers wounded of my regiment ; Captain Talbott in left side, and Lieutenant Hawley in shoulder.

Enclosed herewith you will find copy of the reports of my battalion commanders to me. Aell of which is most respectfully submitted.

I am, sir, with great respect, your obedient servant,

GEORGE L. SHOUP,
*Colonel 3d Colorado Cavalry.*

Colonel J. M. CHIVINGTON, *Commanding District of Colorado.*

## Report of Lieutenant Colonel Bowen.

SANDY CREEK, *November* 30, 1864.

SIR: I have the honor to enclose you the reports of the company commanders of the first battalion, commanded by myself, in the action of yesterday. I fully indorse all contained in these reports; all behaved well, each vieing with the other as to who could do the enemy the most injury. This, I think, can truly be said of the whole regiment. I was in position during the action to see most of the regiment, and did not see one coward. Permit me to congratulate you upon the signal punishment meted out to the savages on yesterday, "who so ruthlessly have murdered our women and children," in the language of the colonel commanding, although I regret the loss of so many brave men. The third regiment cannot any longer be called the " bloodless third."

From the most reliable information, from actual count and positions occupied, I have no doubt that at least one hundred and fifty Indians were killed by my battalion.

I cannot speak in terms of too high praise of all the officers and men under my command.

The war flag of this band of Cheyennes is in my possession, presented by Stephen Decatur, commissary sergeant of company C, who acted as my battalion adjutant.

Very respectfully,

LEAVITT L. BOWEN,
*Lieut. Col. 3d Colorado Cavalry, Commanding 1st Battalion.*
Colonel GEORGE L. SHOUP,
*Third Regiment Colorado Cavalry.*

---

## Report of Major Sayr.

CAMP ———, *December* 6, 1864.

SIR: I have the honor to submit the following report of the part taken by my battalion in the action of November 29, on Sand creek. The battalion consisted of company B, Captain H. M. Orahood, First Lieutenant Charles H. Hawley, Second Lieutenant Harry Richmond, and sixty-four men; company I, Captain John McCannon, First Lieutenant Thomas J. Davis, and fifty-three men; company G, Captain O. H. P. Baxter, Second Lieutenant A. J. Templeton, and forty men; company K, Lieutenant W. E. Grinnell, and twenty-one men; making a total of 178 men. Company I was sent at the beginning of the action to the west of the field, where they remained during the day, much of the time sustaining a heavy fire from the enemy, who were secreted under a high bank, on the south side of Sand creek. This company did good service in preventing the escape of the Indians to the west. Companies B, G, and K, moved across the creek and went into the action on the north side of the creek and west of the Indian town, where they remained for several hours, doing good service, while under a heavy fire from the enemy, who were concealed in rifle-pits in the bed of the creek.

The action became general, and lasted from 6.30 a. m. until 1 p. m., when the companies divided into small squads and went in pursuit of the Indians, who were now flying in every direction across the plains, and were pursued until dark.

Both officers and men conducted themselves bravely. The number of Indians killed by the battalion, as estimated by company commanders, is about 175 to

200.  Company B, Lieutenant Hawley, wounded in shoulder; private Marrion wounded in thigh; company I, three killed and three wounded; company G, none killed or wounded; company K, two killed and two wounded ; making a total of five killed and seven wounded.

Hoping the above will meet your approval, I am, colonel, very respectfully, &c.,

HAL. SAYR,
*Major Commanding 2d Battalion, 3d Colorado Cavalry.*

Colonel GEORGE L. SHOUP,
*Commanding Third Colorado Cavalry.*

---

*Report of Captain Cree.*

CAMP SKEDADDLE, *December* 6, 1864.

SIR : I have the honor to report to you the part taken by the third battalion in the fight of the 29th of November.  They first formed on the left of the regiment, in the rear of the village, then removed upon the right bank of the creek, near one-half mile; there dismounted and fought the red-skins about an hour, where the boys behaved like veterans.

After finding that we had done all the good that we could do there, removed companies D and E, (company F having gone with Colonel Bowen's battalion,) and moved to the right, across the hill, for the purpose of killing Indians that were making their escape to the right of the command, in which movement we succeeded in killing many.  I then made a detail from company D, of fifteen (15) men, and sent them to capture some twenty (20) ponies, which I could see some four (4) miles to the right of the village; but before they reached the ponies some twenty Indians attacked them, when a fierce fight ensued, in which private McFarland was killed in a hand-to-hand engagement; but, like true soldiers, they stood their ground, killing five (5) Indians, and wounding several others. The Indians finding it rather warm to be healthy, left.  The boys pursued them some eight or ten miles, and finding that they could not overtake them, returned, bringing with them the ponies they were sent for.  I then returned with the command to the village to take care of their killed and wounded companions.

Company E lost one killed and one wounded ; company D, two killed and one wounded.

As for the bravery displayed by any one in particular, I have no distinctions to make.  All I can say for officers and men is, that they all behaved well, and won for themselves a name that will be remembered for ages to come.

The number of Indians killed by my battalion is sixty (60.)

I am, colonel, yours truly,

T. G. CREE,
*Captain Commanding 3d Battalion, 3d Colorado Cavalry.*

Colonel GEORGE L. SHOUP.

---

*Report of Major Anthony.*

HEADQUARTERS, IN THE FIELD,
*Battalion First Colorado Cavalry, December 1, 1864.*

SIR : I have the honor to report that I left Fort Lyon, Colorado Territory, with detachments from companies D, G, and H; 1st Colorado cavalry, numbering one hundred and twenty-five men, and two howitzers, and joined Colonel Chivington's brigade one mile below Fort Lyon, at 8 o'clock p. m., November 28, and proceeded with his command, on Indian expedition, in a northeasterly direction, striking Sand creek at daylight of the 29th November, forty miles from

Fort Lyon, when we came upon a herd of Indian horses, and I was sent forward with my battalion to capture stock. After proceeding about one mile we came in sight of an Indian camp, some two miles further. I immediately sent word to the colonel commanding that an lndian camp was in sight, and proceeded with my command in the direction of the camp, which I reached just before sunrise. I found Lieutenant Wilson, with a detachment of 1st Colorado cavalry, upon the right and south of the camp, and Lieutenant Dunn, with a detachment of the 1st Colorado cavalry, posted upon the west bank of Sand creek, and opposite the camp, both commands keeping up a brisk fire upon the camp. Upon my nearing the camp upon the west side I was attacked by a small force of Indians posted behind the bank of the creek, who commenced firing upon me with arrows, and who had collected on the opposite side of camp. Colonel Chivington coming up at this time with Colonel Shoup's regiment, 3d Colorado cavalry, and two howitzers, charged through the camp, driving the Indians completely out of their camp and into the creek, in holes or rifle-pits dug in the sand. The fighting now became general. The Indians fought desperately, apparently resolved to die upon that ground, but to injure us as much as possible before being killed. We fought them for about six hours, along the creek for five miles.

The loss to my command was one killed and three wounded. The loss to the entire command, ten killed and forty wounded. Lieutenant Baldwin, commanding the section of howitzers, attached to my battalion, had a fine private horse shot from under him. Seven horses were killed from my command. The loss to the Indians was about three hundred killed, some six hundred ponies, and one hundred and thirty lodges, with a large quantity of buffalo robes, and their entire camp equipage.

The camp proved to be Cheyenne and Arapahoe Indians, and numbered about 1,100 persons, under the leadership of Black Kettle, head chief of the Cheyenne tribe. Black Kettle and three other chiefs were killed.

All the command fought well, and observed all orders given them. We camped upon the ground occupied by the Indians the day before, destroyed the entire camp of the Indians, and then pushed rapidly in a southeasterly direction, in pursuit of Little Raven's camp of Arapahoes, reported to be on the Arkansas river.

I am, sir, with much respect, your obedient servant,

SCOTT J. ANTHONY,
*Major First Colorado Cavalry, Commanding Battalion.*

A. A. A. General Colonel CHIVINGTON'S
*Brigade, Indian Expedition.*

---

*Report of Lieutenant Kennedy.*

HEADQUARTERS Co. C, FIRST COLORADO CAVALRY,
*Camp, South Bend of Big Sandy, November 30, 1864.*

COLONEL : I have the honor to make the following report of company C, 1st cavalry of Colorado, on the expedition against the Cheyenne Indians, in pursuance of special orders from headquarters, district of Colorado, No. 132, of November 13, 1864.

I left camp Wheeler, Colorado Territory, on the 20th of November, 1864, with forty-two men of company C, 1st cavalry of Colorado, en route for Fort Lyon, Colorado Territory, a distance of two hundred and forty miles, at which place I arrived on the 28th of November, 1864. I left Fort Lyon at eight (8) o'clock p. m the same day, with thirty-five (35) men of C company, under command of First Lieutenant Luther Wilson, commanding battalion 1st cavalry

60

of Colorado, made a march of forty miles to South Bend of Big Sandy, Colorado Territory, at which place I arrived a little after daybreak on the morning of the 29th, where we came upon a large village of hostile Cheyenne Indians, numbering from nine hundred to one thousand, which we immediately attacked; after which a general engagement ensued, which lasted until 3 o'clock p. m., in which the Indians were defeated and nearly annihilated; after which we returned to the Indian village, which we helped to destroy, and then went into camp.

I had one private, Oliver Pierson, mortally wounded, (who has since died;) two privates, August Mettze and John B. Calhoun, severely wounded; Sergeant M. H. Linnell, saddler Elias South, and privates C. J. Ballou and William Boyls, slightly wounded. And I would most respectfully acknowledge to the colonel commanding the services rendered by my platoon commanders, sergeant John C. Turner and M. H. Linnell, and recommend them for their bravery during the entire engagement.

I am, sir, very respectfully, your obedient servant,
J. J. KENNEDY,
*Second Lieut. 1st Colorado Cavalry, Commanding Co. C.*
Colonel J. M. CHIVINGTON,
*Commanding Indian Expedition.*

*Report of Lieutenant Dunn.*

HEADQUARTERS CO. E, FIRST COLORADO CAVALRY,
*Camp South Bend of Big Sandy, C. T., November 30, 1864.*

COLONEL: I have the honor to make the following report of company E, 1st cavalry of Colorado, on an expedition against Indians.

On the 25th instant I left Camp Fillmore with my company, pursuant to Special Order No. 3, headquarters, District of Colorado, dated in the field November 23, 1864. I joined the column then in the field the same evening at Spring Bottom, thirty miles distant. I continued the march the next day under command of Lieutenant Wilson, commanding battalion of the 1st cavalry of Colorado. We reached Fort Lyon, seventy miles further down the Arkansas, on the 28th instant, about noon. About 7 o'clock the same evening I started from that place with eighteen men of my company, taking three days' cooked rations on our horses, and travelled in a northeasterly course. At daylight we came in sight of a large village of hostile Indians, Cheyennes and Arapahoes, numbering nine hundred or one thousand, nearly two miles north of us. We immediately proceeded to the attack by moving down a small ravine and making a charge on the village from the north side, taking the Indians completely by surprise. They rallied immediately and the engagement became general, and lasted till afternoon, when they were utterly routed and half their number left dead on the field.

We continued the pursuit till 3 o'clock p. m., when our horses being much fatigued, and our ammunition nearly exhausted, we returned to the village, which we helped to destroy, and then went into camp for the night.

I lost no men killed, and but two wounded. Sergeant Jackson had his hip broken, and private Mull was shot through the leg.

I am, sir, very respectfully, your obedient servant,
CLARK DUNN,
*Second Lieut. 1st Colorado Cavalry, Commanding Co. E.*
Colonel CHIVINGTON,
*First Colorado Cavalry.*

*Editorial articles from the Rocky Mountain News, the organ of Governor Evans, and edited by Mr. William N. Byers, P. M. at Denver.*

### THE BATTLE OF SAND CREEK.

Among the brilliant feats of arms in Indian warfare, the recent campaign of our Colorado volunteers will stand in history with few rivals, and none to exceed it in final results. We are not prepared to write its history, which can only be done by some one who accompanied the expedition, but we have gathered from those who participated in it, and from others who were in that part of the country, some facts which will doubtless interest many of our readers.

The people of Colorado are well aware of the situation occupied by the third regiment during the great snow-storm which set in the last of October. Their rendezvous was in Bijou Basin, about eighty miles southeast of this city, and close up under the foot of the Divide. That point had been selected as the base for an Indian campaign. Many of the companies reached it after the storm set in ; marching for days through the driving, blinding clouds of snow and deep drifts. Once there, they were exposed for weeks to an Arctic climate, surrounded by a treeless plain covered three feet deep with snow. Their animals suffered for food and with cold, and the men fared but little better. They were insufficiently supplied with tents and blankets, and their sufferings were intense. At the end of a month the snow had settled to the depth of two feet, and the command set out upon its long contemplated march. The rear guard left the Basin on the 23d of November. Their course was southeast, crossing the Divide and thence heading for Fort Lyon. For one hundred miles the snow was quite two feet in depth, and for the next hundred it ranged from six to twelve inches. Beyond that the ground was almost bare and the snow no longer impeded their march.

On the afternoon of the 28th the entire command reached Fort Lyon, a distance of *two hundred and sixty miles, in less than six days,* and so quietly and expeditiously had the march been made that the command at the fort was taken entirely by surprise. When the vanguard appeared in sight it was reported that a body of Indians were approaching, and precautions were taken for their reception. No one upon the route was permitted to go in advance of the column, and persons who it was suspected would spread the news of the advance were kept under surveillance until all danger from that source was past.

At Fort Lyon the force was strengthened by about two hundred and fifty men of the first regiment, and at nine o'clock in the evening the command set out for the Indian village. The course was due north, and their guide was the Polar star. As daylight dawned they came in sight of the Indian camp, after a forced midnight march of forty-two miles, in eight hours, across the rough, unbroken plain. But little time was required for preparation. The forces had been divided and arranged for battle on the march, and just as the sun rose they dashed upon the enemy with yells that would put a Comanche army to blush. Although utterly surprised, the savages were not unprepared, and for a time their defence told terribly against our ranks. Their main force rallied and formed in line of battle on the bluffs beyond the creek, where they were protected by rudely constructed rifle-pits, from which they maintained a steady fire until the shells from company C's (third regiment) howitzers began dropping among them, when they scattered and fought each for himself in genuine Indian fashion. As the battle progressed the field of carnage widened until it extended over not less than twelve miles of territory. The Indians who could, escaped or secreted themselves, and by three o'clock in the afternoon the carnage had ceased. It was estimated that between three and four hundred of the savages got away with their lives. Of the balance there were neither wounded nor prisoners. Their strength at the beginning of the action was estimated at nine hundred.

Their village consisted of one hundred and thirty Cheyenne and eight Arapahoe lodges. These, with their contents, were totally destroyed. Among their effects were large supplies of flour, sugar, coffee, tea, &c. Women's and children's clothing were found; also books and many other articles which must have been taken from captured trains or houses. One white man's scalp was found which had evidently been taken but a few days before. The chiefs fought with unparalleled bravery, falling in front of their men. One of them charged alone against a force of two or three hundred, and fell pierced with balls far in advance of his braves.

Our attack was made by five battalions. The first regiment, Colonel Chivington, part of companies C, D, E, G, H and K, numbering altogether about two hundred and fifty men, was divided into two battalions; the first under command of Major Anthony, and the second under Lieutenant Wilson, until the latter was disabled, when the command devolved upon Lieutenant Dunn. The three battalions of the third, Colonel Shoup, were led, respectively, by Lieutenant Colonel Bowen, Major Sayr, and Captain Cree. The action was begun by the battalion of Lieutenant Wilson, who occupied the right, and by a quick and bold movement cut off the enemy from their herd of stock. From this circumstance we gained our great advantage. A few Indians secured horses, but the great majority of them had to fight or fly on foot. Major Anthony was on the left, and the third in the centre.

Among the killed were *all* the Cheyenne chiefs, Black Kettle, White Antelope, Little Robe, Left Hand, Knock Knee, One Eye, and another, name unknown. Not a single prominent man of the tribe remains, and the tribe itself is almost annihilated. The Arapahoes probably suffered but little. It has been reported that the chief Left Hand, of that tribe, was killed, but Colonel Chivington is of the opinion that he was not. Among the stock captured were a number of government horses and mules, including the twenty or thirty stolen from the command of Lieutenant Chase at Jimmy's camp last summer.

The Indian camp was well supplied with defensive works. For half a mile along the creek there was an almost continuous chain of rifle-pits, and another similar line of works crowned the adjacent bluff. Pits had been dug at all the salient points for miles. After the battle twenty-three dead Indians were taken from one of these pits and twenty-seven from another.

Whether viewed as a march or as a battle, the exploit has few, if any, parallels. A march of 260 miles in but a fraction more than five days, with deep snow, scanty forage, and no road, is a remarkable feat, whilst the utter surprise of a large Indian village is unprecedented. In no single battle in North America, we believe, have so many Indians been slain.

It is said that a short time before the command reached the scene of battle an old squaw partially alarmed the village by reporting that a great heard of buffalo were coming. She heard the rumbling of the artillery and tramp of the moving squadrons, but her people doubted. In a little time the doubt was dispelled, but not by buffaloes.

A thousand incidents of individual daring and the passing events of the day might be told, but space forbids. We leave the task for eye-witnesses to chronicle. All acquitted themselves well, and Colorado soldiers have again covered themselves with glory.

### THE FORT LYON AFFAIR.

The issue of yesterday's News, containing the following despatch, created considerable of a sensation in this city, particularly among the Thirdsters and others who participated in the recent campaign and the battle on Sand creek :

# MASSACRE OF CHEYENNE INDIANS.

"WASHINGTON. *December* 20, 1864.

"The affair at Fort Lyon, Colorado, in which Colonel Chivington destroyed a large Indian village, and all its inhabitants, is to be made the subject of congressional investigation. Letters received from high officials in Colorado say that the Indians were killed after surrendering, and that a large proportion of them were women and children."

Indignation was loudly and unequivocally expressed, and some less considerate of the boys were very persistent in their inquiries as to who those "high officials" were, with a mild intimation that they had half a mind to "go for them." This talk about "friendly Indians" and a "surrendered" village will do to "tell to marines," but to us out here it is all bosh.

The *confessed* murderers of the Hungate family—a man and wife and their two little babes, whose scalped and mutilated remains were seen by all our citizens—were "friendly Indians," we suppose, in the eyes of these "high officials." *They* fell in the Sand creek battle.

The confessed participants in a score of other murders of peaceful settlers and inoffensive travellers upon our borders and along our roads in the past six months must have been *friendly,* or else the "high officials" wouldn't say so.

The band of marauders in whose possession were found scores of horses and mules stolen from government and from individuals; wagon loads of flour, coffee, sugar and tea, and rolls of broad cloth, calico, books, &c , robbed from freighters and emigrants on the plains; underclothes of white women and children, stripped from their murdered victims, were probably peaceably disposed toward *some* of those "high officials," but the mass of our people "can't see it."

Probably those scalps of white men, women and children, *one of them fresh, not three days taken,* found drying in their lodges, were taken in a *friendly,* playful manner; or possibly those Indian saddle-blankets trimmed with the scalps of white women, and with braids and fringes of their hair, were kept simply as mementoes of their owners' high affection for the pale face. At any rate, these delicate and tasteful ornaments could not have been taken from the heads of the wives, sisters or daughters of these "high officials."

That "surrendering" must have been the happy thought of an exceedingly vivid imagination, for we can hear of nothing of the kind from any of those who were engaged in the battle. On the contrary, the savages fought like devils to the end, and one of our pickets was killed and scalped by them the next day after the battle, and a number of others were fired upon. In one instance a party of the vidette pickets were compelled to beat a hasty retreat to save their lives, full twenty-four hours after the battle closed. This does not look much like the Indians had surrendered.

But we are not sure that an investigation may not be a good thing. It should go back of the "affair at Fort Lyon," as they are pleased to term it down east, however, and let the world know who were making money by keeping those Indians under the sheltering protection of Fort Lyon; learn who was interested in systematically representing that the Indians were friendly and wanted peace. It is unquestioned and undenied that the site of the Sand creek battle was the rendezvous of the thieving and marauding bands of savages who roamed over this country last summer and fall, and it is shrewdly suspected that somebody was all the time making a very good thing out of it. By all means let there be an investigation, but we advise the honorable congressional committee, who may be appointed to conduct it, to get their scalps insured before they pass Plum creek on their way out.

64

# MASSACRE OF CHEYENNE INDIANS.

*Extract from the message of Hon. S. H. Elbert, acting governor of Colorado Territory.*

### INDIAN WAR.

The before unbroken peace of our Territory has been disturbed, since the last spring, by an Indian war. Allied and hostile tribes have attacked our frontier settlements, driven in our settlers, destroyed their homes, attacked, burned, and plundered our freight and emigrant trains, and thus suspended agricultural pursuits in portions of our country, and interrupted our trade and commerce with the States. This has for the time seriously retarded the prosperity of our Territory.

At the commencement of the war the general government, taxed to the utmost in subduing the rebellion, was unable to help us, and it became necessary to look to our own citizens for protection. They everywhere responded with patriotism and alacrity. Militia companies were organized in the frontier counties, and secured local protection. Much credit is due to Captain Tyler's company of militia for the important service they rendered in opening and protecting our line of communication with the States.

In response to the call of the governor for a regiment of cavalry for hundred-day service, over a thousand of our citizens—the large majority of them leaving lucrative employment—rapidly volunteered, and in that short time, despite the greatest difficulties in securing proper equipments, organized, armed, made a long and severe campaign amid the snows and storms of winter, and visited upon these merciless murderers of the plains a chastisement smiting and *deserved.* The gratitude of the country is due to the men who thus sacrificed so largely their personal interests for the public good, and rendered such important service to the Territory; and their work, if it can be followed up with a vigorous winter campaign, would result in a permanent peace.

The necessity of such a campaign, and the imperative demand for immediate and complete protection for our line of communication with the States, has been, and is now being, earnestly urged on the government at Washington, and with a prospect of success. These efforts should be seconded by your honorable body with whatever influence there may be in resolution or memorial, setting forth the facts and necessities of our situation.

---

## PAPERS FROM THE WAR DEPARTMENT.

War Department, Adjutant General's Office.
*Washington, March 28, 1865.*

Sir: In reply to your letter of the 15th instant, addressed to the Secretary of War, I have the honor to transmit herewith copies of the orders and reports called for in relation to Indian affairs in the department of Kansas, when commanded by Major General Curtis.

I am, sir, very respectfully, your obedient servant,

E. D. TOWNSEND,
*Assistant Adjutant General.*

Hon. D. W. Gooch,
*Acting Chairman Committee on Conduct of the War.*

COLORADO SUPERINTENDENCY,
*Denver, C. T., June 16, 1864.*

SIR : You will immediately make necessary arrangements for the feeding and support of all the friendly Indians of the Cheyenne and Arapahoe Indians at Fort Lyon, and direct the friendly Comanches and Kiowas, if any, to remain at Fort Larned. You will make a requisition on the military commander of the post for subsistence for the friendly Indians of his neighborhood.

If no agent there to attend to this, deputize some one to do it. These friendly bands must be collected at places of rendezvous, and all intercourse between them and tribes or individuals engaged in warfare with us prohibited; this arrangement will tend to withdraw from the conflict all who are not thoroughly identified with the hostile movement, and, by affording a safe refuge, will gradually collect those who may become tired of war and desire peace.

The war is opened in earnest, and upon your efforts to keep quiet the friendly, as nucleus for peace, will depend its duration to some extent at least. You can send word to all these to come as directed above, but do not allow the families of those at war to be introduced into the camp. I have established a camp for our northern friendly bands on Cache-la-Poudre, and as soon as my plan is approved by the military I will issue a proclamation to the Indians ; please spare no effort to carry out this instruction, and keep me advised by every mail of the situation.

Very respectfully, your obedient servant,

JOHN EVANS,
*Governor and Ex-Officio Superintendent Indian Affairs.*
Major S. G. COLBY, *Fort Lyon, Colorado Territory.*

A true copy:

W. W. DENISON,
*Second Lieutenant 1st Colorado Veteran Cavalry, and*
*Acting Regimental Adjutant.*

U. S. MILITARY TELEGRAPH.

[By Telegraph from ——————————, 186—.]

To ———— ————.

George Evans to Major Colby, at Fort Lyon, instructing him to make arrangements for feeding friendly Indians near Fort Lyon. General instructions about collecting together all friendly Indians at places of rendezvous, as a measure to stop the war with the red skins. Thinks by affording refuge of this kind that those at war now may become tired, and collect at those places, and sue for peace, &c.

ADJUTANT GENERAL'S OFFICE, *March —,* 1865.
Official:

————— —————,
*Assistant Adjutant General.*

EXECUTIVE DEPARTMENT, COLORADO TERRITORY,
*Denver, June 29, 1864.*

DEAR SIR : I enclose a circular to the Indians of the plains. You will, by every means you can, get the contents to all these Indians, as many that are now hostile may come to the friendly camp, and when they all do, the war will

66

be ended. Use the utmost economy in providing for those who come in, as the Secretary of the Interior confines me to the amount of our appropriations, and they may be exhausted before the summer is out.

You will arrange to carry out the plan of the circular at Lyon and Larned.

You will use your utmost vigilance to ascertain how many of your Indians are hostile, where they are, and what plans they propose, and report to me by every mail at least. For this purpose you will enlist the active aid of Mr. John Smith and his son, and of such other parties as you may judge can be of essential service. Mr. C. A. Cook reports to me that Mr. Bent has given you important information in regard to the plans and strength of the hostile combinations on the plains.

Please be careful and report to me in detail all the reliable information you can get promptly, as above directed.

I have the honor to be, respectfully, your obedient servant,

JNO. EVANS,
*Governor Colorado Territory and Superintendent Indian Affairs.*

Major S. G. COLBY,
*U. S. Indian Agent, Fort Lyon, Colorado Territory.*


A true copy :

W. W. DENISON,
*Second Lieutenant, 1st Colorado Veteran Cavalry,*
*Acting Regimental Adjutant.*

---

COLORADO SUPERINTENDENCY, INDIAN AFFAIRS,
*Denver, June 27, 1864.*

*To the friendly Indians of the plains :*

Agents, interpreters, and traders will inform the friendly Indians of the plains that some members of their tribes have gone to war with the white people; they steal stock and run it off, hoping to escape detection and punishment.

In some instances they have attacked and killed soldiers and murdered peaceable citizens. For this the Great Father is angry, and will certainly hunt them out and punish them; but he does not want to injure those who remain friendly to the whites. He desires to protect and take care of them. For this purpose I direct that all friendly Indians keep away from those who are at war, and go to places of safety.

Friendly Arapahoes and Cheyennes belonging on the Arkansas river will go to Major Colby, United States Indian agent, at Fort Lyon, who will give them provisions, and show them a place of safety. Friendly Kiowas and Comanches will go to Fort Larned, where they will be cared for in the same way.

Friendly Sioux will go to their agent at Fort Laramie for directions. Friendly Arapahoes and Cheyennes of the Upper Platte will go to Camp Collins, on the Cache-la-Poudre, where they will be assigned a place of safety, and provisions will be given them.

The object of this is to prevent friendly Indians from being killed through mistake; none but those who intend to be friendly with the whites must come to these places. The families of those who have gone to war with the whites must be kept away from among the friendly Indians.

The war on hostile Indians will be continued until they are all effectually subdued.

JOHN EVANS,
*Governor of Colorado and Superintendent of Indian Affairs.*

A true copy:

W. W. DENISON,
*Second Lieutenant 1st Colorado Veteran Cavalry,*
*Acting Regimental Adjutant.*

ADJUTANT GENERAL'S OFFICE, *March —,* 1865.
Official:

—————  —————,
*Assistant Adjutant General.*

———

FORT RILEY, *July* 23, 1864.

Major General H. W. HALLECK:

The Indian difficulties west of this point are serious, and I have come here to rally a force on the borders to repress the mischief. The stages not coming through, we have not definite intelligence. We only know that they have run off our stock from Larned and Walnut creek, murdering some men. Small parties of Indians have come within thirty miles of this place. I have ordered the quartermaster to buy horses to mount dismounted cavalry, and requested militia colonels to call out seven hundred militia to join me. In this way I hope to raise a thousand men. I go on to Saline to-morrow. I think stealing is the main object of the Indians.

S. R. CURTIS, *Major General.*

HEADQUARTERS OF THE ARMY, *March* 18, 1865.
Official:

D. C. WAGER, *A. A. G.*

———

SALINE, KANSAS, *July* 26, 1864, *via Leavenworth.*

General H. W. HALLECK:

The stage has just arrived from Laramie. The damage done by Indians amounts to ten teamsters killed, five wounded, two of them scalped, and the stealing of about three hundred cattle. Our posts are safe.

S. R. CURTIS, *Major General.*

HEADQUARTERS OF THE ARMY, *March* 18, 1865.
Official:

D. C. WAGER, *A. A. G.*

———

FORT LEAVENWORTH, *August* 8, 1864.

Major General HALLECK, *Chief of Staff:*

I have returned from Upper Arkansas. At Larned divided my force in all directions, going myself with those scouting southward towards Red river. Could not overtake Indians, but scared them away from Santa Fé route, where

68

stages and trains move regularly. Have made district of Upper Arkansas, assigning General Blunt to command. Have increased and improved the organization of troops, giving stringent orders against allowing Indians inside of our line. Discharged militia, and directed continual caution. The Kiowas, Comanches and Big Mouth Arapahoes are evidently determined to do all the mischief they can. I hope no favor will be offered them by authorities at Washington till they make ample remuneration for their outrages.

S. R. CURTIS,<br>
*Major General.*

Official:

HEADQUARTERS ARMY, *March* 18, 1865.

D. C. WAGER, *A. A. G.*

FORT LEAVENWORTH, *August* 10, 1864.

Major General HALLECK, *Chief of Staff:*

Indians have attacked and killed inhabitants on Little Blue, this side Fort Kearney, on overland stage route. Stage just arrived at Atchison without passengers. I have requested governor to send militia after them, and telegraphed commander of Kearney to come down on them if he has force, but forces are scarce in that region. Cannot some of General Sully's command move to Nebraska?

S. R. CURTIS,<br>
*Major General.*

HEADQUARTERS ARMY, *March* 18, 1865.

Official:

D. C. WAGER, *A. A. G.*

HEADQUARTERS OF THE ARMY,<br>
*Washington, D. C., August* 13, 1864.

Major General CURTIS, *Fort Leavenworth:*

The contractor of the overland mail line has represented through the Post Office Department that more protection against Indians is required along the line, and that two armed men should accompany each coach. He also asks that orders be given to the military not to use the grain, forage, and stores of the line.

Please see that these requests are carried out as far as you are able.

H. W. HALLECK,<br>
*Major General and Chief of Staff.*

HEADQUARTERS OF THE ARMY, *March* 18, 1865.

Official:

D. C. WAGER, *A. A. G.*

69

FORT LEAVENWORTH, *August* 13, 1864.

General HALLECK :

Your despatch just received, and telegraphed to General Curtis, at Omaha. The following has just been received from General Mitchell, commanding district of Nebraska, to General Curtis, Fort Leavenworth :

"Just heard from a company of militia sent up the Little Blue from Kearney. They scoured the country for forty miles up and down the stream; found no Indians. I have parties out in every direction from each post chasing Indians. Everything will be done that I can do with my present force. I am raising militia as fast as I can ; the governor has authorized the raising of twelve companies. I have received to-day —— toward one company in this vicinity, of staunch men.

"B. B. MITCHELL, *Brigadier General.*"

C. S. CHARLOTTE,

*Major, A. A. G., Department of Kansas.*

HEADQUARTERS ARMY, *March* 18, 1865.

Official :

D. C. WAGER, *A. A. G.*

---

OMAHA, *August* 16, 1864.

Major General H. W. HALLECK, *Chief of Staff:*

Yours of the 13th, concerning the furnishing of escorts for overland mail line to defend it against Indians, will be complied with. I am here to look after Indian troubles that are quite extensive on the line and against the border settlements. I have troops arriving on the Blue, where the mischief was greatest. General Mitchell telegraphs from Fort Kearney that he thinks that region is threatened by a large force of Indians collecting on the Republican. I am sending out militia in small parties to join forces which I have gathered below, and will soon be upon them, be they many or few.

S. R. CURTIS, *Major General.*

HEADQUARTERS ARMY, *March* 18, 1865.

Official:

D. C. WAGER, *A. A. G.*

---

OMAHA, *August* 18, 1864.

Major General H. W. HALLECK :

General Mitchell telegraphs from Fort Kearney that Captain Mussey encountered five hundred well-armed Indians on Elk creek, near Republican; had a fight; killed ten Indians, and lost two soldiers ; drove Indians ten miles, but had to fall back, pursued by Indians, thirty miles.

S. R. CURTIS, *Major General.*

HEADQUARTERS ARMY, *March* 18, 1865.

Official

D. C. WAGER, *A. A. G.*

DENVER, *August* 18, 1864.

Hon. EDWIN M. STANTON, *Secretary of War:*

Extensive Indian depredations, with murder of families, occurred yesterday thirty miles south of Denver. Our lines of communication are cut, and our crops, our sole dependence, are all in exposed localities, and cannot be gathered by our scattered population. Large bodies of Indians are undoubtedly near to Denver, and we are in danger of destruction both from attack of Indians and starvation. I earnestly request that Colonel Ford's regiment of 2d Colorado volunteers be immediately sent to our relief. It is impossible to exaggerate our danger. We are doing all we can for our defence.

JNO. EVANS, *Governor.*

HEADQUARTERS ARMY, *March* 18, 1865.

Official :

D. C. WAGER, *A. A. G.*

----

DENVER, *August* 22, 1864.

E. M. STANTON, *Secretary of War:*

No government saddles within seven hundred miles from here; no government horses to mount hundred-days regiment of cavalry, nearly full. Unlimited information of contemplated attack by a large body of Indians, in a few days, along the entire line of our settlements. Order Captain Mullin, quartermaster here, to purchase horses, and Lieutenant Hawley, district ordnance officer, to purchase horse equipments. Necessity imperative.

JNO. EVANS,
*Governor of Colorado Territory.*

This application should be granted at once.

J. M. CHIVINGTON,
*Colonel Commanding.*

HEADQUARTERS ARMY, *March* 18, 1865.

Official:

D. C. WAGER, *A. A. G.*

----

HEADQUARTERS OF THE ARMY,
*Washington, D. C., August* 23, 1864.

Governor JOHN EVANS, *Denver, Colorado Territory:*

The Secretary of War directs me to say that a recent law requires all cavalry horses to be purchased under directions of Colonel Ekin, of the quartermaster's department. If there is such a pressing necessity that purchases cannot be made in time, the military authorities can resort to impressment. General Curtis is the proper judge of such necessity in his department.

H. W. HALLECK,
*Major General, Chief of Staff.*

HEADQUARTERS ARMY, *March* 18, 1865.

Official :

D. C. WAGER, *A. A. G.*

DEPARTMENT OF KANSAS,
Fort Kearney, August 28, 1864.

Major General HALLECK, Chief of Staff:

Indians in small bands continue to commit depredations, but seem more cautious moving westward. Have effectually scoured the country east of 99th meridian. Indians going west of settlements. Overland mail agents have withdrawn stock and gone east. I think they can run through with such escorts as I can furnish. Militia very tardy in coming forward, many turning back before reaching this point.

Some fifty murders have been committed by Indians on this line, and considerable private stock stolen, but government has lost but little.

S. R. CURTIS, Major General.

Official:

HEADQUARTERS ARMY, March 18, 1865.

D. C. WAGER, A. A. G.

_____

HEADQUARTERS OF THE ARMY,
Washington, D. C., September 3, 1864.

Major General CURTIS, Fort Kearney:

The civil officers of Montana have asked for military escort to that Territory. The Secretary of War authorizes you to give such escort, if, in your opinion, you can spare troops for that purpose; but, first of all, the overland mail route and the frontier posts require protection from the Indians.

The Secretary of War authorizes you to raise hundred-days men in Nebraska, without bounties.

H. W. HALLECK,
Major General, Chief of Staff.

Official:

HEADQUARTERS ARMY, March 18, 1865.

D. C. WAGER, A. A. G.

_____

DENVER, September 7, 1864.

Hon. EDWIN M. STANTON, Secretary of War:

Pray give positive orders for our second Colorado cavalry to come out. Have notice published that they will come in detachments to escort trains up the Platte on certain days. Unless escorts are sent thus we will inevitably have a famine in addition to this gigantic Indian war. Flour is forty-five dollars a barrel, and the supply growing scarce, with none on the way. Through spies we got knowledge of the plan of about one thousand warriors in camp to strike our frontier settlements, in small bands, simultaneously in the night, for an extent of 300 miles. It was frustrated at the time, but we have to fear another such attempt soon. Pray give the order for our troops to come, as requested, at once, as it will be too late for trains to come this season.

JOHN EVANS, Governor.

Official:

HEADQUARTERS ARMY, March 18, 1865.

D. C. WAGER, A. A. G.

## MASSACRE OF CHEYENNE INDIANS.

CAMP OF SOLOMON'S RIVER,
*Via Lawrence, Kansas, September* 16, 1864.

Major General HALLECK, *Chief of Staff:*

I struck this river near 100th parallel; sent scouts south to head of Saline, finding no large body of Indians. Divided command; sent large portion up valley, to strike Ofallon's bluff; with remainder, two hundred and eighty-five, came down, scouring the country on all sides. Buffalo plenty. Indians only in small parties, escaping south. Shall reach settlements on Smoky Hill river to-morrow. No signs of great concentration of Indians. Bands of hunters steal and scalp, but can be routed by small armed force. Stage stations, ranches, and settlements must have enclosures for themselves and stock, and a few troops, carefully distributed, can protect settlements and lines of commerce.

S. R. CURTIS, *Major General.*

HEADQUARTERS ARMY, *March* 18, 1865.

Official:

D. C. WAGER, *A. A. G.*

---

HEADQUARTERS DEPARTMENT OF KANSAS,
*Fort Leavenworth, September* 19, 1864.

I am in receipt of a copy of letters from the honorable Secretary of the Interior and Commissioner of Indian Affairs, with your indorsement to take such action as I may "deem best." It is stated that I have ordered the Indians not to make their usual hunt. This is erroneous. I may have suggested that it would be dangerous for our friendly Indians to go, but I have desired the Pawnees to follow and operate when I had driven away the hostile bands. Yet I see great difficulty in discriminations, and also fear that some bands of our friendly Indians might mingle with foes if they come in proximity. If the friendly Indians could be united for the purpose of hunting and fighting with our troops, it would be easy to organize and so equip them as to avoid difficulty. In my recent reconnoissance I took about seventy-five Pawnees with me as scouts; and, to avoid mistakes, dressed them with a blowse and hats. It gave them a distinctive and graphic appearance, which could not be mistaken. Any other than an associate arrangement seems almost impossible.

I appreciate the importance of allowing or aiding the friendly Indians to hunt buffalo; but any general movement by them would lead to confusion and difficulty, not only with my troops, but with the border settlements; for the people, being terribly alarmed, would make very little difference in their resentment and raids.

I will do all I can to favor the friendly Indians in any rational arrangement to hunt the buffalo, and believe, with the honorable Secretary, that, properly associated with the troops, they would strengthen our efforts to suppress the hostile tribes.

I have the honor to be, general, your obedient servant,

S. R. CURTIS,
*Major General.*

Major General H. W. HALLECK, *Chief of Staff, Washington.*

HEADQUARTERS ARMY, *March* 18, 1865.

Official copy:

J. C. KELTON, *A. A. G.*

DENVER, *September* 19, 1864.

Hon. E. M. STANTON, *Secretary of War*:

Train with ordnance and ordnance stores en route to New Mexico, with mules, stolen by Indians at Fort Lyon, Colorado. We need such stores for 3d regiment Colorado volunteers, cavalry, one hundred day men, now full. Authorize me by telegraph to take them. Will not be used, if reach New Mexico, before next year. Indian warriors congregated eighty miles from Lyon, three thousand strong.

J. M. CHIVINGTON,
*Colonel Commanding, District Colorado.*

HEADQUARTERS ARMY, *March* 18, 1865.

Official :

D. C. WAGER, *A. A. G.*

---

HEADQUARTERS OF THE ARMY,
*Washington, D. C., September* 20, 1864.

Colonel CHIVINGTON, *Denver City*:

The chief of ordnance objects to the diversion of the train sent to New Mexico. You must make requisition for your wants in the usual way.

H. W. HALLECK,
*Major General, Chief of Staff.*

HEADQUARTERS ARMY, *March* 18, 1865.

Official :

D. C. WAGER, *A. A. G.*

---

DENVER CITY, *September* 22, 1864.

Major General HALLECK, *Chief of Staff*:

Have regiment 100 days men ready for field. Train on the way from Fort Leavenworth, but cannot get here in time because of the Indian troubles on the Platte route. Are four hundred miles back, and laid up. The time of this regiment will expire and Indians will still hold road. This is no ordinary case.

J. M. CHIVINGTON,
*Colonel Commanding.*

HEADQUARTERS ARMY, *March* 18, 1865.

Official :

D. C. WAGER, *A. A. G.*

---

HEADQUARTERS OF THE ARMY,
*Washington, D. C., September* 23, 1864.

Colonel CHIVINGTON, *Denver City*:

You will communicate' your wants to your superior officer, General Curtis, at Fort Leavenworth.

H. W. HALLECK,
*Major General, Chief of Staff.*

HEADQUARTERS ARMY, *March* 18, 1865.

Official :

D. C. WAGER, *A. A. G.*

74

HEADQUARTERS OF THE ARMY,
*Washington, D. C., September* 24, 1864.
Major General CURTIS, *Fort Leavenworth:*
General Rosecrans has been directed to give you the regiment of Colorado cavalry at or near Kansas city. All your available forces, not required against western Indians, should be thrown south on the Fort Scott route. Large reenforcements have been sent to the Arkansas river to cut off the enemy's retreat.
H. W. HALLECK,
*Major General, Chief of Staff.*

HEADQUARTERS ARMY, *March* 18, 1865.
Official:
D. C. WAGER, *A. A. G.*

FORT LEAVENWORTH, *September* 26, 1864.
Major General HALLECK:
Despatch received. Had already begun moving troops and supporting my southeast. But a full regiment of hundred-days men and part of the 1st Colorado going out this week. My main dependence must be in militia. If Price's forces come westward the militia are notified to be ready.
S. R. CURTIS, *Major General.*

HEADQUARTERS ARMY, *March* 18, 1865.
Official:
D. C. WAGER, *A. A. G.*

FORT LEAVENWORTH, *October* 7, 1864.
Major General HALLECK, *Chief of Staff*:
General Blunt came upon a party of Arapahoes and other hostile Indians, supposed to be four thousand, with fifteen hundred warriors, on the twenty-fifth ultimo. This was about one hundred miles west of Larned, in Pawnee fork. The Indians overpowered the advance, but the main force coming up routed and pursued them. Ninety-one dead Indians were left, and we lost two killed and seven wounded. General Blunt's force was less than five hundred. He pursued for several days.
S. R. CURTIS, *Major General.*

HEADQUARTERS ARMY, *March* 18, 1865.
Official:
D. C. WAGER, *A. A. G.*

HEADQUARTERS OF THE ARMY,
*Washington, D. C., October* 16, 1864.
Brigadier General CONNER, *Salt Lake City:*
Give all the protection in your power to the overland route between you and

Fort Kearney, without regard to department lines. General Curtis's forces have been diverted by rebel raids from Arkansas.

H. W. HALLECK,
*Major General, Chief of Staff.*

HEADQUARTERS ARMY, *March* 18, 1865.

Official:

D. C. WAGER, *A. A. G.*

---

HEADQUARTERS, *Fort Lyon, C. T., November* 6, 1864.

SIR: I have the honor to report that I arrived at this post and assumed command November 2, in obedience to Special Orders No. 4, headquarters of district, October 17, 1864. Major E. W. Wynkoop, 1st cavalry of Colorado, was in command of the post. One hundred and thirteen lodges of Arapahoe Indians, under their chiefs Little Raven, Left Hand, Nervah, Storms, and Knock Knee, and numbering, in men, women and children, 652 persons, were encamped in a body about two miles from the post, and were daily visiting the post, and receiving supplies from the commissary department, the supplies being issued by Lieutenant C. M. Copett, assistant commissary of supplies, under orders from Major E. W. Wynkoop, commanding post.

I immediately gave instructions to arrest all Indians coming within the post, until I could learn something more about them. Went down and met their head chiefs, half way between the post and their camp, and demanded of them by what authority and for what purpose they were encamped here. They replied that they had always been on peaceable terms with the whites, had never desired any other than peace, and could not be induced to fight. That other tribes were at war, and, therefore, they had come into the vicinity of a post, in order to show that they desired peace, and to be where the travelling public would not be frightened by them, or the Indians be harmed by travellers or soldiers on the road.

I informed them that I could not permit any body of armed men to camp in the vicinity of the post, nor Indians visit the post, except as prisoners of war. They replied that they had but very few arms and but few horses, but were here to accept any terms that I proposed. I then told them that I should demand their arms and all the stock they had in their possession which had ever belonged to white men; they at once accepted these terms. I then proceeded with a company of cavalry to the vicinity of their camp, leaving my men secreted, and crossed to their camp, received their arms from them, and sent out men to look through their herd for United States or citizens' stock, and to take all stock except Indian ponies; found ten mules and four horses, which have been turned over to the acting assistant quartermaster. Their arms are in very poor condition, and but few, with little ammunition. Their horses far below the average grade of Indian horses. In fact, these that are here could make but a feeble fight if they desired war. I have permitted them to remain encamped near the post, unarmed, as prisoners, until your wishes can be heard in the matter; in the interval, if I can learn that any of their warriors have been engaged in any depredations that have been committed, shall arrest them, and place all such in close confinement.

I am of opinion that the warriors of the Arapahoes, who have been engaged in war, are all now on the Smoky Hill, or with the Sioux Indians, and have all the serviceable arms and horses belonging to the tribe, while these here are too poor to fight, even though they desired war.

76

Nine Cheyenne Indians to-day sent in, wishing to see me. They state that 600 of that tribe are now 35 miles north of here, coming towards the post, and 2,000 about 75 miles away, waiting for better weather to enable them to come in. I shall not permit them to come in, even as prisoners, for the reason that if I do, I shall have to subsist them upon a prisoner's rations. I shall, however, demand their arms, all stolen stock, and the perpetrators of all depredations. I am of the opinion that they will not accept this proposition, but that they will return to the Smoky Hill. They pretend that they want peace, and I think they do now, as they cannot fight during the winter, except where a small band of them can find an unprotected train or frontier settlement. I do not think it is policy to make peace with them now, until all perpetrators of depredations are surrendered up to be dealt with as we may propose.

The force effective for the field at the post is only about 100, and one company, (K, New Mexico volunteers,) sent here by order of General Carlton, commanding department of New Mexico, were sent with orders to remain sixty days, and then report back to Fort Union. Their sixty days will expire on the 10th of November (instant.) Shall I keep them here for a longer period, or permit them to return?

The Kiowas and Comanches, who have all the stock stolen upon the Arkansas route, are reported south of the Arkansas river and towards the Red river. The Cheyennes are between here and the Smoky Hill; part of the Arapahoes are near this post ; the remainder north of the Platte. With the bands divided in this way, one thousand cavalry could now overtake them and punish some of them severely, I think, but with the force here it can only be made available to protect the fort. I shall not permit the Cheyennes to camp here, but will permit the Arapahoes now here to remain in their present camp as prisoners until your action is had in the matter.

I have the honor to be, very respectfully, your obedient servant,

SCOTT I. ANTHONY,
*Major 1st Cavalry of Colorado, Commanding Post.*

To ——————————,
*A. A. A. G. District of Upper Arkansas, Fort Riley, Kansas.*

—

[Indorsed.]

HEADQUARTERS DISTRICT OF UPPER ARKANSAS,
*Fort Riley, November 22, 1864.*

Respectfully forwarded for the information of the general commanding, respectfully asking for instruction in regard to the Arapahoe Indians kept and fed as prisoners at Fort Lyon. Major Anthony has been instructed to carry out general field order No. 2, July 31, 1864, fully, until further instructions from department headquarters. I would also state that I have learned, unofficially, that on Saturday, the 12th instant, two white men were killed and five wagons destroyed near Fort Larned by a party of Indians numbering about thirty. Have written to commanding officer at Fort Larned in reference to it, and instructed him to report all cases of Indian depredations that may come to his knowledge.

B. I. HENNING,
*Major 3d Wisconsin Cavalry, Commanding District.*

FORT LEAVENWORTH, *December* 1, 1864.

Major General H. W. HALLECK, *Chief of Staff:*

I am informed by telegraph from Neosho crossing, about one hundred and twenty miles below Fort Scott, that the train carrying supplies to Fort Gibson is halted because of a large rebel force in front. This is beyond my department lines, and I am unable to do much, but have ordered a regiment of my troops under Colonel Moonlight to support the escort commanded by Major Phillips in going forward or back as circumstances seem to require. Indian troubles now demand all my force, and large numbers are crowding into Fort Lyon as prisoners of war, while others in small bands are attacking stages and trains. Under these circumstances, I cannot furnish escorts to carry provisions for Indians and troops beyond my department lines ; and your attention is called to the necessity of furnishing General Steele with forces sufficient and in position to guard the lines to Fort Gibson and Fort Scott, or have the troops and Indians now there to fall back where they get provisions.

S. R. CURTIS, Major General.

Official :

HEADQUARTERS ARMY, March 18, 1865.

D. C. WAGER, A. A. G.

---

FORT LEAVENWORTH, *December* 8, 1864.

Major General H. W. HALLECK, *Chief of Staff:*

Colonel Chivington, after a march of three hundred miles in ten days, on the 29th returned. He came upon a Cheyenne camp of one hundred and thirty lodges at the south bend of Big Sandy, Cheyenne county, Colorado. He attacked at daylight, killing over four hundred Indians and capturing the same number of ponies. Among the killed are chiefs Black Kettle, White Antelope, and Little Robe. Our loss is nine killed and thirty-eight wounded. Our troops encountered snow two feet deep.

S. R. CURTIS,<br>Major General, Commanding.

Official :

HEADQUARTERS ARMY, March 18, 1865.

D. C. WAGER, A. A. G.

---

### HEADQUARTERS DEPARTMENT OF KANSAS,
*Fort Leavenworth, December* 30, 1864.

Several papers have been referred to me concerning irregularities charged on General Blunt and others before I came in this command, and entirely useless. Yet, as some of the parties are in my command, I may do something if I can get men disconnected with Kansas affairs and worthy of credence. There is so much political and personal strife in our service, it is almost impossible to get an honest, impartial determination of facts.

A shift of troops, so as to put officers and men out of their own home localities, would greatly improve my command, and I wish especially that some of my Kansas regiments may be sent to the front and troops of other States sent to me. I have ordered the 11th Kansas to Colorado, far enough from their homes, but the 15th and 16th Kansas might well be changed.

The 1st Colorado, the 3d Colorado, and many companies of other regiments, have to be mustered out under the provisions of Circular No. 36.

I am also informed that Fort Smith and Fayetteville, in the department of Arkansas, are being evacuated. Fort Gibson, in the same department, is garrisoned with dismounted Indian troops, so that my southern border is more exposed than formerly.

The Indians on the plains continue to act in bands of fifty or one hundred at various points, and I desire to make new efforts to crush them during the latter part of winter. Under these circumstances, I feel it my duty to urge the sending of more troops of other States to aid in keeping open the overland lines, escort trains, put down the Indians, and strengthen the defences which overlook the enemy's approaches from Texas.

I have the honor to be, general, your obedient servant,

S. R. CURTIS, *Major General.*

Major General H. W. HALLECK,
    *Chief of Staff, Washington, D. C.*

Official copy:

HEADQUARTERS ARMY, *March* 18, 1865.

J. C. KELTON, *A. A. G.*

---

HEADQUARTERS OF THE ARMY,
    *Washington, D. C., January* 3, 1865.

GENERAL: Your communications proposing a winter's campaign against the Indians, and asking for more troops, were sent to General Grant immediately on their receipt. If he has acted on the matter, his orders have gone directly to you, as nothing on the subject has been received here.

I write this to inform you that the matter was duly attended to by me.

Very respectfully, your obedient servant,

H. W. HALLECK,
*Major General, Chief of Staff.*

Major General CURTIS,
    *Fort Leavenworth, Kansas.*

Official copy:

HEADQUARTERS ARMY, *March* 18, 1865.

J. C. KELTON, *A. A. G.*

---

[Dated Denver, January 8, 1865.—Received January 9, 3 p. m ]

J. B. CHAFFEE, 45 *William:*

Urge the government to send troops on Platte route. Indians burning trains and slaying emigrants.

GEO. E. CLARK,
CHAS. A. COOK.

Official copy:

HEADQUARTERS ARMY, *March* 18, 1865.

J. C. KELTON, *A. A. G.*

NEW YORK, *January* 10, 1865.

DEAR JUDGE: I received the enclosed despatch this a. m. You cannot be too urgent with the Secretary of War, or the President, about our Indian troubles. Unless something is done to settle this trouble, we are virtually killed as a Territory. You can hardly realize, without seeing it, the large amount of machinery en route for our Territory to work the mines with. Everything in the

way of supplies is exorbitantly high, all on account of the hazard of transportation. Emigration is limited on account of the danger of travel. It is peculiarly disastrous to us now because so many eastern capitalists have been and are investing in our mines, and are preparing to open and develop them.
I am inclined to the opinion that our administration, both civil and military, have failed to comprehend the situation. I mean Evans and Chivington. I think this whole difficulty could have been arrested; but this is nothing to the case now. This must be attended to immediately, or our prospects are blasted for some time to come, and the development of a rich mining country indefinitely postponed. For God's sake, urge some action. I can't come over just now, or I would give you my views regarding what action ought to be taken; but anything, so that some steps are taken to protect the line of travel.
There is no use to depend on General Curtis, Evans, Chivington, or any other politician.
Yours of the 9th received this morning.
Truly, &c.,

J. B. CHAFFEE.

HEADQUARTERS ARMY, *March* 18, 1865.
Official copy:

J. C. KELTON, *A. A. G.*

HEADQUARTERS OF THE ARMY,
*Washington, D. C., January* 11, 1865.
Major General CURTIS, *Fort Leavenworth:*
Statements from respectable sources have been received here that the conduct of Colonel Chivington's command towards the friendly Indians has been a series of outrages calculated to make them all hostile. You will inquire into and report on this matter, and will take measures to have preserved and accounted for all plunder taken from the Indians at Fort Lyons and other places.
H. W. HALLECK,
*Major General, Chief of Staff.*

HEADQUARTERS ARMY, *March* 18, 1865.
Official:

D. C. WAGER, *A. A. G.*

WAR DEPARTMENT, *January* 11, 1865.
Judge Bennet, delegate from Colorado Territory, presents a letter and telegram from J. B. Chaffee relative to the Indian depredations on the mail route to Colorado, and the general unsettled condition of the country, owing to the active hostility of the Indians, incited mainly by the recent attack of Colonel Chivington at Fort Lyons. The attention of the government is called to the immediate necessity of sending additional troops to that region to protect the route.
Respectfully referred to General Halleck.
By order of the Secretary of War.
JAS. A. HARDIE,
*Colonel and Inspector General.*

HEADQUARTERS ARMY, *March* 18, 1865.
Official copy:

J. C. KELTON, *A. A. G.*

MASSACRE OF CHEYENNE INDIANS.

HEADQUARTERS DEPARTMENT OF KANSAS,
*Fort Leavenworth, January* 12, 1865.

GENERAL: Your despatch of yesterday, directing me to investigate Colonel Chivington's conduct towards the Indians, is received, and will be obeyed. Colonel Chivington has been relieved by Colonel Moonlight, and is probably out of the service, under provisions of Circular No. 36, War Department.

Although the colonel may have transgressed my field orders concerning Indian warfare, (a copy of which is here enclosed,) and otherwise acted very much against my views of propriety in his assault at Sand creek, still it is not true, as Indian agents and Indian traders are representing, that such extra severity is increasing Indian war. On the contrary, it tends to reduce their numbers, and bring them to terms. Their bands are more united, perhaps, at this time than during the summer, but this results from their necessities and surroundings. They are in a destitute condition, and must, at this season of the year, resort to desperate measures to procure horses and provisions; hence we see a continual effort to overpower our little posts, or our trains and stages. Their lodges are now between the Arkansas and Platte, and they shift their assaults so as to attack to the best advantage. I am collecting and arranging troops near Fort Riley, but need more force to make another effort to destroy them. I will be glad to save the few honest and kindly disposed, and protest against the slaughter of women and children; although, since General Harney's attack of the Sioux many years ago at Ash Hollow, the popular cry of settlers and soldiers on the frontier favors an indiscriminate slaughter, which is very difficult to restrain. I abhor this style, but so it goes from Minnesota to Texas. I fear that Colonel Chivington's assault at Sand creek was upon Indians who had received some encouragement to camp in that vicinity under some erroneous supposition of the commanding officer at Lyon that he could make a sort of "city of refuge" at such a point. However wrong that may have been, it should have been respected, and any violation of known arrangements of that sort should be severely rebuked. But there is no doubt a portion of the tribe assembled were occupied in making assaults on our stages and trains, and the tribes well know that we have to hold the whole community responsible for acts they could restrain, if they would properly exert their efforts in that way. It is almost impossible to properly try officers in my command, if they have a high rank, my troops all being widely scattered and much employed.

I have the honor to be your obedient servant,

S. R. CURTIS, *Major General.*

HEADQUARTERS OF THE ARMY,
*Washington, March* 18, 1865.

Official copy:

——— ———, *A. A. G.*

GENERAL FIELD ORDERS No. 1.

[Extract.]

HEADQUARTERS DEPARTMENT OF KANSAS,
*In the Field, Fort Ellsworth, July* 27, 1864.

\* \* \* \* \* \* \*

II. Hunters will be detailed for killing game, but the troops must not scatter and break down stock to chase buffalo. Indians at war with us will be the object of our pursuit and distinction, but women and children must be spared. All horses, ponies, and property taken will be placed in charge of Quartermas-

81

ter P. C. Taylor, who will have it properly collected. or sent back to safe place for future disposition ; this is necessary to prevent the accumulation of useless baggage.

\* \* \* \* \* \* \*

By order of Major General Curtis.

JOHN WILLIAMS,
*Assistant Adjutant General.*

Official copy :
JOHN WILLIAMS, *A. G. A.*

HEADQUARTERS OF THE ARMY,
*Washington, March* 18, 1865.

Official copy :
———— ————, *A. A. G.*

---

GENERAL FIELD ORDERS No. 2.

HEADQUARTERS DEPARTMENT OF KANSAS,
*In the Field, Fort Larned, July* 31, 1864.

I. At all military posts or stations west of the Kansas and Nebraska settlements in this department, stockades or abatis enclosures must be made for the troops and stock, and animals must be kept in such enclosures at night, and never herded during the day without distant and careful pickets, who can give warning of approaching enemies in time to preserve the stock from surprise.

II. Indians and their allies or associates will not be allowed within the forts except blindfolded, and then they must be kept totally ignorant of the character and number of our forces. Neglect of this concealment will be followed by the most severe and summary punishment.

Commanders of forts and stations will furnish escorts according to their best judgments, keeping in view the safety of their own posts, the stage or public property to be guarded, and the preservation of the horses.

These precautions must not be relaxed without permission of the commander of the department, and all officers, of whatever grade, will report promptly to the nearest and most available assistance, and to district and department headquarters, any patent neglect of this order, or any palpable danger to a command.

The industry and skill displayed by Lieutenant Ellsworth, and the troops under his command, in the erection of a block-house and other protection for his troops and animals at Smoky Hill crossing, deserve special commendation, while the negligence exhibited elsewhere, especially at this post, while under its former commander, is deprecated and denounced.

By command of Major General S. R. Curtis.

JOHN WILLIAMS,
*Assistant Adjutant General.*

Official :
JOHN WILLIAMS, *A A. G.*

HEADQUARTERS OF THE ARMY,
*Washington, March* 18, 1865.

Official copy :
———— ————, *A. A. G.*

---

HEADQUARTERS DEPARTMENT OF KANSAS,
*Fort Leavenworth, January* 30, 1865.

GOVERNOR : Yours of the 20th is just received, and I telegraph the latest news. I was provoked at the course taken by the commanding officer at Julesburg, who took his entire force to escort prisoners through, leaving that post for a few days entirely vacated. I have telegraphed a proper rebuke, and trust this will not again occur. None of my military stations have been disturbed. They are all intact, and generally too strong to be taken by assault. All we need is three or four regiments, which it seems to me will be sufficient. Most of these I would keep moving in the country infested by foes. I fear your Interior Department will make me trouble, by proposing military evolutions which conflict with my own. After traversing most of the plains last summer, up the Arkansas, up the Platte, and near the head of every stream between these rivers, my personal knowledge, coupled with that obtained from my officers, is abundant to enable me to understand the matter, and I am only desirous of doing what I consider necessary to make a finish, as near as may be, of these troubles. But I cannot carry on war on other people's plans. I want no fancy movements, such as occurred last summer, when one of your militia companies marched down the line, passing my troops, and claiming to have "opened the overland route," as though others had not been over most of the places on the Blue, and on Plum creek and elsewhere, where most of the losses had transpired. This move of Chivington against the bands that had been congregated on Sand creek, at the instance of Major Wynkoop, was also an inspiration of over-zeal which did not emanate from my headquarters. I name these things, governor, to secure unity of action, not to find fault.

On every occasion last summer I took the field promptly, and, although I did not get to Denver, I was at the slaughter-ground near Larned on the Arkansas, and on the Plum and Blue on the Platte, making overland journeys between, with active, efficient forces extending over two thousand miles; so that my zeal and energy cannot be doubted. I protest my desire to pursue and punish the enemy everywhere, in his lodges especially; but I do not believe in killing women and children who can be taken, and, if need be, camped east of the Mississippi, where they can be kept and cared for. I always did and do consider the Ash Hollow massacre a monstrous outrage, but the promotion and laudation that followed that transaction should excuse the indiscretion and cruelty of excited and outraged frontier soldiers, who have always heard Ash Hollow warfare extolled as the very brilliant point of glorious Indian warfare.

In my first movement last summer, when in pursuit of the Indians, I tried to restrain this plan of warfare, by issuing an order against the massacre of women and children, believing that taking such captive and bringing them away would just as effectually mortify and annoy the Indian robbers and warriors. Let me say, too, that I see nothing new in all this Indian movement since the Chivington affair, except that Indians are more frightened and keep further away. By pushing them hard this next month, before grass recruits their ponies, they will be better satisfied with making war and robbery a business. I would send into their lines some friendly, reliable Arapahoes and Cheyennes, and separate tribes, so as to save such as may be willing to make peace and fight the bad Indians.

Such are my views. I am not anxious to have the job of operating matters; but while I have command, I want unity of action, or no cross or counter currents. I have written this, because I see by telegraph that matters are spoken of as being organized at Washington, where I fear less is known of details.

I am, governor, yours truly,

S. R. CURTIS, *Major General.*

His Excellency Governor JNO. EVANS, *Washington, D C.*

HEADQUARTERS OF THE ARMY,
*Washington, March* 18, 1865.

Official copy:

——— ———, *A. A. G.*

83

HEADQUARTERS DEPARTMENT OF KANSAS,
*Fort Leavenworth, January 30, 1865.*

GENERAL: Governor Evans writes me, that he fears Chivington's conduct at Sand creek may embarrass military matters on the plains. I have written him fully, and enclose you a copy of my letter.

There is no new feature in these Indian troubles, except that Indians seem more frightened. More forces and more prudence will keep the lines open and subdue the hostile tribes. Some accounts of great combinations go the rounds; but I put no confidence in such stories.

The Indians of the plains are generally robbers and murderers, and act only from motives of hunger and avarice in their assaults, and by fear in their forbearance.

Settlements have increased, and our lines of communication have become more convenient for their assaults, till they become more troublesome and venturesome. The carelessness of emigration invited their assaults. It is folly to attribute the Indian troubles to the wrongs committed by white men. While we may condemn these, it is really more indulgence than cruelty that endured and continues their warfare. They have no great armies; they are not combined; their action is in separate bands of separate tribes. A thousand men with light artillery can whip their greatest possible combinations; but it is desirable to have three or four more regiments, so that a movable force of say two thousand can take a shifting attitude, going to a central point and throwing out detachments as circumstances seem to require. Such a force must follow the buffalo, as the Indians do, and must not go beyond reasonable proximity to the lines of travel, but remain near enough to the little posts that guard the travel and trains that follow the routes up the Platte and up the Arkansas.

I send you a map of the overland route to the mountains with stations marked. I have required our troops to erect defences against Indian assaults, and a few men can in this way hold position, and a few more accompany the stage or train to adjacent stations. Such forts cost nothing of consequence, and have already saved men and stores in several instances.

Forces are necessary on these lines and in the edge of settlements; but a movable force generally stationed between the Platte and Arkansas, as I have suggested, and nearest the eastern settlements where it can be most economically supplied, will, in my judgment, be the proper organization for the country. I have in a former letter expressed my purpose to do all I can to continue the campaign during the winter.

I specially urge the extension of the telegraph at least to Riley. The advantage will, in my judgment, greatly exceed the cost. I need connexion with the Indian and buffalo range, so I can direct matters on the Platte to correspond with intelligence arriving from the Santa Fe route. Our telegraph company can extend the line with only a cost of about ten thousand dollars; but it is proper to say my request last season was disapproved by the honorable the Secretary of War, and this is a renewal of the request.

I have the honor to be, general, your obedient servant,

S. R. CURTIS,
*Major General.*

Major General H. W. HALLECK,
*Chief of Staff, Washington, D. C.*

P. S.—*February 2.*—I delayed this for the map, which does not satisfy me, and will be delayed a few days for revision. I have ordered all possible force to Julesburg, where Indian difficulties continue. I have information, also, that a council of the chiefs have determined to try to draw off troops from the Arkansas line, by attacking the Platte line. I have to act in view of their shifting assaults.

S. R. CURTIS, *Major General.*

HEADQUARTERS OF THE ARMY,
*Washington, March* 18, 1865.

Official copy :

---

HEADQUARTERS OF THE ARMY,
*Washington, D. C., February* 1, 1865.

GENERAL : I transmit herewith a copy of a letter from General Conner in regard to the defence of the overland mail route, and also several papers from General Curtis on this subject.

These papers and others were, on their receipt, forwarded to Lieutenant General Grant, and have been returned without any instructions from him, so far as I am informed.

It is therefore presumed that he deems the large cavalry force in the department of Kansas as sufficient for present purposes, without taking others from active duty in the field.

It is proper to state in this connexion, that others report these stories of Indian hostilities as greatly exaggerated, if not mostly gotten up for purposes of speculation ; and respectable authorities assert that they are encouraged by the agents of the Overland Mail Company, in order to cover their frequent failure to transport the mails according to contract.

Be this as it may, it is highly important that the roads to New Mexico, Colorado, Utah and Idaho should be properly protected from Indian hostilities, so that there may be no interruption in the transmission of supplies and the mails.

You will transmit these papers, with the necessary instructions, to General Dodge, who will give the whole matter his immediate care and attention.

Very respectfully, your obedient servant,

H. W. HALLECK,
*Major General, Chief of Staff.*

Major General JOHN POPE,
*St. Louis, Missouri.*

HEADQUARTERS ARMY, *March* 18, 1865.

Official copy :

J. C. KELTON, *A. A. G.*

SENATE CHAMBER,
*February* 13, 1865.

SIR : We are appointed by the Committee on Indian Affairs of the Senate a sub-committee to confer with the President and yourself on the subject of transferring the Indian country, with one tier of counties of western Arkansas, to the Missouri–Kansas Department. We refrain from giving reasons or argument, believing you are already of opinion the change should be promptly made, and merely submit the request.

Yours, &c.,

JAMES HARLAN,
J. H. LANE.

Hon. E. M. STANTON,
*Secretary of War.*

N. B.—I saw General Grant Saturday night, who informed me he had no objection to the change.

J. H. LANE.

We earnestly recommend that the Indian troops now in the service in the Indian country be mustered out of the service with their arms in time to raise a crop for their destitute families this season, if other troops are substituted.

JAMES HARLAN,
J. R. DOOLITTLE,
M. S. WILKINSON,
B. GRATZ BROWN,
C. R. BUCKALEW,
*Committee on Indian Affairs.*

HEADQUARTERS ARMY, *March* 18, 1865.

Official copy :

J. C. KELTON, *A. A. G.*

WAR DEPARTMENT,
*January* 23, 1865.

Case of application of Ben Holladay that General Curtis may be ordered to re-enforce Julesburg (crossing of the Platte) immediately.
Referred to Major General Halleck, chief of staff.
By order of the Secretary of War.

JAMES A. HARDIE,
*Colonel and Inspector General.*

HEADQUARTERS OF THE ARMY,
*March* 18, 1865.

Official copy :

J. C. KELTON,
*Colonel and Assistant Adjutant General.*

[From Julesburg, dated 14.—Received January 16, 1865.]

BEN HOLLADAY :

I arrived here to-day with fifteen (15) men ; shall try and hold station ; soldiers all gone ; only the wounded ; station badly torn up ; messenger robbed ; great deal of property destroyed.

R. R. THOMAS,
*Division Adjutant.*

HEADQUARTERS OF THE ARMY,
*March* 18, 1865.

Official copy :

J. C. KELTON,
*Colonel and Assistant Adjutant General.*

[Dated New York 21, 1865.—Received Washington, January 21, 1865.]

(Care of Senator POMEROY, 15th and F sts.)
Reuben Thomas telegraphs cannot hold Julesburg. If he does not the In-

86

dians have conquered the country, from Kearney to Denver, beyond hope this winter.

BEN HOLLADAY.

HEADQUARTERS OF THE ARMY,
*March* 18, 1865.

Official copy:

J. C. KELTON,
*Colonel and Assistant Adjutant General.*

[Dated New York 21, 1865, 11 o'clock.—Received Washington, January 21, 1865.]

To GEORGE B. JOLIS, care of Senator POMEROY:

Try to have order sent to Curtis or Mitchell to help them at Julesburg, or he will abandon.

B. HOLLADAY.

HEADQUARTERS OF THE ARMY,
*March* 18, 1865.

Official copy:

J. C. KELTON,
*Colonel and Assistant Adjutant General.*

---

FORT LYON, COLORADO TERRITORY,
*January* 15, 1865.

SIR: In pursuance of Special Order No. 43, headquarters, district of Upper Arkansas, directing me to assume command of Fort Lyon, as well as to investigate and immediately report in regard to late Indian proceedings in this vicinity, I have the honor to state that I arrived at this post on the evening of the 14th of January, 1865, assumed command on the morning of the 15th of January, 1865, and the result of my investigation is as follows:

As explanatory, I beg respectfully to state that, while formerly in command of this post, on the 4th day of September, 1864, and after certain hostilities on the part of the Cheyenne and Arapahoe Indians, induced, as I have had ample proof, by the overt acts of white men, three Indians (Cheyennes) were brought as prisoners to me, who had been found coming toward the post, and who had in their possession a letter written, as I ascertained afterwards, by a half-breed in the Cheyenne camp, as coming from Black Kettle and other prominent chiefs of the Cheyenne and Arapahoe nations, the purport of which was that they desired peace, had never desired to be at war with the whites, &c., as well as stating that they had in their possession some white prisoners, women and children, whom they were willing to deliver up providing that peace was granted them. Knowing that it was not in my power to insure and offer them the peace for which they sued, but at the same time anxious, if possible, to accomplish the rescue of the white prisoners in their possession, I finally concluded to risk an expedition with the command I could raise, numbering one hundred and twenty-seven men, to their rendezvous, where I was informed they were congregated to the number of two thousand, and endeavor by some means to procure the aforesaid white prisoners, and to be governed in my course in accomplishing the same entirely by circumstances. Having formerly made lengthy reports in regard to the details of my expedition, I have but to say that I succeeded, pro-

Part VI——6

cured four white captives from the hands of these Indians, simply giving them in return a pledge that I would endeavor to procure for them the peace for which they so anxiously sued, feeling that, under the proclamation issued by John Evans, governor of Colorado and superintendent of Indian affairs, a copy of which becomes a portion of this report, even if not by virtue of my position as a United States officer, highest in authority in the country included within the bounds prescribed as the country of the Arapahoe and Cheyenne nations, I could offer them protection until such time as some measures might be taken by those higher in authority than myself in regard to them.  I took with me seven of the principal chiefs, including Black Kettle, to Denver city, for the purpose of allowing them an interview with the governor of Colorado, by that means making a mistake of which I have since become painfully aware—that of proceeding with the chiefs to the governor of Colorado Territory, instead of to the headquarters of my district, to my commanding officer.  In the consultation with Governor Evans, the matter was referred entirely to the military authorities.  Colonel J. M. Chivington, at that time commander of the district of Colorado, was present at the council held with these Indian chiefs, and told them that the whole matter was referred to myself, who would act toward them according to the best of my judgment, until such time as I could receive instructions from the proper authorities.  Returning to Fort Lyon, I allowed the Indians to bring their villages to the vicinity of the post, including their squaws and pappooses, and in such a position that I could at any moment, with the garrison I had, have annihilated them, had they given any evidence of hostility of any kind, in any quarter.

I then immediately despatched my adjutant, Lieutenant W. W. Denison, with a full statement, to the commanding general of the department, asking for instructions; but in the mean while various false rumors having reached district headquarters in regard to my course, I was relieved from the command of Fort Lyon, and ordered to report at headquarters.  Major Scott J. Anthony, 1st cavalry of Colorado, who had been ordered to assume command of Fort Lyon, previous to my departure held a consultation with the chiefs, in my presence, and told them that though acting under strict orders, under the circumstances, he could not materially differ from the course which I had adopted, and allowed them to remain in the vicinity of the post, with their families, assuring them perfect safety until such time as positive orders should be received from headquarters in regard to them.  I left the post on the 25th day of November, for the purpose of reporting at district headquarters.  On the second day after leaving Fort Lyon, while on the plains, I was approached by three Indians, one of whom stated to me that he had been sent by Black Kettle to warn me that about two hundred Sioux warriors had proceeded down the road between where I was and Fort Larned, to make war, and desired that I should be careful; another evidence of these Indians good faith.  All of his statement proved afterwards to be correct.  Having an escort of twenty-eight men, I proceeded on my way, but did not happen to fall in with them.

From evidence of officers at this post, I understand that on the 27th day of November, 1864, Colonel J. M. Chivington, with the 3d regiment of Colorado cavalry (one-hundred-days men) and a battalion of the 1st Colorado cavalry, arrived at Fort Lyon, ordered a portion of the garrison to join him, under the command of Major Scott J. Anthony, and against the remonstrance of the officers of the post, who stated to him the circumstances of which he was well aware, attacked the camp of friendly Indians, the major portion of which were composed of women and children.  The affidavits which become a portion of this report will show, more particularly than I can state, the full particulars of that massacre.  Every one whom I have spoken to, either officer or soldier, agrees in the relation that the most fearful atrocities were committed that ever were heard of.  Women and children were killed and scalped, children shot at their mothers' breasts, and all the bodies mutilated in the most horrible manner. Numerous eye-witnesses have described scenes to me, coming under the eye of Colonel Chivington, of the most disgusting and horrible character; the dead bodies of females profaned in such a manner that the recital is sickening; Colonel J. M. Chivington all the time inciting his troops to these diabolical outrages. Previous to the slaughter commencing he addressed his command, arousing in them, by his language, all their worst passions, urging them on to the work of committing all these atrocities. Knowing himself all the circumstances of these Indians resting on the assurances of protection from the government, given them by myself and Major Scott J. Anthony, he kept his command in entire ignorance of the same; and when it was suggested that such might be the case he denied it, positively stating that they were still continuing their depredations, and laid there threatening the fort. I beg leave to draw the attention of the colonel commanding to the fact established by the enclosed affidavits, that two-thirds or more of that Indian village were women and children, and he is aware whether or not the Indians go to war taking with them their women and children. I desire also to state that Colonel J. M. Chivington is not my superior officer, but is a citizen mustered out of the United States service; and also, that at the time this inhuman monster committed this unprecedented atrocity he was a citizen, by reason of his term of service having expired, he having lost his regulation command some months previous.

Colonel Chivington reports officially that between five and six hundred Indians were left dead upon the field. I have been informed by Captain Booth, district inspector, that he visited the field and counted but sixty-nine bodies, and by others who were present that but a few, if any, over that number were killed, and that two-thirds of them were women and children. I beg leave to further state, for the information of the colonel commanding, that I have talked to every officer in Fort Lyon, and many enlisted men, and that they unanimously agree that all the statements I have made in this report are correct.

In conclusion, allow me to say that from the time I held the consultation with the Indian chiefs on the head-waters of Smoky Hill, up to the date of the massacre by Colonel Chivington, not one single depredation had been committed by the Cheyenne and Arapahoe Indians. The settlers of the Arkansas valley had returned to their ranches from which they had fled, had taken in their crops, and had been resting in perfect security under assurances from myself that they would be in no danger for the present, by that means saving the country from what must inevitably become almost a famine were they to lose their crops; the lines of communication were opened and travel across the plains rendered perfectly safe through the Cheyenne and Arapahoe country. Since this last horrible murder by Colonel Chivington the country presents a scene of desolation. All communication is cut off with the States except by sending large bodies of troops, and already over a hundred whites have fallen as victims to the fearful vengeance of these betrayed Indians. All this country is ruined. There can be no such thing as peace in the future but by the total annihilation of all the Indians on the plains. I have the most reliable information to the effect that the Cheyennes and Arapahoes have allied themselves with the Kiowas Comanches, and Sioux, and are congregated to the number of five or six thousand on the Smoky Hill.

Let me also draw the attention of the colonel commanding to the fact stated by affidavit, that John Smith, United States interpreter, a soldier, and a citizen, were present in the Indian camp, by permission of the commanding officer of this post—another evidence to the fact of these same Indians being regarded as friendly; also, that Colonel Chivington states, in his official report, that he fought from nine hundred to one thousand Indians, and left from five to six hundred dead upon the field, the sworn evidence being that there were but five hundred souls in the village, two-thirds of them being women and children, and that there were but from sixty to seventy killed, the major portion of whom were women and children.

It will take many more troops to give security to travellers and settlers in this country, and to make any kind of successful warfare against these Indians. I am at work placing Fort Lyon in a state of defence, having all, both citizens and soldiers, located here employed upon the works, and expect soon to have them completed, and of such a nature that a comparatively small garrison can hold the fort against any attack by Indians.

Hoping that my report may receive the particular attention of the colonel commanding, I respectfully submit the same.

Your obedient servant,

E. W. WYNKOOP,
*Major Com'g 1st Colorado Cavalry and Fort Lyon.*

Lieutenant J. E. TAPPAN,
*Act'g Ass't Adj't General, District of Upper Arkansas.*

ADJUTANT GENERAL'S OFFICE, *March*, 1865.

Official:

———— —————,

*Assistant Adjutant General.*

————————

FORT LYON, COLORADO TERRITORY,
*January* 15, 1865.

Personally appeared before me John Smith, United States Indian interpreter, who, after being duly sworn, says :

That on the 4th day of September, 1864, he was appointed Indian interpreter for the post of Fort Lyon, and has continued to serve in that capacity up to the present date; that on the 4th day of September, 1864, by order of Major E. W. Wynkoop, commanding post of Fort Lyon, he was called upon to hold a conversation with three Cheyenne Indians, viz: One Eye, and two others, who had been brought in to the post that day; that the result of the interview was as follows : One Eye, Cheyenne, stated that the principal chiefs and sub-chiefs of the Cheyenne and Arapahoe nations had held a consultation and agreed to a man, of the chiefs and sub-chiefs, to come or send some one who was well acquainted with the parties at the post, and finally agreed to send himself, One Eye, with a paper written by George Bent, half-breed, to the effect that they, the Cheyennes and Arapahoes, had and did agree to turn over to Major E. W. Wynkoop, or any other military authority, all the white prisoners they had in their possession, as they were all anxious to make peace with the whites, and never desired to be at war. Major E. W. Wynkoop then asked One Eye, he having lived among whites, and known to have always been friendly disposed towards them, whether he thought the Indians were sincere, and whether they would deliver the white prisoners into his (Major Wynkoop's) hands. His reply was, that at the risk of his life he would guarantee their sincerity. Major Wynkoop then told him that he would detain him as a prisoner for the time, and if he concluded to proceed to the Indian camp he would take him with him and hold him as a hostage for their (the Indian's) good faith.

One Eye also stated that the Cheyenne and Arapahoe nations were congregated, to the number of two thousand, on the head-waters of the Smoky Hill, including some forty lodges of Sioux; that they had rendezvoused there, and brought in their war parties for the purpose of hearing what would be the result of their message by which they had sued for peace, and would remain until they heard something definite. Major Wynkoop told One Eye that he would proceed to the Indian camp and take him with him. One Eye replied that he was perfectly willing to be detained a prisoner, as well as to remain a hostage for the good faith of the Indians, but desired the major to start as soon as possible, for fear the Indians might separate.

On the 6th day of September I was ordered to proceed with Major Wynkoop and his command in the direction of the Indian encampment. After a four days' march, came in sight of the Indians, and one of the three Indians before mentioned was sent to acquaint the chiefs with what was the object of the expedition, with the statement that Major Wynkoop desired to hold a consultation with the chiefs. On the 10th day of September, 1864, the consultation was held between Major Wynkoop and his officers, and the principal chiefs of the Cheyenne and Arapahoe nations. Major Wynkoop stated through me, to the chiefs, that he had received their message; that acting on that, he had come to.talk with them; asked them whether they all agreed to and indorsed the contents of the letter which he had in his possession, and which had been brought in by One Eye. Receiving an answer in the affirmative, he then told the chiefs that he had not the authority to conclude terms of peace with them, but that he desired to make a proposition to them to the effect that if they would give him evidence of their good faith by delivering into his hands the white prisoners they had in their possession, he would endeavor to procure for them peace, which would be subject to conditions that he would take with him what principal chiefs they might select, and conduct them in safety to the governor of Colorado, and whatever might be the result of their interview with him, return them in safety to their tribe.

Black Kettle, the head chief of the Cheyenne nation, replied as follows:

That the Cheyenne and Arapahoe nations had always endeavored to observe the terms of their treaty with the United States government; that some years previously, when the white emigration first commenced coming to what is now the Territory of Colorado, the country which was in possession of the Cheyenne and Arapahoe nations, they could have successfully made war against them, the whites. They did not desire to do so—had invariably treated them with kindness, and had never, to their knowledge, committed any destruction whatever; that until the last few months they had gotten along in perfect peace and harmony with their white brethren, but while a hunting party of their young men were proceeding north, in the neighborhood of the South Platte river, having found some loose stock belonging to white men, which they were taking to a ranch to deliver them up, they were suddenly confronted by a party of United States soldiers and ordered to deliver up their arms. A difficulty immediately ensued, which resulted in the killing and wounding several on both sides.

A short time after this occurrence took place, a village of pappooses, squaws and old men, located on what is known as the Cedar cañon, a short distance north of the South Platte river, who were perfectly unaware of any difficulty having occurred between any portion of their tribe, Cheyenne, and the whites, were attacked by a large party of soldiers, and some of them killed and their ponies driven off. After this, while a body of United States troops were proceeding from the Smoky Hill to the Arkansas river, they reached the neighborhood of Sean Bears' band of the Cheyenne nation. Sean Bears', second chief of the Cheyennes, approached the column of troops alone, his warriors remaining off some distance, he not dreaming that there was any hostility between his nation and the whites. He was immediately shot down, and fire opened upon his band; the result of which was a fight between the two parties. Presuming from all these circumstances that war was inevitable, the young men of the Cheyenne nation commenced to retaliate by committing various depredations all the time, which he, Black Kettle, and other principal chiefs of the Cheyenne nation, was opposed to, and endeavored by all means in their power to restore pacific relations between that tribe and their white brethren, but at various times, when endeavoring to approach the military post for the purpose of accomplishing the same, were fired upon and driven off. In the mean time, while their brothers and allies, the Arapahoes, were on perfectly friendly terms with the whites, and Left Hand's band of that nation were camped in close vicinity to Fort Larned, Left Hand, one of the principal chiefs of the Arapahoe nation, learning that it was the intention of the Kiowas on a certain day to drive off the stock from Fort Larned, proceeded to the commanding officer of that post and informed him of the fact. No attention was paid to the information he gave, and on the day indicated the Kiowas run off the stock. Left Hand again approached the post with a portion of his warriors, for the purpose of offering his services to the commanding officer there to pursue and endeavor to regain the stock from the Kiowa Indians, when he was fired upon and was obliged hastily to leave.

The young men of the Arapahoe nation, supposing it was the intention of the whites to make war upon them as well as the Cheyennes, also commenced retaliating as they were able, and against the desire of most of their principal chiefs, who, as well as Black Kettle and other chiefs of the Cheyennes, were bitterly opposed to hostility with the whites.

He then said that he had lately heard of a proclamation issued by the governor of Colorado, inviting all friendly disposed Indians to come in to the different military posts, and that they would be protected by the government. Under these circumstances, although he thought the whites had been the aggressors and forced the trouble upon the Indians, and anxious for the welfare of his people, he had made this last effort to communicate again with the military authority, and he was glad he succeeded.

He then arose, shook hands with Major Wynkoop and his officers, stating that he was still, as he always had been, a friend to the whites, and, as far as he was concerned, he was willing to deliver up the white prisoners, or anything that was required of him, to procure peace, knowing it to be for the good of his people, but that there were other chiefs who still thought that they were badly treated by the "white brethren," who were willing to make peace, but who felt unwilling to deliver up the prisoners simply on the promise of Major Wynkoop that he would endeavor to procure them peace. They desired that the delivering up the white prisoners should be an assurance of peace. He also went on to state that even if Major Wynkoop's proposition was not accepted there by the chiefs assembled, and although they had sufficient force to entirely overpower Major Wynkoop's small command, from the fact that he had come in good faith to hold this consultation, he should return unmolested to Fort Lyon.

The expressions of other chiefs were to the effect that they insisted upon peace as the conditions of their delivering up the white prisoners.

Major Wynkoop finally replied that he repeated what he had said before, that it was not in his power to insure them peace, and that all he had to say in closing was that they might think about his proposition, that he would march to a certain locality, distant twelve miles, and there await the result of their consultation for two days, advising them at the same time to accede to his proposition as the best means of procuring that peace for which they were anxious.

The white prisoners were brought in and turned over to Major Wynkoop before the time had expired set by him, and Black Kettle, White Antelope, and Bull Bear, of the Cheyenne nation, as well as Nevah Nattanee, Borcu, and Heap Buffalo, of the Arapahoe nation, all chiefs, delivered themselves over to Major Wynkoop. We then proceeded to Fort Lyon, and from there to Denver, Colorado Territory, at which place Governor Evans held a consultation with these chiefs, the result of which was as follows :

He told them he had nothing to do with them; that they would return with Major Wynkoop, who would reconduct them in safety, and they would have to await the action of military authorities. Colonel Chivington, then in command of the district, also told them that they would remain at the disposal of Major Wynkoop until higher authority had acted in their case. The Indians appeared to be perfectly satisfied, presuming that they would eventually be all right as soon as these authorities could be heard from, and expressed themselves so. Black Kettle embraced the governor and Major Wynkoop, and shook hands with all the other officials present, perfectly contented, deeming that the matter was settled. On our return to Fort Lyon I was told by Major Wynkoop to say to the chiefs that they could bring their different bands, including their families, to the vicinity of the post until he had heard from the big chief; that he preferred to have them under his eye and away from other quarters, where they were likely to get into difficulties with the whites.

The chiefs replied that they were willing to do anything Major Wynkoop might choose to dictate, as they had perfect confidence in him. Accordingly, the chiefs went after their families and villages and brought them in; they appeared satisfied that they were in perfect security and safety after their villages were located, and Major Wynkoop had sent an officer to headquarters for instructions. He, Major Wynkoop, was relieved from command of the post by Major Scott J. Anthony, and I was ordered to interpret for him, Major Anthony, in a consultation he desired to hold with these Indians. The consultation that then took place between Major Anthony and these Indians was as follows:

Major Anthony told them that he had been sent here to relieve Major Wynkoop, and that he would from that time be in command of this post; that he had come here under orders from the commanders of all the troops in this country, and that he had orders to have nothing to do with Indians whatever, for they heard at headquarters that the Indians had lately been committing depredations, &c., in the very neighborhood of this post, but that since his arrival he had learned that these reports were all false; that he would write to headquarters himself and correct the rumor in regard to them, and that he would have no objection to their remaining in the vicinity of Sand creek, where they were then located, until such a time as word might be received from the commander of the department; that he himself would forward a complete statement of all that he had seen or heard in regard to them, and that he was in hopes that he would have some good news for the Indians upon receiving an answer, but that he was sorry that his orders were such as to render it impossible for him to make them any issues whatever.

The Indians then replied that it would be impossible for them to remain any great length of time, as they were short of provisions. Major Anthony then told them that they could let their villages remain where they were and send their young men out to hunt buffalo, as he understood that the buffaloes had lately come close in. The Indians appeared to be a little dissatisfied with the change in the commanders of the post, fearing that it boded them no good; but having received assurances of safety from Major Anthony, they still had no fears of their families being disturbed.

On the 26th of November I received permission from Major Scott J. Anthony, commanding post, to proceed to the Indian village on Sand creek for the purpose of trading with the Indians, and started, accompanied by a soldier named David Louderback, and a citizen, Watson Clark. I reached the village and commenced to trade with them. On the morning of the 29th of November the village was attacked by Colonel J. M. Chivington with a command of from nine hundred to one thousand men. The Indian village numbered about one hundred lodges, counting altogether five hundred souls, two-thirds of whom were women and children. From my observation, I do not think there were over sixty Indians that made any defence. I rode over the field after the slaughter was over and counted from sixty to seventy dead bodies, a large majority of which were women and children, all of whose bodies had been mutilated in the most horrible manner. When the troops first approached, I endeavored to join them, but was repeatedly fired upon, as also the soldier and the citizen with me.

When the troops began approaching, I saw Black Kettle, the head chief, hoist the American flag over his lodge, as well as a white flag, fearing there might be some mistake as to who they were. After the fight Colonel Chivington returned with his command in the direction of Fort Lyon, and then proceeded down the Arkansas river.

JOHN S. SMITH,<br>
U. S. Interpreter.

Sworn and subscribed to at Fort Lyon, Colorado Territory, this 27th day of January, 1865.

W. P. MINTON,<br>
Second Lieut. 1st New Mexico Vols., Post Adjutant.

ADJUTANT GENERAL'S OFFICE,<br>
March —, 1865.

Official :

—— ——, A. A. G.

---

FORT LYON, COLORADO TERRITORY,<br>
January 16, 1865.

Personally appeared before me Lieutenant James D. Cannan, 1st New Mexico volunteer infantry, who, after being duly sworn, says:

That on the 28th day of November, 1864, I was ordered by Major Scott J. Anthony to accompany him on an Indian expedition as his battalion adjutant. The object of that expedition was to be a thorough campaign against hostile Indians, as I was led to understand. I referred to the fact of there being a friendly camp of Indians in the immediate neighborhood, and remonstrated against simply attacking that camp, as I was aware that they were resting there in fancied security, under promises held out to them of safety from Major G. W. Wynkoop, from commander of the post of Fort Lyon, as well as by Major S. J. Anthony, then in command. Our battalion was attached to the command of Colonel J. M. Chivington, and left Fort Lyon on the night of the 28th of November, 1864. About daybreak on the morning of the 29th of November we came in sight of the camp of the friendly Indians aforementioned, and was ordered by Colonel Chivington to attack the same, which was accordingly done. The command of Colonel Chivington was composed of about one thousand men. The village of the Indians consisted of from one hundred to one hundred and thirty lodges, and, as far as I am able to judge, of from five hundred to six hundred souls, the majority of whom were women and children.

In going over the battle-ground the next day, I did not see a body of man, woman, or child but was scalped; and in many instances their bodies were mutilated in the most horrible manner, in men, women, and children—privates cut out, &c. I heard one man say that he had cut a woman's private parts out, and had them for exhibition on a stick; I heard another man say that he had cut the fingers off of an Indian to get the rings on the hand. According to the best of my knowledge and belief, these atrocities that were committed were with the knowledge of J. M. Chivington, and I do not know of his taking any measures to prevent them. I heard of one instance of a child a few

94

months old being thrown in the feed-box of a wagon, and after being carried some distance, left on the ground to perish. I also heard of numerous instances in which men had cut out the private parts of females, and stretched them over the saddle-bows, and wore them over their hats, while riding in the ranks. All these matters were a subject of general conversation, and could not help being known by Colonel J. M. Chivington.

JAMES D. CANNAN,
*First Lieutenant 1st Infantry, New Mexico Volunteers.*

Sworn and subscribed to before me this 27th day of January, 1865, at Fort Lyon, Colorado Territory.

W. P. MINTON,
*Second Lieut., 1st New Mexico Vols., Post Adjutant.*

---

*Deposition of Lieutenant Cannan, 1st New Mexico Volunteers.*

Was ordered by Major Anthony to accompany him as his adjutant on an Indian expedition—object, thorough campaign. States that he referred to the camp of friendly Indians, and remonstrated against attacking that camp.

About daybreak, November 29, Colonel Chivington ordered the attack; gives particulars of the barbarities of our men, cutting out *privates, &c.*

ADJUTANT GENERAL'S OFFICE, *March* —, 1865.

Official:

—————— ——————,
*Assistant Adjutant General.*

---

FORT LYON, COLORADO TERRITORY,
*January 16, 1865.*

Personally appeared before me Captain R. A. Hill, 1st New Mexico volunteer infantry, who, after being duly sworn, says:

That, as an officer in the service of the United States, he was on duty at Fort Lyon, Colorado Territory; at the time there was an understanding between the chiefs of the Arapahoe and Cheyenne nations and Major E. W. Wynkoop with regard to their resting in safety with their villages in the vicinity of Fort Lyon until such time as orders in regard to them could be received from the commanding general of the department; that after Major Wynkoop being relieved from the command of Fort Lyon, Colorado Territory, the same understanding existed between Major Scott J. Anthony and the aforesaid Indians; that, to the best of his knowledge and belief, the village of Indians massacred by Colonel J. M. Chivington on the 29th day of November, 1864, were the same friendly Indians heretofore referred to.

R. A. HILL,
*Captain 1st Infantry, New Mexico Volunteers.*

Sworn and subscribed to before me this 27th day of January, 1865.

W. P. MINTON,
*Second Lieut. 1st Infantry, New Mexico Vols. Post Adjutant.*

95

## MASSACRE OF CHEYENNE INDIANS.

*Deposition of Captain R. A. Hill, 1st New Mexico infantry.*

Was on duty at Fort Lyon at time these Indians were camping near said fort; that they were then, by permission of Major Wynkoop and Major Anthony, waiting until instructions could be received from headquarters how to act in their case.

To the best of his knowledge, these Indians were the same massacred by Colonel Chivington November 29.

ADJUTANT GENERAL'S OFFICE, *March* —, 1865.

Official:

—————— ——————,

*Assistant Adjutant General*

—————————

FORT LYON, COLORADO TERRITORY,
*January* 27, 1865.

Personally appeared before me Second Lieutenant W. P. Minton, first regiment, New Mexico infantry volunteers, and Lieutenant C. M. Cossitt, first cavalry of Colorado, who, after being duly sworn, say:

That on the 28th day of November, 1864, Colonel J. M. Chivington, with the third regiment of Colorado cavalry (one-hundred-days men) and a battalion of the first cavalry of Colorado, arrived at this post, and on the 29th of November attacked a village of friendly Indians in this vicinity, and, according to representations made by others in our presence, murdered their women and children, and committed the most horrible outrages upon the dead bodies of the same; that the aforesaid Indians were recognized as friendly by all parties at this post, under the following circumstances, viz:

That Major E. W. Wynkoop, formerly commander of the post, had given them assurances of safety until such time as he could hear from the commanding general of the department in consequence of their having sued for peace, and given every evidence of their sincerity by delivering up the white prisoners they had in their possession, by congregating their families together and leaving them at the mercy of the garrison of Fort Lyon, who could have massacred them at any moment they felt so disposed; that upon Major Wynkoop being relieved from the command of Fort Lyon and Major Scott J. Anthony assuming command of the same, it was still the understanding between Major Anthony and the Indians that they could rest in the security guaranteed them by Major Wynkoop.

Also, that Colonel J. M. Chivington, on his arrival at the post of Fort Lyon, was aware of the circumstances in regard to these Indians, from the fact that different officers remonstrated with him, and stated to him how these Indians were looked upon by the entire garrison; that, notwithstanding these remonstrances, and in the face of all these facts, he committed the massacre aforementioned.

W. P. MINTON,
*Second Lieut. 1st Infantry, New Mexico Volunteers.*
C. M. COSSITT,
*First Lieutenant 1st Cavalry of Colorado.*

Sworn and subscribed to before me this 27th day of January, 1865.

W. W. DENISON,
*Second Lieutenant 1st Colorado Veteran Cavalry,*
*Acting Regimental Adjutant.*

ADJUTANT GENERAL'S OFFICE, *March* —, 1865.

Official:

—————— ——————,

*Assistant Adjutant General.*

96

# MASSACRE OF CHEYENNE INDIANS.

Fort Lyon, Colorado, *January* 27, 1865.

Personally appeared before me Samuel G. Colley, who, being duly sworn, on oath deposes and says:

That he is now, and has been for the past three years, United States agent for the Arapahoe and Cheyenne Indians.

That in the month of June last he received instructions from Hon. John Evans, governor and ex-officio superintendent Indian affairs for Colorado Territory, directing him to send out persons into the Indian country to distribute printed proclamations, (which he was furnished with,) inviting all friendly Indians to come in to the different places designated in said proclamation, and they would be protected and fed. That he caused the terms of said proclamation to be widely disseminated among the different tribes of Indians under his charge, and that in accordance therewith a large number of Arapahoes and Cheyennes came into this post, and provisions were issued to them by Major E. W. Wynkoop, commanding, and myself.

That on the 4th day of September last two Cheyenne Indians (One Eye and Manimick) came into this post with information that the Arapahoes and Cheyennes had several white prisoners among them that they had purchased, and were desirous of giving them up and making peace with the whites.

That on the 6th day of September following Major E. W. Wynkoop left this post with a detachment of troops to rescue said prisoners, and that after an absence of several days he returned, bringing with him four white prisoners which he received from the Arapahoe and Cheyenne Indians. He was accompanied on his return by a number of the most influential men of both tribes, who were unanimously opposed to war with the whites, and desired peace at almost any terms that the whites might dictate.

That immediately upon the arrival of Major Wynkoop at this post large numbers of Arapahoes and Cheyennes came in and camped near the post.

Major Wynkoop selected several of the most prominent chiefs of both nations and proceeded to Denver to council with Superintendent Evans; after his return he held frequent councils with the Indians, and at all of them distinctly stated that he was not empowered to treat with them, but that he had despatched a messenger to the headquarters of the department, stating their wishes in the matter, and that as soon as he received advices from there he would inform them of the decision of General Curtis respecting them.

That until that time, if they placed themselves under his protection, they should not be molested. That the Indians remained quietly near the post until the arrival of Major Anthony, who relieved Major Wynkoop.

Major Anthony held a council with the Indians, and informed them that he was instructed not to allow any Indians in or near the post, but that he had found matters here much better than he had expected, and advised them to go out and camp on Sand creek until he could hear from General Curtis. He wished them to keep him fully advised of all the movements of the Sioux, which they promptly did.

He also promised them that as soon as he heard from General Curtis he would advise them of his decision.

From the time that Major Wynkoop left this post to go out to rescue the white prisoners until the arrival of Colonel Chivington here, which took place on the 28th of November last, no depredations of any kind had been committed by the Indians within two hundred miles of this post.

That upon Colonel Chivington's arrival here with a large body of troops he was informed where these Indians were encamped, and was fully advised under what circumstances they had come in to this post, and why they were then on Sand creek. That he was remonstrated with both by officers and civilians at

97

this post against making war upon those Indians. That he was informed and fully advised that there was a large number of friendly Indians there, together with several white men who were there at the request of himself (Colley) and by permission of Major Anthony. That notwithstanding his knowledge of the facts as above set forth, he is informed that Colonel Chivington did, on the morning of the 29th of November last, surprise and attack said camp of friendly Indians, and massacre a large number of them, (mostly women and children,) and did allow the troops under his command to mangle and mutilate them in the most horrible manner.

S. G. COLLEY,
*United States Indian Agent.*

Sworn and subscribed to before me this 28th day of January, 1865, at Fort Lyon, Colorado Territory.

W. P. MINTON,
*Second Lieut. 1st Infantry, New Mexico Vols., Post Adjutant.*

---

HEADQUARTERS DEPARTMENT OF THE MISSOURI,
*St. Louis,* —— —, 186—.

Deposition of Samuel G. Colley, United States agent for the Arapahoe and Cheyenne Indians, says that in June last, obedient to instructions from Governor Evans, Colorado Territory, he distributed printed proclamations through the Indian country, inviting all friendly Indians to come to the different places designated in said proclamation. That the Indians in question came to Fort Lyon; provisions were issued to them by Major Wynkoop. That two of the chiefs reported they had several white prisoners which they purchased, and which they wished to give up. That Major Wynkoop, on the 6th of September, went and rescued the prisoners. On his return, was accompanied by influential men of both tribes unanimously for peace at any terms almost the whites might dictate. Major Wynkoop proceeded with the chiefs to council with Governor Evans. Major Wynkoop repeatedly stated that he had not the power to treat with them, but was waiting instructions from General Curtis, and until that time he would protect them. These Indians kept the commander of the post fully advised of the movements of the Sioux. No depredations were committed within two hundred miles of the post while these Indians were in the vicinity of the post. Upon Colonel Chivington's arrival he was informed where the Indians were and advised of the circumstances that brought them. He was remonstrated with by officers and civilians against making war. Notwithstanding Colonel Chivington's knowledge of these facts, on the 29th November he surprised and attacked said camp of friendly Indians, killed a large number, mostly women, and allowed his troops to mangle and mutilate bodies.

---

*Deposition of Lieutenants Minton and Cossitt.*

Colonel Chivington, with 3d Colorado cavalry and battalion of 1st Colorado cavalry, attacked, on the 29th November, a village of friendly Indians, and, according to representation, murdered women and children in horrible manner. Indians were recognized friendly. They were there and on assurance from

98

Major Wynkoop of safety. Indians earned the friendship by giving up white prisoners. Colonel Chivington was acquainted with circumstances, and was remonstrated with against, &c.

ADJUTANT GENERAL'S OFFICE, March —, 1865.

Official :

————————— —————————,<br>Assistant Adjutant General.

---

FORT LYON, COLORADO TERRITORY,<br>January 27, 1865.

Personally appeared before me Private David Louderback, 1st cavalry of Colorado, and R. W. Clark, citizen, who, after being duly sworn, say :

That they accompanied John Smith, United States Indian interpreter, on the 26th day of November, 1864, by permission of Major Scott J. Anthony, commanding post of Fort Lyon, Colorado Territory, to the village of the friendly Cheyenne and Arapahoe Indians, on Sand creek, close to Fort Lyon, Colorado Territory, he, John Smith, having received permission to trade with the aforesaid friendly Indians ; that on the morning of the 29th day of November, 1864, the said Indian village was attacked, while deponents were in the same, by Colonel J. M. Chivington, with a command of about 1,000 men ; that, according to their best knowledge and belief, the entire Indian village was composed of not more than 500 souls, two-thirds of which were women and children ; that the dead bodies of women and children were afterwards mutilated in the most horrible manner ; that it was the understanding of the deponents, and the general understanding of the garrison of Fort Lyon, that this village were friendly Indians ; that they had been allowed to remain in the locality they were then in by permission of Major Wynkoop, former commander of the post, and by Major Anthony, then in command, as well as from the fact that permission had been given John Smith and the deponents to visit the said camp for the purpose of trading.

R. W. CLARK,<br>DAVID H. LOUDERBACK.

Sworn and subscribed to before me this 27th day of January, 1865.

W. P. MINTON,<br>Second Lieut. New Mexico Vols., Post Adjutant.

—

*Deposition of David Louderback, 1st Colorado cavalry, and R. W. Clark, citizen.*

They were in camp of Indians with John Smith, interpreter, who had permission to trade with the Indians. On the morning of 29th November camp was attacked by Colonel Chivington's command of 1,000 men, while they were in camp ; dead bodies of women and children were horribly mutilated ; that it was their understanding, and general understanding of garrison Fort Lyon, that these Indians were friendly ; that they were allowed to remain there by Major Wynkoop and Major Anthony.

ADJUTANT GENERAL'S OFFICE, March —, 1865.

Official :

————————— —————————,<br>Assistant Adjutant General.

99

WAR DEPARTMENT, *February* 14, 1865.

Resolutions of Kansas legislature, requesting the Secretary of War to place a sufficient force under General Curtis to enable him to protect the Kansas frontier and the overland and Santa Fé routes.

Referred to General HALLECK, chief of staff, February 14, 1865.

Copy sent to General GRANT some days ago.

H. W. HALLECK,
*Major General, and Chief of Staff.*

HEADQUARTERS OF THE ARMY,
*March* 18, 1865.

Official :

J. C. KELTON, *Colonel, A. A. G.*

CONCURRENT RESOLUTIONS in relation to the overland travel and the settlers upon the frontier.

Whereas the Indian massacres which occurred upon the border of our State during the summer and fall of 1864, and which are now being re-enacted by the hostile tribes of Indians upon the overland route to California, Nevada, and New Mexico, and the Territories of Colorado and Idaho, interfere and retard the settlement and development of the mineral resources of these Territories, and interrupt the overland communication to and from the Pacific and the Territories of Colorado and Idaho; and whereas the military force on said route is entirely inadequate and insufficient to chastise the hostile tribes of Indians, and to keep them from committing their murderous attacks upon emigrants to those Territories and Pacific States, and to keep the line of communication open from the Missouri river, in the State of Kansas, to said States of California and Nevada, and Territories of Colorado and Idaho and New Mexico; and whereas it is necessary to the settlement of the northern and western portion of our State that the hostile tribes of Indians be prevented, if possible, from committing their murderous attacks upon our frontier settlers and the overland mail : Therefore

*Be it resolved by the house of representatives of the State of Kansas,* (the senate concurring therein,) That the Secretary of War be, and he is hereby, requested to place a sufficient military force in the hands of Major General Curtis, commanding this department, to enable him to give sufficient and ample protection to the frontier of Kansas and the overland and Santa Fé routes.

*Resolved,* That the secretary of state be instructed to forward copies of this preamble and resolution to the Secretary of War and our senators and representatives in Congress.

Passed by both houses.

D. M. EMMERT, *Chief Clerk.*

I, R. A. Barker, secretary of state, do hereby certify that the above is a true and correct copy of a concurrent resolution, the original of which is on file in my office.

In testimony whereof, I have set my hand and affixed the official seal of my office this 21st day of January, A. D. 1865.

R. A. BARKER,
*Secretary of State.*

HEADQUARTERS OF THE ARMY, *March* 18, 1865.

Official copy:

J. C. KELTON,
*Colonel and Assistant Adjutant General.*

---

HEADQUARTERS DISTRICT OF COLORADO,
*Denver, February* 13, 1865.

GENERAL: The condition of military affairs in this Territory for the last three months has caused quite a stir at home, and a very great commotion abroad, and justly so. To enable you to properly appreciate the wants and necessities of this people, so as to apply a remedy; to arrive at a desirable conclusion as to the cause of existing hostilities on the part of the Indians; to define my position as district commander, and to lay before you the many difficulties and embarrassments which I have had to contend against since assuming command, as well as to inform you of the steps taken, and the means provided for carrying out the behests of the government and protection of this Territory, I deem it my duty, *first duty*, to give you a concise history of events which may be relied upon for present information and future guidance. Had I been possessed of certain facts from *reliable sources* when I assumed command of this district, on the 4th of January, but a little over a month ago, it might have been possible to arrange matters so as to have fended off part, at least, of the present troubles, which will have (if not, indeed, already) one good effect, viz: to change the policy of the government respecting the treatment of the Indians on the plains. Whatever may have been the origin of the present difficulties, whether the white men or the red were the aggressors, matters not now. We are in every respect the superior of the Indians, and can afford to wage a war of their own choosing, even to extermination.

When I assumed command of this district there were but about two hundred (200) men all told, and they were scattered over an area of three hundred (300) miles, and yet with this command, I was expected to protect the route from Denver to Julesburg, a distance of one hundred and ninety (190) miles, while only forty (40) of the two hundred (200) soldiers were on that line, stationed forty (40) miles from Denver. The balance were on the Arkansas river and at Fort Garland. My district extends about sixty (60) miles on the overland route from Denver, and yet I am called upon to protect as far as Julesburg, in the northeast corner of Colorado Territory, with no troops at my command, while on the north there are plenty, as also from Julesburg to Kearney, which, in my opinion, from what I have seen of them, and heard from reliable sources, had better be sent to some new field of operations. I have special reference to the stations from Kearney to Julesburg. I cannot say who is to blame for this, but it is not the less true. I see every reason why the district of Colorado should embrace the Territory, and none for it being as it now stands defined. Fort Lyon was not in my command when I arrived here, and has but lately been added, which gives me about two hundred and fifty (250) more effective men in the district, but not for operations on the overland route, as they are needed in the southern portion of the Territory to protect the Santa Fé route.

About the end of December, 1864, the 3d regiment Colorado cavalry (one-hundred-days men) were mustered out of the service, thus denuding the district of troops, and at a time, too, when the Indians had suffered an overwhelming defeat, or been subjected to a wholesale massacre at the hands of Colonel Chivington, then commanding district; (I give you these distinctions, as the people here are divided on the question;) at a time when the Indians were burning for revenge on the white men, women, and children, in retaliation for the killed by Colonel Chivington, commanding, for it is useless to deny this fact; at a time when the severity of the winter prevented the making of a campaign with any hope of success on our side, even had the troops been at my command. In view of these facts, and knowing, as he did, that the Territory would be exposed to Indian assaults and depredations, while denuded of troops, I question much the policy and propriety of the Sand creek battle fought by Colonel Chivington on the 29th of November, 1864. This matter is now under investigation by a commission appointed under instructions from Major General Curtis, so that in course of time it will speak for itself.

After having become possessed of all these facts, I looked around to see what could be done in the premises to save the country. I first made a statement to Major General Curtis, which, by the way, has never been acknowledged, and impressed upon him the necessity for making certain changes and of hurrying out re-enforcements. Finding no response or relief from that quarter, I next called upon the governor regarding the turning out of the militia, which was deemed impracticable, owing to the fact that the law has so many defections. I then suggested to the legislature, which was in session, the propriety of amending the militia law, but no answer came or action taken. In consultation with the governor and other prominent men of the Territory, it was deemed most expedient and best to urge the passage of a bill issuing territorial bonds, which could be cashed at par by moneyed men, and the same used to pay volunteers a bounty for three (3) months' service, and purchase horses on which to mount them, (for there are none in the quartermaster's hands, nor any money to purchase them with;) and these men were to be placed under my command, and used in opening and keeping open the overland stage route. The house and council could not agree on this bill; so after over two weeks' delay, and no good resulted from their action, I was compelled to proclaim martial law, shut up all houses of business, stop all labor and traffic, and keep matters so until they furnished me three hundred and sixty (360) mounted men, which I would arm and equip. These men are now being raised, and I expect by the 20th to have the most of them in the field. My position has been, and is, anything but a pleasant one—isolated from all support, a stranger in the land, cut off from all communication, threatened and attacked by hostile Indians, being in a community divided against itself, and compelled to proclaim martial law, with not a man at my back to enforce obedience to the same; yet I have succeeded by first stirring up the public mind, and preparing it for the result which had to follow, unless I chose to back down, and yield my authority, which no living soldier will do.

I enclose, for your information on this subject, copies of a correspondence between myself, the governor, and the legislature on these troubles, also an article from the Journal, a newspaper published in the mountains, which will define to you my position, and show you what I have had to contend with. I made it my business to visit the mountains officially on the very day when excitement was at the highest pitch. On the day but one after that article was written I addressed a meeting of about fifteen hundred (1,500) citizens, in which I pointed out to them at whose door the blame lay, the duties they owed themselves and the government, and my reasons for proclaiming martial law. I was unanimously sustained, and that night one hundred and twenty (120) men were sworn in for three months. This was the quota required by the governor to fill my call.

I enclose you a copy of the order establishing martial law, as also the governor's call in accordance therewith. To assert your authority *here*, in trying cases, is very different from asserting it in any other portion of the Union.

Men of influence and wealth in the east are interested to a very great amount in the mining companies, so that they readily obtain an official ear in Washington to a one-sided story, which invariably works injustice to those in authority and responsible. I therefore respectfully ask, general, that you forward this, or a copy, to Washington, that I may stand right on the record.

I am not afraid to assume any responsibility commensurate with the surrounding circumstances, and which is for the good of the service; but I *am* afraid of the snake-like winding of *hypocrisy*, backed by a grovelling, sensual desire. If men will adhere to truth, I will cheerfully abide every issue.

In the hope this will prove satisfactory and of use to you in your administration, and satisfy your mind regarding my position and the steps I have taken in the premises,

I have the honor to remain, very respectfully, your obedient servant,

T. MOONLIGHT,
*Colonel 11th Kansas Cavalry, Commanding.*

Major General G. M. DODGE,
*Commanding Department of the Missouri,*
*Fort Leavenworth, Kansas.*

---

HEADQUARTERS DISTRICT OF COLORADO,
*Denver, January 7, 1865.*

SIR: As matters now stand in this district (having in a manner no troops) there is great danger of being overrun by the Indians. Troops could at the present time be raised better than at any other time, and now is the time we require them. Will you, as acting governor, communicate with the authorities on the subject (the governor being in Washington) to obtain this authority? It is of immense importance to the Territory, and the only way to receive speedy relief from the danger surrounding, and prevent starvation.

I submit this for your consideration and action, and my name may be used by you in this connexion on your despatches.

Very respectfully, your obedient servant,

T. MOONLIGHT,
*Colonel 11th Kansas Cavalry, Commanding.*

Hon. SAMUEL H. ELBERT.

---

HEADQUARTERS DISTRICT OF COLORADO,
*Denver, C. T., January 8, 1865.*

SIR: Owing to the depredations of Indians, we are, at present, shut up from telegraphic communications with the east, and, therefore, beyond the reach of immediate support from any quarter, leaving us to ourselves to act in the premises. Should the troubles continue, I will be constrained to call on the ablebodied men to muster for the protection of the line of transportation. If you have any special views on the subject, I would be pleased to have them.

Very respectfully, your obedient servant,

T. MOONLIGHT,
*Colonel 11th Kansas Cavalry, Commanding.*

Hon. S. H. ELBERT,
*Secretary and Acting Governor.*
Part VI——7

HEADQUARTERS DISTRICT OF COLORADO,
*Denver, January* 9. 1865.

GENTLEMEN : Learning that the legislative body of Colorado Territory is now in session, I respectfully suggest for your consideration the propriety of immediately reorganizing the militia law. Your country is in a manner isolated from the balance of the federal government, on which you depend for supplies Your line of transportation is now inoperative, and it devolves upon you, th<sup>e</sup> representatives of the people, to take a step in a direction that will insure you at least, an active and efficient militia force to guard over your interests. As, matters now stand, the militia must be called out sooner or later, and I make these suggestions that there may be no misunderstanding between the civil and military.

Gentlemen, pardon my intrusion, I mean it for your good.

Very respectfully, your obedient servant,

T. MOONLIGHT,
*Colonel* 11*th Kansas Cavalry, Commanding.*

SPEAKER OF THE HOUSE OF REPRESENTATIVES,
*Colorado City, Colorado Territory.*

---

HEADQUARTERS DISTRICT OF COLORADO,
*Denver, January* 17, 1865.

SIR : By reason of the scarcity of troops in th is district, our natural enemies the Indians, have possessed themselves of our lines of communication. They have burned ranches, killed innocent women and children, destroyed government property wherever it was found, driven off the stage stock, killed the drivers and passengers travelling on the coaches ; in short, they are making it a war of extermination. We may look in vain for such timely military assistance as will protect the lives and property of settlers ; nor can we hope for an eastern communication this winter, unless the citizens of the Territory band themselves together in a military organization, and spring to arms at your call as chief executive. The blood of the innocent and unoffending martyrs cries aloud for vengeance, and starvation stares in the face the living. You nor I cannot longer remain inactive, and be considered guiltless. It devolves upon the militia, as matters now stand to open the overland route, and keep it open until troops can be had from the east to make war on these savages of the plains, until there remains not a vestige of their originality. On behalf of the general government, and on my own responsibility, (trusting to the justice of the cause for my own protection,) I will furnish carbines to the first mounted and accepted company, and rifled weapons of improved pattern to all the balance ; also, rations for the same as United States troops, and forage for the animals, with the proper allowance of transportation, and also horse equipments. My scouts inform me that the Indian spies are now prowling around the very skirts of this place, so that, in addition to your call for militia for field service, the city companies should at once be placed on a war footing, having daily drills, with appointed places of rendezvous, that we may not be caught napping.

I am, very respectfully, your obedient servant,

T. MOONLIGHT,
*Colonel* 11*th Kansas Cavalry, Commanding.*

Hon. S. H. ELBERT,
*Acting Governor, Colorado Territory.*

MASSACRE OF CHEYENNE INDIANS.

HEADQUARTERS DISTRICT OF COLORADO,
*Denver, January 25, 1865.*

SIR : I have the honor to acknowledge the receipt of your communication of yesterday, from Golden City, making inquiries as to the number of troops in this district, and the disposition made of them. I will cheerfully give you the desired information.

At Fort Lyon, which has lately been placed in my district, there are about 300 men. The mustering officer, Captain J. C. Anderson, has but returned after completing the organization of the 1st regiment, by consolidating it into six maximum companies. About forty men are at Fort Garland, but these now will be increased to 100. About forty men are at Camp Fillmore, but these will be increased to 100 also, as companies will be stationed together at posts so remote. One company will be stationed here of 100 men in place of the stragglers now doing duty. One company will be divided and stationed at Bijou Basin and Living Springs. This leaves only two companies at Fort Lyon. In addition to these, there are about seventy-five (75) recruits of the 2d Colorado ; part of them are now at or near Junction, and the balance will join in a few days. There are about sixty men now at Valley Station, but these must be changed, owing to the new organization. There are about 500 men, all told, for duty, scattered from Fort Lyon, *via* Garland, Fillmore, Denver, and on route to Valley Station, a distance of about 450 miles.

The committee will see from this that so widely spread are the troops, that, even in a case of emergency, it would not be possible to get together more than 200 men in thirty-six hours.

Trusting this may be of service to you in your proceedings, I remain, very respectfully, your obedient servant,

T. MOONLIGHT,
*Colonel 11th Kansas Cavalry, Commanding.*

D. H. NICHOLS,
*Chairman of Committee on Military Affairs.*

---

HEADQUARTERS DISTRICT OF COLORADO,
*Denver, January 31, 1865.*

SIR : I have been looking eagerly and waiting patiently for the passage of the bill which was designed to relieve the people of this Territory from the ravages of the Indians. That bill was introduced at my suggestion, as the most feasible of all plans to raise troops rapidly and voluntarily for the opening of the overland route, and the keeping of it open until succor could arrive from the States. The Indians are every day becoming more desperate, and to-day there stands not a ranch, out of the many that were between Valley Station and Julesburg, and but very few on this side, and all since the introduction of that bill. I trusted implicitly in the patriotism and fidelity of the legislature, and that their wisdom and judgment would at once foresee the necessity of taking steps to defend their homes, their little ones, and the property of the people whom they represent. Am I mistaken ? God forbid ! Yet every indication of late seems to blight my fondest hopes. I cannot longer await the action of your honorable body, for this night's despatches from Junction inform me that about three thousand (3,000) Indians are marching up the Platte on both sides. Unless the legislature, within forty-eight hours, does something to relieve suffering humanity, and save this country from ruin and devastation, I will be compelled, much against my will, to proclaim martial law, shut up all houses of business, and force every man able to bear arms into the ranks, and send them

105

out to protect their brethren, kill off the Indians, and establish permanent communication with the east. I cannot quietly look on and perform my duty to *this people, my country, and my God.*

I have weighed this matter well in my own mind, and what I have stated is my firm resolve, with a lingering hope that your honorable body will yet, and immediately, save this Territory from destruction, and themselves from the indignation of an infuriated people.

I have the honor to remain, very respectfully, your obedient servant,
T. MOONLIGHT,
*Colonel 11th Kansas Cavalry, Commanding.*
SPEAKER OF THE HOUSE OF REPRESENTATIVES, *Golden City.*

---

HEADQUARTERS DISTRICT OF COLORADO,
*Denver, February 4, 1865.*

DEAR SIR: I send this communication by special messenger, and respectfully ask that an answer to this, as well as that of January 31, ultimo, be returned. Time passes, and the danger increases—hence the urgency of my request.

I have been informed from various sources that a portion of the house took exceptions to my letter of the 31st of January, as being threatening and coercive in its tone. Permit me to say that nothing was further from my mind or intention. Liberty is a boon I prize too highly to wilfully deprive others of its blessing, and the course that I fear I must pursue for the salvation of this people is forced upon me by a combination of circumstances which, in my humble opinion, the legislature might, within the past two weeks, have scattered to the winds. This they have not done; therefore I must do something.

On invitation of your honorable body, and on the speaker's stand, in their presence, did I make known my feelings on the Indian question. There I urged the passage of that bill, and there I told them that I was opposed to martial law. My acts have not belied my words; but the time has come when "patience ceases to be a virtue," and when inactivity is a wilful "dereliction of duty." So far, I have been patient in the extreme, though not inactive. I have nothing to retract in my letter of January 31, but will adhere closely to my decision. I may err in addressing the house, and not the council. Should such be the case, it must be attributed to my ignorance of parliamentary rules, for I suppose that a measure of this kind would be acted upon in joint ballot.

I have the honor to be, very respectfully, your obedient servant,
T. MOONLIGHT,
*Colonel 11th Kansas Cavalry, Commanding.*
Hon. SPEAKER OF HOUSE OF REPRESENTATIVES,
*Golden City, Colorado Territory.*

---

HEADQUARTERS DISTRICT OF COLORADO,
*Denver, Colorado Territory, February 6, 1865.*

SIR: I have the honor to acknowledge the receipt of your communication of the 4th instant, (in behalf of the house of which you are an honorable member,) in which I am informed that the bill authorizing the issuing of $200,000 bonds for the purpose of mounting the militia called for, paying the bounty, &c., was *not* likely to pass; and also that a bill was likely to pass, (superseding the bond bill,) giving bounties to men who would enlist in the two Colorado regiments now in the field, and also that it had been represented to the house, as coming from me, that a sufficient number of men could be obtained in this way, so as to avoid the necessity of proclaiming martial law.

In reply, I would state that I am very sorry the bond bill did not pass over two weeks ago, for, to my mind, it was the surest and most honorable way that men could be raised and horses procured. I have never stated that a sufficient number of men could be enlisted for the old regiments, so as to meet the exigencies of the case; and even could these men be persuaded to enlist, I have not at present the horses on which to mount them. I should be pleased to see a bill pass authorizing the payment of a liberal bounty to recruits for the 1st and 2d Colorado regiments, for I think the regiments might be recruited up to the maximum; but I am sorry to say that such a bill at this late hour would not meet the necessities of the times. Men and horses must be had immediately, or else we must yield ourselves living sacrifices to inhuman savages; and who of us all are prepared to do this? I beg of you not to defeat the bounty bill because of the lateness of the hour which gave it birth, for, in my estimation, it will be of great assistance and good. I am more than sorry that I have now no other alternative but to proclaim martial law and suspend all business until a sufficient number of men (mounted) are had to open the overland road and protect the frontier settlers of the Territory. When I modified martial law, as it existed under the former district commander, I never expected to be compelled to recreate it with renewed severity.

Accept my thanks for your courtesy, and believe me, with esteem and respect, your obedient servant,

T. MOONLIGHT,
*Colonel 11th Kansas Cavalry, Commanding.*

Hon. E. T. HOLLAND,
*Chairman of Military Committee.*

HEADQUARTERS DEPARTMENT OF THE MISSOURI,
*St. Louis, Missouri, March 9, 1865.*

A true copy:

J. F. BENNETT, *A. A. G.*

ADJUTANT GENERAL'S OFFICE, *March —, 1865.*

Official:

—— ——, *A. A. G.*

*Testimony of Colonel J. M. Chivington.*

Interrogatories propounded to John M. Chivington by the Joint Committee on the Conduct of the War, and answers thereto given by said Chivington reduced to writing, and subscribed and sworn to before Alexander W. Atkins, notary public, at Denver, in the Territory of Colorado.

1st question. What is your place of residence, your age and profession?

Answer. My place of residence is Denver, Colorado; my age, forty-five years; I have been colonel of 1st Colorado cavalry, and was mustered out of the service on or about the eighth day of January last, and have not been engaged in any business since that time.

2d question. Were you in November, 1864, in any employment, civil or military, under the authority of the United States; and if so, what was that employment, and what position did you hold?

Answer. In November, 1864, I was colonel of 1st Colorado cavalry, and in command of the district of Colorado.

3d question. Did you, as colonel in command of Colorado troops, about the 29th of November, 1864, make an attack on an Indian village or camp at a place known as Sand creek? If so, state particularly the number of men under your command; how armed and equipped; whether mounted or not; and if you had any artillery, state the number of guns, and the batteries to which they belonged.

Answer. On the 29th day of November, 1864, the troops under my command attacked a camp of Cheyenne and Arapaho Indians at a place known as Big Bend of Sandy, about forty miles north of Fort Lyon, Colorado Territory. There were in my command at that time about (500) five hundred men of the 3d regiment Colorado cavalry, under the immediate command of Colonel George L. Shoup, of said 3d regiment, and about (250) two hundred and fifty men of the 1st Colorado cavalry; Major Scott J. Anthony commanded one battalion of said 1st regiment, and Lieutenant Luther Wilson commanded another battalion of said 1st regiment. The 3d regiment was armed with rifled muskets, and Star's and Sharp's carbines. A few of the men of that regiment had revolvers. The men of the 1st regiment were armed with Star's and Sharp's carbines and revolvers. The men of the 3d regiment were poorly equipped; the supply of blankets, boots, hats, and caps was deficient. The men of the 1st regiment were well equipped; all these troops were mounted. I had four 12-pound mountain howitzers, manned by detachments from cavalry companies; they did not belong to any battery company.

4th question. State as nearly as you can the number of Indians that were in the village or camp at the time the attack was made; how many of them were warriors; how many of them were old men, how many of them were women, and how many of them were children?

Answer. From the best and most reliable information I could obtain, there were in the Indian camp, at the time of the attack, about eleven (11) or twelve (12) hundred Indians: of these about seven hundred were warriors, and the remainder were women and children. I am not aware that there were any old men among them. There was an unusual number of males among them, for the reason that the war chiefs of both nations were assembled there evidently for some special purpose.

5th question. At what time of the day or night was the attack made? Was it a surprise to the Indians? What preparation, if any, had they made for defence or offence?

Answer. The attack was made about sunrise. In my opinion the Indians were surprised; they began, as soon as the attack was made, to oppose my troops, however, and were soon fighting desperately. Many of the Indians were armed with rifles and many with revolvers; I think all had bows and arrows. They had excavated trenches under the bank of Sand creek, which in the vicinity of the Indian camp is high, and in many places precipitous. These trenches were two to three feet deep, and, in connexion with the banks, were evidently designed to protect the occupants from the fire of an enemy. They were found at various points extending along the banks of the creek for several miles from the camp; there were marks of the pick and shovel used in excavating them; and the fact that snow was seen in the bottoms of some of the trenches, while all snow had disappeared from the surface of the country generally, sufficiently proved that they had been constructed some time previously. The Indians took shelter in these trenches as soon as the attack was made, and from thence resisted the advance of my troops.

6th question. What number did you lose in killed, what number in wounded, and what number in missing?

Answer. There were seven men killed, forty-seven wounded, and one was missing.

7th question. What number of Indians were killed; and what number of the killed were women, and what number were children?

Answer. From the best information I could obtain, I judge there were five hundred or six hundred Indians killed; I cannot state positively the number killed, nor can I state positively the number of women and children killed. Officers who passed over the field, by my orders, after the battle, for the purpose of ascertaining the number of Indians killed, report that they saw but few women or children dead, no more than would certainly fall in an attack upon a camp in which they were. I myself passed over some portions of the field after the fight, and I saw but one woman who had been killed, and one who had hanged herself; I saw no dead children. From all I could learn, I arrived at the conclusion that but few women or children had been slain. I am of the opinion that when the attack was made on the Indian camp the greater number of squaws and children made their escape, while the warriors remained to fight my troops.

8th question. State, as nearly as you can, the number of Indians that were wounded, giving the number of women and the number of children among the wounded.

Answer. I do not know that any Indians were wounded that were not killed; if there were any wounded, I do not think they could have been made prisoners without endangering the lives of soldiers; Indians usually fight as long as they have strength to resist. Eight Indians fell into the hands of the troops alive, to my knowledge ; these, with one exception, were sent to Fort Lyon properly cared for.

9th question. What property was captured by the forces under your command ? State the number of horses, mules and poneys, buffalo robes, blankets, and also all other property taken, specifying particularly the kinds, quality, and value thereof.

Answer. There were horses, mules, and poneys captured to the number of about six hundred. There were about one hundred buffalo robes taken. Some of this stock had been stolen by the Indians from the government during last spring, summer and fall, and some of the stock was the property of private citizens from whom they had been stolen during the same period. The horses that belonged to the government were returned to the officers responsible for them ; as nearly as could be learned, the horses and mules that were owned by private citizens were returned to them on proof of ownership being furnished ; such were my orders at least. The poneys, horses, and mules for which no owner could be found, were put into the hands of my provost marshal in the field, Captain J. J. Johnson, of company E, 3d Colorado cavalry, with instructions to drive them to Denver and turn them over to the acting quartermaster as captured stock, taking his receipt therefor. After I arrived in Denver I again directed Captain Johnson to turn these animals over to Captain Gorton, assistant quartermaster, as captured stock, which I presume he did. Colonel Thos. Moonlight relieved me of the command of the district soon after I arrived in Denver, that is to say, on the —— day of ——, A. D. 186–, and I was mustered out of the service, the term of service of my regiment having expired. My troops were not fully supplied with hospital equipage, having been on forced marches. The weather was exceedingly cold, and additional covering for the wounded became necessary ; I ordered the buffalo robes to be used for that purpose. I know of no other property of value being captured. It is alleged that groceries were taken from John Smith, United States Indian interpreter for Upper Arkansas agency, who was in the Indian camp at the time of the attack, trading goods, powder, lead, caps, &c., to the Indians. Smith told me that these groceries belonged to Samuel G. Colby, United States Indian agent. I am not aware that these things were taken ; I am aware that Smith and D. D. Colby, son of the Indian agent, have each presented claims against the government for these articles. The buffalo robes mentioned above were also claimed by Samuel G. Colby, D. D. Colby and John Smith. One bale of buffalo robes was marked S. S. Soule, 1st Colorado cavalry, and I am informed that one bale was marked Anthony, Major Anthony being in command of Fort Lyon at that time. I cannot say what has been done with the property since I was relieved of the command and mustered out of service. There was a large quantity of Indian trinkets taken at the Indian camp which were of no value. The soldiers retained a few of these as trophies; the remainder with the Indian lodges were destroyed.

10th question. What reason had you for making the attack? What reasons, if any, had you to believe that Black Kettle or any other Indian or Indians in the camp entertained feelings of hostility towards the whites? Give in detail the names of all Indians so believed to be hostile, with the dates and places of their hostile acts, so far as you may be able to do so.

Answer. My reason for making the attack on the Indian camp was, that I believed the Indians in the camp were hostile to the whites. That they were of the same tribes with those who had murdered many persons and destroyed much valuable property on the Platte and Arkansas rivers during the previous spring, summer and fall was beyond a doubt. When a tribe of Indians is at war with the whites it is impossible to determine what party or band of the tribe or the name of the Indian or Indians belonging to the tribe so at war are guilty of the acts of hostility. The most that can be ascertained is that Indians of the tribe have performed the acts. During the spring, summer and fall of the year 1864, the Arapaho and Cheyenne Indians, in some instances assisted or led on by Sioux, Kiowas, Comanches and Apaches, had committed many acts of hostility in the country lying between the Little Blue and the Rocky mountains and the Platte and Arkansas rivers. They had murdered many of the whites and taken others prisoners, and had destroyed valuable property, probably amounting to $200,000 or $300,000. Their rendezvous was on the headwaters of the Republican, probably one hundred miles from where the Indian camp was located. I had every reason to believe that these Indians were either directly or indirectly concerned in the outrages which had been committed upon the whites. I had no means of ascertaining what were the names of the Indians who had committed these outrages other than the declarations of the Indians themselves; and the character of Indians in the western country for truth and veracity, like their respect for the chastity of women who may become prisoners in their hands, is not of that order which is calculated to inspire confidence in what they may say. In this view I was supported by Major Anthony, 1st Colorado cavalry, commanding at Fort Lyon, and Samuel G. Colby, United States Indian agent, who, as they had been in communication with these Indians, were more competent to judge of their disposition towards the whites than myself. Previous to the battle they expressed to me the opinion that the Indians should be punished. We found in the camp the scalps of nineteen (19) white persons. One of the surgeons informed me that one of these scalps had been taken from the victim's head not more than four days previously. I can furnish a child captured at the camp ornamented with six white women's scalps; these scalps must have been taken by these Indians or furnished to them for their gratification and amusement by some of their brethren, who, like themselves, were in amity with the whites.

11th question. Had you any, and if so, what reason, to believe that Black Kettle and the Indians with him, at the time of your attack, were at peace with the whites, and desired to remain at peace with them?

Answer. I had no reason to believe that Black Kettle and the Indians with him were in good faith at peace with the whites. The day before the attack Major Scott J. Anthony, 1st Colorado cavalry, then in command at Fort Lyon, told me that these Indians were hostile; that he had ordered his sentinels to fire on them if they attempted to come into the post, and that the sentinels had fired on them; that he was apprehensive of an attack from these Indians, and had taken every precaution to prevent a surprise. Major Samuel G. Colby, United States Indian agent for these Indians, told me on the same day that he had done everything in his power to make them behave themselves, and that for the last six months he could do nothing with them; that nothing but a sound whipping would bring a lasting peace with them. These statements were made to me in the presence of the officers of my staff whose statements can be obtained to corroborate the foregoing.

12th question. Had you reason to know or believe that these Indians had sent their chief and leading men at any time to Denver city, in order to take measure in connection with the superintendent of Indian affairs there, or with any other person having authority, to secure friendly relations with the whites?

Answer. I was present at an interview between Governor Evans on the part of the whites, and Black Kettle and six other Indians, at Camp Weldmar, Denver, about the 27th of September, 1864, in which the Indians desired peace, but did not propose terms. General Curtis, by telegraph to me, declined to make peace with them, and said that there could be no peace without his consent. Governor Evans declined to treat with them, and as General Curtis was then in command of the department, and, of course, I could not disobey his instructions. General Curtis's terms of peace were to require all bad Indians to be given up, all stock stolen by the Indians to be delivered up, and hostages given by the Indians for their good conduct. The Indians never complied with these terms.

13th question. Were those Indians, to your knowledge, referred by the superintendent of Indian affairs to the military authorities, as the only power under the government to afford them protection?

Answer. Governor Evans, in the conference mentioned in my last answer, did not refer the Indians to the military authorities for *protection*, but for *terms* of *peace*. He told the Indians "that he was the peace chief, that they had gone to war, and, therefore, must deal with the war chiefs." It was at this time I gave them the terms of General Curtis, and they said they had not received power to make peace on such terms, that they would report to their young men and see what they would say to it; they would like to do it, but if their young men continued the war they would have to go with them. They said there were three or four small war parties of their young men out on the war path against the whites at that time. This ended the talk.

14th question. Did the officer in command of Fort Lyon, to your knowledge, at any time extend the protection of our flag to Black Kettle and the Indians with him, and direct them to encamp upon the reservation of the fort?

Answer. Major E. W. Wynkoop, 1st cavalry, Colorado, did, as I have been informed, allow some of these Indians to camp at or near Fort Lyon, and did promise them the protection of our flag. Subsequently he was relieved of the command of Fort Lyon, and Major Anthony placed in command at that post, who required the Indians to comply with General Curtis's terms, which they failed to do, and thereupon Major Anthony drove them away from the post.

15th question. Were rations ever issued to those Indians either as prisoners of war or otherwise?

Answer. I have been informed that Major Wynkoop issued rations to the Indians encamped near Fort Lyon while he was in command, but whether as prisoners of war I do not know. I think that Major Anthony did not issue any rations.

16th question. And did those Indians remove, in pursuance of the directions, instructions, or suggestions of the commandant at Fort Lyon, to the place on Sand creek, where they were attacked by you?

Answer. I have been informed that Major Anthony, commandant at Fort Lyon, did order the Indians to remove from that post, but I am not aware that they were ordered to go to the place where the battle was fought, or to any other place.

17th question. What measures were taken by you, at any time, to render the attack on those Indians a surprise?

Part VI——8

111

_Answer._ I took every precaution to render the attack upon the Indians a surprise, for the reason that we had been chasing small parties of them all the summer and fall without being able to catch them, and it appeared to me that the only way to deal with them was to surprise them in their place of rendezvous. General Curtis, in his campaign against them, had failed to catch them; General Mitchel had met with no better success; General Blunt had been surprised by them, and his command nearly cut to pieces.

18th question. State in detail the disposition made of the various articles of property, horses, mules, ponies, buffalo robes, &c., captured by you at the time of this attack, and by what authority was such disposition made?

_Answer._ The horses and mules that had been stolen from the government were turned over to the officer who had been responsible for the same; and the animals belonging to Atzins was returned to them upon proof being made of such ownership. The animals not disposed of in this way were turned over to Captain S. J. Johnson, 3d regiment Colorado cavalry, with instructions to proceed with the same to Denver, and turn them into the quartermaster's department. After the command arrived in Denver, I again directed Captain Johnson to turn over the stock to Captain C. L. Gorton, assistant quartermaster, at that place. The buffalo robes were turned into the hospital for use of the wounded as before stated.

19th question. Make such further statement as you may desire, or which may be necessary to a full understanding of all matters relating to the attack upon the Indians at Sand creek.

_Answer._ Since August, 1863, I had been in possession of the most conclusive evidence of the alliance, for the purposes of hostility against the whites, of the Sioux, Cheyennes, Arapahoes, Camanche river, and Apache Indians. Their plan was to interrupt, or, if possible, entirely prevent all travel on the routes along the Arkansas and Platte rivers from the States to the Rocky mountains, and thereby depopulate this country. Rebel emissaries were long since sent among the Indians to incite them against the whites, and afford a medium of communication between the rebels and the Indians; among whom was Gerry Bent, a half-breed Cheyenne Indian, but educated, and to all appearances a white man, who, having served under Price in Missouri, and afterwards becoming a bushwhacker, being taken prisoner, took the oath of allegiance, and was paroled, after which he immediately joined the Indians, and has ever since been one of their most prominent leaders in all depredations upon the whites. I have been reliably informed that this half-breed, Bent, in order to incite the Indians against the whites, told them that the Great Father at Washington having all he could do to fight his children at the south, they could now regain their country.

When John Evans, governor of Colorado Territory, and ex officio superintendent of indian affairs, visited by appointment the Cheyenne Indians on the Republican fork of the Kansas river, to talk with them in regard to their relations with the government, the Indians would have nothing to say to him, nor would they receive the presents sent them by the government, but immediately on his arrival at the said point the Indians moved to a great distance, all their villages appearing determined not to have any intercourse with him individually or as the agent of the government.

This state of affairs continued for a number of months, during which time white men who had been trading with the Indians informed me that the Indians had determined to make war upon the whites as soon as the grass was green, and that they were making preparations for such an event by the large number of arrows they were making and the quantity of arms and ammunition they were collecting; that the settlers along the Platte and Arkansas rivers should be warned of the approaching danger; that the Indians had declared their intention to prosecute the war vigorously when they commenced. With very few troops at my command I could do but little to protect the settlers except to collect the latest intelligence from the Indians' country, communicate it to General Curtis, commanding department of Missouri, and warn the settlers of the relations existing between the Indians and the whites, and the probability of trouble, all of which I did.

Last April, 1864, the Indians, Cheyennes, Arapahoes, and others, commenced their depredations upon the whites by entering their isolated habitations in the distant parts of this territory, taking therefrom everything they desired, and destroying the balance; driving off their stock, horses, mules and cattle. I sent a detachment of troops after the Indians to recover the stolen property, when the stock, &c., being demanded of them they (the Indians) refused to surrender the property so taken from the whites, and stated that they wanted to fight the troops. Again, when a few weeks after the country along the Platte river, near Fremont's orchard, became the theatre of their depredations, one Ripley, a ranchman, living on the Bijon creek, near camp Sanborn, came into camp and informed Captain Sanborn, commanding, that his stock had all been stolen by the Indians, requesting assistance to recover it. Captain Sanborn ordered Lieutenant Clark Dunn, with a detachment of troops, to pursue the Indians and recover the stock; but, if possible, to avoid a collision with them. Upon approaching the Indians, Lieutenant Dunn dismounted, walked forward alone about fifty paces from his command, and requested the Indians to return the stock, which Mr. Ripley had recognized as his; but the Indians treated him with contempt, and commenced firing upon him, which resulted in four of the troops being wounded and about fifteen Indians being killed and wounded, Lieutenant Dunn narrowly escaping with his life. Again, about one hundred and seventy-five head of cattle were stolen from Messrs. Irwin and Jackman, government freighters, when troops were sent in pursuit toward the headwaters of the Republican. They were fired upon by the Indians miles from where the Indians were camped. In this encounter the Indians killed one soldier and wounded another. Again, when the troops were near the Smoky Hill, after stock, while passing through a canon, about eighty miles from Fort Larned, they were attacked by these same Cheyenne Indians, and others, and almost cut to pieces, there being about fifteen hundred Indians. Again, when on a Sunday morning the Kiowas and Camanches were at Fort Larned, to obtain the rations that the commanding officer, on behalf of the government, was issuing to them, they, at a preconcerted signal, fired upon the sentinels at the fort, making a general attack upon the unsuspecting garrison, while the balance of the Indians were driving off the stock belonging to the government, and then as suddenly departed, leaving the garrison afoot excepting about thirty artillery horses that were saved; thus obtaining in all about two hundred and eighty head of stock, including a small herd taken from the suttler at that post.

Again, a few days after this, the Cheyennes and Arapahoes Indians, with whom I had the fight at Sand creek, meeting a government train bound for New Mexico, thirty miles east of Fort Larned, at Walnut creek, who, after manifesting a great deal of friendship by shaking hands, &c., with every person in the train, suddenly attacked them, killing fourteen and wounding a number more, scalping and mutilating in the most inhuman manner those they killed, while they scalped two of this party alive, one a boy about fourteen years of age, who has since become an imbecile. The two persons that were scalped alive I saw a few days after this occurred. Though it occurred within sight of Fort Zarah, the officer commanding considered his command entirely inadequate to render any assistance. But we think we have related enough to satisfy the most incredulous of the determined hostility of these Indians; suffice it to say that during the spring, summer, and fall such atrocious acts were of almost daily occurrence along the Platte and Arkansas routes, till the Indians becoming so bold that a family, consisting of a man, woman, and two children, by the name of Hungate, were brutally murdered and scalped within fifteen miles of Denver, the bodies being brought to Denver for interment. After seeing which, any person who could for a moment believe that these Indians were friendly, to say the least must have strange ideas of their habits. We could not see it in that light.

This last atrocious act was referred to by Governor Evans in his talk with the Cheyennes and Arapahoes Indians on about the 27th day of September, 1864, at Denver, Colorado Territory. The Indians then stated that it had been done by members of their tribe, and that they never denied it. All these things were promptly reported to Major General S. R. Curtis, commanding department, who repeatedly ordered me, regardless of district lines, to appropriately chastise the Indians, which I always endeavored to do. Major General S. R. Curtis himself and Brigadear General R. B. Mitchell made campaigns against the Indians, but could not find them; the Indians succeeded in keeping entirely from their view. Again, Major General J. P. Blunt made a campaign against the Indians; was surprised by them, and a portion of his command nearly cutto pieces.

Commanding only a district with very few troops under my control, with hundreds of miles between my headquarters and rendezvous of the Indians, with a large portion of the Sante Fe and Platte routes, besides the sparsely settled and distant settlements of this Territory, to protect, I could not do anything till the 3d regiment was organized and equipped, when I determined to strike a blow against this savage and determined foe. When I reached Fort Lyon, after passing over from three to five feet of snow, and greatly suffering from the intensity of the cold, the thermometer ranging from 28 to 30 degrees below zero, I questioned Major Anthony in regard to the whereabouts of hostile Indians. He said there was a camp of Cheyennes and Arapahoes about fifty miles distant; that he would have attacked before, but did not consider his force sufficient; that these Indians had threatened to attack the post, &c., and ought to be whipped, all of which was concurred in by Major Colley, Indian agent for the district of the Arkansas, which information, with the positive orders from Major General Curtis, commanding the department, to punish these Indians, decided my course, and resulted in the battle of Sand Creek, which has created such a sensation in Congress through the lying reports of interested and malicious parties.

On my arrival at Fort Lyon, in all my conversations with Major Anthony, commanding the post, and Major Colley, Indian agent, I heard nothing of this recent statement that the Indians were under the protection of the government, &c.; but Major Anthony repeatedly stated to me that he had at different times fired upon these Indians, and that they were hostile, and, during my stay at Fort Lyon, urged the necessity of my immediately attacking the Indians before they could learn of the number of troops at Fort Lyon, and so desirous was Major Colly, Indian agent, that I should find and also attack the Arapahoes, that he sent a messenger after the fight at Sand creek, nearly forty miles, to inform me where I could find the Arapahoes and Kiowas; yet, strange to say, I have learned recently that these men, Anthony and Colly, are the most bitter in their denunciations of the attack upon the Indians at Sand creek. Therefore, I would, in conclusion, most respectfully demand, as an act of justice to myself and the brave men whom I have had the honor to command in one of the hardest campaigns ever made in this country, whether against white men or red, that we be allowed that right guarranteed to every American citizen, of introducing evidence in our behalf to sustain us in what we believe to have been an act of duty to ourselves and to civilization.

We simply ask to introduce as witnesses men that were present during the campaign and know all the facts.

J. M. CHIVINGTON,
*Lieu't Col. 1st Cavalry of Colorado, Com'd'g Dist. of Colorado.*

Sworn and subscribed to before me this 26th day of April, 1865.
ALEXANDER W. ATKINS,
*Notary Public.*

# APPENDIX.

## THE CHIVINGTON MASSACRE.

WASHINGTON, *Tuesday, March* 7, 1865.

Samuel G. Colley sworn and examined.

By Mr. DOOLITTLE :

Question. What is your age ?

Answer. I was fifty-seven last December.

Question. Are you agent for the Cheyennes and Arapahoes ?

Answer. I am.

Question. How long have you acted as such ?

Answer. My commission dates from July, 1861. I filed my bonds October, 1861.

Question. When did you go upon the ground where they are located ?

Answer. I went upon the ground in August, 1861.

Question. Have you been in charge of those Indians, as agent, ever since ?

Answer. I have.

Question. State in brief terms about where they are located.

Answer. Their reservation commences at a point fifteen miles south of Fort Lyon ; thence up the Arkansas river north to a point on the north bank of the Arkansas, some twenty-five miles above Fort Lyon ; it then runs down till it strikes the old line of New Mexico, follows that line due north till it intersects a certain line described in the treaty, thence north till it strikes Sand creek, thence down Sand creek to the place of beginning, including the fort. The reservation is in the form of a triangle.

Question. Have the Arapahoes a reservation adjoining the Cheyennes?

Answer Yes ; the tract which I have described is divided in two, half for the Cheyennes and half for the Arapahoes, the Cheyennes taking the west part of it.

Question. About how many of those Cheyennes are there, according to your best estimate?

Answer. I have enumerated them as well as I could. We have had, when I have given them some presents, between 200 and 300 lodges of Cheyennes there at a time, and something over 200 lodges of Arapahoes. There is another band that were not satisfied with the treaty who ran north of the Platte and have never come down there to mingle with these Indians much. Some of them may have been on the reservation, but they do not claim that as their reservation ; they claim land north.

Question. Are those Cheyennes or Arapahoes ?

Answer. A band of each.

Question. Do the Cheyennes and Arapahoes, any of them, live in houses ?

Answer. No ; they live wild.

Question. Do they have any kind of tents or skins, or anything of that sort, for shelter?

Answer. They build a tent of buffalo skins on lodge poles, very much like a Sibley tent.

Question. They move about from place to place ?

Answer. Yes ; they move about ; wherever the game goes they go.

Question. They are nomadic ?

Answer. Entirely so. They break up into parties of twenty or thirty.

Question. What was the occasion of the recent difficulty between our people and the Cheyennes and Arapahoes ?

Answer. It commenced early last spring on the Platte. There was a collision there between the Indians and the soldiers. I am not able to say which party was the aggressor ; the claim there is differently made, the Indians claiming one way and the soldiers the other.

Question. Was there much fighting then ?

Answer. Not much fighting ; they were small parties. I think Major Downing went out first and destroyed a few lodges, and killed one man and took some of their ponies. I heard immediately that there had been a fight there, and knowing that it is very difficult to keep one party of Indians from fighting when their brethren are at it, I went 240 miles to find the Arapahoes and Cheyennes. I found the former, and explained as well as I could that there had been trouble between some soldiers and Indians, and asked them if they knew anything about the cause of it. They said they did not ; they had not heard of it. They told me at that time that they did not want any trouble with the whites ; that if there had been trouble over there they were not to blame for it. They called those Indians that ran north their dog soldiers. They did not pretend to have much control over them. They pledged me solemnly that if the whites would not follow them up and fight them they would remain peaceable and quiet. Coming back I met a party of Cheyennes and told them the same. They said they would go over towards the Platte and get those Indians in, and get them away. I told them to go over on the Arkansas, their country, and if they behaved them-

115

selves they should be protected as far as I could protect them. The very day that I saw them there another party of soldiers came out from Denver, some of the first Colorado regiment, that were sent out by Colonel Chivington, I suppose, and they followed up these Indians some 200 miles, and came in collision with them over on Smoky Hill, in the buffalo country. They had quite a fight there, the Indians claiming that they were attacked, and the soldiers claiming that they were attacked. I do not know how that was. One of their main chiefs was killed at that time. After that there were depredations committed.

Question By the Indians upon the whites?

Answer. Yes; they came up to work the reservation. Some parties came up, drove in the stock of the contractor, killed two of his men. We supposed at that time the Indians were united against us, that the whole country was going to be at war, and they would unite. Previous to this, however, some Sioux Indians had been laboring with the Cheyennes and Arapahoes to get them to join them, but they disclaimed any idea of it. I got a circular from Governor Evans, in June, requesting me to send out runners and invite all friendly Indians of the Cheyennes and Arapahoes who belonged to the southern bands, as he called them, and to my band, into Fort Lyon, and there feed and protect them. I did so. I sent out one particular Indian who remained there all the while, only as I sent him out. I sent out my interpreter. I sent out Colonel William Bent, who has a wife, a Cheyenne squaw. He has been in that country thirty or forty years. He came back and said that he had seen Black Kettle, the head chief of the Cheyennes, and that they had promised to come in; that they did not want any trouble; were willing to cease hostilities and get all the war parties in that were out and would come up. In the last of September the one-eyed Indian whom I had sent out came in. He said the Indians had three or four white prisoners with them whom they wanted to give up, and if we would go out we could get them. Major Wynkoop went out with a command of 100 men, had an interview with them, brought in their main chief, and brought in four prisoners whom they had, one young lady and three children. They expressed a desire to be friendly. Major Wynkoop went to Denver, took them up to Governor Evans, and had an interview ; I was not present. They came back again; they went out to their lodges towards Smoky Hill ; brought in about 100 lodges of Cheyennes, and about the same number of Arapahoes came into Fort Lyon ; and Major Wynkoop issued them half rations for a time  Soon General Curtis relieved Major Wynkoop, ordered him to report to headquarters at Leavenworth or Fort Riley, I am not sure which, and placed Major Anthony in command, with orders to fight these Indians ; that there could be no peace until they were chastised, as I understood the order. Major Anthony came up, looked the matter over, and said, "It is different from what I expected here ; I supposed these Indians were riding in here making demands, and you were obliged to give in to them. I cannot fight them." He called a council of them. He told them what his orders were, and told them he wanted them to give up their arms and their stolen horses. They came in about two hours, having seen their tribes, and gave up their bows and arrows and perhaps four or five field guns, and a dozen or fifteen government horses and mules ; and he fed them for fifteen days, I think, on prisoners' rations. He considered them his prisoners and gave them prisoners' rations. This continued for some days. Not hearing from General Curtis he got a little afraid, and told them to go down to Sand creek until he heard from General Curtis. They were in frequently ; Black Kettle was in three days before the attack, and Major Anthony and I made up a purse and bought tobacco for them, thinking it was better to keep them peaceable. We had them right there, and there was no use going to fight those Indians at that time, as they were friendly. There they remained till Colonel Chivington came down with his regiment.

Question. When was that?

Answer. It was the 28th of November, 1864, I think.

By Mr. NESMITH :

Question. How many of the Indians were there, and did the number embrace both Cheyennes and Arapahoes?

Answer. About one-half of each tribe were there.

Question. Where were the rest?

Answer. They were, I suppose, on Smoky Hill—I know some of them were—and scattered around through the country.

Question. Were any still up on the emigrant route on the Platte?

Answer. I suppose there might have been some on the Platte. We did not know that Colonel Chivington was coming there until the morning he came in. We had had no mail from Denver for over three weeks, I think. We did not know what trouble there was, and were afraid the Indians had gone off and cut off the settlements above. The evening before he came in some one came down and said he had seen some camp-fires above, and he thought they were the Kioway Indians. He knew they were not our Indians, for if

APPENDIX.

they were they would have come to see him. He came down and reported to the major that camp-fires were there, and he was fearful the Kioway Indians had come in. The major sent out scouts and found that it was Colonel Chivington's command coming from Denver. He came in in the morning, and that evening marched for their camp at 8 o'clock. The results I do not know personally. I was not there

Question. In the mean time did any orders come from General Curtis?

Answer. Not that I know of. I did ask Colonel Chivington that night if there was no hope that peace could be made with these Indians He informed me that General Curtis had telegraphed him that it might be done on certain conditions ; that is to say, they should deliver up property they had stolen, make restitution in ponies for those they had not got, and deliver up their desperadoes who had been making raids.

By Mr. DOOLITTLE :

Question. You think about one-half of the Cheyennes and one-half of the Arapahoes were there in camp ?

Answer. Yes, sir.

Question. Of these, what proportion were of their warriors ?

Answer. I should think an equal portion of their warriors were with them.

By Mr. Ross :

Question. Half of the warriors of the two tribes?

Answer. I should think there were. So far as I know, the young men of the bands who were with them were there. There were warriors, and women and children too.

By Mr. DOOLITTLE :

Question. The warriors belonging to these particular bands were not away ?

Answer. Not to my knowledge. The other Indians, those who were away, were away with their families.

Question. Do they always take their women and children with them ?

Answer. Not always. They leave their women and children when they go out on a war expedition. They were encamped at that time about eighty miles from the others on the Smoky Hill, in the buffalo country.

By Mr. HUBBARD :

Question. When they go on a hunt, do they take their squaws and children ?

Answer. They move their squaws and children to the buffalo country when they go to hunt. When they go on a war party they leave them behind.

By Mr. Ross :

Question. When you speak of a lodge, you mean a family ?

Answer. Yes ; a lodge will contain five on an average. We call a lodge five souls.

By Mr. NESMITH :

Question. Do you know anything about the attack ?

Answer. I was not there. I only know what I heard from officers who were there.

Question. How did you regard those Indians who were in that encampment ?

Answer. I regarded them as at that time friendly.

Question. What had been their conduct previous to that ? Had they been murdering settlers, and robbing, and committing depredations ?

Answer. These Cheyennes had not. They might have had some among them that had been.

Question. Colonel Chivington spoke to you of some desperadoes among the Indians ; did you know of any of that character there ?

Answer. I did not know of any of that character. There might have been some who were out with the Arapahoes. It was said there had been some there that were out.

Question. Was it your understanding that they made restitution of all stolen property prior to the attack ?

Answer. The Arapahoes said they gave up all their government property. I think they had property belonging to citizens which they did not give up.

Question. Did they give up all their arms ?

Answer. I am not able to say. I think it is doubtful whether they did. We did not think, at the time, that they did give up all their arms.

Question. How many guns did they give up?

Answer. But very few. They had not many guns. I thought they had more guns than they brought in and gave up.

117

APPENDIX.

**By Mr. Hubbard :**

Question. Even if these desperate Indians were there among them, you would hardly have known it yourself?

Answer. No ; I did not know who were there, only as the chiefs informed me.

**By Mr. Nesmith :**

Question. Were those Indians, who gave up the young lady and three children, in that encampment?

Answer. One was there and was killed. The other was in the employ of the government at the time.

Question. Do you know that young lady's name?

Answer. Ropers.

**By Mr. Doolittle :**

Question. Did any facts come to your knowledge as to the attack?

Answer. I have heard all the officers repeat it who were there.

Question. Give the current version.

Answer. I can state, according to the received version, that the command marched at 8 o'clock in the evening from Fort Lyon. They attacked the village, which was 30 miles distant, and fired into it about daylight. The Indians, for a while, made some resistance. Some of the chiefs did not lift an arm, but stood there and were shot down. One of them, Black Kettle, raised the American flag, and raised a white flag. He was supposed to be killed, but was not. They retreated right up the creek. They were followed up and pursued and killed and butchered. None denied that they were butchered in a brutal manner, and scalped and mutilated as bad as an Indian ever did to a white man. That is admitted by the parties who did it. They were cut to pieces in almost every manner and form.

Question. How many were killed there, according to the reports?

Answer. I will tell you how I got my information. There was a young half-breed who had been in Kansas. He had been educated here, and came out last summer, for the first time in a good many years, to the Indians. He had been about Fort Lyon a good portion of the summer. When the command came down there, my first impulse was to get him to go up and tell these Indians that the troops were coming up there and might attack them, but he had gone, the day before, out to their camp. He made an attempt to reach the command when they began to fire, but was deterred, fell back and jumped on to a pony, behind a squaw, and rode till he overhauled a drove of ponies that they were driving off. He rode with them to the camp and was with them 14 days after they got together on Smoky Hill. He said there were 148 missing when they got in. After that quite a number came in ; I cannot tell how many. There were eight who came into Fort Lyon to us, reducing it down to about 130 missing, according to the last information I had.

**By Mr. Nesmith :**

Question. Were you on the ground after the battle?

Answer. I was not.

**By Mr. Doolittle :**

Question. Did you understand that any women or children were killed?

Answer. The officers told me they killed and butchered all they came to. They saw little papooses killed by the soldiers. Colonel Shupe was in command of the regiment ; Colonel Chivington in command of the whole force.

**By Mr. Ross :**

Question. Who commanded the troops when this massacre took place?

Answer. Colonel Chivington was in chief command.

**By Mr. Higby :**

Question. Who was in immediate command of the party where the butchery took place? Who led the expedition?

Answer. Colonel Chivington led the expedition. I do not think there was anybody in command ; the soldiers appear to have pitched in without any command.

**By Mr. Nesmith :**

Question. What troops were they, and where were they raised?

Answer. They were the one-hundred-day regiment raised in Denver, with a portion of the first Colorado regiment. The one hundred-day men were Shupe's command as immediate colonel ; Chivington was colonel of the first regiment, and took command of the whole force.

118

# APPENDIX.

### By Mr. DOOLITTLE :

Question. As you learned, was it the first Colorado regiment that joined in this massacre, or was it the one-hundred-day men that were raised ?

Answer. Officers of the first regiment told me they did not fire a gun, and would not or could not ; some of their soldiers undoubtedly did.

Question. Were the men who actually made a rush on the village the one-hundred-day men ?

Answer. That was so understood.

### By Mr. Ross :

Question. Do I understand you that the officers had nothing to do with it ?

Answer. I was told by the officers that Colonel Chivington told the men to remember the wrongs the Indians had inflicted on the whites and to pitch in, and they just went at it pell-mell ; forty of our troops were killed and wounded ; fourteen died. The Indians would get their families ahead of them and then they would fall back, fighting as they went.

### By Mr. DOOLITTLE :

Question. What about the property ?

Answer. From five hundred to six hundred ponies were said to be brought in, having been taken from the Indians, and their whole property was destroyed and they left perfectly destitute without hardly even their clothing.

### By Mr. NESMITH :

Question. Did you see any of the property brought in ?

Answer. Yes, sir.

Question. What did it consist of?

Answer. It consisted of ponies principally, and Indian dresses, and the fixings natural about those wild Indians. They make their dresses out of skins and bead them off very nicely. The dresses were sold for from twenty to thirty dollars the dress.

Question. Was any of this property recognized as property stolen from the whites ?

Answer. There were one or two things I saw that I knew had been stolen.

Question. Was any of the other property recognized as stolen property ?

Answer. I saw a horse or two and a mule or two that were branded other brands than Indians'. Those Indians pick up a great many horses there, and sometimes they bring them in, but sometimes they do not. When they steal a horse their usual custom is to trade it right off to somebody else.

Question. Were there any Mexican dollars among that property ?

Answer I do not know anything about that ; I did not see any ; they might have had some ; I do not know. It must be a mistake to suppose, as has been said, that there were as many Mexican dollars as a mule could carry.

### By Mr. DOOLITTLE :

Question. What is the condition of those tribes now ?

Answer. I have not been able to see any of them, but this young man says they are all imbittered against the whites. He says that Black Kettle, the leading chief, laughed at him when he went out ; said to him, " You are an old fool ; you ought to have stood and been shot down as the rest of us " He made a great deal of fun of him for coming out there and coming under our protection. Two or three of their war councils said they had agreed first to strike the Platte and clean that out, and then strike towards Denver. They told him he had better leave the country there and get home as soon as possible, and furnished him a horse in the night to come home. This was the half-breed who was out this summer, of whom I have spoken.

### By Mr. NESMITH :

Question. What was his name?

Answer. Edward Guerrier ; and Major Wynkoop has his statement in writing, and I suppose it has been forwarded to the War Department.

### By Mr. DOOLITTLE :

Question. What there is left of the tribe that escaped has gone north on to the Platte ?

Answer. I suppose so.

### By Mr. Ross :

Question. Is that outside of the reservation ?

Answer. Yes, sir ; these Indians have not been on the reservation much ; they only come in and see us ; there is no camp there ; they cannot live there ; they have to go out and hunt, for in that country there is no settlement between the Platte and the Arkansas, and

119

none for two hundred and forty miles below us on the Arkansas, and none south of the Platte from us, clear to Texas; it is a buffalo country; they roam there in bands and hunt and come into the agency two or three times a year.

By Mr. DOOLITTLE:

Question. What do you say of the reservation which has been set apart for the Arapahoes and Cheyennes?

Answer. I think we can never get them on to it again; they were killed there on it, and they are superstitious. The reservation is the best tract of land we have in Colorado for agricultural purposes, I think.

By Mr. ROSS:

Question. How is it as to hunting and game?

Answer. There is no hunting there and no game on it, only a few animals. No buffalo have been seen there for three or four years.

By Mr. DOOLITTLE:

Question. From your knowledge of the Arapahoes and Cheyennes and their character, do you think they can be brought to settle down and live a life of agriculture?

Answer. I do not think the present generation can, to any extent. Some few of them want to come in and live with the whites, but as a general thing they are opposed to settling down. They say their fathers hunted, lived, and roamed over the country; the country was all theirs, and they had plenty, but the white man has come and taken it. I think they have gone north now with their families toward the Yellowstone.

Question. Have you an idea that they are uniting with the Sioux?

Answer. I think they are. The Sioux undoubtedly have been wanting them to unite the last two years. They have told me so. They have always disclaimed it and said they would not. They said they did not want to fight; the whites treated them well, and there was no use of their fighting. After the first fight of which I have spoken, they told me that if the whites let them alone they would be peaceable; that there was no object in fighting; but still they said there were young men in the party whom they could not control, which is the fact. The better portion of them cannot control all the young warriors, who are somewhat a political class of men and who make their capital out of their bravery, and if they have no Indians to fight they will fight somebody else.

By Mr. ROSS:

Question. I understood you to say that before this massacre there was a collision, and you could not tell which party commenced it; do you not know who shed blood first?

Answer. I heard officers there say that the Indians commenced it; and I heard others say they did not. I do not know. The Indians say they did not. They said they disarmed it; they came up and shook hands, and took their arms away, and that is like taking their life. That is their notion of it.

By Mr. DOOLITTLE:

Question. How many were in the camp that was attacked?

Answer. About 500. There were only a few lodges of the Arapahoes that were attacked, and before Chivington got there with his command they heard from those who escaped and got away. Only a few of the Arapahoes that were camped with the Cheyennes were attacked—eight lodges. Part of them have now escaped and gone to the Kioways and Comanches, south of Arkansas.

Question. Have you any other statement to make?

Answer. There was a good deal of misunderstanding among us there. At one time we supposed the Indians were all against us, and expected that they were. Indians would come in and try to get into the camp and see us, and see what was the matter, and after we got them in we learned these facts. An Indian whom I had two years ago, who speaks English, rode up to Fort Lyon, and he saw a soldier; he hallooed to that soldier and said he wanted to see Major Colley. He wanted to know what the fighting all meant, and to make peace. The soldier reported that he had been chased by an Indian and saw a number of others. We supposed they were coming to commit depredations and sent a command after them, who overhauled them, and got near enough to fire into them, but not near enough to hurt them. Since he has come in he has told me that he is the Indian who came there to throw down his bow and arrow and talk to me. We did not understand, and supposed he was coming with hostile designs. Then there is another thing. The people of Colorado are very much down on the Indians. As a general thing they want their land. They are coming in contact universally with them. If they take anything to make a fire with, a conflict grows up. My opinion is that white men and wild Indians cannot live in the same country in peace.

120

Question. Are there any of the Indians in Colorado that you know who can be induced to live on and cultivate the soil ?

Answer. I do not know much about the Utes. There is a tribe of Utes over there that I know nothing about. They are west of me in the mountains. I do not know whether they would cultivate the soil or not.

Question. But you think it would be next to impossible to get this generation of these Indians of the plains to settle down to cultivate the soil ?

Answer. I do. They will stay with you if you feed them all the time, and there will be no trouble ; but they will not work. The squaws do all their work that is done.

Question. Do the squaws of these nomadic tribes raise any corn or anything ?

Answer. They do not raise anything. They depend on the buffalo. That is their great staple.

Question. What vegetables, if any, do they eat ?

Answer. They like corn in any way, but they do not raise any. They are fond of pumpkins and potatoes ; they will eat them when you give them to them, but they never raise anything. We attempted to get them to work on the reservation. We laid out a good deal of money in getting a farmer there last spring, and the crops looked very fine until this trouble broke out.

Question. How do you cultivate the crops there on the reservation ; by irrigation ?

Answer. By irrigation. We had 250 acres broken in corn on the Arkansas.

Question. Is it a country where you have no rains during the summer season?

Answer. It rains in July. There are showers almost every day for a month.

Question. Cannot the country be cultivated without irrigation ?

Answer. No, sir. Last season wheat might have been raised without irrigation, but there is no safety in it. As a general thing there is no attempt to raise anything without irrigation.

Question. At what time does the spring open there ?

Answer. Earlier than in Wisconsin. We have but very little snow there. We have late frosts there. We can plant in April or the first of May.

Question. Do you have frosts late enough to injure corn planted as early as that ?

Answer. We have not had.

Question. How early do the frosts come in the fall ?

Answer. About as early as they do in Wisconsin —the last of September or first of October.

Question. With irrigation what productions can you raise : for instance, on the Arapaho and Cheyenne reservation ?

Answer. Wheat, corn, oats, potatoes, barley, all kinds of vegetables.

Question. How is it as to fruit ?

Answer. It has never been tried. Wild fruit is abundant ; plums, wild grapes, and cherries.

Question. Would it be a good country for vines ?

Answer. I think it would.

Question. Which way do your rains come from ?

Answer. Our storms in winter come from the northeast altogether. Our rains are all showers coming from the mountains west and north.

By Mr. NESMITH :

Question. How is this reservation for timber ?

Answer. There is very little of it ; nothing for fencing or building, but enough for firewood. It is cottonwood entirely. There is beautiful stone, as handsome a stone quarry as I have ever seen, there, and plenty all along. We burnt lime last year. It was supposed to be sandstone, but we found it made excellent lime.

By Mr. DOOLITTLE :

Question. Are there any white settlers there ?

Answer. A hundred miles above the reservation it is settled up the Arkansas towards Denver.

By MR. WINDOM:

Question. How far is the reservation from Denver ?

Answer. The head of it is 150 miles.

By Mr. DOOLITTLE :

Question. Are the streams about there plenty ?

Answer. There is hardly any stream that has any running, permanent water.

Question. So that it is only upon the Arkansas that you can irrigate ?

Answer. We cannot on the reservation, except on the Arkansas.

Question. Is the country about there capable of a large settlement, a heavy population, in your opinion?

Answer. It is from the lower end of the reservation to the mountains on those streams. For stock-growing it is the best country I have ever seen. We do not feed at all in winter. The stock keep fat all winter without feeding—those that are not worked.

Question. How is it for sheep?

Answer. There is no finer country in the world for sheep, I think.

Question. Are the winters dry?

Answer. Very dry.

Question. But cold?

Answer. We have some cold days. A snow-storm lasts a day or so, but it is not wet snow; it is dry.

Question. How low does the thermometer go?

Answer. It has been as low as 20 degrees below zero. This winter more than half the time we slept with our doors and windows open. The nights are cool.

Question. So far as health and salubrity are concerned, what do you think of it for a people?

Answer. It cannot be beat in the United States for our white people. There is hardly anybody sick there, and I have known a great many cured of asthma and lung complaints.

Question. What is the nature of the country between this reservation and the Kansas settlements?

Answer. It is rather barren. There is hardly any timber after you get 50 miles below Fort Lyon.

Question. Is that barrenness from a want of rain, or in the nature of the soil itself?

Answer. For want of rain. I say it is barren, although it produces grass. It is a good stock-growing country.

Question. Are there streams sufficient for stock growing purposes?

Answer. On the Arkansas, and as you go north on the Republican and the Smoky Hill, you find water there, and between that and the Platte.

Question. Do you think that all that country which we generally call the plains is adapted to a pastoral people and large stock-growing?

Answer. No doubt of it.

Question. And will hold a tolerably dense population?

Answer. It takes more country to grow stock there, than it would in Wisconsin. You could have larger establishments.

By Mr. Higby:

Question. You say that through winter, stock lives well?

Answer. Yes, sir.

Question. When do the grasses of which you speak spring? Through what months do they grow, and when do they mature?

Answer. They commence in April. The grasses on the high lands generally mature in July, or soon after the rains. That which we call the buffalo and the gramma grass, the bunch grass here, is a different grass from any I have seen in the western country. They spring a little earlier than in other places.

Question. I understand you that there is no rain except in July?

Answer. I have known some in the fore part of August, but generally July is the rainy month.

Question. Then at the time your grasses spring there are no rains?

Answer. None.

Question. Is not that a natural vegetation?

Answer. It appears to be natural to that country; it grows every year.

Question. Do you say a crop cannot be raised annually with the season without irrigation?

Answer. They say that when the white man settles up a country it rains more.

Question. Have you tested it with the natural season by putting in agricultural seeds at the time of the springing of the natural vegetation?

Answer. They have done so about Denver and above me, and sometimes they raise a crop and sometimes they do not.

By Mr. Doolittle:

Question. Is there any coal on the Arapaho reservation?

Answer. Yes, sir; plenty of it on Sand creek. General Pierce, the surveyor general of the Territory, informed me that as he struck the creek he saw plenty of coal.

Question. What would you suggest or propose to do with these Indians?

Answer. My opinion is that they might have a hearing; that we might get at them in

3

APPENDIX

some way, and if we could make them believe what we told them they would be willing to go to some other country. There is a large country south of the Arkansas, between there and Texas, where the Kioways and Comanches roam. The Arapahoes might go there; I think the Cheyennes would want to go where they came from, towards the Sioux.

Question. Are the Arapahoes and the Comanches and Kioways friendly?
Answer. Yes, sir.
Question. Do they speak the same language?
Answer. Not the same language, but they can understand each other.
Question. Have they ever lived or hunted together?
Answer. They have always hunted together and have intermarried.
Question. What is your suggestion as to the best thing to be done with them?
Answer. It was my opinion after this affair that they would have to be annihilated; that we could not get at them; but Colonel Leavenworth tells me that he has seen the Kioways and Comanches, and they are willing yet to come into terms of peace and arrangement.
Question. Is there any other fact or suggestion which you desire to make in relation to the matter?
Answer. The only fact is that, as I told you, the Colorado people are very much opposed to having peace with these Indians. It is almost as much as a man's life is worth to speak friendly of an Indian, and for that reason I do not believe they can live in that country.

By Mr. HUBBARD:

Question. From what does that feeling arise? Does it arise from the depredations and murders which the Indians have committed heretofore, or is it a natural antipathy which the whites there have against Indians?
Answer. There was a natural antipathy, and then the depredations and murders they have committed this year have outraged the people, and they think an Indian ought to be killed anyhow. It is my opinion that they cannot be got on to that reservation again. It is a pity the work was commenced there. Some came and complained that the government had not complied with treaty stipulations in building houses and completing the farm, and we were induced to commence last year.

By Mr. HIGBY:

Question From what you gathered, from all the information you received, did it seem to be a general desire among those engaged in the expedition to make the slaughter, or were they inflamed to it by some of their leaders?
Answer. The officers at Fort Lyon were opposed to going out, and represented to Colonel Chivington that they considered any men who would go out to fight those Indians, knowing the circumstances as they knew them, to be cowards.
Question. Did they so express themselves to Chivington and those men?
Answer. Yes, sir.
Question. What answer, if any, was given?
Answer. Chivington threatened to put the officers under arrest. That was the answer, I believe.
Question. Were the officers who made those remarks officers of his command who did finally go with him?
Answer. Some of them did finally go with him. They said that at Fort Lyon before they started.

By Mr. DOOLITTLE:

Question. In addition to your business as Indian agent, have you been prosecuting any other business there, and any private business, farming, or anything of that sort?
Answer. None at all. My son is settled there; he went there in 1859, and put up some hay at Fort Lyon last summer.
Question. What has been usually the amount of annuities or presents that have passed through your hands to these Indians?
Answer. The treaty of 1851 gave them about $17,000—I think that was the amount of it—in presents for the right of way through their country. In 1861 they made a permanent treaty and this reservation was assigned to them. By that treaty, under the direction of the Interior Department, they were to have $30,000 a year for fifteen years, to be expended in improvements, opening farms, building houses, and so on. Whether any of that has been given to them in goods or not, I do not know. We still continue to give them under the first treaty, which is not yet out, about $17,000 in the shape of presents.
Question. Of that appropriation of $17,000 a year, how much actually gets to and reaches the Indians and is distributed among them?
Answer. The whole of it, so far as I know; all that comes to me does.

123

Question. But where are the purchases made?

Answer. In New York, and the goods are shipped to Colorado.

Question Shipped by the overland route?

Answer. Contracts are made, and they are shipped by freighters from Atchison to Colorado. The bills of lading are sent on. The prices of the goods seem fair.

Question. How do they compare with the prices of the goods as sold in the markets of Colorado?

Answer. ·A great deal less than goods sold there.

Question. Are they furnished to the Indians cheaper than they could be purchased of dealers in Colorado?

Answer. A great deal cheaper.

### By Mr. HUBBARD:

Question. Of what descriptions are the goods?

Answer. Blankets, sugar, coffee, flour, and some kinds of cloths, calicoes, and so on.

Question. Is much hardware sent out?

Answer. Not a great deal.

Question. Trinkets?

Answer. Yes; generally a little paint and a few beads.

### By Mr. ROSS:

Question. Who fixes the prices?

Answer. I understand that the money is laid out in New York, and the government transports the goods to the Indians free of expense to them. The transportation does not come out of the annuities; it is let by contract.

### By Mr. DOOLITTLE:

Question. The goods are purchased in New York, and the transportation is let by the government by contract?

Answer. Yes; the government contracts for hauling them to the agency.

### By Mr. NESMITH:

Question. Have you been in the habit of receiving goods there for disbursement yourself?

Answer. I have received two parcels since I have been there. Last year I received none for these Indians.

Question. Have you ever made a requisition on the department here for goods?

Answer. Yes; every year I consult the Indians and see what they want, and make a requisition on the government, and send it on here.

### By Mr. ROSS:

Question. You spoke of a price being fixed; is that the price of the goods when given by the government to the Indians?

Answer. I understand they have so much money to be expended for them, and the money is laid out in New York, and the goods are transported by the government.

Question. Then the goods would only be for distribution; there would be no price to be fixed?

Answer. There is no price fixed on the goods; we just give them to the Indians. When they come on I generally take them out of the wagons and tell the chiefs to give them to whom they belong, and they divide them up among their families.

### By Mr. NESMITH:

Question. Have the goods generally been furnished according to the requisition you made?

Answer. Sometimes they say it is too large, and costs too much money.

Question. I mean in kind; do they send you what you ask for?

Answer. Yes, sir; they send the same articles.

### By Mr. DOOLITTLE:

Question. As an illustration of the prices, what do blankets cost apiece out there?

Answer. So far as my knowledge extends, and I have seen the prices, they have been furnished cheaper than they could be bought there. Blue blankets, three-point as they call them, that Indians want, used to come at about $12 a pair in New York; I think they are higher now. They send out a good blanket; it is different from a soldier's blanket. I used to look over to see how the prices compared, and I always thought the prices were no higher than the goods were bought at.

Question. What kind of blankets did you get in fact?

Answer. Good blankets; I think the price two years ago—there were none sent last year—was $12 a pair. Since the trouble broke out it has not been safe to send them.

By Mr. Ross :

Question. Did those Indians get anything last year?
Answer. Nothing at all.

By Mr. Doolittle :

Question. What was the occasion of that?
Answer. I suppose on account of the troubles, and because they were fighting the whites there. The articles sent are good fair articles.
Question. What does it cost a pound to get sugar there to the Indians?
Answer. The contract for freights was low. Two years ago I think it was five or six cents a pound. Freights now are higher than that.

By Mr. Nesmith :

Question. What is the difference between the contract price the government pays and private freight?
Answer. It was no higher than private freights, but generally lower, I think. I believe the freights on Indian goods were less than on soldiers' goods. I do not remember the amounts.

By Mr. Doolittle :

Question. What has been spent of the money provided by the treaty?
Answer About $20,000 has been expended in breaking up the land and building a house and warehouse at the reservation on the Arkansas, and for an acequia. Whether there has been any of that expended in goods sent out there I do not know.
Question. You think the Indians really will never live on the reservation?
Answer. I do not believe we can get them to live there now.
Question. What kind of a building has been made there?
Answer They built a house for a blacksmith, that was about completed; then they were to build a house for the agent, and in that house there was to be a council-room, and also a store or warehouse, and that is about up to the windows. It is made of stone. It remains unfinished. They have broken the windows out of the blacksmith's house and out of the blacksmith's shop which was built. About 250 acres, or a little over, were broken up. The acequia was built also. We had a fine crop of corn there, which would have produced well if it had been taken care of.

By Mr. Ross :

Question. Was it contemplated that the Indians themselves would work the land?
Answer. It was thought some would come in to work. We thought we could get some of them in to learn. The object was to teach and show them how to work.

Jesse H. Leavenworth sworn and examined.

By Mr. Doolittle :

Question. Have you lived in Colorado?
Answer. Yes, sir.
Question. For what length of time?
Answer. I went to Colorado in 1860, and I was there until 1862, when I was authorized to raise the second regiment of Colorado volunteers, and was there till the fall of 1863 in command of that regiment on the frontier.
Question. What is about your age?
Answer. Near fifty.
Question. Are you the son of General Leavenworth?
Answer. Yes, sir ; of General Henry Leavenworth, of the United States army.
Question. Did you graduate at West Point?
Answer. I did.
Question. During your father's lifetime, when he was in command upon the frontier, did you become well acquainted with Indian life and character on the border?
Answer. I did.
Question. During your stay in Colorado and since, have you become acquainted with the Cheyennes, Arapahoes, Kioways, Comanches, and Apaches?
Answer. Yes, sir ; I believe I have a thorough acquaintance with each and every one of those tribes.
Question. Do you speak the language?
Answer. No, sir ; I do not speak their language, but I talk with them by signs, more or less. I have no difficulty in communicating with them.
Question. From the best information you have, what do you estimate to be the number of the Arapahoes?

*Answer.* I think there is not to exceed from 1,500 to 1,700 of them. There is a band of Arapahoes that claim not to be connected with those of the Upper Arkansas—the North Platte Arapahoes. With that band I am not much acquainted ; but with the Arapahoes of the Upper Arkansas, who have a reservation with the Cheyennes at Fort Lyon, I am well acquainted. I think there are about 2×0 lodges of them—that is the number I have counted many times—and I think there are from 1,500 to 1,700 of them, all told, men, women, and children.

*Question.* How many of the Cheyennes?

*Answer.* I have supposed there was about the same number, with the addition of eighty lodges of what are called Dog Soldiers, who have never associated much with the Indians of the Arkansas, but have kept aloof from them.

*Question.* What is the character of those who are called the Dog Soldiers?

*Answer.* They are a warlike, high-minded, savage people. They separated from the others on account of the Fort Lyon reservation, with which they were dissatisfied. They went north, and said they would never live on the reservation. They were dissatisfied with the treaty and went off on to the Smoky Hill, and kept between the Smoky Hill and the Powder river.

*Question.* How many of the Kioways do you estimate that there are ?

*Answer.* I think there is just about the same number of them as there is of Cheyennes and of Arapahoes. I do not think there is much difference ; there may be a hundred either way. There are from 1,500 to 1,700 of them.

*Question.* How many Apaches?

*Answer.* Forty lodges, and they average from four to five to a lodge.

*Question.* What is the character of the Apaches?

*Answer.* The Apaches are a small band of docile Indians dependent on their neighbors for protection. They first associated with the Arapahoes, but they thought the Arapahoes were not strong enough to protect them, and they separated from them and now run mostly with the Kioways, more for protection than anything else. They are led partly by the Kioways. For two years that I was in command of the southwestern frontier they would look upon the trains, but I never heard of any depredations committed. They would beg, but they would not do any wrong. They apparently felt their weakness and did not like to get into any trouble.

*Question.* What is the number of the Comanches ?

*Answer.* There are nine bands of Comanches. Eight of them are what we call Union Comanches ; the ninth band is the southern Comanches, residing in Texas, who are friendly with the Texans. I know that eight of the bands are friendly to the United States ; the ninth band has never been north.

*Question.* How many of them are there ?

*Answer.* I cannot state the exact number, but from the best information I can get they average from 500 to 700 warriors to a band. The old men, women, and children will average from three to five to each warrior. Mawwee has the largest band. It is a band composed mostly of young men. He has about 700 warriors, the largest band of all.

*Question.* You think, then, there would be about 3,500 souls in the largest bands, and that there are nine bands of them ; would your estimate be that they amount altogether to about 30,000 ?

*Answer.* Not so many as that—from eighteen to twenty thousand, all told. I should like to state where I get most of my information about the Comanches. In 1834 my father went into the Comanche country with General Dodge, afterwards Governor Dodge, of Wisconsin, the commanding officer of the 1st regiment of dragoons. My father was the second officer in command. He went there to form a treaty, under General Jackson's orders, with the Comanches. On that expedition he died. He had with him a man by the name of Jesse Chisom, as guide and interpreter. Jesse Chisom has been with these Indians almost all the time since. He has been upon that frontier ; he has traded with them ; he speaks their language perfectly ; and he is now my guide and interpreter for these Indians, and has helped me more since last fall than any one else in keeping them quiet and protecting them. His information in regard to them is perfect and complete, and I get most of my information from him. I have had a great deal to do myself with many of the bands, but my information is principally from him.

*Question.* Are all these bands, the Cheyennes, Arapahoes, Apaches, Kioways, and Comanches, of the nomadic tribes ?

*Answer.* They are. They all live in lodges and move from place to place constantly over the plains. Wherever the grass fails them they remove to some other point. Where game is plenty they stay, and when it becomes scarce they move to some other point. They are the wild Arabs of America.

*Question.* Have the Comanches many horses?

*Answer.* A great many.

Question. In their movements do they go on foot or on horseback?

Answer. On horseback. A Comanche never moves except on horse, unless he is compelled to do so.

Question. Are they fine horsemen?

Answer. Splendid. There are no better horsemen in the world. They ride from the moment they can sit up straight. They are tied on the horse by the mother and the mother leads the horse, and that is the way they move from place to place.

Question. Are the Comanches a warlike people?

Answer. The most warlike we have on the continent, I think. They have fought the Texans for a great many years. Since the massacre at San Antonio—I do not remember in what year that was—they have been constantly at war with the Texans, and they are at war with them now. They have a great many Mexicans with them now as prisoners and servants or slaves.

Question. State the disposition of the Kioways, Comanches, and Apaches towards the United States at the present time.

Answer. Last summer I was appointed agent for the Kioways, Comanches, and Apaches, with instructions by the Indian department to meet them and to preserve peace between them and the United States, if possible. Owing to business outside of that I was unable to reach my agency until October. In October I arrived at Council Grove, the last town there is on the verge of civilization in the western part of Kansas. The Kioways, or the wild tribes, I cannot tell who they were, had ranged down within twenty miles of Council Grove last summer; had driven off stock and killed it, but committed no murders. General Curtis, a short time before that, had issued an order that no Indian should approach a military post. My headquarters were at Fort Larned, 240 miles east of Fort Lyon. Knowing that no Indian could approach Fort Larned, and having been in command of that frontier, and knowing all the chiefs and a great many of the braves of the Indian tribes, I felt very anxious to get in communication with them. To do it, it was impossible for me to go into their country with soldiers, because I could not approach any Indian in that way; and if I went alone, they, not knowing who was coming towards them, would of course ambush me; so that it was a very dangerous business. I therefore went south, down on to the Osage lands, where there were bands of Towacaros, Wacos, Keitchies, Wichitas, and Caddoes. These were Indians who had been run out of Texas some years ago, and when this war broke out were called refugee Indians. They had had more or less communication with the Comanches and were most of them very friendly with them. I went to them for the purpose of getting runners to go into the Comanche country and communicate with them, which was the only safe way I had to get to them. I made arrangements for some fifteen or twenty to go out. They started out and were gone a few days, and came back and said they had met some Osages, and the Osages had six spare horses and told them that they had killed six Comanches, and that if they, living on the Osage lands, went out the Comanches would kill them, and they did not dare to go. Before I could get another party started, the massacre at Fort Lyon, under Colonel Chivington, occurred, and then the Indians refused to go at all. They said there was treachery on the part of the whites, and if they went and anything should occur they would be blamed. I had some old acquaintances with the Caddoes. One was Jim Parkman, the chief, who was a very excellent, good man. He told them that he was well acquainted with me, and had been for a number of years; that whatever I might say they might rely upon; it was all straight. I finally succeeded in getting the Waco chief, with three or four of his brothers, two Towacaros, and a Keitchi to go out. They were gone twenty days, and came in with 96 Kioways and Comanches, and 9 Arapahoes that had escaped from Colonel Chivington's massacre. Little Raven's band of Arapahoes got away and six Apaches. When they came in and found who wanted to see them, they told me that they did not want to fight the whites, and had no wish to fight them, but were compelled to go to war. They said they would agree not to go into the Santa Fé road; they would not molest any more white men; they would get all the Indians together and meet me in four weeks and make a peace, and it should be a permanent peace; they did not want a war, but if the whites were determined to fight them on the Santa Fé road or above, they would join hands with the Texans, and go south. I agreed to meet them in four weeks. I came out to Council Grove, and from there to Fort Riley, and saw Colonel Ford, who commands the district. He at once agreed with me that it was right to make peace with them and stop the war. He sent my letter that I addressed to him to General Dodge, at St. Louis, who commanded the department, and telegraphed to him. General Dodge telegraphed back to Colonel Ford that the military have no authority to make peace with Indians; their duty is to make them keep peace by punishing them for hostility; and to keep posted as to their location, so that when they were ready they could strike them. Having been down there as a white man, and almost the only white man that had spoken to these Indians for nearly eight or ten months, I felt that I was doing wrong to the red man to get him to stop his war and then let the whites jump upon him, as Colonel Chivington had upon the Cheyennes, and I immediately started for Washington, in hopes that the military might be stopped and that the Indians might be protected. They do not want a war; they do not want to fight the whites; they want to be let alone.

Question. Have you a copy of the order of General Dodge?

Answer. I have. I have not a copy of my letter to Colonel Ford. I gave it to Colonel Ford for some purpose. I do not remember for what he wanted it.

Question. Will you please read General Dodge's telegraph?

Answer. It is—

"FEBRUARY 23, 1865.

"[By telegraph from St. Louis.]

"To Colonel Ford, Fort Riley:

"The military have no authority to treat with Indians. Our duty is to make them keep the peace by punishing them for their hostility. Keep posted as to their location, so that as soon as ready we can strike them. 400 horses arrived here for you.

"G. M. DODGE, Major General."

I will say that, with all the information I can get, I have not learned that the Comanches have raised a hand hostile to the whites the past season. I know from report that Mawwee and Little Buffalo, the two leading chiefs of two bands, were at Fort Larned at the time the outbreak occurred between the Kioways and the post, and they immediately took their bands and went south, and I have no evidence that any Comanche has been north of the Arkansas this summer; I do not believe any of them have been. In conversation with General Curtis when I first got there, he told me that he did not think the Comanches had committed any depredations, and I do not think they have. I cannot learn that they have committed a single depredation. I think that all the depredations have been committed by Kiowas and Cheyennes, with the Sioux from the north, and probably some Arapahoes, but I do not believe that any of the bands as a tribe have been united in a general war.

Question. Suppose that yourself and Major Colley were authorized to go out and meet these Indians and to make some presents to show the amicable feelings of the United States, rather than hostile feelings on the part of the government, do you believe you could reach them in a way to negotiate or to come to peace with them without any further hostilities?

Answer. In 1862 I was in command of the Santa Fé road from the Great Bend of the Arkansas to the Rattoon mountains, a distance of nearly 700 miles. I was sent there by General Blunt, with all the force at my command, to protect the frontier. I had 102 infantry and one section of artillery, and these were recruits. There were 18 men, all told, at Fort Lyon at the time I arrived there. Major Colley was then the Indian agent. I arrived there about the last of June. I had occasion to go south to Santa Fé to co-operate with General Canby, and I got back to Fort Lyon on the 31st of July. On the 1st day of August Major Colley received an express from Fort Larned saying that the Kioways, Comanches, Apaches, Arapahoes, and Cheyennes were in full force at Fort Larned, and that they had corralled a government train of goods, and asking for re-enforcements. I had no men that I could send. I started with Major Colley and his interpreter, and I went to Fort Larned and found that there was not one dozen of those Indians with whom I was acquainted; they were strangers to me. With the assistance of Major Colley and John Smith, the interpreter, in three days' time I had every one of those Indians off to their hunting-grounds, and the train was started under an escort of twenty men and went through to Fort Lyon, with the Indians camping almost every night around it, in perfect safety; and for two years those Indians never committed a depredation that I know of, and neither the government nor any individual lost a dollar by them. I left there in October, and the outbreak occurred in May following. I have not seen these Indians since I left there, until the 15th of February. I know them well. When I met them they agreed at once to quit hostilities. They said they did not want to fight; that I might make the road and they would travel it. I feel now that I can say with safety that I can go to them with Major Colley, and in thirty days the war will be ended, and it will save millions of money. I say it also because Major Whalley, of the regular army, wrote, last spring, to the department that if Colonel Chivington was not stopped in his course the government would be involved in a war that would cost millions of money. It has occurred. I told the department, last spring, that if Lieutenant Ayres was not stopped in hunting the Cheyennes from camp to camp they would get into a war. It has come. I know all the chiefs and a great many of the braves; I know them to be kind-hearted. I know there are bad men among them, but I know the Cheyennes so well that I am satisfied they can rule those bad men, and there is no necessity for this war. If the soldiers are stopped from hunting the Indians, I will guarantee peace in thirty days, and I will not ask $50,000 to do it with. They want to know that their Great Father will protect them. They want some man that they have confidence in to say that they shall be righted. They never came to me with a complaint that I did not right them if possible.

Question. As our white men are going and gathering into that country, and travelling all around about it, is not the game becoming scarcer ?

Answer. It is.

Question. As the game diminishes, what do you suggest is to be done with the wild hunting Indians?

Answer. There is the finest country in the world for agricultural purposes south of the Arkansas, on the Red river, near Fort Cobb and the Wichita mountains, on the north fork of the Red river, where they can live and raise almost anything they want It is now literally alive with cattle. They can go there now, and if the whites are kept away from them, with the abundance of cattle they can live without coming in contact with the whites All along under the Staked Plain, in the northern part of Texas and eastern New Mexico, there is fine water and fine grazing.

Question. What is your opinion, based on your practical knowledge and experience of this matter? What would you advise the government to do ?

Answer. I would advise them to let some individual in whom these Indians have confidence go there and tell them that they shall be protected ; take them down south, where I have got Kioways, Comanches, and two bands of Arapahoes now, and let them remain there. I think the Cheyennes can be induced to go down there ; but they will never go on to their reservation again.

Question. Do you think the Kioways and Comanches who live down there would be willing to let the Arapahoes and Cheyennes go among them ?

Answer. Yes. sir ; they would have no objection The head chief of the Arapahoes is a half-Comanche ; he speaks the Comanche language just the same as he does the Arapaho.

Question. From your knowledge of all these tribes of Indians, do you think they could be induced to abandon the hunter's life and live by pasturage or by cultivation of the soil ?

Answer. They cannot at present. They may live by grazing, and gradually come into it ; but at present it would be out of the question.

Question. They would be like the Arabs in that respect ?

Answer. Yes ; they would have to come to it gradually, and they may come to raising cattle, and as the buffalo disappeared begin upon the beef. I think they would make excellent graziers.

Question. Do you mean that they should be put in that part of Kansas, as well as the Indian Territory and Texas, that lies south of the Arkansas ?

Answer. I would not bring them anywhere near Kansas if I could help it. There is a little band of refugee Indians called the Caddoes, who, when the rebellion broke out, were driven from Fort Cobb up north and came in almost to Fort Lyon. They came in destitute, freezing, and almost perishing. They brought a few cattle with them, a few hens, a few pigs, and a few calves. Major Colley received them. They were loyal ; they were half-civilized ; they lived in houses ; and a better set of men I never met in my life, well-disposed, kind-hearted. They are like the Pueblos of Mexico. They were more than half-civilized. Their women dressed in long dresses, the same as our American women do ; they made good bread ; everything was neat and clean about them. They lived at Fort Larned. The government gave them $5,000 annuity two years ago. Last year the government authorized me to issue to them some goods to the amount of $5,000. I found them at the mouth of the Arkansas river. Last year they lost over 100 by small-pox. There were only 425 of them when they first came up. Parkman, their head chief, is one of the most intelligent men I ever met ; he is correct in every particular. He told me that he could not live on the borders there ; that the whites were stealing his horses all the time, and he moved across the Arkansas, on to what is called the Minisqua, and they followed him over there and stole quite a number of his horses there. He then moved on to the Chickasaqua. Since this Chivington massacre he has become alarmed, and he is now living with his little band away down between the Salt Plains and the Brushy mountains, as near Texas as he can go. Parkman, if he dared to return to the rebel States to-morrow, would be killed ; he dare not return there, and he dare not come back here, the whites abuse him so and steal his horses. He has nothing left but a few ponies, and his men are suffering ; they are dying almost every day from small-pox. John Leonard, the doctor and priest, died since I left, and his wife too. This is an illustration of the way they are treated.

129

# APPENDIX.

WASHINGTON, *Wednesday, March* 8, 1865.

John S. Smith sworn and examined.

By Mr. DOOLITTLE :

Question. What is your age?
Answer. I was born in December, 1810.
Question. How long have you lived in the country west of Kansas, in Colorado?
Answer. I went to that country first in 1830.
Question. Do you know the language of the Arapahoes and Cheyennes?
Answer. I do that of the Cheyennes.
Question. Have you acted as interpreter for the Indian agent to the Cheyennes?
Answer. I have.
Question. Were you in the Indian camp of the Cheyennes when Colonel Chivington made his attack upon it?
Answer. I was.
Question. State when it was.
Answer. I left Fort Lyon for the Cheyenne village on the 26th of November; on the 27th I reached the village; on the 28th I remained there; and on the 29th the attack was made.
Question. How many Indians were there in camp?
Answer. I think about 500, men, women, and children.
Question. What number of warriors or men?
Answer. About 200. They will average two warriors to a lodge, and there were 100 lodges.
Question. What portion of the Cheyenne tribe was that?
Answer. The southern band, led by the main chief of the nation, Black Kettle.
Question. Where was the northern band at this time?
Answer. They were supposed to be over on the North Platte, between the North Platte and the Smoky Hill.
Question. What time in the day or night was the attack made?
Answer. Between daybreak and sunrise.
Question. State now the circumstances of the attack; just describe them in brief words.
Answer. As soon as the troops were discovered, very early in the morning, about daybreak, the Indians commenced flocking to the head chief's lodge, about the camp where I was—the camp over on Sand creek; it is called Big Sandy, about forty miles northeast of Fort Lyon. When the attack was made the Indians flocked around the camp of the head chief and he ran out his flag. He had a large American flag which was presented to him, I think, by Colonel Greenwood some years ago, and under this American flag he had likewise a small white flag.
Question. Was it light, so that the flags could be plainly seen?
Answer. Yes; they could be plainly seen.
Question. How long was this before any firing was heard?
Answer. A very few minutes; they were but a short time coming into camp after they were first discovered. They came on a charge. When I first saw them they were about three-quarters of a mile from the camp, and then the flag was run up by Black Kettle.
Question. Go on and state what occurred.
Answer. The firing commenced on the northeast side of Sand creek; that was near Black Kettle's lodge. The men, women, and children rushed to the upper end of the village, and ran to the lodge of another chief at the other end, War Bonnet.
Question. Were the Indians then armed?
Answer. Some of them were; some of them left their arms in their lodges; some few picked up their bows and arrows and lances as they left their lodges; the younger men did.
Question. Did they form in any battle array or with a view to oppose the charge?
Answer. No, sir; they just flocked in a promiscuous herd, men, women, and children together. The bed of Sand creek ran right up; there was little or no water in it at this place. Then they came to some breaks in the banks about where the troops overtook them, and the slaughter commenced; I suppose about three hundred yards above the main village. White Antelope was the first Indian killed, within a hundred yards of where I was in camp at the time. They fought them from very early in the morning, as I have stated, until about eleven o'clock that day before they all got back together in camp. The troops then returned to the Indian village, followed the Indians up the creek two or three miles firing on them, then returned back to the Indian camp and destroyed everything there was there—the entire village of one hundred lodges. I had a son there, a half-breed; he gave himself up. In this stampede of the Indians he started to go with them,

130

but when he found there was a fair show for him he turned around and came back to our camp where the troops were. I made several efforts to get to the troops, but was fired on myself by our own troops. My son stayed in the camp of our soldiers one day and a night, and then was shot down by the soldiers. My life was threatened, and they had to put a guard around me to save my life.

Question. After you surrendered to the troops?

Answer. Yes, sir.

Question. How many were killed?

Answer. I think about seventy or eighty, including men, women, and children, were killed; twenty-five or thirty of them were warriors probably, and the rest women, children, boys, and old men.

Question. Were any Indian barbarities practiced?

Answer. The worst I have ever seen.

Question. What were they in fact?

Answer. All manner of depredations were inflicted on their persons; they were scalped, their brains knocked out; the men used their knives, ripped open women, clubbed little children, knocked them in the head with their guns, beat their brains out, mutilated their bodies in every sense of the word.

Question. Do you know which troops those were that actually did this work; whether they were the hundred-day men who came from Denver, or the regular first Colorado regiment?

Answer. I am not able to say; they were all in a body together, between eight hundred and one thousand men I took them to be. It would be hard for me to tell who did these things; I saw some of the first Colorado regiment committing some very bad acts there on the persons of Indians, and I likewise saw some of the one-hundred-day men in the same kind of business.

Question. You say the troops pursued the Indians until about eleven o'clock, the Indians fleeing all the while?

Answer. Yes, sir.

Question. When they came back to the Indian village were there any of the Indians there, men, women, or children, left?

Answer. No, sir; they were all gone except a few children who came into our camp an hour after we had all returned to this Indian camp. There were a couple of women there, white men's women, Indian women who had married white men, and they were not hurt. I think there were seven in number saved from the entire village, women and children, and they were taken to Fort Lyon.

Question. When those Indians were there in camp do you know in what relation they were to our forces at Fort Lyon?

Answer. Yes, sir; some of them had just returned from an interview with Governor Evans and Colonel Chivington at Denver city. We had seven of the chiefs up there with us at Denver city; I went as interpreter with them. They returned and were sent out for their families to move in near Fort Lyon, where they could be protected and taken care of; they were told that if the troops from Denver city or the Platte should meet them over in that direction they would probably hurt them, and it was supposed they would be better off in the vicinity of Fort Lyon, where they could be watched, than out further north, and they went there with all the assurances in the world of peace promised by the commanding officer, Major Wynkoop.

Question. Did he, in the mean time, issue some rations to them?

Answer. Yes, sir.

Question. Did they, so far as you know, remain there?

Answer. They did.

Question. And you, as interpreter of the United States, were in camp with them?

Answer. I was in camp with them at the time.

Question. Had this band, so far as you know, committed any depredations on our people after this interview at Denver?

Answer. None that I heard of; I heard of none until after this raid of Colonel Chivington.

Question. From your knowledge of these Indians, and all about them, and of that place which is set apart as their reservation, do you think they can be brought to settle down upon that Cheyenne reservation?

Answer. Yes, sir; with diligent workers there with them it could be done in some time; probably it would take all summer to do it.

Question. Do you think those Indians could be induced to leave off their wild hunting life and go into agricultural pursuits or the raising of cattle?

Answer. Not all of them; there are a few that are best acquainted with the whites who would be willing to do it; they have told us so; I think that in time, with encouragement, they could be brought to it. I have been twenty-seven successive years with the Cheyennes myself.

Question. During those twenty-seven years how have they been as a tribe generally towards our citizens?

Answer. They have been very peaceable until quite recently. In 1857 they had some trouble over on the Platte, but I never understood the particulars of it; that was when Colonel Sumner went out and had a little fight with them, but they came to immediately, and from that time until about twelve months ago, when they had a falling out with white settlers in the vicinity of Denver and below Denver on the Platte, they were peaceable; but this thing has been growing ever since that time, until Chivington made this raid. They have been followed up from the Platte to the Smoky Hill, and from the Smoky Hill to the Arkansas, and south of the Arkansas river; they went clear over south of Salt Springs, where Colonel Leavenworth is acquainted. Governor Evans then issued some circulars that were taken to them there, and explained to them that if they wanted to return in peace they could do so; that those who were friendly disposed could return to their reservation. As soon as they learned this, the body of them returned. This band that I speak of, that purchased some white prisoners from the Sioux and some of the northern band of Cheyennes, sent us word at Fort Lyon that if we would go out to them they would turn them over to us. I went with Major Wynkoop there as his interpreter, and they turned over four of them, whom they had got from the Sioux and from the northern band of Cheyennes

Question. Even now what is your opinion? Do you think, for instance, that if persons like Major Colley, yourself, or Colonel Leavenworth were to go to these Indians now, peaceable relations could be established between them and the United States, notwithstanding all that has occurred?

Answer I say yes; I think so from the fact that they never wanted to fight the whites. They have lost certainly a great deal of the confidence that they used to have in the white man, but with proper exertions I think they might be brought back, with correct assurances.

Question. Did they have many ponies and horses?
Answer. Yes, sir.
Question. How many were taken away from them?
Answer. About six hundred head.
Question. And all their lodges?
Answer. Everything they had.
Question. These lodges of theirs are made of skins?
Answer. Of buffalo hides; a lodge is made after the pattern of a Sibley tent; when they move from one place to another they take their tents or lodges with them.
Question. Would you feel yourself any personal apprehensions if you were sent to go among them and converse with them?
Answer. I would not like to go without some Indian protectors; I could get some of our other friendly Indians and would readily go with them, sending them on probably as runners ahead of me, so as to let them know my business, and then I would not feel at all apprehensive of losing my life.
Question. But you think the result has been such that now they would kill any white man they should see.
Answer. Yes, sir; anybody.
Question. What is the number of the Cheyennes?
Answer. There are about four hundred and eighty or five hundred lodges, and they will average five souls to a lodge; there are about two thousand five hundred Cheyennes altogether; this includes the northern band.
Question. Is the northern band the same that are commonly called the Dog soldiers?
Answer. No, sir; the Dog soldiers are mixed up promiscuously; this is a band that has preferred the North Platte and north of the North Platte, and lives over in what is called the bad land, *mauvais terre.*
Question. How long have you been with these Indians?
Answer. Since I went there I have resided with these Indians off and on every year; I have generally been employed as United States interpreter; prior to that I was a trader in that country for St. Vrain & Co., and in that way I first learned the Cheyenne language.

John Evans sworn and examined.

By Mr. DOOLITTLE:

Question. Are you governor of the Territory of Colorado?
Answer. I am.
Question. How long have you been in that Territory?
Answer. Since the spring of 1862. I went there in May of that year.

Question. What is the state of the Indian tribes generally in your Territory at this time?

Answer. There are three tribes or bands of Utes which are in the mountains west of us, the Tabahuaches, the Uintas, and the Yampah or Bear River Indians. These Indians have not committed any depredations since the summer of 1863. They committed depredations upon the overland stage line between Denver and Salt lake at that time. In fact, they attacked a party of soldiers who went after them to procure some stock stolen from the stage stations, and killed two or three of the soldiers. I think the Indians did not get worsted any; perhaps one or two were wounded, but they made their escape with the stock, a portion of which, however, has since been returned by them.

Question. What is the condition of the Tabahuache bands?

Answer. They were together at this time.

Question. Are they now in peaceable relations with us?

Answer. Yes, they all have been since that time. Just before that treaty, Major Wynkoop went after them, at the time they made this raid upon the stage line, with quite a large expedition, and followed them down the San Luis valley. He followed their trail, but did not overtake them; ran out of subsistence, and returned. In the mean time I informed Agent Head, the agent of the Tabahuaches, of the difficulty. He had just returned from Washington with a party of chiefs of that band, who had been on a visit here, and he was instructed to get information to these Indians as rapidly as possible, and try to satisfy them until an explanation could be made in regard to this pursuit. They came down there very much alarmed, and at the same time intent upon going to war, and went to the Capotes and Muhuaches, who were near neighbors just over the line in New Mexico, asking them to join and go to war. Agent Head sent immediately to them the chiefs who had been here, and one of those chiefs, Ura, who is a very intelligent and very sharp and shrewd Indian, who speaks the English language fluently, went among them and explained to them the folly of going to war. He and his associates had seen the army of the Potomac, and one of his strong points with the Indians was, that the whites had soldiers enough to surround all their country and close them in and wipe them out. Through the representations of these chiefs difficulty was prevented, and they were induced to meet in council for the purpose of making the treaty of Conejos. That was the treaty with the Tabahuache band. That treaty was amended by the Senate, and last fall I met the band again in council to ratify the Senate amendments, and succeeded after a great deal of earnest effort to get their assent to the diminution of their hunting-grounds, all of which is matter of record. The Uintas, immediately subsequent to this expedition, were seen by Major Whitely and his interpreter, and they made an appointment with them last fall to have some presents for them this summer. They agreed to be peaceable and friendly and meet him in the spring. The waters, however, were so high and the snows were so deep that they could not meet him at the time appointed; they could not get there, nor could he, in the Middle Park, to the place appointed; but afterwards the major went over and found them and induced them to meet at the council ground of Conejos with the other tribes, to receive presents, in conjunction with the Tabahuache band, which they did, and went away very abundantly satisfied. We gave them a very nice distribution of goods. I gave them a lecture on obedience to their chiefs and on the necessity of going immediately to the agent as soon as any difficulty occurred, to report it to him and have it adjusted, instead of committing depredations or exciting any spirit of hostility amongst their men, which they were all satisfied with.

Question So far as they are concerned, do you think they are on friendly terms now?

Answer. They are; and I understand that since my absence they have been down and offered their services to the commander of the department, if he should need them, as soldiers in the war against the Cheyennes.

Question. Are the Tabahuaches hostile to the Cheyennes and Arapahoes?

Answer The Indians in the mountains all through New Mexico and Colorado have been at war with the Indians on the plains, as classes, from time immemorial; whenever they meet they fight.

Question. Is that so when they go to hunt on common hunting-grounds?

Answer. They get up their war parties. When I first went there I thought it would be a very humane and good idea to get those Indians to quit fighting one another, and I gave them a great many lectures on the impropriety of these war parties, but I found, after I had done it, that it gave a great deal of offence to them. One of them said he had been brought up to war, and to quit fighting was a thing he could not think of, and he thought it was an unworthy interference on my part. They were for non intervention. I found that my plan was not working well, and I concluded to let them alone.

Question Now, to come down more particularly to the difficulties with the Cheyennes and Arapahoes, will you state, in as brief terms as you can, your view of the matter and all you know about it; how the difficulty arose: how it has been managed, and the part the force of Chivington took in it?

133

APPENDIX.

Answer. When I went there, the first band of Indians that I met was a band of Arapahoes, under the command of Little Owl. They came in and gave me a visit; we had a friendly smoke, and they went off with this dissatisfaction : They said that the white people had taken their gold—this was Little Owl's speech ; I do not know but that I have a copy of it. He said the white people had taken their gold and their lands ; that they wanted their own lands, they did not care about the gold particularly. I told them that they had made a treaty at Fort Wise. He claimed that he was not there, and a good many of his party said they were not there, but some of them had been there I told them that that treaty provided for their joining in the benefits that were conferred by the government. He said they would not settle on the Arkansas. There is mention in the treaty of one of the bands not being present. He and his band were perhaps as friendly then, and are now, as any other of the Indians of the plains. Friday, who was the chief talker of his band, had been brought up by Major Fitzpatrick, one of the old Indian agents there, and lived in St. Louis for some time, and he speaks English very well. He has, during all the difficulties, with a portion of his band, remained friendly. He came in and remained at Camp Collins under our protection, and has been subsisted by the government to a large extent, because it was unsafe for him to go out and hunt. Another portion of that band was among those young men who wanted to fight. In 1863, the spring next after my arrival, and after this interview, the head man after Little Owl's death—he died the winter after I arrived there—came in and told me there was a party of Sioux who had been down with them and had held a council, in which the question of driving the whites out of the country was the topic of discussion. The Sioux are at the Fort Laramie agency, which is not in Colorado Territory, but the Indians are in the habit of passing to and fro. These Indians are entirely nomadic ; they have no definite home ; they range generally in certain parts of the Territory, but they interchange in their hunts extensively. He told me that the Sioux had been down with them and they had held a council on Horse creek, as he reported, in which the question of driving the whites out of the country and preventing them from settling was the chief discussion. His claim was that he and a good portion of his band were opposed to anything of the kind, but some of them were very much in favor of going to war. Soon after that, Major Lorey, the agent of the Sioux Indians, came to Denver and saw me in regard to the same thing. He said there was dissatisfaction among the Indians ; that he was satisfied that it was important to get them together and hold a council, or they would go to war. They were committing occasional depredations at that time which were reported, and which, in my report for 1863 to the Indian Bureau, are mentioned. I saw the impending danger from the talk I had had with the Arapahoes ; I was satisfied that a portion of them did not feel well, and a portion of the Cheyennes had been in to see me once, some of the Dog soldiers on a war party, and they had gone after the Utes. I advised them not to go. That was at the time I was trying to make friends among them. They promised me that they would not, and started off as though they were going back to their own hunting-grounds, took a circuitous route, and in a day or two the settlers on the road to the South Park, in the southern mines, as they are called, came in and reported that this war party were committing depredations ; they had outraged a woman at one of the ranches, and were in the habit generally of going to a ranch and taking what they wanted without injuring anybody, but they treated one hotel-keeper's wife very improperly. The man happened to be away, and they went into her bed-room and proposed to make her get up out of a sick-bed and get them something to eat, which was their custom. The settlers sent in for defence ; they were alarmed and anticipated an attack. A squad of some half a dozen soldiers went after the Indians ; Captain Wagner commanded the soldiers, but the Indians fled more rapidly than he pursued ; he did not see them. He went up to get them to come out of the settlement and go back to their hunting-grounds again, but he saw no Indians, and while he came out at Colorado City, seventy-five miles south of Denver, the Indians went out on their way to the plains again. That was in July, 1862.

Question. Did any troubles occur in 1863 ?

Answer. This should have been told prior to what I have stated in regard to Little Owl's reporting to me the proposition to go to war. I will return now to that. In 1863, upon Major Lorey's representation, I wrote a letter, a very urgent letter, to the department here for active measures to try to prevent these Indians from becoming hostile and going to war, showing them the danger, that the Sioux Indians were in connexion with the hostile Sioux of Minnesota. A party from Minnesota had been with these Indians at the council on Horse creek. I sent Agent Lorey a despatch and got him to come in person to the Secretary of the Interior. He did so, and laid the matter before the department, with my letter, and they appointed a commission, consisting of Agent Colley, Agent Lorey, and myself, to get the Arapahoes and Cheyennes in council, and especially the northern bands, for the purpose of making an adjustment. I got his return and got the commission, I think in July, 1863. I sent for Major Colley, and we arranged for a council on the head

134

of the Republican in the fall of 1863, on the 1st day of September, or thereabouts. I employed Elbridge Gerry, who has been about twenty-five years among them and has a Cheyenne wife, (and, by the way, he is a grandson of Elbridge Gerry who signed the Declaration of Independence, and a scholar and a man of very good mind,) and Antoine Jaunice, to go to the Indians on the head of the Republican and on the Platte, and up and above Major Lorey's agency, to find all the Arapahoes and Cheyennes they could. They started and notified them of the council and induced them to agree to come. They spent the time up to the 1st of September in these efforts. They met various bands and got promises from them to be at the council. Major Colley and Mr. Smith, together, undertook to notify the Indians of the Arkansas, the Arapahoes and Cheyennes, of this council, and induce them to come. They went in person and visited their principal bands and urged the importance and necessity of coming. At the time of the council, however, they declined to come, on account of their horses being poor, they being at work making their lodges, and the journey being such a long one. It was supposed to be about a medium ground between the different bands, so that we could get them all together. That was advised by Gerry and others, as will be seen in his report of this expedition. Mr. Gerry met the Cheyennes more particularly, where nearly all their chiefs were together, at the head of the Smoky Hill, on Beaver creek, and they promised to meet him at the time. He came out to the Platte river and escorted us to the Upper Timber, on the Rickaree fork of the Platte river, where we went; and after he had escorted us so that he could give us directions to find the place within two days' travel, he left us, in order to conduct the Indians to the same place. We waited two weeks for the Indians and Mr. Gerry's return, and we got quite uneasy about his safety. He came in finally with a report, which is published in my annual report for 1863, showing the reasons why they declined to come. I think all or nearly all the chiefs that signed the treaty of Fort Wise were in the party at the time. Mr. Gerry says that one of them, Bull Bear by name, agreed to come in on his promising to give him a horse if he would do so, but they held a council and decided that he should not do it; that they did not want anything more to do with the whites; that they did not want any presents, but they wanted their lands, and would have their lands. Mr. Gerry argued very sensibly, as will be seen by referring to his statement, which I hope the committee will read. After his report we had nothing to do. The chief of one of the northern bands, Spotted Horse, came in. Major Lorey saw Friday, and he promised to come, but did not get there. I saw several small parties of Cheyennes myself, who told me that they had decided not to hold a council. One was Yellow Wolf's band that I met on the Platte as I was on this expedition. They said, however, they meant to be friendly; they did not mean to fight, but they meant to have their lands. They took the ground that they had never sold their lands. Mr. Gerry argued with them that they had better recognize that, but the chiefs who signed that treaty told Gerry that they were obliged to repudiate the signing of that treaty of Fort Wise, or the Dog soldiers would kill them.

I returned home and was under the necessity of going as far in the opposite direction to meet the Tabahuache band of Utah Indians, which I had made arrangements to meet on the 1st of October. After I got back from Conejos, which took me until the latter part of October, I think the 16th or 20th of October, a party of Indians near Denver made a raid, and they stole Mr. Van Wirmer's horses. I sent out for them to come in and see me, counselled them against difficulty, and told them they must give up the horses they had stolen and try to remain peaceful. I sent to the department statements of these matters, which were published in the report for 1863. These were Arapahoes, I think, altogether; I do not think there were any Cheyennes among them. I sent for the Indians to come in, and they gave up the horses that had been stolen, or made recompense for them to Mr. Van Wirmer. I found a white man, Mr. North, among them, who had been living with them for years and had a squaw wife, who sent me word that he could give me some advice that would be very important. I sent for him to come in, and his statement as made to me I communicated to the Interior Department and to the War Department at the time, and it will be found in my report for this year. His statement that a council of war had been held, and a confederation of the Indians had agreed to go to war in the spring, was laid before the War Department, and a request made that our military posts be strengthened instead of withdrawing troops, as the War Department was then withdrawing them on account of the danger. In the spring these Indians stole 175 head of cattle from Irvin & Jackman, government contractors, about thirty-five or forty miles from Denver, where they were herding them.

Question. What Indians took those cattle?

Answer. They were Cheyennes, I suppose. That is, the Indians who came in to make peace with Major Wynkoop gave me the statement of the particular bands that had committed the depredations, a memorandum of which I have. I do not recollect the facts well enough to state which Indians they were, but I can furnish them in detail as reported by the Indians themselves in this council. I got Major Whitely to take a record of the sayings of the council when they were at Denver, when Colonel Chivington and Colonel Shoop and other officers were present. That is the same council referred to by Captain Smith. Very nearly at the same time they committed the depredations on the Platte, and there were several depredations of this kind committed on the Arkansas and at different points, in pursuance of the arrangement that they had made with one another. The plan was laid down in Mr. Nórth's statement. Wherever there were depredations the people were alarmed and ran in for military protection, and the soldiers went off while there were any to send. But early in the spring not only were our posts not re-enforced, but General Curtis ordered our troops all to Kansas, to rendezvous in the southeast corner of the Territory, on the Arkansas, with the understanding that they were to go to Kansas. as the general said, to fight rebels. I not only made application for re-enforcements, but protested against this. as I knew that the Indians, seeing the troops going away, would become more troublesome and we should have more difficulty in keeping them quiet. Major Colley labored very earnestly to try to pacify and keep them quiet; but these circumstances emboldened them. You will find a portion of my correspondence on the subject in my annual report for this year. I was unable to collect the facts as to all the depredations that were committed at various points. They were not all reported to my office, and I made application at the office of the commander for the information so as to embody it in my report—I mean the depredations that we had heard of as occurring at various points during the spring and summer—and the commander said he was not allowed to furnish the evidence. I suppose the reports will be found on the files of the War Department.

Question. At the time of the interview at Denver, when these chiefs were up there in behalf of the Cheyennes, were assurances given by you and Colonel Chivington that if they returned and went into camp in the neighborhood of Fort Lyon and did not commit depredations, they would have no difficulty?

Answer. After a long talk, by which I endeavored to get all the information that was practicable in regard to who had been doing mischief and what mischief they had been doing, I asked them what assurance they would give that they were going to be friendly. I said that it was no part of our intention to continue a war; that their disposition to be friendly was manifested by their coming up, but I wanted to know what they were willing to do to assure us of their continued friendship; whether they would be willing to join us in fighting the Sioux, a large party of whom, from the north of the Platte, they told us, were then threatening the Platte river, and were on the head of the Republican. I have here the minutes of that council at Denver, as taken down by Major Whitely.

Question. For a more specific statement you may refer to the minutes; but you can give us now the substance of the thing, and subsequently furnish the minutes if you wish.

Answer. After a talk the Indians said they desired to make peace, and they asked if I could give them any assurance that their band, which was on the head of the Republican, would be safe. I told them that I could not; that the soldiers might come across them there and attack them; I could not say anything about that; that their best course would be to get out of the way—to bring them in. In general terms they were advised that they had been at war; that they had been committing a great many depredations by their own confession; that I was not the peace-making power; that the War Department claimed the right to say when the troops should make war and when they should make peace, and that I turned them over to the War Department for this purpose. They professed to be willing not only to make peace, but to join with the whites in fighting the Sioux, the Kioways, and the Comanches, all of whom had been with them in their war parties.

Question. Was it not said by Colonel Chivington and yourself that if they would withdraw out of the way and go into the neighborhood of Fort Lyon they would be safe?

Answer. No, sir.

Question. What was the substance of what you told them on that subject?

Answer. The substance of my assurance was that they should show their peaceable intentions, and that I had little doubt they would be able to make and retain friendly relations with the military department.

Question. Was it not suggested to them to go to the neighborhood of Fort Lyon with their camp?

Answer. Colonel Chivington was there; he was commanding the district. Fort Lyon was not in his district. I asked him if he had anything to say, and he simply remarked to them that his way of making peace was for them to lay down their arms; that the soldiers were still out on the war-path. That, I think, was about the substance of his expression. That is also found in Major Whitely's report. Colonel Chivington simply remarked that they were out of his command; that Major Wynkoop would take them back and that he was competent to take care of them, or something to that effect.

Question. Was Major Wynkoop there with them?

136

Answer. He was there at the council. Immediately after that council I suggested to Major Wynkoop, through Colonel Shoop—I did not see him myself—that my judgment was, that for the time being it was better to treat them as prisoners of war, surrendered prisoners. I had no business to advise him about it; it was simply an extra-official suggestion that I made. I understood, however, that Major Wynkoop did treat them in that way.

By Mr. Ross:

Question Did these men come in by your request?

Answer. No. The council was held by my request, as I before stated. These were brought in by Major Wynkoop, who went out to their camp to rescue some white prisoners from them, and when he got there he suggested to them to make peace and come in, and they came with him to see me.

By Mr. Doolittle:

Question. Looking at the whole transaction as it was, did you not understand that when these Indians came and proposed to surrender the white prisoners, it was an overture on their part to do something to try and make peace with us?

Answer. I did.

Question. Did you not understand from what occurred at the council when Major Wynkoop was there, and on their going back, that, as they had surrendered these white prisoners, if they went back and remained where they were located, they were to have peace?

Answer. I supposed that they were.

Question. Major Wynkoop so understood, as far as you know?

Answer. Yes, sir; I supposed they were to have peace. What occurred after they went away from Denver I have nothing but flying rumors about. The next day after that council I started for the Conejos treaty-ground, 250 miles off.

By Mr. Ross:

Question. Can you give us any explanation of the orders under which the massacre occurred?

Answer. In regard to the massacre I gave no orders. I came away from the Territory before it occurred, and had no knowledge of any intention to make such an attack. I knew the soldiers were to go after the hostile Indians, but that they were actually going I had no knowledge whatever.

Question Did you, as governor, make any order about following them up?

Answer. I made no orders except what will be found in my annual reports. There is a proclamation there to which some have taken exception. I will simply say in regard to it that it was at a time when our troops were all taken away or under orders to go away. The last company was on the march down to the Arkansas when several murders of families and burnings of houses occurred close to the capital. The people were terribly excited and making a great cry that I did not do anything for them. It was impossible to secure the militia. It was out of the question, on account of the state of the militia law, to get the militia out. We had no means of equipping such as would volunteer to go. In that state of the law, as the only means I could think of to justify the people in defending themselves was to issue a proclamation authorizing them to do, so I issued the proclamation, and it is part of my report. I may say further in regard to it that, in reference to pursuing, capturing, and destroying the enemy, I quoted the language of the Secretary of War in his complimentary order to General Rosecrans. The same language which he used in regard to the rebels I used in regard to the Indians. There was nothing said about massacring. The troops were strictly prohibited from interfering with friendly Indians, as will be seen by the document That proclamation was issued before we commenced raising the third regiment, which I subsequently got authority from the Secretary of War to do. I had made application a month before for authority to raise them, but did not get it until this time. At the time I issued this proclamation I renewed my application to him for the means of defending ourselves, and he granted the privilege of raising a regiment, which was done very promptly by our people, for there was a great state of alarm and excitement at the time.

Question. Had you anything to do with directing the troops when this attack was made?

Answer. Nothing. I had no more command of those troops than I had of the army of the Potomac. I did not advise it in any way. Whenever anybody has said anything to me about troops, I have said that what they were raised for was to fight the Indians. I never had any knowledge that that particular attack was contemplated or that it occurred until I was in the States, after having left the Territory.

By Mr. Windom:

Question. Do you know of any palliation or excuse for that massacre except what you have stated before in general terms?

137

*Answer.* There are two stories in regard to it. I do not know what the testimony brought before you is in reference to it, but I see by my Denver papers and some others which I have received that they justify the attack on the ground that those Indians had left the fort and gone off with hostile intentions. I have seen one letter of that kind in the Denver papers.

*Question.* But you do not know any facts yourself?

*Answer.* I know no facts either justifying or condemning it except what I have heard here to-day—some of the statements made by Captain Smith. It would be a matter of interest, I have no doubt, to the committee if we were to collect a statement of the progress of the war so as to give the depredations committed, and show the inauguration of it. I have no doubt, as is stated in my annual report, that emissaries from the hostile tribes who were driven out of Minnesota have got us into these difficulties. The restlessness that is among our Indians would probably have amounted to nothing if it had not been for those Sioux coming down there and telling them—this is their common expression—"Now, whilst the whites are fighting among themselves, we can join together and drive them out of this country." I think that is a very general opinion among the Indians.

---

FORT LYON, C. T., *January* 15, 1865.

Personally appeared before me John Smith, Indian interpreter, who, after being duly sworn, says: That on the fourth day of September, 1864, he was appointed Indian interpreter for the post of Fort Lyon, and has continued to serve in that capacity up to the present date; that on the fourth day of September, 1864, by order of Major E. W. Wynkoop, commanding post of Fort Lyon, he was called upon to hold a conversation with three Cheyenne Indians, viz, One Eye and two others, who had been brought into the post that day; that the result of the interview was as follows: One Eye, Cheyenne, stated that the principal chiefs and sub-chiefs of the Cheyenne and Arapaho nations had held a consultation and agreed to send in himself, One Eye, with a paper written by George Bent, half-breed, to the effect that they, the Cheyennes and Arapahoes, had and did agree to turn over to Major E. W Wynkoop, or any military authority, all the white prisoners they had in their possession, as they were all anxious to make peace with the whites, and never desired to be at war.

Major E W. Wynkoop then asked One Eye, he having lived among whites and known to have always been friendly disposed toward them, whether he thought the Indians were sincere, and whether they would deliver the white persons into his (Major Wynkoop's) hands. His reply was, that at the risk of his life he would guarantee their sincerity.

Major Wynkoop then told him that he would detain him as a prisoner for the time, and if he concluded to proceed to the Indian camp, he would take him out with him and hold him as a hostage for their (the Indians') good faith.

One Eye also stated that the Comanche and Arapaho nations were congregated to the number of two thousand on the headwaters of the Smoky Hill, including some forty lodges of Sioux; that they had rendezvoused there and brought in their war parties for the purpose of hearing what would be the result of their message, by which they had sued for peace, and would remain until they heard something definite.

Major Wynkoop told One Eye that he would proceed to the Indian camps and take him with him. One Eye replied that he was perfectly willing to be detained a prisoner, as well as to remain a hostage for the good faith of the Indians, but desire I the major to start as soon as possible for fear the Indians might separate. On the sixth day of September I was ordered to proceed with Major Wynkoop and his command in the direction of the Indian encampment. After a four days' march we came in sight of the Indians, and one of the three Indians before mentioned was sent to acquaint the chiefs with what was the object of of the expedition, with the statement that Major Wynkoop desired to hold a consultation with the chiefs

On the tenth day of September the consultation was held between Major Wynkoop and his officers and the principal chiefs of the Cheyenne and Arapaho nations. Major Wynkoop stated through me to the chiefs apart that he had received their message; that acting on that, he had come up to talk with them; asked them whether they had all agreed to and indorsed the contents of the letter which he had in his possession, and which had been received from One Eye. Receiving an answer in the affirmative, he then told the chiefs that he had not the authority to conclude terms of peace with them, but he desired to make a proposition to them to the effect that if they would give him evidence of their good faith by delivering into his hands the white prisoners they had in their possession, he would endeavor to procure for them peace, which would be subject to conditions;

4

that he would take with him what principal chiefs they might select and conduct them in safety to the governor of Colorado, and, whatever might be the result of their interview with him, return them safely to their tribe.

Black Kettle, the head chief of the Cheyenne nation, replied as follows : That the Cheyenne and Arapaho nations had always endeavored to observe the terms of their treaty with the United States government; that some years previously, when the white emigration first commenced coming to what is now the Territory of Colorado, the country which was in possession of the Cheyenne and Arapaho nations, they could have successfully made war against them ; they did not desire to do so ; had invariably treated them with kindness, and had never to their knowledge committed any destruction whatever ; that until the last two months they had gotten along in perfect peace and harmony with their white brethren ; but while a hunting party of their young men were proceeding north, in the neighborhood of the South Platte river, having found some loose stock belonging to white men, which they were taking to a ranch to deliver them up, they were suddenly confronted by a party of United States soldiers and ordered to deliver up their arms. A difficulty immediately ensued, which resulted in the killing and wounding of several on both sides. A short time after this occurrence took place a village of papooses and squaws and old men, located on what is known as the Cedar cañon, a short distance north of the South Platte river, who were perfectly unaware of any difficulty having occurred between any portion of their tribe (Cheyennes) and the whites, was attacked by a large party of soldiers, and some of them killed, and their ponies driven off. After this, while a body of United States troops were proceeding from the Smoky Hill to the Arkansas river, they reached the neighborhood of Lean Bear's band of the Cheyenne nation. Lean Bear, second chief of the Cheyennes, approached the column of troops, alone, his warriors remaining off some distance, he not dreaming that there was any hostility between his nation and the whites. He was immediately shot down, and fire opened upon his band, the result of which was a fight between the two parties. Presuming from all the circumstances that war was inevitable, the young men of the Cheyenne nation commenced to retaliate by committing various depredations ; all the time of which he, Black Kettle, and other principal chiefs of the Cheyenne nation, were opposed to war, and endeavored by all means in their power to restore pacific relations between that tribe and their white brethren ; but at various times, when endeavoring to approach the military post for the purpose of accomplishing the same, were fired upon and driven off. In the mean time, while their brothers and allies. the Arapahoes, were on perfectly friendly terms with the whites, and Left Hand's band of that nation were camped in close vicinity of Fort Larned, Left Hand, one of the principal chiefs of the Arapaho nation, learning that it was the intention of the Kioways on a certain day to drive off the stock from Fort Larned, proceeded to the commanding officer of that post and informed him of the fact. No attention was paid to the information he gave, and on the day indicated the Kioways ran off the stock. Left Hand again approached the post with a portion of his warriors for the purpose of offering his services to the commanding officer there to pursue and endeavor to regain the stock from the Kioway Indians, when he was fired upon and obliged hastily to leave.

The young men of the Arapaho nation, supposing it was the intention of the whites to make war upon them, as well as the Cheyennes, also commenced retaliating as well as they were able, and against the desire of most of their principal chiefs, who, as well as Black Kettle, and other chiefs of the Cheyennes, were bitterly opposed to hostilities with the whites.

He then said that he had lately heard of a proclamation issued by the Governor of Colorado, inviting all friendly-disposed Indians to come in to the different military posts, and that they would be protected by the government. Under these circumstances, and although he thought the whites had been the aggressors and forced the trouble upon the Indians, yet, anxious for the welfare of his people, he had made this last effort to communicate again with the military authority, and he was glad he had succeeded.

He then arose, shook hands with Major Wynkoop and his officers, stating that he was still what he had always been, a friend to the whites, and, as far as he was concerned, he was willing to deliver up the white prisoners, or do anything that was required of him, to procure peace, knowing it to be for the good of his people ; but that there were other chiefs who still thought they were badly treated by their white brethren, who were willing to make peace, but who felt unwilling to deliver up the prisoners simply on the promise of Major Wynkoop that he would endeavor to procure them peace. They desired that the delivering up of the white prisoners should be an assurance of peace. He also went on to state that, even if Major Wynkoop's propositions were not accepted then by the chiefs assembled, and although they had sufficient force to entirely overpower Major Wynkoop's small command, yet, from the fact that he had come in good faith to hold this consultation, he should return unmolested to Fort Lyon.

APPENDIX.

The expressions of other chiefs were to the effect that they insisted upon peace as the condition of their delivering up the white prisoners.

Major Wynkoop finally replied that he repeated what he had said before—that it was not in his power to insure them peace, and that all he had to say in the closing was, that they might think about his proposition ; that he would march to a certain locality distant twelve miles, and there await the result of their consultation two days, advising them at the same time to accede to his proposition, as the best means of procuring that peace for which they were anxious.

The white prisoners were brought in and turned over to Major Wynkoop before the time had expired set by him ; and Black Kettle, White Antelope and Bullbeef, of the Cheyenne nation, as well as Nevah Nattune, Bovea, and Hieys Buffalo, of the Arapaho nation, all these chiefs, delivered themselves over to Major Wynkoop. We then proceeded to Fort Lyon, and from there to Denver, Colorado Territory, at which place Governor Evans held a consultation with the chiefs, the result of which was as follows : He told them he had nothing to do with them ; that they would return with Major Wynkoop who would reconduct them in safety, and they would have to await the action of the military authorities. Colonel Chivington, then in command of the district, also told them that they would remain at the disposal of Major Wynkoop until higher authority had acted in their case  The Indians appeared perfectly satisfied, presuming that they would eventually be all right as soon as those authorities could be heard from, and expressed themselves so.  Black Kettle embraced the governor and Major Wynkoop, and shook hands with all the other officials present, perfectly contented, deeming that the matter was settled.  On our return to Fort Lyon I was told by Major Wynkoop to say to the chiefs that they could bring their different bands, including their families, to the vicinity of the post until he had heard from the big chief ; that he preferred to have them under his eye and away from other quarters where they were likely to get into difficulties with the whites.  The chiefs replied that they were willing to do anything Major Wynkoop might choose to dictate, as they had perfect confidence in him.  Accordingly the chiefs went after their families and villages and brought them in.  They seemed satisfied that they were in perfect security and safety.  After their villages were located and Major Wynkoop had sent an officer to headquarters for instructions, he (Major Wynkoop) was relieved from command of the post by Major Scott J. Anthony, and I was ordered to interpret for him (Major Anthony) in a consultation he desired to hold with the Indians.  The consultation that there took place between Major Anthony and the Indians was as follows : Major Anthony told them that he had been sent here to relieve Major Wynkoop, and that he would from that time be in command of this post ; that he had come here under orders from the commander of all the troops in this country, and that he had orders to have nothing to do with Indians whatever, for they had heard at headquarters that the Indians had lately been committing depredations, &c , in the very neighborhood of this post ; but that, since his arrival, he had learned that these reports were all false ; that he would write to headquarters himself and correct the rumor in regard to them, and that he would have no objection to their remaining in the vicinity of Sand creek, where they were then located, until such a time as word might be received from the commander of the department ; that he himself would forward a complete statement of all that he had seen or heard of them, and that he was in hopes that he would have some good news for the Indians upon receiving an answer ; but he was sorry that his orders were such as to render it impossible for him to make them any issues whatever.  The Indians then replied that it would be impossible for them to remain any great length of time, as they were short of provisions.  Major Anthony then told them they could let their villages remain where they were, and could send their young men out to hunt buffalo, as he had understood that the buffalo had lately come close in  The Indians appeared to be a little dissatisfied at the change in commanders of the post, fearing that it boded them no good ; but, having received assurances of safety from Major Anthony, they still had no fears of their families being disturbed.

On the twenty-sixth of November I received permission from Major Scott J. Anthony, commanding post, to proceed to the Indian villages on Sand creek, for the purpose of trading with the Indians, and started, accompanied by a soldier named David Louderbeck, and a citizen, Watson Clark.  I reached the village and commenced to trade with them. On the morning of the twenty-ninth of November the camp was attacked by Colonel J. M. Chivington, with a command of from nine hundred to one thousand men.  The Indian village numbered about one hundred lodges, counting altogether about five hundred souls, two-thirds of whom were women and children, all of whose bodies had been mutilated in the most horrible manner. When the troops first approached, I endeavored to join them, but was repeatedly fired upon ; also the soldier and citizen with me.  When the troops began approaching, I saw Black Kettle, the head chief, hoist the American flag, fearing there might be some mistake as to who they were.

140

After the fight Colonel Chivington returned with his command in the direction of Fort Lyon, and then proceeded down the Arkansas river.

JOHN S. SMITH, *United States Interpreter.*

Sworn and subscribed to at Fort Lyon, C. T., this 27th day of January, 1865.

W. P. MINTON,
*Second Lieutenant First New Mexico Volunteers, Post Adjutant.*

A true copy :

J. E. TAPPAN,
*Acting Assistant Adjutant General*

---

FORT LYON, COLORADO, *January* 27, 1865.

Personally appeared before me Samuel G. Colley, who, being duly sworn, on oath deposes and says : That he is now, and has been for the past three years, United States agent for the Arapahoes and Cheyenne Indians ; that in the month of June last he received instructions from Hon. John Evans, governor and ex-officio superintendent of Indian affairs for Colorado Territory, directing him to send out persons into the Indian country to distribute printed proclamations (which he was furnished with) inviting all friendly Indians to come into the different places designated in said proclamation, and they would be protected and fed ; that he caused the terms of said proclamation to be widely disseminated among the different tribes of Indians under his charge, and that in accordance therewith a large number of Arapahoes and Cheyennes came into this post, and provisions were issued to them by Major E. W. Wynkoop, commanding, and myself ; that on the 4th day of September last two Cheyenne Indians (One-Eye and Manimick) came into this post with information that the Arapahoes and Cheyennes had several white prisoners among them that they had purchased, and were desirous of giving them up and making peace with the whites; that on the 6th day of September following Major E. W. Wynkoop left this post with a detachment of troops to rescue said prisoners, and that, after an absence of several days, he returned, bringing with him four white prisoners, which he received from the Arapaho and Cheyenne Indians ; he was accompanied on his return by a number of the most influential men of both tribes, who were unanimously opposed to war with the whites, and desired peace at almost any terms that the whites might dictate ; that immediately upon the arrival of Major Wynkoop at this post, large numbers of Arapahoes and Cheyennes came in and camped near the post ; Major Wynkoop selected several of the most prominent chiefs of both nations and proceeded to Denver to counsel with Superintendent Evans ; after his return he held frequent councils with the Indians, and at all of them distinctly stated that he was not empowered to treat with them, but that he had despatched a messenger to the headquarters of the department stating their wishes in the matter, and that as soon as he received advices from there he would inform them of the decision of General Curtis respecting them ; that until that time, if they placed themselves under his protection, they should not be molested ; that the Indians remained quietly near the post until the arrival of Major Anthony, who relieved Major Wynkoop ; Major Anthony held a council with the Indians and informed them that he was instructed not to allow any Indians in or near the post, but that he had found matters here much better than he expected, and advised them to go out and camp on Sand creek until he could hear from General Curtis; he wished them to keep him fully advised of all movements of the Sioux, which they promptly did ; he also promised them that as soon as he heard from General Curtis he would advise them of his decision ; from the time that Major Wynkoop left this post to go out to rescue the white prisoners until the arrival of Colonel Chivington here, which took place on the 28th of November last, no depredations of any kind had been committed by the Indians within two hundred miles of this post ; that upon Colonel Chivington's arrival here with a large body of troops he was informed where these Indians were encamped, and was fully advised under what circumstances they had come into this post, and why they were then on Sand creek ; that he was remonstrated with both by officers and civilians at this post against making war upon these Indians ; that he was informed and fully advised that there was a large number of friendly Indians there, together with several white men, who were there at the request of himself (Colley) and by permission of Major Anthony ; that notwithstanding his knowledge of the facts as above set forth, he is informed that Colonel Chivington did, on the morning of the 29th of November last, surprise and attack said camp of friendly Indians and massacre a large number of them, (mostly women and children,) and did allow the troops of his command to mangle and mutilate them in the most horrible manner.

S. G. COLLEY, *United States Indian Agent.*

# APPENDIX.

Sworn and subscribed to before me this 28th day of January, 1865, at Fort Lyon, Colorado Territory.

W. P. MINTON,
*Second Lieutenant First New Mexico Volunteers, Post Adjutant.*

A true copy :

J. E. TAPPAN,
*Acting Assistant Adjutant General.*

---

FORT LYON, COLORADO TERRITORY, *January* 16, 1865.

Personally appeared before me Lieutenant James D. Connor, first New Mexico volunteer infantry, who, after being duly sworn, says : That on the 28th day of November, 1864, I was ordered by Major Scott J. Anthony to accompany him on an expedition (Indian) as his battalion adjutant ; the object of that expedition was to be a thorough campaign against hostile Indians, as I was led to understand  I referred to the fact of there being a friendly camp of Indians in the immediate neighborhood, and remonstrated against simply attacking that camp, as I was aware that they were resting there in fancied security under promises held out to them of safety from Major E. W. Wynkoop, former commander of the post of Fort Lyon, as well as by Major S. J. Anthony, then in command. |Our battalion was attached to the command of Colonel J. M Chivington, and left Fort Lyon on the night of the 28th of November, 1864 ; about daybreak on the morning of the 29th of November we came in sight of the camp of the friendly Indians aforementioned, and were ordered by Colonel Chivington to attack the same, which was accordingly done.  The command of Colonel Chivington was composed of about one thousand men ; the village of the Indians consisted of from one hundred to one hundred and thirty lodges, and, as far as I am able to judge, of from five hundred to six hundred souls, the majority of which were women and children ; in going over the battle-ground the next day I did not see a body of man, woman, or child but was scalped, and in many instances their bodies were mutilated in the most horrible manner—men, women, and children's privates cut out, &c ; I heard one man say that he had cut out a woman's private parts and had them for exhibition on a stick ; I heard another man say that he had cut the fingers off an Indian to get the rings on the hand ; according to the best of my knowledge and belief these atrocities that were committed were with knowledge of J. M Chivington, and I do not know of his taking any measures to prevent them ; I heard of one instance of a child a few months old being thrown in the feed-box of a wagon, and after being carried some distance left on the ground to perish ; I also heard of numerous instances in which men had cut out the private parts of females and stretched them over the saddle-bows, and wore them over their hats while riding in the ranks.  All these matters were a subject of general conversation, and could not help being known by Colonel J. M. Chivington.

JAMES D. CONNOR,
*First Lieutenant First Infantry New Mexico Volunteers.*

Sworn and subscribed to before me this 27th day of January, 1865, at Fort Lyon, Colorado Territory.

W. P. MINTON,
*Second Lieutenant First New Mexico Volunteers, Post Adjutant.*

A true copy :

J. E. TAPPAN,
*Acting Assistant Adjutant General United States Volunteers.*

---

FORT LYON, COLORADO TERRITORY, *January* 27, 1865.

Personally appeared before me Private David Lauderbock, first cavalry of Colorado, and R. W. Clark, citizen, who, after being duly sworn, say : That they accompanied John Smith, United States Indian interpreter, on the 26th day of November, 1864, by permission of Major Scott J. Anthony, commanding post, Fort Lyon, Colorado Territory, to the village of the friendly Cheyenne and Arapaho Indians, on Sand creek, close to Fort Lyon, Colorado Territory, he, John Smith, having received permission to trade with the aforesaid friendly Indians ; that on the morning of the 29th day of November, 1864, the said Indian village was attacked while deponents were in the same, by Colonel J. M Chivington, with a command of about one thousand (1,000) men ; that according to their best knowledge and belief the entire Indian village was composed of not more than five hundred (500) souls, two-thirds of which were women and children ; that the dead bodies of women and children were afterwards mutilated in the most horrible manner ; that it was the understanding of the deponents, and the general understanding of the garrison of Fort Lyon, that this vil-

142

APPENDIX.

lage were friendly Indians; that they had been allowed to remain in the localities they were then in by permission of Major Wynkoop, former commander of the post, and by Major Anthony, then in command, as well as from the fact that permission had been given John Smith and the deponents to visit the said camp for the purpose of trading.

DAVID H. LAUDERBOCK.
R. W. CLARK.

Sworn and subscribed to before me this 27th day of January, 1865.

W. P. MINTON,
*Second Lieutenant New Mexico Volunteers, Post Adjutant.*

A true copy :

J. E TAPPAN,
*Acting Assistant Adjutant General.*

---

FORT LYON, COLORADO TERRITORY, *January* 27, 1865.

Personally appeared before me Second Lieutenant W. P. Minton, first regiment New Mexico infantry volunteers, and Lieutenant C. M. Cossitt, first cavalry of Colorado, who, after being duly sworn, say : That on the 28th day of November, 1864, Colonel J. M. Chivington, with the third regiment of Colorado cavalry, one-hundred-day men, and a battalion of the first cavalry of Colorado, arrived at this post, and on the 29th of November attacked a village of friendly Indians in the vicinity, and, according to representations made by others in our presence, murdered their women and children, and committed the most horrible outrages upon the dead bodies of the same ; that the aforesaid Indians were recognized as friendly by all parties of this post, under the following circumstances, viz : that Major E. W. Wynkoop, formerly commander of the post, had given them assurances of safety until such time as he could hear from the commanding general of the department, in consequence of their having sued for peace and given every evidence of their sincerity by delivering up the white prisoners they had in their possession, by congregating their families together, and leaving them at the mercy of the garrison at Fort Lyon, who could have massacred them at any moment they felt so disposed ; that upon Major Wynkoop's being relieved from the command of Fort Lyon, and Major Scott J. Anthony's assuming command of the same, it was still the understanding between Major Anthony and the Indians that they could rest in the security guaranteed them by Major Anthony ; also that Colonel J. M. Chivington, on his arrival at the post of Fort Lyon, was aware of the circumstances in regard to the Indians, from the fact that different officers remonstrated with him, and stated to him how these Indians were looked upon by the entire garrison ; that notwithstanding these remonstrances, and in the face of all these facts, he committed the massacre aforementioned.

W. P. MINTON,
*Second Lieutenant First New Mexico Volunteers.*
C. M. COSSITT,
*First Lieutenant First Cavalry of Colorado.*

Sworn and subscribed to before me this 27th day of January, 1865.

W. W. DENNISON,
*Second Lieutenant First Colorado Veteran Cavalry,*
*Acting Regimental Adjutant.*

A true copy :

J. E. TAPPAN,
*Acting Assistant Adjutant General.*

---

FORT LYON, COLORADO TERRITORY, *January* 16, 1865.

Personally appeared before me Captain R A. Hill, first New Mexico volunteer infantry, who, after being duly sworn, says : That, as an officer in the United States service, he was on duty at Fort Lyon, Colorado Territory, at the time there was an understanding between the chiefs of the Arapaho and Cheyenne nations and Major E W. Wynkoop, with regard to their resting in safety with their villages in the vicinity of Fort Lyon until such time as orders in regard to them could be received from the commanding general of the department ; that after Major Wynkoop being relieved from the command of Fort Lyon, Colorado Territory, the same understanding existed between Major Scott J. Anthony and the afore-

143

APPENDIX.

said Indians ; that to the best of his knowledge and belief the village of Indians massacred by Colonel J. M. Chivington on the 29th day of November, 1864, were the same friendly Indians heretofore referred to.

R. A. HILL,
*Captain First New Mexico Volunteers.*

Sworn and subscribed to before me this 27th day of January, 1865.
W. P. MINTON,
*Second Lieut. First Infantry New Mexico Volunteers, Post Adjutant.*

A true copy :
J. E. TAPPAN,
*Acting Assistant Adjutant General.*

EXECUTIVE DEPARTMENT, COLORADO TERRITORY,
*Denver, June 29, 1864.*

DEAR SIR: I enclose a circular to the Indians of the plains. You will, by every means you can, get the contents to all these Indians, as many that are hostile may come to the friendly camp, and when they all do the war will be ended. Use the utmost economy in providing for those that come in, as the Secretary of the Interior confines me to the amount of our appropriations, and they may be exhausted before the summer is out. You will arrange to carry out the plan of the circular at Lyon and Larned.

You will use your utmost vigilance to ascertain how many of your Indians are hostile, where they are, and what plans they propose, and report to me by every mail at least. For this purpose you will enlist the active aid of Mr. John Smith and his son, and of such other parties as you may judge can be of essential service. Mr. C. A. Cook reports to me that Mr. Bent has given you important information in regard to the plans and strength of the hostile combinations on the plains. Please be careful and report to me in detail all of the reliable information you can get, promptly, as above directed.

I have the honor to be, respectfully, your obedient servant,
JOHN EVANS,
*Governor of Colorado Territory and Sup't Indian Affairs.*

Major S. G. COLLEY,
*United States Indian Agent, Fort Lyon, C. T.*

A true copy:
W. W. DENNISON,
*2d Lieut. 1st Colorado Vet. Cavalry, Act'g Regt'l Adj't.*

A true copy :
J. E. TAPPAN,
*Acting Assistant Adjutant General.*

COLORADO SUPERINTENDENCY OF INDIAN AFFAIRS,
*Denver, June 27, 1864.*

*To the friendly Indians of the plains :*

Agents, interpreters, and traders will inform the friendly Indians of the plains that some members of their tribes have gone to war with the white people. They steal stock and run it off, hoping to escape detection and punishment ; in some instances they have attacked and killed soldiers, and murdered peaceable citizens. For this the Great Father is angry, and will certainly hunt them out and punish them, but he does not want to injure those who remain friendly to the whites ; he desires to protect and take care of them. For this purpose I direct that all friendly Indians keep away from those who are at war, and go to places of safety.

Friendly Arapahoes and Cheyennes, belonging to the Arkansas river, will go to Major Colley, United States Indian agent, at Fort Lyon, who will give them provisions and show them a place of safety. Friendly Kiowas and Comanches will go to Fort Larned, where they will be cared for in the same way. Friendly Sioux will go to their agent at Fort Laramie for directions. Friendly Arapahoes and Cheyennes of the Upper Platte will go to Camp Collins, on the Cache-la-Poudre, where they will be assigned a place of safety, and provisions will be given them. The object of this is to prevent friendly Indians from being killed through mistake ; none but those who intend to be friendly with the whites

144

must come to these places. The families of those who have gone to war with the whites must be kept away from the friendly Indians. The war on hostile Indians will be continued until they are all effectually subdued.

JOHN EVANS,
*Governor of Colorado and Superintendent of Indian Affairs.*

A true copy:

W. W. DENNISON,
*2d Lieut. 1st Colorado Vet. Cavalry, Act'g Regt'l Adj't.*

A true copy:

J. E. TAPPAN,
*Acting Assistant Adjutant General.*

COLORADO SUPERINTENDENCY,
*Denver, C. T., June 16, 1864.*

SIR: You will immediately make necessary arrangements for the feeding and support of all the friendly Indians of the Cheyenne and Arapaho Indians at Fort Lyon, and direct the friendly Comanches and Kiowas, if any, to remain at Fort Larned ; you will make a requisition on the military commander of the post for subsistence for the friendly Indians o his neighborhood. If there is no agent there to attend to this, deputize some one to do it. These friendly Indians must be collected at places of rendezvous, and all intercourse between them and tribes or individuals engaged in warfare with us prohibited.

This arrangement will tend to withdraw from the conflict all who are not thoroughly identified with the hostile movement, and, by affording a safe refuge, will gradually collect those who may become tired of war and desire peace.

The war is opened in earnest, and upon your efforts to keep quiet the friendly Indians, as nucleus for peace, will depend its duration to some extent at least. You can send word to all these tribes to come as directed above, but do not allow the families of those at war to be introduced into the friendly camp I have established a camp for our northern friendly bands on Cache-la-Poudre, and as soon as my plan is approved by the military I will issue a proclamation to the Indians.

Please spare no effort to carry out this instruction, and keep me advised by every mail of the situation.

Very respectfully, your obedient servant,

JOHN EVANS,
*Governor and Ex officio Sup't Indian Affairs.*

A true copy:

W. W. DENNISON,
*2d Lieut. 1st Colorado Vet. Cavalry, Act'g Regt'l Adj't.*

A true copy:

J. E. TAPPAN,
*Acting Assistant Adjutant General.*

FORT LYON, COLORADO TERRITORY, *January 16, 1865.*

Personally appeared before me Private David Louderback, 1st cavalry of Colorado, and R. W. Clark, citizen, who, after being duly sworn according to law, say: That they accompanied John Smith, Indian interpreter, on the 26th day of November, 1864, by permission of Major Scott J. Anthony, commanding post of Fort Lyon, to the village of the friendly Indians, Cheyennes and Arapahoes, on Sand creek, close to Fort Lyon, he, John Smith, having received permission to trade with the aforesaid Indians ; that on the morning of the 29th of November the said Indian village, while the deponents were in the same, was attacked by Colonel J. M. Chivington with a command of about one thousand men ; that, according to their best knowledge and belief, the entire Indian party was composed of not more than five hundred souls, two-thirds of which were women and children ; that the dead bodies of children were afterwards mutilated in the most horrible manner ; that this village were friendly Indians ; that it was the understanding of the deponents, and the general understanding of the garrison at Fort Lyon, they were allowed to remain in the locality they were then in by Major E. W. Wynkoop, former commander of the post, and by Major Scott J. Anthony, then in command, as well as from the fact that permission had been given to John Smith and the deponents to visit the said camp for the purpose of trading.

DAVID LOUDERBACK.
R. W. CLARK.

Sworn and subscribed to before me this 16th day of January, 1865.

W. P. MINTON, *Post Adjutant.*

# APPENDIX.

FORT LYON, COLORADO TERRITORY, *January* 16, 1865.

Personally appeared before me Lieutenant James D. Cannon, 1st New Mexico volunteer infantry, who, after being duly sworn, says: That on the 28th day of November, 1864, I was ordered by Major Scott J. Anthony to accompany him on an Indian expedition as his battalion adjutant; the object of the expedition was to be a thorough campaign against hostile Indians, as I was led to understand. I referred to the fact of there being a friendly camp of Indians in the immediate vicinity, and simply remonstrated against attacking that camp, as I was aware that they were resting there in fancied security, under promises held out to them of safety by Major E. W. Wynkoop, formerly commander of Fort Lyon, and by Major Scott J. Anthony, then in command. Our battalion was attached to the command of Colonel J. M. Chivington, and left Fort Lyon on the night of the 28th of November, 1864; about daybreak on the morning of the 29th of November came in sight of the camp of friendly Indians aforementioned, and was ordered by Colonel Chivington to attack the same, which was accordingly done. The command of Colonel Chivington was composed of about one thousand men; the village of Indians consisting of from one hundred to one hundred and thirty lodges, and, as far as I am able to judge, of from five to six hundred souls, the majority of them were women and children. In going over the battle-ground the next day I did not see a body of man, or woman, or child, but what was scalped, and in many instances their bodies were mutilated in the most horrible manner—men, women and children's privates cut out. I heard one man say that he had cut a woman's private parts out and had them for exhibition on a stick; I heard another man say that he had cut the fingers off of an Indian to get the rings on his hands. According to the best of my knowledge and belief, these atrocities that were committed were with the knowledge of Colonel J. M. Chivington, and I do not know of him taking any measure to prevent them. I heard of one instance of a child, a few months old, being thrown into the feed-box of a wagon, and after being carried some distance, left on the ground to perish; I also heard of numerous instances in which men had cut out the private parts of females and stretched them over their saddle-bows, and some of them over their hats. While riding in ranks, all these matters were a subject of general conversation, and could not help being known to Colonel J. M. Chivington.

JAMES D. CANNON.

Sworn and subscribed to before me this 16th day of January, 1865.

W P. MINTON, Post Adjutant.

---

FORT LYON, COLORADO TERRITORY, *January* 16, 1865.

Personally appeared before me Captain R. H. Hill, 1st New Mexico volunteer infantry, who, after being duly sworn, says: That, as an officer in the service of the United States, he was on duty at Fort Lyon, Colorado Territory, at the time there was an understanding between the chiefs of the Arapahoes and Cheyenne nation and Major Wynkoop with regard to their resting in safety with these villages in the vicinity of Fort Lyon until such a time as orders in regard to them could be received from the commanding general of the department; that after Major Wynkoop being relieved from the command of Fort Lyon, the same understanding existed between Major S. J. Anthony and the aforementioned Indians; that, to the best of his belief, the village of Indians massacred by Colonel J. M. Chivington, on the 29th day of November, 1864, were the same friendly Indians heretofore referred to.

R. H. HILL.

Sworn and subscribed to this 16th day of January, 1865.

W. P. MINTON, Post Adjutant.

---

FORT LYON, COLORADO TERRITORY, *January* 16, 1865.

Personally appeared before me Second Lieutenant W. P. Minton, 1st New Mexico volunteer infantry, and Lieutenant C. M. Cossitt, 1st cavalry of Colorado, who, after being duly sworn, says: That on the 28th day of November, 1864, Colonel J. M. Chivington, with the 3d regiment Colorado cavalry, (one-hundred-days men,) and a battalion of the 1st cavalry of Colorado, arrived at this post, and on the 29th day of November, 1864, attacked a village of friendly Indians in the vicinity, and, according to representations made by others in our presence, murdered their women and children, and committed the most horrible outrages upon the dead bodies of the same; that the aforesaid Indians were recognized as friendly Indians by all parties at this post, under the following circumstances, viz: That

146

Major E. W. Wynkoop, formerly commander of the post, had given them assurances of safety until such a time as he could hear from the commanding general of the department, in consequence of their having sued for peace, and given every evidence of their sincerity, by delivering up white prisoners they had in their possession, by congregating their families together and leaving them at the mercy of the garrison of Fort Lyon, Colorado Territory, who felt so disposed; that upon Major Wynkoop being relieved of the command of Fort Lyon, Colorado Territory, and Major Scott J. Anthony assuming command of the same, it was still the understanding between Major Anthony and the Indians that they could rest in that security guaranteed them by Major E. W. Wynkoop; also that Colonel J. M Chivington, on his arrival at the post of Fort Lyon, Colorado Territory, was made aware of the circumstances in regard to these Indians, from the fact that different officers remonstrated with him and stated to him how these Indians were looked upon by the entire garrison; that notwithstanding these remonstrances, and in the face of all true facts, he committed the massacre aforementioned.

C. M. COSSITT.
W. P. MINTON.

Sworn and subscribed to before me this 16th day of January, 1865.

W. W. DENNISON,
*Acting Regimental Adjutant.*

---

FORT LYON, COLORADO TERRITORY, *January* 16, 1865.

Personally appeared before me John Smith, United States Indian interpreter, who, after being duly sworn, says : That on the 4th day of September, 1865, he was appointed Indian interpreter for the post of Fort Lyon, Colorado Territory, and has continued to serve in that capacity up to the present time ; that on the 4th day of September, 1865, by order of Major E. W. Wynkoop, commanding post of Fort Lyon, he was called upon to hold a conversation with three Cheyenne Indians, "One Eye" and two others, who had been brought into the fort that day ; that the result of the interview was as follows : "One Eye" (Cheyenne) stated that the principal chiefs and sub-chiefs of the Cheyenne and Arapaho nations had held a consultation and agreed, to a man, of the chiefs and sub-chiefs to come or send in some one who was well acquainted with parties at the post, and finally agreed to send in himself, "One Eye," with a paper, written by George Bent, half-breed, to the effect that the Cheyenne and Arapaho chiefs would and did agree to turn over to Major E. W. Wynkoop or any other military commander all the white prisoners they had in their possession, as they were anxious to make peace with the whites, and never desired to be at war. Major Wynkoop then asked "One Eye," he having lived among the whites and known to have always been friendly disposed towards them, whether they would deliver the prisoners into his (Wynkoop's) hands; his reply was that, at the risk of his life, he would guarantee their sincerity. Major Wynkoop then told him that he would deliver him as a prisoner for the time, and if he concluded to go to the Indian camp he would take him along as a hostage for their (the Indians') good faith. "One Eye" also stated that the Cheyenne and Arapaho nation were congregated, to the number of two thousand Indians, on the headwaters of Smoky Hill, including some forty lodges of Sioux ; that they had rendezvoused there and brought in their war parties for the purpose of hearing what would be the result of their message by which they had sued for peace, and would remain until they heard something definite. Major Wynkoop told "One Eye" that he would proceed to the Indian camp and take him with him. "One Eye" replied that he was perfectly willing to remain a prisoner, as well as a hostage for the good faith of the Indians, but desired the major to start as soon as possible for fear the Indians might separate. On the 26th day of September I was ordered by Major Wynkoop to proceed, with his command, in the direction of the Indian encampment. After a four days' march we came in sight of the Indians, and one of the three Indians aforementioned was sent to acquaint the chiefs with what was the object of the expedition, with the statement that Major Wynkoop desired to hold a consultation with them (the chiefs) on the 10th day of September, 1864. The consultation was held between Major Wynkoop and his officers and the principal chiefs of the Cheyenne and Arapaho nations. Major Wynkoop stated, through me, to the chiefs, that he had received their message ; that acting on that he had come to talk with them ; asked them whether they all agreed to and indorsed the contents of the letter which he had in his possession, and which had been brought in by "One Eye." Receiving an answer in the affirmative, he then told the chiefs that he had not the authority to conclude terms of peace with them, but that he desired to make a proposition to them to the effect that if they would give him evidence of their good faith by delivering into his hands the white prisoners they had in their possession he would endeavor to procure for them peace, which would be subject to conditions; that he would take with him what principal chiefs they might select, and conduct them in safety to the governor of Colorado, and whatever might be the result of their interview, he would conduct them in safety to their tribe. "Black Kettle," the head chief of the Cheyenne nation, replied as follows: that the Cheyenne and Arapaho nation had always endeavored to observe the terms of their treaty with the United States government; that some years previously, when the whole emigration first commenced coming to what is now the Territory of Colorado, the country which was in possession of the Cheyenne and Arapaho nations, they could have successfully made war against them, the whites; they did not desire to do so; had invariably treated them with kindness, and have never, to his knowledge, committed any depredations whatever; that until within the last few months they had got along in perfect peace and harmony with their white brethren; but while a hunting party of their young men were proceeding north, in the neighborhood of the South Platte river, having found some lost stock belonging to white men, which they were driving to a ranch to deliver up, they were suddenly confronted by a party of United States soldiers and ordered to deliver up their arms; a difficulty immediately ensued, which resulted in killing and wounding several on both sides. A short time after an occurrence took place at a village of pappooses, squaws, and old men, located in what is known as the "Cedar cañon," a short distance north of the South Platte, who were perfectly unaware of any difficulty having occurred between the whites and a portion of their tribe, (Cheyenne;) were attacked by a large body of United States soldiers, some of them killed and their ponies driven off. After this, while a body of soldiers were proceeding from the Smoky Hill to the Arkansas, they reached the neighborhood of "Lou. Bear's" band of Cheyennes. "Lou. Bear," 2d chief of the Cheyenne nation, approached the column of troops alone, his warriors remaining off some distance, he not deeming that there was any hostility between his nation and the whites; he was immediately shot down and fire opened upon his band, the result of which was a fight between the two parties. Presuming from all these circumstances that war was inevitable, the young men of the Cheyenne nation commenced to retaliate by committing various depredations at all times, which he, "Black Kettle," and other principal chiefs of the Cheyenne nation, were opposed to, and endeavored by all the means in his power to restore pacific relations between that tribe and their white brethren. but at various times, when endeavoring to approach military posts for the purpose of accomplishing the same, was fired upon and driven off. In the meanwhile their brothers and allies, the Arapahoes, were on perfectly friendly terms with the whites, and Left Hand, one of the principal chiefs of the Arapaho nation, learning that it was the intention of the Kioways on a certain day to run off the stock from Fort Larned, proceeded to the commanding officer of that post and informed him of the fact. No attention was paid to the information he gave, and on the day anticipated the stock was run off by the Kioways. Left Hand again approached the post with a portion of his warriors for the purpose of offering his services to the commanding officer to pursue and endeavor to regain the stock from the Kioways, when he was fired upon and obliged hastily to leave. The young men of the Arapaho nation supposing it was the intention of the whites to make war upon them as well as the Cheyennes, also commenced retaliating as well as they were able. and against the desire of most of their principal chiefs, who, as well as Black Kettle and other chiefs of the Cheyennes, were bitterly opposed to hostilities with the whites He then said that he had lately learned of the proclamation issued by the governor of Colorado, inviting all friendly disposed Indians to come to the different military posts and they would be protected by the government. Under these circumstances, notwithstanding he thought the whites had been the aggressors and had forced the trouble on the Indians, anxious altogether for the welfare of his people, he had made this last effort to communicate again with the military authorities, and he was glad to have succeeded. He then arose, shook hands with Major Wynkoop and his officers, stating that he was still, as he had always been, a friend to the whites, and that, as far as he was concerned, he was willing to deliver up the white prisoners or do anything that was required of him to procure "peace," knowing it to be for the best of his people; but that there were other chiefs who still thought that they were badly treated by their brethren, but who were willing to make peace, but who felt unwilling to deliver up the white prisoners simply upon the promise of Major Wynkoop that he would endeavor to procure them peace; they desired that the condition of their delivering up the white prisoners would be an assurance of peace; he also stated that even if Major Wynkoop's propositions were not accepted then by the chiefs assembled, and although they had sufficient force to entirely overpower Major Wynkoop's small command, that from the fact that he had come in good faith to hold a consultation in consequence of the letter received, he should return to Fort Lyon, Colorado Territory, without being molested. The expressions of the other chiefs were to the effect that they insisted upon peace on the condition of their delivering up the white

prisoners. Major Wynkoop finally replied, that he repeated what he had said, that it wa
out of his power to insure them peace, and that all he had to say was, that they might
think about his proposition ; that he would march to a certain locality, distant twelve
miles, and there await the result of their consultation for two days, advising them at
the same time to accede to his proposition as the best means of procuring that peace for
which they were anxious. The white prisoners were brought in and delivered up before
the time had expired set by him, and Black Kettle, White Antelope, and Bull Bear, of
the Cheyenne nation, as well as Nevah, Natanee, Boisee, and Hip Buffalo, chiefs of the
Arapahoes, delivered themselves over to Major Wynkoop. We then proceeded to Fort Lyon,
and from thence to Denver, at which place Governor Evans held a consultation with the
chiefs, the result of which was as follows : He told them they could return with Major
Wynkoop, who would reconduct them in safety, and they would have to await the action of
the military authorities. Colonel Chivington, then in command of the district of Colorado, also told them that they would 'remain at the disposal of Major Wynkoop until
higher authorities had acted in their case. The Indians appeared to be perfectly satisfied,
presuming that they would eventually be all right, as soon as those authorities could be
heard from, and expressed themselves so. Black Kettle embraced the governor and
Major Wynkoop, and shook hands with all the other officers present, perfectly contented,
deeming the matter was settled. On our return to Fort Lyon I was told by Major Wynkoop to say to the chiefs that they could bring their different bands, including their families, to the vicinity of the post until he had heard from the big chief ; that he preferred to have them under his eye, and away from other quarters where they were likely to
get into difficulty with the whites. The chiefs replied that they were willing to do anything that Major Wynkoop might choose to dictate, as they had perfect confidence in him,
and accordingly immediately brought their villages, their squaws, and pappooses, and
appeared satisfied that they were in perfect safety. After their villages were located here,
and Major Wynkoop had sent an officer to headquarters for instructions, then Major Wynkoop was relieved from command of the post by Major Scott J. Anthony, and I was ordered
to interpret for him (Major Anthony) in a consultation he desired to hold with these
Indians  The consultation that then took place between Major Anthony and these Indians
was as follows : Major Anthony told them that he had been sent here to relieve Major
Wynkoop, and that he would be from that time in command of the post ; that he had
come here under orders from the commander of all the troops in this country, and that he
had orders to have nothing to do with the Indians whatever, as they had heard at headquarters that they had been committing depredations, &c., in the neighborhood of this
post ; but that, since his arrival, he had learned that these reports were all false ; that he
would write to headquarters himself and correct these errors in regard to them, and that
he would have no objections to their remaining in the vicinity of Sand creek, where they
were located, until such time as word might be received from the commander of the department ; that he himself would forward a complete statement of all that he had seen
and heard, and that he was in hopes that he would have some good news for the Indians
upon receiving an answer ; but that he was sorry that his orders were such as to render it
impossible for him to make them any issues whatever. The Indians then replied that it
would be impossible for them to remain where they were located any length of time, as
they were short of provisions. Major Anthony then told them that they could let their
villages remain where they were, and could send their young men out to hunt buffaloes, as
he understood that the buffalo had lately come in very close. The Indians appeared to be
a little dissatisfied in regard to the change of the commanders of the post, fearing that it
boded them no good ; but, having received assurances of safety from Major Anthony, they
still had no fear of their families being disturbed. On the twenty-sixth day of November,
1864, I received permission of Major Scott J. Anthony, commander of the post, to proceed
to the Indian village on Sand creek for the purpose of trading with the Indians, and started,
accompanied by a soldier named Daniel Louderback and a citizen, Watson Clark. I reached
the village and commenced to trade with them. On the morning of the twenty-ninth of
November, 1864, the village was attacked by Colonel J. M. Chivington, with a command
of from nine hundred to one thousand men. The Indian village was composed of about
one hundred lodges, numbering altogether some five hundred souls, two-thirds of which
were women and children. From my observation I do not think there were over sixty
warriors that made any defence. I rode over the field after the slaughter was over and
counted from sixty to seventy bodies of dead Indians, a large majority of which were
women and children, all of whose bodies had been mutilated in the most horrible manner.
When troops first appeared I endeavored to go to them, but was repeatedly fired upon ;
also the soldier and citizen that were with me. When the troops began approaching in a
hostile manner. I saw Black Kettle hoist the American flag over his lodge, as well as a
white flag, fearing that there might be some mistake as to who they were. After the

fight Colonel Chivington returned with the command in the direction of Fort Lyon, and then proceeded by the road down the Arkansas river.

JOHN SMITH.

Sworn and subscribed to before me this sixteenth day of January. 1865.

W. P. MINTON, Post Adjutant.

---

FORT LYON, COLORADO TERRITORY, April 20, 1865.

Personally appeared before me Lieutenant James Olney, veteran battalion first Colorado cavalry, who, after being duly sworn, deposes and says: That he was present at the massacre of the Indians at Sand creek by Colonel Chivington, on the twenty-ninth day of November, 1864 ; that during that massacre he saw three squaws and five children, prisoners in charge of some soldiers ; that, while they were being conducted along, they were approached by Lieutenant Harry Richmond, of the third Colorado cavalry ; that Lieutenant Richmond thereupon immediately killed and scalped the three women and the five children while they (the prisoners) were screaming for mercy ; while the soldiers in whose charge these prisoners were shrank back, apparently aghast.

JAMES OLNEY.

Sworn and subscribed to before me at Fort Lyon, Colorado Territory, this twentieth day of April, 1865

CHARLES WHEELER,<br>Adjutant Veteran Battalion First Colorado Cavalry, Adjutant Fort Lyon.

Official copy respectfully furnished to headquarters, Fort Lyon, Colorado Territory, eleventh June, 1865.

CHARLES WHEELER,<br>First Lieutenant Veteran Battalion First Colorado Cavalry, Adjutant Fort Lyon.

---

FORT LYON, COLORADO, January 27, 1865.

Personally appeared before me Samuel G. Colley, who being duly sworn, on oath deposes and says: That he is now, and has been for the past three years, United States agent for the Arapaho and Cheyenne Indians ; that in the month of June last he received instructions from honorable John Evans, governor and ex officio superintendent of Indian affairs for Colorado Territory, directing him to send out persons into the Indian country to distribute printed proclamations, (which he was furnished with,) inviting all friendly Indians to come into the different places designated in said proclamation, and they would be protected and fed ; that he caused the terms of said proclamation to be disseminated among the different tribes of Indians under his charge, and that in accordance therewith a large number of Arapahoes and Cheyennes came in to this post, and provisions were issued to them by Major E. W. Wynkoop, commanding, and myself ; that on the fourth day of September last two Cheyenne Indians (One Eye and Manimick) came in to this post with information that the Arapahoes and Cheyennes had several white prisoners among them that they had purchased, and were desirous of giving them up and making peace with the whites ; that on the sixth day of September following Major E. W. Wynkoop left this post with a detachment of troops to rescue said prisoners, and that after an absence of several days he returned, bringing with him four white prisoners, which he received from the Arapaho and Cheyenne Indians. He was accompanied on his return by a number of the most influential men of both tribes, who were unanimously opposed to war with the whites, and desired peace at almost any terms that the whites might dictate ; that immediately upon the arrival of Major Wynkoop at this post large numbers of Arapahoes and Cheyennes came and camped near the post Major Wynkoop selected several of the most prominent chiefs of both nations and proceeded to Denver to counsel with Superintendent Evans. After his return he held frequent councils with the Indians, and at all of them distinctly stated that he was not empowered to treat with them ; but that he had despatched a message to the headquarters of the department, stating their wish in the matter, and that as soon as he received advices from there he would inform them of the decision of General Curtis respecting them ; that until that time, if they placed themselves under his protection they should not be molested ; that the Indians remained quietly near the post until the arrival of Major Anthony, who relieved Major Wynkoop. Major Anthony held

150

a council with the Indians and informed them that he was instructed not to allow any Indians in or near the post, but that he had found matters much better here than he had expected, and advised them to go out and camp on Sand creek until he could hear from General Curtis. He wished them to keep him fully advised of all the movements of the Sioux, which they promptly did. He also promised them that as soon as he heard from General Curtis he would advise them of his decision. From the time that Major Wynkoop left this post to go out to rescue the white prisoners until the arrival of Colonel Chivington here, which took place on the twenty-eighth day of November last, no depredations of any kind had been committed by the Indians within two hundred miles of this post; that upon Colonel Chivington's arrival here with a large body of troops, he was informed where the Indians were encamped, and was fully advised under what cirumstances they had come in to this post, and why they were then on Sand creek; that he was remonstrated with, both by officers and civilians at this post, against making war upon these Indians; that he was informed and fully advised that there was a large number of friendly Indians there, together with several white men, who were there at the request of himself (Colley) and by permission of Major Authony; that notwithstanding his knowledge of the facts as above set forth, he is informed that Colonel Chivington did, on the morning of the twenty-ninth day of November last, surprise and attack said camp of friendly Indians and massacre a large number of them, mostly women and children, and did allow the troops under his command to mangle and mutilate them in the most horrible manner.

S. G. COLLEY,
*United States Indian Agent.*

Sworn and subscribed to before me this twenty-eighth day of January, at Fort Lyon, Colorado Territory.

W. P. MINTON,
*Second Lieutenant New Mexico Volunteers and Post Adjutant.*

FORT LYON, COLORADO TERRITORY. *January* 16, 1865.

SIR: In pursuance of Special Order No. 43, headquarters district of the Upper Arkansas, directing me to assume command of Fort Lyon, Colorado Territory, as well as to investigate and immediately report in regard to late Indian proceedings in this vicinity. I have the honor to state that I arrived at this post on the evening of the 14th of January, 1865, assumed command on the morning of the 18th, and the result of my investigation is as follows, viz:

As explanatory, I beg respectfully to state, that while formerly in command of this post, on the 4th day of September, 1864, and after certain hostilities on the part of the Cheyenne and Arapaho Indians, induced, as I have had ample proof, by the overt acts of white men, three Indians, Cheyennes, were brought as prisoners to myself, who had been found coming towards the post, and who had in their possession a letter, written, as I ascertained afterwards, by a half-breed in the Cheyenne camp, as coming from Black Kettle and other prominent chiefs of the Cheyenne and Arapaho nation, the purport of which was that they desired peace, had never desired war with the whites, and as well as stating they had in their possession some white prisoners, women and children, whom they were willing to deliver up, providing that peace was granted them; knowing that it was not in my power to insure and offer them peace for which they sued, and at the same time anxious, if possible, to accomplish the rescue of the white persons in their possession, I finally concluded to risk an expedition, with a small command I could raise, numbering one hundred and twenty-seven men, to the rendezvous where I was informed they were congregated to the number of two thousand, and endeavor by some means to procure the aforesaid white persons, and to be governed in my course of accomplishing the same entirely by circumstances, having formerly made a lengthy report in regard to the same. In my expedition I have but to say that I succeeded, procuring four white captives from the hands of these Indians, simply giving them, in return, a pledge that I would endeavor to procure for them the peace for which they so anxiously sued; feeling that under the proclamation issued by John Evans, governor of Colorado and superintendent of Indian affairs, a copy of which becomes a portion of this report, by virtue of my position as a United States officer highest in authority in the country included within the bounds prescribed as the country of the Arapaho and Cheyenne nations, I could offer them protection until such time as some measures might be taken by those higher in authority than myself in regard to them. I took with me seven of the principal chiefs, including Black Kettle, to Denver City for the purpose of allowing them an interview with the governor of Colorado, by that means making a mistake of which I have since become painfully aware, that of proceeding with these chiefs to the governor of Colorado Territory instead of to the headquarters of my district to my commanding officer. In the consultation with Governor Evans the matter was referred entirely to the military authorities. Colonel J. M. Chivington, at that time commander of the district of Colorado, was present at the council held with these Indian chiefs, and told them that the whole matter was referred to myself, who would act towards them according to the best of my judgment, until such time as I could receive instructions from the proper authority. Returning to Fort Lyon, Colorado Territory, I allowed the Indians to bring their villages to the vicinity of the fort, including their squaws and papooses, and in such a position that I could at any moment, with the garrison, have annihilated them had they given any evidence of hostility of any kind in any quarter.

I then immediately despatched my adjutant, Lieutenant W. W. Dennison, with a full statement, to the commanding general of the department, asking for instructions, but in the meanwhile various false rumors having reached district headquarters in regard to my course, I was relieved from the command of Fort Lyon, Colorado Territory, and ordered to report to district headquarters ; Major Scott J. Anthony, 1st cavalry of Colorado, who had been ordered to assume command of Fort Lyon, Colorado Territory, previous to my departure, held a consultation with the chiefs in my presence, and told them that though acting under strict orders, under the circumstances, could not materially differ from the course which I had adopted, and allowed them to remain in the vicinity of the post with their families, assuring them of perfect safety until such time as positive orders should be received from headquarters in regard to them. I left the fort on the 26th of November, 1864, for the purpose of reporting to district headquarters ; on the second day after leaving Fort Lyon, while on the plains, I was approached by three Indians, one of whom stated to me that he had been sent by Black Kettle to warn me that about two hundred Sioux warriors had proceeded down the road between where I was and Fort Larned to make war, and desired that I should be careful, another evidence of these Indians' good faith ; all of his statement proved afterwards to be correct. Having an escort of twenty-eight men, I proceeded on my way, but did not happen to fall in with them.

From evidence of officers at this post I understand that on the 28th day of November, 1864, Colonel J. M Chivington, with the 3d regiment of Colorado cavalry (one-hundred-days men) and a battalion of the 1st Colorado cavalry arrived at this post, ordered a portion of the garrison to join him, under the command of Major Scott J. Anthony, against the remonstrances of the officers of the post, who stated circumstances of which he was well aware, attacked the camp of friendly Indians, the major portion of which were composed of women and children. The affidavits which become a portion of this report will show more particulars of that massacre ; any one whom I have spoken to, whether officers or soldiers, agree in the relation that the most fearful atrocities were committed that was ever heard of ; women and children were killed and scalped, children shot at their mother's breast, and all the bodies mutilated in the most horrible manner. Numerous eye-witnesses have described scenes to me, coming under the notice of Colonel Chivington, of the most disgusting and horrible character, the dead bodies of females profaned in such a manner that the recital is sickening. Colonel J. M. Chivington all the time inciting his troops to these diabolical outrages previous to the slaughter ; commencing, he addressed his command, arousing in them, by his language, all their worst passions, urging them on to the work of committing all these diabolical outrages, knowing himself all the circumstances of these Indians resting on the assurances of protection from the government given them by myself and Major S. J. Anthony ; he kept his command in entire ignorance of the same, and when it was suggested that such might be the case, he denied it positively, stating that they were still continuing their depredations and lay there threatening the fort. I beg leave to draw the attention of the colonel commanding to the fact, established by the enclosed affidavits, that two-thirds or more of that Indian village were women and children. I desire also to state that Colonel J. M. Chivington is not my superior officer, but is a citizen mustered out of the United States service, and also to the time this inhuman monster committed this unprecedented atrocity he was a citizen by reason of his term of service having expired, he having lost his regulation command some months previous. Colonel Chivington reports officially that between five and six hundred Indians were left dead upon the field. I have been informed by Captain Booth, district inspector, that he visited the field and counted but sixty-nine bodies, and by others who were present, but that few, if any, over that number were killed, and that two-thirds of them were women and children. I beg leave to further state, for the information of the colonel commanding, that I talked to every officer in Fort Lyon, and many enlisted men, and that they unanimously agree that all the statements I have made in this report are correct. In conclusion, allow me to say that from the time I held the consultation with the Indian chiefs, on the headwaters of Smoky Hill, up to the date of the massacre by Colonel Chivington, not one single depredation had been committed by the Cheyenne and Arapaho Indians ; the settlers of the Arkansas valley had returned to their camps and had been resting in perfect security, under assurances from myself that they would be in no danger for the present, by that means saving the country from what must inevitably become a famine were they

APPENDIX.

to lose their crops; the lines of communication to the States were opened, and travel across the plains rendered perfectly safe through the Cheyenne and Arapaho country. Since this last horrible murder by Chivington the country presents a scene of desolation; all communication is cut off with the States, except by sending large bodies of troops, and already over a hundred whites have fallen as victims to the fearful vengeance of these betrayed Indians. All this country is ruined; there can be no such thing as peace in the future but by the total annihilation of all these Indians on the plains. I have most reliable information to the effect that the Cheyennes and Arapahoes have allied themselves with the Kiowas, Comanches and Sioux, and are congregated to the number of ——— thousand on the Smoky Hill. Let me also draw the attention of the colonel commanding to the fact stated by the affidavits, that John Smith, United States interpreter, a soldier and citizen were presented in the Indian camp by permission of the commanding officer of this camp, another evidence to the fact of these same Indians being regarded as friendly Indians; also, that Colonel Chivington states in his official report that he fought from nine hundred to one thousand Indians, and left from five to six hundred dead upon the field, the sworn evidence being that there were but five hundred souls in the village, two thirds of them being women and children, and that there were but from sixty to seventy killed, the major portion of whom were women and children. It will take many more troops to give security to the travellers and settlers in this country and to make any kind of successful warfare against the Indians. I am at work placing Fort Lyon in a state of defence, having all, both citizens and soldiers located here, employed upon the works, and expect to have them soon completed and of such a nature that a comparatively small garrison can hold the fort against any attack by Indians. Hoping that my report may receive the particular attention of the colonel commanding, I respectfully submit the same.

Your obedient servant,

E. W. WYNKOOP,
*Major, Com'dg 1st Veteran Cavalry and Fort Lyon, C. T.*

Lieutenant J. E. TAPPAN,
*A. A A. General, District of Upper Arkansas.*

---

FORT LARNED, *May* 31, 1865.

Colonel Ford sworn:

I am colonel of the 2d Colorado regiment of cavalry and brevet brigadier general in command of the district of the Upper Arkansas. I have been in command since about the 1st of September last. I relieved Major Henning. From the best of my information all the tribes of Indians are hostile The Kioways, Cheyennes, Comanches, Arapahoes, and parts of other tribes, with their families, are now south of the Arkansas, on the Red river, which is one of its tributaries. In February last a large number of them were about one hundred and fifty miles west of south of this point. From the best information I can get, there are about seven thousand warriors well mounted, some on fleet Texan horses. On horseback they are the finest skirmishers I ever saw. How large a force, mounted and infantry, would be required to defend the Santa Fé road and wage a successful war against the Indians south of the Arkansas? It would require at least ten thousand men—four thousand constantly in the field, well mounted; the line of defence to extend from Fort Lyon to Fort Riley and south about three hundred miles. All supplies would have to come from the States. Contract price for corn delivered at this point was $5.26 per bushel. I do not know how the Indian difficulties originated. I believe the Cheyennes are trying to keep all the Indian tribes in hostility. I have no doubt the attack of Colonel Chivington on the Cheyennes had a very bad effect. There are no Indians north of the Arkansas in my district except some small roving bands. I think, without moving south of the Arkansas, it would require four thousand men to defend the line of this road. I could not swear what Indians have committed the hostilities. Colonel Leavenworth has, in my opinion, the only feasible plan for procuring an interview with the hostile tribes. I received my information from some Mexicans who were trading with the Indians under a pass from General Carleton If a treaty were made by which the Indians would agree to keep south of the Arkansas and east of Fort Bascom, would it protect this route? It would if the northern Indians did not come on to the road. The time has been when travelling over these plains was safe; the travel was as great then as now. There seems to be no reason why that state of affairs could not be brought about by making or conquering a treaty of peace. I think the mouth of Cow creek would be a good point to meet the Indians. General Dodge's orders were to the effect that the military authorities were not to make peace, but to punish the offenders. I am of the opinion that no permits to trade with the Indians should be given while we are carrying on hostilities against them ; and no presents should be given by the agent without the concurrence of the military authorities.  I am of the opinion that if a peace could be made by which the Indians would agree to keep south of the Arkansas it would be better than to conquer one.  My plan of operations would be to capture their villages, women and children, killing the warriors found.  I understand Kit Carson last winter destroyed an Indian village.  He had about four hundred men with him, but the Indians attacked him as bravely as any men in the world, charging up to his lines, and he withdrew his command.  They had a regular bugler, who sounded the calls as well as they are sounded for troops.  Carson said if it had not been for his howitzers few would have been left to tell the tale.  This I learned from an officer who was in the fight.  From information I learn that Captain Parmeter, at Fort Larned, ordered soldiers to fire on Left Hand and party when they came to offer their services to recover the stock run off by other Indians.  There is a general order in this district that no Indian shall be permitted to enter any fort or post without being blindfolded.  I am satisfied that the Sand creek affair has made the Indians more bitter and harder to get at.

---

FORT LARNED, *May* 31, 1865.

John T. Dodds affirms :

I am fifty-four years old.  Have spent six years among the Indians of Ohio and seven years here.  Have been engaged, in company with another man, trading with the Indians.  The Cheyennes complain that the Great Father was to give them a certain amount for the privilege of passing through their country.  Heretofore they have had their presents delivered to them at a point designated by themselves ; that they requested their agent, Major Colley, to make the delivery at Walnut creek, but instead the agent carried them on to Fort Lyon ; that they could not go there for them without losing more horses than the goods were worth.  Part of the Arapahoes, under Little Raven, went to Fort Lyon, but lost their ponies ; and they all complain that if the Great Father intends giving them anything he should give it when it arrives in their country, and not put them to so much trouble.  They complain further that they have to pay for the goods intended by the Great Father to be given them.  The above is the statement of Black Kettle, Lean Bear, Left Hand, and Raven.  They complain generally that the whites are encroaching on their lands and killing their buffalo.  I think that before the Sand creek affair they were willing to settle on their reservations ; but they now feel that they have been badly treated.  The Comanches claim that until lately they have been at peace.  A Kioway chief stated that if they went to war the Comanches would join them.  Stante stated that the Kioways divided with the Comanches the stock run off from Fort Larned.  I think if Satank and Stante, of the Kioways, were out of the way there would be peace, but not until.  After the stock was run off from Fort Larned, Lean Bear started to go into the fort under a flag of truce, but was fired on by order of Captain Parmeter.  He left, tearing up his flag.  Mauwee, One-Eye, Lou Bears, and Two Buttes, chiefs of the Comanche tribe, were present at the fort when the stock was run off, and have not since been seen.

---

FORT RILEY, *May* 25, 1865.

Edmond G. Guerrier, being duly sworn, says :

I am the person referred to by Mr. Mayer in his statement.  I speak English well ; I can speak Cheyenne some, though from long absence I have forgotten a good deal of Cheyenne.  My father was a Frenchman and my mother a Cheyenne.  I am twenty-five years of age.  I was in the camp of the Cheyennes when Chivington made his attack upon them.  I had been with them about three days before the attack.  There were, I think, about eighty lodges ; there are four or five in a lodge on the average ; can't tell precisely the number.  After the attack I remained with them about four weeks.  I do not know how many warriors were in the lodges.  I do not think there were over two hundred warriors in the camp.  Last spring I met John Smith, the interpreter, to go out with him ; about the time we got out there the Cheyennes were at war with the whites ; but the Kioways, Comanches, and Arapahoes were friendly to the whites.  I drove team out for Major Colley, the Indian agent.  I took my discharge at Fort Lyon, came back to Fort Larned and hired to another man to trade with the Indians, and lay in camp at Walnut creek and Fort Garah a few days after the Kioways, Comanches, and Arapahoes broke out into hostilities, and came into our camp at Fort Garah.  There were two Cheyennes in the camp with us that night, and they saved us, saved our lives, myself and a trader.  That night I left with the two Cheyenne Indians.  This was in July some time.  I was out with them

5

until September, when they sued for peace. I wrote the propositions for them to send into Fort Lyon, as the terms of peace. Major Colley, the Indian agent, was there. Major Wynkoop, then in command of Fort Lyon, came out into the prairie and met the Indians. Before he came he replied to my letter. His letter was directed to the chiefs. I read the letter to the chiefs. I think they have the letter still if it was not lost at the fight. The substance of the letter which I wrote and signed by order of the chief was this : That the Indians held some prisoners, three women and four children, and that they were ready to surrender them ; that the Indians desired peace, and to have all the other Indians come too, and have a general peace. He does not now remember all the contents of the letter. One thing more I remember about the prisoners; they had heard there were some Indian prisoners at Denver, and they wanted to have them given up also. The substance of Wynkoop's letter, as I now recollect, was this : He stated there were no Indian prisoners, to his recollection or knowledge, at Denver ; that he would come out to talk with the Indians, and wanted them to meet him on one of the branches of the Smoky Hill ; he did not come out to fight, but to talk, and wanted them to bring the priscners along. I read the letter to the Indians ; they saddled up their horses and started immediately and met him that night, but had no interview until the next morning. He told them he was not big chief enough to make a treaty ; he had no orders of that kind, but told them he would do all he could, and use his influence if some of the chiefs would go to Denver and see the governor, and told them that by giving up their prisoners to him it would go to show they were in earnest for peace. The Indians agreed to do so, and started the same day to go after the prisoners. In three days they brought in one young woman, and in a day or two after that brought in three children ; the other three had gone north with another party of the band on to the Powder river. The chiefs who brought in the prisoners went with Wynkoop to see the governor at Denver. After Wynkoop and the chiefs returned, Wynkoop desired that the Indians who wished to be friendly should all come in and camp near Fort Lyon. If they did so it would show, if there were depredations committed they had no part in them ; and if they did so, as long as they would behave, he would issue them rations. He was expecting some expeditions, and if they were found outside they would be treated by them like hostile Indians. He told them as long as they would stay there and behave themselves he would protect them and see that no troops should hurt them. I am sure and positive of this. Black Kettle and White Antelope, Cheyenne chiefs, also told me that Wynkoop had promised protection if they would come in, and they had promised to do so ; and that Wynkoop had acted like a gentleman, more so than any other white man who had dealt with them, and they had promised to come in, and they did so. Before they came in Wynkoop was relieved of his command, and Major Anthony took command. Wynkoop left and came east. They were encamped on Sand creek, about twenty-five or thirty miles from Fort Lyon. A few days after Wynkoop left I went out with John Smith from Fort Lyon to the camp to trade. Smith had a Cheyenne wife at the camp ; he also had a son with him, full grown. About three days after that the camp was attacked early in the morning. David Louderback was also in the camp ; also a young man by the name of Watt Clark ; these were white men. I was, at the time of the attack, sleeping in a lodge. I heard, at first, some of the squaws outside say there were a lot of buffalo coming into camp ; others said they were a lot of soldiers. The squaws in my lodge looked out and then called to me to get up ; "there were a lot of soldiers coming." I did so, went out, and went towards Smith's tent, where he traded ; I ran and met him. Louderback, the soldier, proposed we should go out and meet the troops. We started ; before we got outside the edge of the tent I could see soldiers begin to dismount. I thought they were artillerymen and were about to shell the camp. I had hardly spoken when they began firing with their rifles and pistols. When I saw I could not get to them, I struck out; I left the soldier and Smith ; I went to the northeast ; I ran about five miles, when I came across an Indian woman driving a herd of ponies, some ten or fifteen. I got a pony. She was a cousin of mine—one of White Antelope's daughters. I went on with her to Smoky Hill. I saw as soon as the firing began, from the number of troops, that there could be no resistance, and I escaped as quick as I could. From all I could learn at the council held by the Indians, there were one hundred and forty-eight killed and missing ; out of the one hundred and forty-eight, about sixty were men—the balance women and children. From all I heard before and after the attack, I am sure that the Indians were encamped at the place where they were attacked in full faith and assurance that they would be protected as friendly Indians. George Bent, a half-Cheyenne, helped me in writing the letter to Wynkoop to make terms of peace.

E. G. GUERRIER.

Henry F. Mayer:

I am sutler to the post, and have been such for two and a half years. I am forty-seven years of age. I know Edmond G. Guerrier, a son of William Guerrier, formerly an Indian trader, a Frenchman, and trader at Fort Laramie, by a Cheyenne woman. He is now about twenty-five years of age. I know him intimately. I was the executor of his father's estate, and am his guardian. His father died in February, 1858. Edmond has been with me most of the time since I know him to be an upright, intelligent, correct young man. He is entirely reliable. I trust every word he says.

H. F. MAYER.

Sworn to this 25th day of May, 1865, before me.

J. R. DOOLITTLE.

---

Captain L. Wilson, 1st Colorado cavalry, sworn:

I arrived in Colorado in May, 1860, from Omaha, Nebraska ; was raised in Pennsylvania ; I have been in the service since August, 1861 ; I entered the service as a private, was promoted to second lieutenant, and then to captain. The only fight with Indians I have been engaged in was the Sand creek affair. I was first lieutenant commanding a battalion at Sand creek ; I think there were about eight hundred troops engaged, under the command of Colonel Chivington. The fight occurred on the 29th of November, 1864 ; the column concentrated at Fort Lyon and moved from there. No pickets were thrown around the post by the command, and nothing done to prevent any one from passing out. We reached Fort Lyon about 10½ o'clock on the morning of the 28th ; we received no information that the Indians at Sand creek were considered under the protection of the government. Major Scott Anthony was in command of the post ; the column moved about 9½ o'clock in the evening ; the command was composed of cavalry with six pieces of 12-pound howitzers. We reached the Indian village at daybreak the next morning, surprising the Indians. I was ordered with my battalion to cut the Indians off from their ponies. The advance was made from the southeast side by the whole column. My orders from Colonel Chivington were to cut the herd off, and in doing that I was compelled to fire on the Indians. The first firing was by our troops ; I detached H company of my battalion, which was engaged some five minutes before the action became general. The artillery opened on the Indians, who had approached me under a bank as if they were going to fight. The Indians returned our first fire almost instantaneously. I was wounded in the early part of the action ; the general action lasted about two hours. I saw no flag of any kind among the Indians. I heard the loss of the enemy estimated by some of the officers engaged at from 300 to 500 ; I should judge there were from 600 to 800 Indians in all. I heard no orders given in relation to taking prisoners, but it was generally understood among the officers and men, that no prisoners would be taken. Young Jack Smith and young Bent, half-breeds and two or three squaws, were the only prisoners taken. Young Bent was sent as a prisoner to Fort Lyon ; Jack Smith was afterwards killed in camp. The squaws and pappooses followed the column to Fort Lyon ; one young infant was picked up on the field ; when we got into camp it was given to one of the squaws, but afterwards died and was buried. I saw some Indians that had been scalped, and the ears were cut off of the body of White Antelope. One Indian who had been scalped had also his skull all smashed in, and I heard that the privates of White Antelope had been cut off to make a tobacco bag out of. I heard some of the men say that the privates of one of the squaws had been cut out and put on a stick. There was a herd of about 600 ponies, mules and horses captured, whose average value per head was, I think, about $100 ; the Indians did not succeed in getting away with more than half a dozen of them. The herd was placed in charge of Captain Johnson, provost marshal of the column, and sent into Fort Lyon. When I reached Fort Lyon, I heard from the quartermaster that the main portion of the herd had been stolen by the troops ; there were about 250 head recovered and brought to Denver with the command. Of the whole number captured the government derived no benefit, the stock being stolen and generally distributed throughout the country. In the Indian camp I saw one new scalp, a white man's, and two old ones. Some clothing was found, women's shoes and dresses, and officers' uniforms and other articles. The men helped themselves to what they wanted, and the balance was burned in the village. All the force, with the exception of about two hundred and forty of the veteran battalion, were one-hundred-days men ; this was their only engagement. I do not know of its being an Indian custom to scalp their own dead, but am of the opinion, that the Indians at Sand creek were scalped by our soldiers.

# APPENDIX.

Pressly Talbott sworn:

Have resided in the Territory since 1859 ; I came from Kentucky ; have become pretty well acquainted with Indian affairs ; the difficulties arise from depredations committed by the Indians. The first year I was here there was no difficulty with the Indians ; since then they have been committing depredations. I entered the service as captain in the 3d regiment Colorado one-hundred-days men ; the only battle I was engaged in was at Sand creek. I was at Fort Lyon the day before the battle ; I had a conversation with Major Anthony, who expressed himself glad that we had come, saying that he would have attacked the Indians himself had he had sufficient force. I did not understand from any source that the Indians had been placed there at Sand creek under the protection of the government. Colonel Chivington gave orders that no parties, either military or civil, should be allowed to leave or enter Fort Lyon without his consent, and he stationed pickets to enforce the order. I believe the object of the order was to prevent any one from giving the Indians information that troops were coming. I think we moved from Fort Lyon with about 650 men and four pieces of artillery, passing a distance of about forty-five miles, reaching the Indian village about sun up, surprising the Indians; Colonel Chivington ordering that the ponies be first secured, and Captain Wilson was intrusted with stampeding the ponies with Colonel Shoup. I received orders to march up the right side of the creek and attack, which I obeyed ; the troops on the other side of the creek had commenced firing before ; the artillery was also playing on the Indians. My company was permitted to charge the banks and ditches. No orders were given about taking prisoners. I was wounded and taken from the field about half an hour after the battle began, and know nothing of the fight after that time ; I was shot through with a bullet. I did not see any flags displayed by the Indians. I do not know what disposition was made of the captured stock. I occupied a room while wounded adjoining the room of Major Colley, and was shown papers by John Smith against the government for 105 buffalo robes, two white ponies, and a wagon-load of goods. This account was made out in favor of Smith and Colley for $6,000. They claimed they had other demands against the government, and Smith said they would realize $25,000 out of it, and damn Colonel Chivington. They were very bitter in their denunciations of Colonel Chivington and Major Downing. Private Louderback swore to the accounts ; he was detailed as a nurse for me, but did writing for Smith and Colley.

---

DENVER, *July* 21, 1865.

Jacob Downing sworn:

I have resided in Colorado since the spring of 1860 ; am a native of Albany, New York, a lawyer by profession, and about thirty-three years of age. I was major of the first cavalry of Colorado ; was in service from August, 1861, to January, 1865. A portion of the time I acted as inspector of the district of Colorado. The first collision between the troops and the Indians was at Fremont's orchard, near Camp Sanborn, on the north side of the South Platte river, about the twelfth of April, 1864. I was at Camp Sanborn, inspecting troops. In the evening, about 9 o'clock, a man by the name of Ripley, a ranchman on the Kioway creek, came into Camp Sanborn and stated that the Indians had taken from him all his stock, and that he had narrowly escaped with his life. He did not know what tribe of Indians, and said that they were driving the people off from the Kioway, Bijout, and other creeks. He requested Captain Sanborn, the commander of the post, to give him the assistance of a few troops, stationed there, to recover the stock, saying that he knew the Indians ; that they would go north, and he thought he could find them. Captain Sanborn consented. Next morning Lieutenant Dunn, with about forty men, was ordered to go in pursuit and recover the stock, if possible, taking Mr. Ripley as guide ; with instructions also, as I understood, to disarm the Indians if he found them in possession of the stock, but to use every means to avoid a collision with them. He started that morning and returned about ten o'clock that evening, stating that he had had a fight with the Indians ; that they first fired upon him. After marching until four o'clock in the afternoon he came in sight of the Indians, near Fremont's orchard. He was then on the south side of the Platte ; the Indians were crossing to the north side, some of whom were driving a herd of stock—horses, mules, &c. In the river he halted his command to allow the horses to drink, they not having had water since morning, when Mr. Ripley and a soldier went ahead of the command to see what the Indians were driving, and to see if they could see Ripley's stock in the herd of the Indians. They soon returned, when Ripley stated that he recognized the Indians as those who drove off his stock, and had seen his horses in their herd, which they were rapidly driving towards the bluffs. The soldier stated that he thought the Indians intended to fight ; that they were loading their rifles. When Lieutenant Dunn arrived on the north bank of the Platte, where he could see the Indians, he found them with their bows strung and their rifles in their hands. He directed

157

Mr. Ripley and four soldiers to stop the herd the Indians were driving, halted his command, and alone rode forward to meet the Indians; talked with them, endeavoring to obtain the stock without any difficulty, and requested one or two of the Indians to come forward and talk with him. They paid no attention to him, but together and in line rode towards him. Finding them determined not to talk with him, he rode slowly back to his command, and when the Indians were within about six or eight feet, he ordered his men to dismount and disarm the Indians. As soon as his men had dismounted the Indians fired upon them, and a fight commenced, which lasted about an hour. He succeeded in driving them into the bluffs, and followed them that night about twenty miles. He had four wounded, two of whom afterwards died. He thought he killed a number of Indians. The Indians, being greatly superior in numbers, succeeded in getting their dead and wounded away. At the commencement of the fight a small party of Indians drove the stock into the bluffs, and Ripley's stock was never recovered. He afterwards learned they were southern Cheyennes. He learned it from spears, bows, arrows, and other things left on the ground where the fight occurred, and by statements of some of the Indians of the Cheyennes; this is hearsay. Major Whitely took the statement of Indians at Camp Welles. Lieutenant Dunn had separated his command, and had only sixteen men with him. He thought there were from eighty to one hundred Indians. He returned to camp, and next morning, having obtained a man named Geary as a guide, with a fresh-mount, he started in pursuit. It having snowed in the night, the trail was obliterated so they could not follow it. The next was a fight I had with them at Cedar Bluffs. I came to Denver and requested Colonel Chivington to give me a force to go against the Indians. He did so. I had about forty men. I captured an Indian and required him to go to the village, or I would kill him. This was about the middle of May. We started about eleven o'clock in the day; travelled all day and all that night. About daylight I succeeded in surprising the Cheyenne village of Cedar Bluffs, in a small cañon about sixty miles north of the South Platte river. We commenced shooting; I ordered the men to commence killing them. We soon found a cañon on the edge of the brinks, occupied by warriors with rifles. I arranged my men the best, as I thought, under the circumstances, and commenced shooting at them, and they at us. The fight lasted about three hours. They put their dead under the rocks. They lost, as I was informed, some twenty-six killed and thirty wounded. My own loss was one killed and one wounded. I burnt up their lodges and everything I could get hold of. There were fifteen large lodges and some smaller ones, but I was informed that there were some warriors who had no lodges. I took no prisoners. We got out of ammunition and could not pursue them. There were women and children among the Indians, but, to my knowledge, none were killed. We captured about one hundred head of stock, which was distributed among the boys. The stock consisted of ponies, for which I would not have given $5 per head. They were probably worth in this market $15 per head. I distributed the stock among the men for the reason that they had been marching almost constantly day and night for nearly three weeks, and with the understanding that if Major General Curtis, commanding the department, would not consent to it, they would turn the stock over to the government—having seen such things done in New Mexico, under the command of General Canby, commanding the department. General Curtis would not allow this to be done, and I ordered the men to turn the ponies over to Lieutenant Chase, acting battalion quartermaster, which, to the best of my knowledge and belief, was done; and by Lieutenant Chase, as I was informed, the ponies were turned over to the government. About the same time I heard Lieutenant Ayres had a collision with the Indians. I made my attack on the Indians from the fact that constant statements were made to me by the settlers of the depredations committed by the Indians on the Platte, and the statements of murders committed; and I regarded hostilities as existing between the whites and Cheyennes before I attacked them at Cedar Bluffs, and before Lieutenant Dunn had a collision with them; and continue up to the present time. I was under Colonel Chivington when he went to Fort Lyon, and when he made the attack at Sand creek. I have no knowledge of what occurred between the Indians and Major Wynkoop, commander of the post of Fort Lyon, but heard Major Anthony's statement. Colonel Chivington marched with about five hundred men from Camp Fillmore; upon arriving at Fort Lyon he surrounded the place with pickets to prevent any one from leaving. He met Major Anthony at the officers' quarters. I was not present at the commencement of the interview, but came up soon after. I heard Colonel Chivington ask Major Anthony how the Indians were. The major said he wished Colonel Chivington would go out and attack them; that every man in Fort Lyon would go with him that had the opportunity; that he would have attacked them long before if he had had a sufficient number of troops. He stated that the Indians were on Sand creek, about twenty miles from Fort Lyon; but afterwards understood that he was mistaken, as they were about forty miles from Fort Lyon. He urged an immediate attack upon the Indians, stating that he would like to save out of the number a few who he believed to be good Indians; mention-

APPENDIX.

ing the names of One Eye, Black Kettle, and one other, stating that the rest ought all to be killed. He said, in substance, that he had ordered the Indians at one time to give up their arms, and that he had intended to treat them as prisoners of war ; that they gave him a few bows and arrows used by boys, and perfectly useless for warriors ; that they gave up a Hawkins rifle without any lock on it ; and, in fact, all the arms they surrendered were useless. Then, believing that they were insincere in their professions of friendship, he had returned their arms, ordered them away from the post, and directed the guard to fire upon them if they attempted to come into the fort. In fact, all his statements were urging Colonel Chivington to attack the Indians ; that they were hostile. The command arrived at Fort Lyon in the forenoon, and that evening about 9 o'clock Colonel Chivington's command started for Sand creek. I should judge he took with him some one hundred or one hundred and twenty men from Fort Lyon. We reached Sand creek about sunrise next morning. A battalion was immediately ordered to place themselves between the village and the ponies ; the other battalions were brought up and nearly surrounded the village. The horse of a man named Pierce was apparently running away with him ; the horse ran into the village and fell, but got up ; when an Indian fired and killed Pierce ; this was the first shot fired, to my knowledge. I rode forward to the village at the head of what was left of my battalion, some having been sent away, and when near the village an Indian fired at me from under the bank of the creek. After looking at the arrangement of the village, I went back to Major Anthony, who had his battalion in line, and, under the supposition that he was going to charge the village with his cavalry, advised him not to do it, believing that the horses were liable to become entangled among the ropes and fall. Immediately after Pierce was killed the battalion on the right commenced firing into the village. Major Anthony was on the east of the village, on the north side of the creek ; most of the command were dismounted, and fought in that way. The Indians took refuge in trenches under the banks, which had evidently been dug before our arrival. The fighting became general ; we killed as many as we could ; the village was destroyed and burned. The surgeon informed me that some forty were killed and wounded in Colonel Chivington's command. My own belief is, that there were some five hundred or six hundred Indians killed ; I counted two hundred and odd Indians within a very short distance of where their village stood, most of whom were in these trenches, and Indians were killed five and six miles from the village ; but of the two hundred killed, I counted about twelve or fifteen women and a few children, who had been killed in the trenches. I did not see any flag over the village, but afterwards saw a man with a small flag, who said he got it out of a lodge ; I saw no person advancing with a white flag, but think I should have seen it had it happened. The Indians were not buried by our men. I saw no soldier scalping anybody, but saw one or two bodies which had evidently been scalped. I understand two or three squaws were taken prisoners, and carried to Fort Lyon. A half breed named Smith was taken prisoner, but was afterwards shot, the man who shot him afterwards deserting. I remember seeing John Smith after the attack was made. Major Anthony ordered his men to cease firing, and called to Smith to come towards him. I saw no mutilated bodies besides scalping, but heard that some bodies were mutilated. I don't know that I saw any squaw that had been scalped. I saw no scalps or other parts of the person among the command on our return I saw no papoose in a feed-box. I think I saw one with a squaw the night of our first camp, but understood they abandoned it the next morning, when the command moved. I heard Colonel Chivington give no orders in regard to prisoners. I tried to take none myself, but killed all I could ; and I think that was the general feeling in the command. I think and earnestly believe the Indians to be an obstacle to civilization, and should be exterminated. I think there were some five hundred or six hundred head of ponies, horses, and mules. Colonel Chivington ordered the provost marshal, Captain J. J. Johnson, to take charge of them and turn them over to the quartermaster at Denver. Captain Johnson took charge of them and, I think, turned them over. I do not know of any being distributed among the men. I acted as attorney for Colonel Chivington in the late investigation.

DENVER, *July* 27, 1865.

Oliver A. Williard :

Is a clergyman of the Methodist Episcopal church, residing in Denver, and have resided here three years nearly ; I know Colonel Chivington, and also Governor Evans ; I have had conversation with Colonel Chivington more than once upon the subject of Governor Evans's connexion with the affair at Sand creek last year ; Colonel Chivington said that Governor Evans had no knowledge of when he was to strike, or where, nor what was the object of his expedition ; he said this more than once ; he said it was necessary to keep secrecy in such expeditions, and the governor knew nothing of it when he went to the States ; the governor was absent when the attack took place ; both Colonel Chivington and Governor Evans are my friends, and members of my church.

# APPENDIX.

## Major Simeon Whitely sworn:

I have resided in Colorado since April, 1863 ; I came here from Wisconsin ; there was no outbreak among the Plain Indians until a year ago last spring ; since then there has been continual trouble ; I was present at a council held between Governor Evans and seven or nine chiefs of the Cheyenne and Arapaho tribes in September, 1864 ; copies of what was said at the council are on file in the Senate Committee on Indian Affairs, and in the commission to investigate the conduct of Colonel Chivington ; the original draught is in the possession of Governor Evans ; I did not hear Governor Evans say that he did not want to see the Indians, or to make peace with them ; he told them that the power to make peace had passed out of his hands ; I did not hear him at any time say that if he made peace he would not know what to do with the regiment he had raised ; in making the report of what transpired at the council I took great pains, and am sure that it is a correct and truthful account of the whole transaction ; when the third Colorado regiment came back from Sand creek I saw in the hands of a good many of the privates a great many scalps, or parts of scalps, said to have been taken in that fight ; at a theatrical performance held in this city I saw a great many scalps exhibited ; at various times in the city I must have seen as many as a hundred scalps.

## S. E. Browne sworn:

I have lived in Colorado since May, 1862, during which time have been United States attorney for the Territory ; I have no doubt that if the military and civil management of Indian affairs were in discreet and competent hands Indian difficulties might be avoided ; I personally know of no frauds or peculations committed against the government or Indians by any civil or military officers ; in February last I was elected colonel of a mounted regiment raised in this Territory to serve for ninety days ; late in the month of February I was in General Moonlight's headquarters, who was in command of the district of Colorado at that time, and heard him say that from the first and third Colorado cavalry then mustered out, and the horses and ponies taken at Sand creek, there were two thousand two hundred head to be accounted for to the government, but of that number only four hundred and twenty-five or four hundred and seventy-five had been accounted for, leaving a deficit of over seventeen hundred that he knew not what had become of ; a comparatively small number, I have been informed, have since been recovered ; I have seen over a hundred scalps in the city and through the country, said to have been taken at Sand creek; early in September or late in August last I heard Colonel Chivington in a public speech announce that his policy was to "kill and scalp all, little and big ; that nits made lice ;" one of the main causes of our difficulties with the Indians comes from the delay in paying the Indians their annuities according to law.

## Colonel Potter sworn:

Am colonel of the sixth United States volunteers ; I have been in Colorado nearly two months ; am in command of the south sub-district of the plains ; off from the stage lines I have received no reports ; on the line south to Forts Garland and Fillmore, and the line into the States, I have had no difficulty, but on the line to Green river, towards Salt lake, the Indians have been troublesome, killing men, &c. ; the Indians, as near as I can find out, are the Arapahoes, who have committed depredations between Fort Collins and the North Platte ; they have driven off stage stock from some of the stations, and have also killed one sergeant and five men, burnt Foot's ranch, attacked a train near the ranch, capturing two wagons and running off some sixty head of stock ; the train was escorted by soldiers, who fought as well as men could until their ammunition gave out ; it requires from twenty-five to thirty men to guard the stage from Virginia Dale to the North Platte ; these depredations I believe to have been committed by the Arapahoes, who, while their families are fed and protected by the government, prey upon the trains ; I know of no other Indians who have committed depredations this side of the North Platte ; north of the North Platte depredations have been committed by the Sioux and Cheyennes ; General Connor, commanding the district, is now at Fort Laramie ; I do not know the strength of his force ; I have at present twelve hundred and eighty-eight men under my command ; I don't think there is any possibility of making any lasting peace with the Indians ; I think there is only one of three things to do—either abandon the country to the Indians, forcibly place the tribes on reservations surrounded by soldiers, or exterminate them ; my orders are to kill every male Indian over twelve years of age found north of the South Platte, but to disturb no women and children ; as far as I know the policy of the military department here, it is to exterminate the Indians ; Utah is within General Connor's district ; I know of no depredations committed in Utah.

Dr. Caleb S. Birtsell sworn :

I have resided in Colorado since 1859 ; I came from Ohio originally ; I was at the battle of Sand creek as assistant surgeon of the third Colorado cavalry ; it commenced by our men corralling the ponies ; Colonel Chivington and Colonel Shoup gave orders to form in line of battle, but it could not be kept ; firing commenced, and I was soon after engaged attending to the wounded ; I saw very little of what occurred ; I reserved some of the lodges for hospital tents, and my time was occupied that day and night and the next day caring for the wounded ; on the afternoon of the 29th of November, while in one of the lodges dressing wounded soldiers, a soldier came to the opening of the lodge and called my attention to some white scalps he held in his hand ; my impression, after examination, was that two or three of them were quite fresh ; I saw in the hands of soldiers silk dresses and other garments belonging to women ; I saw some squaws that were dead, but did not go over the ground ; I did not see any Indians scalped, but saw the bodies after they were scalped ; I saw no other mutilations ; I did not see any kind of a flag in the Indian camp ; there were none left wounded on the field ; I know of none being killed after being taken prisoner ; soon after the battle, on the march, and here in Denver, I have seen soldiers with Indian scalps ; of the stock captured a great many died, and some were distributed among the troops, and some, I think, were sold ; I heard Major Anthony say that he had given the Indians back what arms they had delivered up, and told them they must take care of themselves—that he would issue no more provisions to them—and that they dared let the soldiers out to fight ; my impression is that orders were given to take no prisoners ; I think Colonel Chivington was in a position where he must have seen the scalping going on.

---

Asbury Bird, company D, 1st Colorado cavalry, sworn :

I was present at the engagement between Lieutenant Ayres and the Indians, composed of Cheyennes, Arapahoes, and some Kioways. There was some cattle stolen on the head of Beaver creek. We were sent to recover it ; encountered a band of five lodges ; two of the Indians came towards us armed with rifles ; when about sixty yards off we hollered "how" to them, and they to us ; before we got clear up to them they saw the command about half a mile in rear of us coming up on a lope, and put off to their village and took their squaws and left. Lieutenant Ayres took round a hill to catch the Indians. On our left there was one Indian, and Lieutenant Ayres sent two men to capture him ; but the Indian shot one of the men and the other ran off. The ground being too rough to get the artillery up, we returned to the Indian camp, took all the meat, &c., and burned the lodges. We got on the Indian trail the next morning and pressed them so close they abandoned many things, and we recovered twenty of the stolen cattle. We then returned to Denver. We were ordered out again ; met some Indians of the Sioux tribe ; held a talk with them ; they said they did not wish to fight ; did not feel strong enough ; they stayed in our camp that night, we sharing our provisions with them. The next morning, about 9 o'clock, we were attacked by about seven hundred Indians, and fought them until dark ; we lost four men killed. We had no interpreter along with us. When the two Indians came to meet me they appeared friendly, but when they saw the command coming on a lope, they seemed frightened and ran off. No effort was made by Lieutenant Ayres to hold a talk with the Indians. I was with the train at Sand creek, but did not see the fight. I went over the ground soon after the battle. I should judge there were between 400 and 500 Indians killed. I counted 350 lying up and down the creek. I think about half the killed were women and children. Nearly all, men, women, and children, were scalped. I saw one woman whose privates had been mutilated. The scalps were carried away mostly by the 3d regiment, one-hundred-day men. I saw but one Indian infant killed. Two children were brought to the fort. I think about 500 head of stock was taken ; about 400 were turned over to the quartermaster at Fort Lyon. A great portion of all the stock became scattered through the country. In a conversation with Dick Colley, in the month of November, 1864, he told me they had sent $2,000 worth of the Indian goods to Denver, and expected the money every day. I heard John Smith say he had some goods that did not cost him anything ; that he was going to trade with the Indians, and if he lost them would not be out anything.

---

Mr. Bouser sworn :

The first difficulty between the Cheyennes and Arapahoes and whites occurred on the 11th day of April, 1864. A white man came into Camp Sanborn and reported that he had cattle stolen. A detail of twenty men was sent after the Indians to get the cattle. The commander of the detail, Lieutenant Clark Dunn, had orders to disarm and fetch in the Indians ; if they refused, to sweep them off the face of the earth. A fight occurred, and some Indians were wounded, also four soldiers, two of whom afterwards died. There was no interpreter along with the detail. The Indians, so Lieutenant Dunn told me, shook hands, and appeared as though they wanted to say or do anything. I know an Indian named Spotted Horse, part Cheyenne and part Sioux ; he is now dead ; he told me that he was in the affair with Lieutenant Dunn. He said the Indians took three head of cattle ; there were 100 warriors. There was snow on the ground, and the Indians were hungry and took the cattle ; they would have come into Denver if their horses had been in condition. They went south of the river with the cattle, intending if the soldiers came after them to settle for the cattle by giving some of their ponies. Before they had time to cross the river and kill the cattle the soldiers overtook them. The soldiers had no interpreter, held no talk with the Indians, gave them no time even to deliver the cattle, but pitched into them. He also told me that had he been up in time, as he speaks English, or had there been an interpreter, the whole matter might have been settled without a fight. As it was, the Indians rode up close to the soldiers, dismounted, and shook hands with them. Lieutenant Dunn's men then took hold of some of the Indians' weapons and tried to wrest them away. The Indians did not know what it meant, and refused to give up their arms, when they were fired upon by the soldiers. Spotted Horse, seeing that there was going to be a war, threw up his chieftainship, and with it some one hundred head of ponies, and came in to Governor Evans. I acted as interpreter, and he told substantially to Governor Evans the above. This same chief traded four of his ponies to ransom a white woman— Mrs. Kelly. The next collision was under Major Downing, at Cedar cañon. I have a Brulé Sioux woman for a wife. I am of opinion that a lasting peace could be made with all the southern Sioux without any more fighting.

FORT LYON, COLORADO TERRITORY.

Lieutenant Cramer sworn :

I am stationed at this post, 1st lieutenant company C, veteran battalion Colorado cavalry. I was at this post when Colonel Chivington arrived here, and accompanied him on his expedition. He came into the post with a few officers and men, and threw out pickets, with instructions to allow no one to go beyond the line. I was then in command of company K. He brought some eight or nine hundred men with him, and took from this post over a hundred men, all being mounted. My company was ordered along to take part. We arrived at the Indian village about daylight. On arriving in sight of the village a battalion of the 1st cavalry and the Fort Lyon battalion were ordered on a charge to surround the village and the Indian herd. After driving the herd towards the village, Lieutenant Wilson's battalion of the 1st took possession of the northeast side of the village, Major Anthony's battalion took position on the south, Colonel Chivington's 3d regiment took position in our rear, dismounted, and after the fight had been commenced by Major Anthony and Lieutenant Wilson, mounted, and commenced firing through us and over our heads. About this time Captain John Smith, Indian interpreter, attempting to come to our troops, was fired on by our men, at the command of some one in our rear, "To shoot the damned old son of a bitch." One of my men rode forward to save him, but was killed. To get out of the fire from the rear, we were ordered to the left. About this time Colonel Chivington moved his regiment to the front, the Indians retreating up the creek, and hiding under the banks. There seemed to be no organization among our troops ; every one on his own hook, and shots flying between our own ranks. White Antelope ran towards our columns unarmed, and with both arms raised, but was killed. Several other of the warriors were killed in like manner. The women and children were huddled together, and most of our fire was concentrated on them. Sometimes during the engagement I was compelled to move my company to get out of the fire of our own men. Captain Soule did not order his men to fire when the order was given to commence the fight. During the fight, the battery on the opposite side of the creek kept firing at the bank while our men were in range. The Indian warriors, about one hundred in number, fought desperately ; there were about five hundred all told. I estimated the loss of the Indians to be from one hundred and twenty-five to one hundred and seventy-five killed ; no wounded fell into our hands, and all the dead were scalped. The Indian who was pointed out as White Antelope had his fingers cut off. Our force was so large that there was no necessity of firing on the Indians. They did not return the fire until after our troops had fired several rounds. We had the assurance from Major Anthony that Black Kettle and his friends should be saved, and only those Indians who had committed depredations should be harmed. During the fight no officer took any measures to get out of the fire of our own men. Left Hand stood with his arms folded, saying he would not fight the white men, as they were his friends. I told Colonel Chivington of the position in which the officers stood from Major Wynkoop's pledges to the Indians, and also Major Anthony's, and that it would be murder, in every sense of the word, if he attacked those Indians. His reply was, bringing his fist down close to my face, "Damn any man who sympathizes with Indians." I told him what pledges were given the Indians. He replied, " That he had come to kill Indians, and believed it to be honorable to kill Indians under any and all circumstances ;" all this at Fort Lyon. Lieutenant Dunn went to Colonel Chivington and wanted to know if he could kill his prisoner, young Smith. His reply was, " Don't ask me ; you know my orders; I want no prisoners." Colonel Chivington was in position where he must have seen the scalping and mutilation going on. One of the soldiers was taking a squaw prisoner across the creek, when other soldiers fired on him, telling him they would kill him if he did not let her go. On our approach to the village I saw some one with a white flag approaching our lines, and the troops fired upon it ; and at the time Captain Smith was fired upon, some one wearing a uniform coat was fired upon approaching our lines. Captain Smith was wearing one. After the fight I saw the United States flag in the Indian camp. It is a mistake that there were any white scalps found in the village. I saw one, but it was very old, the hair being much faded. I was ordered to burn the village, and was through all the lodges. There was not any snow on the ground, and no rifle-pits. I was present at the interview on the Smoky Hill between Major Wynkoop and the Indians, and it is correctly set out in his report, which I have read. I was also present at the interview between the Indian chiefs and Major Anthony, after he had assumed command. The chiefs desired to come into the post for protection, as they had heard through the Sioux that the 3d regiment Colorado troops was advancing in their direction. Major Anthony declined to permit them, saying he had not provisions to feed them. They must stay where they were, and their young men must go out and hunt buffalo. This was only three days before the massacre.

---

FORT LYON, COLORADO TERRITORY.

C. M. Cossitt :

Is acting quartermaster at this post ; was here when Colonel Chivington came in from Sand creek after the fight or massacre there. He used to stop with me when he came here. In my room several present, among others Major Colley, Indian agent. He thought he had done a brilliant thing which would make him a brigadier general. I think the expression was, "that he thought that would put a star on his shoulder." This would do for a second Harney as an Indian fighter. This is the substance of the conversation.

C. M. COSSITT,
*Lieut. Vet. Battalion 1st Colorado Cavalry, A. A. Q. M.*

---

Lucien Palmer sworn:

Am sergeant of company C, veteran battalion 1st Colorado cavalry. I was such at the time of the attack on the Cheyennes by Chivington ; I was in the midst of the fight; I counted 130 bodies, all dead ; two squaws and three papooses were captured and brought to Fort Lyon. I think among the dead bodies one-third were women and children. The bodies were horribly cut up, skulls broken in a good many ; I judge they were broken in after they were killed, as they were shot besides. I do not think I saw any but what was scalped ; saw fingers cut off, saw several bodies with privates cut off, women as well as men. I saw Major Sayre, of the 3d regiment, scalp an Indian for the scalp lock ornamented by silver ornaments ; he cut off the skin with it. He stood by and saw his men cutting fingers from dead bodies. This was the morning after the fight. All I saw done in mutilating bodies was done by the members of the 3d regiment. I counted the number of dead bodies, but did not count the women and children separate from the men to learn the proportion of each. I speak only from my impression as to the women and children being one-third of the number killed. I was with the battery.

---

Amos C. Miksch sworn:

Am a corporal in company E, veteran battalion, 1st Colorado cavalry ; was born in Pennsylvania, but my home is in Ohio. I was in the battery ; did not see the first attack ; after we came up we opened on the Indians ; they retreated and we followed and stayed until all were killed we could find. Next morning after the battle I saw a little boy covered up among the Indians in a trench, still alive. I saw a major in the 3d regiment take out his pistol and blow off the top of his head. I saw some men unjointing fingers to get rings

163

off, and cutting off ears to get silver ornaments. I saw a party with the same major take up bodies that had been buried in the night to scalp them and take off ornaments. I saw a squaw with her head smashed in before she was killed. Next morning, after they were dead and stiff, these men pulled out the bodies of the squaws and pulled them open in an indecent manner. I heard men say they had cut out the privates, but did not see it myself. It was the 3d Colorado men who did these things. I counted 123 dead bodies; I think not over twenty-five were full-grown men; the warriors were killed out in the bluff; altogether I think there were about 500. There were 115 lodges, from four to five in a lodge. In the afternoon I saw twenty-five or thirty women and children; Colonel Chivington would not allow them to come in; a squad of the 3d Colorado was sent out; I don't know what became of them; it was about four miles off. The Indians were generally scalped as they fell. Next day I saw Lieutenant Richmond scalp two Indians; it was disgusting to me; I heard nothing of a fresh white scalp in the Indian camp until I saw it in the Dunn papers. There was no snow on the ground; there were no rifle-pits except what the Indians dug into the sand-bank after we commenced firing. I saw them digging out sand with their hands while firing was going on; the water came into the trenches they dug in this manner.

FORT LYON, *June* 9, 1865.

Major Wynkoop sworn :

I am in command of this post; I was in command in May, 1864, and until within a short time previous to the Sand creek affair.

Question. Do your report and the accompanying affidavits state the facts of that affair ?

Answer. They do so far as they go. I have been a resident of this Territory since October, 1858. I have been familiar with the state of affairs with the Cheyenne and Arapaho Indians. Previous to the Chivington affair hostilities were open about four months. From my own personal knowledge I have no doubt that the hostilities were commenced by a detachment of soldiers under the command of Lieutenant Dunn, who was sent in search of some cattle supposed to have been stolen and driven away by some Cheyenne Indians. A conflict occurred between Lieutenant Dunn and the Indians. Captain Sanborn sent out the detachment. A rumor had reached district headquarters that the cattle had been stolen by the Indians, and Colonel Chivington issued orders that a detachment should be sent out to recover the stock and disarm the Indians. The attempt to disarm the Indians resulted in a conflict ; there was one killed and three wounded on our side. That was the first difficulty I know of between the Cheyennes, Arapahoes and whites since my residence in the country, seven years. The next difficulty was an attack on a Cheyenne village by Major Downing, under Chivington's orders. The major reported he had killed over forty warriors, but the Cheyenne chiefs stated to me that their loss consisted of two squaws and two pappooses. Our loss was one killed. Lieutenant Ayres, of the Colorado battery, had the next conflict with the Indians. He had been ordered by Colonel Chivington, as he stated to me, to kill all Indians he came across. He marched from Fort Larned, about forty miles, until he came to Lean Bear's band of Cheyennes, a few of whom were some distance from the column, hunting buffalo. Sergeant Fribbley was approached by Lean Bear, and accompanied by him into our column, leaving his warriors at some distance. A short time after Lean Bear reached our command he was killed, and fire opened upon his band. I am not aware of any hostilities committed by Lean Bear's command previous to this time. A running fight for a couple of hours ensued, in which we lost several killed, the Indians getting possession of the bodies. My information has been derived from information received and reports made to me, also from the Cheyennes. At and previous to the fight of Lieutenant Ayres, a band of Arapahoes were situated about twenty-five miles from here, on Sand creek ; they had been in the habit of coming into the fort frequently, and having communication with their agent, Major Colley, and myself. I had been in the habit of issuing rations to them when I found them in want. They had given every evidence of friendship for the whites, and were in the habit of bringing in and delivering to me government stock found loose on the prairie. In consequence of this friendly feeling on their part, and desirous to keep them friendly, as we were at war with the Cheyennes. I issued rations to them every ten days. About this time I made the proposition to them. Colonel Chivington was temporarily at this post, and in the presence of several officers I submitted the proposition to him, and he heartily indorsed the same, and was present at one or two issues. This post was then in the district of the Upper Arkansas ; Colonel Chivington was here, but dated his orders headquarters in the field. Left-Hand's band was at this time camped near Fort Larned ; near them was a band of Kiowas. Left-Hand, who had always been friendly to the whites, learned that the Kiowas, on a certain day, intended to run off the stock from Fort Larned, and he accordingly stated that fact to the commanding officer of that post, Captain Parmeter. No apparent attention was paid to the

164

information given by Left-Hand, and on the day indicated by him the stock was driven off by the Kiowas. Immediately after this Left-Hand and his band approached the post to offer his services and the services of his young men to pursue the Kiowas and recover the stock. Meeting a soldier a short distance from the post, he requested him to state to the commanding officer his object. I am personally acquainted with Left-Hand ; he speaks English. Left-Hand continued to approach the post, at the same time exhibiting a white flag, when fire was opened upon them by the battery, which drove them off After sufficient time had elapsed for the news to reach this vicinity, the band of Arapahoes camped here suddenly disappeared. Not a great while afterwards a citizen, a quartermaster's teamster, and his wife, while travelling from Denver here, were attacked by Indians ; the man killed and the woman carried off  I have reliable information that this act was committed by Little Raven's band of Arapahoes. A short time after that, two citizens on their way to this post to testify before a military commission, sixteen miles from here, were attacked by Indians and killed. My information is, that this outrage was committed by Little Raven's band. I know of no outrages committed by any of Left-Hand's band. While a small detachment of my regiment, some thirty men, were encamped near the mouth of the Cimarron crossing, their stock was run off. Lieutenant Chase, encamped at Jimmy's camp, had his stock driven off The letter I received from the Indians is correctly printed in the Commissioner's report. I do know that the Indians encamped on Sand creek felt that they were under the protection of the government, and were friendly ; have driven my family down to their camp and sat in their lodges, without an escort. Colonel Chivington had no orders to attack the Cheyenne camp ; I never have received any instructions in regard to Indians and their treatment. Since the Sand creek affair there has existed the deadliest hostility between those tribes and the whites ; they have killed many persons on the Platte, and captured and destroyed much property. I know of no depredations committed on this route by the Cheyennes and Arapahoes since ; I have reason to know that the Kiowas and Comanches have joined them in hostilities ; I know that the Sioux are anxious, with the other tribes, to make peace, if the Cheyennes and Arapahoes do, and I think before the Sand creek affair a lasting peace could have been made with all the Indians. Since the massacre I have not been able to hold any communication with the Indians. I have in my possession a statement made by a half-breed, who had been in their camp since the massacre. He was in during the attack, and was among those who escaped ; he was also in their camp when the remnant of the tribe got together on the Smoky Hill. Black Kettle, head chief of the Cheyennes, was there, but in disgrace with his tribe ; was recognized no longer, and was taunted for having, by putting too much faith in the white man, their women and children murdered. They insulted him and threatened his life, asking him why he did not stay and die with his brother, White Antelope. The Indians told him that altogether there were one hundred and forty missing, but some wounded afterwards came in. Black Kettle is the only chief left who was in favor of peace. White Antelope folded his arms stoically and was shot down, refusing to leave the field, stating that it was the fault of Black Kettle, others, and himself that occasioned the massacre, and he would die. Black Kettle refusing to leave the field, was carried off by his young men. I gave to the head chiefs of the Cheyennes and Arapahoes a written statement that I had, in consequence of their delivering up some white prisoners, come to an understanding as a United States officer to cease hostilities until such a time as something definite could be concluded by the proper authorities, and warned all officers from interfering with them in a hostile manner, until such time should elapse. I pledged myself to give them an interview with the governor of Colorado, and, whatever might be the result, I would return them in safety. This post, at the time of Chivington's attack, was not in his department ; but he went out of his district to make the attack. There was force enough at this post, if necessary, to have whipped the Indians  I do not think this reservation is very good, not as good as on the Beaver creek or Smoky Hill Fork. The latter place is midway between the travelled routes, and the Indians would much prefer land there. There is a great scope of country south of the Arkansas ; the Smoky Hill is the best section of country for the buffalo. In 1858 I travelled with one companion down the Platte, through all the tribes, and was fed and lodged in their camps, encountering no difficulty. I think we might make peace if we could meet the Indians, with the exception of the Dog soldiers of the Cheyennes. But it would be difficult, in consequence of the massacre, to obtain their confidence. I think it a matter of justice to the Indians, and of a decent self-respect to the government, that an effort should be made to make peace. At the time I met the Indians I had but 130 men, and the Indians had some 700 armed warriors. I think had a fight occurred I should have been defeated  After Major Anthony assumed command of the post, he proceeded with a command of cavalry to an Arapaho village, containing the bands of Little Raven and Left-Hand. I had gone down to the village simply as a looker-on, and was there when Major Anthony arrived. He told Little Raven and Left-Hand that he had come for the purpose of taking their arms, as it became necessary to consider them prisoners ; he did not wish any of them to leave camp without permission from him ; he said he would count the number of souls in their camp, and would send an officer every day to verify their presence. The chiefs both appeared willing to deliver up their arms, Little Raven stating he did not desire to be at war with the whites, but was willing to submit to whatever Major Anthony might impose on him. Left-Hand coincided, but requested that he would like to have the Indian boys retain their bows and arrows, as they were in the habit of shooting prairie dogs and jack rabbits, which proved of benefit to them in consequence of their destitute situation. Major Anthony refused to accede to his request, and ordered all the arms to be turned over to him, which was accordingly done, and I saw them placed in a wagon and conveyed to Fort Lyon. This occurred about ten days previous to the fight on Sand creek ; Left-Hand joining the Cheyennes, and Little Raven going to Camp Wynkoop.

I proceeded from this post with a detachment of cavalry under charge of Lieutenant Cramer. At Booneville I left the detachment, and proceeded ahead with the white prisoners, expecting the cavalry having the Indian chiefs in charge would reach Denver two days after my arrival. My object in proceeding ahead was to have an interview with Governor John Evans, ex-officio superintendent of Indian affairs, previous to the arrival of the chiefs. On my arrival I was informed that the governor was sick in bed, and on that evening I did not see him. The next morning he called on me at my hotel. Upon entering the parlor I found him in conversation with Dexter Colley, son of the Indian agent for the Cheyennes and Arapahoes, who was present during our whole interview. I told the governor I had come up in accordance with my report ; had brought the rescued white prisoners with me, and that the chiefs would be in a few days, for the purpose of having an interview with him. He intimated that he was sorry I had brought them ; that he considered he had nothing to do with them ; that they had declared war against the United States, and he considered them in the hands of the military authorities ; that he did not think, anyhow, it was policy to make peace with them until they were properly punished, for the reason that the United States would be acknowledging themselves whipped. I said it would be strange if the United States would consider themselves whipped by a few Indians, and drew his attention to the fact that, as a United States officer, I had pledged myself to these Indians to convey them to Denver, to procure an interview with himself, being the Indian superintendent, upon conditions communicated to him in my report ; that I had brought these Indians a distance of nearly four hundred miles from their village with that object in view ; and desired that he would furnish them an audience. He replied querulously that he was to start next day to visit the Ute agency on business ; besides, he did not want to see them, anyhow. I endeavored to explain to him the position in which I was placed, and earnestly requested that he would await their arrival. He then referred to the fact that the third regiment of one-hundred-day men having been raised, and in camp, were nearly ready to make an Indian campaign. He further said that the regiment was ordered to be raised upon his representations to Washington that they were necessary for the protection of the Territory, and to fight hostile Indians ; and now, if he made peace with the Indians, it would be supposed at Washington that he had misrepresented matters in regard to the Indian difficulties in Colorado, and had put the government to a useless expense in raising and equipping the regiment ; that they had been raised to kill Indians, and they must kill Indians. Several times in our conversation in regard to the object of the Indians who were coming to see him, he made the remark, "What shall I do with the third regiment, if I make peace?"

I have recently been over the battle-field of Sand creek : I saw no evidences of any intrenchments. I do not think the location is suitable for defence.

---

DENVER, COLORADO TERRITORY, *September* 13, 1865.

DEAR SIR : Enclosed please find a copy of my reply to the "Committee on the Conduct of the War." I hope you will find in it a vindication against their unjust implication of my name in the "Sand creek affair."

I fain would hope that, in your report, my administration of Indian affairs might have such mention as the faithfulness of which I am conscious entitles me to receive. I ask nothing but justice, and feel confident that I shall receive this. But the circumstances in which I am placed by the Committee on the Conduct of the War make me anxious for more at the hands of your committee than a mere passing notice. If there is any point in my administration not fully and satisfactorily explained I shall be happy to give the facts as they are.

I have, from what was said to me, assumed that the account of my stewardship was satisfactory to you. I trust I have not been hasty in this.

APPENDIX.

I am gratefully obliged for the kind words in my behalf you were pleased to express at Washington, which have been communicated to me by a friend.

I have the honor to be, very respectfully, yours, &c.,

JOHN EVANS.

Hon. J. R. Doolittle.

---

*Reply of Governor Evans, of the Territory of Colorado, to that part, referring to him, of the report of the "Committee on the Conduct of the War," headed "Massacre of Cheyenne Indians."*

EXECUTIVE DEPARTMENT AND SUPERINTENDENCY OF INDIAN AFFAIRS, C. T.,
*Denver, August 6, 1865.*

*To the Public:*

I have just seen, for the first time, a copy of the report of the Committee on the Conduct of the War! headed "Massacre of Cheyenne Indians."

As it does me great injustice, and by its partial, unfair, and erroneous statements will mislead the public, I respectfully ask a suspension of opinion in my case until I shall have time to present the facts to said committee or some equally high authority, and ask a correction. In the mean time I desire to lay a few facts before the public.

The Committee on the Conduct of the War, as shown by the resolution of the House of Representatives heading the report, had power "to inquire into and report all the facts connected with the late attack, by the 3d regiment Colorado volunteers, under Colonel Chivington, on a village of the Cheyenne tribe of Indians, near Fort Lyon."

They had no power to inquire into my management of Indian affairs except in so far as it related to this battle; and the chairman of the committee assured me that they would not inquire into such general management. Having no connexion whatever with the battle, and, at the time, knowing nothing of the immediate facts connected therewith, I so stated to the committee, and, relying upon the above assurance of the chairman, addressed myself to another committee which had been appointed to investigate the management of Indian affairs generally in the United States. Of this committee, Senator Doolittle was chairman, and to it, I believe, I have rendered a satisfactory account of my stewardship.

The Committee on the Conduct of the War, however, have seen fit to go beyond the scope of their powers, and to enter into a hasty and general investigation of Indian affairs in this superintendency, and in their report attack matters occurring at remote periods from, and entirely disconnected with, the subject-matter of investigation.

Under these circumstances, having been censured unheard, I claim the privilege of presenting proof of the falsity of their charges, in order that, so far as it can be done, the committee, or equally high authority, may repair the great injury done me. And I pledge myself to prove, by official correspondence and accredited testimony, to their satisfaction, and that of all fair-minded men, the truth and justice of my complaint.

I do not propose to discuss the merits or demerits of the Sand creek battle, but simply to meet the attempt, on the part of the committee, to connect my name with it, and to throw discredit on my testimony. I shall not ask the public to take my assertions, except so far as I shall sustain them by undoubted authority, a large part of which is published in government documents by the authority of the honorable body of which the committee are members. The report begins:

"In the summer of 1864 Governor Evans, of Colorado Territory, as acting superintendent of Indian affairs, sent notice to the various bands and tribes of Indians within his jurisdiction that such as desired to be considered friendly to the whites should repair to the nearest military post in order to be protected from the soldiers who were to take the field against the hostile Indians."

This statement is true as to such notice having been sent, but conveys the false impression that it was at the beginning of hostilities, and the declaration of war. The truth is, it was issued by authority of the Indian department months after the war had become general, for the purpose of inducing the Indians to cease hostilities, and to protect those who had been or would become friendly, from the inevitable dangers to which they were exposed. This "notice" may be found published in the report of the Commissioner of Indian Affairs for 1864, page 218.

The report continues:

"About the close of the summer some Cheyenne Indians, in the neighborhood of the Smoky Hill, sent word to Major Wynkoop, commanding at Fort Lyon, that they had in their possession, and were willing to deliver up, some white captives they had purchased

167

of other Indians. Major Wynkoop, with a force of over one hundred men, visited those Indians and recovered the white captives. On his return he was accompanied by a number of the chiefs and leading men of the Indians, whom he had brought to visit Denver for the purpose of conferring with the authorities there in regard to keeping the peace. Among them were Black Kettle and White Antelope, of the Cheyennes, and some chiefs of the Arapahoes. The council was held, and these chiefs stated that they were friendly to the whites and had always been."

Again they say :

" All the testimony goes to show that the Indians under the immediate control of Black Kettle and White Antelope, of the Cheyennes, and Left-Hand, of the Arapahoes, were and had always been friendly to the whites, and had not been guilty of any acts of hostility or depredations."

This word which the committee say was sent to Major Wynkoop was a letter to United States Indian Agent Major Colley, which is published in the report of the Commissioner of Indian Affairs for 1865, page 233, and is as follows :

" CHEYENNE VILLAGE, *August* 29, 1864.

"MAJOR COLLEY: We received a letter from Bent, wishing us to make peace. We held a council in regard to it. All come to the conclusion to make peace with you, providing you make peace with the Kiowas, Comanches, Arapahoes, Apaches, and Sioux. We are going to send a messenger to the Kiowas and to the other nations about our going to make peace with you. We heard that you have some [prisoners] in Denver. We have seven prisoners of yours which we are willing to give up, providing you give up yours. There are three war parties out yet, and two of Arapahoes. They have been out some time and expected in soon. When we held this council there were few Arapahoes and Sioux present. We want true news from you in return. That is a letter.

" BLACK KETTLE, *and other Chiefs.*"

Compare the above extract from the report of the committee with this published letter of Black Kettle and the admission of the Indians in the council at Denver.

The committee say, the prisoners proposed to be delivered up were *purchased of other Indians.* Black Kettle, in his letter, says: "We have seven prisoners of yours, which we are willing to give up, providing you give up yours."

They say nothing about prisoners whom they had *purchased.* On the other hand, in the council held in Denver, Black Kettle said :

" Major Wynkoop was kind enough to receive the letter, and visited them in camp, to whom they delivered four white prisoners, one other (Mrs. Snyder) having killed herself ; that there are two women and one child in their camp whom they will deliver up as soon as they can get them in ; Laura Roper, 16 or 17 years ; Ambrose Asher, 7 or 8 years ; Daniel Marble, 7 or 8 years ; Isabel Ubanks, 4 or 5 years. The prisoners still with them [are] Mrs. Ubanks and babe, and a Mrs. Norton, who was taken on the Platte. Mrs. Snyder is the name of the woman who hung herself. The boys were taken between Fort Kearney and the Blue."

Again : they did not deny having captured the prisoners, when I told them that having the prisoners in their possession was evidence of their having committed the depredations when they were taken. But White Antelope said : " We (the Cheyennes) took two prisoners west of Kearney, and destroyed the trains." Had they *purchased* the prisoners they would not have been slow to make it known in this council.

The committee say the chiefs went to Denver to confer with the authorities about *keeping the peace.* Black Kettle says : " All come to the conclusion to *make peace* with you providing you will *make peace* with the Kiowas, Comanches, Arapahoes, Apaches, and Sioux."

Again, the committee say :

" All the testimony goes to show that the Indians under the immediate control of Black Kettle and White Antelope, of the Cheyennes, and Left-Hand, of the Arapahoes, *were, and had been, friendly to the whites, and had not been guilty of any acts of hostility or depredations* "

Black Kettle says, in his letter : " We received a letter from Bent, wishing us to make peace." Why did Bent send a letter to *friendly* Indians, and want to make peace with Indians "*who had always been friendly ?*" Again, they say, "We have held a council in regard to it." Why did they hold a council in regard to making peace, when they were already peaceable ? Again, they say, "All come to the conclusion to *make peace* with you, *providing* you make peace with the Kiowas, Comanches, Arapahoes, Apaches, and Sioux. We have seven prisoners of yours, which we are willing to give up, providing you give up yours. There are three *war* [not *peace*] *parties* out yet, and two of Arapahoes."

APPENDIX.

Every line of this letter shows that they were and had been at war. I desire to throw additional light upon this assertion of the committee that these Indians "were and had been friendly to the whites, and had not been guilty of any acts of hostility or depredations;" for it is upon this point that the committee accuse me of prevarication.

In the council held at Denver, White Antelope said: "We (the Cheyennes) took two prisoners west of Kearney, and destroyed the trains." This was one of the most destructive and bloody raids of the war. Again, Neva (Left-Hand's brother) said: "The Comanches, Kiowas, and Sioux have done much more harm than we have."

The entire report of this council, which is hereunto attached, shows that the Indians had been at war, and had been "guilty of acts of hostility and depredations."

As showing more fully the status and disposition of these Indians, I call attention to the following extract from the report of Major Wynkoop, published in the report of the Commissioner of Indian Affairs for 1864, page 234, and a letter from Major Colley, their agent; same report, page 230. Also statement of Robert North; same report, page 224.

"FORT LYON, COLORADO TERRITORY, September 18, 1864.

"SIR :    o    o    o    o    o    o    Taking with me, under strict guard, the Indians I had in my possession, I reached my destination, and was confronted by from six to eight hundred Indian warriors, drawn up in line of battle, and prepared to fight.

"Putting on as bold a front as I could under the circumstances, I formed my command in as good order as possible for the purpose of acting on the offensive or defensive, as might be necessary, and advanced towards them, at the same time sending forward one of the Indians I had with me, as an emissary, to state that I had come for the purpose of holding a consultation with the chiefs of the Arapahoes and Cheyennes, to come to an understanding which might result in mutual benefit; that I had not come desiring strife, but was prepared for it if necessary, and advised them to listen to what I had to say, previous to making any more warlike demonstrations.

"They consented to meet me in council, and I then proposed to them that if they desired peace to give me palpable evidence of their sincerity by delivering into my hands their white prisoners. I told them that I was not authorized to conclude terms of peace with them, but if they acceded to my proposition I would take what chiefs they might choose to select to the governor of Colorado Territory, state the circumstances to him, and that I believed it would result in what it was their desire to accomplish—'peace with their white brothers.' I had reference, particularly, to the Arapaho and Cheyenne tribes.

"The council was divided—undecided—and could not come to an understanding among themselves. I told them that I would march to a certain locality, distant twelve miles, and await a given time for their action in the matter. I took a strong position in the locality named, and remained three days. In the interval they brought in and turned over four white prisoners, all that was possible for them at the time being to turn over, the balance of the seven being (as they stated) with another band far to the northward.
o    o    o    o    o    o    o    o    o    o    o    o

"I have the principal chiefs of the two tribes with me, and propose starting immediately to Denver, to put into effect the aforementioned proposition made by me to them.

"They agree to deliver up the balance of the prisoners as soon as it is possible to procure them, which can be done better from Denver City than from this point.

"I have the honor, governor, to be your obedient servant,
"E. W. WYNKOOP,
"Major First Col. Cav., Comd'g Fort Lyon, C. T.

"His Excellency JOHN EVANS,
"Governor of Colorado, Denver, C. T."

"FORT LYON, COLORADO TERRITORY, July 26, 1864.

"SIR : When I last wrote you I was in hopes that our Indian troubles were at an end. Colonel Chivington has just arrived from Larned, and gives a sad account of affairs at that post. They have killed some ten men from a train, and run off all the stock from the post.

"As near as they can learn, all the tribes were engaged in it. The colonel will give you the particulars. There is no dependence to be put in any of them. I have done everything in my power to keep the peace; I now think a little powder and lead is the best food for them.

"Respectfully, your obedient servant,
"S. G. COLLEY, United States Indian Agent.

"Hon. JOHN EVANS,
"Governor and Superintendent Indian Affairs."

169

The following statement, by Robert North, was made to me :

"NOVEMBER 10, 1863.

"Having recovered an Arapaho prisoner (a squaw) from the Utes, I obtained the confidence of the Indians completely. I have lived with them from a boy, and my wife is an Arapaho.

"In honor of my exploit in recovering the prisoner, the Indians recently gave me a 'big medicine dance,' about fifty miles below Fort Lyon, on the Arkansas river, at which the leading chiefs and warriors of several of the tribes of the plains met.

"The Comanches, Apaches, Kiowas, the northern band of Arapahoes, and all of the Cheyennes, with the Sioux, have pledged one another to go to war with the whites as soon as they can procure ammunition in the spring. I heard them discuss the matter often, and the few of them who opposed it were forced to be quiet, and were really in danger of their lives. I saw the principal chiefs pledge to each other that they would be friendly and shake hands with the whites until they procured ammunition and guns, and so to be ready when they strike. Plundering, to get means, has already commenced ; and the plan is to commence the war at several points in the sparse settlements early in the spring. They wanted me to join them in the war, saying that they would take a great many white women and children prisoners, and get a heap of property, blankets, &c. ; but while I am connected with them by marriage, and live with them, I am yet a white man, and wish to avoid bloodshed. There are many Mexicans with the Comanche and Apache Indians, all of whom urge on the war, promising to help the Indians themselves, and that a great many more Mexicans would come up from New Mexico for the purpose in the spring."

In addition to the statement showing that all the Cheyennes were in the alliance, I desire to add the following frank admission from the Indians in the council :

"Governor Evans explained that smoking the war-pipe was a figurative term, but their conduct had been such as to show they had an understanding with other tribes.

"SEVERAL INDIANS. We acknowledge that our actions have given you reason to believe this "

In addition to all this, I refer to the appended statement of Mrs. Ewbanks. She is one of the prisoners that Black Kettle, in the council, said they had. Instead of *purchasing* her, it will be observed that they first *captured* her on the Little Blue, and then *sold* her to the Sioux.

Mrs. Martin, another rescued prisoner, was *captured* by the *Cheyennes* on Plum creek, *west of Kearney*, with a boy nine years old. These were the prisoners of which White Antelope said, in the council, "We took two prisoners west of Kearney, and destroyed the trains." In her published statement she says the party who captured her and the boy killed eleven men and destroyed the trains, and were mostly *Cheyennes*.

Thus I have proved, by the Indian chiefs named in the report, by Agent Colley and Major Wynkoop, to whom they refer to sustain their assertion to the contrary, that these Indians had "been at war, and had committed acts of hostility and depredations."

This documentary evidence could be extended much further, but enough has been produced to show the utter recklessness of their statements ; and because I would not admit, in the face of these published facts, that these Indians "were, and always had been, friendly, and had not been guilty of any acts of hostility or depredations," the committee accuse me of "prevarication." They say that I prevaricated "for the evident purpose of avoiding the admission that he was fully aware that the Indians massacred so brutally at Sand creek were then, *and had been, actuated by the most friendly feelings towards the whites.*"

I had left the Indians in the hands of the military authorities, as I shall presently show. There were many conflicting rumors as to the disposition made of them. I was absent from the Territory, and could state nothing positive in regard to their status after the council.

In regard to their status prior to the council at Denver, the foregoing public documents which I have cited show how utterly devoid of truth or foundation is the assertion that these Indians "had been friendly to the whites, and had not been guilty of any acts of hostility or depredations." Ignorance of the facts contained in the report of the Commissioner of Indian Affairs for 1864 is inexcusable on the part of the committee, for I particularly referred them to it.

I am obliged to the committee, however, for stating wherein I prevaricated, for I am thus enabled to repel their gross attack on my character as a witness, by showing that they were *mistaken* and I was *correct* in my testimony.

The next paragraph of the report is as follows :

"A northern band of the Cheyennes, known as the 'Dog Soldiers,' had been guilty of acts of hostility ; but all the testimony goes to prove that they had no connexion with

6

Black Kettle's band, and acted in spite of his authority and influence. Black Kettle and his band denied all connexion with, or responsibility for, the Dog Soldiers, and Left-Hand and his band were equally friendly.''

The committee and the public will be surprised to learn the fact that these Dog Soldiers, on which the committee throw the *slight* blame of acts of hostility, were really among Black Kettle and White Antelope's own warriors, in the "*friendly*" camp to which Major Wynkoop made his expedition, and their head man, Bull Bear, was one of the prominent men of the deputation brought in to see me at Denver. By reference to the accompanying report of the council with the chiefs, to which I referred the committee, it will be observed that Black Kettle and all present based their propositions to *make peace* upon the assent of *their bands*, and that these Dog Soldiers were especially referred to.

The report continues:

"These Indians, at the suggestion of Governor Evans and Colonel Chivington, repaired to Fort Lyon and placed themselves under the protection of Major Wynkoop,'' &c.

The connexion of my name in this is again wrong. As will be seen by the accompanying report of the council, to which I referred in my testimony, I simply left them in the hands of the military authorities, where I found them, and my action was approved by the Indian bureau.

The following extracts from the accompanying report of the council will prove this, conclusively. I stated to the Indians:

o o o "Another reason that I am not in a condition to make a treaty is, that the war is begun, and the power to make a treaty of peace has passed from me to the great war chief.''

I also said: "Again, whatever peace they may make must be with the soldiers, and not with me.''

And again, in reply to White Antelope's inquiry, "How can we be protected from the soldiers on the plains?'' I said: "You must make that arrangement with the military chief.''

The morning after this council I addressed the following letter to the agent of these Indians, which is published in the report of the Commissioner of Indian Affairs for 1864, page 220:

"COLORADO SUPERINTENDENCY INDIAN AFFAIRS,
"*Denver, September* 29, 1864.

"SIR: The chiefs brought in by Major Wynkoop have been heard. I have declined to make any peace with them, lest it might embarrass the military operations against the hostile Indians of the plains. The Arapaho and Cheyenne Indians being now at war with the United States government, must make peace with the military authorities. Of course this arrangement relieves the Indian bureau of their care until peace is declared with them; and as these tribes are yet scattered, and all except Friday's band are at war, it is not probable that it will be done immediately. You will be particular to impress upon these chiefs the fact that my talk with them was for the purpose of ascertaining their views, and not to offer them anything whatever. They must deal with the military authorities until peace, in which case, alone, they will be in proper position to treat with the government in relation to the future.

"I have the honor to be, very respectfully, your obedient servant,

"JOHN EVANS,
"*Governor Colorado Territory and ex-officio Superintendent Indian Affairs.*

"Major S. G. COLLEY,
"*United States Indian Agent, Upper Arkansas.*''

That this course accorded with the policy of the military authorities was confirmed by a telegram from the department commander, sent from headquarters at Fort Leavenworth to the district commander, on the day of the council, in which he said: "I fear agent of the Interior Department will be ready to make presents too soon. It is better to chastise, before giving anything but a little tobacco to talk over. No peace must be made without my directions.''

It will thus be seen that I had, with the approval of the Indian bureau, turned the adjustment of difficulties with hostile Indians entirely over to the military authorities; that I had instructed Agent Colley, at Fort Lyon, that this would relieve the bureau of further care of the Arapahoes and Cheyennes, until peace was made, and having had no notice of such peace, or instructions to change the arrangement, the status of these Indians was in no respect within my jurisdiction or under my official inspection.

In the face of all these facts —matters of public record—the committee attempt to make me responsible for the care of these Indians at the time of the battle.

171

It may be proper for me to say, further, that it will appear in evidence that I had no intimation of the direction in which the campaign against the hostile Indians was to move, or against what bands it was to be made, when I left the Territory last fall, and that I was absent from Colorado when the Sand creek battle occurred.

The report continues :

"It is true that there seems to have been excited among the people inhabiting that region of country a hostile feeling towards the Indians. Some had committed acts of hostility towards the whites, but no effort seems to have been made by the authorities there to prevent these hostilities, other than by the commission of even worse acts."

"*The people inhabiting that region of country !*" A form of expression of frequent occurrence in the reports of exploring expeditions, when speaking of savages and unknown tribes, but scarcely a respectful mode of mention of the people of Colorado.

"*Some had committed acts of hostility towards the whites !*" Hear the facts : In the fall of 1863 a general alliance of the Indians of the plains was effected with the Sioux, and in the language of Bull Bear, in the report of the council, appended, "Their plan is to clean out all this country."

The war opened early in the spring of 1864. The people of the east, absorbed in the greater interest of the rebellion, know but little of its history. Stock was stolen, ranches destroyed, houses burned, freight trains plundered, and their contents carried away or scattered upon the plains; settlers in the frontier counties murdered, or forced to seek safety for themselves and families in block-houses and interior towns; emigrants to our Territory were surprised in their camps, children were slain, and wives taken prisoners; our trade and travel with the States were cut off ; the necessaries of life were at starvation prices ; the interests of the Territory were being damaged to the extent of millions; every species of atrocity and barbarity which characterizes savage warfare was committed. This is no fancy sketch, but a plain statement of facts, of which the committee seem to have had no proper realization. All this history of war and blood—all this history of rapine and ruin—all this story of outrage and suffering on the part of our people—is summed up by the committee, and given to the public, in one mild sentence, " *Some* had committed acts of hostility against the whites."

The committee not only ignore the general and terrible character of our Indian war, and the great sufferings of our people, but make the grave charge that "no effort seems to have been made by the authorities there to prevent all these hostilities."

Had the committee taken the trouble, as they certainly should have done before making so grave a charge, to have read the public documents of the government, examined the record and files of the Indian bureau of the War Department, and of this superintendency, instead of adopting the language of some hostile and irresponsible witness, as they appear to have done, they would have found that the most earnest and persistent efforts had been made on my part to prevent hostilities. The records show that, early in the spring of 1863, United States Indian Agent Loree, of the Upper Platte agency, reported to me in person that the Sioux under his agency, and the Arapahoes and Cheyennes, were negotiating an alliance for war on the whites. I immediately wrote an urgent appeal for authority to avert the danger, and sent Agent Loree as special messenger with the despatch to Washington. In response, authority was given, and an earnest effort was made to collect the Indians in council. The following admission, in the appended report of the council, explains the result :

"GOVERNOR EVANS. ○ ○ ○ Hearing last fall that they were dissatisfied, the Great Father at Washington sent me out on the plains to talk with you and make it all right. I sent messengers out to tell you that I had presents, and would make you a feast ; but you sent word to me that you did not want to have anything to do with me, and to the Great Father at Washington that you could get along without him. Bull Bear wanted to come in to see me, at the head of the Republican, but his people held a council and would not let him come.

"BLACK KETTLE. That is true.

"GOVERNOR EVANS. I was under the necessity, after all my trouble, and all the expense I was at, of returning home without seeing them. Instead of this, your people went away and smoked the war pipe with our enemies."

Notwithstanding these unsuccessful efforts, I still hoped to preserve peace.

The records of these offices also show that, in the autumn of 1863, I was reliably advised from various sources that nearly all the Indians of the plains had formed an alliance for the purpose of going to war in the spring, and I immediately commenced my efforts to avert the imminent danger. From that time forward, by letter, by telegram, and by personal representation to the Commissioner of Indian Affairs, the Secretary of War, the commanders of the department and district ; by travelling for weeks in the wilderness of the plains ; by distribution of annuities and presents ; by sending notice to the Indians

APPENDIX.

to leave the hostile alliance ; by every means within my power, I endeavored to preserve peace and protect the interests of the people of the Territory. And in the face of all this, which the records abundantly show, the committee say : " No effort seems to have been made by the authorities there to prevent these hostilities, other than by the commission of even worse acts."

They do not point out any of these acts, unless the continuation of the paragraph is intended to do so. It proceeds:

" The hatred of the whites to the Indians would seem to have been inflamed and excited to the utmost. The bodies of persons killed at a distance—whether by Indians or not is not certain—were brought to the capital of the Territory and exposed to the public gaze, for the purpose of inflaming still more the already excited feeling of the people."

There is no mention in this of anything that was done by authority, but it is so full of misrepresentation, in apology for Indians, and unjust reflection on a people who have a right, from their birth, education, and ties of sympathy with the people they so recently left behind them, to have at least a just consideration. The bodies referred to were those of the Hungate family, who were brutally murdered by the Indians, within twenty-five miles of Denver. No one here ever doubted that the Indians did it, and it was admitted by the Indians in the council. This was early in the summer, and before the notice sent in June to the friendly Indians. Their mangled bodies were brought to Denver for decent burial. Many of our people went to see them, as any people would have done. It did produce excitement and consternation, and where are the people who could have witnessed it without emotion? Would the committee have the people shut their eyes to such scenes at their very doors?

The next sentence, equally unjust and unfair, refers to my proclamation, issued two months after this occurrence, and four months before the " attack" they were investigating, and having no connexion with it or with the troops engaged in it. It is as follows :

"The cupidity was appealed to, for the governor, in a proclamation, calls upon all, either individually, or in such parties as they may organize, to kill and destroy, as enemies of the country, wherever they may be found, all such hostile Indians ; authorizing them to hold, to their own use and benefit, all the property of said hostile Indians they may capture. What Indians he would ever term friendly it is impossible to tell."

I offer the following statement of the circumstances under which this proclamation was issued, by the Hon. D. A. Chever. It is as follows :

" EXECUTIVE DEPARTMENT, COLORADO TERRITORY, *August* 21, 1865.

" I, David A. Chever, clerk in the office of the governor of the Territory of Colorado, do solemnly swear that the people of said Territory, from the Purgatoire to the Cache a la Poudre rivers, a distance of over two hundred miles, and for a like distance along the Platte river, being the whole of our settlements on the plains, were thrown into the greatest alarm and consternation by numerous and almost simultaneous attacks and depredations by hostile Indians early last summer ; that they left their unreaped crops, and, collecting into communities, built block-houses and stockades for protection at central points throughout the long line of settlements ; that those living in the vicinity of Denver City fled to it, and that the people of said city were in great fear of sharing the fate of New Ulm, Minnesota ; that the threatened loss of crops, and the interruption of communication with the States by the combined hostilities, threatened the very existence of the whole people ; that this feeling of danger was universal ; that a flood of petitions and deputations poured into this office, from the people of all parts of the Territory, praying for protection, and for arms and authority to protect themselves ; that the defects of the militia law and the want of means to provide for defence was proved by the failure of this department, after the utmost endeavors, to secure an effective organization under it ; that reliable reports of the presence of a large body of hostile warriors at no great distance east of this place were received, which reports were afterwards proved to be true, by the statement of Elbridge Gerry, (page 232, Report of Commissioner of Indian Affairs for 1864 ;) that repeated and urgent applications to the War Department, for protection and the authority to raise troops for the purpose, had failed ; that urgent applications to department and district commanders had failed to bring any prospect of relief, and that in the midst of this terrible consternation, and apparently defenceless condition, it had been announced to this office, from district headquarters, that all the Colorado troops in the service of the United States had been peremptorily ordered away, and nearly all of them had marched to the Arkansas river, to be in position to repel the threatened invasion of the rebels into Kansas and Missouri ; that reliable reports of depredations and murders by the Indians, from all parts of our extended lines of exposed settlements, became daily more numerous, until the simultaneous attacks on trains along the overland stage line were reported by telegraph, on the 8th of August, described in the letter of George K. Otis, su-

173

perintendent of overland stage line, published on page 254 of Report of Commissioner of Indian Affairs for 1864. Under these circumstances, on the 11th of August, the governor issued his proclamation to the people, calling upon them to defend their homes and families from the savage foe ; that it prevented anarchy ; that several militia companies immediately organized under it, and aided in inspiring confidence ; that under its authority no act of impropriety has been reported, and I do not believe that any occurred ; that it had no reference to or connexion with the third regiment one-hundred-days men that was subsequently raised by authority of the War Department, under a different proclamation, calling for volunteers, or with any of the troops engaged in the Sand creek affair, and that the reference to it in such connexion, in the report of the Committee on the Conduct of the War, is a perversion of the history and facts in the case.

"DAVID A. CHEVER.

"TERRITORY OF COLORADO, *Arapaho County, City of Denver, ss :*

"Subscribed and sworn to before me this 21st day of August, A. D. 1865.

"ELI M. ASHLEY, *Notary Public.*"

I had appealed by telegraph, June 14, to the War Department, for authority to call the militia into the United States service or to raise one-hundred-day troops ; also had written to our delegate in Congress to see why I got no response, and had received his reply to the effect that he could learn nothing about it ; had received a notice from the department commander, declining to take the responsibility of asking the militia for United States service, throwing the people entirely on the necessity of taking care of themselves.

It was under these circumstances of trial, suffering and danger on the part of the people, and of fruitless appeal upon my part to the general government for aid, that I issued my proclamation of the 11th August, 1864, of which the committee complain.

Without means to mount or pay militia, and failing to get government authority to raise forces, and under the withdrawal of the few troops in the Territory, could any other course be pursued ?

The people were asked to fight on their own account—at their own expense—and in lieu of the protection the government failed to render. They were authorized to kill only the Indians that were murdering and robbing them in hostility, and to keep the property captured from them. How the committee would have them fight these savages, and what other disposition they would make of the property captured, the public will be curious to know. Would they fight without killing ? Would they have the captured property turned over to the government, as if captured by United States troops ? Would they forbid such captures ? Would they restore it to the hostile tribes ?

The absurdity of the committee's saying that this was an "appeal to the cupidity," is too palpable to require much comment. Would men leave high wages, mount and equip themselves at enormous expense, as some patriotically did, for the poor chance of capturing property, as a mere speculation, from the prowling bands of Indians that infested the settlements and were murdering their families ? The thing is preposterous.

For this proclamation I have no apology. It had its origin and has its justification in the imperative necessities of the case. A merciless foe surrounded us. Without means to mount or pay militia, unable to secure government authority to raise forces, and our own troops ordered away, again I ask, could any other course be pursued ?

Captain Tyler's and other companies organized under it, at enormous expense, left their lucrative business, high wages and profitable employment, and served without other pay than the consciousness of having done noble and patriotic service ; and no act of impropriety has ever been laid to the charge of any party acting under this proclamation. They had all been disbanded months before the "attack" was made that the committee were investigating.

The third regiment was organized under authority from the War Department, subsequently received by telegraph, and under a subsequent proclamation issued on the 13th of August, and were regularly mustered into the service of the United States about three months before the battle the committee were investigating occurred.

Before leaving this subject, I desire to call attention to the following significant fact ; the part of my proclamation from which the committee quote reads as follows :

"Now, therefore, I, John Evans, governor of Colorado Territory, do issue this, my proclamation, authorizing all citizens of Colorado, either individually or in such parties as they may organize, to go in pursuit of all hostile Indians on the plains, *scrupulously avoiding those who have responded to my call to rendezvous at the points indicated.* Also to kill and destroy, as enemies of the country, wherever they may be found, all such hostile Indians."

The language which I have italicised in the foregoing quotation shows that I forbade, in this proclamation, the disturbance of the friendly Indians and only authorized killing the hostile.

174

The committee, in their censorious mention of the proclamation, omit this sentence which I have italicised, although they quote the language immediately in connexion with it, and add the exclamation, "What Indians he would ever term friendly it is impossible to tell." Had they not suppressed this sentence their exclamation would have been awkward. Had they not suppressed it, its appearance in its proper connexion would have answered one of their most serious charges against me.

Why is this? Does it not look like a persistent determination on their part to place me before the public in an improper and unjust position? If such a thing is possible, from so high a source, where is there any safety for the character of public men?

Before closing this reply, it is perhaps just that I should say that when I testified before the committee the chairman and all its members, except three, were absent, and I think, when the truth becomes known, this report will trace its parentage to a single member of the committee.

I have thus noticed such portions of the report as refer to myself, and shown conclusively that the committee, in every mention they have made of me, have been, to say the least, mistaken.

*First.* The committee, for the evident purpose of maintaining their position that these Indians had not been engaged in the war, say the prisoners they held were purchased. The testimony is to the effect that they captured them.

*Second.* The committee say that these Indians were and always had been friendly, and had committed no acts of hostility or depredations. The public documents to which I refer show conclusively that they had been hostile, and had committed many acts of hostility and depredations.

*Third.* They say that I joined in sending these Indians to Fort Lyon. The published report of the Commissioner of Indian Affairs, and of the Indian council, show that I left them entirely in the hands of the military authorities.

*Fourth.* They say nothing seems to have been done by the authorities to prevent hostilities. The public documents and files of the Indian bureau, and of my superintendency, show constant and unremitting diligence and effort on my part to prevent hostilities and protect the people.

*Fifth.* They say that I prevaricated for the purpose of avoiding the admission that these Indians "were and had been actuated by the most friendly feelings towards the whites." Public documents cited show conclusively that the admission they desired me to make was false, and that my statement, instead of being a prevarication, was true, although not in accordance with the preconceived and mistaken opinions of the committee.

Those who read this will be curious for some explanation of this slanderous report. To me it is plain. I am governor of Colorado, and, as is usual with men in public position, have enemies. Many of these gentlemen were in the city of Washington last winter, endeavoring to effect my removal, and were not particular as to the character of the means they employed, so that the desired result was accomplished. For this purpose, they conspired to connect my name with the Sand creek battle, although they knew that I was in no way connected with it. A friend in that city, writing to me in regard to this attempt, and mentioning the names of certain of these gentlemen, said: "They are much in communication with ———, a member of the committee charged with the investigation of the Chivington affair." These gentlemen, by their false and unscrupulous representations, have misled the committee.

I do not charge the committee with any intentional wrong. My charge against the committee is that they have been culpably negligent and culpably hasty; culpably negligent in not examining the public documents to which I called their attention, and which would have exonerated me, and saved them from many serious, unjust and mistaken representations; culpably hasty in concluding that I had prevaricated, because my statement did not agree with the falsehoods they had embraced.

If my statement did not agree with what they supposed to be the truth, my position was such as to demand that they should at least go to the trouble of investigating the public documents to which I called their attention before publishing a report containing charges of so grave a character.

That the Committee on the Conduct of the War should have published a report containing so many errors is to be regretted. It is composed of honorable gentlemen—members of the Congress of the United States—to whom have been intrusted duties of the gravest character, and from whom is expected, first, thorough investigation, and then careful statement, so that their reports may be relied upon as truth, so far as truth is ascertainable by human means.

This report, so full of mistakes which ordinary investigation would have avoided; so full of slander, which ordinary care of the character of men would have prevented, is to be regretted, for the reason that it throws doubt upon the reliability of all reports which have emanated from the same source, during the last four years of war.

I am confident that the public will see, from the facts herein set forth, the great injustice done me ; and I am further confident that the committee, when they know these and other facts I shall lay before them, will also see this injustice, and, as far as possible, repair it.

Very respectfully, your obedient servant,

JOHN EVANS,

*Governor of the Territory of Colorado and ex-officio Sup't Ind. Affairs.*

---

*Report of council with Cheyenne and Arapaho chiefs and warriors, brought to Denver by Major Wynkoop ; taken down by United States Indian Agent Simeon Whiteley as it progressed.*

CAMP WELD, DENVER, *Wednesday, September 28, 1864.*

Present : Governor John Evans ; Colonel Chivington, commanding district of Colorado ; Colonel George L. Shoup, third Colorado volunteer cavalry ; Major E. Wynkoop, Colorado first ; S. Whiteley, United States Indian agent ; Black Kettle, leading Cheyenne chief ; White Antelope, chief central Cheyenne band ; Bull Bear, leader of Dog Soldiers, (Cheyenne;) Neva, sub-Arapaho chief, (who was in Washington ;) Bosse, sub-Arapaho chief ; Heap of Buffalo, Arapaho chief ; Na-ta-nee, Arapaho chief ; (the Arapahoes are all relatives of Left-Hand, chief of the Arapahoes, and are sent by him in his stead ;) John Smith, interpreter to the Upper Arkansas agency ; and many other citizens and officers.

His Excellency Governor Evans asked the Indians what they had to say.

Black Kettle then said : On sight of your circular of June 27, 1864, I took hold of the matter, and have now come to talk to you about it. I told Mr. Bent, who brought it, that I accepted it, but it would take some time to get all my people together—many of my young men being absent—and I have done everything in my power, since then, to keep peace with the whites. As soon as I could get my people together we held a council, and got a half-breed, who was with them, to write a letter to inform Major Wynkoop, or other military officer nearest to them, of their intention to comply with the terms of the circular. Major Wynkoop was kind enough to receive the letter, and visited them in camp, to whom they delivered four white prisoners—one other (Mrs. Snyder) having killed herself ; that there are two women and one child yet in their camp, whom they will deliver up as soon as they can get them in—Laura Roper, sixteen or seventeen years ; Ambrose Asher, seven or eight years ; Daniel Marble, seven or eight years ; Isabel Ubanks, four or five years. The prisoners still with them [are] Mrs. Ubanks and babe, and a Mrs. Morton, who was taken on the Platte. Mrs. Snyder is the name of the woman who hung herself. The boys were taken between Fort Kearney and the Blue. I followed Major Wynkoop to Fort Lyon, and Major Wynkoop proposed that we come up to see you. We have come with our eyes shut, following his handful of men, like coming through the fire. All we ask is that we may have peace with the whites. We want to hold you by the hand. You are our father. We have been travelling through a cloud. The sky has been dark ever since the war began. These braves who are with me are all willing to do what I say. We want to take good tidings home to our people, that they may sleep in peace. I want you to give all these chiefs of the soldiers here to understand that we are for peace, and that we have made peace, that we may not be mistaken by them for enemies. I have not come here with a little wolf bark, but have come to talk plain with you. We must live near the buffalo or starve. When we came here we came free, without any apprehension, to see you, and when I go home and tell my people that I have taken your hand, and the hands of all the chiefs here in Denver, they will feel well, and so will all the different tribes of Indians on the plains, after we have eaten and drank with them.

Governor Evans replied : I am sorry you did not respond to my appeal at once. You have gone into an alliance with the Sioux, who were at war with us. You have done a great deal of damage—have stolen stock, and now have possession of it. However much a few individuals may have tried to keep the peace, as a nation you have gone to war. While we have been spending thousands of dollars in opening farms for you, and making preparations to feed, protect, and make you comfortable, you have joined our enemies and gone to war. Hearing, last fall, that they were dissatisfied, the Great Father at Washington sent me out on the plains to talk with you and make it all right. I sent messengers out to tell you that I had presents, and would make you a feast, but you sent word to me that you did not want to have anything to do with me, and to the Great Father at Washington that you could get along without him. Bull Bear wanted to come in to see me at the head of the Republican, but his people held a council and would not let him come.

BLACK KETTLE. That is true.

APPENDIX.

GOVERNOR EVANS. I was under the necessity, after all my trouble and all the expense I was at, of returning home without seeing them. Instead of this, your people went away and smoked the war-pipe with our enemies.

BLACK KETTLE. I don't know who could have told you this.

GOVERNOR EVANS. No matter who said this, but your conduct has proved to my satisfaction that was the case.

SEVERAL INDIANS. This is a mistake; we have made no alliance with the Sioux or any one else.

Governor Evans explained that smoking the war-pipe was a figurative term, but their conduct had been such as to show they had an understanding with other tribes.

SEVERAL INDIANS. We acknowledge that our actions have given you reason to believe this.

GOVERNOR EVANS. So far as making a treaty now is concerned, we are in no condition to do it. Your young men are on the war-path. My soldiers are preparing for the fight. You, so far, have had the advantage; but the time is near at hand when the plains will swarm with United States soldiers. I understand that these men who have come to see me now have been opposed to the war all the time, but that their people have controlled them and they could not help themselves. Is this so?

ALL THE INDIANS. It has been so.

GOVERNOR EVANS. The fact that they have not been able to prevent their people from going to war in the past spring, when there was plenty of grass and game, makes me believe that they will not be able to make a peace which will last longer than until winter is past.

WHITE ANTELOPE. I will answer that after a time.

GOVERNOR EVANS. The time when you can make war best is in the summer-time; when I can make war best is in the winter. You, so far, have had the advantage; my time is just coming. I have learned that you understand that as the whites are at war among themselves, you think you can now drive the whites from this country; but this reliance is false. The Great Father at Washington has men enough to drive all the Indians off the plains, and whip the rebels at the same time. Now the war with the whites is nearly through, and the Great Father will not know what to do with all his soldiers, except to send them after the Indians on the plains. My proposition to the friendly Indians has gone out; shall be glad to have them all come in under it. I have no new propositions to make. Another reason that I am not in a condition to make a treaty is that war is begun, and the power to make a treaty of peace has passed from me to the great war chief. My advice to you is to turn on the side of the government, and show by your acts that friendly disposition you profess to me. It is utterly out of the question for you to be at peace with us while living with our enemies, and being on friendly terms with them.

INQUIRY MADE BY ONE INDIAN. What was meant by being on the side of the government? Explanation being made, all gave assent, saying: "All right."

GOVERNOR EVANS. The only way you can show this friendship is by making some arrangement with the soldiers to help them.

BLACK KETTLE. We will return with Major Wynkoop to Fort Lyon; we will then proceed to our village and take back word to my young men every word you say. I cannot answer for all of them, but think there will be but little difficulty in getting them to assent to help the soldiers.

MAJOR WYNKOOP. Did not the Dog Soldiers agree, when I had my council with you, to do whatever you said, after you had been here?

BLACK KETTLE. Yes.

Governor Evans explained that if the Indians did not keep with the United States soldiers, or have an arrangement with them, they would be all treated as enemies. You understand, if you are at peace with us it is necessary to keep away from our enemies. But I hand you over to the military, one of the chiefs of which is here to-day, and can speak for himself to them, if he chooses.

WHITE ANTELOPE. I understand every word you have said, and will hold on to it. I will give you an answer directly. The Cheyennes, all of them, have their eyes open this way, and they will hear what you say. He is proud to have seen the chief of all the whites in this country. He will tell his people. Ever since he went to Washington and received this medal, I have called all white men as my brothers. But other Indians have since been to Washington and got medals, and now the soldiers do not shake hands, but seek to kill me. What do you mean by us fighting your enemies? Who are they?

GOVERNOR EVANS. All Indians who are fighting us.

WHITE ANTELOPE. How can we be protected from the soldiers on the plains?

GOVERNOR EVANS. You must make that arrangement with the military chief.

WHITE ANTELOPE. I fear that these new soldiers who have gone out may kill some of my people while I am here.

177

GOVERNOR EVANS. There is great danger of it.

WHITE ANTELOPE. When we sent our letter to Major Wynkoop, it was like going through a strong fire or blast for Major Wynkoop's men to come to our camp; it was the same for us to come to see you. We have our doubts whether the Indians south of the Arkansas, or those north of the Platte, will do as you say. A large number of Sioux have crossed the Platte, in the vicinity of the Junction, into their country. When Major Wynkoop came, we proposed to make peace. He said he had no power to make a peace, except to bring them here and return them safe.

GOVERNOR EVANS. Again, whatever peace they make must be with the soldiers, and not with me. Are the Apaches at war with the whites?

WHITE ANTELOPE. Yes, and the Comanches and Kiowas as well; also a tribe of Indians from Texas, whose names we do not know. There are thirteen different bands of Sioux who have crossed the Platte, and are in alliance with the others named.

GOVERNOR EVANS. How many warriors with the Apaches, Kiowas, and Comanches?

WHITE ANTELOPE. A good many; don't know.

GOVERNOR EVANS. How many of the Sioux?

WHITE ANTELOPE. Don't know; but many more than of the southern tribes.

GOVERNOR EVANS. Who committed the depredation on the trains near the Junction about the first of August?

WHITE ANTELOPE. Do not know; did not know any was committed; have taken you by the hand and will tell the truth, keeping back nothing.

GOVERNOR EVANS. Who committed the murder of the Hungate family on Running creek?

NEVA. The Arapahoes; a party of the northern band, who were passing north. It was Medicine Man, or Roman Nose, and three others. I am satisfied from the time he left a certain camp for the north, that it was this party of four persons.

AGENT WHITELEY. That cannot be true.

GOVERNOR EVANS. Where is Roman Nose?

NEVA. You ought to know better than me; you have been nearer to him.

GOVERNOR EVANS. Who killed the man and boy at the head of Cherry creek?

NEVA. (After consultation.) Kiowas and Comanches.

GOVERNOR EVANS. Who stole soldiers' horses and mules from Jimmy's camp twenty-seven days ago?

NEVA. Fourteen Cheyennes and Arapahoes together.

GOVERNOR EVANS. What were their names?

NEVA. Powder Face and Whirlwind, who are now in our camp, were the leaders.

COLONEL SHOUP. I counted twenty Indians on that occasion.

GOVERNOR EVANS. Who stole Charley Autobee's horses?

NEVA. Raven's son.

GOVERNOR EVANS. Who took the stock from Fremont's orchard and had the first fight with the soldiers this spring north of there?

WHITE ANTELOPE. Before answering this question I would like for you to know that this was the beginning of war, and I should like to know what it was for. A soldier fired first.

GOVERNOR EVANS. The Indians had stolen about forty horses; the soldiers went to recover them, and the Indians fired a volley into their ranks.

WHITE ANTELOPE. This is all a mistake; they were coming down the Bijou, and found one horse and one mule. They returned one horse before they got to Geary's to a man, then went to Geary's expecting to turn the other one over to some one. They then heard that the soldiers and Indians were fighting somewhere down the Platte; then they took fright and all fled.

GOVERNOR EVANS. Who were the Indians who had the fight?

WHITE ANTELOPE. They were headed by the Fool Badger's son, a young man, one of the greatest of the Cheyenne warriors, who was wounded, and though still alive he will never recover.

NEVA. I want to say something; it makes me feel bad to be talking about these things and opening old sores.

GOVERNOR EVANS. Let him speak.

NEVA. Mr. Smith has known me ever since I was a child. Has he ever known me commit depredations on the whites? I went to Washington last year; received good counsel; I hold on to it. I determined to always keep peace with the whites. Now, when I shake hands with them, they seem to pull away. I came here to seek peace, and nothing else.

GOVERNOR EVANS. We feel that they have, by their stealing and murdering, done us great damage. They come here and say they will tell me all, and that is what I am trying to get.

NEVA. The Comanches, Kiowas, and Sioux have done much more injury than we have. We will tell what we know, but cannot speak for others.

APPENDIX.

GOVERNOR EVANS. I suppose you acknowledge the depredations on the Little Blue, as you have the prisoners then taken in your possession.

WHITE ANTELOPE. We (the Cheyennes) took two prisoners west of Fort Kearney, and destroyed the trains.

GOVERNOR EVANS. Who committed depredations at Cottonwood?

WHITE ANTELOPE. The Sioux ; what band, we do not know.

GOVERNOR EVANS. What are the Sioux going to do next?

BULL BEAR. Their plan is to clean out all this country ; they are angry, and will do all the damage to the whites they can. I am with you and the troops, to fight all those who have no ears to listen to what you say. Who are they? Show them to me. I am not yet old ; I am young. I have never hurt a white man. I am pushing for something good. I am always going to be friends with the whites ; they can do me good.

GOVERNOR EVANS. Where are the Sioux?

BULL BEAR. Down on the Republican, where it opens out.

GOVERNOR EVANS. Do you know that they intend to attack the trains this week?

BULL BEAR. Yes ; about one-half of all the Missouri River Sioux and Yanktons, who were driven from Minnesota, are those who have crossed the Platte. I am young and can fight. I have given my word to fight with the whites. My brother (Lean Bear) died in trying to keep peace with the whites. I am willing to die in the same way, and expect to do so.

NEVA. I know the value of the presents which we receive from Washington ; we cannot live without them. That is why I try so hard to keep peace with the whites.

GOVERNOR EVANS. I cannot say anything about those things now.

NEVA. I can speak for all the Arapahoes under Left-Hand. Raven has sent no one here to speak for him. Raven has fought the whites.

GOVERNOR EVANS. Are there any white men among your people?

NEVA. There are none except Keith, who is now in the store at Fort Larned.

COLONEL CHIVINGTON. I am not a big war chief, but all the soldiers in this country are at my command. My rule of fighting white men or Indians is to fight them until they lay down their arms and submit to military authority. They are nearer Major Wynkoop than any one else, and they can go to him when they get ready to do that.

The council then adjourned.

I certify that this report is correct and complete ; that I took down the talk of the Indians in the exact words of the interpreter, and of the other parties as given to him, without change of phraseology or correction of any kind whatever.

SIMEON WHITELEY.

*Statement of Mrs. Ewbanks, giving an account of her captivity among the Indians. She was taken by the Cheyennes, and was one of the prisoners proposed to be given up by Black Kettle, White Antelope and others, in the council at Denver.*

JULESBURG, COLORADO TERRITORY, *June* 22, 1865.

Mrs. Lucinda Ewbanks states that she was born in Pennsylvania ; is 24 years of age ; she resided on the Little Blue, at or near the Narrows. She says that on the 8th day of August, 1864, the house was attacked, robbed, burned, and herself and two children, with her nephew and Miss Roper, were captured by the Cheyenne Indians. Her eldest child, at the time, was three years old ; her youngest was one year old ; her nephew was six years old. When taken from her home was, by the Indians, taken south across the Republican, and west to a creek the name of which she does not remember. Here, for a short time, was their village or camping place. They were travelling all winter. When first taken by the Cheyennes she was taken to the lodge of an old chief whose name she does [not] recollect. He forced me, by the most terrible threats and menaces, to yield my person to him. He treated me as his wife. He then traded me to Two Face, a Sioux, who did not treat me as a wife, but forced me to do all menial labor done by squaws, and he beat me terribly. Two Face traded me to Black Foot, (Sioux,) who treated me as his wife, and because I resisted him his squaws abused and ill-used me. Black Foot also beat me unmercifully, and the Indians generally treated me as though I was a dog, on account of my showing so much detestation towards Black Foot. Two Face traded for me again. I then received a little better treatment. I was better treated among the Sioux than the Cheyennes—that is, the Sioux gave me more to eat. When with the Cheyennes I was often hungry. Her purchase from the Cheyennes was made early last fall, and she remained with them until May, 1865. During the winter the Cheyennes came to buy me

179

and the child, for the purpose of burning us, but Two Face would not let them have me. During the winter we were on the North Platte the Indians were killing the whites all the time and running off their stock. They would bring in the scalps of the whites and show them to me and laugh about it. They ordered me frequently to wean my baby, but I always refused; for I felt convinced if he was weaned they would take him from me, and I should never see him again. They took my daughter from me just after we were captured, and I never saw her after. I have seen the man to-day who had her; his name is Davenport. He lives in Denver. He received her from a Dr. Smith. She was given up by the Cheyennes to Major Wynkoop, but from injuries received while with the Indians, she died last February. My nephew also was given up to Major Wynkoop, but he, too, died at Denver. The doctor said it was caused by bad treatment from the Indians. While encamped on the North Platte, Elston came to the village, and I went with him and Two Face to Fort Laramie. I have heard it stated that a story had been told by me to the effect that Two Face's son had saved my life. I never made any such statement, as I have no knowledge of any such thing, and I think if my life had been in danger he would not have troubled himself about it.

LUCINDA EWBANKS.

Witness :
J. H. TRIGGS, *1st Lieut. Comd'g Co. D, 7th Iowa Cavalry.*
E. B. ZABRISKIE, *Capt. 1st Cav. Nev. Vol., Judge Advocate Dis't of the Plains.*

SENATOR : Since you were here I have had another talk with Major Anthony, who was in command of Fort Lyon at the time Colonel Chivington arrived there, having relieved Major Wynkoop. He says, among a great many other things :

" As I told you before, but two days before Colonel Chivington came down, they [Cheyennes] sent word to me, *after I had fired on them,* that if that little G—d d—d red-eyed [Major Anthony's eyes and eyelids are red from having had the scurvy] chief wanted a fight out of them, if he would go up to their camp they would give him all he wanted."

And Major Anthony says to me : " I told Colonel Chivington I was glad he had come ; that I would have gone before and cleaned out the sons of guns if I had had force enough ; but there were some of them I should have saved if possible."

Again, he says : " This whole row has been caused by jealous officers and civilians who conspired to get ' Old Chiv.' out of the way."

I have no note or comment to make on this, only that it is a repetition of what the major said to me on the cars last spring, between Atchison and Leavenworth, and accords with what officers in Denver say he told them before the battle.

Truly yours,

SIMEON WHITELEY.

Hon. J. R. DOOLITTLE, *U. S. Senate.*

---

EXTRACTS FROM THE ROCKY MOUNTAIN NEWS, DECEMBER, 1864.

*Despatch from Colonel Chivington.*

HEADQUARTERS DISTRICT OF COLORADO,
*Denver, December 7, 1864.*

EDITORS NEWS : The following despatch has been received at this office and forwarded to department headquarters :

HEADQUARTERS DISTRICT OF COLORADO, IN THE FIELD,
*Cheyenne Country, South Bend, Big Sandy, November 29.*

GENERAL : In the last ten days my command has marched three hundred miles—one hundred of which the snow was two feet deep. After a march of forty miles last night, I, at daylight this morning, attacked a Cheyenne village of one hundred and thirty lodges, from nine hundred to one thousand warriors strong. We killed chiefs Black Kettle, White Antelope, and Little Robe, and between four and five hundred other Indians ; captured between four and five hundred ponies and mules. Our loss is nine killed and thirty-eight wounded. All did nobly. I think I will catch some more of them about eighty miles on Smoky Hill. We found a white man's scalp, not more than three days old, in a lodge.

J. M. CHIVINGTON,
*Colonel, Commanding District of Colorado and First Indian Expedition.*

Major General S. R. CURTIS, *Fort Leavenworth.*

I am, gentlemen, very respectfully, your obedient servant,

CHARLES WHEELER,
*A. A. A. General.*

# APPENDIX.

*Letter from Colonel Shoup—About the big fight.*

[The following private letter from Colonel Shoup was politely handed us for publication.

SOUTH BEND OF BIG SANDY, BATTLE GROUND,
*Cheyenne Country, December* 3, 1864.

DEAR SIR : I have the pleasure of informing you that we engaged the Indians on yesterday, on the Big Sandy, about forty (40) miles north of Fort Lyon. The engagement commenced at sunrise, and lasted to about 2½ o'clock p. m., completely routing the Indians.

Our loss is eight (8) killed, one missing, and about forty wounded. The Indian loss is variously estimated at from 300 to 500—I think about 300—between 500 and 600 Indian saddles, and over 100 lodges, with all their camp equipage. Black Kettle, White Antelope, One Eye, and other chiefs, are among the killed. I think this the severest chastisement ever given to Indians in battle on the American continent.

Our men fought with great enthusiasm and bravery, but with some disorder. There are plenty more Indians within a few days' march. I fear, however, they will lose their assumed bravery when they hear of the defeat of their allies in arms. The story that Indians are our equals in warfare is nailed. This story may do to tell to down-easters, but not to Colorado soldiers. About one hundred and seventy-five men of the first Colorado, a small detachment of the first New Mexico, and about six hundred and fifty of my regiment were in the engagement. I might, if time would permit, give you many interesting incidents that came under my notice during the battle, but I will have to close. Your son, the lieutenant, behaved well in the fight, and came out without a wound.

Your friend,

GEO. L. SHOUP.

Captain SOPRIS.

—

*Letter from Major Anthony—About the Indian fight.*

[The following from the major to his brother, in this city, we are permitted to publish:]

SAND CREEK, 25 MILES ABOVE FORT LYON,
*December* 1, 1864.

DEAR WEBB : I am here with the command. We have just had, day before yesterday, an Indian fight. We have nearly annihilated Black Kettle's band of Cheyennes and Left-Hand's Arapahoes.

                                        

I did my share, and I think my command did as well as any in the whole brigade, notwithstanding I lost one man killed and two slightly wounded ; I was one of the first in the fight and among the last to leave, and my loss is less than any other battalion. We have forty-seven persons killed and wounded.

                                        

I will give particulars when I see you. We start for another band of red-skins, and shall fight differently next time. I never saw more bravery displayed by any set of people on the face of the earth than by those Indians. They would charge on a whole company singly, determined to kill some one before being killed themselves. We, of course, took no prisoners, except John Smith's son, and he was taken suddenly ill in the night, and died before morning.

Lieutenant Baldwin, of my command, lost his horse. I had one horse shot under me, but came off with a whole " hide." I did not sleep for three days and two nights until last evening.

S. J. ANTHONY.

—

*Additional about the Indian fight.*

HEADQUARTERS DISTRICT OF COLORADO, IN THE FIELD,
*On Big Bend of Sandy Creek, Colorado Territory, November* 29, 1864.

SIR : I have not the time to give you a detailed history of our engagement of to-day, or to mention those officers and men who distinguished themselves in one of the most bloody Indian battles ever fought on these plains. You will find enclosed the report of my surgeon in charge, which will bring to many anxious friends the sad fate of loved ones, who are and have been risking everything to avenge the horrid deeds of those savages we have so severely handled. We made a forced march of forty miles and sur-

181

prised, at break of day, one of the most powerful villages of the Cheyenne nation, and captured over five hundred animals ; killing the celebrated chiefs One Eye, White Antelope, Knock-Knee, Black Kettle, and Little Robe, with about five hundred of their people, destroying all their lodges and equipage, making almost an annihilation of the entire tribe.

I shall leave here, as soon as I can see our wounded safely on the way to the hospital at Fort Lyon, for the villages of the Sioux, which are reported about eighty miles from here on the Smoky Hill, and three thousand strong—so look out for more fighting. I will state for the consideration of gentlemen who are opposed to fighting these red scoundrels, that I was shown by my chief surgeon the scalp of a white man, taken from the lodge of one of the chiefs, which could not have been more than two or three days taken : and I could mention many more things to show how these Indians, who have been drawing government rations at Fort Lyon, are and have been acting.

Very respectfully, your obedient servant,

J.. M. CHIVINGTON,
*Colonel, Commanding Colorado Expedition against Indians on Plains.*

CHARLES WHEELER,
*A. A. A. General, Headquarters District of Colorado, Denver.*

---

Colonel Bent sworn:

Having been living near the mouth of the Purgatoire on the Arkansas river in Colorado Territory for the last thirty-six years, and during all that time have resided near or at what is known as Bent's Old Fort, I have had considerable experience in Indian affairs from my long residence in the country. Since I have been there nearly every instance of difficulties between the Indians and the whites arose from aggressions on the Indians by the whites. Some of these aggressions are of recent date. About three years ago the Arapahoes were encamped near Fort Lyon ; a soldier had obtained some whiskey and went to the Arapaho village after dark ; he met an Indian or two outside and told them he wanted a squaw for the whiskey ; that is, he wanted a squaw to sleep with for the whiskey. The Indian told him that if he would give him the whiskey he would get him a squaw ; he gave him the whiskey, and the Indian started off and went into a lodge of his friends, and commenced drinking the whiskey with them, without bringing the squaw. The soldier started on a search for the Indian and whiskey, and found them in a lodge. The Indian refused to return the whiskey, when the soldier pulled out his revolver, fired and broke the Indian's arm : the soldier then made his escape and could never be identified by his officers or by the Indians. The matter created great confusion among the Indians, but was finally settled without a fight. I understood from some officers under Colonel Chivington that the hostiliti. s between the Cheyennes and the whites were commenced by Colonel Chivington's orders, who sent an officer down the Platte to see some Indians who, it was said, had stolen some stock, with orders to disarm all the Indians he met. The officer procee led until he met some Indians coming in with some animals they had found, belonging to the whites ; he rode up to the Indians in what they thought to be a friendly manner, and, I think, shook hands with the Indians, and after doing that, he and his men made a grab for the Indians' arms. The Indians tried to run ; the soldiers fired at them, wounding two ; one fell from his horse, but the Indians rallied and got him off before the whites could get hold of them. This was a party of Cheyennes, I think seven in number. This was the first actual conflict between this tribe and the whites. Very soon after Lieutenant Ayres was sent down to pursue the Cheyennes ; to continue down the Republican and Smoky Hill fork to Fort Larned. He met a party of Cheyennes on Smoky Hill, who were going out on a hunt ; they had just left Fort Larned. One of the chiefs who had been on to Washington the spring previous was with the party. He went up to the soldiers, shook hands with them, showed the lieutenant the medal he got from the President, stating that his Great Father, when giving him the medal, told him to be always friendly to the whites. This chief, Lean Bear, was then shot by one of the soldiers ; a fight then commenced ; there were two other Indians killed, three soldiers killed and ten or twelve wounded. The troops then commenced retreating, and a running fight was kept up for ten or fifteen miles ; the Indians finally left them, the soldiers going to Fort Larned. Lieutenant Ayres left his troops at Fort Larned and started for Fort Lyon. I met him on my way to the States, near Fort Lyon. He told me he had had a fight with the Cheyennes, and some Sioux connected with them, on the Smoky Hill, killing some seventeen of them. I continued on my journey the next morning and met an express from the Indian village, where the fight was, stating they had had a fight on the Smoky Hill, but did not know what it was about or for, and that they would like to see me and converse with me on the subject. I sent the express back, stating I would meet the chief on Coon creek. Seven days after this I met the chief on Coon creek ; he stated to me that he did not know the cause of the attack ; that it was not his intention or wish to fight the whites ; that he wanted to be friendly and peaceable and keep his tribe so. He felt he was not able to fight the whites, and wanted to live in peace. I then asked him if he would prevent his young men from committing any depredations for twenty days, by which time I thought I should be able to go to Leavenworth, see General Curtis, then in command of the department, and return. After leaving the chief I altered my mind, and concluded I could do better by seeing the authorities in Colorado at Fort Lyon. I returned next morning towards Fort Lyon. On my arrival there I met Colonel Chivington, related to him the conversation that had taken place between me and the Indians, and that the chiefs desired to be friendly. In reply he said he was not authorized to make peace, and that he was then on the war path—I think were the words he used. I then stated to him that there was great risk to run in keeping up war ; that there were a great many government trains travelling to New Mexico and other points, also a great many citizens, and that I did not think there was sufficient force to protect the travel, and that the citizens and settlers of the country would have to suffer. He said the citizens would have to protect themselves. I then said no more to him. I then went up to my ranch, twenty-five miles from Fort Lyon ; was there about seven days, when I received a letter from Major Colley, the Indian agent, stating he wished to see me immediately on business. I went to the fort, and he (Major Colley) showed me Governor Evans's proclamation, also a letter from Governor Evans to him, directing him to get some one to go immediately to the different tribes of Indians and fetch all of the different tribes of Indians into the forts, Lyon and Larned—that is, all who desired to be friendly ; that they should be protected by the government of the United States, and at the same time have rations issued to them. Governor Evans at that time was ex-officio superintendent of Indian affairs. I immediately started on my way in search of the Indians, alone ; I found all the different tribes in the vicinity of Fort Larned ; the Cheyennes, Arapahoes, Kiowas, Comanches, and Apaches. I then immediately brought the Cheyenne chiefs within four miles of Fort Larned, they being at war with the whites ; the other tribes were at peace. I had an interview with the Cheyennes—translated to them the governor's proclamation ; they expressed a great desire to make peace and to keep it, and appeared to be perfectly well satisfied with the governor's proclamation. They went up with me the next morning and had an interview with the commanding officer of the post, and everything was settled satisfactorily on both sides. The Indians then returned to their villages on the Arkansas, some twenty-five miles from Fort Lyon. I then mentioned to the commanding officer that I thought from the movements and actions of the Kiowas they would break out in a short time, which proved to be the case. In two or three days afterwards the Kiowas went up to Fort Larned and ran off the stock, at the same time wounding a sentinel. They resorted to a stratagem to obtain the stock : the squaws went into the fort and commenced a dance to attract the attention of the troops, while the war party got the horses, and when the alarm was given the squaws jumped on their horses and ran off. The Arapaho chief, Left-Hand, then took twenty-five of his men and went to Fort Larned, with the intention of offering his services to the United States, to assist them in fighting the Kiowas and recovering the stolen stock. He got within four hundred yards of the fort, met a soldier, and sent him to the commanding officer, to state that he wished to have an interview with him, but the first salute he received was a cannon shot fired at himself and party. Left-Hand carried a white flag, and could speak English very well. He was afterwards killed in the massacre on Sand creek. This was the commencement of the Arapaho war. The Arapahoes, who had committed no hostile acts previously, now commenced and committed more depredations than the Cheyennes. From information, I know of what occurred in the Sand creek fight ; I had two sons in the village, and one who acted as guide and interpreter for the government, and was with Colonel Chivington. The attack at Sand creek on the Indians produced great excitement among them ; they even deposed their head chief, Black Kettle, stating that he had brought them in there to be betrayed ; they also stated that they had always heard that white men would not kill women and children, but they had now lost all confidence in the whites. Since that time the Cheyennes, Arapahoes, Kiowas, and a portion of the Comanches, have been at war with the whites. I have no doubt but for the firing on the Arapahoes at Fort Larned, and the affair at Sand creek, we might have had peace with all the Indians on the Arkansas. I have no doubt if proper persons (and by proper persons I mean those who would be honest and not try to defraud the Indians or the government, and they should be acquainted with the Indian character) were appointed agents, and if officers from the regular army, with troops from the same, were stationed at the posts near the Indians, I think there would be no difficulty. Volunteer officers, the Indians can see, have no control over their men—no discipline, and the soldiers cannot be punished for abusing the Indians. The last great difficulty previous to the one I have mentioned, grew out of the Sioux war. This war originated as follows : Some Mormons on their way to Salt lake were driving some stock ; either a cow or an ox gave out, the Indians killed the animal, and the Mormons reported the fact to the commanding officer at Fort Laramie ; the officer sent down for the Indian who killed the animal, but the Indians refused to send him, as he was not present and could not be found, offering at the same time to pay for the animal killed ; the officer then sent Lieutenant Grattan, with eighteen men, to the Indian camp, where there were some three hundred warriors, to fetch the Indian away ; he demanded that the Indian should be delivered in fifteen minutes, or he would fire on them ; the Indian not being forthcoming at the time, Lieutenant Grattan fired on the Indians, and in a few minutes he and his command were all massacred. This occurred in 1854, and was the commencement of the Sioux war, which lasted some time, the Cheyenne band of the North Platte becoming involved in it. Two campaigns were carried on against them ; one under General Harney, and the other under Colonel Sumner. In answer to your inquiry, I must say there have been a good many goods sent by the government to the Indians which never were delivered. These goods are withheld in various ways. For instance, an Indian will come in and make the agent a present of a poney another will make him a present of a mule, another will present four or five buffalo robes, all of which the agent will receive to himself, when he has no right to. The agent then pays these Indians out of the annuity goods, which causes a great deal of dispute among the other Indians, who see the goods which ought to come to them given in payment to other Indians. The Indians never make presents without expecting to receive something more than its value in return, so in the long run it is nothing more nor less than a trade. I believe there are agents, or agents' relatives, in this country who have made very good speculations. The son of Major Colley, the Indian agent of the Cheyennes and Arapahoes, was an Indian trader for the Cheyennes, Arapahoes, Kiowas, and Comanches. He came to this country the fall after his father was appointed agent. When he first came here he could not have had property of the value to exceed fifteen hundred dollars, which consisted of some thirty or forty head of cows. From what he said to me he must have made twenty-five or thirty thousand dollars in the two or three years he was trading with the Indians. John Smith acted as the Indian trader, and was considered as a partner in the business. It is hard to identify Indian goods, but I am satisfied that a portion of the goods traded with the Indians were annuity goods. From comparison of the goods traded and the annuity goods, I am satisfied they were identically the same goods. The Indians knew they were purchasing their own goods, but did not complain about it. At the time I was trading in the same village with Mr. Colley, one of my men went into his lodge and brought back to me a top of a box marked " U. S. Upper Arkansas Agency." I have heard it stated that sometimes agents give the Indian goods to white traders in the country to trade them on shares. To procure vouchers for the goods the agent will send out to have the tribe come in and get their annuity goods. The goods thought proper to be given them are piled in a heap on the prairie, the Indians sit round in a large circle, and the agent then tells them, " There are your annuity goods—divide them among yourselves." The agent then gets four or five of the principal chiefs to come in and sign the vouchers ; as a matter of course the Indians do not know what or how much they are signing for. I would suggest that the Indians be allowed by law to select some white man to be present at the distribution, with power to examine all bills and vouchers, and see that the Indians are not defrauded. All the agents on the Arkansas have been in the habit of distributing the goods in the manner above described, and the poor and needy Indians do not get their share, which falls to the richer and more powerful ones. If the matter were left to me I would guarantee with my life that in three months I could have all the Indians along the Arkansas at peace, without the expense of war. These would include the Cheyennes, Arapahoes, Kiowas, Comanches, and Apaches. Some Cheyennes in whom I have confidence stated to me that they had no confidence in Major Colley, knowing he was swindling them out of their goods, and they did not care to come in and receive them, but when Major Fitzpatrick was their agent they had confidence and always came in for their annuities. There was a treaty made between the Cheyennes and Arapahoes and Colonel Boone. In my opinion the reservation now set apart for the Cheyennes and Arapahoes is not suitable. The best place for a reservation for them, in my opinion, would be on Beaver creek, between the Smoky Hill and the Republican. This would be in their own country, where the buffalo abound, and where they will probably last be seen. This reservation would be off from all the roads and all the great thoroughfares, and distant from all settlements. The land would be suitable for them, but not for the whites, and contains no minerals. On this reservation the agency should be established, and the agent should always be with them ; grass and timber abound.

--------

Robert Bent sworn :

I am twenty-four years old ; was born on the Arkansas river. I am pretty well acquainted with the Indians of the plains, having spent most of my life among them. I was employed as guide and interpreter at Fort Lyon by Major Anthony. Colonel Chiving-

184

ton ordered me to accompany him on his way to Sand creek. The command consisted of from nine hundred to one thousand men, principally Colorado volunteers. We left Fort Lyon at eight o'clock in the evening, and came on to the Indian camp at daylight the next morning. Colonel Chivington surrounded the village with his troops. When we came in sight of the camp I saw the American flag waving and heard Black Kettle tell the Indians to stand round the flag, and there they were huddled—men, women, and children. This was when we were within fifty yards of the Indians. I also saw a white flag raised. These flags were in so conspicuous a position that they must have been seen. When the troops fired the Indians ran, some of the men into their lodges, probably to get their arms. They had time to get away if they had wanted to. I remained on the field five hours, and when I left there were shots being fired up the creek. I think there were six hundred Indians in all. I think there were thirty-five braves and some old men, about sixty in all. All fought well. At the time the rest of the men were away from camp, hunting. I visited the battle-ground one month afterwards ; saw the remains of a good many ; counted sixty-nine, but a number had been eaten by the wolves and dogs. After the firing the warriors put the squaws and children together, and surrounded them to protect them. I saw five squaws under a bank for shelter. When the troops came up to them they ran out and showed their persons to let the soldiers know they were squaws and begged for mercy, but the soldiers shot them all. I saw one squaw lying on the bank whose leg had been broken by a shell ; a soldier came up to her with a drawn sabre ; she raised her arm to protect herself, when he struck, breaking her arm ; she rolled over and raised her other arm, when he struck, breaking it, and then left her without killing her. There seemed to be an indiscriminate slaughter of men, women, and children. There were some thirty or forty squaws collected in a hole for protection ; they sent out a little girl about six years old with a white flag on a stick ; she had not proceeded but a few steps when she was shot and killed. All the squaws in that hole were afterwards killed, and four or five bucks outside. The squaws offered no resistance. Every one I saw dead was scalped. I saw one squaw cut open with an unborn child, as I thought, lying by her side. Captain Soulé afterwards told me that such was the fact. I saw the body of White Antelope with the privates cut off, and I heard a soldier say he was going to make a tobacco-pouch out of them. I saw one squaw whose privates had been cut out. I heard Colonel Chivington say to the soldiers as they charged past him, " Remember our wives and children murdered on the Platte and Arkansas." He occupied a position where he could not have failed to have seen the American flag, which I think was a garrison flag, six by twelve. He was within fifty yards when he planted his battery. I saw a little girl about five years of age who had been hid in the sand ; two soldiers discovered her, drew their pistols and shot her, and then pulled her out of the sand by the arm. I saw quite a number of infants in arms killed with their mothers. There were trading in the village at the time John Smith, a soldier named Louderback, and a teamster of young Colley's named Clark. They were trading goods said to belong to Dexter Colley and John Smith. The goods traded were similar to those they had been in the habit of trading before. I have heard the Indians charge Major Colley with trading their own goods to them.

---

Colonel Kit Carson sworn :

I have heard read the statement of Colonel Bent, and his suggestions and opinions in relation to Indian affairs coincide perfectly with my own. I came to this country in 1826, and since that time have become pretty well acquainted with the Indian tribes, both in peace and at war. I think, as a general thing, the difficulties arise from aggressions on the part of the whites. From what I have heard, the whites are always cursing the Indians, and are not willing to do them justice. For instance, at times large trains come out to this country, and some man without any responsibility is hired to guard the horses, mules, and stock of the trains ; these cattle by his negligence frequently stray off ; always, if anything is lost, the cry is raised that the Indians stole it. It is customary among the Indians, even among themselves, if they lose animals, as Indians go everywhere, if they bring them in they expect to get something for their trouble. Among themselves they always pay ; but when brought in to this man, who lost them through his negligence, he refuses to pay, and abuses the Indians, striking or sometimes shooting them, because they do not wish to give up the stock without pay ; and thus a war is brought on. That is the way in which difficulties frequently arise. I have heard read the statement of how the Sioux war arose, which agrees word for word with what I have heard, and what I believe to be the facts. And in relation to the war with the Cheyennes, I have heard it publicly stated that the authorities of Colorado, expecting that their troops would be sent to the Potomac, determined to get up an Indian war, so that the troops would be compelled to remain. I know of no acts of hostility on the part of the Cheyennes and Arapahoes committed previous to the attacks made upon them, as stated by

APPENDIX.

Colonel Bent. In 1830, or '31, I was one of a party who made peace with the Arapahoes, and since that time I know of no difficulty with them until that described by Colonel Bent. I know of no other great difficulties on the Arkansas route than the Sioux war and the present war. I think the Kiowas are hostile against the government without cause. The other tribes, I think, are rather compelled to be so. Most of the Comanches, I think, are friendly disposed. I think if proper men were appointed and proper steps taken, peace could be had with all the Indians on and below the Arkansas, without war. I believe that, if Colonel Bent and myself were authorized, we could make a solid, lasting peace with those Indians. I have much more confidence in the influence of Colonel Bent with the Indians than in my own. I think if prompt action were taken the Indians could be got together by the tenth of September. I know that even before the acquisition of New Mexico there had about always existed an hereditary warfare between the Navajoes and Mexicans ; forays were made into each other's country, and stock, women, and children stolen. Since the acquisition, the same state has existed ; we would hardly get back from fighting and making peace with them before they would be at war again. I consider the reservation system as the only one to be adopted for them. If they were sent back to their own country to-morrow, it would not be a month before hostilities would commence again. There is a part of the Navajoes, the wealthy, who wish to live in peace ; the poorer class are in the majority, and they have no chiefs who can control them. When I campaigned against them eight months I found them scattered over a country several hundred miles in extent. There is no suitable place in their own country—and I have been all over it—where more than two thousand could be placed. If located in different places, it would not be long before they and the Mexicans would be at war. If they were scattered on different locations, I hardly think any number of troops could keep them on their reservations. The mountains they live in in the Navajo country cannot be penetrated by troops. There are cañons in their country thirty miles in length, with walls a thousand feet high, and when at war it is impossible for troops to pass through these cañons, in which they hide and cultivate the ground. In the main Cañon de Chelly they had some two or three thousand peach trees, which were mostly destroyed by my troops. Colonel Sumner, in the fall of 1851, went into the Cañon de Chelly with several hundred men and two pieces of artillery ; he got into the cañon some eight or ten miles, but had to retreat out of it at night. In the walls of the cañon they have regular houses built in the crevices, from which they fire and roll down huge stones on an enemy. They have regular fortifications, averaging from one to two hundred feet from the bottom, with portholes for firing. No small-arms can injure them, and artillery cannot be used. In one of these crevices I found a two-story house. I regard these cañons as impregnable. General Canby entered this cañon, but retreated out the next morning. When I captured the Navajoes I first destroyed their crops, and harassed them until the snow fell very deep in the cañons, taking some prisoners occasionally. I think it was about the 6th of January, after the snow fell, that I started. Five thousand soldiers would probably keep them on reservations in their own country. The Navajoes had a good many small herds when I went there. I took twelve hundred sheep from them at one time, and smaller lots at different times. The volunteers were allowed one dollar per head for all sheep and goats taken, which were turned over to the commissary. I think General Carleton gave the order as an encouragement to the troops. I think from fifteen hundred to two thousand could subsist themselves in the Valley de Chelly. At this point it took me and three hundred men most one day to destroy a field of corn. I think probably fifteen hundred could subsist on the northeastern slope of the Tunacha mountain. I know of no other place near by where any considerable number could subsist themselves. I was in the valley of the San Juan, but can give no idea of the number that could subsist themselves in it. While I was in the country there was continual thieving carried on between the Navajoes and Mexicans. Some Mexicans now object to the settlement of the Navajoes at the Bosque, because they cannot prey on them as formerly. I am of the opinion that, in consequence of the military campaign and the destruction of their crops, they were forced to come in. It appears to me that the only objection to the Bosque is on account of the wood, which consists of mesquite roots ; but I am not sufficiently acquainted with the character of it to give an opinion of it, and the time it would last, but it is rather hard to dig. Many of the Apaches understand farming, and they should be put on a reservation. I think the Jicarrilla Apaches would object to being put on the Bosque. The Apaches in Arizona, I think, would make very little objection to being placed on a reservation. With the Utes it would be more difficult, as they know nothing of planting, and when spoken to on the subject have invariably objected. They are a brave, warlike people ; they are of rather small size, but hardy, and very fine shots. I would advise, however, that they be put on a reservation, as they cannot live much longer as now ; they are generally hungry, and killing cattle and sheep, which will bring on a war. They are now at peace, and it would be the wiser

7

186

policy to remain at peace with them. I think there is a good place for a reservation north of the San Juan in Utah. I think that justice demands that every effort should be made to secure peace with the Cheyennes and Arapahoes before any war was prosecuted against them, in view of the treatment they have received.

---

HEADQUARTERS DISTRICT OF NEW MEXICO,
*Santa Fé, New Mexico, October 22, 1865.*

SIR: I have the honor herewith to enclose for the information of the congressional committee, of which you are the chairman, letters of instruction and advice from myself to various commanders and to different departments of the public service in relation to Indians, Indian wars, &c., &c., within my official jurisdiction and controlled by myself.

Among these letters will be found two or three relating to the wealth of this part of the country in precious metals. These are sent to you in order that the committee may see the national importance of settling Indians upon reservations, so that the country now inhabited by many bands of them may be left open to the enterprise and skill of the miner. The Indians will not themselves work the mines : they should not be permitted to lie in wait to murder the prospecter who comes with much toil and many privations to explore their country for its hidden wealth. This they will surely do unless they are exterminated or placed upon reservations. The miners *will* go to their country, and the question which comes up is, shall the miners be protected and the country be developed, or shall the Indians be suffered to kill them and the nation be deprived of its immense wealth ?

In all that I have had to do in this command, so far as the Indians are concerned, I have endeavored to treat them justly, and I point to this record of over three years of anxiety and toil, mostly on their account, as one of which I do not feel ashamed.

I have the honor to be, very respectfully. your obedient servant,

JAMES H. CARLETON,
*Brigadier General. Commanding.*

Hon. JAMES R. DOOLITTLE,
*United States Senate, Washington, D. C.*

---

# LETTERS RELATING TO INDIAN AFFAIRS IN THE DEPARTMENT OF NEW MEXICO DURING THE YEARS 1862 AND 1863.

[Extract.]

HEADQUARTERS DEPARTMENT OF NEW MEXICO,
*Santa Fé, N. M., September 30, 1862.*

GENERAL: I have the honor to inform you that I relieved General Canby in the command of this department on the 18th instant, and he left this city for Washington, D. C., four days afterwards. I find that during the raid which was made into this Territory by some armed men from Texas, under Brigadier General Sibley, of the army of the so-called Confederate States, the Indians, aware that the attention of our troops could not, for the time, be turned toward them, commenced robbing the inhabitants of their stock, and killed, in various places, a great number of people ; the Navajoes on the western side, and the Mescalero Apaches on the eastern side of the settlements. both committing these outrages at the same time, and during the last year that has passed have left the people greatly impoverished. Many farms and settlements near Fort Stanton have been entirely abandoned.

To punish and control the Mescaleros, I have ordered Fort Stanton to be reoccupied. That post is in the heart of their country, and hitherto when troops occupied it those Indians were at peace. I have sent Colonel Christopher Carson, (Kit Carson,) with five companies of his regiment of New Mexican volunteers, to Fort Stanton. One of these companies, on foot, will hold the post and guard the stores, while four companies mounted, under Carson, will operate against the Indians until they have been punished for their recent aggressions. The lieutenant colonel, with four companies of the same regiment, will move into the Navajo country and establish and garrison a post on the Gallo, which was selected by General Canby ;. it is called Fort Wingate. I shall endeavor to have this force, assisted

# REPORT OF THE SECRETARY OF WAR

39th Congress, Second Session
Senate Executive Document 26
Washington, D.C., 1867

# REPORT

OF

# THE SECRETARY OF WAR,

COMMUNICATING,

*In compliance with a resolution of the Senate of February 4, 1867, a copy of the evidence taken at Denver and Fort Lyon, Colorado Territory, by a military commission, ordered to inquire into the Sand Creek massacre, November, 1864.*

---

FEBRUARY 14, 1867.—Read, referred to the Committee on Indian Affairs, and ordered to be printed.

---

WAR DEPARTMENT,
*Washington City, February 12, 1867.*

SIR: I have the honor to transmit herewith a communication from the Adjutant General, of this date, covering a report of the Sand Creek massacre in November, 1864, called for by a resolution of the Senate dated February 4, 1867.

Very respectfully, sir, your obedient servant,

EDWIN M. STANTON,
*Secretary of War.*

Hon. L. F. S. FOSTER,
*President of the Senate.*

---

WAR DEPARTMENT, ADJUTANT GENERAL'S OFFICE,
*Washington, February 12, 1866.*

SIR: In compliance with your instructions of the 4th instant, I have the honor to submit herewith a copy of the "evidence taken at Denver and Fort Lyon, Colorado Territory, by a military commission, of which Colonel S. F. Tappan, veteran battalion first Colorado cavalry, was president, ordered to inquire into and report all the facts connected with the so-called Sand Creek massacre in November, 1864," called for by Senate resolution of the 4th of February, 1867.

I have the honor to be, sir, very respectfully, your obedient servant,

E. D. TOWNSEND,
*Assistant Adjutant General.*

Hon. E. M. STANTON,
*Secretary of War.*

191

SAND CREEK MASSACRE.

PROCEEDINGS OF A MILITARY COMMISSION CONVENED BY SPECIAL OR-
DERS No. 23, HEADQUARTERS DISTRICT OF COLORADO, DENVER, COL-
ORADO TERRITORY, DATED FEBRUARY 1, 1865, IN THE CASE OF COLONEL
J. M. CHIVINGTON, FIRST COLORADO CAVALRY.

DENVER, COLORADO TERRITORY,
May 30, 1865.

Proceedings of a military commission convened by Special Orders No. 23,
current series, headquarters district of Colorado, date February 1, 1865.

SAM. F. TAPPAN,
*Lieut. Colonel Veteran Battalion, First Colorado Cavalry.*

GEO. H. STILWELL,
*Capt. Vet. Batt. First Col. Cav., Recorder of Military Commission.*

[Special Order No. 23.—Extract.]

HEADQUARTERS DISTRICT OF COLORADO,
*Denver, Colorado Territory, February 1, 1865.*

\* \* \* \* \* \* \* \* \*

II. In obedience to instructions from the major general commanding department, a military commission is hereby convened, to meet in Denver City, Colorado Territory, on the 9th instant, to investigate the conduct of the late Colonel
J. M. Chivington, first regiment Colorado cavalry, in his recent campaign against
the Indians, in the months of October, November, and December, 1864. This
includes the amount and disposition made of all property captured from the Indians, or otherwise, obtained during the campaign.

*Detail for the commission.*

1. Lieutenant Colonel Sam. F. Tappan, veteran battalion first Colorado cavalry.
2. Captain Ed. A. Jacobs, veteran battalion first Colorado cavalry.
3. Captain Geo. H. Stilwell, veteran battalion first Colorado cavalry.

III. In view of the press of business and the necessities of the case, the commission will sit without regard to hours. The junior member will record the
proceedings.

By order of Colonel T. Moonlight, eleventh regiment Kansas cavalry :

IRA I. TABER,
*First Lieutenant and Acting Assistant Adjutant General.*

DENVER, COLORADO TERRITORY,
*February 9, 1865—2 p. m.*

Commission met pursuant to foregoing order.

Present : Lieutenant Colonel S. F. Tappan, veteran battalion first Colorado
cavalry ; Captain E. A. Jacobs, veteran battalion first Colorado cavalry ; Captain Geo. H. Stilwell, veteran battalion first Colorado cavalry, recorder.

Order convening commission read in the presence of J. M. Chivington, late
colonel first Colorado cavalry.

Question raised by members as to the construction to be put upon the order
convening this commission, which was determined to decide before organization.

The commission was cleared for discussion, pending which, adjourned until
10 o'clock a. m. to-morrow, February 10, 1865.

192

SAND CREEK MASSACRE.

SECOND DAY.

FEBRUARY 10, 1865—10 o'clock a. m.

Commission met pursuant to adjournment.
Present : Lieutenant Colonel S. F. Tappan, veteran battalion first Colorado cavalry ; Captain E. A. Jacobs, veteran battalion first Colorado cavalry ; Captain George H. Stilwell, veteran battalion first Colorado cavalry, recorder.
The question under discussion at adjournment was resumed, pending which, adjourned until 2 o'clock p. m. this day.
*Two o'clock p. m.*—Commission met pursuant to adjournment.
Present, all members and recorder.
The question under discussion at adjournment was resumed, pending which, adjourned until 10 o'clock a. m. to-morrow, February 11, 1865.

THIRD DAY.

FEBRUARY 11, 1865—10 o'clock a. m.

Commission met pursuant to adjournment. Present, all members and recorder.
The question under discussion at adjournment yesterday was resumed, pending which, adjourned until 2 o'clock p. m. this day.
*Two p. m.*—Commission met pursuant to adjournment. Present, all members and recorder.
Adjourned until 10 o'clock a. m. Monday, February 13, 1865.

FOURTH DAY.

FEBRUARY 13, 1865—10 a. m.

Commission met pursuant to adjournment. Present, all members and recorder.
Adjourned until 2 p. m. this day.
*Two p. m.*—Commission met pursuant to adjournment. Present, all members and recorder.
Additional orders or instructions from Colonel T. Moonlight, commanding district Colorado, marked A, and appended to these proceedings.

A.

HEADQUARTERS DISTRICT OF COLORADO,
*Denver, Colorado Territory, February 12, 1865.*

SIR : The commission, of which you are president, convened by Special Orders No. 23, current series, from these headquarters, in obedience to instructions from department headquarters, is convened for the purpose of investigating all matters connected with the action between Colonel Chivington and the Indians, known as the Sand Creek fight, to ascertain, as far as possible, who are the aggressors, whether the campaign was conducted by Colonel Chivington according to the recognized rules of civilized warfare, and whether based upon the law of equity from the commencement of Indian hostilities to the present time.
It is also important to understand whether the Indians were under the protection of the government, and by what authority, or through what influence, they were induced to place themselves under that protection ; whether Colonel Chivington was knowing to this fact ; and whether, or not, the campaign was forced upon the Indians by the whites, knowing their helpless condition ; and whether the Indians were in a state of open hostility and prepared to resist any and all of the United States troops.
Whether any prisoners were taken by Colonel Chivington's command, and the disposition made by the same.

193

If the proper steps were taken by the colonel to prevent unnatural outrages by his command, and punish the transgressors, if such there were.

A special point in your investigation should be as to the amount, kind, and quality of property captured by Colonel Chivington and command; the disposition made of that property, and the steps taken by the colonel to protect the government and insure justice to all parties, and whether he gave this matter any special attention. Also, regarding the treatment of government property, such as horses and mules in the service, during the campaign, and until relieved from duty.

This commission is not intended for the trial of any person, but simply to investigate and accumulate facts called for by the government, to fix the responsibility, if any, and to insure justice to all parties. Colonel Chivington, under these circumstances, has not the right of challenge, and I have been careful to appoint a commission composed of officers not engaged in the operations they are called upon to investigate.

The commission will be sworn in presence of Colonel Chivington, under the 93d article of war, and he will be permitted to have such legal assistance as the commission may deem proper in the premises.

The sessions may be public or private, as the members deem prudent and right.

The commission has power to call for witnesses, and compel attendance. These instructions will be appended to the proceedings, and the whole forwarded through these headquarters.

I have been thus explicit, that the commission may have full sweep, and act without embarrassment.

Respectfully, your obedient servant,

T. MOONLIGHT,
*Colonel Eleventh Kansas Cavalry, Commanding.*

Lieutenant Colonel S. F. TAPPAN,
*President of Military Commission.*

Read in the presence of J. M. Chivington, late colonel first Colorado cavalry, who made application for a copy of said instructions, which was given him

The following request was also made by J. M. Chivington, late colonel first Colorado cavalry:

"I would most respectfully request the commission to delay their organization until I can prepare objections to their organization of the court as a commission, and to object to one of the members, on the grounds of prejudice open and avowed, as I have only this minute heard what the instructions of the colonel commanding were, and what the court intended to investigate."

The rooms were cleared for discussion.

Rooms again opened.

J. M. Chivington, late colonel first Colorado cavalry, called in.

The request was not complied with.

The commission proceeded to organize.

The members and recorder were duly sworn in presence of J. M. Chivington, late colonel first Colorado cavalry.

Asked permission to be granted until to-morrow morning, 10 o'clock, to file certain papers containing his objections to the organizing of the commission, which was granted.

The following request was also made by J. M. Chivington, late colonel first Colorado cavalry, viz:

"I would most respectfully request that the proceedings of this commission be public, and the daily or other papers be allowed, if they desire, to have reporters present;" which was decided to answer to-morrow.

The commission adjourned until 10 a. m. to-morrow, February 14, 1865.

FIFTH DAY.

FEBRUARY 14, 1865, 10 *a. m.*

Commission met pursuant to adjournment.   Present, all members and recorder.
Foregoing proceedings read in presence of J. M. Chivington, late colonel first
Colorado cavalry.

Documents marked in red letters, B, C, D, and E, and appended to these proceedings, presented to the commission by J. M. Chivington, late colonel first
Colorado cavalry.

B.

*To the president and members of the military commission, convened as per Special
Orders No.* 23, *Headquarters District of Colorado, February* 1, 1865:

GENTLEMEN : I would most respectfully object to Lieutenant Colonel S. F.
Tappan, first veteran battalion Colorado cavalry, being a member of the commission, for the following reasons, to wit:

1st. That the said Lieutenant Colonel S. F. Tappan is, and for a long time
past has been, my open and avowed enemy.

2d. That the said Lieutenant Colonel S. F. Tappan has repeatedly expressed
himself very much prejudiced against the killing of the Indians near Fort Lyon,
Colorado Territory, commonly known as the battle of " Sand Creek," and has
said that it was a disgrace to every officer connected with it, and that he
( Tappan ) would make it appear so in the end.

3d. That I believe, from a full knowledge of his character, that he cannot
divest himself of his prejudices sufficiently to render an impartial verdict, and is,
therefore, not such a judge as the law contemplates when it directs that all
men shall be tried by an impartial tribunal. To sustain the above, you will
please notice accompanying affidavits, marked A and B.

J. M. CHIVINGTON,
*Late Colonel First Cavalry of Colorado.*

———

C.

John M. Chivington, being first duly sworn, deposes and says, that he is well
acquainted with Lieutenant Colonel S. F. Tappan, first cavalry Colorado ; that
said Lieutenant Colonel Tappan should not be permitted to remain as a member
of the military commission convened for the investigation of the " Sand Creek
affair," or, properly, of the battle between the troops under Colonel John M.
Chivington and the Cheyenne Indians, fought November 29, 1864, about forty
miles north of Fort Lyon, on the south branch of the Big Sandy, for the following reasons, to wit :

That the said Tappan is, and for a long time past has been, an avowed
enemy of the said John M. Chivington ; that the said Tappan has repeatedly
stated that the " Sand Creek affair " was a disgrace to every officer connected
with it ; and upon one occasion said Lieutenant Colonel Tappan stated that he
would make it appear so in the end.

J. M. CHIVINGTON.

Subscribed and sworn to before me, as witness my hand and notarial seal, on
this 9th day of February, A. D. 1865.

[SEAL.]

JOHN Q. CHARLES,
*Notary Public.*

## D.

Joseph S. Maynard, being first duly sworn, deposes and says, that he is well acquainted with Lieutenant Colonel S. F. Tappan, first cavalry, Colorado; that he has heard said Tappan say that the battle of "Sand Creek," or, more properly, the battle fought between the troops under Colonel John M. Chivington, first cavalry Colorado, and the Cheyenne Indians, fought November 29, 1864, about forty miles north of Fort Lyon, Colorado Territory, was one of the greatest blunders ever committed, and one that would cost thousands of lives, and the government a great deal of treasure. Further the deponent saith not.

J. S. MAYNARD.

Sworn and subscribed to before me this 9th day of February, 1865, as witness my hand and notarial seal.

[SEAL.]

JOHN Q. CHARLES,<br>Notary Public.

## E.

*To the president and members of the military commission convened pursuant to Special Orders No. 23, Headquarters District of Colorado, dated February 1, 1865, Denver, Colorado Territory:*

John M. Chivington, late colonel first cavalry, Colorado, most respectfully objects that this commission has not power and authority to inquire concerning his official acts as specified in the order concerning this commission, for the following reasons:

1st. That the subject-matter which this commission is directed to investigate should be submitted to a court of inquiry, and not to a military commission.

2d. That this court, although denominated a military commission, has been organized as a court of inquiry, using the forms prescribed for the organization of such courts.

3d. That the instructions accompanying the order convening this commission clearly show that the duties of a court of inquiry are imposed upon this commission.

4th. That the colonel commanding this district has no authority to convene a court of inquiry, or any tribunal which shall perform the duties of a court of inquiry, except by order of the President, or request of the officer accused.

5th. That there are no charges or specifications filed with the commission, and that the order and instructions are couched in such general language that they do not apprise him of the nature of the accusations against him.

6th. According to the provisions of General Orders No. ——, dated Washington, D. C., 1864, the colonel commanding the district of Colorado, the number of troops in the district and under his command, are not sufficient to authorize the said colonel commanding to convene a military commission.

J. M. CHIVINGTON,<br>Late Colonel First Cavalry of Colorado.

Read to commission. The commission was then cleared for discussion. Adjourned until 2 p. m. this day.

*Two p. m.*—Commission met pursuant to adjournment. Present, all members and recorder.

The following reply to J. M. Chivington's request was made by the commission, and read in his presence:

In reply to the request of Colonel J. M. Chivington, late colonel first Colorado cavalry, that the sessions of this commission be opened to the public, and a reporter be allowed to report and publish the proceedings in the daily papers, the commission not being able to determine who may be required as witnesses during this investigation, and believing that the exigencies* of the public service do not demand, and that no one can be benefited by such publicity, decides that until further orders the sessions of the commission shall be private ; this order not to be construed in such a manner as to prevent the attendance of Colonel Chivington and his attorneys. Commission was cleared for further discussion. J. M. Chivington, late colonel first Colorado cavalry, was then called in and the following decision read in his presence :

In reply to the objections of Colonel Chivington, late colonel first Colorado cavalry, as to the jurisdiction of this commission, the commission is of opinion that it is competent for the commander of the district, or department, to order an officer, or officers, to take depositions, or collect evidence upon any matter of public interest that may have taken place in his district, or department, and to give said officer, or officers, instructions as to what facts he or they are to elicit, to indicate the form of an oath such officer or officers may take, and designate such officer or officers as a commission, or military commission ; the instructions giving the proper interpretation of the term binding upon the commission, and to declare that no person or persons shall have the privilege of objecting to the proceedings of such commission as long as its members confine themselves to the order, instructions, and the common rules for taking evidence. In this case Colonel Chivington is expected to be present during the sessions of the commission, to introduce evidence and cross-question witnesses, in order that all the facts may be collected, and justice done to all parties. The order and instructions convening the commission specify our duties. No one is arraigned before us on trial, no charges alleged and placed in possession of the commission ; but the said commission is merely called upon to receive and methodize information only, and in this case to give no opinion on the same, as we are not required to make a report, save that of submitting the evidence in accordance with instructions, as the commission is instructed to collect evidence, information, and facts only. It does not feel authorized to prevent the introduction of evidence bearing upon the subject to be investigated, provided it is pertinent and not merely accumulative.

Adjourned until 10 a. m. to-morrow, February 15, 1865.

SIXTH DAY.

FEBRUARY 15, 1865.

Commission met pursuant to adjournment. Present, all members and recorder.

Proceedings of yesterday read and approved.

The following communication was read to commission and in presence of J. M. Chivington, late colonel first Colorado cavalry :

I hereby give notice that during the day, or to-morrow, I will file an answer to the statement of Colonel Chivington in reference to myself, and desire that it be made a part of the record.

SAMUEL F. TAPPAN,
*Lieut. Colonel Veteran Battalion, First Colorado Cavalry,*
*President of Commission.*

The following communications were read to commission :

I respectfully request a copy of my objection and the reply thereto, that I may refer the matter to the major general commanding department of Missouri, for his decision.

J. M. CHIVINGTON,
*Late Colonel First Colorado Cavalry.*

197

*To the President and members military commission :*

GENTLEMEN : I would most respectfully protest against Lieutenant Colonel S. F. Tappan, veteran battalion first Colorado cavalry, filing a reply to my objections after the court commences taking evidence, as the court did not allow me time to file objections, and I think they cannot reasonably claim that which they do not grant.

J. M. CHIVINGTON,
*Late Colonel First Colorado Cavalry.*

The commission was cleared for discussion. Commission adjourned until 2 p. m. this day.

*Two p. m.*—Commission met pursuant to adjournment. Present, all members and recorder.

J. M. Chivington, late colonel first Colorado cavalry, called, and the following decision of commission read in his presence :

Request of John M. Chivington, late colonel first Colorado cavalry, for copy of certain papers, not complied with as requested. The commission has no objections to furnishing a copy of the said papers, if asked for, without reference to the disposition to be made of them.

In reply to objections of J. M. Chivington, late colonel first Colorado cavalry, to my being a member of this commission, I desire to state, and have this statement made a part of the record : The colonel misunderstood me to have said that "I would make it appear so in the end," referring to my statement that the affair at Sand creek was a disgrace to the officers connected with it. I said "it would appear so," not having any desire or expectation that I should ever be called upon to prosecute the matter, but confident government would take action on the subject, and the facts elicited would make it appear disgraceful.

The statement of Captain Maynard is substantially correct. A few days after the affair of Sand creek I remarked to Captain Maynard that from what I could hear, the attack on the Indians at Sand creek was the greatest military blunder of the age, and fatal in its consequences.

As to my alleged prejudice and alleged personal enmity, even if true, I should not consider them at all influencing me in performing the duties assigned me in this commission, especially after taking the oath required as a member.

SAMUEL F. TAPPAN,
*Lieut. Colonel Veteran Battalion, First Colorado Cavalry,*
*President Commission.*

Captain S. S. SOULE, veteran battalion first Colorado cavalry, called in to give evidence by the commission, having been duly sworn according to law, in presence of J. M. Chivington, testified as follows :

By the COMMISSION :

Question. Your full name, age, and rank in the army?

Answer. Silas S. Soule; twenty-six years of age; captain company D, veteran battalion first Colorado cavalry, and assistant provost marshal general, district of Colorado.

Question. How long have you been an officer in the first regiment Colorado volunteers?

Answer. Since December 11, 1861.

Question. Were you on duty at Fort Lyon in August and September?

Answer. I was.

Question. Did you accompany Major Wynkoop's command to an Indian camp on the Smoky Hill about that time?

Answer. I did.

Question. How large a command had Major Wynkoop, and what was the object of the expedition?

Answer. Between one hundred and twenty and one hundred and thirty men; for rescuing some white captives the Indians had in their possession.

Question. Did you find the camp? how many Indians were in it, and what was done by Major Wynkoop?

Answer. We did not find the camp; we found where they camped the night before. The Indians were there, I think about five hundred or six hundred warriors; their women and children were removed. He told them he wanted to talk to them, and their chiefs came into our camp and held a council. Major Wynkoop asked them to give up the white prisoners in their possession. They said they were desirous of making peace with the whites. Major Wynkoop told them he had not the power to make peace, but if they would give up the white prisoners he would take them to Denver before the governor, and pledged himself to protect them to Denver and back; whether they made peace or not they should be safely returned. Black Kettle, their principal chief, said the white prisoners were some distance from their camp, and wanted us to move one or two days' march nearer Fort Lyon, and wait there two days (I think) and he would bring the white prisoners to us. They brought a white woman into our camp the same day, and the second day they brought in three children. We then went to Fort Lyon with about fifty of their Indians, and from there to Denver with seven Indians and the captives.

Question. How far was the camp from Fort Lyon?

Answer. About eighty or ninety miles.

Question. What tribes composed the Indian forces?

Answer. Cheyennes and Arapahoes.

Question. Who were those seven Indians that came to Denver with you?

Answer. Black Kettle, Bull Bear, Boisee, White Antelope, Neva, Notanee; I do not remember the name of the other.

Question. Were these all chiefs of the tribes that were where you first found the Indians?

Answer. They were.

Question. State what was done after reaching Denver.

Answer. Major Wynkoop asked the governor, Colonel Chivington, and some others to meet in council at Camp Weld, to hear their propositions for peace. They had a talk with the chiefs. The Indians seemed very anxious to make peace. The governor told them that he could not make peace with them. They must look to military power for protection. Colonel Chivington told them that he left the matter with Major Wynkoop; if they wanted peace they must come into the post and subject themselves to military law. There was a great deal more said, but I don't remember what it was.

Question. What was done after the council in Denver?

Answer. We returned with the chiefs to Fort Lyon. Major Wynkoop told them to bring in the Indians of their tribe who were anxious for peace to Fort Lyon, and camp near the post, (just below,) and he would immediately send to General Curtis and see if peace could not be made. He immediately sent Lieutenant Denison to General Curtis. The Indians came in and complied with Wynkoop's orders, and camped near the post.

Question. Did the Indians, in council, manifest a desire for peace, and a willingness to comply with the conditions of Colonel Chivington?

Answer. They did.

Question. How many Indians came into the fort, and what tribes were they?

Answer. There were one hundred and six lodges came into the post. Arapahoes and Cheyennes—mostly Arapahoes.

Question. Were all the chiefs with them, those who had been to Denver?

Answer. Black Kettle, their principal chief, and Bull Bear went out to their tribes to bring in more Cheyennes, and brought in a number of Cheyenne families. I have forgotten how many, probably three hundred Indians. I think they all remained at the post with the exception of three—Black Kettle, Bull Bear, and some other one I don't know; I think there were three chiefs went out.

Question. Were they all there after Bull Bear and Black Kettle returned?

Answer. They were all there, I think, with the exception of Bull Bear.

Question. State how long the Indians remained at Fort Lyon, and what was done concerning them.

Answer. I should think that they remained at the post about two weeks, until Major Anthony came from Denver and relieved Major Wynkoop from command at Fort Lyon. Major Anthony told the Indians that they must give up their arms, and horses and mules which belonged to the government or to the whites. This he told to Little Raven, (Arapahoe chief,) then in command of the village near the post. Little Raven gave up three rifles, one pistol, and I think about sixty bows and quivers; nine horses and mules.

Question. Was the same demand made upon Black Kettle?

Answer. No; it was not made to my knowledge.

Question. Was the demand on Little Raven repeated by Major Anthony?

Answer. No, it was not.

Question. What was the understanding with the Indians while in and about Fort Lyon?

Answer. That they were to be protected by the troops there until the messenger returned from General Curtis.

Question. Did a messenger arrive at the fort from General Curtis prior to the first of December, 1864?

Answer. There was not.

Question. Were you at Fort Lyon on or about the 27th of November? If so, what happened there on that day?

Answer. I was there on the 27th of November, at Fort Lyon. About that time Major Wynkoop left Fort Lyon. On the evening of the 27th, Lieutenant Minton and myself discovered some horsemen about fifteen miles above Fort Lyon; supposed them to be Indians. We returned to the fort and reported to Major Anthony. Major Anthony ordered me to take twenty men and go after them, supposing them to be hostile Indians. I proceeded up the Arkansas, and about sunrise I met a mule team; inquired if there were Indians ahead, and the driver told me that Colonel Chivington had ten or twelve companies of *"one hundred-daysers." On, about two miles further, I went, and met Colonel Chivington and about, I suppose, one thousand men (soldiers.) Colonel Chivington asked me if they knew he was coming at Fort Lyon. I told him they did not, and that I had learned from the person with the mule team, two miles below, that he was coming. Colonel Chivington then rode ahead of the command to Fort Lyon. I remained and came in with the third regiment, or a little ahead of them.

Question. Did Colonel Chivington ask you if the Arapahoes and Cheyennes were still in Fort Lyon?

Answer. I think Colonel Chivington asked me if there were any Indians at Fort Lyon; it might have been some of his staff who were with him.

Question. What answer did you make?

Answer. I said that there were some Indians camped near the fort, below the fort, but they were not dangerous; that they were waiting to hear from General Curtis. They were considered as prisoners; some one made answer that they wouldn't be prisoners after they got there.

Question. Did the command go on to the fort and camp?

Answer. No; they camped a mile below the fort, below the commissary.

Commission adjourned until 9½ o'clock a. m. to-morrow, February 16, 1865.

---

* Third regiment, Colorado cavalry, (one hundred-days men.)

FEBRUARY 16, 1865—9½ a. m.

Commission met pursuant to adjournment. Present, all members and recorder. Proceedings of yesterday read and approved.

Captain Silas S. Soule, veteran battalion first Colorado cavalry, recalled by the commission, and, in presence of J. M. Chivington, testified as follows:

By COMMISSION:

Question. Did Colonel Chivington say anything to the Indians while in council near Denver? If so, what did he say?

Answer. Said his business was not to talk, but to fight; that he was a man of few words. He said but little; I do not remember all that was said. He gave them to understand that he was the man, and not Governor Evans, for them to talk to; that he left the matter with Major Wynkoop; that is about all I recollect of it.

Question. State what was done after the command of Colonel Chivington reached Fort Lyon?

Answer. There was a guard stationed around the post, before the regiment arrived there—before I got in—with orders to allow no person to pass out. Major Anthony ordered myself and company to join the colonel's command with three days' cooked rations, and twenty uncooked. I joined Colonel Chivington's command that evening about 8 o'clock, in company with companies G and K, under Major Anthony. I immediately marched about north, marched all night, arrived at the village of Cheyennes and Arapahoes just before sunrise. Major Anthony's battalion was ordered by Colonel Chivington to move across below the Indian camp to cut off a herd of ponies. Lieutenant Wilson, with a battalion of two or three companies, crossed the creek ahead of us, and opened fire on the village. Major Anthony then moved our battalion to within about one hundred yards of the lodges, and ordered us to open fire; some firing done, when the battery came up in our rear with the third regiment and prepared for action. Major Anthony ordered my company, which was directly in line of fire of the battery, to move down into the creek, with orders to move up the creek and for the purpose of killing Indians which were under the banks. Before I got into the creek there were troops upon both sides firing across. It was unsafe for me to take my command up the creek. I crossed over to the other side and moved up the creek. The battery and the first and third regiments kept up firing until all the Indians were killed they could get at; until about 2 o'clock. About 3 o'clock I received orders from Major Anthony to accompany him with my company to escort a supply train on their way from Fort Lyon. I was not back to the battle-ground again that day. Met Colonel Chivington's command returning the next day; they went into camp with us, and the next day we marched to the mouth of Sand creek, about eighteen miles from Fort Lyon; started out that same night, and marched all night on the Santa Fé road, toward the States; laid over the next day in camp; Colonel Chivington ordered me on a scout with twenty-odd men; I saw nothing more of his command until two days after, I think; I came across their camp about eighty miles below Fort Lyon; laid in camp, I believe, one day, and moved back in company with their command to Fort Lyon.

Question. Have you been at Sand creek since; if so, what did you see there, and who went with you?

Answer. I went to Sand creek on the last of December with about thirty men, accompanied by Captain Booth, inspecting officer and chief of cavalry, district of the upper Arkansas. Saw sixty-nine dead Indians and about one hundred live dogs, and two live ponies and a few dead ones. I believe that is about all.

Question. How long have you been provost marshal of the district?

Answer. Since about the 20th of January. I don't remember the exact date

Question. How many horses, ponies, and mules have you taken for the government from private persons ?

Answer. I don't know exactly. The guards have brought in a good many, and were turned in to the quartermaster.

Question. Do you know what became of the horses furnished the third regiment by the government, and the stock captured at Sand creek by Colonel Chivington's command ?

Answer. I do not; except I saw bills of sale of some signed by Captain Johnson, third regiment.

Question. What was the form of those bills of sale, and how signed, and to whom were they given ?

Answer. I don't remember the form ; I have one at the office, I think, given to a man on West Plum creek.

Question. Do you know of any ponies that were captured at Sand creek being driven north of Denver, fifty or a hundred miles, and left upon the ranch of Mason & Maynard, by Captain Johnson ?

Answer. I have seen a note from Mr. Mason, stating that he, Mason, had sent a herd; that they were on their way to Denver.

Objection by J. M. CHIVINGTON :

I object to the answer on the ground that it is not responsive to the question and irrelevant to the subject-matter of inquiry, and not evidence that the court should receive, being hearsay.

(Objection sustained.)

By COMMISSION :

Question. Have you any information in your possession as provost marshal, that a herd of stock was left on Mr. Mason's ranch by Captain Johnson, and that it is there now ?

Answer. I have information that a herd of stock was left there or sent there by Captain Johnson.

Objection by J. M. CHIVINGTON:

I object to the question and answer because it does not adduce facts, within the knowledge of the witness.

Commission was cleared for discussion. Adjourned until 2 p. m. this day.

*Two p. m.*—Commission met pursuant to adjournment. Present, all members and recorder.

Decision of commission in relation to the last objection of J. M. Chivington, relative to question by commission and answer by witness : The objection is sustained.

Captain Silas S. Soule, veteran battalion first Colorado cavalry, recalled by commission, and in presence of J. M. Chivington testified as follows :

By COMMISSION :

Question. At what time on the 28th of November did Colonel Chivington leave Fort Lyon, how far did he march to reach the Indian camp on Sand creek, and what was his order of march ?

Answer. He left camp about 8 o'clock in the evening, and arrived at the Indian camp between daylight and sunrise ; distance about forty-five miles; marched in column of fours. Major Anthony's battalion I think was on the right. Lieutenant Wilson's battalion was in the rear of us, as near as I can recollect, between Anthony's battalion and the third regiment.

Question. Did you know before leaving Fort Lyon, to join Colonel Chivington's command, that he was going to attack Black Kettle's band of Indians ?

Answer. I heard so before the order was given, from Lieutenant Cramer.

202

Question. Did you inform Colonel Chivington of the relations existing between the officers at Fort Lyon and the Indians?

Answer. I did not inform him personally, but I requested Major Anthony to inform him; I also wrote a note to an officer of the third regiment to give to him, (Chivington.)

Question. Did you protest to your commanding officer against attacking those Indians?

Answer. I did.

Question. Who was your commanding officer?

Answer. Major Anthony.

Question. Did you inform Major Anthony of the relations existing with Black Kettle's Indians?

Answer. I did. He knew the relations; I frequently talked to him about it.

Question. What answer did Major Anthony make to your protest?

Answer. He told me that we were going on the Smoky Hill to fight the hostile Indians; he also said that he was in for killing all Indians, and that he was only acting or had been only acting friendly with them until he could get a force large enough to go out and kill all of them—"all the Indians," or words to that effect.

Question. On arriving near the camp of Black Kettle, what was the order of attack?

Answer. We went on a gallop in column of fours, for about two miles. Lieutenant Wilson's battalion went ahead, crossed Sand creek, and opened the attack on the lower end of camp. Major Anthony's battalion took nearly the same as Wilson's and opened fire to the left, before we got to Wilson's battalion. The battery opened fire in rear of Anthony's battalion; they prepared for action in rear of Anthony's battalion, and moved forward before firing to about where Anthony's battalion had been; after that, I could see no order to the battle. The command was scattered and every man firing on his own hook on both sides of the creek.

Question. What is the general course of Sand creek at the point Black Kettle was encamped?

Answer. At the camp, I think it was about northeast and southwest; the creek takes a bend there where the battle-ground was. The general course of the creek I think is about northwest and southeast.

Question. Did Lieutenant Wilson's battalion approach the camp in line?

Answer. They were in line when they opened fire.

Question. From what point of the compass did Lieutenant Wilson's battalion face the camp?

Answer. Faced the camp from the northeast and fired in a southwesterly direction.

Question. At the time Lieutenant Wilson's battalion opened fire, was Major Anthony's battalion in line? If so, from what point of the compass did he face the camp?

Answer. We were not in line when Wilson commenced firing, but were in line soon after, and opened fire from the south or southeast.

Question. At any time during the fight was a portion of Colonel Chivington's command under the fire of another portion?

Answer. They were.

Question. State how it was.

Answer. The troops were on both banks of the creek firing across at Indians under both banks, and if they over-shot they were liable to hit our own men.

Question. Did your squadron become separated from Major Anthony's battalion during the fight? If so, how did it happen?

Answer. It did when he ordered me into the creek. I kept my squadron together, and crossed over to the opposite bank, and followed up the creek one or two miles—about two miles, I guess. I didn't see the balance of the battalion together till after the fight. I saw a number of Anthony's battalion, but not together.

Question. At the time of the attack, were there any white men in the Indian camp? If so, who were they?

Answer. There were: John Smith, Indian interpreter, Fort Lyon; David H. Louderback, private company G, first cavalry of Colorado, and a driver of Major Colley's; I don't think of his name. They had an ambulance; this was the driver of the ambulance.

Question. How came they there, and how did they escape?

Answer. They went out by permission of Major Anthony to do some trading with the Indians. It is a hard matter to tell how they did escape. Louderback escaped toward the command with some cloth or handkerchief on a stick. He had a white rag on a stick. I would not swear it was white, but thought it was. It was a rag or piece of cloth. I did not see how the others escaped. John Smith attempted to come to Anthony's battalion, but the fire was so hot he went back into a lodge.

Question. Did any of Colonel Chivington's command fire upon John Smith?

Answer. I think they did. I think they were fired on by Anthony's battalion and Wilson's.

Question. Did any of the Indians advance towards Colonel Chivington's command, making signs that they were friends?

Answer. I saw them advance towards the line, some of them holding their hands up.

Question. Was any demand made upon the Indians prior to the attack, and any attention paid to their signs that they were friends?

Answer. Not to my knowledge.

Question. Were the women and children shot while attempting to escape by Colonel Chivington's command?

Answer. They were.

Question. Were the women and children followed while attempting to escape, shot down and scalped, and otherwise mutilated, by any of Colonel Chivington's command?

Answer. They were.

Question. Were any efforts made by the commanding officers, Colonels Chivington, Shoup, and Major Anthony, to prevent these mutilations?

Answer. Not that I know of.

Commission adjourned until 9½ a. m. to-morrow, February 17, 1865.

EIGHTH DAY.

FEBRUARY 17, 1865—9.30 a. m.

Commission met pursuant to adjournment. Present, all members and recorder.

Journal of yesterday read, amended as follows, and approved:

Instead of reading (wherever it occurs) "Captain Silas S. Soule, veteran battalion, first Colorado cavalry, recalled by the commission," read, the examination of Captain Soule continued, &c.

The examination of Captain S. S. Soule (in presence of J. M. Chivington) continued:

By COMMISSION:

Question. Did you witness any scalping and otherwise mutilating of the dead during and after the engagement on Sand creek?

Answer. I did.

Question. Did you see any officer engage in this business of scalping and mutilating the dead?

Answer. I cannot say that I did.

204

Question. Were any prisoners taken by Colonel Chivington's command? If so, what was done with them?

Answer. There were three squaws taken, son of Colonel Bent, John Smith's son, and two children with the squaws. Smith's son was killed in camp. I took Bent's son with me. Sent him to Fort Lyon. The squaws went to Fort Lyon at the time the command went back from Sand creek. There were two other prisoners besides those—two children. They were kept by the third regiment. They are now in the mountains.

Question. Are you acquainted with the circumstances of Jack Smith's death?

Answer. Not of my own knowledge.

Question. On your second visit to Sand creek, did you find that the dead had been scalped and otherwise mutilated?

Answer. I did.

Question. All of them—men, women, and children?

Answer. All, with the exception of Jack Smith, (old man Smith's son,) and one squaw that was burnt in a lodge. I could not tell whether she was scalped or not.

Question. Did you discover any indications of rifle-pits or earthworks that had been thrown up by the Indians prior to the attack on the 29th of November?

Answer. I didn't then see any that were thrown up by the Indians at that time. I saw holes under the banks in the sand that I think were dug the day of the fight.

Question. What was the object of the scout upon which you were sent with twenty-odd men?

Answer. To see if there was a camp of Indians on the Aubrey road about fifty miles south of the river, and to see if I could discover Indians anywhere south of the Arkansas river.

Question. Had the Indians committed any depredations in the vicinity of Fort Lyon, and on the road to Larned, during the three months prior to the 29th of November?

Answer. Not to my knowledge.

Question. Do you know what became of the stock and other property taken from the Indians on Sand creek?

Answer. I know some of the stock and other property taken there is in the hands of persons that took it; members of the third regiment and first regiment also.

Question. State who has the property, and describe it?

Answer. I know of probably two hundred who have or had some of the property in their possession; nearly every man in the command had some. Lieutenant Antoby, third regiment, had a lot of stock. He had a number of ponies in his possession. Hank Lathrop, of the third. He sold one pony which he had in his possession on the way up. (Sold to a citizen.) Lieutenant Hardin's wife had one pony given her by one of the third regiment. I think it was given by Lieutenant Antoby. Lieutenant Baldwin, of the independent battery, had some ponies from there. Captain Evans, eleventh Ohio cavalry, of Camp Collins, took five ponies from Mason's ranch, on Cache le Poudre. Major Anthony has trophies. Lieutenant Cannon, of the first New Mexico volunteers, has got some Indian clothing. Major Anthony has, or had when I left there, an Indian shield, squaw's dress, and some other property of little value. I don't remember the articles. It is hard to enumerate these things. I know of a good many soldiers who have property of this kind. I have taken, as provost martial, considerable of this stock, and turned it in to the quartermaster.

Adjourned until 2 p. m. this day.

*Two p. m.*—Commission met pursuant to adjournment. Present, all members and recorder.

The examination of Captain S. S. Soule continued.

Cross-examined by J. M. CHIVINGTON, late colonel first Colorado cavalry:

Question. In what military district was Fort Lyon, and the place where the battle of Sand creek occurred, at the time said battle took place?

Answer. District of the Upper Arkansas.

Question. State, if you know, who had command of that district?

Answer. I think the district was in command of Major B. F. Henning, third Wisconsin cavalry.

Question. Do you know whether Major Wynkoop was ordered or directed by the commander of the district of Upper Arkansas, or any superior officer, to go out upon the expedition of which you speak in your direct examination?

Answer. I do not know that he had any orders.

Question. State, if you know, whether Major Wynkoop was ordered to go out upon that expedition, or to treat with the Indians, by the governor of Colorado, or the commander of the district of Colorado?

Answer. Not to my knowledge.

Question. Did or did not the Indians manifest any hostility towards Major Wynkoop's command upon that expedition?

Answer. They did when we met them. They met us in line of battle.

Question. What acts of hostility did the Indians show towards Major Wynkoop's command?

Answer. They were in line of battle; we were the same. They asked Major Wynkoop what he came there for. They were answered that we came there to talk. They asked Major Wynkoop why we came there with soldiers and cannon, in form of battle, if Major Wynkoop's intentions were peaceable. Major told them that he came prepared to defend himself in case of any treachery. They surrounded us, and marched about two miles, encircling our flanks and rear until we got to their camp. We met them two or three miles from their camp. While we were in they were saucy. There were some cases of them putting their hands in soldiers' pockets to get tobacco. After we were in camp they closed around us as though they meant to gobble us up, i. e., we expected an attack, until one of their chiefs, (One-Eye,) who went out with us from Fort Lyon, told the Indians that he had promised us protection, and if they fired on us, or attempted to kill us, he would join the whites and fight against them. One-Eye (and some other chiefs) made a speech to them. Black Kettle and One-Eye were the principle ones. They then left us. Black Kettle and One-Eye ordered us to leave and go a day or two's march nearer Fort Lyon, and go in camp, and wait for them to bring in the white prisoners. During the council Lieutenant Hardin, of the "first," was officer of the day. He came in to the camp and complained to the major that the Indians were crowding in on him, and he could not keep them out. I think he said they (the Indians) had possession of the cannon, and were sitting on them. Then Major Wynkoop told the chiefs in council that they must keep their men out of camp, and One-Eye and others made speeches to the Indians. The Indians then left our camp.

Question. How far from the place where the council was held did Major Wynkoop's command march towards Fort Lyon on the day after the council?

Answer. On the day of the council we marched back about eight miles. The day after the council we laid in camp, and the day after that we marched about twenty miles.

Question. At what time in the day was the council with the Indians held?

Answer. I should think it was about 10 o'clock in the forenoon. It might not have been that late.

Question. At what time did Major Wynkoop's command leave Fort Lyon, and of what troops was his command composed, and what subordinate officers were in command of such troops?

Answer. I think the fore part of September, or in September—I cannot recollect clearly—company D, company G, and company K, first cavalry of Colorado. I commanded D company; Lieutenant Hardin commanded company G. I don't recollect who was in command of company K. Lieutenants Phillips and Cramer were along. The officers present were Major Wynkoop, myself, and Lieutenants Hardin, Phillips, and Cramer.

Question. Were there any Indians at Fort Lyon when Major Wynkoop's expedition left there? If so, to what tribe did they belong, and give the names of any whom you may know?

Answer. I think there were none at the fort except those that went with us.

Question. What Indians went with Major Wynkoop's expedition, and to what tribe did they belong?

Answer. One-Eye and his squaw, and Min-im-mie. They were Cheyennes, There was one other, a Cheyenne also.

Question. Were there any Indians at Fort Lyon other than those you have named, shortly before Major Wynkoop's expedition left there? If so, how long before that time were they there, and what was the number of them?

Answer. None at the post. We had a fight about two weeks before, near there, with fourteen Indians, supposed to be Arapahoes. The fight was about ten or fifteen miles from the post. They chased in a soldier, within a mile or two of the post. Then Lieutenant Cramer pursued them. Overtook them probably about ten miles from the post, and had a running fight with them, probably five miles.

Question. Was there an election held by the command under the laws of the Territory, while out on the expedition?

Answer. We held an election the day after the council on the Smoky Hill; it was for officers of State, &c.

Question. Did the Indians commit any acts of hostility against the whites in the vicinity of Fort Lyon prior to the time when Major Wynkoop's expedition left there?

Answer. They had. They killed two men about two miles from the post. I don't remember the exact time, but I think about two weeks before Wynkoop's expedition went out. These men were on their way from Point of Rocks to Fort Lyon, as witnesses for a military commission.

Question. Was there any whiskey, or other intoxicating beverages, used by the men or officers of Major Wynkoop's command on the day on which the council with the Indians was held?

Answer. I think there was. I saw some.

Question. State if you know whether any of the men or officers of Major Wynkoop's command were intoxicated at the time the council with the Indians was held.

(Objections to question by Lieutenant Colonel Tappan, president of the commission.

Commission was cleared for discussion.

Commission opened.

The objection sustained by the commission, on the ground that it is not pertinent to the subject-matter of this investigation. Some men in difficult situations become very much excited, and it would be unjust to accuse them of being intoxicated. The action of the officers on that occasion is a proper subject of investigation; but opinion of witnesses as to the impulses or influences under which they acted determines nothing.)

Cross-examination continued:

Question. State, if you know, whether Major Wynkoop and other officers of his expedition acted as men having full control of their reasoning faculties at the time the council with the Indians took place.

Answer. I think they all did, except Lieutenant Hardin, who was excited.

Ex. Doc. 26——2

Question. State, if you know, whether the Indians of whom you have spoken in your direct examination, in council or elsewhere, stated by what Indians the captives of whom you have spoken were captured.

Answer. They spoke of them as being captured by the Cheyennes.

Question. Did the Indians of whom you have spoken state how many white prisoners they then had in their possession?

Answer. They said they had seven.

Question. Did they or did they not promise to deliver to Major Wynkoop all the white captives they then had in their possession?

Answer. They promised to give them all up as soon as they could get them. They were sold in different tribes (scattered.)

Question. State whether they did deliver all the white captives that they admitted were in their possession, and how many they delivered in accordance with their promise?

Answer. They delivered all but three; they delivered four.

Question. Did the Indians, in council or elsewhere, state when and where they had captured the white prisoners of whom you have spoken?

Answer. I don't know as the Indians did.

Question. Did the white captives state where and when they were captured and by whom? If so, what statement did they make respecting the time when, place where, and Indians by whom they were captured?

Answer. They stated they were captured some time in August, on the Little Blue river, Kansas, by Cheyennes.

Question. Did or did not the Indians state that they had captured Mrs. Snider a few miles below Booneville?

Answer. I believe they did.

Commission adjourned until to-morrow morning, 9½ o'clock, February 18, 1865.

### NINTH DAY.

FEBRUARY 18, 1865.

Commission met pursuant to adjournment. Present, all members and recorder.

Yesterday's proceedings read and approved.

Cross-examination of Captain Silas S. Soule by J. M. Chivington, late colonel, &c., continued:

Question. Did or did not Major Wynkoop represent to the Indians in council that any person had power to make peace with them on behalf of the government? And if so, what statement did he make?

Answer. He told them that no one but the governor had the right; that he (Wynkoop) could not make peace with them.

Question. After the council with the Indians on the Smoky Hill, did they return in force to Major Wynkoop's command? If so, in what number did they return?

Answer. They did not.

Question. Who were present at the council between the Indians and the governor, at Camp Weld, near Denver?

Answer. Colonel Chivington, Major Wynkoop, myself, J. Bright Smith, Amos Steck, John Smith, Indian interpreter; I think Lieutenant Hawley, first regiment. There were a good many there; I don't remember all of them.

Question. Were the proceedings of the council at Camp Weld recorded or reduced to writing at the time such council was held; if so, by whom?

Answer. They were, I think, by Major Whitely, Indian agent of the Utes.

Question. State if you know whether orders or directions were received by Colonel Chivington from Major General Curtis, commanding department of Kansas, at the time or before the council at Camp Weld was held, in relation to treating with the Indians; if so, state if you know what those orders or directions were.

Answer. I do not know.

Question. Did or did not the Indians in council at Camp Weld, or elsewhere, represent that they had power to act for the Arapahoe and Cheyenne tribes?

Answer. They did, I think.

Question. After Major Wynkoop's return to Fort Lyon from the Camp Weld council, did or did not the Indians represent that they would bring in the entire Arapahoe and Cheyenne tribes to Fort Lyon?

Answer. They would if they could. They would bring in all who would comply with the orders of Major Wynkoop.

Question. Was there anything said by Major Wynkoop to the Indians after the Camp Weld council, as to furnishing provisions to those Indians who should come in and camp near Fort Lyon?

Answer. He furnished them provisions, but I did not hear him tell them he would furnish provisions.

Question. State as nearly as you can the quantity of provisions furnished by Major Wynkoop to the Indians.

Answer. He furnished prisoners' allowance for ten days—I think, for five hundred Indians.

Question. At the time these provisions were furnished, had any communication been received by Major Wynkoop in reply to that sent with Lieutenant Dennison to General Curtis?

Answer. There had not.

Question. State, if you know, the number of Indians that came in and camped near Fort Lyon, in obedience to Major Wynkoop's orders.·

Answer. There were about one hundred and twenty lodges, or about six hundred Indians.

Question. When did Major Anthony assume command at Fort Lyon?

Answer. I don't remember the date; I should think about the first of November, 1864.

Question. Did or did not Major Anthony order or direct the Indians to remove from Fort Lyon, soon after he assumed command?

Answer. He directed or advised them to move out on Sand creek. He could not furnish them provisions, and wanted them to remove where they could kill buffalo.

Question. State the number of Indians encamped near Fort Lyon, at the time Major Anthony required them to deliver up their arms, and the horses and mules belonging to the whites.

Answer. I should think there were about six hundred Indians.

Question. Where were Black Kettle and Bull Bear at the time Major Anthony required the Indians to deliver up their arms?

Answer. Out after the Cheyennes.

Question. Did Black Kettle and Bull Bear, or either of them, subsequently bring in other Indians?

Answer. They did.

Question. How many Indians did they bring in after that time?

Answer. I do not know; their camp was on Sand creek. They were not allowed to come to the post with their village.

Question. Were any steps taken by Major Anthony to secure all the arms the Indians had, other than the mere request that they should deliver them up?

Answer. There were steps taken to get all the arms from the band, besides the mere request.

Question. What steps were taken, as stated in your last answer?

Answer. He ordered me to count all the Indians in the village, and to take all arms that could be found.

Question. State if you know whether the arms received from the Indians were ever returned to them; if so, when and by whom?

Answer. They were returned by me, by Major Anthony's order, about the middle of November, 1864, I think.

Question. Did all the Indians of the Arapahoe and Cheyenne tribes come in and camp near Fort Lyon, in compliance with Major Wynkoop's order.

Answer. They did not all come in, none of the Dog * soldiers came in, I think, and not all of the fighting men of the Arapahoes; about forty or fifty, I should think, came in; they are not organized as their soldiers.

Question. Was there anything said in the council at Camp Weld about furnishing provisions to those Indians that should come in and camp near Fort Lyon?

Answer. There was something said, but I don't remember what it was.

Question. Were the squaws and children of the Arapahoe and Cheyenne warriors among those Indians that came in and camped near Fort Lyon?

Answer. I don't know; I don't think the squaws came in without their warriors did.

Question. What proportion of the Arapahoe and Cheyenne Indians, came in and camped near Fort Lyon?

Answer. I do not know; I don't know their strength; I think nearly all of the Arapahoes in that section of the country.

Question. State your means of knowledge as to the understanding between the Indians and the officers at Fort Lyon, as to the protection to be furnished said Indians.

Answer. I heard Major Wynkoop tell the chiefs that he would protect them until the messenger returned from General Curtis. Major Anthony and all the officers at the post signed a document to General Curtis, indorsing Wynkoop's action.

Question. State, if you know, whether Lieutenant Dennison, bearer of despatches from Major Wynkoop, ever returned with orders from the latter officer.

Answer. He returned after Major Wynkoop left, but I do not know whether he brought orders or not.

Question. How long after Lieutenant Dennison was sent as messenger to General Curtis, did Major Wynkoop remain in command at Fort Lyon?

Answer. I think about two weeks.

Question. By whom was Major Wynkoop relieved of the command at Fort Lyon, and by whose order was he relieved?

Answer. He was relieved by Major Anthony, by the order of General Curtis.

Question. At what time did the Indians remove from the immediate vicinity of Fort Lyon?

Answer. Shortly after Major Anthony's arrival. I should think it was a long about the middle of November.

Question. Who, if any one, was present at the conversation held by you with Colonel Chivington, when you met him with the command above Fort Lyon?

Answer. I don't remember certain who they were. There were a number present. I think some of the soldiers of my command heard the conversation.

Question. Did you converse with Colonel Chivington prior to the arrival of the command at Fort Lyon?

Answer. Yes.

Question. What statement did Colonel Chivington make to you in that conversation?

Answer. He asked me if they knew at Fort Lyon that he was coming. He asked me how far ahead the mule team was I met. He asked me if I would

---

* Fighting men of the Cheyenne tribe regularly organized.

ride ahead with him into the post. I think he asked me in regard to the Indians that had been there. I cannot remember all of the conversation.

Question. Did Colonel Chivington in that conversation state to you the object of his expedition?

Answer. He did not, I think.

Question. State, if you know, whether any officer at Fort Lyon objected to joining Colonel Chivington's command; and if so, to whom such objection was made.

Answer. Objection was made to Major Anthony by officers at the post. I think objections were made at the post to Colonel Chivington, also by officers, and to several officers belonging to the expedition under Chivington.

Question. What are your means of knowledge respecting objections having been made to Colonel Chivington personally?

Answer. Lieutenant Cramer and some one else told me that day that they objected to Colonel Chivington personally, and I was warned by Major Anthony, Lieutenant Cramer, and some others not to go to the camp where Colonel Chivington was; that he had made threats against me for language I had used that day against Colonel Chivington's command going out to kill those Indians on Sand creek.

Question. To whom did you deliver the note which you addressed to Colonel Chivington, for the purpose of being delivered to the latter? and state if you know that note was delivered to Colonel Chivington.

Answer. I delivered the note to Captain Talbert, third regiment, and Colonel Chivington came into camp, and Talbert returned the note to me. I think Colonel Chivington knew the contents, although I did not deliver it.

Question. By whom was the plan of attack on the Indian village at Sand creek arranged or directed?

Answer. By Colonel Chivington, I think.

Question. By whom were you ordered to move up Sand creek after the battle began?

Answer. By Major Anthony.

Question. After you crossed Sand creek, did you or did you not return to your superior officer for further orders? and did you receive any further or other orders during the progress of the fight?

Answer. I met Major Anthony about 12 o'clock, and asked what I should do with my company. He told me to put them on guard over some wounded men and property belonging to our men and officers.

Commission adjourned at 1 p. m. to meet again Monday morning, February 20, 1865, at 9½ o'clock.

TENTH DAY.

FEBRUARY 20, 1865.

Commission met pursuant to adjournment. Present, all members and recorder.

Proceedings of Saturday last read and approved.

Cross-examination of Captain Silas S. Soule continued:

Question. Did you receive any orders other than those you have mentioned, during the fight at Sand creek?

Answer. Not that I remember.

Question. Did the squadron or company under your command remain together in rank and under your supervision during the fight?

Answer. They did.

Question. State, if you know, whether Colonel Chivington or any officer at the battle of Sand creek ordered the men to disperse and conduct the fight without regard to order, or gave any order to the effect that the men should fight singly.

Answer. Not that I know of.

Question. State, if you know, whether any company, battalion, squadron, or other military organization engaged in the battle of Sand creek, remained in rank and conducted the battle as a military organization during the progress of the battle.

Answer. Not to my knowledge, except what I took to be a squadron about three miles to the northwest of the Indian village.

Question. After the battle began, did the officers retain control of the men under their command?

Answer. I think not.

Question. What was the extent or area of the battle-ground where the battle of Sand creek was fought?

Answer. I should think about four or five miles up the creek, and one or two each side.

Question. Were all the forces under the command of Colonel Chivington engaged in the battle?

Answer. I do not know.

Question. What part of the battle-field did you occupy during the battle?

Answer. I commenced at the lower end of the battle-ground, crossed the creek south, moved up the creek about two miles, crossed it to the north, and down the creek again to the village where the battle commenced.

Question. What forces were upon the northeastern bank of the creek when you were there?

Answer. Men of the first and third mixed together.

Question. What was the number of soldiers upon the northeastern bank of the creek when you were there?

Answer. I should think about four hundred.

Question. How long did you remain upon the northeastern bank of the creek?

Answer. Three or four hours.

Question. What time in the day did you cross from the northeastern to the southwestern bank of the creek?

Answer. Early in the morning at the commencement of the fight, and remained on the southwestern side till nearly noon.

Question. What time in the day did you cross from the southwestern to the northeastern bank of the creek?

Answer. Nearly noon; probably between 11 and 12 o'clock.

Question. Was the battle still progressing when you crossed, as stated in your last answer?

Answer. It was both above and below me.

Question. Did you see Colonel Chivington or communicate with him after the battle began, and before the close thereof?

Answer. I did. I saw him (Colonel Chivington) during the progress of and before the battle closed and communicated with him.

Question. What was that communication, and in what time in the day was it made?

Answer. It was about two o'clock. I asked him if I could send Colonels Bent's son Charles, who was taken prisoner with Jack Smith, to his home. Colonel Chivington said that his (Bent's) brother Robert did not care about having him taken back, and the colonel told me he guessed I better not take or send him back; and then, again, he said he had no objections.

Question. Did you see Major Anthony or communicate with him after the battle began and before the close thereof?

Answer. I did.

212

Question. What were those communications, and at what time in the day were they respectively made?

Answer. I think about twelve or one o'clock. I asked him what I should do with my command. He told me to put them on guard over some wounded men and baggage. I received orders I should think between two and three o'clock to get my command ready to go back that night with him to escort a supply train.

Question. Was the battle still progressing when you received the order from Major Anthony, about one o'clock in the day?

Answer. It was. The battle was still progressing when I received the last order.

Question. What time did you leave the battle-field?

Answer. I should think between two and three o'clock p. m.

Question. State if you know whether any of the Indians escaped from the battle-field on the day of the battle.

Answer. I know I saw some escape.

Question. If you know, state whether orders were given by any officer at the battle of Sand creek, or prior thereto, to the effect that Indians killed should be scalped or mutilated.

Answer. Not that I know of.

Question. Do you state that Indian children were scalped or mutilated by soldiers at the battle of Sand creek?

Answer. They were scalped I know; I saw holes in them, and some with their skulls knocked in, but cannot say how they were mutilated.

Question. Did you see any soldiers in the act of scalping or mutilating Indian children?

Answer. I think not. I saw soldiers with children's scalps during the day, but did not see them cut them off.

Question. To what company, regiment, or military organization did the soldiers mentioned in your last answer belong?

Answer. They belonged to Colonel Chivington's command.

Commission adjourned until 2 p. m. this day.

*Two p. m.*—Commission met pursuant to adjournment. Present, all members and recorder.

Cross-examination of Captain Silas S. Soule continued:

Question. How many soldiers did you see with the scalps of Indian children?

Answer. I could not tell for certain.

Question. How high were the banks of Sand creek at the place where the battle occurred?

Answer. All the way from two to fifteen and twenty feet.

Question. Where was the Indian camp with reference to Sand creek—in the bend of the creek or on the banks thereof?

Answer. On the banks.

Question. On which bank of the creek was the Indian camp located?

Answer. On the northern banks.

Question. How high were the banks of the creek at the place where the camp was located?

Answer. The bank I should say was from two to five feet high.

Question. State if you know whether Colonel Chivington ordered portions of his command to occupy each bank of the creek.

Answer. I do not know. I know that the regimental color-bearer of the third, with the flag, was on the south side of the creek.

Question. How long after the battle began was it that the soldiers arranged themselves on each bank of the creek, so that those upon one bank were under the fire of those on the opposite bank?

213

Answer. Immediately after the battle opened—before I got across with my company.

Question. Do you know whether the soldiers who occupied the banks of the creek, in the manner stated in the last question, assumed those positions in obedience to the command of any officer?

Answer. I do not.

Question. Did they assume those positions in rank and by companies, or battalions, or in a disorderly manner?

Answer. In a disorderly manner.

Question. Did they not assume those positions for the purpose of driving the Indians from under the banks of the creek?

Answer. I suppose they assumed those positions to kill the Indians under the banks of the creek. They were not much on the drive.

Question. Were the positions of the soldiers upon the banks of the creek such that shots fired by those upon one bank at the Indians under the opposite bank would take effect upon the soldiers upon the opposite bank?

Answer. They were very apt to if they fired too high.

Question. Did you discover any Indians when you went upon the scout, immediately after the battle?

Answer. I did, what I supposed to be Indians.

Question. Where did you discover those Indians?

Answer. I discovered signal fires about forty miles south of the Arkansas, and about east of those, within about ten miles of the river, I came across what I supposed to be a village of Indians, in the vicinity of the signal fires to the east about eight or ten miles from the river.

Question. How near did you approach to the village mentioned in your last answer?

Answer. In less than a quarter of a mile.

Question. What reasons had you for supposing that it was an Indian village?

Answer. Their camp-fires were burning. The dogs barked at us. I heard the voices of Indians, and thought I saw Indians walking by the fire.

Question. What was the number of lodges in the village?

Answer. I could not tell; it was in the night. I did not think, from the appearance of the fires, that their lodges were up.

Question. How long before the battle of Sand creek did the Indians remove from Fort Lyon?

Answer. I don't exactly remember; about two weeks.

Question. How long did the conversation between yourself and Colonel Chivington, when you met him with the command above Fort Lyon, continue?

Answer. Not long; a very few minutes.

Question. Did Colonel Chivington halt and remain with you while the conversation was being carried on?

Answer. He halted a moment. I rode on a little piece with him in the direction of Fort Lyon.

Question. How far above Fort Lyon is the place where this conversation took place?

Answer. About ten or twelve miles, at the head of the Big Bottom, near the watering place.

Question. State your means of knowledge as to permission being granted by Major Anthony to the persons who were in the Indian camp at Sand creek to go to that place.

Answer. The persons themselves told me the day before that they had permission. I also heard Major Anthony speak of these men having gone to the Indian camp.

Question. Give the names of the persons to whom such permission was granted by Major Anthony.

Answer. John Smith, Indian interpreter, David L. Louderback, company G, first cavalry of Colorado, and teamster—I do not recollect his name.

Question. State if you know whether the authority given them by Major Anthony was verbal or in writing.

Answer. I do not know.

Question. If you know, state how long the persons last named by you had been in the Indian camp.

Answer. I think two days. They started, I think, the day Major Wynkoop started for the States.

Question. If you know, state what articles those persons were authorized to deal in, in trading with the Indians.

Answer. I don't know.

Question. Do you state that any portion of Colonel Chivington's command fired on John Smith; and if they did so, was such firing done by command of any officer?

Answer. I think not. Firing was done, but not by orders of any officer. I heard Lieutenant Cramer sing out that it was John Smith, and tell him to come to company K.

Question. Did you hear any plans suggested by officers at Fort Lyon after the battle of Sand creek for prosecuting Colonel Chivington for the part he had taken in the battle?

Answer. I don't know that I heard any plan of prosecution. They all denounced him there.

Question. Did you hear any of the officers at Fort Lyon say that they would prosecute Colonel Chivington for the part he had taken in the battle of Sand creek?

Answer. I don't know that I heard them say they would do it. I heard them say that he ought to be prosecuted, and that, when the facts got to Washington, he was liable to be, or words to that effect.

Question. Who were the officers who made these declarations?

Answer. It was the general talk among the officers at the post. I think I heard Major Anthony say so, and Lieutenant Baldwin, Lieutenant Cramer, Lieutenants Cannon and Minton, and Captain Hill. I don't remember all. Lieutenant Colonel Tappan, too, I think.

Question. Do you know whether Major Anthony made any statements to Colonel Chivington respecting the propriety at attacking the Indians on Sand creek after Colonel Chivington's command arrived at Fort Lyon, and before the battle of Sand creek?

Answer. I did not hear him make any.

Question. Do you know whether Major Anthony made any statements to any persons as to the propriety of attacking the Indians on Sand creek after Colonel Chivington's command arrived at Fort Lyon and before the battle of Sand creek? If so, state if you know what those statements were.

Answer. I talked to Anthony about it, and he said that some of those Indians ought to be killed; that he had been only waiting for a good chance to pitch into them. I reminded him of the pledges he had made them, and he said that Colonel Chivington had told him that those Indians he had pledged the soldiers and white men in the camp should not be killed; that the object of the expedition was to go out the Smoky Hill and follow the Indians up. Anthony told me that I would not compromise myself by going out, as I was opposed to going.

Question. Did or did not Major Anthony seek to convince you that the Indians at Sand creek should be attacked?

Answer. He tried to convince me that a good many of them should be killed and some of them saved, and among them he mentioned Black Kettle, One-Eye, White Antelope, Left-Hand, and some others, that should not be killed.

215

Question. Who accompanied you on the scout south of the Arkansas river?
What troops were in your command on that expedition?

Answer. Between twenty and thirty soldiers from K and D, first regiment.
There was a Dutch Jew by the name of Meyer accompanied me.

Question. What subordinate officers were in your command on that occasion?

Answer. I had none.

Question. How far south of the Arkansas river did you proceed on that occasion?

Answer. About thirty miles.

Cross-examination closed.

Commission adjourned until 9½ a. m. to-morrow, February 21.

### ELEVENTH DAY.

FEBRUARY 21, 1865.

Commission met pursuant to adjournment. Present, all members and recorder.

Proceedings of yesterday read and approved, with the following amendments:
Page 87, 3d line, in 3d answer, amended so as to read "thirty miles east, &c."
Page 91, 4th line, 3d answer, amended so as to read "and teamsters who
drove Major Colley's ambulance."

Page 94, 18th line, in first answer, amended so as to read "Anthony told me
this to induce me to go out, as I was opposed, &c."

Re-examination of Captain Silas S. Soule, veteran battalion first Colorado
cavalry, by the commission.

### By COMMISSION:

Question. In what direction was Major Wynkoop marching with his command
when he came upon the Indians on the Smoky Hill?

Answer. In a northeasterly direction.

Question. After meeting the Indians in what direction did he continue his
march to reach their camp?

Answer. About the same direction—a little more to the east.

Question. While marching with the Indians on your flanks and rear did they
make any hostile demonstrations?

Answer. They kept up a howl. I asked one of our party what it meant by
such howling, and he said they were singing for grub. A good many had bows
strung and arrows in their hands; some of them had guns. I think they fired
two or three shots at a dog in our command, and at a hawk.

Question. Did the Indians request, advise, or order Major Wynkoop to move
two days' march nearer Fort Lyon?

Answer. They advised him to go nearer the fort, for the reason, I think, that
there were thirteen hundred lodges of Sioux within about thirty miles of us.

Question. While Major Wynkoop was in council with the Indians on Smoky
Hill did the Indians get the advantage by surrounding the camp?

Answer. They got into the camp while we were in council. The officer of
the day seemed to be alarmed, and came to the council and told Major Wynkoop
that he could not keep them out of camp.

Question. Was Lieutenant Hardin instructed not to permit the Indians to
come in and about the camp?

Answer. He was.

Question. Was it Lieutenant Hardin's fault that the Indians got into the camp?

Answer. It was; if he had obeyed his orders they would not have got in
without a fight.

Question. Was it the personal influence, appeals, and efforts of Black Kettle,
White Antelope, One-Eye, and other Indians that prevented an attack upon
Wynkoop's command?

216

Answer. It think it was Black Kettle, One-Eye, aud other chiefs. I am not so sure about White Antelope.

Question. Was it these same Indians who afterwards, while in camp on Sand creek, were attacked by Colonel Chivington's command and some of them killed?

Answer. It was.

Question. At the time Major Wynkoop went to the Smoky Hill was he in command of the post and troops at Fort Lyon?

Answer. He was.

Question. When the Indians drove the soldier into the post did they fire upon him?

Answer. They did not.

Question. Did you hear some of the chiefs say in council at Camp Weld or Denver that the Indians who pursued the soldier threw down their arms and were trying to overtake him in order to send by him a friendly message into Fort Lyon?

Answer. They told us in council at Smoky Hill that they were trying to get letters to the commanding officer at Fort Lyon.

Question. What did Black Kettle and White Antelope say had been done with the three prisoners whom they had failed to deliver Major Wynkoop?

Answer. They had been sold or traded out of their village to some other tribe or village.

Question. While in council at Camp Weld or Denver did Major Whiteley record all that was said by parties in council?

Answer. I do not know.

Question. Were the Indians permitted to make statements of what they had suffered by the depredations of the whites in that council?

Answer. I think not. There were other questions put to them while they were telling of the outrages that had been committed upon them, or words to that effect. They were led from the suhject by other questions.

Question. When Major Anthony ordered the Indians to surrender themselves and give up their arms, did he do it to completely disarm them, or merely to give them an opportunity to acknowledge their submission to the government—make manifest their compliance with the demands of Major Wynkoop and their desire for peace?

(J. M. Chivington respectfully objects to the question for the reason that it is leading, suggesting to the witness the answer which the commission seeks to elicit. Objection sustained by the commission.)

Question. Did Major Anthony completely disarm the Indians at Fort Lyon?

Answer. He did.

Question. Did he refuse to issue them rations until they had surrendered their arms?

Answer. I believe he did.

Question. Did he afterwards return arms he had taken from these Indians?

Answer He did.

Question. Did Majors Wynkoop and Anthony tell the Indians that no advantage should be taken of their submission to the military authorities if General Curtis should not approve what they, Wynkoop and Anthony, had done respecting them?

Answer. I think they did.

Question. How near Fort Lyon were the citizens murdered by Indians?

Answer. About sixteen or eighteen miles.

Question. Was it known at Fort Lyon at the time, or afterwards, what Indians murdered these men?

Answer. Afterwards.

Question. Did War Bonnet, one of the chiefs of the Cheyennes, come into Fort Lyon a few days before the attack on Black Kettle's camp and request of

Major Anthony that the interpreter, John Smith, be permitted to go out to Sand creek and trade with them?

Answer. War Bonnet came in, but I don't know what was said.

Question. What field officers were present at the fight on Sand creek?

Answer. Colonel Chivington, Colonel Shoup, Lieutenant Colonel Bowen, Major Anthony, Major Downing, Major Sayer.

Question. Did either or any of them attempt to rally their men, and relieve them from being shot by each other.

Answer. Major Downing advised, or told, me to move my command out of fire of the men on the opposite bank.

Question. Did any of these officers appear to exercise a general supervision of the command and control it during the attack on Black Kettle's camp?

Answer. I could not tell. I don't think they did.

Question. Did you hear Colonel Chivington, either prior to or during the attack on the Indian camp, make any remarks or give any orders to the command? If so, what were they?

Answer. I don't remember.

Question. Did you hear any officer converse with Colonel Chivington in reference to the disposal of Charles Bent or other prisoners?

Answer. I heard Lieutenant Dunn ask Colonel Chivington if he had any objections to having Jack Smith killed. Colonel Chivington said that he need not ask him about it; he knew how he (Chivington) felt about it, or words to that effect.

Question. Did you join Colonel Chivington's command with the understanding that all Indians to whom pledges of protection had been given should not be molested?

Answer. I think I did. I believed until after the firing commenced that we would not attack the village.

Commission adjourned until 2 p. m. this day.

*Two p. m.*—Commission met pursuant to adjournment. Present, all members and recorder.

Re-examination of Captain S. S. Soule continued.

By J. M. CHIVINGTON:

Question. You state that Jack Smith was killed after he was taken prisoner. Do you know how he was killed, and by whom, and at what time, and where he was killed?

Answer. I saw the body of Jack Smith, when I was out to the battle-ground last December, lying in the place of, or near, the lodge where I saw him before I left the field the day of the battle, and I think Lieutenant Dunn acknowledged that a man of his company, E, shot Jack Smith. All I know is from hearsay, except seeing the dead body.

Question. What means were adopted to prevent the Indians from detailing what they suffered at the hands of the whites at the Camp Weld council?

Answer. By questions on other subjects.

Question. What are your means of knowledge as to Majors Wynkoop and Anthony having told the Indians at Fort Lyon that no advantage should be taken of them if General Curtis should not approve the action of those officers?

Answer. I heard Wynkoop tell some of the chiefs, I think Black Kettle or Left-Hand, that—in case he got word from Curtis not to make peace with them, that he would let them know, so that they could remove out of the way and get to their tribe; then he should fight them if he had orders to, or words to that effect.

Question. Did you hear Major Anthony make any statements to the Indians similar to that mentioned in your last answer?

Answer. I don't think I heard him make the statement to the Indians, but he (Anthony) indorsed Wynkoop's course.

Question. Who propounded questions on the part of the whites at the Camp Weld council?

Answer. Mostly by Governor Evans. I think Colonel Chivington and others propounded questions.

Question. What questions did Colonel Chivington propound?

Answer. I think he asked them who killed some white people on the Platte.

Question. Did Colonel Chivington ask any other questions than that mentioned in your last answer? If so, what were they?

Answer. I don't remember. He had but little to say during the council.

By COMMISSION:

Question. When you last saw Jack Smith on the day of the fight, was he alive and a prisoner in Colonel Chivington's camp?

Answer. He was alive and in a lodge with soldiers—in and about the lodge. I don't know that he was under guard.

Examination of Captain Silas S. Soule closed.

Commission adjourned until 9½ a. m. to-morrow, February 22, 1865.

TWELFTH DAY.

FEBRUARY 22, 1865.

Commission met pursuant to adjournment. Present, all members and recorder. Proceedings of yesterday read and approved, with the following amendments: Page 103, beginning of third answer, to read "except Major Downing," &c. Commission adjourned until 9½ a. m. to-morrow, February 23, 1865.

THIRTEENTH DAY.

FEBRUARY 23, 1865.

Commission met pursuant to adjournment. Present, all members and recorder. Yesterday's proceedings read and approved.

Lieutenant JOSEPH A. CRAMER, veteran battalion first Colorado cavalry, called in to give evidence by the commission, having been duly sworn according to law, in presence of J. M. Chivington, testified as follows:

By COMMISSION:

Question. What is your full name, age, and rank is the army?

Answer. Josesh A. Cramer; 29 years old; second lieutenant company D veteran battalion first Colorado cavalry.

Question. How long have you been in the public service as an officer?

Answer. A year and nearly four months.

Question. Did you accompany Major Wynkoop to meet the Indians in council, on the Smoky Hill, last August or September?

Answer. I did, in September, 1864.

Question. State the object of the expedition, and what was done in council with the Indians.

Answer. The object of the expedition, as stated by Major Wynkoop, was for the recovery of some white prisoners held by the Indians. Seven, I think, was the number stated by the Indians—to be recovered by peaceable means if possible, and forcible means if necessary. The council was composed of the principal chiefs, on the part of the Indians, being Black Kettle, Big or White Wolf; I think Bull Bear, Left-Hand or Nor-wan-che, Little Raven, Neva, White Antelope, Big Mouth, were there, and other Indians. When the council was called, Major Wynkoop stated his object: that, on receiving the letter written by George Bent, and brought to the fort by One-Eye and Min-im-mie, and from conversation held with One-Eye and Min-im-mie at Fort Lyon he thought that

219

they (the Indians) were acting in good faith, and that he had come out there with his men to have a talk with them, to see if an understanding could be brought about between them and the whites, or their white brethren, or something of that kind. I think that the Indians said if he had come to talk peace to them why had he brought his men and guns, or words to that effect. Major Wynkoop's reply was that, relying on the words of the chief, he had come out with but few men, but knowing that there were some bad Indians among them he had brought sufficient number to fight them if they did not act in good faith, but he hoped they could understand each other so that they would have no trouble, and he could take the white prisoners to Fort Lyon and return them to their homes. I think, at that time, he told the chiefs that he would listen to them. I think Bull Bear (Cheyenne) spoke first. He stated that he had tried to live in good faith with the whites, and a party of soldiers had come out into their country, on the Smoky Hill, and had killed his brother; his name, I think, was Sitting Bear; that before his brother was killed he went to them and told them not to fire on his young men, as they did not wish to fight the whites, but wanted to live in peace with them; and that while so talking he was killed by the soldiers. He wound up his remarks by saying that he thought the Indians were not to blame. Left Hand, (Arapahoe chief,) when he spoke, said that he had always been friendly with the whites, and had no difficulty with them until the present season. He spoke of the trouble or difficulty between him and the commanding officer of Fort Larned—the date I have forgotten; that at the time, the Kiowas and Comanches run off the stock at Fort Larned; that he had first sent word in to the commander that he wished to take his tribe and recover, or help to recover, the stock; that he afterwards tried to get into the fort himself for the purpose of making the same proposals, carrying at the time a white flag, and upon approaching the fort he was fired upon and could not get in, and had to run, or words to that effect. Soon after this occurrence at Fort Larned, some of his young men had joined in with the Dog soldiers, (a renegade band of the Cheyennes,) or the Kiowas, and had been out on scouting or war parties, and at that time he had done all he could to prevent their doing so, and thought and said that an understanding could be brought about with the whites, and that he did not wish to fight them, if he could get word to Major Colley, Indian agent, that he could bring about a big peace, but was unable to restrain a few of his young braves; that he had repeatedly tried to get a message to Major Colley, or the forts, but had not been able to do so; that his men had been fired on while approaching the forts. At the time Bull Bear was speaking, he said that he thought the whites were foxes, and no peace could be brought about with them, and that the only way the Indians could do was to fight; that was the substance of it. I think Little Raven (Arapahoe chief) spoke next; spoke but little, and indorsing what had been said by Bull Bear. He stated in his remarks that he had lived several years among the whites; that he had always lived friendly with them, and that he had always loved the whites and would like to shake hands with them, (their term of friendship was shaking hands,) but was afraid that no peace could be brought about, or words to that effect. That is all I recollect at present in regard to what he said. I think I have stated the times in which the chiefs spoke wrong. I think One-Eye (Cheyenne chief) spoke immediately after Bull Bear. One-Eye stated that he had been sent into Fort Lyon with a letter, written by the chiefs, at the risk of his life, but that he was willing to run such risk if, by so doing, he could bring about a peace or an understanding with the whites; that on his starting for Fort Lyon he had supposed that the chiefs were acting in good faith, and that they would do as they had agreed, and believing that the Cheyennes did not lie, that he had offered himself to Major Wynkoop as a pledge of their good faith, so that if the Indians did not act in good faith his life should be forfeited, as he did not wish to live when Cheyennes broke their word; that he

220

SAND CREEK MASSACRE.

was ashamed to hear such talk in the council as that uttered by Bull Bear. He then appealed to the other chiefs to know if they would act like men and fulfil or live up to their word; that he had been sent by them to Fort Lyon and had taken their message to Major Wynkoop, (or their tall chief,) and that he believing them to be honest had come from Fort Lyon to talk with them; that he had pledged Major Wynkoop his word and his life, and the word of his, or their big chief, (I suppose referring to Black Kettle,) and that he should stand by his word, (or fulfil his word,) and that if the chiefs did not act in good faith he should go with the whites and fight with them, and that he had a great many friends who would follow him; that he was ashamed of their council to hear chiefs get up and make a fuss about a few horses, or ponies and mules, or words to that effect, and that he was willing to divide with them or give them the best stock that he had if they would say no more in council. This is all I remember except, I think, Bull Bear accepted his proposition and took two of the best horses he had in his herd, and had no more to say. Black Kettle (principal chief of the Cheyennes) next spoke; stated that he had sent One-Eye and Min-im-mie into Fort Lyon; had authorized the letter to be written, and was glad that it resulted as it had in bringing Major Wynkoop out; that he was glad to hear his brother chief speak as he had; he was glad to know that Cheyennes fulfilled their word, and that if Major Wynkoop did as he (Wynkoop) proposed, he, with his friends, would go with us. These remarks were in reference to what One-Eye had said. The most of the remarks which followed were in reply to Major Wynkoop at the opening of the council, which were as follows: Major Wynkoop told them that he had come for peace and not for war and that if they would give up their prisoners it would be an evidence in their favor in the eye of their Great Father at Denver and Washington; that if they would give up their prisoners and go with him he would take them to Denver, to have a talk with the Great Father in Denver, and he had no doubt but what peace would be made, and that he would return them in safety to their tribes; that he was not great enough chief himself to make any treaty with them that would be binding, but that he would pledge them his word that they should be protected on their way to Denver and return, and that he wished their principal chiefs to go with him and that they should take their families into Fort Lyon and leave them there until their return from Denver in compliance with the governor's proclamation. He then read them the proclamation. He stated that he knew nothing about the whites holding any prisoners spoken of in the letter, and that if the authorities at Denver held any he could make no pledges to give them up; that he was acting upon his own responsibility and would pledge them nothing but what he knew he could fulfil; that chiefs bigger than he would have to decide that matter in Denver—that, is in relation to giving up the Indian prisoners; that what he had told them they could rely upon; that his life was a pledge for his words, and that the officers and the men who were with him would sustain him. He then asked each officer in the council if he indorsed what had been said and the pledges that had been made, all replying that they did. The officers present were Captain S. S. Soule, Lieutenant Charles Phillips, Interpreter John Smith, and myself. I don't recollect any more that Wynkoop said at the opening of the council. Black Kettle, in his reply, said he was glad to hear his white brother talk; that he believed he was honest in what he said, and that he welcomed us as friends; that he believed that their troubles were over if they would follow the advice of the tall chief, meaning Major Wynkoop; that there were bad white men and bad Indians, and that the bad men on both sides had brought about this trouble; that some of his young men had joined in with them; that he was opposed to fighting and had done everything in his power to prevent it; that he believed that the blame rested with the whites; that they had commenced the war and forced the Indians to fight. He then gave an account of the first difficulties that occurred last winter

221

or spring. At first a good deal of stock was stolen from the Indians by the whites, over on or out near the Platte country. Previous to the fight with the soldiers in the vicinity of the Platte, (by description supposed to be the command of Lieutenant Dunn,) that they were travelling from the Smoky Hill country and found some loose stock, I think, on the Beaver or Box Elder, and took it with them to leave at Geary's ranch, and on arriving there found no one at home and took the stock with them. Soon after this they were overtaken by a party of soldiers who appeared to be friendly, but demanded the stock which they had in their possession——

Commission adjourned until 2 p. m. this day.

*Two p. m.*—Commission met pursuant to adjournment. Present, all members and recorder.

Examination of Second Lieutenant Joseph A. Cramer, veteran battalion first Colorado cavalry continued.

By the COMMISSION :

——which they were willing to give up, and offered to do so with the exception of one horse or mule, which they stated to the chief of the soldiers one of the Indians had off on a hunt and would be back in a day or two, and as soon as he returned, the mule or horse should be given up. The chief of the soldiers still demanded the mule or horse, at the same time taking from the Indians their arms, which the Indians supposed were merely to look at. One of the Indians refused to let him take his arms, when he undertook to take them by force. I am not positive that the Indians fired first, but my impression is that he said the Indians fired first after the attempt to take the arms by force. I think that the Indians stated that there were three killed or wounded. The Indians then went to the Cedar Bluffs immediately after this occurrence. Soon after they were attacked by another party of soldiers. Before the attack and while in camp at or near Cedar Bluffs, one of their herders, a boy, was killed, and another captured—I do not know whether it was a boy or not—and a number of their herd of stock; I think he said near a hundred head. It may have been more or less; but my impression is that it was about a hundred. The Indians then became convinced the whites were going to make war on them and prepared to go to the Arkansas valley; had left a good deal of their property; had rolled up what they could and hid them in the rocks, and while preparing to start were attacked by a party of soldiers, killing one. I do not recollect that he said any were wounded or not; that he thought the soldiers were firing on the buffalo-robes in the rocks, and not at the Indians; that they immediately after started for the Arkansas valley, or words to that effect. I think he also stated that he was near the Indians at the time of the fight with the soldiers on the Smoky Hill, or but a few days afterwards; that he had prevented them from fighting the whites, as were their intentions; then told them, could they but see the Indian agent at Fort Lyon it would be made all right; and he kept most of these Indians with him until his arrival at or near Fort Larned; then they were misused by the commander of the post. They often tried to warn the garrison that the Kiowas intended to attack the post and run off the herd; that Min-im-mie, one of their chiefs, had warned the commander of the post and settlers below the post that on a certain day, naming the day also, the Kiowas would attack them and take their herds. Still the commanding officer would not believe them and still mistrusted them. Some of the young men of the Cheyenne tribe, thinking that no understanding could be brought about between them and the whites, had joined in with the Kiowas, and on the day named by Min-im-mie helped take the stock; after this he and Left-Hand both tried to have a talk with the commander of the post and were fired on in attempting to get into the post. Left-Hand had sent in word that he with his band of warriors would go

222

with the soldiers or go alone to recover the stock, and heard nothing from the commander of the post, and then attempted to get in himself with a white flag, when he was fired upon. He then started up the river with most of his tribe. Some of his young men, whom he could no longer restrain, started out in war parties and committed some depredations. He, with his main band, kept away from them, refusing to fight the whites, still believing that the difficulty could be settled upon hearing the proclamation of the big chief at Denver. He had made every effort to comply with it; that he thought the big chief at Denver was acting in good faith; that he had repeatedly attempted to communicate with the chief of the soldiers at Lyon and at Larned, but had been unable to accomplish it or to have any talk; that the men he had sent in had been fired upon, and that he had taken his tribe back to the Smoky Hill, and had there camped for the purpose of hunting; that after arriving there he had sent Neva, (an Arapahoe sub-chief,) and fourteen others, who were well known at or near Fort Lyon, for the purpose of getting word to the commander of the post that they did not wish to fight; that they never had, nor would not unless attacked; that Neva succeeded in getting within a mile or so of the post, and close enough to a soldier to halloo to him and show him a letter he had for Major Colley, Indian agent. The soldier ran into the post, and soon afterwards a party of soldiers came out and run them for twenty or twenty-five miles before overtaking them, and upon overtaking them firing on them and doing no damage. That night the Indians came back, during a severe rain-storm, for the purpose of fighting us, and Neva would not let them do it. Neva thought he could kill us all, but did not wish to fight, as he was sent out on a peace mission. As soon as they returned to the Smoky Hill he (Black Kettle) made every effort to get these war parties to come in, and succeeded in getting them all but two or three small parties. He then sent in One Eye and Min-im-mie with the letter to Major Wynkoop, also one to Colonel Bent, and that they had succeeded in getting into the fort, and that he was glad that Major Wynkoop had trusted them and came out to have a talk with them; that they were willing to do all and more than he had asked of them; that they would go with him to Denver and trust to his word, and that they would make all reparation in their power in order that a good peace might be established, so that they and the whites might be brothers; that they would give up what prisoners they had and try and get them all, most of which were with the Sioux, if the major would give them time, which he (Wynkoop) agreed to do, he giving them three or four days in which to accomplish their object. Black Kettle stated that he would be back at the required time if possible; and if he could not, and the major had gone on to the fort, he would bring them in to Fort Lyon himself. He stated also that he would have to buy part of these prisoners from the Sioux, and that he might have difficulty in procuring them, and he (Black Kettle) could make no pledges. Black Kettle also stated that the Sioux did not wish the Cheyennes to make any treaty with the whites in which they (the Sioux) were not included.

I think that immediately after this speech most of the chiefs expressed their satisfaction in regard to what he had said, and agreed to be guided by his action. The arrangements were then perfected for going to Denver, provided the Indians complied with what Major Wynkoop demanded.

Question. What chief appeared to have the most influence in the council with Major Wynkoop?

Answer. Black Kettle and One-Eye.

Question. Did the chiefs in council with Major Wynkoop on the Smoky Hill say they could, in behalf of the tribes they represented, (Cheyennes and Arapahoes,) make a treaty with the whites?

Answer. They did; and that the action would be bound by Black Kettle.

Question. Did Black Kettle and other chiefs advise Major Wynkoop to move with his command, two days' march nearer Fort Lyon? If so, what reasons did they give for such advice?

Answer. As I understood it, they advised him to move about a half a day's march—twelve or fourteen miles—while the arrangements were being made; and at the last of the council I was absent from the council, and in camp, and could not state what passed. I am of the impression that after the council Black Kettle advised him to move his command to where there was wood and water, to avoid any difficulty which might occur with his young braves.

Commission adjourned until 9½ a. m. to-morrow, February 24, 1865.

## FOURTEENTH DAY.

FEBRUARY 24, 1865.

Commission met pursuant to adjournment. Present, all members and recorder. Proceedings of yesterday read and approved with the following amendments: On page 122, 18th line, the word mistrusted to read misused.

The witness, J. A. Cramer, stated that he was unwell, and unable to attend the session of the commission, and asked to be excused. He was excused by the commission.

Adjourned until 2 p. m. this day.

*Two p. m.*—Commission met pursuant to adjournment· Present, all members and recorder.

The witness, Lieutenant Joseph Cramer, being too unwell to attend the commission to give his evidence, his further examination is postponed for the present.

First Lieutenant C. C. HAWLEY veteran battalion, first Colorado cavalry, called in by commission to give evidence, being duly sworn according to law, in presence of J. M. Chivington, testified as follows:

Question. Your full name, age, and rank in the army?

Answer. Charles C. Hawley; aged 25 years; first lieutenant veteran battalion, first Colorado cavalry, and acting ordnance officer district of Colorado.

Question. How long have you been ordnance officer of the district?

Answer. About seventeen months.

Question. Were you on duty in the district as ordnance officer at the time of and after the organization of the third regiment Colorado cavalry.

Answer. Yes.

Question. For how long a time was that regiment raised, and how long was it in the service?

Answer. I could not tell how long it was in the service. It was raised for a hundred days.

Question. Did you furnish the third regiment with arms and other ordnance stores?

Answer. Yes.

Question. State the number, kind, and quality of the ordnance stores issued to the regiment.

Answer:

772 (seven hundred and seventy-two) rifles; calibre, 54.
224 (two hundred and twenty-four) muskets; calibre, 69.
16 (sixteen) muskets; calibre, 71.
1,012 (one thousand and twelve) cartridge boxes, infantry.
1,105 (one thousand one hundred and five) cap pouches and picks.
1,019 (one thousand and nineteen) waist-belts and plates.
633 (six hundred and thirty-three) gun-slings.
620 (six hundred and twenty) cartridge-box belts.

224

650 (six hundred and fifty) screw-drivers and cone wrenches.
28 (twenty-eight) Sharp's carbines.
58 (fifty-eight) Starr's carbines.
29 (twenty-nine) Starr's revolvers.
2 (two) Colt's army revolvers.
72 (seventy-two) Whitney revolvers.
82 (eighty-two) carbine slings and swivels.
63 (sixty-three) carbine cartridge boxes.
39 (thirty-nine) brush wipers with thongs.
107 (one hundred and seven) pistol-belt holsters.
71 (seventy-one) pistol cartridge pouches.
5 (five) Colt's repeating rifles.
7 (seven) cavalry sabres.
122 (one hundred and twenty-two) sabre-belts and plates.
527 (five hundred and twenty-seven) saddles complete, (pattern of 1859.)
527 (five hundred and twenty-seven) curb-bridles.
376 (three hundred and seventy-six) watering bridles.
500 (five hundred) halters and straps.
624 (six hundred and twenty-four) saddle blankets.
426 (four hundred and twenty-six) surcingles.
515 (five hundred and fifteen) spurs and straps.
562 (five hundred and sixty-two) horse-brushes.
565 (five hundred and sixty-five) currycombs.
354 (three hundred and fifty-four) lariats.
354 (three hundred and fifty-four) picket pins.
500 (five hundred) links.
146 (one hundred and forty-six) nose bags.
245 (two hundred and forty-five) wipers.
14 (fourteen) spring vices.
12,000 (twelve thousand) cartridges; calibre, 71.
9,000 (nine thousand) cartridges; calibre, 69.
11,000 (eleven thousand) cartridges ; calibre, 58.
66,000 (sixty-six thousand) cartridges ; calibre, 54.
22,500 (twenty-two thousand five hundred) cartridges ; calibre, 44.
15,700 (fifteen thousand seven hundred) cartridges ; calibre, 36.
1,500 (one thousand five hundred) pounds of lead.
20 (twenty) kegs powder.
15 (fifteen) quires cartridge paper. I believe that is all issued to the third regiment.

Question. Were these articles, as enumerated by you, new when issued to the third regiment ?

Answer. The saddles were very nearly all new ; a portion of them had seen service, but were in a serviceable condition. The arms, I believe, had also seen service. The accoutrements were nearly all new ; some of them might have seen service.

Question. State the time these stores were issued.

Answer. Most of the horse equipments were issued in November, 1864. The guns and accoutrements were issued, some of them in September, and some in October, 1864. I don't recollect that any were issued in November, 1864.

Question. Why were not the horse equipments issued earlier ?

Answer. Because I did not have them on hand. They were issued immediately after being received from Leavenworth arsenal.

Question. Have the officers of the third regiment, responsible for these stores, been mustered out of the public service ?

Answer. I presume they have; I have no official information that they have been mustered out.

Question. Have you, before and since the muster out of these officers, received ordnance stores from them?

Answer. Those responsible turned in their ordnance stores on hand to me.

Question. State the kind, quality, and condition of the ordnance and ordnance stores received by you from the third regiment Colorado cavalry.

Answer:

493 (four hundred and ninety-three) rifles; calibre, 54.

92 (ninety-two) muskets; calibre, 69.

8 (eight) muskets; calibre, 71. As far as the arms are concerned they were in a serviceable condition, but rusty.

658 (six hundred and fifty-eight) cartridge boxes, infantry.

455 (four hundred and fifty-five) cap pouches and picks.

523 (five hundred and twenty-three) waist belts and plates.

358 (three hundred and fifty-eight) gun slings.

279 (two hundred and seventy-nine) cartridge-box plates.

160 (one hundred and sixty) screw-drivers and cone wrenches.

17 (seventeen) Sharp's carbines.

169 (one hundred and sixty-nine) Starr's carbines.

19 (nineteen) Starr's revolvers.

2 (two) Colt's army revolvers.

12 (twelve) Whitney's revolvers.

114 (one hundred and fourteen) carbine slings and swivels.

16 (sixteen) carbine cartridge boxes.

49 (forty-nine) brush wipers and thongs.

43 (forty-three) pistol belt-holders.

5 (five) pistol cartridge pouches.

13 (thirteen) cavalry sabres.

59 (fifty-nine) sabre belts and plates.

412 (four hundred and twelve) saddles complete; pattern 1859.

382 (three hundred and eighty-two) curb bridles.

275 (two hundred and seventy-five) watering bridles.

225 (two hundred and twenty-five) halters and straps.

80 (eighty) saddle blankets.

239 (two hundred and thirty-nine) surcingles.

193 (one hundred and ninety-three) spurs and straps, (pairs.)

321 (three hundred and twenty-one) horse brushes.

342 (three hundred and forty-two) currycombs.

50 (fifty) lariats.

64 (sixty-four) picket pins.

139 (one hundred and thirty-nine) links.

22 (twenty-two) wipers.

4 (four) spring vices.

1,000 (one thousand) cartridges; calibre, 54.

17,050 (seventeen thousand and fifty) cartridges; calibre, 52.

11,000 (eleven thousand) cartridges; calibre, 44.

1,000 (one thousand) cartridges; calibre, 69.

10,000 (ten thousand) cartridges; calibre, 71.

1,000 (one thousand) cartridges; calibre, 36.

700 (seven hundred) pounds of lead.

12 (twelve) kegs powder.

Question. State the deficiency of ordnance stores.

Answer:

279 (two hundred and seventy-nine) rifles; calibre, 54.

132 (one hundred and thirty-two) muskets; calibre, 69.

226

8 (eight) muskets; calibre, 71.
354 (three hundred and fifty-four) cartridge boxes, infantry.
650 (six hundred and fifty) cap pouches and picks.
496 (four hundred and ninety-six) waist belts and plates.
275 (two hundred and seventy-five) gun slings.
341 (three hundred and forty-one) cartridge-box plates.
490 (four hundred and ninety) screw-drivers and cone wrenches.
11 (eleven) Sharp's carbines.
10 (ten) Starr's revolvers.
60 (sixty) Whitney's revolvers.
3 (three) carbine cartridge boxes.
64 (sixty-four) pistol belt-holders.
66 (sixty-six) pistol cartridge pouches.
5 (five) Colt's repeating rifles.
63 (sixty-three) sabre belts and plates.
115 (one hundred and fifteen) saddles, complete; pattern of 1859.
145 (one hundred and forty-five) curb bridles.
101 (one hundred and one) watering bridles.
275 (two hundred and seventy-five) halters and straps.
544 (five hundred and forty-four) saddle blankets.
187 (one hundred and eighty-seven) surcingles.
322 (three hundred and twenty-two) pairs spurs and straps.
241 (two hundred and forty-one) horse-brushes.
223 (two hundred and twenty-three) currycombs.
304 (three hundred and four) lariats.
290 (two hundred and ninety) picket pins.
371 (three hundred and seventy-one) links.
146 (one hundred and forty-six) nose bags.
223 (two hundred and twenty-three) wipers.
10 (ten) spring vices.
65,000 (sixty-five thousand) cartridges; calibre, 54.
11,500 (eleven thousand five hundred) cartridges; calibre, 44.
8,000 (eight thousand) cartridges; calibre, 69.
2,000 (two thousand) cartridges; calibre, 71.
14,700 (fourteen thousand seven hundred) cartridges; calibre, 36.
11,000 (eleven thousand) cartridges; calibre, 58.
800 (eight hundred) pounds lead.
8 (eight) kegs of powder.
15 (fifteen) quires cartridge paper.

Question. State the time when you received ordnance and ordnance stores from officers of the third regiment.

Answer. In the latter part of December, 1864, between the 20th and 31st.

Direct examination closed. Cross-examination by J. M. Chivington, late colonel, &c. :

By J. M. CHIVINGTON :

Question. Were any of the arms mentioned by you as having been issued to the third regiment Colorado cavalry returned to you, and others issued instead thereof ?

Answer. Yes; I believe Captain Johnson turned in some arms and received carbines instead.

Question. Does the list of ordnance and ordnance stores comprise all the ordnance and ordnance stores issued by you to the third regiment?

Answer. It does, I believe, with the exception of ammunition issued to Captain Morgan of the battery, and two howitzers and their equipments.

Question. Is the list of property returned all the property returned, or is it a list of that only returned when the third regiment was mustered out?

Answer. It is a complete list with that exception, Captain Morgan's battery.

Question. Was not some of the ordnance and ordnance stores just mentioned by you exchanged by officers of the third regiment, invoiced and receipted for as original issues?

Answer. Not to my knowledge; I have no record of that kind in my office.

Question. Were you able to fill all the requisitions made by officers of the third regiment for ordnance and ordnance stores?

Answer. I was not.

Question. Had the third regiment cannon or howitzers; if so, from whom did they get them?

Answer. I stated before that Captain Morgan drew two from me.

Question. What was the date of the shipment of the horse equipments mentioned by you, from Leavenworth, and when did they arrive at Denver?

Answer. To the best of my belief they were shipped on the first of August and arrived at Denver, I think, the latter part of October or the beginning of November. That was the first shipment of saddles.

Question. Do you know whether any of the officers of the third regiment turned in or over any of their ordnance or ordnance stores to any person besides yourself?

Answer. I do not.

Question. Do you know whether any of the deficient ordnance or ordnance stores were charged to the enlisted men of the third regiment on their muster rolls?

Answer. I do not. Those that made their returns sent them in to my office, of which I took a copy. I never examined them, and cannot tell whether any ordnance or ordnance stores were charged to the men.

Question. Will you state why powder and lead were issued to the officers of the third regiment, in some instances, instead of cartridges?

Answer. Because I had no cartridges to issue.

Question. Please state the date of the order, and from whom received, directing the officers of the third regiment to turn in their ordnance and ordnance stores.

Answer. The order was received from Colonel Chivington, commanding district of Colorado. I do not recollect the exact date.

Question. What was the date of the issue to the third regiment of the last of the ordnance or ordnance stores received by the third regiment?

Answer. I cannot tell the exact date; it was just previous to the departure of the third regiment for Fort Lyon.

By the COMMISSION :

Question. Did you issue ordnance and ordnance stores to officers of the third regiment as fast and as soon as you received the same from the east?

Answer. Yes.

Question. What is your means of knowledge as to the officers of the third regiment having been mustered out of service?

Answer. I know from hearsay.

Cross-examination of First Lieutenant Charles C. Hawley closed.

Commission adjourned until 9½ a. m. to-morrow, February 25, 1865.

FIFTEENTH DAY.

FEBRUARY 25, 1865.

Commission met pursuant to adjournment. Present, all members and recorder.

Proceedings of yesterday read and approved, with the following amendments: On page 135, first line to third question, "quality" to read "quantity."

Re-examination of First Lieutenant Charles C. Hawley, veteran battalion first Colorado cavalry, in presence of J. M. Chivington:

By the COMMISSION:

Question. You spoke of some ordnance or ordnance stores being exchanged by officers of the third regiment, when such articles were brought in to be exchanged. Did you give receipts and receive invoices for them; and when you issued others in their stead did you give receipts and take invoices for them?
Answer. I did.
Re-examination of First Lieutenant Charles C. Hawley closed.

A. STOCK, esq., called in by commission to give evidence, being duly sworn according to law, in presence of J. M. Chivington, late colonel, &c., testified as follows:

By the COMMISSION:

Question. Your full name, residence, and profession?
Answer. Amos Stock; residence, Denver, and by profession an attorney-at-law.
Question. How long have you been a resident of Colorado?
Answer. Five years last May.
Question. Were you present at a council last summer, at Camp Weld, (near Denver,) with certain Indian chiefs?
Answer. No; I was not present last summer at any council of that kind, and know of none at that time. I was present at a council with the Indians on or about the 27th of last September, at Camp Weld, near the city of Denver.
Question. Who were present at that council?
Answer. I am not able to tell who all of those were that were present. But on the part of the Indians there were Black Kettle, White Antelope, and Bull Bear, representing the Cheyennes; and Neva, Heap Buffalo, Knock Knee, and another Indian and brother of Knock Knee and Heap Buffalo, all half-brothers of Left Hand, as I understood from the interpreter, Governor Evans, and the whole audience. On the part of the whites there was Governor Evans, who conducted most of the business of the interview at that time. There were also present Simeon Whiteley, James McNassar, Captain J. Bright Smith, Sheriff Robert S. Wilson; I believe they were all the civilians present. Of the military present whom I recognized and now remember, were Colonel John M. Chivington, Major Wynkoop, Captain Sam. Robbins, Captain S. S. Soule, Captain Sanborn, Lieutenant Hawley, Lieutenant Cramer, and the rest of the military I do not remember. There were several others. John Smith was present as interpreter; also, I think, Sam. Ashecraft. Simeon Whiteley acted as secretary, at the instance of the governor. How fully he took the notes I am not able to state.
Question. Who did the talking and business there transacted on the part of the whites?
Answer. Mainly Governor Evans; also Colonel Chivington and Major Wynkoop. The latter interposed one remark at the instance of the governor. My impression is that was all that was said by him (Wynkoop.)
Question. Who on the part of the Indians?
Answer. Black Kettle, White Antelope, Bull Bear, and Neva spoke on behalf of their people. The other three said nothing.
Question. State what was said and done by the parties present at the council?
(John M. Chivington respectfully objects to the introduction of oral testimony concerning the proceedings of the council between Indians of the Arapahoe and Cheyenne tribes and Governor Evans and others, held at Camp Weld on or about the 27th September, 1864, for the reason that it appears from the evi-

229

dence of Captain Silas S. Soule and Amos Stock, esq., that the proceedings of that council were reduced to writing by Simeon Whiteley, acting as secretary to Governor Evans, and such record is, therefore, the best evidence of the proceedings of that council, and should be introduced, or its absence accounted for, before secondary evidence is offered. For this reason I object to the question.)
Commission cleared for discussion.

Commission adjourned until 2 p. m. this day.

*Two p. m.*—Commission met pursuant to adjournment. Present, all members and recorder.

*Decision of commission relative to the objection of J. M. Chivington to the last question before adjournment.*

It appearing from the evidence of Captain Soule that the Indian chiefs, while in council at Camp Weld, near Denver, last September, were not permitted to state their grievances, and that they had suffered by the depredations of the whites, and it not appearing to the satisfaction of the commission that the said Simeon Whiteley was sworn to make a faithful record of the proceedings, having the same submitted for the approval of the members of the said council; also, a majority of the commission having, since the adjournment, called upon the acting governor of the Territory, and being informed by him that he understood the notes made by Simeon Whiteley to be merely a private memorandum, made for the use of the governor, and not a matter of record in the executive office, except the pencilled notes of the said Whiteley, which were on file; the commission is of opinion that there is no official record of the proceedings of that council, and therefore overrule the objections of John M. Chivington, and decide to introduce oral testimony to have what was said and done in the council at the place and time aforesaid.

Examination of Amos Stock, esq., continued:

Answer. It was mainly said, not done. The Indians shook hands with everybody in the room, and smoked their pipe, which was passed from one to another, immediately after which the governor requested of Interpreter Smith to ask the Indians what they had to say; whereupon Black Kettle began his speech, and said, in substance, that he had seen Major Wynkoop and his command out in the Indian country when he had come and met him and his people, and that he had come to reclaim some prisoners which they had in their possession, and who had been captured somewhere on the Platte and down on the Blue; that he held a parley with Major Wynkoop, and desired him to make peace with the whites and his people. He said he was anxious for peace, and would deliver up the prisoners they had in their possession, and did deliver them, I believe he stated; but Wynkoop told them that he was not authorized to make any peace, but would guarantee their safe conduct to Denver, to the governor of the Territory, with such of his chiefs as might go along. He said that he had great apprehensions, in agreeing to the proposal of Major Wynkoop, for his and their personal safety in leaving his people to come to Denver to see the governor, but that he relied upon his good faith; that he would see them through safely, and that if a peace could not be made, Wynkoop had promised to conduct them back to their own people, and that they should not be harmed. He said that their people had been living under a cloud, and that he and his brothers had come to hear the word of the governor that would dispel those clouds and let the light of peace shine upon them again. He said that such were his fears for their personal safety on this trip that it was like passing through a flame of fire, but that he had closed his eyes and passed through the fire, and was now here to know if the Great Father would not make peace with them and their people. There was a great deal more poetry about it, but it has

SAND CREEK MASSACRE.

escaped me, but those two similes I recollect well. He said frequently in the course of his speech that he was anxious for peace, and the people whom those men then represented were also anxious for peace with the white men. My impression now is that, before he made his speech, one of the Indians—I think it was Bull Bear—or it may have been some time afterwards, during that interview, said that they had counseled together, and had all agreed that whatever Black Kettle said and agreed to in that council, that they would all agree to; that they understood his views and fully assented to them. After Black Kettle had closed his speech the governor replied that he at one time was fully authorized to make peace with their two tribes, (the Cheyennes and Arapahoes;) that he had endeavored to do so; that he knew that there had been much discontent among them towards the whites; and that for the purpose of making peace, he had gone down into their country about a year previously, on to the Republican, and had sent word to their chiefs and headmen to come in and make peace, but that they had refused to do so; that Bull Bear sent him word when down in that country that he was willing himself to make peace, but that his young men said that they could live without their great father, or any assistance from him. Bull Bear immediately interposed, and said that's true. The governor said, I could then have made a peace with you, but I have no authority to do so now, and I fear that what you want is peace during the winter which is coming on, and that in the spring, when the grass grows, you will again begin to plunder our people and kill our settlers; that they had murdered our people and run off their cattle and stock, and would do so again in the spring; that up to this time you (the Indians) have killed more of our people than our soldiers have killed of you; that you have the advantage of us in that because we were not ready to fight you; but now we are ready.

He said that he had issued a proclamation, which he had sent out by runners to their people, telling them to come in to the military posts and they had not done so. That the great father was determined to punish them. That he had soldiers to put down this rebellion and to put them down too, and that he assuredly meant to do it. That soon the plains would swarm with soldiers and they might rest assured that they would be punished. That all that were friendly disposed towards the whites, by his proclamation were required to come in to the military post, and those that would not would be hunted out and punished.

He said that all he could tell them was that all who were friendly disposed to the whites should do as he had told them in the proclamation. The conversation became desultory during the governor's speech, and continued so till the close of the interview between Governor Evans and them. They said (which one I don't remember) in reply to what the governor had said about coming to the post under his proclamation, that as soon as it was read to them by a half-breed that was among them, they wrote a paper, which Bull Bear's brother carried to commander of soldiers that had come into their country, and that he got off his horse, and tied him to one of the wagons of the command, and was advancing unarmed, with the paper in his hand, towards the military, when he was shot down and killed. The governor made no inquiry concerning this killing, no allusion whatever, but said you must go to the military posts and lay down your arms and submit to the military authorities. One of them said in reply to that, "How are we to subsist ourselves and people?" that "we must be fed and provided for at the posts if we come in with our people," or we must live on the edge of the buffalo country in order to subsist our people. The governor said that he left that to them and the military authorities. They said that they would endeavor to bring in their people to the military posts. That they wanted peace, and the governor said that you must not only go to the military posts and lay down your arms, but you must also show your good faith and desire for peace with the whites by joining the soldiers to punish the Indians

231

that were hostile—those that would not come in and lay down their arms. And they said they would do it. The governor inquired of them "who killed the Hungate family?" Neva promptly answered "the Arapahoes did it." He, the governor, explained to them that it was out on Running creek, about twenty-five or thirty miles from Denver. The governor then inquired particularly what Indians did it. Neva said it was Big Roman Nose and some two or three others. He then asked them "where is Roman Nose?" He said that he had gone off north somewhere, and that he had not seen him, but knew that he did it, and his people knew that he did it. The governor inquired about a depredation, as I understood it, down on the Fontaine-que-buille, and the Cheyennes (either Bull Bear or White Atelope) said they did it. White Antelope or Bull Bear said that a long time before that, while crossing from their country, crossing down toward the Platte via the Bizyou, they found a horse and a mule—I think they said a white horse—that had strayed away in the bluffs, far beyond the care of their owners, and that going on down towards the Platte they met a man to whom they gave the horse, and that afterwards when they got to Geary's they left the mule with Geary and passed on. A short time afterwards they were attacked by some military command and one of their greatest braves was shot in the hip; and he said that he won't die, but that he was crippled for life, and was no use, and would be a charge on our people for life. Immediately after that was said, and upon the instant, White Antelope said, "There, governor, is the beginning of this war." The governor made no inquiry respecting it—made no answer. They appeared anxious to tell it, but the subject was changed, and the governor directed the interpreter to inquire in regard to other matters. The governor told them that we have just to-day received news of a great victory in the east, and that the rebellion would be put down, and that they (the Indians) would be put down too. By that time it began to get late in the day, and the conversation began to get so desultory between the governor and the Indians as to somewhat weary me with the interview, so that I stepped out. In a moment or two afterwards I saw Colonel Chivington take his position in the middle of the floor, standing up, as I moved to the door, and he told Smith that they must go down to the military posts and lay down their arms and submit to the authorities as the governor had told them. He said : tell them that the soldiers in all this country are under my command; that he was not much of a speech-maker, but that his business was to fight. He said that was all he had to say. Immediately after the whole interview terminated. During the interview, when the governor was making inquiries who committed the depredations at various places, Neva said "We haven't come here to talk about the past; we have been fighting you, and are willing that bygones should be bygones; what we want is peace for the future," and Bull Bear said that he might be killed in endeavoring to make peace as his brother had been, but that he was ready to die if peace could be had for his people. This last matter of Neva and Bull Bear should have been mentioned in the body of my testimony. That constitutes all I know in answer to that question. They also said that they were willing to exchange the property that they had taken for the property taken from them.

By COMMISSION :

Question. What did Governor Evans say to the Indian chiefs in council they must do in order to secure peace with the whites ?

(J. M. Chivington objects to the question for the reason that the question suggests to the witness the answer which the commission seeks to draw from him, and for the reason that the witness has already stated all that he can recollect that was said by Governor Evans.

Objection overruled by the commission.)

Answer. He said that all those who were friendly to the whites must come in to the military and lay down their arms, and that they must also show their sincerity by joining the soldiers in punishing the Indians who would not do so, and they agreed to do it.

By COMMISSION:

Question. What did Colonel Chivington tell them they must do in order to secure a peace with the whites?

(J. M. Chivington respectfully objects to the question for the reasons that it has not been shown that Colonel Chivington made any statement such as is assumed to have been made by the language of the question, and for the reason that the witness has already given the language used by Colonel Chivington. Objection overruled by the commission.)

Answer. I have already told substantially all that he said.

Commission adjourned until 9½ a. m., February 27, 1865.

SIXTEENTH DAY.

FEBRUARY 27, 1865.

Commission met pursuant to adjournment. Present, all the members and recorder.

Proceedings of Saturday read and approved with the following amendments:

Page —, line —, words "I think" to be omitted. In — line to second answer, "at the instance of the governor," to read, "by permission of the governor." Page —, line —, after the word "Smith" insert "to tell the Indians." Page —, line —, in second answer, after the word "military," insert the word "posts."

Recorder stated to the commission that he was unwell, and not able to record the proceedings, and requested an adjournment until 9½ a. m. to-morrow.

Commission adjourned until 9½ a. m., February 28, 1865.

SEVENTEENTH DAY.

FEBRUARY 28, 1865.

Commission met pursuant to adjournment. Present, all the members and recorder.

Proceedings of yesterday read and approved.

Examination of AMOS STEEK in presence of J. M. Chivington continued.

Amos Steek, esq., stated that he forgot to mention in the body of his evidence that the chiefs White Antelope, Bull Bear, and Neva stated that two thousand or twenty-five hundred hostile Sioux Indians had crossed the Platte towards the south, and I think they said were on the Republican. That was in reply to a question asked by Governor Evans at the council at Camp Weld.

Direct examination of Amos Steek, esq., closed.

Cross-examination of Amos Steek, esq., by J. M. Chivington, late colonel, &c.

Question. In the council had by Governor Evans, with the Indians at Camp Weld, did any person attempt to stop the Indians from telling all they desired in regard to their difficulties?

Answer. No, I do not know that anybody stopped them—don't think anybody did. Neva said that they did not come to talk of bygones and was willing to let bygones be bygones—that they desired to talk of the future. This was in response to some inquiry of the governor relative to some depredations committed by them. They admitted that they (their people) had been fighting the whites. They neither admitted nor denied that they themselves, as individuals, committed any depredations.

Question. Did they say to what tribe the Indians belonged who stole the government stock from Lieutenant Chase on the head of Squirrel creek or Jemmey's ranch in September?

Answer. I do not know that any time was mentioned, but it is the same event of which I spoke in the body of my testimony as having taken place down south near the "Fountain-qui-bouit," as I thought, and they answered the Cheyennes did it. I think it was Bull Bear who answered.

Cross-examination of Amos Steek, esq., by J. M. Chivington, closed.

Re-examination of Amos Steek, esq.

By COMMISSION :

Question. Was the interpreter, John Smith, stopped when he attempted to make known what the Indian chiefs had said in council in reference to what they had suffered by the whites ?

Answer. He began to tell something once—it may have been twice—which they had said, and directions were given to him to ask some question by the governor, but what they had said which Smith was about to tell I do not know, and it was at the time they were telling about the attack made upon them after they had left the mule at Geary's, and after they had told about Bull Bear's brother being shot down when he had the paper in his hand; and, further, at the time when this occurred the conversation had become very desultory.

Re-examination of Amos Steek, esquire, closed; commission adjourned until 2 p. m. this day.

*Two p. m.*—Commission met pursuant to adjournment. Present, all members and recorder.

Second Lieutenant Joseph A. Cramer recalled by the commission and in presence of J. M. Chivington, late colonel, &c., testified as follows :

By the COMMISSION :

Question. Did Black Kettle and other chiefs of the Cheyennes in council with Major Wynkoop say the Dog soldiers of their tribe were under their control and subject to their (the chiefs) orders ?

Answer. I don't recollect; I think Black Kettle stated the Dog soldiers were renegades from the different bands of Cheyennes and Arapahoes, whom they were not able to control. It may have been the interpreter or others who made this statement.

Question. How many of the Cheyenne tribe are known as Dog soldiers ?

Answer. I do not know.

Question. Did Black Kettle afterwards bring the white prisoners into Fort Lyon ? If so, what did he say respecting them ?

Answer. He brought three, and Left-Hand one, into our camp, and then accompanied us to Fort Lyon.

Question. What did the white prisoners say of their treatment by the Indians while in their possession ?

Answer. That they had been treated well after the first two or three days. The only mistreatment they complained of was in being obliged to ride night and day for two or three days.

Question. When the chiefs, Black Kettle of the Cheyennes and Left-Hand of the Arapahoes, brought the white prisoners into camp, what did they say respecting them ?

Answer. Black Kettle stated he had brought some of them—I don't recollect how many—from the Sioux, and the Sioux had taken the others on to the Republican, and from the time given by Major Wynkoop he was not able to go there after them. Left-Hand brought in one the first day, this young woman, (Laure Roper,) and stated that he was glad to give her up, and wanted to see her go back to her friends. She also stated that he had promised before our coming to the Smoky Hill to take her to her friends, if the whites would make a treaty. Those prisoners who came in with Black Kettle were too small to say much. The oldest said that he had just as lief stay with the Indians as not.

234

# SAND CREEK MASSACRE.

Question. Did you accompany Major Wynkoop and Indian chiefs to Denver and return with them to Fort Lyon?

Answer. I did. I accompanied the major and the chiefs up here and back as far as Coberly's, when Major Wynkoop went on ahead to Fort Lyon.

Question. While in Denver, did you attend the council held with the Indian chiefs at Camp Weld?

Answer. I did.

Question. In that council what did the Indian chiefs say in reference to peace with the whites?

Answer. That they had come up here to talk or make peace with the whites; that they did not wish to fight nor would not, and would do what was required of them in order to make peace. I think that is about the substance of it all. They also stated that they had not come to state their grievances or to tell of their misdeeds, but for peace.

Question. In that council who spoke on behalf of the government?

Answer. Governor Evans and Colonel Chivington. I think Major Wynkoop did too.

Question. What did Governor Evans, Colonel Chivington, and Major Wynkoop tell them they must do in order to secure peace with the whites?

(J. M. Chivington objects to the question, for the reason that it assumes that Governor Evans, Colonel Chivington, or Major Wynkoop told the Indians that they must do something to secure peace with the whites. The witness may be asked what those persons said at the council, but it cannot be assumed that a specific statement was made, and the witness then asked what that statement was.

Objection sustained by commission.)

Question. How were their proposals for peace received by those who spoke in behalf of the whites?

Answer. By Major Wynkoop favorably; by Governor Evans and Colonel Chivington mixed. Major Wynkoop I think stated in council that an understanding had been made between himself and the Indians, whereby he could use them to fight the other hostile Indians. I think the Kiowas and Comanches were the tribes mentioned, provided that a peace could be made favorable to the whites and Indians. I am not quite positive that Major Wynkoop stated this in council, but think he did. I know it was talked of by him, and think he stated it in council. He also stated that he believed it to be policy to make a treaty with them, as we were not prepared to fight them, and that he believed they had and would act in good faith. Governor Evans, I believe, made no direct propositions, but stated that it was in the hands of the military authorities, and that he did not wish to interfere until he could hear from the authorities east; but that he would advise them to go back with Major Wynkoop, and remain with him, and be good Indians, and he (Major Wynkoop) would care for them or take care of them as he had been doing. I think that is the substance of what he (the governor) stated. Colonel Chivington stated that he believed it to be policy to delay the thing until such time as we could get troops here to fight them. That they had been bad Indians, and should be punished; that they should be required to give up their stock, and that the bad Indians should be punished, or words to that effect; that he could make them no promises until he heard from the east; that they would go back with Major Wynkoop, who were the tribes mentioned, provided that a peace could be made favorable to the would treat them as he had been doing, I think—or as prisoners, I am not certain which. The understanding that I had of Colonel Chivington's talk in council was that he had indorsed the actions of Major Wynkoop. Part or all of this statement may have been between himself, Colonel Shoup, and Governor Evans. I am not certain that he made his statement direct to the Indians,

235

but the substance of it I think was interpreted by the interpreter to theIndians That is all I recollect, that I am positive of.

Question. Did the Indian chiefs in council manifest willingness to comply with the terms proposed in order to secure peace?

Answer. They did.

Question. Were you present in the council during its entire session?

Answer. Not all the time.

Question. Upon the return of the Indian chiefs to Fort Lyon, were any more councils held with them prior to the 29th of November, 1864?

Answer. There were several.

Question. Were you present at either or all of these councils? If so, state their object and what was done?

Answer. I was present to only one—that is, after my return to Fort Lyon. That one was held by Major Anthony, commanding Fort Lyon. The proceedings in this council were in connection with a council held with Majors Anthony and Wynkoop; prior to this, Black Kettle with the Cheyennes had just returned from the Smoky Hill in order to comply with instructions or an understanding between himself and the commander of the post to camp his' band near the fort for protection, so that all travellers might know that they were friendlyIndians. At this council, which I attended, Major Anthony told them that it would be impossible to feed them, and that they had better camp on Sand creek, and there remain until he heard from General Curtis or Washington; to let their young men go out and hunt buffalo, but not to come on to the Arkansas river, for they might get into difficulty with trains or soldiers, and as soon as he heard from General Curtis or Washington he would let them know and, if possible, would let them come in near the fort. I think that they were all of the Cheyenne tribe in that council. Black Kettle or some of his chiefs expressed dissatisfaction that the commanding officer had not complied with the previous understanding so as to allow him to come in to the fort, for he was afraid that the soldiers from Denver and the east might come across some of his young men while hunting and kill them, and then he would be unable to restrain his men. Major Anthony told them that they would be perfectly safe, and that he did not think it would be more than a few days before he would hear from General Curtis or Washington and that he was sure it would be all right. That is about all I recollect in regard to it now.

Question. Were you at Fort Lyon on duty on or about the 28th of November, 864?

Answer. I was, I think.

Question. State what transpired at Fort Lyon on the 28th of November, 1864?

Answer. Colonel Chivington's command arrived there in the morning about 9 o'clock. Went into camp below the commissary about 1 o'clock. I received an order from Major Anthony, commanding post, to report at 7 or 8 o'clock at night with every available man in my command with three days' cooked rations in their saddle-bags, and two hundred rounds of ammunition. I reported between 7 and 8 with forty-four men to Major Anthony, and soon after joined Colonel Chivington's command, and started from Fort Lyon in a northerly direction. Marched forty or forty-five miles, and between daylight and sunrise came upon an Indian village consisting of about one hundred lodges.

Question. Did you converse with Major Anthony prior to leaving Fort Lyon on the eve of the 28th of November, relative to a contemplated attack upon the Indians?

Answer. I did.

Question. What did you say to him and what reply did he make?

Answer. I stated to him that I was perfectly willing to obey orders, but that. I did it under protest, for I believed that he directly, and all officers who accompanied Major Wynkoop to the Smoky Hill indirectly, would perjure themselves both as officers and men; that I believed it to be murder to go out and kill those Indians, as I felt that Major Wynkoop's command owed their lives to this same band of Indians. Major Anthony in his reply stated that he had made no pledges that would compromise his honor; that the promise he had given the Indians he did not consider binding, inasmuch as he had not heard from General Curtis or Washington, and that was as far as his argument extended, to let them know when he did hear. He also stated that he was opposed to killing those Indians if it went no further, but the intention was to go on to the Sioux camp; and if they did that, he was in favor of killing everything they come to. I told him that I thought that Black Kettle and his tribe had acted in good faith; that they had saved the lives of one hundred and twenty of our men and the settlers in the Arkansas valley, and that he with his tribe could be of use to us to fight the other Indians, and that he (Black Kettle) was willing to do so. He (Anthony) stated that Black Kettle would not be killed; that it was a promise given by Colonel Chivington or an understanding between himself and Colonel Chivington that Black Kettle and his friends should be spared; that the object of the expedition was to surround the camp and take the stolen stock and kill the Indians that had been committing depredations during the last spring and summer. I told him that on those grounds I was perfectly willing to go. I do not recollect whether all of this conversation occurred before we started for Sand creek or not; most of it did, I know.

Commission adjourned until 9½ a. m. to-morrow, March 1, 1865.

EIGHTEENTH DAY.

MARCH 1, 1865.

Commission met pursuant to adjournment. Present, all members and recorder. Proceedings of yesterday read and approved.

Examination of Second Lieutenant Joseph A. Cramer, veteran battalion first Colorado cavalry, by the commission, in presence of J. M. Chivington, late colonel, &c., continued.

By the COMMISSION:

Question. Did you have any further conversation with officers at Fort Lyon in reference to the contemplated attack upon Black Kettle's camp? If so, state who the officers were, and what was said.

Answer. I had some conversation with Major Downing, Lieutenant Maynard, and Colonel Chivington. I stated to them my feelings in regard to the matter; that I believed it to be "murder," and stated the obligations that we of Major Wynkoop's command were under to those Indians. To Colonel Chivington I know I stated that Major Wynkoop had pledged his word as an officer and a man to those Indians, and that all officers under him were indirectly pledged in the same manner that he was, and that I felt it was placing us in very embarrassing circumstances to fight the same Indians that had saved our lives, as we all felt they had. Colonel Chivington's reply was, that he believed it to be right or honorable to use any means under God's heaven to kill Indians that would kill women and children, and "damn any man that was in sympathy with Indians," and such men as Major Wynkoop and myself had better get out of the United States service. I think that Major Downing said he would not advise me to go, if I felt as I said, or words to that effect. I do not know that Lieutenant Maynard made any reply. I also stated to Major Anthony that I believed it to be his duty to let these Indians know what was going on, according to the agreement he had made with them, and that an officer who would disregard his honor was a disgrace to the United States uniform. That is about all I recollect at present. There were several remarks passed between Captain Soule, Lieutenant Baldwin, and myself, but it was all a one-sided affair, as we all agreed.

Question. In your conversation with officers at Fort Lyon, was anything said in reference to the white men in Black Kettle's camp?

Answer. There was, either at Fort Lyon or on the road.

Question. What was said?

Answer. Major Anthony stated that arrangements had been made with Colonel Chivington to get them out of the Indian camp before there was any fighting done.

Question. Did you join Colonel Chivington's column in the attack upon Black Kettle's camp? If so, state what was your understanding of the object of the attack.

Answer. I did join it, the object of which was to take the stock and kill and punish the Indians who had committed the depredations in this Territory during last winter, spring and summer, and to save Black Kettle and his friends.

Question. Had the Indians committed any depredations in the vicinity of Fort Lyon for three months prior to the 29th of November, 1864?

Answer. To the best of my knowledge, none that I ever heard of or know of.

Question. What was the last depredation committed by the Indians near Fort Lyon during the summer of 1864?

Answer. It was the killing of two men—the names I have forgotten—I think about the 17th of August. They were on their way to Fort Lyon as witnesses in the Haynes case before a military commission. I do not know what Indians they were. Mr. Combs and one of the first Colorado battery boys found them while on their road up to the Indian agency, (it is called the Upper Arkansas Indian agency.) They saw Indians ahead of them, and returned to Fort Lyon. I do not recollect whether they reported that the Indians fired on them or not.

Question. What Indians were reported on the Arkansas, above and below Fort Lyon, during the summer of 1864?

Answer. Kiowas, Arapahoes, Cheyennes, and Sioux.

Question. Did the Indian chiefs in any council refer to the killing of the two men near Fort Lyon?

Answer. I think they did, but am not positive. I think it was in the Smoky Hill council. I am not positive that I heard it from Indians at all.

Question. State what was done on the arrival of Colonel Chivington's command at Black Kettle's camp on the morning of 29th November, 1864.

Answer. We had a fight. Lieutenant Wilson's battalion, consisting of parts of three companies of the first cavalry of Colorado, on our approach to the Indian village, made a charge for the Indians' herd, from one-half to a mile east of the Indian village, and drove their herd in towards the village; Major Anthony's battalion, from Fort Lyon, following, consisting of parts of three companies of the first cavalry. G company had a battery of two twelve-pounder mountain howitzers, and on approaching the village Lieutenant Wilson's battalion took a position on the north side of the village and Sand creek, and immediately opened fire on the Indians. Major Anthony's battalion took a position on the southeast side, I should judge, and there waited for Colonel Shoup's third regiment to come up, (the third regiment, as I understand it, were volunteer cavalry enlisted for one hundred days,) as he (Major Anthony) said he did not wish to open the ball, but wanted to see Colonel Chivington do so. The third regiment took up their first position in rear and to the right of the Fort Lyon battalion, dismounted part or all of their men for some purpose, I don't know what, and, mounting again and moving to the front, commenced firing, some of them firing over or through our ranks. On reporting this fact to Major Anthony I was ordered to move my company to the left, down to the bank of Sand creek. Previous to our moving, John Smith, Indian interpreter, came out, and when within from thirty to fifty paces several hallooed out "Shoot the old son of a bitch," and commenced firing on him; he then ran back to his lodge or tepe. About that same time some one came out with a white flag, going towards the head of the column, and was fired upon, and immediately ran back; I do not know who he was, but supposed him to be David Louderback, a soldier of G company, first cavalry of Colorado, or a teamster, who had driven John Smith, Indian interpreter, out there, as he had on a government overcoat. George Pierce, a member of F company, attached to my company, in attempting to save the life of John Smith, was killed, I think, by the third regiment, or Lieutenant Wilson's battalion, as they were firing at the time, and I saw no Indians firing at the time and in that direction. In the position first taken one battalion, I think, of the third regiment took position on the south side of Sand creek, and opposite to the village and almost directly opposite to Lieutenant Wilson's battalion; they, at the same time, were firing. Immediately after firing upon John Smith, the Fort Lyon battalion opened fire; several Indians were killed while running towards the troops with both hands raised, one of whom I think was White Antelope, a Cheyenne chief. During this time the Indians had been running up the creek, and the whole command moved forward and took such positions as best suited them, as there appeared to be no general organization, and no one to command, and at different periods of the fight they were in such positions that I thought and said they were firing on each other; the fight continued until about between 12 and 2, I should judge; we then went back to the Indian village.

Question. At any time during the attack upon the Indian camp at Sand creek was the command of Colonel Chivington, or any portion of it, so situated or so scattered as to be in danger of being shot by each other?

Answer. They were, I should judge. Men were directly opposite each other, on both sides of the creek, and were firing towards each other, and several times during the fight I ordered my men to cease firing, owing to the position in which our troops were placed, and fearful of killing some of our own men.

Question. State how long they were so scattered or so situated?

Answer. During the whole fight, after the first hour or one-half hour.

Question. Did the commanding officer make any efforts to rally the command and place it in a position where they would not be in danger of being shot by our own men?

Answer. Not that I know of.

Commission adjourned until 2 p. m. this day.

*Two p. m.*—Commmission met pursuant to adjournment. Present, all members and recorder.

Examination of Second Lieutenant Joseph A. Cramer, by commission, in presence of J. M. Chivington, late colonel, &c., continued.

Question. What field officers, besides Colonel Chivington, were present at and during the attack on Black Kettle's camp?

Answer. Colonel Shoup, of the third regiment; Lieutenant Colonel Bowen, third regiment; Major Sayre, third regiment; Major Anthony, first regiment; Major Downing, first regiment.

Question. Who of these officers you have mentioned attempted to rally the men and save them from the danger of each other's fire?

Answer. None that I know of.

Question. Were the two mountain howitzers brought into action at Sand creek? If so, state what was done with them.

Answer. They were brought into action, took position to the left of where the Fort Lyon battalion first took position, and opened fire, doing but little execution—that is, I should judge so, firing up the creek until the Indians were out of range—then took position further up the creek, firing across into the opposite bank. They were in action throughout the fight in several different positions

Ex. Doc. 26——4

I think I am mistaken about the Fort Lyon howitzers firing into the opposite bank; I think it was the third regiment howitzers.

Question. Were there any other howitzers than these you have mentioned, engaged in the attack at Sand creek? If so, state what was done with them.

Answer. There were two twelve-pounder howitzers with the third regiment, commanded by Captain Morgan; the third regiment took position to the rear of our first position and opened fire, then following up the Indians, taking several different positions, doing but little or no execution, to the best of my knowledge.

Question. At the time the four howitzers were engaged were any of Colonel Chivington's command on the opposite bank of the creek and exposed to their fire?

Answer. Part of his command were on the opposite bank shooting over the bank at Indians below them, and I thought they were in great danger from the fire of the howitzers, at the time they were firing across the creek. I think only two guns were in action; they belonged to the third regiment. The Fort Lyon howitzers, I think, at that time were out of ammunition.

Question. Was there, at any time during the attack, an American flag displayed over the Indian camp?

Answer. I saw none during the fight; I saw one in the camp after the fight, reported to have been over Black Kettle's lodge.

Question. Do you know of any one giving Black Kettle an American flag, and instructing him what to do with it if soldiers should be seen approaching his camp?

Answer. No, I do not. Major Wynkoop gave him instructions in regard to some signal, but do not know whether it was the flag or not.

Question. Do you know what instructions were given Black Kettle in reference to a signal?

Answer. One was, that in approaching troops or a soldier's camp, to use a white flag or white blanket; that is all the instructions I heard given.

Question. At what time did you leave Sand creek on the day of the attack upon Black Kettle's camp?

Answer. I should judge it was between 3 and 4 o'clock.

Question. Prior to your leaving did you ride over the field? If so, state what you saw.

Answer. I did; saw some dead Indians at that time; I estimated them at one hundred and seventy-five or one hundred and eighty; I do not think there were that many; I do not recollect of seeing one but what was scalped; that is about all. I did not see any rifle-pits.

Question. Were most of the Indians killed and scalped at Sand creek warriors?

Answer. They were not; I should think two-thirds were women and children.

Question. Did any of the Indians escape during the attack upon Black Kettle's camp?

Answer. I should judge they did, a good many.

Question. Were the chiefs, White Antelope, Black Kettle, One-Eye, and Neva, in camp at time of attack?

Answer. Black Kettle, White Antelope, and One-Eye, I think, were; Neva was not.

Question. Were these the same chiefs that were in council with Major Wynkoop on the Smoky Hill?

Answer. They were.

Question. At any time during the attack on Black Kettle's camp did the Indians appear in line of battle?

Answer. Not that I saw.

Question, How did the Indians resist the attack upon them?

Answer. By fighting back. They fought singly or a few in a place when the ground would give them shelter from our fire, and fought bravely. A great many started towards our lines with hands raised, as if begging for us to spare them.

Question. Were the Indians followed and killed while attempting to escape?

Answer. They were, some of them.

Question. Were any of the Indian women and children killed and mutilated while attempting to escape?

Answer. They were; they were followed and killed, but I do not know when they were mutilated. They were mutilated, though.

Question. Were any prisoners taken at Sand creek? If so, state what was done with them.

Answer. There were several; there were two women and two children, Charley Bent, a half-breed, son of Colonel Bent, Jack Smith, half-breed, son of John Smith, Indian interpreter. The two women and children were taken into Fort Lyon by company G of the first regiment. Charley Bent was taken in or sent in by Captain S. S. Soule. Jack Smith, I understood, was murdered. There was one little child but a few months old, brought one day's march from Sand creek and then abandoned; so I was told by enlisted men of the command. The third regiment had some Indian prisoners. I know nothing of how they were taken or what was done with them. One old squaw came into the fort for food and protection; she was left by our command at the Indian camp.

Question. What became of the prisoners after being taken to Fort Lyon?

Answer. The three women and two children were sent by the commander of the post (Major Anthony) up to Colonel Bent's, eighteen miles above Fort Lyon. Charley Bent, who was confined in the guard-house, was released by the officer of the day, and I do not know where he went; heard he had gone to New Mexico.

Question. Did you take the prisoners to Colonel Bent's?

Answer. The Indians were sent on in the morning with an escort from Fort Lyon. I was ordered in the afternoon to take an escort of twelve men, I believe, and proceed to Colonel Bent to offer such protection as I might deem necessary. On my arrival there found the river blocked with ice, so that they were enable to cross. Waited until in the night, when the river had frozen over, and then crossed over with the escort and the Indians and delivered them over to Colonel Bent.

Question. Had the lives of those prisoners been threatened by any person or persons?

Answer. They had; also Colonel Bent and family.

Question. State what transpired at Colonel Bent's while you were there;

Answer. Upon my arrival there I found Colonel Bent under guard, left there when the third regiment were going down the country, and in command of Lieutenant Graham, third regiment, who had a guard established over the house and corral. Told Colonel Bent what my instructions were, and quartered my guard in the house. Captain Cree, of the third regiment, arrived that night with a few men and said he had orders from Colonel Shoup to take command of all the troops there, but did not do it, that I know of. Next morning Captain Cree, Lieutenant Graham, and their men left and went up the river on their road to Denver. I remained until the next day and then returned to Fort Lyon.

Question. What did Captain Cree say to you and Colonel Bent he had done to some prisoners?

Answer. That he had killed them, or they had been killed by his command. That he had started from Denver with them to take them to Fort Lyon; that they had attempted to get away from his guard, and he had ordered them that in case they made the attempt to kill them, and they had done so. Most of his guard, and I think himself, were ahead of the prisoners at the time they were killed. I think he also stated that he was acting under orders from Colonel Chivington, commanding the district of Colorado. He also stated that they left them on the

241

plains or prairie, and that Colonel Chivington had issued an order that he would hang any "son of a bitch" who would bury their bodies or bones. I believe that's about all.

Question. Do you know what became of the stock and other property captured at Sand creek by Colonel Chivington's command?

Answer. Part of it I understood was turned in to the quartermaster at Denver. A large portion of it was stolen and run off by officers and men of the third regiment This I learned by report; part of the stock I saw on my trip from Fort Lyon to Denver. The camp plunder that was taken was mostly in the hands of the soldiers, and I do not know what was done with it.

Question. State whether the property captured, excepting the stock, was of any value or not.

Answer. It was. There were a great many buffalo robes—probably two hundred or three hundred—which would be worth from fifteen to twenty dollars apiece. The camp fixings or trinkets were of no real value, but they would have brought a considerable amount of money, could they have been sold at auction. There were some few guns taken which were valuable.

Question. Was the stock at Fort Lyon, taken at Sand Creek, turned over to Captain Johnson, third regiment Colorado cavalry?

Answer. It was.

Question. In whose possession was that stock you saw on your way from Fort Lyon to Denver?

Answer. In the possession of citizens living on the Arkansas and Fountain-qui-bouit; I do not know their names.

Question. Did they say how they came in possession of it?

Answer. They did not. I had no conversation with them in regard to it.

Commission adjourned until 9½ a. m. to-morrow, March 2, 1865.

NINETEENTH DAY.

MARCH 2, 1865.

Commission met pursuant to adjournment. Present, all members and recorder. Proceedings of yesterday read and approved.

On February 28, 1865, Colonel Chivington applied to the commission to obtain for him, from the Indian bureau at Washington, D. C., a copy of Governor Evans's report of proceedings of a council with the Indians at Camp Weld about the 27th of September, 1864, and, on March 1, 1865, from the Adjutant General's office, Washington, D. C., an authenticated copy of General Blunt's report of a battle had by that officer with the Indians about the 25th September, 1864, on or near the headwaters of the Pawnee fork of the Arkansas river. Commission decided to make an application for the papers mentioned, and instructed the recorder to apply for them by letter.

Examination of Second Lieutenant Joseph A. Cramer, veteran battalion first Colorado cavalry, by the commission, in presence of J. M. Chivington, late colonel, &c., continued:

Question. At any time during the summer and fall of 1864 did the Indians send challenges to the commander of Fort Lyon to come out and fight them?

Answer. Not that I heard of. The Sioux, I understood, did. It may not have been considered a challenge. They, I understood, sent in word that they had come to this country to fight, and were going to fight.

Question. Where were the Sioux reported camped in the fall of 1864?

Answer. On a branch of the Smoky Hill.

Question. In what direction, and how far, from Fort Lyon?

Answer. About ninety miles, in a northerly direction.

Question. Did you ever hear of Black Kettle's band of Cheyennes committing depredations upon the lives and property of the whites?

242

Answer. I have, since the fight at Sand creek; before that I did not.

Direct examination of Second Lieutenant Joseph A. Cramer closed.

Cross-examination of Second Lieutenant Joseph A. Cramer, by J. M. Chivington, late colonel, &c.:

Question. State, if you know, whether Major Wynkoop was ordered or directed to go out on Smoky Hill, or to treat with the Indians, by any officer, civil or military, during the summer or fall of the year 1864.

Answer. I think he was not.

Question. State, if you know, whether Major Wynkoop had any information as to the number of Indians he would probably meet on the Smoky Hill expedition, before starting out on that expedition?

Answer. I don't know anything about it, whether he had any of that kind of information or not.

Question. If you know, state what information Major Wynkoop had as to white prisoners being in possession of the Indians, before starting out on the Smoky Hill?

Answer. The information he had he got from a letter written by George Bent by instructions from the chiefs—it was signed by Black Kettle and other chiefs—and what he learned from One-Eye and Min-im-mie.

Question. What was contained in the letter you have mentioned?

Answer. Stating that they held seven (7) white prisoners, and that they wanted to have a talk, or make peace; that we held in Denver some of their Indians prisoners, and that they would give up theirs if we would do the same, and a peace would be made.

Question. What was stated by One-Eye and Min-im-mie?

Answer. The substance was the same as contained in the letter, and that we might hold their lives as pledges that they acted in good faith.

Question. Did the chiefs signing the letter represent therein, or did One-Eye or Min-im-mie pretend that they acted on behalf of, the Sioux?

Answer. Not as I understood it. They were acting in their own behalf. I think that One-Eye stated that, if a treaty was made, the Sioux wanted to be considered in.

Question. Did the letter contain a request, or did One-Eye or Min-im-mie request, that a council should be held by Major Wynkoop with the Indians, for the purpose of discussing the matter referred to in the letter?

Answer. They did; both the letter and the two Indians.

Question. Was any suggestion made in the letter, or by One-Eye or Min-im-mie, respecting the place where, and the time when, the council should be held?

Answer. Not in the letter. I think by Min-im-mie and One-Eye there were.

Question. What were these suggestions?

Answer. That we should either go to the Indian camp, or the Smoky Hill, or if Major Wynkoop would let one of them go ahead to notify the Indians they would come out and meet us.

Question. How were you made acquainted with the object of the expedition of Major Wynkoop?

Answer. By the council of officers held in Major Wynkoop's room, previous to our starting.

Question. What, if any, course was determined upon in that council?

Answer. The course determined on was, to go and hold these Indians as hostages for their good faith.

Question. What number of Indians did Major Wynkoop's command encounter on that expedition?

Answer. I should judge about seven hundred warriors.

Question. To what tribes did the Indians referred to in your answer belong?

Answer. Cheyennes and Arapahoes principally. I think there were some Sioux, but I am not positive about that.

Question. How far was Major Wynkoop's command from Fort Lyon, when the Indians were first met?

Answer. From one hundred and twenty to one hundred and forty miles; probably one hundred and forty miles.

Question. How far from Fort Lyon is the place where the council between the officers of Major Wynkoop's expedition and the Indians was held?

Answer. Held from two to four miles from where we first met the Indians.

Question. Did or did not the Indians make any hostile demonstrations towards Major Wynkoop's command?

Answer. I think they did, until One-Eye was sent on ahead to acquaint them who we were, and that we did not come to fight them.

Question. What were those hostile demonstrations?

Answer. Merely making signs or signals to the Indians in their rear, and riding or remaining in such positions as to be able to fight.

Question. How near was Major Wynkoop's command to the Indians when One-Eye was sent forward to communicate with them?

Answer. About a half or three-quarters of a mile.

Question. Did Major Wynkoop continue his march after One-Eye was sent forward, or did he halt and wait One-Eye's return?

Answer. He halted, formed a line of battle, and there remained until One-Eye had joined the Indians, and then I think moved on.

Question. In what order did Major Wynkoop's command and the Indians proceed from the place where the Indians were first met to the place where the council was held?

Answer. In line of battle part of the way, and part of the way in squadron columns. Some few of the Indians joined us on the march, and showed us where we would find some water.

Question. Did not the Indians encircle the rear of Major Wynkoop's command, and proceed in that way from the place where they were first met to the place where the council was held?

Answer. They did not. But very few Indians came to us that night at all; probably not more than fifty or seventy-five. Some few came up after we had camped, and showed us where we could get water by digging; as Major Wynkoop had not camped where the Indians had told him, there was no water, but took a position so as to be able to defend his command.

Question. Did or did not the Indians make any hostile demonstrations toward Major Wynkoop's command after One-Eye was sent forward to communicate with them?

Answer. Not at that time; not that night.

Question. At what time in the day, and upon what day of the month, was the council held?

Answer. The council was held I think upon the 10th day of September, about 11 o'clock in the day. It may have commenced at 9 a. m.

Question. Did the Indians commit any acts of hostility on the day in which the council was held?

Answer. None that I know of. Their actions were considered hostile, but they claimed them not to be; and after Major Wynkoop had spoken with some of the chiefs, their acts were friendly.

Commission adjourned until 2 p. m. this day.

*Two p. m.*—Commission met pursuant to adjournment. Present, all members and recorder.

Cross-examination of Second Lieutenant Joseph A. Cramer, by J. M. Chivington, continued:

Question. What were the actions of the Indians on the day on which the council was held?

SAND CREEK MASSACRE.

Answer. Singing, and having a general pow-wow, which the chiefs interpreted as their manner of rejoicing, to think that we were going to make a treaty with them. They fired their guns and revolvers in the air.

Question. What were the acts of the Indians which were regarded as acts of hostility by persons in Major Wynkoop's command?

Answer. Those that I have just mentioned, and being drawn up in line of battle, and forming a circle or a partial circle around us, as Major Wynkoop was marching in line of battle with train driven in form of corral. The Indians said that they thought it looked more like fighting than coming to talk, or make peace. But when told by Major Wynkoop if they did not keep further back he would fire on them, we had no further difficulty in making our camp.

Question. Did or did not the Indian warriors come into Major Wynkoop's camp during the time the council was being held?

Answer. They did.

Question. Did their coming into Major Wynkoop's camp cause any apprehensions of danger among the officers of Major Wynkoop's command?

Answer. I can speak only for myself. I thought there was no greater danger then than when marching into camp.

Question. What was the conduct of the Indian warriors when in Major Wynkoop's camp?

Answer. Friendly. At one time when Lieutenant Hardin was attempting to form in line the men of Major Wynkoop's command just outside of the council, the Indians commenced loading their guns and stringing their bows. Lieutenant Phillips acquainted me with the fact of Lieutenant Hardin's actions, and requested me to stop it if possible, which I did. No other acts on the part of the Indians, after this, could be construed as hostile.

Question. What was the object of Lieutenant Hardin's forming line with the troops while the council was going on?

Answer. That is more than I can tell.

Question. Who was the officer of the day at the time the council was held?

Answer. Lieutenant Hardin.

Question. Do you know of any request being made by any of the officers of Major Wynkoop's command to the Indian chiefs in council, that the Indian warriors should withdraw from Major Wynkoop's camp?

Answer. I do not recollect of any until after the council was over. Then, I think, Major Wynkoop told Black Kettle that he had them or part of them go outside. I am not positive that this occurred.

Question. Did you hear Lieutenant Hardin make any statement to the effect that the Indians were in the camp, and that he could not keep them out of the camp?

Answer. After we were on our return to Fort Lyon, I did; while in camp, I think I did not.

Question. State as nearly as you can the number of Indian warriors in Major Wynkoop's camp at the time the council was held.

Answer. All that were present. I have previously stated the number.

Question. Did you hear any of the officers of Major Wynkoop's command, on the day on which the council was held, express any fears of an attack from the Indians? If so, give the names of such officers, and what was said by them.

Answer. I don't think that I heard any one express fears of an attack. At the time that Lieutenant Phillips acquainted me of the fact of Lieutenant Hardin's falling in the men, I think he said that I would have to stop it or we would be massacred, and that our only show now was to show them a reckless indifference. I also told the men of my command that they must take the thing cool, and keep but a few in a place, only a sufficient number to defend themselves, for if we did anything that looked like fighting, I thought it would bring on a fight with the Indians; and also to keep near the wagons so as to use them

245

to fight behind in case we were attacked; that if they would let the Indians see that we did not care which way the thing went, we would have no trouble.

Question. By whose order was the act of Lieutenant Hardin forming the men in line stopped?

Answer. I don't know of anybody but myself; I taking the responsibility of ordering the company which I commanded (K) to disperse and keep near the wagons.

Question. Were you Lieutenant Hardin's superior officer?

Answer. I was not, particularly when he was officer of the day. He was a first lieutenant.

Question. State, if you know, whether Major Wynkoop gave any orders concerning the keeping the Indians out of camp.

Answer. He did. So he stated, and so Lieutenant Hardin admitted.

Question. What were those orders?

Answer. To allow no Indians in camp without his permission. That when the chiefs arrived, to notify him, and he would pass them in with a few of their friends. His orders were to form his guard around the camp and the horses, which were picketed out near the camp.

Question. State if you know whether any of the officers of Major Wynkoop's command entertained any apprehensions of danger from the Indians on the day of the council or the day preceding that day.

Answer. Yes; I think they all did.

Question. Who acted as interpreter to Major Wynkoop on the expedition?

Answer. John Smith; also George Bent, in some instances, as he was asked by Major Wynkoop if the interpretations were correct.

Question. Did John Smith regard the conduct of the Indians as hostile or otherwise?

Answer. I think he regarded it as otherwise. That he expressed no fears until after Bull Bear spoke in council, and then I think he said, I have now got to talk for my life. After Black Kettle spoke I think that he then stated that it was all right.

Question. Did the Indians at any time say that they were prepared to fight Major Wynkoop's command, and willing to do so, or substantially that?

Answer. I think not. Bull Bear may have said it, as he stated that he believed the only thing left for them was to fight; that the whites were not to be trusted.

Question. State whether there was a battery or portion of a battery with Major Wynkoop's command.

Answer. There were two pieces, 12-pounder howitzers, commanded by Lieutenant Hardin.

Question. State, if you know, whether the Indians got possession or control of these howitzers, or either of them, or handled, or in any way interfered with them, or either of them, during or before the time the council was held.

Answer. I don't know anything about it. Heard it reported in camp that one of the Indians attempted to put grapes into the vent of the howitzers, one or both, but was shoved away by the soldiers on guard at the time, and no more allowed to approach near them.

Question. Did Major Wynkoop state to the Indians in council that any person had power to make peace with them on behalf of the government? If so, who did he say had such power?

Answer. Governor Evans, or the authorities east.

Question. Did Major Wynkoop represent to the Indians that it was probable that peace could be made with them?

Answer. He did, if they would do as he proposed.

Question. Did Major Wynkoop desire the Indians to send their chiefs and headmen to Denver with him?

Answer. He did.

Question. Was there anything said in the council between Major Wynkoop and the Indians respecting the terms upon which peace was to be made ?

Answer. I think not. Major Wynkoop proposed to them that if they would give up their prisoners, that would be an evidence of their good faith, and would be instrumental in bringing about a good peace. He stated to them at the opening of the council, that he was not big enough chief to make any peace or promises of a treaty, but that he could use his influence in their favor, providing they did as he wished them to do.

Question. Did the Indians in council make any statements as to how, and when and where they came into possession of the white captives then in their hands? If so, what were these statements ?

Answer. I think they made none, only in regard to the prisoner Laurie Roper, whom they stated they had bought of other Indians. I did not understand what Indians. Part or all of the other prisoners were then in the hands of the Sioux.

Question. Did the Indians in council with Major Wynkoop make any statements as to whether they had ever committed any acts of hostility against the whites, or joined in the commission of such acts ? If so, what were those statements?

Answer. They made a statement in regard to some of the men of their tribes joining with the Kiowas at Fort Larned in taking the stock at that post; also in the fight with Lieutenant Eayres, on the Smoky Hill, and the fight with Lieutenant Dunn. Black Kettle spoke of some of his young men, about the time or after he had left Fort Larned, going off in small war parties and committing some depredations. What they were I did not understand. I think the murdering of Snyder and two other men, near Colonel Boone's, was spoken of. I think it was Little Raven's brother, an Arapahoe, and his party were the ones that killed them. Neva also acknowledged to be the one that was near Fort Lyon, and had the fight with my command, on the 11th of August.

Question. State, if you know, whether the Indians in council with Major Wynkoop did, or did not, represent that they were authorized to act for the entire tribes of Arapahoes and Cheyenne Indians ? If so, what statements were made by them ?

Answer. I think the whole Cheyenne and Arapahoe nations living in that part of the country were represented in that council, and that they were willing and would be guided by Black Kettle's actions.

Question. Were any statements made by any of the Indians in council, or elsewhere, to the effect that any of the Indians of their tribes were then out upon the war path ? If so, what were those statements?

Answer. That there were two or three small war parties still out, and that he was using and would use his utmost endeavors to bring them in. This, I think, was stated by Black Kettle.

Question. At what council was the statement made ?

Answer. Smoky Hill.

Question. State, if you know, whether any of the Dog soldiers were with the band of Indians encountered by Major Wynkoop's command.

Answer. There were. I think their head chief was there. I know his name was Bull Bear, as I understood it.

Question. Was anything said by the chiefs in council with Major Wynkoop as to their ability to control the Dog soldiers ? If so, what was it ?

Answer. That owing to the difficulties that had occurred they had been unable to control all of them, and unless a treaty was made they would be unable to do so.

Question. What proportion do the Dog soldiers bear to the fighting strength of the Arapahoes and Cheyenne Indians ?

Answer. I do not know.

Question. Can you state what number of Dog soldiers were with the band of Indians encountered by Major Wynkoop's command?

Answer. I cannot.

Question. State, if you know, whether the Indians encountered by Major Wynkoop's command had, at that time, their squaws and children with them.

Answer. They had not.

Question. Did the Indians in council with Major Wynkoop make any statement respecting the purpose for which they visited that part of the country?

Answer. They came down there for the purpose of getting plums and grapes, and for grazing their stock.

Question. Were the Indians encountered by Major Wynkoop's command armed? And if so, how were they armed?

Answer. They were armed with bows and arrows, guns, revolvers, and lances.

Question. What proportion of the Indians had guns or revolvers?

Answer. The majority had guns, and a great many revolvers.

Question. Was anything said by the Indians respecting a large band of Sioux being near the place where the council was held? If so, state what was said.

Answer. I think there was; that they had been camped but a few miles—I think they said sixteen miles—from where we were, but had gone over on to the Republican.

Question. If anything was said by the Indians in council with Major Wynkoop relative to peace with the Sioux, state what was said.

Answer. That the Sioux did not wish a peace made unless they were interested in it.

Question. What, if anything, did the Indians say respecting their ability to procure the white captives then in possession of the Sioux?

Answer. That they thought it would be difficult to do so, owing to the fact that Major Wynkoop had excluded them, as he did not feel authorized to make any promises in regard to them.

Question. What, if anything did they say as to the number of white prisoners in their possession and in possession of the Sioux?

Answer. I am not positive that there was but one in possession of the Cheyennes and Arapahoes.

Question. Did the Indians in council make any promises to the effect that they would return all the captives to Major Wynkoop? If so, what were those promises?

Answer. They would return them if they could procure them, and they would do their best to procure them.

Question. Were any reasons assigned by the Indians after bringing in the four captives of whom you have spoken, why they did not bring the other white prisoners?

Answer. Owing to the time given by Major Wynkoop, they were unable to procure them.

Question. What were the terms upon which Major Wynkoop agreed to protect the Indian chiefs to Denver and back, and to use his influence to obtain a treaty of peace?

Answer. That they would deliver up the white prisoners in their possession.

Question. Was anything said as to the number of prisoners which should be so delivered?

Answer. At the time the proposition was made there was not.

Question. Was anything said respecting the number of prisoners to be delivered before or after the time when the proposition was made?

Answer. There was, afterwards. Black Kettle stated that he would procure what he could in the time given, and if he did not procure all of them he would send some of his men over there to buy them, and would have them brought into the fort.

Question. How many white prisoners were delivered in accordance with this arrangement?

Answer. Four.

Question. How long did the council between the Indians and Major Wynkoop continue?

Answer. Until about two p. m., I should judge.

Question. Did the Indian warriors remain in the camp during the whole of the time the council was in session?

Answer. All that did come in I think remained there until a fire broke out near camp, the wind driving it towards our wagons. A great many of them went out and assisted in putting it out.

Question. What reason, if any, was assigned by the Indians for advising Major Wynkoop to move his command nearer Fort Lyon after the council was held?

Answer. For fear a difficulty might occur between some of his young men and the soldiers.

Question. How did it occur that you and the officers of Major Wynkoop's command owed your lives to Black Kettle and his band of Indians, as stated in your direct examination?

Answer. Because if it had not been for them the Indians would have cleaned us out.

Question. If the Indians had given battle to Major Wynkoop's command, what, in your opinion, would have been the result of that battle?

Answer. We would have all been killed.

Question. After the council between the Indians and Major Wynkoop, did the Indians return to Major Wynkoop's camp? and if so, in what number did they return?

Answer. They had not left it after the council.

Question. After Major Wynkoop's command left the place where the council was held, did the Indians return to Major Wynkoop's command? and if so, in what number did they return?

Answer. From twenty to forty families and thirteen chiefs returned.

Commission adjourned until 9½ a. m. to-morrow, March 3, 1865.

TWENTIETH DAY.

MARCH 3, 1865.

Commission met pursuant to adjournment. Present, all members and recorder.

The quartermaster's department having failed to furnish the commission rooms with wood, the commission adjourned until 2 p. m. this day.

*Two p. m.*—Commission met pursuant to adjournment. Present, all members and recorder.

Proceedings of yesterday read and approved, with the following amendments: Page 211, first line to last answer, to read, nearly all, &c.; page 220, fifth line to first answer, to read, "and said that they were willing," &c.

Cross-examination of Second Lieutenant Joseph H. Cramer, veteran battalion, &c., by J. M. Chivington, continued:

Question. State, if you know, whether Lieutenant Hardin made any report to Major Wynkoop respecting the Indians during the time the council was in session.

Answer. I do not know, but think not.

Question. Were there any Indians in Major Wynkoop's camp at the time that Lieutenant Hardin attempted to form the soldiers of the command into line?

Answer. There were—all of them.

Question. Did not Lieutenant Hardin attempt to form the soldiers in line for the purpose of drawing the Indians from the camp?

Answer. I do not know.

Question. Did the Indians in council with Major Wynkoop make any statements as to why they went to Fort Larned before coming to the vicinity of Fort Lyon?

Answer. No, not that I know of.

Question. Do you know whether Major Wynkoop made any statement to the Indians, to the effect that he or the military authorities would take the white prisoners then in their possession by force if they (the Indians) did not give them up voluntarily?

Answer. He did.

Question. What were those statements?

Answer. That he had come to get them by peaceable means, if possible, and forcible means if necessary.

Question. What number of Indians accompanied Major Wynkoop's command to Fort Lyon?

Answer. About from twenty to forty families, and thirteen chiefs.

Question. Did Major Wynkoop make any statements to the Indians to the effect that they were to treat with Colonel Chivington for peace?

Answer. I think not.

Question. Were the proceedings of the council at Camp Weld, near Denver, reduced to writing by any person? If so, by whom?

Answer. There were two or three taking notes; I think Amos Steck and Major Whiteley.

Question. During the time that you were present at the Camp Weld council, did Colonel Chivington make any statements or propound any questions to the Indians?

Answer. I think not. I think that the questions were all asked by the governor.

Question. State if you know whether Colonel Chivington received any orders or instructions from Major General Curtis in relation to treating with the Indians for peace shortly before the Camp Weld council.

Answer. Not that I know of; heard that he received a telegram after the council.

Question. State if you know whether the Indians in council at Camp Weld made any statement to the effect that they had not come to talk of the past, and they were willing to let bygones be bygones. If so, what was that statement?

Answer. I think that they made the statement as the question reads.

Question. What white persons were present at the Camp Weld council?

Answer. Governor Evans, Colonel Chivington, Colonel Shoup, Major Wynkoop, Amos Steck, J. Bright Smith, Captain Wanless, John Smith, Indian interpreter, Captain Rollins; I think James McNassar, Simeon Whiteley; several others—I have forgotten the names.

Question. Were any statements made to the Indians at the Camp Weld council, in your hearing, in relation to treating with the Indians for peace at some time thereafter? If so, by whom were those statements made, and what were they?

Answer. Governor Evans stated that it was in the hands of the military authorities, and he would not interfere until such times as he could hear from the east.

Question. Did any one state to the Indians at the Camp Weld council, in your hearing, that he would use his influence to bring about a treaty between them and the United States, or substantially that? If so, who made such statement?

Answer. Major Wynkoop, I think, told in council of the pledges he had made to the Indians, and, as I understood it, Colonel Chivington indorsed his actions throughout. I think Governor Evans also stated that he would do what he could to have a peace established.

Question. Did Governor Evans make the statement mentioned in your last answer to the Indians?

Answer. To the Indians through the interpreter.

Question. How did you get your understanding as to Colonel Chivington's indorsement of Major Wynkoop's cause?

Answer. From what I heard him say.

Question. Was anything said to the Indians at the Camp Weld council to the effect that Indians who had committed depredations upon the whites would have to be delivered to the whites to be punished? If so, what was it, and who made the statement?

Answer. Colonel Chivington made the remark to them that the stock would have to be given up, and the Indians who had committed the depredations punished, before a peace could be made. I do not recollect whether this was directly to the Indians or not. It might have been between himself, Colonel Shoup, and Governor Evans.

Question. At what time did the Indians who were at the Camp Weld council arrive at Fort Lyon after the council was held?

Answer. I think about the 14th of October, 1864.

Question. Did you find any Indians at Fort Lyon on your return after the Camp Weld council? If so, what was their number, and to what tribe or tribes did they belong?

Answer. There were some there belonging to the Cheyennes and Arapahoes. I do not know how many.

Question. State if you know whether Major Wynkoop gave any directions to the Indians who were at the Camp Weld council, after his return to Fort Lyon. If so, state what those directions were.

Answer. I don't know, as I was not in the council held after their arrival at Fort Lyon.

Question. If you know, state whether any Indians came into Fort Lyon after your return to that place from the Camp Weld council. If so, state the number as near as you can.

Answer. The Arapahoes came in; I think altogether five hundred and fifty-seven.

Question. At what time did the Indians come in, as stated in your last answer, and how long did they remain?

Answer. I think about ten days after my arrival there, and remained until about the 20th of November, 1864.

Question. Were there any Cheyenne Indians, who came into Fort Lyon after the Camp Weld council? If so, state the number as near as you can.

Answer. There were some came in, but cannot tell how many; perhaps fifty lodges.

Commission adjourned until 9½ a. m. to-morrow, March 4, 1865.

### TWENTY-FIRST DAY.

MARCH 4, 1865.

Commission met pursuant to adjournment. Present, all members and recorder. Proceedings of yesterday read and approved.

Cross-examination of Second Lieutenant Joseph A. Cramer, veteran battalion first Colorado cavalry, by J. M. Chivington, late colonel, &c., continued:

Question. Why did the Indians, of whom you have spoken, leave Fort Lyon on or about the 20th November, 1864?

*Answer.* By order of the commander of the post; *i. e.*, in reference to the Cheyennes. I do not know whether the Arapahoes had any such orders or not, but think they did.

*Question.* What time did the Arapahoes leave Fort Lyon?

*Answer.* About the same time the Cheyennes did.

*Question.* Do you know of the commander at Fort Lyon taking any steps to disarm the Indians at Fort Lyon at any time after the Camp Weld council?

*Answer.* Yes.

*Question.* What were the steps taken by him?

*Answer.* Ordered the Indians to give up their arms, and sent one of the officers at Fort Lyon down to their camp to take them.

*Question.* Did the Indians comply with such order, and give up their arms?

*Answer.* They gave up some; I don't know how many.

*Question.* State if you know whether the arms given up by the Indians were ever returned to them by the commander at Fort Lyon. If so, when were they returned?

*Answer.* I do not know of their being returned.

*Question.* Do you know anything as to the commander at Fort Lyon making any demand for stock alleged to have been stolen by the Indians? If so, state what you know.

*Answer.* The demand was made, and all the stock in their possession then was given up.

*Question.* How much stock was given up, as stated in your last answer?

*Answer.* I do not know.

*Question.* State as nearly as you can the number of animals given up.

*Answer.* I have no idea at all about it.

*Question.* State as nearly as you can the number of adult males among the Indians who came in and camped near Fort Lyon.

*Answer.* About one-fifth of the whole number, I should judge.

*Question.* State if you know whether there were any Dog soldiers among the Indians who came in and camped near Fort Lyon. If so, what was the number of Dog soldiers?

*Answer.* I do not know of any being there.

*Question.* How were the Indians subsisted while at Fort Lyon?

*Answer.* The officers at the post made up a contribution for the Cheyennes, and prisoners' rations were issued to the Arapahoes by the commander of the post or Indian agents.

*Question.* How long did Major Wynkoop remain in command at Fort Lyon after the Camp Weld council?

*Answer.* From ten to twenty days after my arrival at Fort Lyon.

*Question.* By whom was he succeeded?

*Answer.* Major Scott J. Anthony, first cavalry of Colorado.

*Question.* Do you know anything of the Indians at Fort Lyon being fired upon by the soldiers while at that post? If so, state what you know.

*Answer.* There was one fired upon by one of the guard, as she did not halt when told to.

*Question.* Did Major Anthony make any statement in your hearing on or about the 28th of November, 1864, as to whether he joined Colonel Chivington's command voluntarily or in obedience to orders? If so, what statement did he make?

*Answer.* He stated that Colonel Chivington wanted him to go; but I do not recollect whether he said he ordered him or not, but think he did not order him. I think he said Colonel Chivington said he did not feel authorized to issue any orders in regard to troops situated at Fort Lyon.

*Question.* Did any person or persons state to you the object of Colonel Chivington's expedition on or about the 28th of November, 1864? If so, who made such statements, and what were they?

Answer. Major Anthony made a statement in regard to the object of the expedition, and that the object of the expedition was to go to the Indian camp, take the stock, and kill the Indians who had committed depredations the previous winter, spring, and summer. To save Black Kettle and his band, and to go to the Sioux Indian camp on the Smoky Hill.

Question. Did Colonel Chivington, at any time prior to the battle of Sand creek, state to you the object of his expedition?

Answer. I heard him say he was in favor of killing all the Indians he came to.

Question. Do you know anything of a messenger being sent from Fort Lyon at or about the 27th or 28th of November, 1864, to Little Raven or his band of Indians, to inform him or them of the presence of Colonel Chivington's command in that vicinity? If so, state what you know?

Answer. I do not know anything about it. This is the first time I heard of such a thing.

Question. Were all the Indians attacked by Colonel Chivington's command on or about the 29th of November, 1864, at any time encamped at Fort Lyon?

Answer. No; there were but very few of them.

Question. What is the course of Sand creek at the place where the battle took place on the 29th of November, 1864?

Answer. About east and west.

Question. On which bank of the creek was the Indian village located?

Answer. On the north bank.

Question. State as near as you can the number of Indians there at the time the fight began, on the 29th of November, 1864.

Answer. About five hundred I should judge.

Question. How many lodges were there? State as near as you can.

Answer. About one hundred. I was told by a man that counted them, there were one hundred or one hundred and three.

Question. To what battalion or military organization did your company belong?

Answer. To the Fort Lyon battalion, commanded by Major Anthony.

Question. Did you receive any orders from Major Anthony, or any other field officer, after the battle began, and before the termination thereof? If so, what were those orders?

Answer. I received orders from Major Anthony to move my company to the left, to the bank of the creek, and there remain until further orders, so as to be out of danger of the fire from Colonel Chivington's command.

Question. State how long after the battle began you received the order mentioned in your last answer.

Answer. But a few minutes.

Question. Did you receive any other orders than that you have mentioned? If so, from whom, and how long after the battle began?

Answer. I received an order from Mr. Gill to burn the Indian village. I received an order from Colonel Chivington to furnish four or five men as messengers back to Fort Lyon or the train. Was hallooed at by some one in the third regiment battery to get out of the road, as they were going to open fire. In the afternoon received an order from Major Anthony to go with my company back to the train. The order of Mr. Gill was received half an hour after the battle began. The order from Colonel Chivington a little before, or about the time the battle closed. The order from Major Anthony about two hours after the fight.

Question. Did you move from the position which you assumed in compliance with Major Anthony's order, first received by you, during the progress of the fight? If so, by whose order did you move?

Answer. I did move from the position. I was hallooed at by some one, (I don't know whether it was an order or not,) to get out of the road, as they were going to fire with the battery.

Question. On which bank of the creek did you first take position after the battle began?

Answer. On the north.

Question. How long did you remain on the north bank of the creek?

Answer. During the fight.

Question. How far did you move from the position first assumed by you, during the fight, and in what direction?

Answer. Up the creek perhaps three or four miles.

Question. How far along the line of the creek did the battle extend?

Answer. Perhaps three or four miles.

Question. Did the men of your company remain in rank, and effect their movements as a military organization throughout the fight?

Answer. They did not.

Question. How long after the battle began did the men of your company remain in rank?

Answer. From one half to one hour.

Question. Did the men of Colonel Chivington's command remain in rank, and conduct the battle in squadrons, companies, battalions, or regiments, throughout the battle, or in a disorderly manner?

Answer. I should call it a disorderly manner.

Question. What were the positions respectively of those bodies of soldiers of whom you have spoken as being endangered by each other's fire?

Answer. On the opposite banks of the creek, nearly opposite each other, and but two hundred or three hundred yards apart, and in no regular order, all appearing to do as they thought best.

Question. Did the bodies of soldiers of whom you have spoken as being under each other's fire assume those positions in ranks and by companies, or in a disorderly manner?

Answer. In a disorderly manner; and partially by companies.

Question. State if you know whether they assumed those positions by order of any field officer, or otherwise.

Answer. I do not know.

Question. At how many different times during the progress of the battle did you see soldiers under the fire of other soldiers, and what was the number of soldiers so under the fire of other soldiers, and how long did they remain in that position? State as nearly as you can.

Answer. After the first hour nearly all the command was in that position throughout the fight.

Question. Upon which side of the creek did John Smith attempt to make his escape in the manner stated by you in your direct examination?

Answer. On the north side.

Question. To what company, battalion or regiment did the soldiers belong who cried out, "shoot the son of a bitch?"

Answer. I should judge, from the third regiment, as it came from our rear.

Question. To what company, regiment, or battalion did the soldiers belong who fired on John Smith and the man with the white flag?

Answer. I should judge from the third regiment, as I saw none of our battalion firing at the time.

Question. What was the position of the third regiment at the time that John Smith and the man with the white flag attempted to approach the command?

Answer. To our right and rear; one battalion of it was across the creek.

Question. On what bank of the creek was the third regiment at that time?

Answer. Part of it on the north and part on the south bank.

Question. Upon which bank of the creek were the men who fired on Smith and the man with the white flag?

Answer. On the north bank I should judge.

254

Question. Upon which bank of the creek was George Pierce at the time he was shot?

Answer. On the north bank.

Question. How far were you from the place where he fell at the time he was shot?

Answer. Fifty or sixty yards.

Question. What efforts did he make to save Smith that led to his being shot?

Answer. He rode his horse around Smith so as to prevent soldiers from shooting in that direction.

Question. When did you return to the battle-field after the battle was ended?

Answer. We were then on the battle-field.

Question. At what time did you leave the battle-field after the battle was ended?

Answer. Between 3 and 4 o'clock.

Question. Did you return to the battle-field after that time? If so, when?

Answer. I did not return.

Question. At what time did you ride over the field after the battle was ended?

Answer. On my way back to the Indian village.

Question. Did you ride over the entire field after the battle was ended?

Answer. I did not.

Question. Over what portion of the field did you pass?

Answer. Nearly all of it; through the centre, down the creek.

Question. How did you pass along the creek in the manner stated in your last answer?

Answer. I stated the whole length from the upper end of the battle-ground to the Indian village.

Commission adjourned until 2 p. m. this day.

*Two p. m.*—Commission met pursuant to adjournment. Present, all members and recorder.

Cross-examination of Second Lieutenant Joseph A. Cramer by J M. Chivington, continued:

Question. State, if you know, whether those Indians who escaped from the Sand Creek battle-field were men or squaws, and to which sex the majority belonged.

Answer. They were men, squaws, and children; the majority of them were squaws and children.

Question. State, if you know, when Major Wynkoop gave Black Kettle instructions as to signals to be used by him.

Answer. The only kind I know anything about was on our Smoky Hill trip; heard that he gave some instructions at Fort Lyon, after our return from Denver.

Question. Who, if any one, gave the white persons who were in the Indian camp at Sand creek permission to go there?

Answer. Major Anthony, I understood; also the Indian agent, Major Colley.

Question. In what military district was Fort Lyon and the place where Major Wynkoop held the council with the Indians on the Smoky Hill and the battle-field of Sand creek at the various times when the events you have mentioned took place?

Answer. District of the Upper Arkansas.

Question. Who was in command of that district at those times?

Answer. Major General Blunt part of the time and Major Henning.

Question. Do you know anything as to any of the troops at Fort Lyon during the summer or fall of 1864 being ordered to assist the Cheyennes and Arapahoes in fighting the Ute Indians?

Answer. No.

Ex. Doc. 26——5

Question. Do you know anything as to troops at Fort Lyon going out to assist Arapahoes or Cheyennes against the Ute Indians?

Answer. No.

Question. Do you state that Captain Cree stated in your presence that he was acting under orders from Colonel Chivington in killing prisoners in his possession?

Answer. I did. After stating the circumstances of the killing of those prisoners, he then said he was acting under orders from Colonel Chivington.

Question. Do you know anything as to officers of Major Wynkoop's expedition giving whiskey to Indians while out on the expedition to the Smoky Hill? If so, state what you know.

Answer. I do not.

Question. State, if you know, whether whiskey or other intoxicating liquor was used by officers of Major Wynkoop's expedition while out upon that expedition. If so, state whether the same was used freely or otherwise.

(Question objected to by Lieutenant Colonel Samuel F. Tappan for the same reason objection was made to a similar question, made during the cross-examination of Captain Silas S. Soule.

Objection sustained by the commission.)

Question. What was your means of knowledge as to stock and other property taken at Sand creek having been stolen by men and officers of the third regiment?

Answer. What I heard reported and what I saw.

Question. From whom did you hear reports and what were those reports respecting such stock and other property?

Answer. I can't tell who I heard them from. One report was that one of the officers of the third regiment, I think a captain, had sold quite a number of the ponies, giving a bill of sale for the property, and that the officers and men on their road to Denver were constantly running off stock, and leaving it at ranches along the route, and a good deal was run off after arriving at Denver.

Question. If you can do so, give the name of the officer or officers of the third regiment concerning whom you heard such report.

Answer. Captain Baxter was one who I heard had a lot of this stock, and that Captain J. J. Johnson, who had the stock in charge, knew of its being run off.

Question. What did you see which led you to believe that such stock and other property had been stolen?

Answer. I saw some of the stock.

Question. Where did you see such stock, and in whose possession did you see it?

Answer. I do not know in whose possession; I saw it on my road from Fort Lyon to Denver, and reported the fact to Colonel Moonlight, commanding district.

Question. At what time did you see it, and how much did you see?

Answer. I saw it in the month of January, 1863; I probably saw from twenty to fifty head.

Question. Where was the stock when you saw it?

Answer. On the Arkansas and Fountain-qui-bouit.

Cross-examination of Second Lieutenant Joseph A. Cramer by J. M. Chivington, closed.

Re-examination of Second Lieutenant Joseph A. Cramer by the commission:

Question. Was Major Wynkoop at the time he started for Indian camp on the Smoky Hill in command of the post and all the troops at Fort Lyon?

Answer. He was.

Question. In what department and district was Fort Lyon at that time?

Answer. Department of Kansas, district of the Upper Arkansas.

Question. State the distance from Fort Lyon to department and district head-quarters.

Answer. About three hundred and fifty miles to district headquarters, and about four hundred and fifty or five hundred miles to department headquarters; district headquarters was at Fort Riley; department headquarters at Fort Leavenworth, Kansas.

Question. State the facilities for communicating at that time with department and district headquarters, and the time necessary to transmit a letter to each and return.

Answer. The facilities were very poor, as we had only a weekly mail, and would take about a month to hear from department headquarters and about three weeks from district headquarters.

Question. Did Black Kettle in council claim that the Dog soldiers of his tribe were under his control?

Answer. He admitted it indirectly by saying that he had been unable to control all of them, and would be unless a treaty was made.

Question. At the time the Indians commenced loading their guns and stringing their bows in camp on Smoky Hill, were the chiefs in council with Major Wynkoop and other officers?

Answer. They were.

Question. Did the chiefs at the time make any efforts to prevent an outbreak or attack by the warriors?

Answer. I do not know, as I was absent from the council at that time.

Question. Did you consider the actions of the Indians while in Major Wynkoop's camp on the Smoky Hill as manifesting a hostile or mischievous spirit?

(J. M. Chivington respectfully objects to the question for the reason that it seeks to draw from the witness his conclusion as to the acts of the Indian chiefs. Witnesses are called upon to testify respecting facts, not to give opinions. Objection sustained.)

Question. Do you know where the white captives were at the time of the council on the Smoky Hill?

Answer. I do not.

Question. Did Governor Evans tell the Indian chiefs in council that he had power to make peace with them?

Answer. I do not recollect whether he did or not.

Question. In the council in Denver or Camp Weld, (held by Governor Evans and others with the Indian chiefs,) was any person appointed as secretary and instructed to keep a record of the proceedings?

Answer. Not that I know of.

Question. Did Colonel Chivington, in the council held at Camp Weld with certain Indian chiefs, make any statements that were interpreted to the Indians?

Answer. He did, I think.

Question. State as nearly as you can the number of warriors in Black Kettle's camp at the time of the attack upon it by Colonel Chivington.

Answer. I do not think there were over one hundred.

Question. State as near as you can the number of warriors killed at the attack upon Black Kettle's camp by Colonel Chivington.

Answer. Probably not over fifty warriors.

Question. State in what capacity Mr. Gill acted, and by what authority he gave you an order to burn the village of Black Kettle, on Sand creek?

Answer. He gave me the order as coming from Colonel Chivington. I do not know in what capacity he was acting. He acted as though he was an aid or assistant.

Question. Were the officers and men who accompanied Major Wynkoop to the Smoky Hill ordered by him to go?

Answer. They were.

257

Question. State if you know of any field officer at Sand creek endeavoring to rally the men from under each other's fire.

Answer. There was none that I know of.

Re-examination of second Lieutenant Joseph A. Cramer, veteran battalion first Colorado cavalry, closed.

Commissioned adjourned until 9½ o'clock a. m. Monday, March 6th, 1865.

### TWENTY-SECOND DAY.

MARCH 6, 1865.

Commission met pursuant to adjournment. Present, all members and recorder. Proceedings of yesterday read and approved with the following amendments : On page 260, first answer to first question, add the following :

" At that time Lieutenant Hardin was forming the men just outside the council, facing towards the council, looking towards the Indians, as if he was going to fire on the chiefs in council. At the time I ordered the men to disperse and keep near the wagons, I believed it to be necessary so to do to prevent a fight with the Indians. Immediately after my actions in regard to the case, I reported what I had done to Major Wynkoop, and I think he approved my actions."

On page 249, answer to last question, add the following :

" When we were first ordered to the front to drive in the Indian stock, a man appeared on the hill, about half a mile south of the village and south of the creek, having a white flag, which he was waving over his head. He was fired upon. By whom I do not know, and I do not know what became of him."

JAMES P. BECKWITH called in by the commission to give evidence.

J. M. Chivington respectfully asks that the witness, James P. Beckwith, may be interrogated as to his belief in the existence of God, who rewards good and punishes evil, before he is sworn.

By COMMISSION :

Question. James P. Beckwith, do you believe in the existence of a Supreme Being, of a God, by whom truth is enjoined and falsehood punished, and do you consider the form of administering an oath as binding upon your conscience ?

Answer. I do.

The oath being administered according to law, in presence of J. M. Chivington, late colonel first Colorado cavalry, James P. Beckwith testified as follows :

Question. Your full name, age, and residence ?

Answer. James Pierson Beckwith. I reside in this city at present. I am in my 69th year.

Question. How long have you resided in what is now known as Colorado Territory ?

Answer. Off and on for forty-nine years. Not in this Territory that long.

Question. Did you accompany Colonel Chivington's command to Sand creek last November ?

Answer. Yes. I started with Colonel Shoup as guide and interpreter ; afterwards Colonel Chivington overtook us, and, I think, assumed command.

Question. Were you present at Sand creek at the time of the attack upon Black Kettle's camp, by Colonel Chivington ?

Answer. Yes, I was present.

Question. Previous to the attack on Black Kettle's village, did you hear Colonel Chivington give any orders or make any remarks to his command ?

Answer. Yes.

Question. What orders did he give, and what remarks did he make to his command ?

Answer. His remark, when he halted us in the middle of Sand creek, was this : " Men, strip for action." He also said, " I don't tell you to kill all ages and sex, but look back on the plains of the Platte, where your mothers, fathers, brothers, sisters have been slain, and their blood saturating the sands on the Platte."

Question. How many lodges did the village of Black Kettle contain at the time of the atttack ?

Answer. I can't tell. I did not count them.

Question. State as near as you can the number of lodges at the time of the attack ?

Answer. From eighty to one hundred, as near as I could guess from the look of them. I did not count them.

Question. State as near as you can of what tribes Black Kettle's camp was composed ?

Answer. Of the Cheyennes and Arapahoes.

Question. Are you acquainted with the manners and customs of the Cheyennes and Arapahoes ?

Answer. Perfectly.

Question. State as nearly as you can the number of Indians of the Cheyennes and Arapahoes usually assigned to each lodge in their winter camps ?

(J. M. Chivington objects to the question because it does not apprear that the witness has any knowledge of the subject-matter of the inquiry, and because he is not asked to give his knowledge, but merely to state as nearly as he can. A person having no knowledge of the subject might answer the question truthfully, and yet the answer would be of no value as testimony.

Objection overruled.)

Answer. I could not, as I have not been with them for the last twelve or fourteen years. I mean I have done no business or trading with them for that length of time.

Question. During the last fourteen years have you passed through the Cheyennes or Arapahoes villages ?

Answer. Yes. Have been in them frequently since.

Question. Have you any acquaintance with the chiefs of the Cheyennes and Arapahoes, and their people ?

Answer. Yes.

Question. Describe an Indian lodge.

Answer. They are generally made of dressed buffalo skins. They are made in such a way that I cannot give the dimensions of them. They are made similar to the round tents. Have poles on the inside of the lodge, and two poles on the outside to turn the two wings of the lodge, to turn the smoke.

Question. State as nearly as you can the number of Indians in the village of Black Kettle at the time of the attack.

(J. M. Chivington objects to the question for the reason that it does not appear that the witness has any knowledge of the subject-matter of the inquiry.

Objection sustained.)

Question. Were there any Indians in the camp of Black Kettle at the time of the attack ? If so, state how many.

Answer. Yes, there were Indians in the camp, but how many it is impossible for me to say.

Question. At what time in the morning did the attack on Black Kettle commence ?

Answer. A little after sunrise.

Question. At what time was the attack over ?

Answer. I think it was between 2 and 3 p. m. when they ceased firing. I had not the time of day with me, but guess it was about that time.

Question. Were any Indians killed ? If so, state how many.

Answer. It is impossible for me to say how many were killed. A great many were killed, but I cannot guess within a hundred how many were killed.

Question. Were those Indians killed on Sand creek, warriors ?

Answer. There were all sexes, warriors, women, and children, and all ages, from one week old up to eighty years.

Question. What proportion of those killed were women and children ?

Answer. About two-thirds, as near as I saw.

Question. Were any of the Indians killed at Sand creek scalped, and otherwise mutilated ?

Answer. They were scalped ; that I know of. White Antelope was the only one I saw that was otherwise mutilated.

Question. Did the Indians at Sand creek, at the time of the attack, form in line of battle to resist Colonel Chivington's command ?

Answer. Not until they had been run out of their village.

Question. What did the Indians do at the time of the attack upon them by Colonel Chivington ?

Answer. They run out of the village, and formed to fight until the shells were thrown among them, and they broke and fought all over the country.

Commission adjourned until 2 p. m. this day.

*Two p. m.*—Commission met pursuant to adjournment. Present, all members and recorder.

Examination of James P. Beckwith, by the commission, in presence of J. M. Chivington, late colonel, &c., continued:

Question. Did any of the Indians make an attempt to reach Colonel Chivington's command at the time of the attack ?

Answer. Yes, one Indian.

Question. Do you know his name ? If so, state it, and what he did

Answer. The name he went by with the Indians was Spotted Antelope, and by the whites, White Antelope. He came running out to meet the command at the time the battle had commenced, holding up his hands and saying " Stop ! stop !" He spoke it in as plain English as I can. He stopped and folded his arms until shot down. I don't know whether the colonels heard it or not, as there was such a whooping and hallooing that it was hard to hear what was said.

Question. Was any attention paid to White Antelope as he advanced towards Colonel Chivington's command ?

Answer. None, only to shoot him, as I saw.

Question. Did White Antelope have anything in his hand as he advanced towards the command ?

Answer. Nothing that I saw.

Question. How near Colonel Chivington's command was White Antelope shot down ?

Answer. As near as I can guess, fifteen or twenty steps.

Question. Was White Antelope scalped and otherwise mutilated ?

Answer. Yes, both.

Question. Did you see any person engaged in scalping White Antelope ?

Answer. I did not. I saw him, though, after this had been done.

Question. State if any others advanced towards the command at the time of the attack.

Answer. Mr. Smith, the United States interpreter, was the only one I saw.

Question. What was done as Mr. Smith advanced towards the command ?

Answer. As close as I recollect I think he spoke to Colonel Chivington, and I cannot recollect what he said. I think Colonel Chivington told him to jump on the artillery carriage, and remain there, which he obeyed as sure as you are born.

Question. Did any of Colonel Chivington's command fire upon John Smith ?

Answer. Not that I saw. The reports were so, but I did not see anybody fire at him.

260

SAND CREEK MASSACRE.

Question. Did you see any of Colonel Chivington's command in the act of scalping the Indians at Sand creek?

Answer. I did; I saw several men scalping, but I know not their names; but there is only one man that I know who scalped an Indian I killed myself.

Question. Did you see any officer of Colonel Chivington's command scalping the Indians at Sand creek?

Answer. No.

Question. Did any officer or officers of Colonel Chivington's command make any efforts to prevent scalping or mutilating of the dead at Sand creek?

Answer. None that I saw or heard. I only saw White Antelope that had been mutilated otherwise than by scalping.

Question. Did Colonel Chivington's command take any prisoners? If so, state what was done with them.

Answer. The prisoners taken was one woman rescued by Charley Antoby, turned over to me, and Colonel William Bent's son Charles (half-breed Cheyenne) begged of me to save his life, and him and the squaw together. I put him in an ambulance with Captain Talburt, who was wounded; sent him to the hospital with Captain Talburt, and told him to stay there until I came; then I took the squaw with a wounded soldier by the name of Metcalf, and got them safe into camp. I did not go on the battle-field until next morning. Charley Bent went off with his brother that night with the ponies.

Question. Were any others taken prisoners than those you have mentioned?

Answer. Yes, there was an old squaw with two children. I do not know as they were taken prisoners, but they were found in camp that evening after the battle. There were two little girls and a boy that were taken prisoners. The oldest girl was between twelve and fourteen years old. The next was between ten and eleven, and the boy between eight and nine years of age. One of the old squaw's daughters had a finger shot off.

Question. Was there any shooting in camp after the attack upon Black Kettle's camp?

Answer. They were shooting all over the country, in camp and out of camp.

Question. Was any person shot in Colonel Chivington's camp after the battle with the Indians?

Answer. Yes.

Question. State who it was.

(J. M. Chivington objects to the question for the reason that it does not appear that the witness has any knowledge upon the subject-matter of inquiry, while the question assumes that he has such knowledge.

Objection not sustained.)

Answer. It was a half-breed, who went by the name of Jack Smith. John Smith's son. He was sitting in the lodge with me; not more than five or six feet from me, just across the lodge. There were from ten to fifteen soldiers came into the lodge at the time, and there was some person came on the outside and called to his father, John Smith. He, the old man, went out, and there was a pistol fired when the old man got out of the lodge. There was a piece of the lodge cut out where the old man went out. There was a pistol fired through this opening and the bullet entered below his right breast. He sprung forward and fell dead, and the lodge scattered, soldiers, squaws, and everything else. I went out myself; as I went out I met a man with a pistol in his hand. He made this remark to me: he said, "I am afraid the damn son of a bitch is not dead, and I will finish him." Says I, "Let him go to rest; he is dead." That is all that occurred at that time. We took him out and laid him out of doors. I do not know what they did with him afterwards.

Question. Who were in the lodge at the time Jack Smith was killed?

Answer. There was a soldier who belongs to the Colorado first and a teamster. I do not know their names, nor the company the soldier belonged to.

261

There were ten or fifteen other soldiers in the tent, but do not know what regiment or company they belonged to. Some of them belonged to the third Colorado cavalry.

Question. Do you know the name of the man you met who had the pistol?
Answer. No, I do not.

Question. Were any efforts made by the commanding officer to ascertain who had killed Jack Smith?
Answer. Not as I know of.

Question. Did you hear any threats made against the life of Jack Smith, previous to his being shot?
Answer. Yes.

Question. What were those threats and by whom made?
Answer. By whom I know not. It was made by soldiers, who said that he should not leave the camp alive.

Question. Where were the wounded taken during the fight?
Answer. They were taken back to a lodge used as a hospital.

Question. In what part of the field was the hospital established for wounded officers and soldiers?
Answer. A little east of north of where we attacked the village.

Question. How early in the fight was the hospital established at the place mentioned?
Answer. I think about three or four hours after the charge and the battery opened. It was after the village was cleaned of the Indians.

Question. Where were the Indians at the time the hospital was established?
Answer. They were beyond the village. The main portion of them were south of the village. The Indians were everywhere.

Question. Had the firing ceased in that part of the village at the time and place where the hospital was established?
Answer. Yes.

Question. Have you seen any of the Cheyennes since the day of the attack on Sand creek?
Answer. Yes.

Question. When and where did you see them?
Answer. I saw them between the 9th and 12th of January, on the White Man's fork. I went into their village in the night. The White Man's fork heads in the vicinity of the Smoky Hill. It used to be called the Box Elder by the trappers.

Question. How large a village was it?
Answer. There were about one hundred and thirty or one hundred and forty lodges. They were then travelling north.

Question. Were they all Cheyennes?
Answer. No, they were mixed up with other tribes, half-breed Cheyennes, Kiowas, and Camanche warriors. There may have been some Arapahoe lodges among them; most of the lodges were Cheyenne.

Question. Were there any chiefs among them? If so, state who they were.
Answer. There were Leg-in-the-Water, who was then acting as chief, (Black Kettle was not there,) and Little Robe, son of the old war chief who was killed at Sand creek.

Question. State what transpired while you were in the village.
(J. M. Chivington objects to the question, for the reason that it seeks to draw from the witness information which was derived from the Indians, and is therefore hearsay. Furthermore, it is sought by this question to make the proceedings at an unauthorized interview with Indians' testimony, to be considered in this investigation, when none of the parties who may be charged as military offenders were present thereat. Again, the interview between the witness and

the Indians occurred after the battle of Sand creek, and therefore it is not a proper subject for investigation under the instructions given the commission.

The commission are instructed to make such investigation as may disclose all the facts connected with the battle of Sand creek, not to inquire concerning the results of that battle.)

Commission was cleared for discussion. Commission adjourned until 9½ a. m. to-morrow, March 7, 1865.

TWENTY-THIRD DAY.

MARCH 7, 1865.

Commission met pursuant to adjournment. Present, all members and recorder.

Proceedings of yesterday read and approved.

The objections by J. M. Chivington, against obtaining from the witness testimony as to what transpired in the camp of the Indians while he was present, are sustained so far as to rule out the question, and all information referring to the probable results of the affair of Sand creek. But in order to do justice to all parties, and in consequence of not being able to procure the attendance to this commission of the surviving Indians who were attacked while in camp on Sand creek, it becomes necessary to question the witness in reference to statements, admissions, &c., made by the Indians to him (the witness) in reference to their (the Indians) understanding of the agreement between them and the military authorities at Fort Lyon, and their (the Indians) admissions to the recapture of stock taken by Colonel Chivington from them at Sand creek, receiving it as information essential to the object of this commission, which is to obtain all facts, and do justice to all parties.

Examination of James P. Beckwith by the commission, in presence of J. M. Chivington, continued:

Question. While in the camp of the Indians on White Man's fork, did you have any conversation with them in reference to Sand creek?

Answer. Yes.

Question. What was said?

(J. M. Chivington respectfully objects to the question. The statements of Indians are never received as evidence even when the Indians are personally present, except in cases where it is specially authorized by statute. In other words, it requires an express congressional enactment to render an Indian a competent witness, as in cases of violation of the Indian intercourse laws. The instructions given the commission do not authorize them to receive hearsay testimony as coming from Indians or whites. The latitude given to the commission is as to the facts concerning which evidence may be received, not as to what shall or shall not be considered evidence. The commission may receive evidence as to any fact deemed material, but all evidence received must be such as is recognized by law as evidence. Objection overruled by a majority of the commission.)

Answer. I went into the lodge of Leg-in-the-Water. When I went in he raised up and he said, "Medicine Calf, what have you come here for; have you fetched the white man to finish killing our families again?" I told him I had come to talk to him; call in your council. They came in a short time afterwards, and wanted to know what I had come for. I told them I had come to persuade them to make peace with the whites, as there was not enough of them to fight the whites, as they were as numerous as the leaves of the trees. "We know it," was the general response of the council. But what do we want to live for? The white man has taken our country, killed all of our game; was not satisfied with that, but killed our wives and children. Now no peace. We want to go and meet our families in the spirit land. We loved the whites

263

until we found out they lied to us, and robbed us of what we had. We have raised the battle-axe until death.

They asked me then why I had come to Sand creek with the soldiers to show them the country. I told them if I had not come the white chief would have hung me. "Go and stay with your white brothers, but we are going to fight till death." I obeyed orders and came back, willing to play quits. There was nothing mentioned about horses or anything that transpired on the battle-field, with the exception of their wives and children.

Question. While in the camp, was anything said in reference to the chief Black Kettle?

Answer. Yes.

Question. What was said?

Answer. That he had gone over to the half-breed Cheyenne village, and Sioux also, to raise the warriors of those two tribes to fight the whites when grass came, (meaning spring.)

Question. You say you are acquainted with the manners and customs of the Cheyennes and Arapahoes. State what is the custom of these Indians in their treatment of women and children taken in battle from their enemies.

(J. M. Chivington objects to the question. Objection not sustained by a majority of the commission.)

Answer. The children are treated kindly; the women are generally violated.

Question. Do they often kill, scalp, and otherwise mutilate women or children taken prisoners by them in battle?

(J. M. Chivington objects to the question. Objection sustained.)

Direct examination of James P. Beckwith closed.

Cross-examination of James P. Beckwith, by J. M. Chivington:

Question. With what company, battalion, and regiment of Colonel Chivington's command were you at the time of the attack on Black Kettle's camp?

Answer. I was with a portion of the third regiment (100-days men.) I could not tell what company or battalion I was with.

Question. Were you under the command of any officer? If so, of whom?

Answer. I was under the command of Colonel Chivington and Colonel Shoup; no other officer had command over me.

Question. Did you participate in the charge made by the third regiment on the Indian village at Sand Creek? If so, what position did you occupy in that charge?

Answer. Yes; I charged with the foremost; I was by the side of Colonel Chivington himself for a little ways; his horse was fleeter than mine.

Question. Who made the noise and confusion of which you speak as occurring at the time of the charge?

Answer. Both officers and men, as I heard, with the exception of Colonels Chivington and Shoup. I could hear them occasionally order the men to be steady. This was while I was in hearing of them, which was but a short time.

Question. Could you hear distinctly all that was said and done at the time that the charge was made?

Answer. No.

Question. How far was White Antelope from you at the time he shouted to the commander to stop?

Answer. He was from fifteen to twenty steps, when I heard him the first time; he was advancing very fast towards the command.

Question. How many feet was White Antelope from you at the time he shouted to the command to stop?

Answer. About sixty feet, probably; that is as near as I can judge.

Question. How many feet was White Antelope from the command at the time he was shot?

Answer. I can't say.

Question. How far did White Antelope advance towards the command after you first saw him, and before he was shot?

Answer. Some three or four paces, and stopped.

Question. Where was he when you first saw him?

Answer. On the outside of the lodges.

Question. How far outside of the lodges?

Answer. I cannot say.

Question. State as nearly as you can.

Answer. I can't, because I don't know; my attention was drawn too far at that time.

Question. How did you recognize him when you first saw him?

Answer. I was intimately acquainted with him.

Question. Do you know of any orders or directions being given by any officer respecting Jack Smith after the battle?

Answer. None.

Question. Do you know of any order being given respecting the lodge in which you say Jack Smith was killed?

Answer. Yes.

Question. What was that order?

Answer. Colonel Shoup himself ordered me to stay there and protect the squaws and John Smith's property; and also sent me a sergeant from some company; I don't know who he was.

Question. How long had Jack Smith been in that lodge at the time you say he was killed?

Answer. He was taken about 10 o'clock in the morning of the day of the battle, and remained in the lodge until early in the morning after sunrise the next day.

Question. Was he or was he not under guard?

Answer. He was not under guard.

Question. Did he remain constantly in the lodge after he fell into the hands of Colonel Chivington's command until he was shot?

Answer. No.

Question. Was the man whom you saw with the pistol after passing out from the lodge an officer or private?

Answer. A private; he had on private's clothing.

Question. How far is it from Denver to the place where you met the Indians on the White Man's fork?

Answer. About eighty-five or ninety miles. It may be a hundred.

Question. When and from where did you start to go there?

Answer. I started from here on the 9th or 10th of the month of January.

Question. Did any one suggest the expediency of going there? If so, who?

Answer. None.

Question. How did you ascertain where you should go in order to find the Indians?

Answer. Because I am acquainted with the country, and from reports, and what I could hear of the depredations they were doing on the road.

Question. How long were you in making the trip?

Answer. Six days and a half going and coming.

Question. Did you go directly from Denver to the place where you met the Indians on White Man's fork?

Answer. Yes, as straight a course as I could go; I struck the trail six or seven miles above where I found the village.

Question. How long were you in going there?

Answer. A little over three days.

Question. Where did you hear that they had committed depredations which led you to suspect the Indians were where you found them?

Answer. I heard it in town here and saw it in the paper.
Question. Where were these depredations committed?
Answer. Down the Platte.
Question. How far down the Platte?
Answer. I don't know; can't say.
Question. What were the depredations of which you have spoken?
Answer. Killing white men and taking their property.
Question. How long before you went out to meet the Indians were these depredations committed?
Answer. I know not. It was an every-day occurrence, from reports.
Question. Are Indians usually found upon White Man's fork, soon after they have committed depredations on the Platte?
Answer. I don't know. They were moving north at the time.
Question. Did you not say you were led to suppose that the Indians were on White Man's fork, from the depredations which had been committed?
Answer. Yes.

Commission adjourned until 2 p. m. this day.

*Two p. m.*—Commission met pursuant to adjournment. Present, all members and recorder.

Cross-examination of James P. Beckwith by J. M. Chivington, late colonel &c., continued:

Question. Where have you resided since the first of January last?
Answer. With the exception of the trip I made out to the Indians, I have resided here in Denver.
Question. Did any one accompany you on the trip to the White Man's fork?
Answer. No.
Question. Is there any enmity existing between yourself and Colonel Chivington?
Answer. None, so help me God.
Question. Have you not used expressions of hostility towards Colonel Chivington within the six months last past?
Answer. Not to my knowledge.
Question. To what race do you belong—the white, black, or Indian?
(Objection to the question by Lieutenant Colonel Samuel F. Tappan, president of the commission. Objection sustained by the commission.)
Question. Were you a chief among the Crow Indians?
Answer. Yes.

Cross-examination of James P. Beckwith by J. M. Chivington closed.
Question raised by recorder. The commission was closed for discussion.

Commission adjourned until 9½ a. m. to-morrow, March 8, 1865.

### TWENTY-FOURTH DAY.

MARCH 8, 1865.

Commission met pursuant to adjournment. Present, all members and recorder.
Proceedings of yesterday read and approved.

Commission adjourned until 2 p. m. this day.

*Two p. m.*—Commission met pursuant to adjournment. Present, all members and recorder.

N. D. SNYDER called in by the commission to give evidence.

The oath being administered according to law, he (Snyder) testified as follows:
Question. Your full name, age, and occupation?
Answer. Naman D. Snyder; nineteen years old; occupation a soldier.
Question. How long have you been in the service as a soldier?

SAND CREEK MASSACRE.

Answer. I enlisted on the thirteenth of December, 1863.
Question. To what regiment and company did you belong in November, 1864?
Answer. Company D of the first regiment Colorado cavalry.
Question. Where was your company stationed during the latter part of November, 1864?
Answer. At Fort Lyon.
Question. Where was your company on the morning of the twenty-ninth of November, 1864?
Answer. Out with Chivington, I believe.
Question. Was your company in the engagement with Indians on Sand creek at that time?
Answer. I don't recollect.
Question. Were you present at the attack on Black Kettle's camp on Sand creek?
Answer. Yes.
Question. At the time of the attack on Black Kettle's camp, did you see any American flag? If so, state where you saw it.
(Colonel John M. Chivington objects to the question. Objection overruled by the commission.)
Answer. Yes, at the lower end of the village. The west end.
Question. Were any Indians killed during the attack upon Black Kettle's camps on Sand creek?
Answer. Yes.
Question. Was anything more done to the Indians? If so, state what it was.
Answer. Nothing more done to the Indians on Sand creek as I saw.
Question. Have you been to Sand creek since?
Answer. Yes.
Question. State the time you went to Sand creek.
Answer. About the fourteenth of January.
Question. Who did you go to Sand creek with?
Answer. Captain Soule, and Captain Boothe, and thirty men of D and K companies.
Question. What did you see there?
Answer. Dead Indians and a desolate looking place.
Question. How many dead Indians did you see at Sand creek on your second viist?
Answer. I saw ninety-eight.
Question. Were the Indians killed at Sand creek in November all warriors?
Answer. No.
Question. What were they?
Answer. Squaws and pappooses, besides the warriors.
Question. What proportion of the whole number killed at Sand creek were women and children?
Answer. Half that were there, as near as I can guess.
Question. Do you know of any scalping being done by Colonel Chivington's command at Sand creek?
(John M. Chivington respectfully objects to the question. Objection overruled by the commission.)
Answer. Yes.
Question. State how you know of scalping being done at Sand creek?
Answer. By seeing it done.
Question. State who you saw engaged in scalping.
Answer. The boys in the third regiment; also the boys in the first regiment.
Question. Were the women and children scalped?

267

(John M. Chivington respectfully objects to the question. Objection overruled by the commission.)
Answer. Yes.
Question. Were any of the Indians otherwise mutilated at Sand creek?
(J. M. Chivington most respectfully objects to the question. Objection overruled by the commission.)
Answer. Yes.
Question. By whom were any otherwise mutilated?
Answer. By a company of Mexicans.
Question. Were the Mexicans a portion of Colonel Chivington's command?
Answer. Yes.
Question. Did any officer of the command attempt to prevent scalping and mutilating?
(J. M. Chivington objects to the question. Objection overruled by the commission.)
Answer. Not that I know of.
Question. Were those you saw engaged in scalping and mutilating the dead, private soldiers?
Answer. Yes.
Question. Were all the Indians killed at Sand creek killed by Colonel Chivington's command?
Answer. Yes.
Question. Were any prisoners taken by Colonel Chivington's command at Sand creek?
Answer. Yes.
Question. How many, and what was done with them?
Answer. To the best of my recollection there were three taken and brought to Denver.
Question. How many dead Indians did you see on the day of the battle at Sand creek? State as near as you can.
Answer. Two hundred.
Direct examination of Naman D. Snyder, a soldier, closed.

Cross-examination of Naman D. Snyder, by J. M. Chivington, late colonel, &c.:
Question. You state, at the time of the attack on the Indian village at Sand creek, you saw an American flag at the western end of the village. Was that the end from which you approached the village? If not, please state from what end you approached the village, and how far this flag was from you?
Answer. We approached the village at the end the flag was. The flag was about twenty-five yards from where we first formed in line.
Question. Did you see the soldier when he placed the flag where you saw it?
Answer. No. I saw him place the white flag.
Question. Can you name any person that you saw scalping Indians?
Answer. I can name no one person.
Question. Was this scalping that you saw done during the fight or after the battle was over?
Answer. During the fight.
Question. How do you know that the men belonged to Colonel Chivington's command, that you saw scalping the Indians?
Answer. Because they were under his command.
Question. Did you ever see Colonel Chivington give them any orders?
Answer. No.
Question. How do you know the Mexicans belonged to Colonel Chivington's command?
Answer. Because they were there at the fight, and under his command as a company.

Question. Do you know that the Mexicans were soldiers, and that Colonel Chivington had a right to command them?

Answer. Yes.

Question. How do you know it?

Answer. I know it because they were raised as a company and brought down there under or with his command.

Question. Was there not a number of citizens accompanying Colonel Chivington's command, over whom Colonel Chivington had no control?

Answer. Not that I know of.

Question. On your second visit to Sand creek, with Captain Soule, did not Captain Soule send a number of his men ahead of his command to Sand creek, with instructions to mutilate the dead, &c.?

Answer. No.

Question. How long did you remain on the field the day the battle of Sand creek was fought?

Answer. From sunrise to two o'clock.

Question. What part of the field were you on? Please describe the field and the place you occupied, with the company to which you belonged.

Answer. Company D was on the southwest part, on west side of the creek, after the battle began. We were first formed on the east side of the creek.

Question. Were you not a great distance, all the time during the fight, from where the fighting was done?

Answer. No.

Question. Were you with company D all the time during the fight at Sand creek?

Answer. No.

Question. Where were you when not with company D?

Answer. With company K.

Question. How many Indians did company K kill in the fight?

Answer. I could not say, not knowing.

Question. Did not Captain Soule direct you to go ahead of his command, on your second visit to Sand creek, and tie up a squaw with your lariat, in such a position that Captain Boothe, inspector, would think she had been hung?

(Objection to question, by Lieutenant Colonel Samuel F. Tappan, president of the commission. Objection sustained.)

*To the president and members of the military commission convened pursuant to Special Orders No. 23:*

John M. Chivington respectfully represents that many of the witnesses whom he desired should testify in his behalf before the commission reside or may now be found in the vicinity of Denver, where the commission is now in session. That some of these witnesses are temporarily in Denver, and do not intend to remain here but a short time. Being informed that it is the intention of the members of the commission to adjourn at an early day and reassemble at Fort Lyon, I request that before such adjournment I may have an opportunity to introduce such witnesses as I may be able to find in the vicinity of Denver, and thus obtain their testimony. As there are no charges or specifications to be sustained by the government, or negatived by the accused in this proceeding, the reasons for requiring all testimony on behalf of the government to be first introduced lose their force. It matters not in what order the testimony may be introduced, since no portion of it can be regarded as rebutting to any other portion. I may be permitted to suggest, further, that much time and expense may be saved to the government by procuring all the testimony obtainable in this vicinity at the present session of the commission, so that it may not be necessary to reassemble at this place at some future day. If it is thought best the testimony taken on my behalf as suggested may be incorporated with such other testimony as may be taken on my behalf after the whole shall have been taken.

Respectfully submitted :

J. M. CHIVINGTON.

MILITARY COMMISSION ROOMS, *March* 8, 1865.

Commission was cleared for discussion. Commission adjourned until 9 a. m. to-morrow, March 9, 1865.

TWENTY-FIFTH DAY.

MARCH 9, 1865.

Commission met pursuant to adjournment. Present, all members and recorder.

Proceedings of yesterday read, amended as follows, and approved : Page 304, third answer to read, "Yes, all but a squaw, who hung herself."

Cross-examination of Naman D. Snyder, by J. M. Chivington, continued :

Question. Has any person spoken to you in regard to the Sand creek fight? If so, what did they say to you and what were their names ?

(Objection to the question by Lieutenant Colonel Samuel F. Tappan, president of the commission. Objection sustained.)

Question. Has any person spoken to you in relation to what you would testify to before this commission in regard to the Sand creek fight? If so, what are their names and what did they say ?

(Objection to the question by Lieutenant Colonel Samuel F. Tappan, president of the commission. Objection overruled.)

Answer. There has been only one person, as I can recollect, who spoke in regard to the matter ; that was in regard to one squaw who hung herself; his name I can't tell; he asked me if there wasn't a squaw hung or not.

Question. Did not some person talk to you this morning about what you testify to, &c., before this commission ?

Answer. Not about anything but what I stated before.

Question. Did not Lieutenant Colonel Tappan talk to you about what you could testify to before this commission ?

Answer. No.

Cross-examination of Naman D. Snyder closed.

Re-examination of Naman D. Snyder :

By COMMISSION :

Question. Has any person attempted to influence you in reference to what you should testify to before this commission ?

(J. M. Chivington most respectfully objects to the question. Objection sustained.)

Question. Was the American flag displayed over Black Kettle's camp before any soldiers of Colonel Chivington's command reached the western end of the village ?

(J. M. Chivington most respectfully objects to the question. Objection overruled by the commission.)

Answer. To the best of my knowledge it was.

Question. On your second visit to Sand creek did you reach the place as soon as any of the command ?

Answer. Yes, before.

Question. Had any person been sent on in advance of Captain Booth ?

(J. M. Chivington most respectfully objects to the question. Objection overruled.)

Answer. Yes.

270

Question. You say you were the first to arrive at Sand creek; how long were you there before the arrival of Captain Booth?

Answer. About fifteen minutes.

Question. Was anything done to the dead àt Sand creek before Captain Booth arrived on the spot?

(J. M. Chivington most respectfully objects to the question. Objection overruled by the commission.)

Answer. No.

By J. M. CHIVINGTON:

Question. How do you know there was nothing done to the dead before Captain Booth arrived at Sand creek?

Answer. Because I was then in charge of the advance guard.

Question. Is this the only reason you have for stating that you know nothing was done to the dead at Sand creek before Captain Booth's arrival?

Answer. Yes.

Re-examination of Naman D. Snyder closed.

Commission rooms were cleared for discussion.

Commission adjourned until 2 p. m. this day.

*Two p. m.*—Commission met pursuant to adjournment. Present, all members and recorder.

Captain L. Mullin called in by the commission to give evidence. The oath being administered according to law, he (Captain Mullin) testified as follows:

Question. Your full name, residence, and occupation?

Answer. Linden Mullin; residence, Denver; assistant quartermaster and mustering and disbursing officer.

Question. Were you ever assistant quartermaster of the district of Colorado?

Answer. Yes.

Question. At what time were you assigned to duty as assistant quartermaster of Colorado district?

Answer. I don't recollect the time of assignment exactly; I think it was some time in May; I took possession here about the fourth of June, 1863; it was some time before that that I was assigned.

Question. How long did you continue to act as assistant quartermaster of this district?

Answer. Until September 15, 1864.

Question. Who relieved you as assistant quartermaster of this district at the time mentioned?

Answer. Captain C. L. Gorton.

Question. Was the third regiment Colorado cavalry organized and equipped during the time you acted as assistant quartermaster of this district?

Answer. A part of them.

Question. Who furnished the horses for that regiment?

Answer. I furnished a part.

Question. Where did you obtain the horses you furnished that regiment?

Answer. Bought them here in Denver, and on Boulder creek.

Question. Did you purchase them in open market or by contract?

Answer. In open market.

Question. How many horses were purchased by you for that regiment?

Answer. Seven hundred and sixty-four.

Question. What was the average cost of the horses purchased, and by whom were they inspected?

(J. M. Chivington objects to the question, for the reason that the facts for which the question calls are shown by the records of the Quartermaster General's office and by his report made in accordance with the regulations of the

Ex. Doc. 26——6

army; therefore such records and reports furnish the best evidence of those facts. Objection overruled.)

Answer. I never footed the average cost; I think it would be about two hundred and twenty-five in vouchers. They were inspected by me—not appointed, but ordered.

Question. Were the horses you purchased of the first quality?

Answer. They were not.

Question. Of what quality were they?

Answer. Some were good; some very poor as cavalry horses.

Question. Were the horses broken down or only poor in flesh?

Answer. Neither to my knowledge.

Question. Were they serviceable horses?

Answer. I considered them so at the time; I afterwards learned that some of them were constitutionally diseased.

Question. What proportion of the whole number did you afterwards learn were constitutionally diseased?

Answer. I did not learn definitely.

Question. To whom did you deliver the horses?

Answer. What I bought I delivered to companies A, B, C, D, E, and F; the balance I turned over to Captain Gorton. They were turned over between the 20th of August and the 15th of September.

Question. How many of the horses did you deliver to Captain Gorton?

Answer. I can't say definitely.

Question. Were all the horses you delivered to the third regiment purchased in open market?

Answer. They were.

Question. Did you receive any of those horses from officers of that regiment after you had invoiced them?

Answer. No.

Question. Did you furnish that regiment with transportation? If so, state how much?

Answer. I furnished the companies that were then full, for company use, six mule teams, and hired the transportation for regiment; September 3, thirty-five four mule-teams; September 6, seven four-mule teams, which were transferred to Captain Gorton September 15.

Question. Was this transportation still in the possession of that regiment at the time you were relieved by Captain Gorton?

Answer. It was still in the service of that regiment.

Question. Who furnished the forage for the third regiment after they had received the horses and transportation?

Answer. I furnished it until the 15th of September; I can't tell who furnished it afterwards.

Direct examination by the commission closed.

Cross-examination of Captain Louden Mullin by J. M. Chivington, late colonel, &c.:

Question. By whom were you ordered to purchase the horses of which you have spoken?

Answer. By Major General Curtis, through headquarters district of Colorado.

Question. What order did you receive as stated in your last answer?

Answer. I was ordered to buy in open market horses, and equip and mount the third regiment, either as soon as possible or as soon as practicable, I don't know which.

Question. Was the third regiment Colorado cavalry organized as a regiment at the time you were relieved by Captain Gorton?

Answer. I think they were; I am not certain they were mustered in at that time.

Question. State, if you know, the number of men in that regiment at that time.

Answer. I don't know ; I think about a thousand.

Question. What use was made of the transportation of which you have spoken, by the companies of the third regiment to which the same was delivered ?

Answer. They used it for hauling forage, rations, and their camp equipage, during the time I had control of them.

Question. Were there any other facilities for transportation accessible to the officers of that regiment, at the time referred to ?

Answer. No, not that I know of.

Cross-examination of Captain L. Mullin closed.

Commission adjourned until 9½ a. m. to-morrow, March 10, 1865.

### TWENTY-SIXTH DAY.

MARCH 10, 1865.

Commission met pursuant to adjournment. Present, all members and recorder.

Proceedings of yesterday read and approved. Commission adjourned until 2 o'clock this p. m.

*Two p. m.*—Commission met pursuant to adjournment. Present, all members and recorder.

The question of adjournment:

The application of John M. Chivington was then considered, and after deliberation it was decided not to comply with it at present, but to proceed without delay to Fort Lyon, and examine such witnesses as may there be introduced, and return to Denver to conclude the labors of the commission.

The commission considers this step necessary on account of the liabilities of the streams becoming at an early day much swollen, rendering travel to Fort Lyon extremely difficult ; and important witnesses are now at Fort Lyon, whose services cannot be dispensed with at that post without detriment to the public service, and their evidence is important to the object for which this commission was convened.

The recorder is instructed to notify John M. Chivington of the adjournment to Fort Lyon.

Commission adjourned, to meet again at Fort Lyon, Colorado Territory, on the 20th instant, or as soon thereafter as practicable.

### TWENTY-SEVENTH DAY.

FORT LYON, COLORADO TERRITORY,
*March* 20, 1865—10 a. m.

Commission met pursuant to adjournment. Present, all members and recorder.

Proceedings of the twenty-sixth day (March 10, 1865) read and approved.

Major E. W. WYNKOOP called in by the commission to give evidence. The oath being administered according to law, he, Major Wynkoop, testified as follows :

By the COMMISSION :

Question. What is your full name and occupation ?

Answer. Edward W. Wynkoop ; occupation a soldier.

Question. What is your rank in the army ?

Answer. Major, veteran battalion first Colorado cavalry.

273

Question. How long have you been an officer?
Answer. Since the 25th of July, 1861.
Question. Upon what duty were you in the spring and summer of 1864?
Answer. I was in command of Fort Lyon during a portion of the spring and summer.
Question. By whose order were you placed in command of Fort Lyon?
Answer. By order of Colonel Chivington, commanding district of Colorado.
Question. Did you, as commander of the post at Fort Lyon, have any dealings with any of the Indians or Indian tribes of the plains?
Answer. I had dealings officially with the Indians.
Question. State what they were.
Answer. The first dealings I had with them officially was on the 4th day of September, 1864. Three Indians were brought in to me as prisoners. Their names were One-Eye, a sub-chief of the Cheyennes, and Min-im-mie, who I believe was also a sub-chief or captain of some kind, and One-Eye's squaw. They were brought to me as prisoners. One-Eye had in his possession two letters, one addressed to Colonel William Bent, the other to Major Colley, Indian agent. He stated that they were written by a half-breed in the Cheyenne camp. They were signed by Black Kettle and other chiefs. One-Eye stated this was written by the direction of Black Kettle and other chiefs of the Arapahoe and Cheyenne tribes. The purport of the letters was, that they desired to have peace; that they had seven white prisoners in their possession whom they would deliver up if peace could be assured them, and in case we would deliver up any Indian prisoners we had in our possession. The letter stated that they thought we had some Indian prisoners in Denver. I questioned One-Eye further, and he said that the Arapahoes and Cheyennes, and forty lodges of Sioux, were congregated together on the headwaters of the Smoky Hill, at a place known as "The bunch of timber;" that they numbered about two thousand. After gaining this information, I held the Indians as prisoners and sent them to the guardhouse, and immediately commenced to make preparations for an expedition to the headwaters of the Smoky Hill, for the purpose of procuring the white prisoners. On the 6th day of September I started with one hundred and twenty-seven mounted men and two howitzers; I took with me the three Indians I held as prisoners, and another Cheyenne Indian who was living with John Vogle, who was living in the vicinity of this post. They called the Indian "The Fool." I told these Indians, whom I stated I would hold as hostages for the good faith of their tribe, that if any treachery was exhibited on the part of their tribe, I would instantly kill them. One-Eye appeared to be perfectly satisfied, and said he was willing to sacrifice his life if his tribe did not act in good faith towards me. After four days' march I came in sight of the Indians, who were located on a tributary of the Smoky Hill. I found about seven hundred or eight hundred warriors drawn up in line of battle, and judged, from their appearance at the time, that they were making hostile demonstrations. I formed my command in as good order as possible, and continued to advance towards them. The same time I sent One-Eye forward, instructing him to state to the chiefs that I had come in accordance with their letter, and in reference to the white prisoners. I still retained One-Eye's squaw, and the other Indian called "Fool." I had sent Min-im-mie off the day before with the same message to the chiefs, previous to our coming in sight of them. One-Eye returned, and told me that Black Kettle and other chiefs were willing to meet me in council. The Indians then fell back, and I advanced and took up a position on the bank of a stream, after which Black Kettle, head chief of the Cheyennes, and Left Hand, of the Arapahoes, and other chiefs of both tribes, entered my camp and a council was held. The council on the part of the Indians was composed of Black Kettle, of the Cheyennes, White Antelope, Bull Bear, Sitting Bear, and other chiefs whom I don't know. On the part of the Arapahoes were Left Hand,

Neva, Little Raven, and other chiefs whom I don't know. On our part it was composed of Captain Soule, Lieutenant Hardin, Lieutenant Cramer, Lieutenant Phillips, and myself. I commenced by showing the letters I had in my possession, purporting to have come from Black Kettle and other chiefs, and asked the chiefs of both tribes whether they indorsed those letters. They answered in the affirmative  I then addressed myself particularly to Black Kettle, through the interpreter. I told him that I had not the power to offer them terms of peace ; that I was not big enough chief; that I had come out there for negotiating with them, if possible, for the return of the white prisoners, and that I had a proposition to make to them, which was, that if they would deliver up the white prisoners they had in their hands, I would use my utmost endeavors to procure peace for them. I stated that I would take any delegation of chiefs that they might select from both tribes with me to the governor of Colorado Territory, who was also Indian superintendent, and that the fact of their having delivered up the white prisoners into my hands would in all probability assist them, it being an evidence that they were sincere. Black Kettle commenced by saying that the Arapahoes and Cheyennes—

(John H. Chivington most respectfully objects to the court receiving from Major Wynkoop as evidence, what Black Kettle and other Indians stated to Major Wynkoop in council or anywhere else, for the reason that it is hearsay and is illegal ; that Major Wynkoop can testify only to facts within his own knowledge, and not to assertions made by others.

Objection overruled by the commission.)

— had always desired to be at peace since their last treaty with the whites. He said that if they had desired to make war with the whites, they had a good opportunity of doing so when the white emigration first came to Colorado, but that a short time before, while a party of his young men were proceeding north on a hunting expedition in the neighborhood of the South Platte river, they found some loose stock on the prairie ; that they had taken them up and were about proceeding to return them to their owners, if they could be found, and while in the act of doing so they were met by a party of United States soldiers, who attempted to deprive them of their arms, which they refused to deliver up, and the consequence was a fight ensued ; that a short time after that, a village that was located in a place called Cedar Cañon, in some locality north of the South Platte river, and who were perfectly unaware that any difficulty had occurred between any portion of their tribe and the whites, were attacked by a body of United States troops, some of them killed, and their ponies run off; that after this occurrence had taken place, while a column of United States troops were proceeding from the Smoky Hill towards the Arkansas, they were approached by Lean Bear, second chief of the Cheyennes, with his band; that Lean Bear, leaving his warriors behind, approached the column alone, with friendly feelings, and was then murdered by our soldiers, as well as his son who had followed him.

Commission adjourned until 2 p. m. this day.

*Two p. m.*—Commission met pursuant to adjournment. Present, all members and recorder.

Direct examination of Major E. W. Wynkoop continued :

He said that after all these occurrences the Cheyennes concluded that war was inevitable, and they immediately commenced to retaliate. He then said that during this time the Arapahoe Indians were on perfectly friendly terms with the whites, but that while Left Hand, one of the principal chiefs of the Arapahoe tribe, was camped in the vicinity of Fort Larned, he understood that the Kiowas were going to run off the stock belonging to the post ; that he notified the commanding officer of that post to that effect ; that no attention was paid to the information given to the commander of the post, and that on the day and hour indicated the stock was run off by the Kiowas; that then Left Hand again approached the post with some of his warriors for the purpose of tendering their services to pursue the Kiowas and recover the stock. He met a soldier outside the post and sent him with the statement to the commanding officer; that he then continued to approach the post, exhibiting a white flag; that he was fired upon from the fort and obliged hastily to leave; that from this circumstance the Arapahoes, presuming it was the intention of the whites to make war on them as well as the Cheyennes, commenced to retaliate, still against the wishes and desires of the principal men of both nations; that after the war had commenced they had heard of a proclamation issued by Governor Evans, inviting all friendly disposed Indians to place themselves under the protection of the United States forts; that they had frequently attempted to do so by approaching the different forts with that view, but had invariably been driven off; that under all these circumstances, they considered that they had been unjustly dealt with by their white brethren. But nothwithstanding that, he himself was willing to do anything for the purpose of procuring peace, knowing it to be for the good of his people; that he was willing to deliver up the white prisoners, but that there were other chiefs there who objected to do so simply on the assurance of myself that I would endeavor to procure them peace. They desired an assurance of peace as an equivalent for delivering up the white prisoners. The Indians then held a consultation among themselves, and, as I learned from the interpreter, were divided as to whether or not they should deliver up the prisoners upon the proposition made by me. On their frequently referring to me and asking whether I could insure them peace, I invariably answered it was out of my power to do so. The council then broke up without coming to any decision on the part of the Indians. Previous to their leaving, I told them that I would march to a certain place, naming the locality, distance about twelve miles, and there await three days the decision from them. Before the time had expired, four of the white prisoners were brought in and delivered over to me, and Black Kettle, who came in with some of them, stated that the other three would be turned over to me as soon as they could be procured; that they were at that time some distance off with a small band, somewhere on the Republican.

Black Kettle, White Antelope, and Bull Bear, principal chiefs of the Cheyennes, as well as Neva, No-ta-ne, Boisee, and Heap Buffalo, chiefs of the Arapahoes, agreed to accompany me in accordance with my proposition; with these chiefs I proceeded to Denver City, where a consultation was held with Governor Evans—Colonel John M. Chivington, commander of that military district, being present. Governor Evans, after asking the Indians numerous questions, finally told the Indians that he could have nothing to do with them; that they had made war against the United States, and that they were in the hands of the military authorities; that they had come up there under the protection of myself, and would return in the same manner, and would be subject to my disposal, until such time as higher authorities might be heard from. Colonel Chivington then got up, and told them that he was the big war chief of this part of the country, and his business was to kill Indians, and not to make peace with them; but that, under these circumstances, they would return with myself to Fort Lyon, and there be disposed of as I thought proper, until such time as a statement of their case had been heard and acted upon by the proper authorities. I returned to Fort Lyon, told the chiefs to bring in their villages, their squaws and pappooses, to the vicinity of the post, where they could be under my own eye, and where I could make them responsible for any depredation that might be committed outside, till such time as I could receive instructions from department headquarters. I then immediately despatched an officer, with a full statement of all the aforementioned facts, to Major General Curtis, commanding the department. In the meanwhile the Indians had brought in their villages to the vicinity of this post, under assurances of perfect safety and protection from the government, given to them by myself, as a United States officer, until such time as I could receive instructions from department headquarters. They were perfectly satisfied with the assurances that I had given them. I at different times, when I considered they were in a destitute condition, issued a limited amount of rations to them. On the 5th day of November, 1864, Major Scott J. Anthony, first cavalry of Colorado, relieved me from the command of Fort Lyon, in pursuance of an order from district headquarters, and I was ordered to report at district headquarters. Major Anthony stated to me, in relieving me in command of the post, that he was under strict instructions to have nothing to do with the Indians, to make them no issue, and to keep them away from the post. But after learning all the circumstances in regard to them, he assured me that, notwithstanding his stringent orders, he was obliged to follow the same course almost that I had adopted. He made issues to these same Indians, and of a greater quantity than ever I had issued; one camp of Arapahoes that were located near the post, he ordered to deliver up their arms, which, without hesitation, they did. The arms were taken possession of by Major Anthony. I also heard Left Hand, the chief of the Arapahoe nation, say that he was willing to submit to anything; that the whites might place him in irons, or kill him, but that he would not fight them. I was afterwards present at a consultation held by Major Anthony with chiefs of the Cheyenne and Arapahoe nation, at which he told them that he was now in command at Fort Lyon, and expected to be some time, but that he would insure them the same protection as I had, until such time as he could hear from the commanding general of the department. He told them to locate their villages close to the post, and to send out their young men to hunt buffalo. He told them that he had written to the big chief himself, since taking command. and told him a great many false reports had been circulated in regard to them, together with what he knew of their case, and that they should be in perfect safety until he got a reply. On the 26th day of November, 1864, I left Fort Lyon for the purpose of proceeding to district headquarters, in accordance with orders received. On the 28th day of November, while on the plains, I was overtaken by three Indians, namely, No-ta-ne (an Arapahoe) and two others. No-ta-ne stated that he had been sent by Black Kettle to overtake me and warn me that some two hundred Sioux had left the headwaters of the Smoky Hill, and had gone down to strike the road between where I was and Fort Larned, for the purpose of making war upon the whites; that, if I had not a sufficient escort, I had better return to Fort Lyon. I, however, proceeded on to Fort Larned without encountering any Indians; and upon my arrival at that post, from all that I could glean, learned that the statement of Black Kettle was correct; that the said body of Sioux, a few days previously, had been seen upon the river. That is all I know from my own personal knowledge. I returned to Fort Lyon on the 15th of January, with orders to assume command of the post, which I accordingly did.

Commission adjourned until 9 a. m. to-morrow, March 21, 1865.

## TWENTY-EIGHTH DAY.

MARCH 21, 1865—9 a. m.

Commission met pursuant to adjournment. Present, all members and recorder.
Proceedings of yesterday read and approved, with the following amendments: Page 326, ninth and tenth lines, omit the words "whom I stated;" page 327, next to bottom line, to read "whose names I don't know;" page 328, second line, to read "whose names I don't know."

Direct examination of Major E. W. Wynkoop, veteran battalion first Colorado cavalry, by the commission, continued:

Question. At the time of your assuming command of Fort Lyon, in 1864, in what department and district was the post then located?
Answer. District of Colorado, department of Kansas.
Question. Who commanded the district at that time, and how far was district headquarters from Fort Lyon?
Answer. Colonel John H. Chivington commanded the district at that time. district headquarters was about two hundred and fifty miles from Fort Lyon.
Question. Was there a change of district lines while you were in command at Fort Lyon?
Answer. There was.
Question. State the time and manner of such change.
Answer. I think the change was made about the middle of July, 1864. Fort Lyon was included in the district of the Upper Arkansas, headquarters at Fort Riley, Kansas, Major General Blunt in command.
Question. Was there any other change in the district lines, or commander, while you were in command of Fort Lyon.
Answer. Yes. Major General Blunt left the district, and command was assumed by Major Henning, headquarters at Fort Riley.
Question. How far from Fort Lyon to headquarters, department of Kansas, and district of the Upper Arkansas? and what facilities had you for communicating with department and district headquarters?
Answer. Distance to district headquarters was about four hundred miles; to department headquarters, about five hundred miles. The opportunities for communicating to district and department headquarters were very bad, in consequence of being obliged to cross the plains through a country which, during a large portion of the time, was troubled with hostile Indians; in fact, the only communication was by means of large bodies of troops.
Question. What tribe of Indians were at that time committing the depredations you speak of on the road?
Answer. It was my understanding the depredations were being committed by the Kiowas, Comanches, Sioux, Arapahoes, and Cheyennes.
Question. How long did they continue to commit depredations on the road?
Answer. Up to within a couple of weeks of the 10th of September, 1864, the date of my consultation on the Smoky Hill. I heard of no depredations being committed between the 10th of September and the 29th of November, 1864, the date of Chivington's massacre at Sand creek.
Question. Were any depredations committed by the Indians west of Fort Lyon, and in the vicinity of the settlements, prior to the 10th of September, 1864?
Answer. Yes, there were depedations committed; there were men killed in the neighborhood of Fort Lyon and further west in the vicinity of the Arkansas settlements.
Question. How long after you received the letter from Black Kettle and other chiefs in reference to certain prisoners did you start for the Smoky Hill with command?
Answer. Two days afterwards. I received the letter on the 4th day of September, 1864, and started on the 6th.
Question. Where were the white prisoners at the time of the council?
Answer. I do not know; when the Indians first saw me, they moved their village and left nothing but warriors behind, and I supposed the white captives to be with the village.
Question. Did Black Kettle and other chiefs in council say they were authorized to act for any other tribes than their own, in making peace with the whites?
Answer. They did not say they were authorized to act for other tribes, but told me that if peace was made with the Cheyennes and Arapahoes, the Sioux,

278

Kiowas, and Comanches wanted peace also. Some of the chiefs said at the time, if they made peace and the whites wanted them to, they would assist in fighting the Kiowas and Comanches.

Question. In the council on Smoky Hill was any reference made to a band of Indians called Dog soldiers.

Answer. Yes, I spoke to Black Kettle and asked him if he could control a portion of his tribe called Dog soldiers. I can't remember whether this conversation occurred at the council, but the conversation I have reference to took place with Black Kettle and Bull Bear, chief of the Dog soldiers, in case peace was made, whether they would submit to such terms as he might accept. He replied in the affirmative. I also understood from Bull Bear (the chief of the Dog soldiers,) that they (the Dog soldiers) would indorse whatever Black Kettle and other chiefs might do, in reference to making peace with the whites.

Question. What did the chiefs say in council on the Smoky Hill, and Denver, they would do in order to secure peace with the whites?

Answer. I do not know of anything particular they said; they appeared willing to submit to anything the whites might impose on them. They also said at different times, (I don't know exactly when and where,) that they were willing to assist the whites in fighting the other Indians who were hostile; they also said that they were willing to go up to their reservation and remain there.

Question. Did you have a conversation with the rescued white prisoners in reference to their capture and treatment by the Indians?

Answer. I had a conversation with the oldest one, a young girl about sixteen or seventeen years old.

Question. By whom did they say they had been taken?

Answer. She stated that herself and two of the children were taken by the Cheyennes.

Question. Did she state the place and circumstances of her capture?

Answer. She did; she said that she was taken on the Blue river, Kansas, from a ranch known as the Liberty Farm; that there were one woman and three children besides herself, taken at the same time and place, and I believe two men killed.

Question. On your return from the council on the Smoky Hill to Fort Lyon, did you make a report of what you had done? If so, state to whom you made it.

Answer. I made two reports; one to Major General Blunt, commanding the district, the other to Governor Evans, of Colorado.

Question. Can you furnish a copy of each of the reports?

Answer. I can, a copy of the report to Major General Curtis in relation to this affair; also the report to Governor Evans; also a report made to Colonel Ford, then commanding the district in which Fort Lyon was included, made in accordance with orders to return to Fort Lyon, assume command of the post, investigate and report in regard to late Indian proceedings in that vicinity. I have not a copy of the report furnished to Major General Blunt, but it was of the same purport of the report furnished to Governor Evans in regard to the details of the expedition. I can furnish copies in two or three days; Major Wynkoop was instructed by the commission to furnish copies of said reports, which will be appended to these proceedings, and marked in red letters F, S, and H.

Question. How long after your return from the council on the Smoky Hill did you leave for Denver, and who accompanied you?

Answer. It was a few days after my return from the Smoky Hill, I left for Denver with the Indian chiefs aforementioned in my testimony by an escort of about forty men, commanded by Lieutenant Cramer and accompanied by Captain Soule and John Smith, United States Indian interpreter.

Question. At that time, had the settlers on the Arkansas left their farms on account of Indian depredations?

Answer. A large majority had. As I passed up through the Arkansas valley

279

I found a great many farms deserted, both on the Arkansas and Fountain-qui-bouit. I found the people congregated together at different points for mutual protection.

Question. On your arrival in Denver to whom did you report?

Answer. I did not report to anybody. I sent a message to the governor of Colorado Territory that I had arrived.

Question. By whom was the council with the Indians convened at Denver?

Answer. Governor Evans.

Commission adjourned until 1½ p. m.

*One and a half p. m.*—Commission met pursuant to adjournment. Present, all members and recorder.

Direct examination of Major E. W. Wynkoop by the commission continued:

Question. Why did you send a message to Governor Evans that you had arrived with cerain Indian chiefs, instead of to the military commander?

Answer. Because Governor Evans was ex officio superintendent of Indian affairs, and because I was not under the command of the commander of the district of Colorado.

Question. Did you have a conversation with Governor Evans in reference to the Indian proposals for peace?

(John M. Chivington most respectfully objects to the question for the reason that it is leading and can be answered by a negative or affirmative, and suggests the answer required.

Objection sustained by the commission.)

Question. Did you, while in Denver, have any conversation with any person or persons, holding an official position, in reference to the subject of your mission to that city?

Answer. I did.

Question. With whom did you have such conversation?

Answer. John Evans, governor of Colorado and ex officio superintendent of Indian affairs.

Question. What was the purport of that conversation?

Answer. I told Governor Evans that I had come to Denver in accordance with the report I had made to him; that I had brought the chiefs with me and desired that he would see them and hear what they had to say. He stated that he did not think he could have anything to do with them officially, as these Indians had declared war against the United States, and he considered that the matter now rested in the hands of the military authorities; besides, even if he could make peace with the Indians, he did not think it would be policy at that present time, for the reason that he had not punished the Indians sufficiently, and that if he made peace with them under these circumstances, the United States government would be acknowledging themselves whipped. He also said that the third regiment (one-hundred-days men) had been raised upon representations made by him to the department that their services were necessary to fight these Indians, and that now, after they had been raised and equipped, if peace was made before they had gone into the field, they would suppose at Washington that he had misrepresented matters, and that there never had been any necessity for the government to go to the expense of raising that regiment; that, therefore, there must be something for the third regiment to do; but he finally consented to see the Indians and talk with them, and he set an hour and day for that purpose. He also said that he gave me a great deal of credit for rescuing those white prisoners, but that he would not have adopted the same means that I had; that he, after finding out where their camp was, would have gone out and fought them and killed them, and made them deliver up the white captives. I reminded the governor then of the fact that all the force I could raise was one hundred and twenty-seven men, after leaving sufficient garrison at Fort Fort Lyon, and that the Indians numbered upwards of two thousand.

Question. How long after this conversation did the council meet? Who were present and what was done?

Answer. I think it was two days after this conversation, the council met; the government officials present, were : Governor Evans, Colonel John M. Chivington, Lieutenant Cramer, Captain Soule, and myself. There were some other officers whom I don't remember, a few citizens, and the United States Indian interpreter, John Smith. The Indians were composed of Black Kettle, White Antelope, and Bull Bear, of the Cheyennes, and Neva, No-ta-ne, Boisee, and Heap Buffalo, of the Arapahoes. At the conclusion of the council the Indians appeared perfectly satisfied with everything that had taken place; they expressed themselves, through the interpreter, that they supposed they were now all right. Black Kettle very affectionately embraced the governor; then he and the balance of the chiefs shook hands with all those assembled.

Question. How long after the council in Denver did you return to Fort Lyon?

Answer. In about five or six days, I think.

Question. On your return did you find the settlers on the Arkansas still absent from their farms?

(John M. Chivington most respectfully objects to the question, for the following reasons : that the question is leading, suggesting the answer required, and may be answered by a negative or affirmative.)

Objection overruled by the commission.)

Answer. No; they had returned to their farms and were taking in their crops. It was just the season of the year when the corn was ripe.

Question. What induced them to return to their farms?

(John M. Chivington most respectfully objects to the question, for the reason that it has not been shown to the court that the witness is acquainted with the causes that actuated the settlers in their removals from and to their farms, and it is not competent for the court to prove conclusions, but only to elicit facts within the knowledge of the witness.

Objection overruled by the commission.)

Answer. Under an assurance from myself of safety; since I had the consultation with the Indians on the headwaters of the Smoky Hill, I told them that they could consider themselves in perfect safety until such time as I could give them warning to the contrary, and told them to return to their ranches and take in their crops, which they were doing upon my return from Denver.

Question. How long after your return to Fort Lyon did you commence issuing provisions to the Indians?

Answer. I don't know how long; it was in a few days after my return; there was a village of Arapahoes that I first issued provisions to.

Question. Did you have any council with the Indians after your return to Fort Lyon?

Answer. I did.

Question. State with whom you had such council?

Answer. It was with Black Kettle and some of the chiefs I took up to Denver, together with Left Hand, chief of the Arapahoes, and Little Raven, of the Arapahoes, at which consultation some of my officers were present—also Colonel William Bent and John Smith, the United States Indian interpreter.

Question. What was the object of the council and what was done?

Answer. I told the chiefs, what I have already stated in my testimony yesterday, to bring in their villages, so that I could have them under my own eye until such time as I could hear from department. headquarters. I also told Black Kettle that I wanted him to bring me in the three remaining white captives as soon as possible, which he promised to do, but said it would take some time, as they were off at a distance, but that he would send Bull Bear (a portion of whose band they were with) after them, with instructions to return as soon as possible. That is about all that occurred, except what I said yesterday in my testimony.

Question. Were the Indian chiefs advised of your sending an officer to department headquarters and the object you had in sending him?

Answer. They were.

Question. What statements did you make to Major Anthony, on his assuming command of Fort Lyons, in reference to the Indians?

Answer. The principal points I have heretofore detailed in my testimony in regard to my relations with the Indians.

Question. How long after being relieved of the command of Fort Lyon did you leave for district headquarters?

Answer. I was relieved from command on the 5th of November, 1864, and started for district headquarters on the 26th of November.

Question. Did you receive any orders on your arrival at district headquarters?

Answer. I did. I received an order placing me on duty at Fort Riley, and assumed command of the post.

Question. Did you make a report to the district or department commander after your arrival at Fort Riley?

Answer. I made a verbal report to the district commander at Fort Riley of my arrival. I also, after assuming command of Fort Riley, wrote a letter to Major General Curtis, commanding department, requesting permission to visit him for the purpose of making certain explanations in regard to my connection with Indian affairs at Fort Lyon, which request was granted, and I proceeded to department headquarters and had an interview with General Curtis.

Question. What explanations or report did you make to department commander?

Answer. I commenced to explain to him the facts that I have heretofore given in my testimony, but before I had finished he intimated to me that he was aware of all the facts, and that he had censured me not for the course I had adopted with the Indians particularly, but for committing an unmilitary act by leaving my district without orders and proceeding to Denver City with the Indian chiefs and white captives to the governor of Colorado instead of coming to himself, and asked what explanation I had to make. I told him that I had since become pretty well convinced that I had made a mistake, but that at the time I thought that Governor Evans was the proper person to refer that matter to, he being governor of Colorado Territory and *ex officio* Indian superintendent; that I had heard of no declaration of war with the United States. I also explained to him the isolated position of Fort Lyon, and how seldom the chances were for communicating with headquarters, and that in consequence, while in command at Fort Lyon, I felt it frequently incumbent upon me to assume responsibilities. I showed him a paper which I had in my possession, addressed to me from the settlers in the Arkansas valley and from the Fountain-qui-bouit and the Huerfano, which paper was to the effect that they were grateful for what I had done in reference to the Indians; complimenting me, and indorsing the course that I had adopted as the best that could have been followed for the interest and welfare of the settlers of Colorado; referring to the fact of my having obtained possession of the prisoners aforementioned, and complimented me for doing so. I also exhibited to the general a document addressed to myself, and signed by all the officers at Fort Lyon, which was to the effect that they indorsed my whole action with regard to the Indians, and thought that I had acted for the best interests of the service as well as for the benefit of the people of the country, which action was indorsed by Major Scott J. Anthony, who agreed with all that was therein stated, and ended by stating that he considered that Major Wynkoop had acted for the best.

Commission adjourned until 9 a. m. to-morrow, March 22, 1865.

## TWENTY-NINTH DAY.

MARCH 22, 1865.

Commission met pursuant to adjournment. Present, all members and recorder.

Proceedings of yesterday read, amended as follows, and approved : On page 347, third line of first answer, to read, "from a ranch near what is known as Liberty farm." Page 351, fourth line from bottom to read, "we had not," &c. Page 360, ninteenth line to read, "that I had heard of no declaration of war declared against these Indians, and did not suppose, as a nation, they were at war with the United States."

Direct examination of Major E. W. Wynkoop, by the commission continued :

Question. Can you furnish copies of the papers you refer to as shown to General Curtis ?

Answer. I can.

Major E. W. Wynkoop produced the papers which are appended to these proceedings, and marked in red letters I and K.

---

I.

FORT LYON, COLORADO,
*November 25, 1864*

DEAR SIR : Having learned with regret that you have been relieved and ordered to Fort Leavenworth to report your official proceedings in regard to Indians while in command of this post, I cannot let the opportunity pass without bearing testimony to the fact that the course adopted and carried out by you was the only proper one to pursue, and has been the means of saving the lives of hundreds of men, women, and children, as well as thousands of dollars' worth of property.

No one can doubt that the lively aid rendered by you (at the risk of your own life as well as the lives of your small command) to the captives among the Arapahoes and Cheyenne Indians, was also the means of saving their lives. For this act alone (even if you had not done more) you should receive the warmest thanks of all men, whether in military or civil life.

Your visit to Denver with some of the principal chiefs of the Arapahoe and Cheyenne tribes was productive of more good to the Indians, and did more to allay the fears of the inhabitants in the Arkansas valley, than all that has been done by all other persons in this portion of the department.

Since that time no depredations have been committed by these tribes, and the people have returned to their houses and farms, and are now living as quietly and peaceably as if the bloody scenes of the past summer had never been enacted.

Hoping that in all things your course will be approved by the commander of this department, and that you will soon be restored to your command in this district, I remain your obedient servant,

JOSEPH A. CRAMER,
*Second Lieut. First Cavalry of Colorado, Commanding Co. K.*

Major E. W. WYNKOOP.

FORT LYON, COLORADO TERRITORY,
*November 25, 1864.*

We, the undersigned, being conversant with all the facts set forth in the fore-going letter, heartily concur in the same.

R. A. HILL,
*Captain First New Mexico Vols.*
JAMES D. CANNON,
*First Lieut. First New Mexico Vols.*
WILLIAM P. MINTON,
*Second Lieut. First New Mexico Vols.*
C. M. COGSIL,
*First Lieut. First Cav. of Colorado.*
S. G. COLBEY,
*United States Indian Agent.*
HORACE W. BALDWIN,
*Lieut. Ind. Battery C. V. A.*
SILAS S. SOULE,
*Captain First Cavalry of Colorado.*
G. H. HARDIN,
*First Lieut. First Cav. of Colorado.*

The above letter was indorsed as follows:

HEADQUARTERS FORT LYON, C. T.,
*November 26, 1864.*

Respectfully forwarded to headquarters district, with the remarks: That it is the general opinion here by officers, soldiers, and citizens, that had it not been for the course pursued by Major Wynkoop towards the Cheyenne and Arapahoe Indians, the travel upon the public road must have entirely stopped and the settlers upon the ranches all through the country must have abandoned them or been murdered, as no force of troops sufficient to protect the road and settlements could be got together in this locality.

I think Major Wynkoop acted for the best in the matter.

SCOTT J. ANTHONY,
*Major First Cavalry of Colorado, Commanding Post.*

FORT LYON, COLORADO TERRITORY,
*November 25, 1864.*

Lieutenant Joseph A. Cramer and other officers of Fort Lyon state that having learned that Major E. W Wynkoop has been relieved from command of Fort Lyon and ordered to Fort Leavenworth to report his official proceedings in regard to Indian affairs while in command of that fort, bear testimony that the plan adopted and carried out by him was the only proper one, and that he has been the means of saving the lives of hundreds of men, women, and children, and thousands of dollars' worth of property, and hope his proceedings will be approved by the department commander.

HEADQUARTERS DISTRICT UPPER ARKANSAS,
*Fort Riley, December 6, 1864.*

Respectfully forwarded to department headquarters.

R. S. HENNING,
*Major Third Wisconsin Cavalry, Commanding District.*

## K.

Major E. W. WYNKOOP, *First Colorado Regiment Volunteers:*

We, the undersigned, citizens of the Arkansas Valley, of Colorado Territory, in view of your recent action in taking certain chiefs of the Arapahoe and Cheyenne tribes of Indians to Denver to have a consultation with the governor of this Territory, and your efforts thereby to effect a treaty of peace and restore pacific relations between us and those tribes who have threatened our peace and safety as settlers of this country, desire to express to you our hearty sympathy in your laudable efforts to prevent further danger and bloodshed, and sincerely congratulate you in your noble efforts to do what we consider right, politic, and just, whether those efforts on your part prove successful or not, sincerely hoping they may prove successful, and peace instead of war reign throughout our land.

In consideration of the danger and risks you have incurred in achieving the rescue of prisoners from those tribes, the hazard to your own life and the lives of the men under your command, we desire to further express our appreciation of your bravery, as well as your sense of right, and earnestly express the hope that the merit which is justly your due may not go unrewarded in official preferment as well as the gratitude of private citizens.

| | |
|---|---|
| A. J. Boone. | Allen A. Bradford. |
| Robt. B. Willis. | P. K. Dobson. |
| W. Craig. | James Chatam. |
| J. B. Rice. | M. Dobson. |
| Z. Gattlen. | J. M. Francisco. |
| Charles Autubees. | W. J. Thompson. |
| N. W. Wellon. | Benj. B. Field. |
| Davy Hayden. | Geo. F. Norris. |
| Wm. Reeker. | M. G. Bradford. |
| A. Sims. | E. R. Cozzens. |
| George F. Hall. | J. A. Betts. |
| J. T. Robinson. | Jno. A. Thatcher. |
| S. S. Smith. | J. T. Smith. |
| A. S. Alexander. | |

Question. How long after your interview with the department commander did you assume command of Fort Lyon?

Answer. I assumed command at Fort Lyon about the 15th day of January. My interview with the department commander took place about the middle of the previous month.

Question. At the time you left Fort Lyon for district headquarters where were the Indians with whom you had been in council?

Answer. One village was located at the Smoky Hill crossing of Sand creek, twenty-five miles from Fort Lyon, and another village was in the neighborhood of Camp Wynkoop, about sixty-five miles below Fort Lyon. The last mentioned village had recently moved from the vicinity of the post.

Question. State the number of Indians who encamped at Sand creek, and of what tribe or tribes were they?

Answer. I could not positively state the number except from hearsay.

Question. Did you while in Denver have conversation with any person or persons occupying official positions as to what you had done in your dealings with Indians?

Answer. Yes, I had with several occupying official positions.

Question. State with whom you had such conversation.

Answer. With Governor John Evans, Colonel John M. Chivington, Major

J. S. Fillmore, and United States Marshal Hunt, and others, but whom I don't remember particularly.

Question. What statement did you make to the persons named, in that conversation?

Answer. In several instances I simply gave a statement in reference to my operation with the Indians, as stated in my testimony. I also, after the council held with the Indians had broken up, when questioned by any of these different persons in regard to what I was going to do in future with these Indians, invariably stated that I would bring them back to Fort Lyon and get them to bring their families into the vicinity of the post, until such time as some action was taken by proper authorities in relation to their proposition for peace. I mentioned this fact particularly to Colonel John M. Chivington, as made to Governor John Evans.

Question. Had you, previous to your council with them on the Smoky Hill, any acquaintance with the Cheyennes and Arapahoes?

(John M. Chivington most respectfully objects to the question, for the following reasons:

The court is convened to investigate certain facts pointed out by the instuctions, &c., and it is not competent to prove any acquaintance the witness may have with the Cheyenne or any other Indians. The question is not of acquaintance, but of guilt or innocence, which can be established only by the establishment of certain facts in a legal and regular manner.

Objection overruled by the commission.)

Answer. I had, and have had upwards of seven years.

Commission adjourned until 1½ this p. m.

*One and a half p. m.*—Commission met pursuant to adjournment. Present, all members and recorder.

Direct examination of Major E. W. Wynkoop by the commission closed.

Cross-examination of Major E. W. Wynkoop by J. H. Chivington, late colonel first Colorado cavalry:

Question. Prior to your expedition to the Smoky Hill, as stated in your examination in chief, what instructions had you received from the commanding officer of the district, or department in which Fort Lyon was located, in regard to your intercourse with the Indians, as commanding officer of Fort Lyon, by order, letter, or otherwise? Please state particularly.

Answer. I had never received any instructions in regard to what the question has reference to. I had received a letter from General Blunt, to the effect that on account of the peculiar position of Fort Lyon, a great deal was left to my discretion, being so far removed from headquarters, and the opportunities for communicating being seldom.

Question. Prior to your expedition to the Smoky Hill, had not Field Order No. 2, headquarters department of Kansas, Major General Curtis commanding, been received at Fort Lyon?

Answer. It had not, to my knowledge.

Question. Who brought in the Indians who carried the letter from the Indians to Major Colby and Colonel William Brent, as stated in your examination in chief?

Answer. Some soldiers brought them in, who were on their way to Denver to be mustered out of service.

Question. Have you ever seen Field Order No. 2, headquarters department of Kansas, 1864, Major General Curtis commanding?

Answer. I have.

Question. When did you first see it?

Answer. I can't remember the date or time, but it was since my expedition to the Smoky Hill.

Question. When was it received at Fort Lyon, and have you a copy of it?

Answer. The first I heard of it being at Fort Lyon was when Major Anthony relieved me from the command on the 5th day of November, 1864. He brought some copies with him. I have not a copy of it.

Question. Do you keep a record of the orders received at Fort Lyon, the time, &c., from whom received, &c.?

Answer. I keep a file of all orders received at Fort Lyon only.

Question. You stated that you received a letter signed Black Kettle and others, desiring to give up some white prisoners, &c., and that they desired peace, &c. Upon first seeing the Indians after leaving Fort Lyon, did they act in a friendly manner towards you, or did they not manifest a disposition to fight rather than treat?

Answer. The manner in which they were drawn up presented a hostile appearance.

Question. What induced you to believe they did not intend to be hostile?

Answer. In the first place the fact of their not making an attack while having greatly superior numbers; and in the next, the fact of their delivering up the white prisoners which they had in their possession, and their chiefs entering my camp and delivering themselves over to me.

Question. After first seeing the Indians, were there not members of your command who expressed to you their fears of the Indians, and for certain causes threatened to return to Fort Lyon?

Answer. There were certain members of my command who expressed to me their fears that the Indians intended treachery, but they did not threaten in my presence to return to Fort Lyon.

Question. In your examination in chief you referred to a memorandum for dates, &c. Is your statement as regards dates from the memorandum or memory?

Answer. From the memorandum taken from my official reports.

Question. You say after meeting the Indians you went into camp on the bank of a creek. Was not your camp on this bank surrounded on three sides by the creek, and was not the brush or willows very thick on the opposite side of the creek, and how far was the centre of your camp to the brush?

Answer. The camp was not surrounded on three sides by the creek. From the centre of camp to the brush I should judge was from four hundred to six hundred yards. The brush or willow was thick on both sides of the creek.

Question. Will you describe your camp, its formation, shape, length, width, &c., how your men were arranged, &c., how large your guard, what their orders were, and if they were immediately on duty when you went into camp, and whether your men were permitted to leave camp when they pleased?

Answer. The camp was formed, cavalry in line, battery in the centre, and wagons coralled in rear of the battery. The camp was as wide as the line occupied, and the depth of the wagons. The line was formed parallel with the creek. The men were not arranged in any particular formation. I don't remember the number on guard. My order to the officer of the day was to deploy the guard at certain intervals around the camp, and not allow any Indians to come into camp without my permission. They were on duty all the time, from the time they were mounted until they were relieved. The men were not permitted to leave camp when they pleased.

Question. Was this camp just referred to the camp first made after first seeing the Indians and in which your council was held, which you referred to in your examination in chief?

Answer. It was the camp in which the council was held. It was made the day I first saw the main body of Indians. I had seen a few Indians the day before.

Question. What officer of your command was officer of the day on the day of the council and during the council, or at any time after first meeting the In-

Ex. Doc. 26——7

287

dians ? Did the Indians behave in a threatening manner towards you ? If so, please state the particulars.

Answer. Lieutenant Hardin was officer of the day. I did not see them make any demonstrations that I considered hostile, except some of those who were present were apparently prepared for strife by having their bows strung and arrows in their hands. On the other hand my men had their loaded carbines in their hands, prepared, at any time to fight.

Question. Was your attention called to any threatening demonstration made by the Indians during the council, and did not the officer of the day once during the council call to the men to fall in for the purpose of fighting the Indians ?

Answer. While in the council I was told that Lieutenant Hardin, for some cause or other, had formed the men in line, and that the Indians seeing it, had made a demonstration as though they were preparing for a fight, but that nothing of this kind had taken place on the part of the Indians until our men had fallen in line.

Question. Did the Indians put any seeds or anything of that description into the vent of your howitzers ?

Answer. I never knew of their doing so.

Question. During the council you state the Indians had among themselves, did not your interpreter inform you that the Indians meditated the destruction of your command ?

Answer. He did not.

Commission adjourned until 9 a m. to-morrow, March 23, 1865.

### THIRTIETH DAY.

MARCH 23, 1865.

Commission met pursuant to adjournment. Present, all members and recorder· Proceedings of yesterday read and approved.

Cross-examination of Major E. W. Wynkoop by J. M. Chivington continued :

Question. At your first camp, where the council with the Indians was held, did not the Indians come into your camp, so that there were a great many more Indians in camp than soldiers of your command?

Answer. They did.

Question. Were not these Indians all armed, and did they not while in camp in many instances behave in a very threatening manner towards the soldiers of your command ; and did not the Indians in some instances abstract the contents of the soldiers' pockets, taking such things as tobacco, &c.?

Answer. They were all armed. As I stated before, I did not see them act in a threatening manner. I never heard of their abstracting the contents of the soldiers' pockets.

Question. You stated that your command numbered one hundred and twenty-seven men ; how many Indians, or about how many, were in camp during the council, or at the time Lieutenant Hardin ordered his men to fall in ?

Answer. I do not know how many; I could not say positively about how many.

Question. Did Lieutenant Hardin, commanding the howitzers that accompanied your expedition, ever inform you of the fact that seed had been placed in the vent of the howitzers by the Indians, or did you ever have any conversation with Lieutenant Hardin, or any other officer of your command, in regard to that fact ?

Answer. I heard that some grapes had been dropped into the vent of the gun. It was told me by some one or other, I don't remember who. That was the cause of a difficulty between the soldier on guard and an Indian. I understood that the soldier pushed the Indian off; that the Indian drew his bow and the soldier his revolver.

288

Question. In your conversation with the Indians in your camp, where the council was held, did you state to Black Kettle, One-Eye, or any other chief, that you were in the power of the Indians, and they could destroy you if they desired, or language to that effect?

Answer. I did not.

Question. Did the Indians state to you, at any conversation you had with them, that they could destroy you if they desired?

Answer. They did not.

Question. In your conversation with the Indians did you promise them subsistence or anything of that kind upon any conditions?

Answer. I did not.

Question. Was the cause of your moving toward Fort Lyon on account of the threatening demonstrations made toward you by the Indians, and the probability that if you remained there, there would be a collision between your command and the Indians?

Answer. My object in removing toward Fort Lyon was for the reason that I had no occasion to go the other way.

Question. Was this the only reason you had in going toward Fort Lyon?

Answer. The reason for moving my camp immediately to another locality was for the purpose of taking a better position, so that, in case the Indians did not accept the proposition I had made to them, and chose to be hostile, I would be in a better position to make a defence.

Question. Was there any act upon the part of the Indians that induced you to believe that they would not accept your proposition and would attack you? If so, what was that act?

Answer. I was induced to believe that my proposition might not be accepted from the fact that a portion of the chiefs composing the council appeared unwilling to deliver up the white prisoners, simply from my statement that I would endeavor to procure them peace  They desired an assurance of peace, which I told them positively I could not give them; and as an officer I took what I deemed to be the necessary precaution.

Question. Did John Smith, United States Indian interpreter, at any time state to you or any officer of your command that he would have to talk for your lives—that the Indians meditated the destruction of yourself and command?

Answer. He made no statement of that kind to me. I do not know of his making any statement to any officer of my command to that effect.

Question. Did Black Kettle or One-Eye at any time address the Indians assembled about your camp, and implore the Indians not to destroy yourself and command?

Answer. I did not know of their doing anything of that kind.

Question. How long after the council you held with the Indians were the white captives brought to you? and who were the Indians that brought in the captives? and did they not state that the Dog soldiers, they feared, could not be controlled?

Answer. One was brought in the next day, and three others the day after. The first was brought in by Left Hand, chief of the Arapahoes, and the other three by Black Kettle, chief of the Cheyennes. They did not state that they feared the Dog soldiers could not be controlled.

Question. Will you explain what the Dog soldiers are, and how they are controlled?

Answer. I understand that the Dog soldiers are a portion of the warriors of the Cheyenne tribe, and presume that they are controlled by the headmen.

Question. Did any of the chiefs, or did John Smith, at any time state to you that they feared the Dog soldiers, as well as the Indian warriors generally, could not be controlled; and did not some of the Indian chiefs advise you to move toward Fort Lyon, fearing a collision between your command and the Indians?

289

Answer. They did not.

Question. You stated in your direct examination that Colonel John M. Chivington said in Denver, at the council with the Indians, that he (Chivington) was the big war chief of this part of the country, &c. Who was present when Colonel Chivington made this statement? and did not Colonel Chivington manifest a desire for peace with the Indians, provided Major General Curtis would consent, and provided a peace could be made that would afford permanent security to the people of Colorado Territory? and did not Colonel Chivington state that he was determined the white people of Colorado should be protected in their lives and property, if he had to kill all the Indians on the plains; and was not all Colonel Chivington's conversation with you manifestly for the whites, regardless of the sympathies that others might have for the Indians?

Answer. All those were present I believe that I have stated were present at the council. I never heard him express himself in that way, manifesting a desire for peace, &c., or heard him make use of the expressions used in the latter part of the question. I had no conversation with him of importance, except what I had done and intended to do. He expressed no opinion particularly on the subject that I can remember, at any time that I was in Denver.

Question. Who was present when this conversation occurred between yourself and Colonel Chivington?

Answer. No person was present but myself.

Commission adjourned until 1½ this p. m.

*One and a half p. m.*—Commission met pursuant to adjournment. Present, all members and recorder.

Cross-examination of Major E. W. Wynkoop by J. M. Chivington continued:

Question. Were you in the council during the whole time of its sitting in Denver?

Answer. I was.

Question. In the council at Denver, did Colonel Chivington at any time encourage the Indians in the belief that peace would be made with them on their own terms? but did he not, on the contrary, treat the Indians in such a manner that they would believe that he (Chivington) would not make peace with them or encourage the making of peace with them?

Answer. All that he did and said is what I have already stated in my direct examination.

Question. From Governor Evans's conversation with the Indians, at the council in Denver, could the Indians believe that peace would be made with them by the government, or did Governor Evans encourage the Indians to believe that peace would be made with them?

Answer. I should not judge from his conversation that he encouraged or discouraged them; but they were under the impression, from some cause or other, that they were all right.

Question. You state that Governor Evans wished the third regiment would do something, so that the government would not think it had been raised without a cause, &c. Did not Governor Evans also say that he believed it to be policy to whip the Indians, as without that being first done nothing could be accomplished that would be a permanent benefit to the government?

Answer. He did state that it would not be policy to make peace with the Indians until they had been punished more.

Question. In the council with the Indians at Denver, did any person attempt to prevent the Indians from telling all they desired in regard to their difficulties with the whites?

Answer. I did not see or hear anybody attempt to prevent them.

Question. On your return to Fort Lyon and after the Indians had brought in their squaws and children, did not the Indians retain in their possession government horses, mules, &c., branded U. S., and evidently stolen from the government, besides other property belonging to the government?

Answer. I understood that the village of Arapahoes that was located in the vicinity of the post had in their possession some government animals, but before I investigated the matter I was relieved from command by Major Scott J. Anthony, who told me afterwards that he had looked for government animals among their herd, but had found none.

Question. Did you not at one time, upon hearing a report that the Utes, who are at peace with the whites, were about attacking the Arapahoes or Cheyennes near Fort Lyon, take the larger portion of your command out to fight the Utes?

Answer. I did not. I heard that the Utes were in the neighborhood of the Arapahoe camp, and heard that the Arapahoes had started out to fight them, and with twenty mounted men I rode out to see what was going on.

Question. Will you state how much subsistence, in quantity and value, you issued to the Indians up to the time that you were relieved from command, and whether Major Anthony did not tell you when he assumed command of Fort Lyon that he would make the issues to the Indians as you had done?

Answer. I don't know how much I issued, and don't remember of Major Anthony mentioning anything particular in regard to issuing rations to Indians.

Question. Was there no account kept of the issues to the Indians, and could you not obtain such account of your assistant commissary of subsistence?

Answer. The issues were made to the Indians on orders issued by myself to the assistant commissary of subsistence, and I presume he could furnish a statement of the amount issued on those orders.

Question. In your interview with the major general commanding (General Curtis) did he express to you his policy in regard to the treatment of Indians, and what orders he had given to Colonel Chivington in regard to their punishment?

Answer. He did not.

Question. During the council on the tributary of the Smoky Hill which you held with the Indians, did the Indians at any time get possession of the howitzers you had with your command, and sit upon them, at the same time manifesting a great deal of contempt for your command, &c.?

Answer. They did not.

Question. You state that persons in your command, while on the expedition to the Smoky Hill, &c., expressed their fears of the Indians' treachery, but no persons of your command threatened to you to return to Fort Lyon; did any person ever inform you that such threats had been made?

Answer. Yes.

Question. By whom were you informed of that fact, and what was the cause of such threats? Please state particularly.

Answer. I don't remember who informed me. I understood that the cause of the threats was, that the men were fearful that the Indians would prove treacherous.

Question. Did One-Eye at any time while on this expedition state to the Indians that you and your command should be protected from all harm from the Indians, and that he had pledged himself to protect you and your command, and that if the Indians harmed you or your command he would go with the whites and fight against the Indians?

Answer. His remarks as interpreted to me by the United States Indian interpreter were to the effect that if they (the Indians) still determined to fight against the whites he would assist the whites.

Question. What was the cause of this remark, and where was it made?

Answer. I don't know what the cause of the remark was. It was made while the council was in session.

Question. Did John Smith, the interpreter, pretend to interpret to you all the Indians said in council ?

Answer. No, that would have been impossible ; he interpreted, as he said, all that was said in reference to the matters for which the council was held.

Cross-examination of Major E. W. Wynkoop by J. M. Chivington closed.

Commission adjourned until 9 a. m. to-morrow, March 24, 1865.

### THIRTY-FIRST DAY.

MARCH 24, 1865.

Commission met pursuant to adjournment.    Present, all members and recorder. Proceedings of yesterday read and approved.

Re-examination of Major E. W. Wynkoop:

By the COMMISSION :

Question. Were the Indians, while in council in Denver, enabled to make a statement of what they had suffered by the depredations of the whites ?

Answer. They were not.   I asked Governor Evans in the council to ask some questions in regard to that, which he did not do.   The principal questions asked were in regard to what they had done, which they answered without hesitation and with apparent truthfulness.

Question. What is the purport of Field Order No. 2, referred to in your cross-examination ?

Answer. One paragraph was to the effect that Indians must not be permitted to enter a post without being blindfolded.   Another paragraph, complimenting Lieutenant Ellsworth for building defences at Smoky Hill crossing, and censuring other post and station commanders for not having done likewise.   There were other things in that order which I don't remember.

Question. Did you, in council with the Indians, after being relieved of the command of Fort Lyon, advise the Indians to depend upon the assurances given them by Major Anthony ?

Answer. In the council held with the Indians by Major Anthony I was present, and requested Major Anthony to allow me to say a few words to the chiefs, which he granted.   I then told them how I was situated, having been relieved from the command by Major Anthony, and that I was no longer in authority, but that Major Anthony, who was now in command, would treat them the same as I had done, until something definite could be heard from proper quarters in regard to them, and advised them to rely upon what he told them ; that he was a good chief.

By J. M. CHIVINGTON :

Question. After your expedition to the tributary of the Smoky Hill, and up to the time of your being relieved from command of Fort Lyon, did you not allow the Indians to visit Fort Lyon as they pleased, and did not large numbers of Indians go into Fort Lyon and have dances on the parade ground of that post ?

Answer. Large numbers of Indians were not allowed to enter Fort Lyon as they pleased.   There were a few Indians at one time that had a dance in front of the United States Indian agent's dwelling, and at the time this occurrence took place I was not aware of the existence of Field Order No. 2.

Question. About how many Indians were there that participated in the dance the Indians had in front of the agent's dwelling ?

Answer. I believe there were about three.

Question. About how many Indians were there present who did not participate in the dance in front of the agent's dwelling ?

Answer. I could not say about how many.

292

Question. Did you see the Indians present who did not participate in the dance in front of the agent's dwelling ?

Answer. I did.

Question. You say that you told the Indians to rely upon what Major Anthony told them. Did Major Anthony hear you tell the Indians this, and did he consent to the assurances you gave the Indians in regard to his treatment of the Indians ?

Answer. Major Anthony was present when I told them, but I don't remember of his making any remarks on the subject, although I had at different times heard him give them assurances of safety.

Re-examination of Major E. W. Wynkoop closed.

JOHN W. PROWERS called in by the commission to give evidence. The oath being administered according to law, he (Prowers) testified as follows:

Question. What is your full name, residence, and occupation ?

Answer. John W. Prowers; Fort Lyon, Colorado Terrritory; government contractor and employé.

Question. How long have you resided in what is known as the Territory of Colorado ?

Answer. Two years in July.

Question. How long have you resided in the Indian country ?

Answer. Ever since I have been here.

Question. Among what tribes of Indians have you resided ?

Answer. Cheyennes and Arapahoes.

Question. Are you familiar with the languages, manners, and customs of the Cheyennes and Arapahoes ?

Answer. Yes, to a considerable extent. I have acted as interpreter here at the post in the last two or three years several times; part of the time regularly employed by the commanding officer, and sometimes, when sent for, acting voluntarily.

Question. How are the Cheyennes and Arapahoes organized and governed among themselves?

Answer. Organized in bands; governed by the head men of the tribes; each band has a chief, separate from the head men of the tribes. When the principal chiefs get together for council, they call the head chiefs of each separate band to sit in council with them.

Question. Is the head chief of each band a "war" or a "council chief?"

Answer. War chief.

Question. Who were the principal chiefs of the Cheyenne and Arapahoe tribes last year ?

Answer. Of the Cheyennes, Black Kettle, White Antelope, Lean Bear, and Jake; of the Arapahoes, Little Raven, Left Hand, Neva.

Question. Who are known as the head war chiefs of each tribe ?

Answer. I do not know the names of the head war chiefs of the tribes. They very often change at different times.

Question. Do you know who were known as the head war chiefs of each tribe last summer and fall ?

Answer. I do not, only of the Dog soldiers: Bull Bear.

Question. Are the Cheyennes divided into different bands ?

Answer. Yes.

Question. Into how many, and how are they or each of them governed ?

Answer. Four or five—five, I think, governed by the principal chiefs of the tribe.

Question. What are known among the Cheyennes as "Dog soldiers?"

Answer. A band that ranges on the Platte. I never have seen them but once at this place. They came here in 1856, and drew their presents from Major

Robert Miller, Indian agent, and have not been back here since. They live most of the time on the Smoky Hill and Republican, and have done their trading altogether on the Platte, sometimes on the North and sometimes on the South Platte. They have done no trading on this river, nor with any one from here, to my knowledge, since 1856. They have been sent for often, but would never come into this place, for some reason of difficulty between themselves and other bands of Cheyennes. They have drawn off from Black Kettle's band, and refused to have anything to do with him, and have appointed their own trading man. They do not claim any connection to Black Kettle's band whatever. They have often tried to persuade Black Kettle's band to go north of the Platte to their old lands between the Platte and the Missouri river. Black Kettle always refused and never would go. They (the Dog soldiers) being a large band, have often threatened to take all the Indians north of the Platte by force. For some reason they never attempted to take them by force. They have often threatened, but never attempted. They (the Dog soldiers) have always been very mean to white traders, always wanting to make the traders trade as they (the Dog soldiers) pleased. They have often thrown the traders' goods into the fire.

Commission adjourned until 1½ this p. m.

*One and a half p. m.*—Commission met pursuant to adjournment. Present, all members and recorder.

Examination of John W. Prowers by the commission continued:

Question. When did the Dog soldiers separate themselves from Black Kettle's band?

Answer. About nine years ago this fall.

Question. What portion of the Cheyenne Indians are known as Dog soldiers?

Answer. A strong band, in the neighborhood of a hundred lodges.

Question. Where were the Dog soldiers last summer and fall?

Answer. On the Smoky Hill and the Republican, I understood; I don't know positively. A portion of them I understood were over there when Wynkoop went over, but only a portion.

Question. Did you accompany Major Wynkoop to the Smoky Hill last September?

Answer. I did not.

Question. Did you see Black Kettle, One-Eye, and other chiefs of the Cheyennes and Arapahoes last September, before or after the council on Smoky Hill?

Answer. I saw One-Eye before the council on the Smoky Hill, and Black Kettle and One-Eye here at the fort after the council.

Question. Did you have any conversation with them in reference to peace?

Answer. Yes; I talked with them some.

Question. What was said in that conversation by yourself, Black Kettle, and One-Eye?

(John M. Chivington most respectfully objects to the question, for the following reasons : That it has not been shown that the witness was an authorized agent of the government, and consequently, whatever conversation occurred between unauthorized parties cannot be used as evidence to show the disposition of the Indians toward the whites; that the statement of an Indian to an acquaintance is not such testimony as the court in our opinion should receive.

Objection overruled by the commission.)

Answer. The talk was at the place known as Caddoe. There they told me that Black Kettle had been to Denver; had seen Governor Evans and Colonel Chivington; that they could not make any treaty of peace with them; that their case had been left in the hands of Major Wynkoop; that any arrangement Wynkoop would make for them they would abide by it. Black Kettle started next

294

day to bring in his village, as Major Wynkoop told him to move in. One-Eye also returned to the camp and brought in his family and lodges, and camped alongside of me.' He left Black Kettle on Sand creek, and came in several days ahead of him. Finally, Black Kettle came in, and I came down from Caddoe to the fort, and here I met Black Kettle and several of the principal men, and by the request of Major Colley and Lieutenant Cossitt I attended council here in the commissary building, when John Smith acted as interpreter. During the absence of Black Kettle Major Wynkoop had been relieved by Major Anthony, in command of the post. Major Wynkoop asked permission of Major Anthony to say a few words to the chiefs, which permission was granted. Major Wynkoop told the Indians that he was no more in command of the post, and he (Wynkoop) could do no more for them. He also told the Indians that they could depend upon what Major Anthony said. Then Major Anthony spoke to them. He said that below here, on his way up, he heard a great many bad reports about Black Kettle's Indians, and that he expected to have a fight with them upon his arrival here. After arriving here I heard things quite different, but was glad to meet them; that he had seen Major Wynkoop's reports to headquarters, and had approved of them; that he would try and do everything he could to have a permanent peace made for the whole tribe, (Black Kettle's band;) that he hoped the day was near at hand when we could visit their villages, and they could visit our camps, and trade their furs for provisions, coffee, flour, &c. For the present he could not issue them any rations, owing to his orders from headquarters; that he hoped in a few days to get news so that he might give them something to eat. He told them to remain on Sand creek, and let their young men go hunting buffalo. He also told them that they could come in at any time when they felt like it, and that he would always be glad to see them. He told them that he expected that the next mail would bring him some news from Leavenworth, and that if it was good or bad he would let them know, agreeable to promise to Major Wynkoop. That was about all that was said by Major Anthony. Black Kettle spoke next, saying that he was perfectly satisfied with what he had heard; that his village would remain on Sand creek, and said that if any news came from the States he would like to know, so as to move his village on to the river. He said that he had intended to move at once on to the Purgatory, but that he was perfectly willing to stop on Sand creek, as Major Anthony had advised them. He then told Major Anthony that they wanted to visit Colonel Bent's ranch at the mouth of the Purgatory. Major Anthony then spoke, saying that he had nothing to give them, and no place to keep them for the night. I then spoke, and asked permission to let them go to my place. The major said that he was glad that I should take them. I asked the Indians to go, and they went with me. I fed them that night, and the next morning Black Kettle and a portion of his band then started for Colonel Bent's. A portion remained at my place, and the next day Black Kettle returned, and remained at my camp that night; sent for me in the tent to come and see them. They said they were perfectly satisfied with the way things were going, and hoped the matter would soon be settled. They said that they were very sorry that Major Wynkoop had been removed, but thought that Major Anthony would do all he could for them, and that they felt perfectly easy. Black Kettle asked me what I thought of the council. I told him that I thought it was all right; that from all I could learn I thought everything favorable. They all appeared much pleased with what I had told them, and hoped that it would all be so. Next morning, before leaving my place, I made them a few presents, sugar, coffee, flour, rice, and bacon. I also gave them some tobacco which had been purchased by the officers at this post, and sent to me to give them. They were well pleased, and thanked the officers for giving them the tobacco, (some of the officers being present,) and shook hands all around. Major Anthony had agreed to come up and see them at my place, and for some reason did not come. He sent John

Smith up to talk for him. John Smith told them that he was sorry that he (Anthony) could not come up to see them, but would be glad at any time to see them at the post, and for them to remain on Sand creek with their lodges; that they should be perfectly safe there. Then they shook hands all around, and the talk broke up, and the Indians left for the camp on Sand creek.

Question. At what time in the year did this last talk take place?

Answer. Some time about the middle of November; I can't recollect the date.

Question. How many Indians encamped on Sand creek with Black Kettle?

Answer. I do not know exactly; I understood something over a hundred lodges—about one hundred and twenty or thirty lodges.

Question. Did any Indians afterwards, and prior to the 29th of November, join Black Kettle on Sand creek?

Answer. Not that I know of.

Question. Did any of the Indians who were encamped on Sand creek with Black Kettle move to some other place prior to the 29th of November, 1864?

Answer. A few lodges had moved up the creek aways; how many I do not know.

Question. How far up the creek?

Answer. I did not learn.

Question. How many Indians usually occupy a Cheyenne lodge when in camp?

(John M. Chivington most respectfully objects to the question, for the reason that the witness evidently knows or has intimated he knew how many Indians there were in Black Kettle's village, and that under the circumstances we think the court should not attempt to apply a general rule of average, when the number can be more closely approximated to by the knowledge of the witness of the exact number of Indians in the village of Black Kettle.

Objections overruled by the commission.)

Answer. About five.

Question. How many warriors usually occupy a Cheyenne lodge when in camp?

(John M. Chivington most respectfully objects to the question, on the grounds that the witness has not stated yet that he did not know how many Indian warriors were in the village of Black Kettle, and that the rule of average will not apply nor should be applied by the court until the witness states that he cannot tell how many were in the village.

Objection sustained by the commission.)

Question. How many warriors encamped with Black Kettle at the time you speak of on Sand creek?

Answer. I do not know.

Question. How many warriors usually occupy a Cheyenne lodge when in camp?

Answer. About three to every two lodges.

Commission adjourned until 9 a. m. to-morrow, March 25, 1865.

### THIRTY-SECOND DAY.

MARCH 25, 1865.

Commission met pursuant to adjournment. Present, all members and recorder. Proceedings of yesterday read and approved.

Examination of John W. Prowers by the commission continued:

Question. At the time the Indians went into camp on Sand creek, did they have any stock?

Answer. I did not see them; they usually have horses, mules, and ponies.

Question. What amount of stock did Black Kettle's band own at or about the time they went into camp on Sand creek?

Answer. I do not know.

Question. What position did Black Kettle and One-Eye hold in the Cheyenne tribe during the latter part of the year 1864 ?

Answer. Black Kettle was the principal man of the tribe, and One-Eye was one of the principal men, but not one of the head chiefs ; he had a great deal of influence with the tribe, and they always listened to his council.

Question. In the council with Majors Wynkoop and Anthony at Fort Lyon did Black Kettle speak for and claim to represent any other tribe than his own ?

Answer. None other that I know of.

Question. Did the Indians known as Black Kettle's band have any other property in their camp of value, excepting stock ?

Answer. Only their fineries, saddles, bridles, blankets, silver tails, worn in the hair, silver breastplates, and must have had considerable clothing, as they had drawn it a few days before from Major Colley—domestic, calico, Indian cloth, beads, knives, axes, sugar, coffee, bacon, flour, and numerous small articles, needles, thread, &c., drawn from Major Colley, Indian agent, a few days before they went into camp, or some time in October ; I don't remember the date.

Question. While in camp on Sand creek, and after the issue you refer to, did Black Kettle's band receive any property of value ?

Answer. Not that I know of.

Question. Where were you during the latter part of November, 1864 ?

Answer. At Caddoe, seven miles above here, herding government beef cattle, horses, and mules, &c.

Question. Did anything happen to you about that time ?

Answer. I was taken prisoner one Sunday evening, about sundown, by men of company E, first cavalry of Colorado, by orders of Colonel Chivington, and my men, seven in number, were all disarmed and not allowed to leave the house for two nights and a day and a half, during which time the horses and cattle scattered for miles.

Question. Were any reasons given for your arrest ? If so, what were they.

Answer. No reasons given whatever ; the men were ordered to disarm us, and would not allow any one to come or go to and from the place.

Question. At what time and by whose orders were you afterwards relieved from arrest ?

Answer. By Captain Cook's orders, two days and a half after I was arrested.

Question. By whose authority did Captain Cook release you ?

Answer. I do not know; he was in command of the post at the time.

Question. You say you were arrested on Sunday at sundown ; at what time were you released by Captain Cook ?

Answer. Wednesday, about noon.

Question. Did you at any time hear the reasons for your being arrested ?

Answer. I understood it was because I had an Indian family. The colonel commanding thought I might communicate some news to the Indians encamped on Sand creek.

Question. What became of Black Kettle's band who had encamped on Sand creek ?

Answer. I do not know.

Direct examination of John W. Prowers by the commission closed.

Cross-examination of John W. Prowers, by J. M. Chivington :

Question. What business first induced you to reside among the Indians ?

Answer. I came out with Robert Mills, Indian agent, as clerk; afterwards clerk to Colonel William Bent. Good wages and situation induced me to reside here.

Question. Are you not married to an Indian girl ? and if so, how long have you been married ?

Answer. Yes ; I have been married four years in January last.

297

Question. Whose daughter did you marry?

Answer. One-Eye's.

Question. On or about the 28th of November last, did you not tell some persons who visited your camp that the Indians were not to be trusted, and that you kept Indians in your camp for the purpose of apprising you if the Cheyennes and Arapahoes attempt to kill or injure you?

Answer. No.

Question. You state in your examination in chief that at the time the Indians went into camp on Sand creek the Indians had mules, horses, &c. Did you see in the camp of the Indians on Sand creek any of the horses, mules, &c., that you have stated were there?

Answer. I was not in their camp, and therefore I did not see any in their camp, but they rode horses and mules to my camp. I think I saw some sixty or seventy horses, ponies, and mules.

Question. You say you were not in the camp of the Indians at Sand creek. How then do you know there were any of the animals you spoke of as being in the possession of the Indians at their camp on Sand creek?

Answer. The Indians told me that they had left a number of their animals in camp that were lame. Heretofore I have known them to have from six to fifteen animals to a lodge, and do not know of their losing any number of horses at any time during the last year or two.

Question. Is this the only way you know that the Indians had animals in their camp at Sand creek?

Answer. It is the only way I know.

Question. You state that Major Colley issued a great many articles of domestics, calicoes, &c., to the Indians. Is this the only way you know that the Indians had these articles at their camp at Sand creek in the latter part of November 1864?

Answer. It is the only way I know. I saw Major Colley issue them to the Indians at Fort Lyon.

Question. Did you ever tell the Indians that in case of any meditated atttack upon them by the whites you would give them warning, if in your power?

Answer. I did not

Question. Did you ever have any conversation with any person in regard to what you would or could testify to before this court? If so, with whom?

Answer. I never had any conversation with any one in regard to what I would or could testify to before this court; nothing more than what I have said, I never made the remark as to what I would or could testify to, to any one. The question has never been asked me.

Commission adjourned until Monday, March 27, 1865, at 9 a. m.

### THIRTY-THIRD DAY.

MARCH 27, 1865.

Commission met pursuant to adjournment. Present, all members and recorder.

Proceedings of Saturday, the 25th ultimo, read, amended as follows, and approved: On page 411, first and second line to read "allowed to leave the house for three nights and two days and a half."

The question of J. M. Chivington, before the adjournment, Saturday is rejected and not placed on the record, because he asked the witness if a certain officer (naming him, a member of this commission) had not conversed with him, the witness, in reference to what he could or should testify to before this commission, and this before it appears that the witness ever had any conversation upon the subject with the officer mentioned, and after the witness has testified that he has had no conversation with any one in regard to what he could or would testify to before this commission, and that he never made the remark as to what he could and would testify to to any one, and that the question had never been asked him.

(John M. Chivington most respectfully protests against the ruling of the court in the case of the last interrogatory, which the court has refused to place on record, for the following reasons : That it is the duty of the court to record all interrogatories filed by J. M. Chivington, that the record of the court may embrace every transaction occurring therein; that placing, as the court has done, a resolution of censure upon the records against John M. Chivington, without also placing upon the records the interrogatory upon which that resolution of censure is based, is not rendering him a fair opportunity with the approving officers to show the motives that prompted him in his conduct before this court; that J. M. Chivington would most respectfully inform this court that it always will be, as it always has been, his intention to behave toward this court with all the respect that the most technical could demand.)

Cross-examination of John W. Prowers, by J. W. Chivington, continued :

Question. Were not the expressions of satisfaction by Black Kettle, One-Eye and other Indians, upon leaving your camp, induced by the presents, &c., you stated you made them, rather than by any reasonable grounds they could have had for supposing that peace would be made with them ?

Answer. Not at all. They would have felt the same if I had not given them anything. What they did say to me they said before I gave them any presents.

Question. Were not the feelings of satisfaction expressed by Black Kettle, One-Eye, and other Indians in regard to peace, made for the purpose of obtaining presents from you, knowing or thinking you were afraid of them ?

Answer. No.

Question. Have you at any time, at any place, or to any person, expressed your distrust of the Arapahoes and Cheyenne Indians' sincerity ?

Answer. Not that I can remember of; at least, I have not within the last year or two, that I know of.

Cross-examination of John W. Prowers, by J. M. Chivington, closed.

Re-examination of John W. Prowers, by the commission :

Question. Have you any doubt as to the truthfulness of Black Kettle and One-Eye ?

(John M. Chivington most respectfully objects to the question, for the following reasons : That it is not competent for the court to prove the veracity of the statement of any party whose evidence has been placed on record ; that the language of Black Kettle and One-Eye being brought before the court as evidence, as being only the statement of Indians who were not at the time under the obligations of an oath, to an unauthorized person, is, in our opinion, not the proper subject to introduce evidence upon, either to show their veracity or mendacity—is irrelevant and irregular.

Objection sustained by the commission.)

Re-examination of John W. Prowers closed.

Lieutenant CANNON called in by the commission to give evidence.

The oath being administered according to law, he (Lieutenant Cannon) testified as follows :

Question. What is your full name and occupation?

Answer. James Dean Cannon; occupation, a soldier or officer in the United States volunteers.

Question. What is your rank in the army, and where are you on duty ?

Answer. My rank is first lieutenant, company K, first New Mexico volunteers. I am on duty at Fort Lyon, Colorado Territory.

Question. How long have you been at Fort Lyon?

Answer. I believe I came here in September last.

Question. State what was done at Fort Lyon during the latter part of November, 1864.

Answer. Along about the middle of November a partial treaty was made with the Arapahoe and Cheyenne Indians. In the latter part of November, Colonel Chivington arrived here with a command. Major Anthony was then in command of the post. I was then in command of company K, first New Mexico volunteers, Captain Hill being absent. Major Anthony came to me on the 28th of November, and asked me if I was willing to go out as adjutant of the Fort Lyon battalion on an Indian expedition. I asked Major Anthony what the object was of this expedition. He told me that it was to be a thorough, vigorous Indian warfare. I told him if such was the case I had no objection to go; that I would do as much and go as far as any person; but that I was fearful that it was only of short duration, as the principal part of Colonel Chivington's command were one-hundred-days men, whose term of service had nearly expired; that I was fearful that all it would amount to was that they would go out there and jump into the band of Indians that we had corralled. He assured me again that it would be a thorough, vigorous warfare; that we would go on to the Smoky Hill and Republican. He then issued an order placing me on duty as adjutant of the Fort Lyon battalion. We started accordingly on the night of the 28th of November, about 8 o'clock in the evening. We marched all night, and a little after daylight, on the morning of the 29th, came in sight of the camp of Indians. The command was halted by Colonel Chivington, in order for the men to strap their overcoats on to their saddles. Before we were ordered to charge, Colonel Chivington addressed his command. He says, "Men, remember the murdered women and children on the Platte." We were then ordered to charge the Indian camp, which we did. As soon as near enough, we opened fire on their camp, the Indians returning the fire and retreating into the bed of Sand creek, and up the creek. A portion of our command was on each side of the creek, the artillery in the bed of the creek. We pursued them a distance of some three or four miles, with almost a continued fire from each on either side. As the Indians would escape from the creek to the bluffs, they were pursued by troops on either side as long as any could be found. That is all I know in regard to the fight.

Commission adjourned until 1½ this p. m.

*One and a half p. m.*—Commission met pursuant to adjournment. Present, all members and recorder.

Examination of James D. Cannon, first lieutenant first New Mexico volunteers, by the commission, continued :

Question. Did you, prior to the attack on Black Kettle's camp, have any conversation with any officer, besides Major Anthony, in reference to the Indians encamped on Sand creek?

Answer. I think I did.

Question. With whom did you have such conversation?

Answer. With Captain Soule, Lieutenant Cramer, and I am not sure but what I did with Major Downing; I think I did.

Question. What orders were given by the commander during the attack on Black Kettle's camp?

Answer. I heard no order except "to charge upon the camp and remember the murdered women and children on the Platte;" that is, I heard no other orders from the commander.

Question. How many Indians were in the camp at the time of the attack upon them?

Answer. As near as I could judge I should say there were from five hundred to six hundred souls, all told. I would state that my opinion is formed from

300

the number of Indians who generally occupy a lodge, and knowing the number of lodges in the camp.

Question. What proportion of the whole number were women and children?

Answer. I would say two-thirds, to the best of my knowledge.

Question. In what order did Colonel Chivington's command move up the creek while attacking the Indians?

Answer. On the northeast side of the creek, being the side I was on. As one company would come up opposite to where the Indians were in the creek they were ordered to dismount by the company commander; they would continue their fire until the Indians would get out of their reach up the creek. Then the cavalry dismounted would be ordered to mount and renew their charge. In the mean time another company would often pass them and get in ahead and dismount to commence their fire the same as before.

Question. Did the Indians try to shelter themselves from the fire of Colonel Chivington's command? If so, in what manner?

Answer. They did; by digging holes under the banks and in the top of the banks in the sand.

Question. How long did the fight continue, and how many Indians were killed?

Answer. The fight, I judge, continued some four or five hours. My estimate of the number of Indians killed was about two hundred, all told.

Question. What proportion of those killed were women and children?

Answer. I would say two-thirds, to the best of my knowledge.

Question. During the fight on Sand creek was any portion of Colonel Chivington's command so situated as to be under the fire of another portion?

Answer. Yes.

Question. Did any Indians escape from Sand creek after the fight commenced?

Answer. I think they did.

Question. Was anything done with or to the Indians killed?

Answer. Yes.

Question. State what was done.

Answer. They were scalped and mutilated in various ways.

Question. Did the commanding officer make any attempt to prevent the scalping and mutilating of the dead?

(J. M. Chivington most respectfully objects to the question, for the following reason: That it has not been shown that the commanding officer had any knowledge that such mutilation was being done.

Objection overruled by the commission.)

Answer. Not to my knowledge.

Question. Did you have any conversation with the commanding officer during or after the fight on Sand creek in reference to that affair?

Answer. I did not during the fight; I did after.

Question. What was said in that conversation?

Answer. He told me that he believed that there were from five hundred to six hundred Indians killed, and that it was the biggest fight on record. That was the purport of the conversation that passed between him and myself.

Question. Did you before or after the fight on Sand creek hear Colonel Chivington make any threats against or curse any person or persons?

(John M. Chivington most respectfully objects to the question, for the following reasons: That the evidence of any threats Colonel Chivington has made is irrelevant to the matter in issue, and should not be received by this court. That the orders of this commission are to examine into the official acts of Colonel Chivington, and not inquire into any private quarrels with any person; that the government can be benefited by, and in our opinion desires only facts in regard to certain official acts of Colonel Chivington, and does not require either his pedigree or history of his relations as a private individual with any man or men.

301

Objection overruled by the commission.)

Answer. I don't know that I did.

Question. Was any property captured from the Indians on Sand creek?

Answer. Yes.

Question. Describe the property and what was done with it.

Answer. I think there were about six hundred ponies and mules captured, principally ponies, and quite a large number of buffalo robes. Some four hundred head of the ponies were sent into Fort Lyon in charge of an officer who was in charge of a Mexican company belonging to the third regiment; his name was Marina Autobees, a lieutenant. The balance was brought in here by the command.

Question. Were any prisoners taken at Sand creek by Colonel Chivington's command? ·

Answer. Yes.

Question. How many and what was done with them?

Answer. There was one man, (half-breed, said to be a son of John Smith,) two squaws, and two or three children; that was all I saw. The man was killed in a lodge there at Sand creek while a prisoner ; two squaws and two of the children were brought into Fort Lyon by company G, first Colorado cavalry.

Question. State how the man was killed.

Answer. He was shot.

Question. Was he under guard at the time he was shot?

Answer. I could not say whether there was a guard posted there or not.

Question. Was he shot by order of any person?

Answer. Not to my knowledge.

Question. Was any attempt made to ascertain who shot him ?

Answer. I think not ; none, however, to my knowledge.

Question. What did the Indians do when Colonel Chivington's command opened fire on them ?

Answer. They fled to the creek; retreated fighting.

Question. Did any of them advance towards Colonel Chivington's command?

Answer. I think there did after the fight commenced. I know some of them came towards me several times.

Question. Were the women and children killed while attempting to escape?

Answer. Yes.

Question. At what time was the scalping and mutilating done?

Answer. I think it was done all through the fight, and after; I think it commenced very soon after the fight commenced.

Question. Who took part in the scalping and mutilating of the dead?

Answer. I don't know as I could tell you who it was. It was very near a general thing.

Question. Did any of the officers encourage scalping by act or word?

(John M. Chivington objects to the question for the following reasons: That the witness has stated that he did not know that he could tell who took part in it. That the question is leading, and directs the witness what to say, and can be answered by a negative or an affirmative, and that it is illegal and irregular to put questions of this kind, particularly when the party asking the questions has introduced the witness.

Objection sustained by the commission.)

Question. Were the parties who did the scalping and mutilating of the dead, soldiers?

Answer. Yes, I think so. There were but few there who were not soldiers.

Commission adourned until 9 a. m. to-morrow, March 28, 1865.

THIRTY-FOURTH DAY.

MARCH 28, 1865.

Commission met pursuant to adjournment. Present, all members and re-corder.

Proceedings of yesterday read and approved.

Direct examination of Lieutenant James D. Cannon by the commission continued:

Question. Did any person, or persons, have any conversation with you after the fight on Sand creek, in reference to the scalping and mutilating of the Indians?

Answer. Yes.

Question. What was that conversation?

Answer. I had some men to tell me that they had scalped, some one, some two, and some three and four Indians.

Question. State particularly what they said.

Answer. I heard one man say that he had cut a squaw's heart out, and he had it stuck up on a stick.

Question. State who the man was and what command he belonged to.

Answer. The man was a soldier; I do not know his name. I could not say whether he was a first or third regiment man, but was with the command of Colonel Chivington.

Question. What was the understanding or partial treaty you refer to, as between the Indians of Black Kettle's band and the officers at Fort Lyon?

(John M. Chivington most respectfully objects to the question, for the following reasons: That it has not been shown that any treaty could be made by the officers of Fort Lyon, but that they had no authority to make such partial treaty, and that the witness has stated what he knew in regard to the transactions at Fort Lyon, and that no knowledge has been brought to the court that the witness knew of any understanding with the officers at Fort Lyon and the Indians, or that any such understanding existed, which it is necessary to prove before the witness can be asked what the understanding was.

Objection overruled by the commission.)

Answer. It was to the effect that the Indians came in here and were ordered to camp down below the commissary. They said they wished to become friendly and make a treaty with the whites. In council with the Indians Major Wynkoop told them that he had no power to make a treaty, but if they would deliver up the government stock which they had, and their arms, they could remain in the vicinity of the post and have protection until he could hear from Washington as to what could be done. Immediately afterwards Major Wynkoop was relieved from command by Major Anthony. There was a council called, and Major Anthony adopted the same policy in regard to the Indians as Major Wynkoop had. Shortly after the Indians came and asked permission of Major Anthony to give them their arms and remove their camp over in the vicinity of the Buffalo range. Their request was granted by Major Anthony, and their arms given up to them.

Direct examination of First Lieutenant James D. Cannon, by the commission, closed.

Cross-examination of First Lieutenant James D. Cannon, by J. M. Chivington:

Question. How far was Colonel Chivington from you when he made the speech referred to by you, before going into battle? What command was you with, and did you yourself hear the speech of Chivington, or was it told to you by some other person?

Ex. Doc. 26——8

Answer. Not far; about fifty feet. I was with the Fort Lyon battalion. I heard it myself.

Question. Who gave the order to charge, and to whom was it given?

Answer. Colonel Chivington gave the order to Major Anthony.

Question. How long did you remain after the fight, and did you not accompany Major Anthony's command back to the train?

Answer. I remained there until Colonel Chivington's command came back. I did not accompany Major Anthony's command back to the train.

Question. How long was one portion of Colonel Chivington's command under fire of another portion, and what portion in number was so under fire of another portion?

Answer. I could not state how long; at different times during the fight. Companies were firing a cross-fire opposite each other.

Question. What part of the field did this occur? Please describe particularly.

Answer. It occurred when the Indians were retreating up Sand creek, the command pursuing them on each side. It was at a bend about a mile and a half above the village.

Question. What reason have you for thinking that Indians escaped after the fight? Please state particularly.

Answer. I saw Indians on the hills. I judge also from the number I was led to believe were there, and the number killed.

Question. Is this all the reason you have for believing Indians escaped? Please state particularly.

Answer. Yes.

Question. Did you see the commanding officer during the fight?

Answer. I did not.

Question. How soon after the fight, and where did you see the commanding officer?

Answer. I saw him immediately after the fight was over; some three or four miles above the village, on the northeast side of the creek.

Question. Did you have any conversation with the commanding officer at the time you saw him after the fight?

Answer. No, not particularly; though I heard a conversation between him and others.

Question. What was that conversation in regard to?

Answer. In regard to the success of the fight.

Question. Was anything else referred to in that conversation?

Answer. Not that I know of.

Question. You state that Indians were scalped, &c. Did you see any person scalping them?

Answer. I did.

Commission adjourned until 1½ o'clock p. m.

*One and a half p. m.*—Commission met pursuant to adjournment. Present, Captain E. A. Jacobs, veteran battalion first Colorado cavalry; Captain Geo. H. Stilwell, veteran battalion first Colorado cavalry, recorder. Absent, Lieutenant Colonel S. F. Tappan, veteran battalion first Colorado cavalry.

Commission adjourned at 3 o'clock, to meet again at 9 a. m. to-morrow, March 29, 1865.

### THIRTY-FIFTH DAY

MARCH 29, 1865.

Commission met pursuant to adjournment. Present, all members and recorder.

Proceedings of yesterday read and approved.

Cross-examination of First Lieutenant James D. Cannon by J. M. Chivington, continued:

Question. You say you saw persons scalping; did you try to stop them, or report the fact to Colonel Chivington, the commanding officer?

Answer. I did not.

Question. Have you had any conversation with any person in regard to the Sand Creek fight? If yes, with whom?

Answer. I have, with different persons; with the officers at Fort Lyon in general, Captain Hill, Captain Soule, Lieutenant Cossitt, Lieutenant Clinton, Captain Jacobs, and with various others. I don't know as I can mention the names of others positively.

Question. Have you given the names of all the officers at Fort Lyon with whom you have had a conversation in regard to the Sand Creek fight? If not, state the names of the other officers.

Answer. I think I had some conversation with Colonel Tappan; also with Lieutenant Marvin and Major Wynkoop.

Question. Were you interrogated by any of these officers particularly in regard to what you know of the Sand Creek fight?

Answer. No.

Question. Did you state particularly what you knew of the Sand Creek fight to any of the Fort Lyon officers?

Answer. I have made statements respecting the Sand Creek fight to nearly all the officers who were not present at the fight. I gave detailed accounts, but could not say that I made particular statements, it being a general topic of conversation.

Cross-examination of First Lieutenant James D. Cannon by J. M. Chivington closed.

Examination of First Lieutenant James D. Cannon by the commission:

Question. You refer to a conversation between Colonel Chivington and others after the fight, in regard to the success of the fight; what was that conversation?

(John M. Chivington most respectfully objects to the question for the following reasons: That in the cross-examination the witness stated that he had stated all he knew in regard to the conversation, &c.; that upon a re-examination it is not proper that the prosecution inquire into statements about which the witness has said he has stated all he knew. That prosecution can only re-examine their own witnesses upon new matter brought out by the defence on cross-examination.

Objection overruled by the commission.)

Answer. That the fight was the most successful thing on record; that we had achieved a glorious victory; that is the purport of the conversation.

Examination of First Lieutenant James D. Cannon closed.

Commission adjourned until 1½ this p. m.

*One and a half p. m.*—Commission met pursuant to adjournment. Present, all members and recorder.

Mr. J. M. Combs called in by the commission to give evidence. The oath being administered according to law, he (Combs) testified as follows:

Question. What is your full name and residence?

Answer. James M. Combs; reside here at present.

Question. How long have you resided at Fort Lyon?

Answer. About the last of August or the 1st of September I moved here.

Question. Where were you during the latter part of November, 1864?

Answer. About the 20th of November I started up the river, and I think about the 5th of December I got back here.

Question. How far up the river did you go?

Answer. I went as far as Pueblo.

Question. On your road up the river did anything happen of an unusual character? If so, state what it was.

Answer. The third night after leaving here I met the command of Colonel Chivington in camp at Spring Bottom. I had some conversation there soon after I got in. I had been in the station but a few minutes, and of course expressed some little astonishment at meeting that command ; some one remarked to Colonel Chivington that here was a man just up from Fort Lyon. Colonel Chivington then commenced to ask me some questions. At first said he : " They don't expect me down there, do they?" I told him no, that I did not think that anybody from there to the post, or at the post, knew of his coming. He says, "No, sir; nor they won't know it till they see me there." After that I think that Major Downing and Colonel Chivington asked me about the Indians, &c., and who was in command of the fort. I told them that at that time Major Anthony was in command, or was at the time I left He (Chivington) wanted to know who was in command before Major Anthony. I told him that Major Wynkoop commanded before Major Anthony was sent here. He says, "Oh! you must be mistaken ; I think that Left Hand was in command before Major Anthony came here." From that I supposed he was talking more for sport than anything else, and made my answers very short after that. Then I think Major Downing asked me the question, why Major Wynkoop was not in command there. I told him that I heard he was ordered to Fort Larned, and started the same morning that I left Lyon. I think then Major Downing asked me what his business was, and what he was going to Larned for. I told him that I knew nothing about it, that I was not posted in military matters, and was not supposed to know anything about it. Colonel Chivington then straightened himself back in the chair, and laughingly said, " I know what he has gone there for; it is to take command of that post," which led me to believe that it was not so. He then said that he (Wynkoop) is a nice commander, and an honor to the Colorado first. Said he : "How do the Indians like Major Anthony down there?" I told him not very well, giving him hard names, calling him the red-eyed chief, and other names. He wanted to know if Major Anthony fed them as well as Major Wynkoop did. I told him I did not know how well either of them had fed them; that I saw them get stores from both. He wanted to know then how far the Indians were from there. I told him that up to the time I left, there was a large party encamped within a mile and a half from there, but that the most of them had got permission from the commanding officer of the post, and had started out on a buffalo hunt, and a part of them were here yet. He wanted to know if they had been allowed around the post much. I told him that they generally went where they chose—one place and another. He wanted to know if they had been troublesome—much stealing and bothering the people here and about here. I told him that they were here about every day, begging and troubling us in that way. He says : " Have they been in as much since Major Anthony has been in command." I told him that some days he would allow them in, and some days he would not. He wanted to know if the officers, soldiers, or citizens visited their camp often. I told him that I was quite sure that more or less of all, from each class, had been there every day. I told him that I had been there several times, and always met some of them there, officers, soldiers, or citizens. He asked me about how many lodges they had, and about how many warriors. I told him that I thought there was at least about two hundred warriors there at one time. He then asked me the question, how I knew, &c. I told him that I had seen them at that time mounted, with their bows, arrows, and spears, as they were coming in from the bluffs, where they had been, as they supposed, to meet a party of Utes. Then they were all armed. They were in line of battle as they were coming in. I suppose that is what you call it ; they were in a long line, about two deep, as they were coming in. He, Colonel Chivington, or some one else asked me if there were any white men there except me. I told him there were some soldiers and officers mounted ; also some citizens were there besides myself. Colonel Chivington asked me if I knew what they were all there for, mounted. I told him that I did not know; that I did not know what was up until I got there, and that I did not know whether the others knew or not. He wanted to know if they appeared perfectly friendly to the party present. I told him they were very friendly. He then inquired about the Utes; if the Utes were down here. I told him that it was a false alarm, and after that nearly all the officers, soldiers, and some citizens started and came up to the post. He asked me then about feeding them—if they got regular rations here. I told him I thought not, as they were all the time trading for provisions of every kind that they could get. He asked me several questions—nothing regular. I was sitting there, and sometimes he would ask me a question. I can remember a good many questions he asked me about Wynkoop going to Larned, the Indians, &c.

There was a promiscuous conversation about scalps, where they were going to arrange them, &c. He (Chivington) spoke up and said that "scalps are what we are after." I told him that I thought he could get, any way, some four hundred or five hundred of them within one day's march of Fort Lyon; that I thought there was about that number, warriors, squaws, and pappooses, in all, and told him that I thought he ought to do it with that party; that there had been no time, for some time past, when they could not have been taken with fifty men; that they had given up their arms to Major Anthony, and were unarmed now. I told him too that they had given up horses and mules, and all government property taken, and told him that they were considered prisoners of war, and that he (Anthony) had allowed them to go on a buffalo hunt for thirty or forty miles. He asked me if they had all gone. I told him no, that part of them were here. Then he wanted to know why they had not all gone. I told him that Left Hand was very sick, and most of his party was here with him. He asked me the direction they had gone. I told him I did not know; that the distance I heard them say, but not the direction. He made the remark that he would give them a lively buffalo hunt. I was there but about half an hour after that. Very little was said to me, as I was eating my supper.

While I was sitting there one remark was made, I think to Major Downing. Colonel Sharp, Mr. Gill, and several officers were present. He (Chivington) drew himself up in his chair, and made this remark : " Well, I long to be wading in gore." I left the room about that time. I think I was about going out when he made the remark.

Question. Was anything further than what you have already stated said by yourself and Colonel Chivington in reference to the Indians being under the protection of the military at Fort Lyon ?

Answer. I don't think anything more than what I have said.

Question. Did you have any further conversation with Colonel Chivington ?

Answer. Not after that time.

Question. Did anything unusual happen on your way back and after your return to Fort Lyon ?

Answer. Nothing unusual on my way back. After I got back there were reports coming in relating to the Indian fight, and men and officers going to and from the battle-ground, for the first few days after I came back, and then the command came in.

Question. Was the conversation with Colonel Chivington at Spring Bottom, to which you have referred, the last you had with him in reference to Indians ?

Answer. Yes, at Spring Bottom station.

Direct examination of James M. Combs by the commission closed.

Cross-examination of James M. Combs by J. M. Chivington :

Question. Give the names of the persons present when you had the conversation with Colonel Chivington in reference to Indians at Spring Bottom, and the name of the person or persons with you.

Answer. Colonel Chivington, (the parties I shall name were with him, but do not know whether they were there all the time or not, but were most of the time,) Major Downing, Colonel Sharp, and at the last part Captain Maynard and Mr. Gill were there in the room, and some officers of the third, whose names I don't know. Two or three were present. Lieutenant Graham was in and out a good deal while I was there, also a man by the name of Robert Wright. The room was full, but I don't know their names. There was a man by the name of Brown travelling with me. He was there through but little of the conversation.

Question. How long did this conversation last, and did you leave the room at any time during the conversation?

Answer. From the time I went in till the time I came out, it lasted altogether about one hour and a half. I don't remember of going out at that time at all; if I did, it was but for a few minutes, but I do not think I went out during that conversation.

Question. Were not the remarks of hatred uttered by Chivington in reply to what you told him in regard to Indians? Thus, for instance, did you not yourself tell Colonel Chivington that the Indians appeared to be running the post, and that the commanding officer was afraid of the Indians?

Answer. No; I never said anything of that kind.

Question. Did you not say that Major Wynkoop and Captain Soule took the larger part of the command at Fort Lyon out to assist the Arapahoe and Cheyenne Indians, or Indians that were camped near the post, and that you entertained a great deal of fear, on the return of Major Wynkoop and command, from the conduct of the Indians, that the Indians would attack Wynkoop's command?

Answer. I told Colonel Chivington and party that, while I was there at the Indian camp, near this post, a party of soldiers, probably twenty—there might be twenty-five men, and Major Wynkoop and Captain Soule, came across the river on horseback, and I inquired of some of the soldiers that were about me what they were there for, (I saw the Indians striking out across the bluffs, armed,) and was told that the chiefs had been to the post and claimed protection; that the Utes were after them in a large body, and, as the Indians were friends, the officers and soldiers here had to protect them. That I saw nothing but what was perfectly friendly; they were all talking together, chiefs and officers. The Indians dismounted, and most of them remained there, and a few Indians and chiefs came to the post. I saw no reason for fear at all.

Question. Did you state, at any time, that Major Wynkoop and Captain Soule went out with a command to assist the Indians encamped near Fort Lyon to fight the Utes?

Answer. No; I have stated just as I said before.

Question. Did you not state to Colonel Chivington that Major Wynkoop, or Captain Soule, ought to be dismissed from the service for their conduct toward the Indians?

(Objection to the question by Lieutenant Colonel S. F. Tappan, president of the commission.

Objection sustained by the commission.)

Commission adjourned until 9 a. m. to-morrow, March 30, 1865.

### THIRTY-SIXTH DAY.

MARCH 30, 1865.

Commission met pursuant to adjournment. Present, all members and recorder.

Proceedings of yesterday read, amended as follows, and approved: On page 449, insert after second line, "he was out most of the time attending to the horses;" on page 450, fifteenth line, to first answer, omit the words "friends," and insert the word "prisoners."

The reports of Major Wynkoop, marked F, G, and H, referred to on page 348, are here appended, and are as follows:

## F.

The following is a report of Major Wynkoop to his excellency John Evans, governor of Colorado Territory, dated September 18, 1864:

FORT LYON, C. T., *September* 18, 1864.

SIR: I have the honor to report that on the 3d instant three Cheyenne Indians were met a few miles outside of this post by some of my men, en route for Denver, and were brought in. They came, as they stated, bearing with them a proposition for peace from Black Kettle and other chiefs of the Cheyenne and Arapahoe nations. Their propositions were to this effect: that they, the Cheyenne and Arapahoes, had in their possession seven white prisoners whom they offered to deliver up in case that we should come to terms of peace with them. They told me that the Arapahoes, Cheyennes, and Sioux were congregated for mutual protection at what is called the Bunch of Timbers, on the headwaters of Smoky Hill, at a distance of one hundred and forty miles northeast of this post, numbering altogether about three thousand warriors, and were anxious and desirous to make peace with the whites.

Feeling extremely anxious at all odds to effect the release of these white prisoners, and my command but just having been re-enforced by General Carlton, commanding department of New Mexico, by a detachment of infantry sent from New Mexico to my assistance, I found that I would be enabled to leave sufficient garrison for this post by taking one hundred and thirty men with me, (including one section of the battery,) and concluded to march to this Indian rendezvous for the purpose of procuring the white prisoners aforementioned, and to be governed by circumstances as to what manner I should proceed to accomplish the same object.

Taking with me under strict guard the Indians I had in my possession, I reached my destination, and was confronted by from six to eight hundred Indian warriors drawn up in line of battle and prepared to fight.

Putting on as bold a front as I could under the circumstances, I formed my command in as good order as possible for the purpose of acting on the offensive or defensive as might be necessary, and advanced towards them, at the same time sending forward one of the Indians I had with me as an emissary, to state that I had come for the purpose of holding a consultation with the chiefs of the Arapahoes and Cheyennes to come to an understanding which might result in mutual benefit; that I had not come desiring strife, but was prepared for it if necessary, and advised them to listen to what I had to say previous to making any more warlike demonstrations.

They consented to meet me in council, and I then proposed to them that if they desired peace to give me palpable evidence of their sincerity by delivering into my hands their white prisoners. I told them that I was not authorized to conclude terms of peace with them, but if they acceded to my proposition I would take what chiefs they might choose to select to the governor of Colorado Territory, state the circumstances to him, and that I believed it would result in what it was their desire to accomplish, "peace with their white brothers." I had reference particularly to the Arapahoe and Cheyenne tribes.

The council was divided, undecided, and could not come to an understanding among themselves. Finding this to be the case, I told them that I would march to a certain locality, distant twelve miles, and await a given time for their action in the matter. I took a strong position in the locality named and remained three days. In the interval they brought in and turned over four white prisoners, all that was possible for them at the time being to turn over, the balance of the seven being, as they stated, with another band far to the northward.

The released captives that I have now with me at this post consist of one female named Laura Roper, aged sixteen, and three children, two boys and one girl, named Isabella Ubanks, Ambrose Usher, and Daniel Marble; the three first named being taken on Blue river, in the neighborhood of what is known as Liberty farm, and the last captured at some place on the South Platte with a train; all the men belonging thereto were murdered.

I have the principal chiefs of the two tribes with me, and propose starting immediately to Denver to put into effect the aforementioned proposition made by me to them.

They agree to deliver up the balance of the prisoners as soon as it is possible to procure them, which can be done better from Denver city than from this point.

I have the honor, governor, to be your obedient servant,

E. W. WYNKOOP,
*Major First Cavalry of Colorado Com'g Fort Lyon., C. T.*

His Excellency JOHN EVANS,
*Governor of Colorado, Denver, C. T.*

A true copy from the published report of the Commissioner of Indian Affairs, 1864.

CHARLES WHEELER,
*First Lt. Vet. Bat. First Col. Cav., Post Adj't Fort Lyon, C. T.*

G.

FORT LYON, COLORADO TERRITORY,
*October 8, 1864.*

SIR : I have the honor to forward, for the consideration of the major general commanding, the following statement in regard to my course with respect to the Arapahoe and Cheyenne tribes of Indians, and respectfully ask for instructions as to what I may do in the future.

On the third day of September last, three Cheyenne Indians were captured who were approaching this post. They came, as they stated, bearing with them a proposition for peace from Black Kettle and other chiefs of the Arapahoe and Cheyenne nations; their proposition was to the effect that they, the Cheyennes and Arapahoes, had in their possession seven white prisoners, whom they offered to deliver up in case that we should come to terms of peace with them; they said the Arapahoes and Cheyenes were congregated together for mutual protection, numbering over two thousand, on the headwaters of the Smoky Hill river, at what is called "Bunch of Timbers," a distance of one hundred and forty miles from this post, and were anxious to make peace with the whites.

Desiring at all odds to effect the release of these white prisoners, and my command having just been re-enforced by a detachment of New Mexican troops sent me by General Carleton, I found that I could leave sufficient garrison for the post, and take with me one hundred and thirty men, and concluded to march to this Indian rendezvous for the purpose of procuring these white prisoners aforementioned, and to be governed by circumstances as to in what manner I should proceed to accomplish the same object.

Taking with me the three Indians I had in my possession, I reached my destination, and was confronted by from six to eight hundred Indian warriors drawn up in line of battle and prepared to fight. Putting on as bold a front as possible under the circumstances, I formed my little command in as good order as possible for the purpose of acting in the offensive or defensive, as might be necessary, and advanced towards them, at the same time sending forward one of the Indians I had with me as an emissary, to state that I had come for the purpose of holding a consultation with the chiefs of the Arapahoe and Cheyenne nations, to endeavor to come to an understanding which might result in mutual *benefit;* that I had not come desiring strife, but was prepared for it if necessary, and advised them to listen to what I had to say previous to their making any more warlike demonstrations. They consented to meet me in council, and I then told them that if they desired peace to give me some palpable evidence of their sincerity, by delivering into my hands their white prisoners. I said I was not authorized to conclude terms of peace with them, but that, if they accepted my proposition, I would take the chiefs they might choose to select to the governor of Colorado Territory, state the circumstances to him, and that I believed it would result in what it was their object to accomplish.

The council were divided, and could not come to an understanding among themselves. Finding this to be the case, I told them I would march to a certain locality, distant twelve miles, and await a given time for their action in the matter.

I took a strong position in the locality named, and remained three days; in the interim they brought and turned over into my possession four white prisoners, all that was possible at the time for them to procure, the balance of the seven, as they stated, being with another band far to the northward.

With three of the principal chiefs of the Cheyenne, and four of the Arapahoe nation, I proceeded to Denver city to see the governor of Colorado Territory; I had, I supposed, sufficient proofs to show that these Indians had respected their treaty until they were provoked and driven to commit these outrages. As far as the Arapahoe tribe are concerned, I know of my own personal knowledge that such is the case; they have never desired war, and are now anxious for peace.

The governor of Colorado refused to have anything to do with the matter, and referred them to the military authorities, and particularly to myself, as having direct jurisdiction over the country through which they ranged. They were perfectly willing to place themselves under my control, for me to dispose of them as I thought proper, when I was shown a telegram from the major general commanding department, to the effect that no peace should be made with these Indians. Presuming that the general commanding was not acquainted with all the circumstances connected with the affair, is why I have entered into this lengthy detail, and now would ask for particular instructions in regard to my future course.

The general commanding will please notice that there are still three white female prisoners in the hands of these savages, whom they have promised to deliver up to me, and whom I am expecting every day, and whom, I presume, were they to know that they could not procure peace, they would instantly sacrifice.

I think that if some terms are made with these Indians, I can arrange matters so, by bringing their villages under my direct control, that I can answer for their fidelity. We are at war with the Sioux, and the Kiowas, and Comanches; these Indians, the Arapahoes and Cheyennes, tell me they are willing to lend me their assistance in fighting the Kiowas and Comanches. It is the universal desire of the settlers of this part of the country for peace. I enclose a copy of a communication received from the settlers to prove that such is the case; and, if I may be pardoned for the suggestion, I deem it the best policy to adopt at present, in consequence of the necessity of the services of our troops elsewhere, and in consequence of having had considerable experience in this country. I know that in a general Indian war it will take more soldiers than we can possibly spare to keep open the two lines of communication, protect the settlements, and make an effective war upon them.

Deeming these matters to be of the utmost importance, and despatch required to bring the same before the major general commanding, I have taken the liberty of ordering an officer to carry this communication, and return with instructions as soon as possible. Hoping that I have not been too bold in the responsibility I have assumed, which may lay me liable to the censure of the commanding general,

I have the honor to remain your obedient servant,

E. W. WYNKOOP,
*Major First Cavalry of Colorado, Com'g Fort Lyon, C. T.*

A true copy:

CHARLES WHEELER,
*First Lieut. and Regimental Adjutant Veteran Battalion First Colorado Cavalry, Post Adjutant Fort Lyon, Colorado Territory.*

The above is a report of Major E. W. Wynkoop, commanding Fort Lyon, to the commander of department of Kansas.

---

H.

FORT LYON, COLORADO TERRITORY,
*January* 15, 1865.

SIR: In pursuance of Special Order No. 43, headquarters district of Upper Arkansas, directing me to assume command of Fort Lyon, as well as to investigate and immediately report in regard to late Indian proceedings in this vicinity, I have the honor to state that I arrived at this post on the evening of the 14th of January, 1865, assumed command on the morning of the 15th, and the result of my investigation is as follows, viz:

As explanatory, I beg respectfully to state that, while formerly in command of this post, on the 4th day of September, 1864, and after cer'ain hostilities on the part of the Cheyenne and Arapahoe Indians, induced, as I have had ample proof, by the overt acts of white men, three Indians (Cheyennes) were brought as prisoners to myself, who had been found coming towards the post, and who had in their possession a letter, written, as I ascertained afterwards, by a half-breed in the Cheyenne camp, as coming from Black Kettle and other prominent chiefs of the Cheyenne and Arapahoe nation; the purport of which was that they desired peace, had never desired to be at war with the whites, &c., as well as stating that they had in their possession some white prisoners, women and children, whom they were willing to deliver up, provided that peace was granted them. Knowing that it was not in my power to insure and offer them the peace for which they sued, but at the same time anxious, if possible, to accomplish the rescue of the white prisoners in their possession, I finally concluded to risk an expedition with the small command I could raise, numbering one hundred and twenty-seven men, to the rendezvous, where I was informed they were congregated to the number of two thousand, and endeavor by some means to procure the aforesaid white prisoners, and to be governed in my course in accomplishing the same entirely by circumstances. Having formerly made lengthy reports in regard to the details of my expedition, I have but to say that I succeeded, procured four white captives from the hands of these Indians, simply giving them in return a pledge that I would endeavor to procure for them the peace for which they so anxiously sued, feeling that under the proclamation issued by John Evans, governor of Colorado and superintendent of Indian affairs, a copy of which becomes portion of this report, even if not by virtue of my position as a United States officer highest in authority in the country included within the bounds prescribed as the country of the Arapahoe and Cheyenne nations, that I could offer them protection until such time as some measures might be taken by those higher in authority than myself in regard to them. I took with me seven of the principal chiefs, including Black Kettle, to Denver City, for the purpose of allowing them an interview with the governor of Colorado—by that means making a mistake, of which I have since become painfully aware, that of

312

proceeding with these chiefs to the governor of Colorada Territory instead of to the headquarters of my district to my commanding officer. In the consultation with Governor Evans the matter was referred entirely to the military authorities. Colonel J. M. Chivington, at that time commander of the district of Colorado, was present at the council held with these Indian chiefs, and told them that the whole matter was referred to myself, who would act towards them according to the best of my judgment until such time as I could receive instructions from the proper authorities. Returning to Fort Lyon I allowed the Indians to bring their villages to the vicinity of the post, including their squaws and pappooses, and in such a position that I could at any moment, with the garrison I had, have annihilated them, had they given any evidence of hostility of any kind in any quarter. I then immediately despatched my adjutant, Lieutenant W. W. Denison, with a full statement to the commanding general of the department, asking for instructions; but in the meanwhile, various false rumors having reached district headquarters in regard to my course, I was relieved from the command of Fort Lyon and ordered to report at district headquarters. Major Scott J. Anthony, first cavalry of Colorado, who had been ordered to assume command of Fort Lyon previous to my departure, held a consultation with the chiefs in my presence, and told them that, though acting under strict orders, under the circumstances, he could not materially differ from the course which I had adopted, and allowed them to remain in the vicinity of the post with their families, assuring them of perfect safety until such time as positive orders should be received from headquarters in regard to them. I left the post on the 26th of November for the purpose of reporting to district headquarters. On the second day after leaving Fort Lyon, while on the plains, I was approached by three Indians, one of whom stated to me that he had been sent by Black Kettle to warn me that about two hundred Sioux warriors had proceeded down the road between where I was and Fort Larned, to make war, and desired that I should be careful—another evidence of these Indians' good faith. All of his statement proved afterwards to be correct. Having an escort of twenty-eight men I proceeded on my way, but did not happen to fall in with them.

From evidence of officers at this post, I understand that on the 28th day of November, 1864, Colonel J. M. Chivington, with the third regiment of Colorado cavalry, (one hundred days' men,) and a battalion of the first Colorado cavalry, arrived at Fort Lyon, ordered a portion of the garrison to join him under the command of Major Scott J. Anthony, and, against the remonstrance of the officers of the post, who stated to him the circumstances, of which he was well aware, attacked the camp of friendly Indians, the major portion of which were composed of women and children. The affidavits which become a portion of this report, will show more particulars of that massacre. Every one whom I have spoken to, either officer or soldier, agrees in the relation that the most fearful atrocities were committed that ever were heard of; women and children were killed and scalped; children shot at their mothers' breast, and all the bodies mutilated in the most horrible manner. Numerous eye-witnesses have described scenes to me, coming under the eye of Colonel Chivington, of the most disgusting and horrible character; the dead bodies of females profaned in such a manner that the recital is sickening; Colonel J. M. Chivington all the time inciting his troops to these diabolical outrages. Previous to the slaughter commencing, he addressed his command, arousing in them by his language all their worst passions, urging them on to the work of committing all these diabolical outrages. Knowing himself all the circumstances of these Indians resting on the assurances of protection from the government given them by myself and Major S. J. Anthony, he kept his command in entire ignorance of the same, and when it was suggested that such might be the case, he denied it positively, stating that they were still continuing their depredations, and lay there threatening the fort.

313

I beg leave to draw the attention of the colonel commanding to the fact established by the enclosed affidavits, that two-thirds or more of that Indian village were women and children, and he is aware whether or not the Indians go to war taking with them their women and children. I desire, also, to state that Colonel J. M. Chivington is not my superior officer, but is a citizen mustered out of the United States service; and, also, at the time this inhuman monster committed this unprecedented atrocity, he was a citizen by reason of his term of service having expired, he having lost his regulation command some months previous.

Colonel Chivington reports, officially, that between five and six hundred Indians were left dead upon the field. I have been informed by Captain Booth, district inspector, that he visited the field, and counted but sixty-nine bodies, and by others who were present, but that few, if any over that number were killed, and that two-thirds of them were women and children. I beg leave to further state, for the information of the colonel commanding, that I have talked to every officer in Fort Lyon, and many enlisted men, and that they unanimously agree that all the statements I have made in this report are true.

In conclusion, allow me to say that from the time I held the consultation with the Indian chiefs on the headwaters of the Smoky Hill, up to the date of the massacre by Colonel Chivington, not one single depredation had been committed by the Cheyenne and Arapahoe Indians; the settlers of the Arkansas valley had returned to their ranches, from which they had fled, had taken in their crops, and had been resting in perfect security, under assurances from myself that they would be in no danger for the present—by that means saving the country from what must inevitably become almost a famine were they to lose their crops. The lines of communication to the State were opened, and travel across the plains rendered perfectly safe through the Cheyenne and Arapahoe country. Since this last horrible murder by Chivington the country presents a scene of desolation; all communication is cut off with the States, except by sending bodies of troops, and already over one hundred whites have fallen as victims to the fearful vengeance of these betrayed Indians. All this country is ruined; there can be no such thing as peace in the future but by the total annihilation of all the Indians on the plains. I have the most reliable information to the effect that the Cheyennes and Arapahoes have allied themselves with the Kiowas, Comanches, and Sioux, and are congregated to the number of five or six thousand on the Smoky Hill.

Let me also draw the attention of the colonel commanding to the fact stated by affidavit, that John Smith, United States interpreter, a soldier, and a citizen, were present in the Indian camp by permission of the commanding officer of this post, another evidence to the fact of these same Indians being regarded as friendly; also, that Colonel Chivington states, in his official report, that he fought from 900 to 1,000 Indians, and left from five to six hundred dead upon the field, the sworn evidence being that there were but 500 souls in the village, two-thirds of them being women and children, and that there were but from sixty to seventy killed, the major portion of which were women and children.

It will take many more troops to give security to the travellers and settlers in this country, and to make any kind of successful warfare against the Indians. I am at work placing Fort Lyon in a state of defence, having all, both citizens and soldiers, located here employed upon the works, and expect to have them soon completed, and of such a nature that a comparatively small garrison can hold the fort against any attack by Indians.

Hoping that my report may receive the particular attention of the colonel commanding, I respectfully submit the same.

Your obedient servant,

E. W. WYNKOOP,
*Major Commanding First Veteran Cavalry and Fort Lyon.*

Lieutenant J. E. TAPPAN,
*Acting Assistant Adjutant General, District Upper Arkansas.*

The above is a report to Colonel Ford, commanding district Upper Arkansas, dated January 15, 1865.

A true copy :

CHARLES WHEELER,
*First Lieut. and Regimental Adj't Vet. Battalion First Colorado Cav., Post Adj't, Fort Lyon, Colorado Territory.*

FORT LYON, COLORADO TERRITORY,
*January* 15, 1864.

Personally appeared before me John Smith, United States Indian interpreter, who, after being duly sworn, says :

That on the fourth day of September, 1864, he was appointed Indian interpreter for the post of Fort Lyon, and has continued to serve in that capacity up to the present date ; that on the fourth day of September, 1864, by order of Major E. W. Wynkoop, commanding post of Fort Lyon, he was called upon to hold a conversation with three Cheyenne Indians, viz., One-Eye and two others, who had been brought into the post that day ; that the result of the interview was as follows : One-Eye (Cheyenne) stated that the principal chiefs and sub-chiefs of the Cheyenne and Arapahoe nations had held a consultation, and agreed to a man, of the chief and sub-chiefs, to come, or send in some one who was well acquainted with parties at this post, and finally agreed to send in himself, (One-Eye,) with a paper written by George Bent, (half-breed,) to the effect that the Cheyenne and Arapahoe chiefs had, and did, agree to turn over to Major Wynkoop, or any other military authority, all the white prisoners they had in their possession, as they were all anxious to make peace with the whites, and never desired to be at war. Major Wynkoop then asked One-Eye, he having lived among the whites, and known to have always been friendly disposed towards them, whether he thought the Indians were sincere, and whether they would deliver the white prisoners into his (Major Wynkoop's) hands. His reply was, that at the risk of his life he would guarantee their sincerity. Major Wynkoop then told him he would retain him as a prisoner for the time, and if he concluded to proceed to the Indian camp, he would take him as a hostage for their (the Indians') good faith.

One-Eye also stated that the Cheyenne and Arapahoe nations were congregated to the number of two thousand on the headwaters of Smoky Hill, including some forty lodges of the Sioux ; that they had rendezvoused there and brought in their war parties for the purpose of hearing what would be the result of their message, by which they had sued for peace, and would remain until they heard something definite.

Major Wynkoop told One-Eye that he would proceed to the Indian camp and take him with him.

One-Eye replied he was perfectly willing to be detained a prisoner as well as remain as hostage for the good faith of the Indians, but desired the major to start as soon as possible, for fear that the Indians might separate. On the sixth day of September I was ordered to proceed with Major Wynkoop and his command in the direction of the Indian encampment. After a four days' march we came in sight of the Indians, and one of the three Indians aforementioned was sent to acquaint the chiefs with what was the object of the expedition, with a statement that Major Wynkoop desired to hold a consultation with them, the chiefs. On the 10th day of September, 1864, the consultation was held between Major Wynkoop and his officers and the principal chiefs of the Cheyenne and Arapahoe nations. Major E. W. Wynkoop stated, through me, to the chiefs that he had received their message ; that, acting on that, he had come to talk with them ; asked them whether they all agreed to and indorsed the contents of the letter which he had in his possession, and which had been brought in by One-Eye, receiving an answer in the affirmative. He then told the chiefs that he had not the authority to conclude terms of peace with them, but that he desired to make a proposition to them, to the effect that if they would give him an evidence of their good faith, by delivering into his hands the white prisoners they had in their possession, he would endeavor to procure for them peace, which would be subject to conditions; that he would take with him what principal chiefs they might select, and conduct them in safety to the governor of Colorado, and, whatever might be the result of their interview with him, return them in safety to their tribe.

Black Kettle, the head chief of the Cheyenne nation, replied as follows: That the Cheyenne and Arapahoe nations had always endeavored to observe the terms of their treaty with the United States government; that some years previous, when the white emigration first commenced coming to what is now the Territory of Colorado, the country which was in the possession of the Cheyenne and Arapahoe nation, they could have successfully made war against them, (the whites.) They did not desire to do so; had invariably treated them with kindness, and never, to his knowledge, committed any depredations whatever; that until within the last few months they had gotten along in perfect peace and harmony with their white brethren; but while a hunting party of their young men were proceeding north in the neighborhood of South Platte river, having found some lost stock belonging to white men, which they were driving towards a ranch to deliver up, they were suddenly confronted by a party of United States soldiers and ordered to deliver up their arms. A difficulty immediately ensued which resulted in killing and wounding several on both sides. A short time after this occurrence took place, a village of squaws, papooses and old men, located at what is known as "Cedar Cañon," a short distance north of the South Platte, who were perfectly unaware of any difficulty having occurred between any portion of their tribe (Cheyenne) and the whites, were attacked by a large party of soldiers and some of them killed and their ponies driven off. After this, while a body of United States troops were proceeding from Smoky Hill to Arkansas river, they reached the neighborhood of Law Bear's band of the Cheyenne nation. Law Bear, second chief of the Cheyenne nation, approached the column of troops alone, his warriors remaining off some distance, he not dreaming that there was any hostility between his nation and the whites. He was immediately shot down and a fire opened upon his band, the result of which was a fight between the two parties. Presuming from all these circumstances that war was inevitable, the young men of the Cheyenne nation commenced to retaliate, committing various depredations all the time, which he (Black Kettle) and other principal chiefs of the Cheyenne nation were opposed to, and endeavored by all means in his power to restore pacific relations between that tribe and their white brethren; but, at various times when endeavoring to approach the military posts for the purpose of accomplishing the same, he was fired upon and driven off. Meanwhile, their brethren and allies, the Arapahoes, were on perfectly friendly terms with the whites, and Left Hand's band of that nation were camped in close vicinity to Fort Larned. Left Hand, one of the principal chiefs of the Arapahoe nation, learning that it was the intention of the Kiowas, on a certain day, to run off the stock from Fort Larned, proceeded to the commanding officer of that post and informed him of the fact; no attention was given to the information he gave, and on the day indicated the stock was run off by the Kiowa Indians. Left Hand again approached the post with a portion of his warriors for the purpose of offering his services to the commanding officer there, to pursue and endeavor to regain the stock from the Kiowa Indians, when he was fired upon and obliged hastily to leave. The young men of the Arapahoe nation, supposing it was the intention of the whites to make war upon them as well as the Cheyennes, also commenced retaliating, as well as they were able, and against the desire of

316

most of their principal chiefs, who, as well as Black Kettle and other chiefs of the Cheyennes, were bitterly opposed to hostilities with the whites. He then said that he had lately heard of a proclamation issued by the Governor of Colorado inviting all friendly disposed Indians to come into the different posts, and that they would be protected by the government. Under these circumstances, although the whites had been the aggressors and had forced this trouble upon the Indians, anxious altogether for the welfare of his people, he had made this last effort to communicate again with the military authorities, and he was glad he had succeeded. He then arose, shook hands with Major E. W. Wynkoop and his officers, stating that he was still, as he always had been, a friend to the whites ; and that so far as he was concerned he was willing to deliver up the white prisoners, or do anything that was required of him to procure peace, knowing it to be for the good of his people; but that there were other chiefs who still thought that they were badly treated by their white brethern, but who were willing to make peace, but who felt unwilling to deliver up the white prisoners simply upon the promise of Major Wynkoop that he would endeavor to procure them peace ; they desired that the condition of their delivering up the white prisoners should be an assurance of peace. He also went on to state, that even if Major Wynkoop's proposition was not accepted by the chiefs assembled, and although they had sufficient force to entirely overpower Major Wynkoop's small command, that from the fact that he had come in good faith to hold his consultation in consequence of the letter received, he should return to Fort Lyon without being molested.

The expressions from the other chiefs were to the effect that they insisted upon peace as the condition of their delivering up the white prisoners. Major Wynkoop finally replied that he repeated what he had said before, that it was out of his power to insure them peace, and that all he had to say in closing was that they might think about his propositions ; that he would march to a certain locality, distant twelve miles, and there await the result of their consultation for two days, advising them at the same time to accede to his propositions, as the best means to procure that peace for which they were anxious. The white prisoners were brought in and delivered over to Major Wynkoop before the time had expired set by him and Black Kettle and White Antelope and Bull Bear, of the Cheyenne nation, and as well as Neva, No-ta-ne, Boisee, and Heap Buffalo, chiefs of the Arapahoes, delivered themselves over to Major Wynkoop. We then proceeded to Fort Lyon, and from there to Denver, at which place Governor Evans held a consultation with the chiefs, the result of which was as follows :

He told them that he had nothing to do with them; that they would return with Major Wynkoop, who would reconduct them in safety and they would have to await the action of the military authorities ; Colonel J. M. Chivington, then in command of the district of Colorado, also told them that they would remain at the disposal of Major Wynkoop, until higher authority had acted in their case. The Indians appeared perfectly satisfied, presuming that they would eventually be all right, as soon as the authorities could be heard from, and expressed themselves so. Black Kettle embraced the governor and Major Wynkoop and shook hands with all the officers present, perfectly contented, deeming that the matter was settled. On our return to Fort Lyon I was told by Major Wynkoop to say to the chiefs that they could bring their different bands, including their families, to the vicinity of the post, until he had heard from the big chief; that he preferred to have them under his eye and away from other quarters where they were likely to get into difficulties with the whites. The chiefs replied that they were willing to do anything Major Wynkoop might choose to dictate, as they had perfect confidence in him, and accordingly immediately brought in their villages, their squaws and pappooses, and appeared satisfied that they were in perfect safety.

After these villages were located and Major Wynkoop had sent an officer to headquarters for instructions, he, Major Wynkoop, was relieved from the command of the post by Major Scott J. Anthony, and I was ordered to interpret for Major Anthony in a consultation he desired to hold with these Indians. The conversation that then took place between Major Anthony and the Indians was as follows:

Major Anthony told them that he had been sent there to relieve Major Wynkoop, and that he would be from that time in command of the post; that he came here under orders from the commander. of all the troops in this country, and that he had orders to have nothing to do with the Indians whatever; that they had heard at headquarters that they had lately been committing depredations, &c., in the neighborhood of this post, but that since his arrival he had learned that these reports were all false; that he would write to headquarters himself and correct the error in regard to them, and that he would have no objections to their remaining in the vicinity of Sand creek, where they were then located, until such time as word might be received from the commander of the department; that he himself would forward a complete statement of all that he had seen and heard, and that he was in hopes he would have some good news for the Indians upon receiving an answer, but that he was sorry that his orders were such as to render it impossible for him to make them any issues whatever; the Indians then replied that it would be impossible for them to remain any great length of time, as they were short of provisions. Major Anthony told them that they could allow their villages to remain where they were then, and could send their young men out to hunt buffaloes, as he understood that the buffaloes had lately come close in. The Indians appeared to be a little dissatisfied in regard to the change in the commander of the post, fearing that it boded them no good, but having received assurances of safety from Major Anthony, they still had no fears of their families being disturbed.

On the 26th of November, 1864, I received permission from Major Scott J. Anthony, commander of the post, to proceed to the Indian village on Sand creek for the purpose of trading with the Indians, and started, accompanied by a soldier named David Lauderback and a citizen, Watson Clark. I reached the village and commenced to trade with them.

On the morning of the 29th of November, 1864, the village was attacked by Colonel J. M. Chivington with a command of 900 to 1,000 men. The Indian village was composed of about one hundred lodges, numbering altogether some five hundred souls, two-thirds of whom were women and children. From my observation, I do not think there were over sixty Indians that made any defence. I rode over the field after the slaughter was over, and counted from sixty to seventy dead bodies, a large majority of which were women and children, all of which bodies had been mutilated in the most horrible manner.

When the troops first approached I endeavored to join them, and was repeatedly fired upon; also the soldier who was with me, and the citizen. When the troops began approaching in a hostile manner, I saw Black Kettle, head chief, hoist the American flag over his lodge, as well as a white flag, fearing that there might be some mistake as to who they were.

After the fight, Colonel Chivington returned with his command in the direction of Fort Lyon, and then proceeded by the road down the Arkansas river.

JOHN SMITH.

Sworn and subscribed to before me, this 15th day of January, 1865.

W. P. MINTON,
*Second Lieutenant First New Mexico Volunteers, Post Adjutant.*

A true copy:

CHARLES WHEELER,
*First Lieut. and Reg'l Adj't Vet. Batt. First Colorado Cavalry,*
*Post Adjutant, Fort Lyon, C. T.*

SAND CREEK MASSACRE.

FORT LYON, COLORADO TERRITORY,
*January* 16, 1865.

Personally appeared before me Captain R. A. Hill, first New Mexico volunteer infantry, who, after being duly sworn, says that, as an officer in the service of the United States, he was on duty at Fort Lyon at the time there was an understanding between the chiefs of the Arapahoe and Cheyenne nations and Major Wynkoop, with regard to their resting in safety in their villages in the vicinity of Fort Lyon until such a time as orders in regard to them could be received from the commanding general of the department; that after Major Wynkoop had been relieved from the command at Fort Lyon, the same understanding existed between Major J. Anthony and the aforementioned Indians; that, to the best of his belief, the village of Indians massacred by Colonel J. M. Chivington, on the 29th day of November, 1864, were the same friendly Indians heretofere referred to.

R. A. HILL.

Sworn and subscribed to, this 16th day of January, 1865
W. P. MINTON, *Post Adjutant.*

FORT LYON, COLORADO TERRITORY,
*January* 16, 1865.

Personally appeared before me Lieutenant James D. Cannon, first New Mexico volunteer infantry, who, after being duly sworn, says, that on the 28th day of November, 1864, I was ordered by Major Scott J. Anthony to accompany him on an Indian expedition, as his battalion adjutant; the object of the expedition was to be a thorough campaign against hostile Indians, as I was led to understand. I referred to the fact of there being a friendly camp of Indians in the immediate vicinity, and remonstrated against simply attacking that camp, as I was aware that they were resting there in fancied security, under promises held out to them of safety by Major E. W. Wynkoop, former commander of Fort Lyon, as by Major Scott J. Anthony, then in command. Our battalion was attached to the command of Colonel J. M. Chivington, and left Fort Lyon on the night of the 28th of November, 1864. About daybreak, on the morning of the 29th of November, we came in sight of the camp of friendly Indians aforementioned, and were ordered by Colonel J. M. Chivington to attack the same, which was accordingly done. The command of Colonel Chivington was composed of about one thousand men. The village of Indians consisted of from one hundred to one hundred and thirty lodges, and, as far as I am able to judge, of from five to six hundred souls; the majority of them were women and children. In going over the battle-ground the next day, I did not see a body of a man, woman, or child but what was scalped, and, in many instances, their bodies were mutilated in a most horrible manner—men, women, and children's privates cut out, &c. I heard one man say that he had cut a woman's private parts out, and had them for exhibition on a stick. I heard another man say that he had cut the fingers off of an Indian, to get the rings on his hand. According to the best of my knowledge and belief, these atrocities that were committed were with the knowledge of Colonel J. M. Chivington. and I do not know of him taking any measures to prevent them. I heard of one instance of a child a few months old being thrown into the feed-box of a wagon, and, after being carried some distance, left on the ground to perish. I also heard of numerous instances in which men had cut out the private parts of females, and stretched them over

Ex. Doc. 26——9

319

their saddle-bows, and some of them over their hats. While riding in ranks, all these matters were a subject of general conversation, and could not help being known to Colonel J. M. Chivington.

JAMES D. CANNON.

Sworn and subscribed to, this 16th day of January, 1865.

W. P. MINTON, *Post Adjutant.*

———

FORT LYON, COLORADO TERRITORY,
*January* 16, 1865.

Personally appeared before me Second Lieutenant W. P. Minton, first New Mexico volunteer infantry, and Lieutenant C. M. Cossitt, first cavalry of Colorado, who, after being duly sworn, say, that on the 28th day of November, 1864, Colonel J. M. Chivington, with the third regiment of Colorado cavalry (one-hundred-days men) and a battalion of the first Colorado cavalry, arrived at this post, and on the 29th of November attacked a village of friendly Indians in this vicinity, and, according to representations made by others in our presence, murdered their women and children, and committed the most horrible outrages upon the dead bodies of the same; that the aforesaid Indians were recognized as friendly by all parties at this post, under the following circumstances, viz:

That Major E. W. Wynkoop, formerly commander of the post, had given them assurances of safety until such time as he could hear from the commanding general of the department, in consequence of their having sued for peace, and given every evidence of their sincerity by delivering up white prisoners they had in their possession, by congregating their families together, and leaving them at the mercy of the garrison of Fort Lyon, who could have massacred them at any moment they felt disposed; that upon Major Wynkoop being relieved of the command of Fort Lyon, Colorado Territory, and Major Scott J. Anthony assuming command of the same, it was still the understanding between Major Anthony and the Indians that they could rest in that security guaranteed them by Major E. W. Wynkoop.

Also, that Colonel J. M. Chivington, on his arrival at the post of Fort Lyon, Colorado Territory, was made aware of the circumstances in regard to these Indians, from the fact that different officers remonstrated with him, and stated to him how these Indians were looked upon by the entire garrison; that, notwithstanding these remonstrances, and in the face of all these facts, he committed the massacre aforementioned.

———

FORT LYON, COLORADO TERRITORY,
*January* 16, 1865.

Personally appeared before me Private David Lauderback, first cavalry of Colorado, and R. W. Clark, citizen, who, after being duly sworn, say, that they accompanied John Smith, Indian interpreter, on the 26th day of November, 1864, by permission of Major Scott J. Anthony, commanding post of Fort Lyon, to the village of the friendly Indians, Cheyennes and Arapahoes, on Sand creek, close to Fort Lyon he, John Smith, having received permission to trade with the aforesaid friendly Indians; that, on the morning of the 29th of November, the said Indian village, while all deponents were in the same, was attacked by Colonel J. M. Chivington, with a command of about one thousand men; that, according to their best knowledge and belief, the entire Indian village was composed of not more than five hundred souls, two-thirds of which were women and children; that the dead bodies of women and children were afterwards mutilated

320

in the most horrible manner; that it was the understanding of deponents, and the general understanding of the garrison at Fort Lyon, that this village were friendly Indians; that they were allowed to remain in the locality they were then in by Major Wynkoop, former commander of the post, and by Major Scott J. Anthony, then in command, as well as from the fact that permission had been given John Smith and the deponents to visit the said camp for the purpose of trading.

DAVID H. LAUDERBACK.<br>
R. W. CLARK.

Sworn and subscribed to before me, this 16th day of January, 1865.

W. P. MINTON, <i>Post Adjutant.</i>

True copies from the records of this post.

CHARLES WHEELER,<br>
First Lieut. and Reg'tal Adj't Vet. Batt. First Col. Cav.,<br>
Post Adjutant.

FORT LYON, COLORADO TERRITORY,<br>
January 27, 1865.

Personally appeared before me Samuel G. Colley, who, being duly sworn, on oath deposes and says, that he is now, and has been for the past three years, United States agent for the Arapahoe and Cheyenne Indians; that in the month of June last he received instructions from Hon. John Evans, governor and *ex officio* superintendent of Indian affairs for Colorado Territory, directing him to send out persons into the Indian country to distribute printed proclamations, (which he was furnished with,) inviting all friendly Indians to come into the different places designated in said proclamation, and they would be protected and fed; that he caused the terms of said proclamation to be disseminated among the different tribes of Indians under his charge; and that, in accordance therewith, a large number of Arapahoes and Cheyennes came into this post, and provisions were issued to them by Major E. W. Wynkoop, commanding, and myself.

That on the 4th day of September last, two Cheyenne Indians (One-Eye and Manimick) came into this post with information that the Arapahoes and Cheyennes had several white prisoners among them, that they had purchased, and were desirous of giving them up and making peace with the whites.

That on the 6th day of September following, Major E. W. Wynkoop left this post with a detachment of troops to rescue said prisoners, and that after an absence of several days he returned, bringing with him four white prisoners, which he received from the Arapahoe and Cheyenne Indians. He was accompanied on his return by a number of the most influential men of both tribes, who were unanimously opposed to war with the whites, and desired peace at almost any terms that the whites might dictate.

That immediately upon the arrival of Major Wynkoop at this post, large numbers of Arapahoes and Cheyennes came in and camped near the post.

Major Wynkoop selected several of the most prominent chiefs of both nations, and proceeded to Denver to council with Superintendent Evans. After his return he held frequent councils with the Indians, and, as all of them distinctly stated, that he was not empowered to treat with them, but that he despatched a messenger to the headquarters of the department, stating their wishes in the matter, and that as soon as he received advices from there he would inform them of the decisions of General Curtis respecting them. That until that time, if they placed themselves under his protection, they should not be molested. That the Indians remained quietly near the post until the arrival of Major Anthony, who relieved Major Wynkoop.

321

Major Anthony held a council with the Indians, and informed them that he was instructed not to allow any Indians in or near the post, but that he had found matters here much better than he had expected, and advised them to go out and camp on Sand creek until he could hear from General Curtis. He wished them to keep him fully advised of all the movements of the Sioux, which they promptly did. He also promised them that as soon as he heard from General Curtis he would advise them of his decisions.

From the time that Major Wynkoop left this post to go out to rescue the white prisoners, until the arrival of Colonel Chivington here, which took place on the 28th day of November last, no depredations of any kind had been committed by the Indians within 200 miles of the post. That upon Colonel Chivington's arrival here with a large body of troops he was informed where these Indians were encamped, and was fully advised under what circumstances they had come into this post, and why they were then on Sand creek. That he was remonstrated with, both by officers and civilians at this post, against making war upon those Indians; that he was informed and fully advised that there was a large number of friendly Indians there, together with several white men, who were there at the request of himself and Colley, and by permission of Major Anthony. That notwithstanding his knowledge of the facts, as above set forth, he is informed that Colonel Chivington did, on the morning of the 29th of November last, surprise and attack said camp of friendly Indians and massacre a large number of them, (mostly women and children,) and did allow the troops under his command to mangle and mutilate them in the most horrible manner.

S. G. COLLEY,
*United States Indian Agent.*

Sworn and subscribed to before me this 28th day of January, 1865, at Fort Lyon, Colorado Territory.

W. P. MINTON,
*Second Lieut. New Mexico Volunteers, Post Adjutant.*

A true copy :

CHARLES WHEELER,
*First Lieut. and Regimental Adj't Vet. Bat. First Col. Cav.,*
*Post Adjutant, Fort Lyon, Colorado Territory.*

The following protest was presented, and the court was cleared for discussion.:

John M. Chivington most respectfully protests against the ruling of the court, for the following reasons :

1st. That in our cross-examination of witnesses introduced by the prosecution, the court does not allow us the right guaranteed to us by law, of asking direct or leading questions, thereby entirely taking from us the only means we have to test the credibility of witnesses introduced by the prosecution. In the last instance we asked a question which we have reason to believe we can prove by other witnesses, but the court overruled the question; that we stated prior to that, that we would have to ask leading questions in relation to what occurred at Spring Bottom, in order to lay the foundation for impeaching the testimony of the witness, but the court has overruled the question, and deprived us of a right without which we are left to the mercy of malice and hatred in a perfectly defenceless condition.

The commission objected to the question on account of its irrelevancy to the subject-matter of this investigation, and after the witness has stated in his direct evidence that Colonel Chivington has manifested a disposition to make sport of him, (the witness,) and that he (the witness,) gave him short answers. Even admitting that the witness made the statement (he was not under oath) that Major Anthony and Captain Soule should be dismissed from the service, for something said or done, it was only the opinion of a citizen, who makes no pretension to a correct knowledge of the duties of military officers, and while in conversation with one whom he considered as making sport of his statements

Cross-examination of Mr. James M. Combs by J. M. Chivington continued:

Question. What did you state to Colonel Chivington regarding the officers at Fort Lyon?

Answer. I don't know as I stated anything except what I stated before; nothing in particular about them any way.

Question. You say that Colonel Chivington stated to you that Left Hand was in command of Fort Lyon. Was it not yourself that made that statement?

Answer. No.

Question. You say that Colonel Chivington told you that Wynkoop was an honor to the Colorado first, &c. Was not that told you in reply to a statement made by you in regard to Major Wynkoop?

Answer. I made no remark concerning Major Wynkoop except what I have heretofore stated.

Question. You stated that you had seen the Indians get stores from both Majors Wynkoop and Anthony. Will you state as near as you are able how much in quantity you have seen the Indians obtain from each of the two officers named?

Answer. I have seen the Indians taking provisions from the commissary when each was in command, and while Major Anthony was in command I saw them haul away a wagon load of flour. That was the most I saw at any one time.

Question. You state that the Indians generally went where they chose. How many Indians have you seen in the post at any one time, and who was in command when the Indians went where they chose?

Answer. I could not state how many I have seen there begging and trading in different houses, and that when each was in command. Sometimes,. while Major Anthony was in command, he would allow them in some days and some days would order them kept out. There was nothing regular about it. I don't know as I ever saw any on the parade ground after he gave the order forbidding them.

Question. You state that a great deal of trouble was experienced from the Indians' begging, &c., at Fort Lyon. Who was in command at that time, and at what time of the year was this?

Answer. It was when each was in command. It was in November and I think the last of October. I think that when they first came in they were more for trading than begging. After that the articles they were trading were small articles, lariats, moccasins, &c., begging more than trading. Before that they traded buffalo robes, &c.

Question. You state that the officers, soldiers and citizens visited the Indian camps at Fort Lyon. At that time how far was the Indian camp from Fort Lyon?

Answer. At that time I should think about a mile and a half. I say at Fort Lyon, for it was considered so when they were camped seven miles below here.

Question. What officers have you seen at the Indian camps at Fort Lyon?

Answer. I have seen Major Wynkoop there; I have seen Captain Soule there, and I think Lieutenant Phillips. I don't think of any others now.

Question. Who was with you when you first heard the news of the Sand creek affair, and did you or did you not express yourself pleased to hear that the Indians had been killed?

Answer. I don't remember where I heard it first. I know I was on my way home when I heard it. I heard it was a party of Sioux warriors that were attacked, and heard they were near Smoky Hill; also heard that several officers were killed at the same time—Captain Baxter and others. I was pleased that they (the Indians) were killed when I first heard the report, and thought they were a party of warriors.

Question. Did you at any time while conversing with Colonel Chivington express to him your opinion as to the propriety of his killing the Indians near Fort Lyon ?

Answer. No. I avoided all conversation of that kind. My opinion I think would not have been worth much.

Question. Who was it that was telling how he was going to arrange his scalps, &c.?

Answer. Different ones ; it was a general conversation with all present. I think that Major Downing had as much to say as any of them. Some said they were going to have Neva's, some Left Hand, &c.

Question. Will you state the names of any of these parties if you remember ?

Answer. It was a general talk ; I don't remember names particularly. They were mostly officers, and of the third, whose names I do not know ; I have named before all that I know.

Question. You state that you told Colonel Chivington that the Indians had given up horses, mules, and all government property taken ; to whom did the Indians give this property, and at what time was it given up ?

Answer. What I saw was turned over to Major Anthony, and was said to be all they had. I should think that what was said to be the last of it was given up between the first and the middle of November.

Question. Did you and your friend or person with whom you were travelling, Mr. Brown, after leaving the house have any conversation in regard to Colonel Chivington, and what had been said in regard to Indians ?

Answer. We might have had ; we probably did ; it was natural to have after what was said in the house ; I don't recollect for certain.

Commission adjourned until 1½ this p. m.

*One and a half p. m.*—Commission met pursuant to adjournment  Present, all members and recorder.

Cross-examination of Mr. James M. Combs by J. M. Chivington closed.

Re-examination of Mr. James M. Combs :
No questions asked.

DAVID H. LOUDERBACK called in by the commission to give evidence.  The oath being administered according to law, he (Louderback) testified as follows :

Question. Your full name and occupation ?

Answer. David Henry Louderback, a soldier.

Question. How long have you been a soldier ?

Answer. Almost four years.

Question. Where were you during the latter part of November, 1864 ?

Answer. I was on Sand creek.

Question. State the time of your going there.

Answer. On the morning of the 26th of November, 1864 ; the same morning that Major Wynkoop left for the States.

Question. Did you go alone, and what induced you to go to Sand creek ?

Answer. I did not go alone. John Smith and a teamster, by the name of Clark, went with me. Major Anthony requested John Smith to go out there and see what the Indians were doing, and gave him permission to take some goods out with him to trade to those Indians on Sand creek. John Smith wanted me to accompany him, and Major Anthony gave me his permission to go out with him.

Question. What did you find there on your arrival?

Answer. I found an Indian village there; about one hundred and twenty lodges altogether.

Question. State whose village it was, and how many Indians were there.

Answer. Black Kettle's band of Cheyennes, and Left Hand's Arapahoes, (eight lodges of Arapahoes;) in all, about five hundred Indians.

Question. State what was done on your arrival at the village.

Answer. We unloaded our goods, put them in the lodge of War Bonnett, and turned our mules loose to let them graze. We eat our dinner after turning the mules loose.

Question. How long did you remain at the village, and what was done with your goods?

Answer. Arrived there on the 27th of November, and we remained at the village until the morning of the following Thursday, December 1, 1864. The goods were traded off for buffalo robes, ponies, and mules.

Question. State the number of ponies, mules, and buffalo robes you received in exchange for your goods.

Answer. Three ponies, one mule, and one hundred and four buffalo robes.

Question. Did anything happen to that village before you left Sand creek?

Answer. Yes; on Tuesday morning, the 29th, a squaw came into the lodge where we were eating breakfast, and said there was a heap of buffaloes coming. A few minutes afterwards, one of the chiefs came in and said there were a lot of soldiers coming.

Question. State what happened on the morning of the 29th November, 1864, at Sand creek.

Answer. John Smith and I started out to see what was the matter. We thought they were Blunt's men from Riley, at first. I wanted Jack Smith (John Smith's son) to get me a horse, so that I could go out and see what they wanted, but he could not get one. The squaws had driven them all away from the village, as soon as they knew there were soldiers coming. The main herd was below the village a mile or two.

The soldiers commenced firing by that time, and I put a white handkerchief on a stick, and started towards the soldiers with it. I got up within a hundred and fifty yards of them, and they commenced firing on John Smith and me. We had to go back to the village; after that, Clark got a tanned buffalo skin and put it on a lodge pole and raised it. He stood on a wagon with it; he had to get down off the wagon with it, as the bullets flew so thick around him, and he and John Smith went into a lodge. I staid outside, sitting on the wagon tongue, until they commenced firing the howitzers.

Then I went into the lodge; I thought it was getting too warm for me outside. I staid inside of the lodge, looking out the door, watching for Colonel Chivington. I saw him crossing the creek, at the lower end of the village. I watched him until he came up within forty or fifty yards of the lodge, and I hallooed to him, calling him by name, and he told me to come on, that I was all right, calling me by name. I went out to him, and in going out a man fired at me. I asked the colonel what they were firing at me for, and he turned around and told them to stop firing. He then told me to fall in rear of the command, that I was all right. I told him to hold on a minute, the lodge was full of white men, pointing a lodge out to him in which John Smith was. Just at this time John Smith came out and called Colonel Chivington. Colonel Chivington told him to bring his friends out, that he was all right; he came out, bringing the teamster and Charley Bent, and they fell in with the command. I had got a horse in the mean time, and gave that to John Smith to ride. I got another one for myself, and went on up to our battery, (our company had a battery at that time.) I went to where they were fighting, and helped them to work their guns, hold horses, &c., until Lieutenant Baldwin's horse was shot. When his horse was shot I went back to the village to get my boots and overcoat. These were in the lodge where I stopped. After putting on my overcoat and boots, I got a saddle and put on my horse, and went back up to where they were fighting.

The fighting was pretty much over, and I came back down to the village. I met Major Downing as I was going down. The major and I rode through the village, and he said he would like to get a good robe. I saw one in a lodge door, and I got off and picked it up and handed it to him. I left Major Downing after that, and met Major Anthony.

He said that he was sorry for getting us in such a scrape as he had got us into. That he had done the best he could to get us out. Then I told him I could see no best about it; that it was the tightest place I was ever in. I told him that I had been in many a tight place, but this beat all of them.

I then left Major Anthony and went to War Bonnet's lodge, where we had been stopping in the village. I found John Smith there, our teamster—and John Smith's squaw in the lodge; she was there all the time during the fight and had not left the lodge; she had her child with her. In about half an hour they brought in a squaw belonging to Charlie Windsor, who used to keep the sutler's store here. In a few minutes after they brought in Jack Smith, who had given himself to a major of the third regiment—I think his name is "Sayre." Along late in the evening they brought into the lodge three young Indian children and a pappoose about a month old. I cooked the supper for them that night and their breakfast next morning. At the time I cooked supper for them I made some coffee for Colonel Chivington and Mr. Gill. Jack Smith and I that night borrowed some coffee for the hospital and Colonel Chivington. They came and got it the next morning. Wednesday morning, after breakfast, some of the men came for our robes that we had baled up, and said that Colonel Chivington had ordered them for the hospital. They took all our robes, blankets, and provisions, and everything we had in the way of clothing, except what we had on our backs. John Smith went up to see Colonel Chivington about it, and remonstrated with him about their taking all his clothing, robes, provisions, &c. Then Colonel Shoup went down to the lodge and put a guard over it, and ordered the guard not to let any person take anything away from the lodge. There was nothing in the lodge at the time except the Indian prisoners, ourselves, and one set of harness. The guard staid there until about 12 o'clock that day; then they left, and were not back there again. In the afternoon there were several men in talking to Jack Smith, and told him he was a son of a bitch, and ought to have been shot long ago. Jack told the man that was talking to him that he did not give a damn; that if he wanted to kill him, shoot him. When Jack said this I thought it was time for me to get out of there, as men had threatened to hang and shoot me as well as uncle John Smith and the teamster that was with us. I went up to Colonel Chivington's headquarters, and had just reached there, when I heard the report of a pistol or gun, I could not tell which, and looking around I saw old uncle John Smith coming up towards Colonel Chivington's headquarters. Colonel Chivington, upon hearing the report, said "Halloo; I wonder what that is." I answered by saying that they had shot Jack Smith, and I thought it was a damned shame the way that they killed him. No matter what a man had done, they ought to give him a show for his life. Upon which some officer—I could not name him, I do not know what his name is—told me I better be careful how I "shot my mouth off" around there about killing Indians. I told him I enlisted as a soldier, and I considered my tongue my own; that I did not consider that it belonged to the government; that I thought I could use it whenever I wanted to. Sergeant Palmer, of our company, was standing near me at the time. He told me I had better go down and stay with the company, or I would get shot yet before I left the village. I told him they could have a chance to shoot me in a few days, as soon as I could go to the fort and back, as I did not have anything to shoot with now. I went down and staid with my company until Thursday morning, when I started to Fort Lyon with two men that were wounded in the fight, (in an ambulance.) I arrived there Friday noon. After turning the men over to Dr. Hamel, I put my team in the quartermaster's corral and reported to the commanding officer of my company at the fort. I drew me a horse and arms and intended to join, when there were orders come in for every man that was fit for duty at the post to report to the command at Sand creek immediately. I left the fort to join the command with Major Anthony about 12 o'clock that night, (Friday night.) We caught the command about ten miles below Salt Bottom, near Camp Wynkoop, about 7 o'clock Saturday morning. On reaching the command I was put on duty as sergeant major of the Fort Lyon battalion. The command proceeded down the river about forty miles below Camp Wynkoop, when they laid-over two days and then returned to the post.

Question. How many Indians were in the village at the time of the attack upon it by Colonel Chivington.

Answer. They were all there that were there when we first went there, five hundred, or very near five hundred.

Question. How many of these were women and children?

Answer. The largest part of them were women and children. There were only a few men there, (warriors.)

Question. Did any of the Indians escape during the attack?

Answer. Yes; a large number of the Indians got away.

Question. How many Indians were killed?

Answer. That I cannot say, as I did not go up above to count them. I saw only eight. I could not stand it; they were cut up too much.

Question. Was anything done to the Indians after they had been killed?

Answer. Yes; they were scalped and cut up in an awful manner; what I saw were.

Question. By whom were they scalped and mutilated?

Answer. By the soldiers; I could not say what regiment they belonged to, or what their names are.

Question. Did you see them scalping and mutilating?

Answer. I did not. I saw the bodies after it was done.

Question. Had the Indians before the attack made any preparations for defence?

Answer. They had not.

Commission adjourned until 9 a. m. to-morrow, March 31, 1865.

### THIRTY-SEVENTH DAY.

MARCH 31, 1865.

Commission met pursuant to adjournment. Present, all members and recorder.

Reading of papers appended to these proceedings, from page 453 to page 494, both inclusive, was dispensed with for the present, by order of the commission. With that exception, the proceedings of yesterday were read, amended as follows, and approved: on page 507, 18th line, insert after the word "saddle," "and bridle."

Direct examination of David H. Louderback (a soldier) by the commission continued :

Question. At the time of the attack, were any of the chiefs in the village? If so, give their names.

Answer. There were; Black Kettle, White Antelope, Stand-in-the-Water, Little Robe, War Bonnet, and Left Hand, of the Arapahoes. Those are all the chiefs I know were there.

Question. What did they they do when the village was attacked?

Answer. White Antelope, Black Kettle, and Stand-in-the-Water started toward the soldiers to tell them they did not want to fight. The troops fired at them, and Black Kettle then started off with the rest of the Indians that left the village; White Antelope and Stand-in-the-Water started to their lodges, got their guns, came back, and commenced firing at the troops. Both of them were

327

killed within fifty yards of each other; White Antelope was killed in the bed of the creek and Stand-in-the-Water was killed right opposite to him, on the left hand side of the creek. After they were killed they were scalped, and White Antelope's nose, ears, and privates were cut off.

Question. What became of the other chiefs you have mentioned?

Answer. I believe they all got away, as I did not see any of them afterwards.

Question. Were all the Indians killed at Sand creek killed by Colonel Chivington's command?

Answer. They were killed by the soldiers under his command. They were all under his command.

Question. Have you been to Sand creek since?

Answer. I have not.

Question. Who threatened to kill John Smith at Sand creek?

Answer. I could not say who they were. They were soldiers; some of the officers said, (while John Smith was trying to get to them,) "Shoot the old son of a bitch; he is no better than an Indian."

Question. What became of the prisoners taken at Sand creek?

Answer. With the exception of Jack Smith, they were all brought into the fort; John Smith's squaw and Charlie Winsor's squaw, with their children, were brought in when I came in first to the post. The three children the third regiment men took care of, and were brought into the post when we returned from down the river below Camp Wynkoop. The pappoose was carried in a feed-box of a wagon a day or a day and a half, and then it was thrown out and left in the road; I do not know whether they killed it or not.

Question. State who it was that threw the pappoose out on the ground.

Answer. I do not know who it was.

Direct examination of David H. Louderback by the commission closed.

Cross-examination of David H. Louderback, by J. M. Chivington:

Question. You say you went to Sand creek with John Smith, who had permission to trade, &c.; did you have any interest in the profits that might accrue from any transactions you might have with the Indians?

Answer. I did not.

Question. You say there were about one hundred and twenty lodges in the village; what was your means of knowledge that there were that number, and did you count them?

Answer. I counted the lodges to the number of one hundred and fifteen. There were some few lodges about half a mile below the main village that I did not count, and concluded there were about one hundred and twenty lodges in all.

Question. How long have you been acquainted with Black Kettle and the other chiefs you have named?

Answer. Since September, 1864.

Question. Have you often since that time been among the Indians trading?

Answer. I have not. It was the only time I ever was among them trading. It is the only time I ever was in an Indian camp. I traded a little with the squaws here at the post, but was never before in their village except at Sand creek.

Question. Upon first learning that the soldiers were coming did not the Indians take from you, or some of you, your arms, and did they not threaten to injure you?

Answer. They did. They threatened to injure me, but they did not threaten to injure uncle John Smith. They took John Smith's and my revolvers from us; but they were not on us. We were outside the lodge, and the revolvers were on the inside of the lodge, on our beds.

Question. Did they (the Indians) at any time threaten to injure John Smith?

Answer. I did not hear the Indians threaten to injure him.

Question. Did you at any time hear John Smith say that the Indians had threatened to injure him?

Answer. I did not.

Question. Why did the squaws drive the herd of ponies, &c., away, when they heard that the soldiers were coming?

Answer. They thought there was something wrong when they first came in sight.

Question. You say you made coffee for Colonel Chivington. Did you make the coffee at his request?

Answer. I did. He requested John Smith to have some made, and John Smith asked me to make it.

Question. Who told you that Colonel Chivington ordered the robes, blankets, and provisions, taken out of John Smith's lodge, to be taken for the hospital? State what your means of knowledge is that Colonel Chivington gave such orders.

Answer. It was a sergeant of the third regiment. He came and said that Colonel Chivington ordered them for the use of the hospital, and ordered the men to take them to the hospital.

Question. You state that there were about five hundred Indians in the village when Colonel Chivington attacked it. How do you know that their number was five hundred; did you count them?

Answer. I had been out at the village at Sand creek there two days and two nights. I knew about the number that had been trading with us.

Question. Was this your only means of knowledge of the number of Indians in the village at Sand creek?

Answer. That was all. I thought I ought to know as I had been there two days trading, &c.

Commission adjourned until 1½ p. m. this day.

*One and a half p. m.*—Commission met pursuant to adjournment. Present, all members and recorder.

Cross-examination of David H. Louderback, by J. M. Chivington, continued:

Question. Were there more women and children in the village at Sand creek than are usually in Indian villages, according to the number of men? You state that two-thirds present were women and children.

Answer. I said the larger number of them were women and children. No, there were not any more women and children in the village at Sand creek than are usually in Indian villages, according to the number of men.

Question. You state that a large number of Indians got away. What is your means of knowledge that they got away; and were you in a position where you could see all that were killed and all that got away?

Answer. I was in such a position that I could see when they got away, as a large number started before the troops commenced firing. I could not see all that were killed. I did not see all that got away. I saw those that got away before the fight commenced.

Question. Were the eight Indians you saw killed all scalped, and otherwise mutilated?

Answer. They were, all but one pappoose, about a year old.

Question. Describe particularly how these Indians were mutilated, and where they laid.

Answer. All but Stand-in-the-Water laid in Sand creek. The creek was very nearly dry, but a very little water running in it. They were all scalped, and in some instances, including White Antelope, had their noses and ears cut off, including their private parts. White Antelope laid in the bed of the creek, opposite the lower end of the main village, and opposite to War Bonnet's lodge. Stand-in-the-Water laid on the left-hand side of the bank, opposite to White Antelope. The others laid between White Antelope and the upper part of the village, where they had the main fight. They all laid in the bed and on the banks of the creek.

Question. Were White Antelope, Stand-in-the-Water, and the other you state were mutilated, so mutilated immediately after they were killed and before the fight had terminated?

Answer. I could not state, as I did not see them until the next day, Wednesday.

Question. Were there not a great many Indian or wild dogs about the village, and might they not have mutilated the bodies?

Answer. There were a great many dogs about the village, but they couldn't mutilate the bodies as I saw them.

Question. You state that when the Indians were attacked, White Antelope, Black Kettle, and Stand-in-the-Water started towards the troops to tell the troops they did not want to fight. Do you understand their language? And how did you know that they went towards the troops to tell the troops they, the Indians, did not want to fight?

Answer. John Smith told me so at the time, when they started toward the troops.

Question. Is this, what John Smith told you, the only means you have of knowing that Black Kettle, White Antelope, and Stand-in-the-Water went toward the troops to tell the troops that they, the Indians, did not want to fight?

Answer. Yes.

Question. Do you know that the person or persons who mutilated the bodies of the Indians were soldiers?

Answer. I do not.

Question. Did you ever see any correspondence between Major Anthony, commanding Fort Lyon, and the commanding officer of the district of the Upper Arkansas? If yes, state the contents particularly.

Answer. I did. Major Anthony stated to the commanding officer that he was keeping these Indians here under promise of peace, but still, if he had one thousand men here ready for the field, after getting some few friendly Indians out of their camp, he would kill the balance of them.

Question. Did you ever see any correspondence between Major Anthony and Colonel Chivington in regard to these Indians? If so, state what it was, particularly.

Answer. He wrote a letter to Colonel Chivington. Contents were about the same as the letter to the commanding officer of the district of the Upper Arkansas.

Question. In that letter to Colonel Chivington, did not Major Anthony state that the Indians had threatened to attack Fort Lyon?

Answer. No, he did not state that; what I saw of the letter didn't; not these Indians.

Question. Do you know that Major Anthony ever stated that the Indians had threatened to attack Fort Lyon?

Answer. I do not; he had never stated the Indians on Sand creek had; but the Indians on Smoky hill had.

Question. Did the Indians that were attacked on Sandy creek ever receive any rations from the government?

Answer. Yes, there were some of them who did—Black Kettle, One-Eye, and Left Hand; that is all I know of those Indians.

Question. Did Black Kettle, One-Eye, and Left Hand simply receive rations for themselves, or for their tribes? State how much in quantity they received, as near as you are able.

Answer. Black Kettle and Left Hand received rations for themselves and families only. One-Eye drew rations from government as a government employé, (a spy.)

Question. You state that the pappoose captured at Sand creek, and carried a day or a day and a half in the feed-box of a wagon, was thrown out and abandoned on the road; what is your means of knowledge that such was the fact?

Answer. Men and officers of the command told me it was thrown out.

Question. Is what the men and officers of the command told you in regard to the abandonment of the pappoose all that you know of the abandonment?

Answer. The Arapahoe squaw that came in here after the command had left for Denver stated to John Smith that she had found the child on the road and cut its throat.

Question. Could the squaw speak English, and did you understand her when she told of cutting the child's throat, or did John Smith tell you that the squaw had told him that she had found the child and cut its throat?

Answer. She couldn't speak English; John Smith and Bob Bent both told me what she said.

Question. Is what you have stated all your means of knowledge that the pappoose was abandoned as you first stated?

Answer. Yes. It never came in here, and I did not see it after I got back to the command.

Cross-examination of David H. Louderback by J. M. Chivington closed.

Re-examination of David H. Louderback by the commission:

Question. Did the Indians give any reasons for disarming you at the time of the attack upon their village by Colonel Chivington? If so, state what they are.

Answer. They did not.

Question. Did they offer you, or those with you, any personal violence at that time?

Answer. They did not offer any violence to any but me.

Question. Did they give any reasons why they had disarmed you? If so, state what they were.

Answer. They thought I was a spy, sent out there by Major Anthony to see what they were doing and leave marks to show the soldiers the way out.

Re-examination of David H. Louderback (a soldier) closed.

Commission adjourned until 9 a. m. to-morrow, April 1, 1865.

THIRTY-EIGHTH DAY.

APRIL 1, 1865.

Commission met pursuant to adjournment. Present, all members and recorder. Proceedings of yesterday read and approved.

GEORGE M. ROAN called in by the commission to give evidence.

The oath being administered according to law, he (Roan) testified as follows:

Question. Your full name and occupation?

Answer. George M. Roan; occupation, a soldier, company C, veteran battalion first Colorado cavalry.

Question. How long have you been a soldier?

Answer. Two years next June.

Question. Where were you during the latter part of November, 1864?

Answer. I was here at this post until I started out to Sand creek, on the 28th, under command of Lieutenant Baldwin, who was under command of Colonel Chivington.

Question. State what you saw on your arrival at Sand creek?

331

Answer. I saw some fighting ; I saw a camp of Indians, and the stars and stripes waving over the camp.

Question. State what was done on arriving at Sand creek.

Answer. There were Indians killed all around over the bluffs ; that is all I saw then ; I saw Jack Smith killed in a lodge.

Question. State who Jack Smith was and how he was killed.

Answer. He was old John Smith's son ; the man who shot Jack Smith was a soldier ; I don't know what his name was. There was a hole cut through the lodge, and a revolver poked through the hole. The man that shot him was on the outside of the lodge.

Question Had any of Colonel Chivington's command reached the Indian village at the time you first saw the stars and stripes ?

Answer. No, they had not.

Direct examination of George M. Roan by the commission closed.

Cross-examination of George M. Roan by J. M. Chivington :

Question. You state that when you first saw the stars and stripes none of Colonel Chivington s command had reached the village. State how you know that none of Colonel Chivington's command reached the village before you did.

Answer. I was on the right of the battalion and in front.

Question. During the march of the battalion in which you were serving, was there no one in advance of the battalion ?

Answer. Yes, I suppose there were men, but they had not arrived at the camp yet.

Question. How many persons were in advance of the battalion in which you were serving, and how far in advance of the battalion were they ?

Answer. I can't state how many ; I did not count them. I should think they were about three-quarters of a mile in advance when I saw them.

Question. Were they not over three-quarters of mile in advance of the battalion ?

Answer. No ; to the best of my knowledge they were not.

Cross-examination of George M. Roan by J. M. Chivington closed.

Re-examination of George M. Roan, a soldier, company C, veteran battalion first Colorado cavalry :

No questions asked.

Sergeant PALMER, veteran battalion first Colorado cavalry, called in by the commission to give evidence. The oath being administered according to law, he (Sergeant Palmer) testified as follows :

Question. Your full name and occupation ?

Answer. Lucian Palmer ; occupation a soldier of company C, veteran battalion first Colorado cavalry.

Question. How long have you been a soldier ?

Answer. A little over three years.

Question. Where were you during the latter part of November, 1864 ?

Answer. On the 28th of November I left Fort Lyon with a command on an expedition against the Indians.

Question. Of whose command were you at that time ?

Answer. Major Anthony's.

Question. Where did you go ?

Answer. To Sand creek.

Question. What did you see on your arrival at Sand creek ?

Answer. I saw a skirmish fight with the Indians.

Question. In what situation were the Indians on your arrival at Sand creek ?

Answer. They were encamped there.

Question. Describe their camp on Sand creek.

Answer. I should judge the camp was a half a mile long, extending up and down the creek, situated between two very high ridges in a valley. Their camp was on the north side of the creek.

Question. State of what their camp consisted.

Answer. Their lodges; I don't know the number.

Question. Did you see anything more than the lodges? If so, state what you saw.

Answer. I don't think I saw anything worth speaking of; I was through their camp but very little.

Question. State what happened on the arrival of the command at the Indian village on Sand creek.

(John M. Chivington most respectfully objects to the question for the following reason: that the witness has stated what occurred on his arrival.

Objection sustained by the commission.)

Question. State the particulars of the skirmish with the Indians—what you saw.

Answer. The first movement that I saw after arriving at the Indian village was to cut off the herd of ponies from the village. Our battery was ordered up by Colonel Chivington to take position near the bank of the creek. On arriving at that position the main body of the Indians were several hundred yards up the creek. We threw several shells, which did not reach them. The third battery threw several shells, some of them falling among the Indians. Several companies of cavalry were upon each side of the creek firing into the Indians. Our battery was then ordered by Colonel Chivington to take another position. We threw several rounds of grape and canister at them when they were intrenching themselves on the opposite side of the creek. All this time the cavalry were firing into them briskly, no respect paid to little or big, old or young. Our battery was then ordered back, where we remained until the skirmish or fight closed. I have stated about all I saw, during the skirmish, I believe.

Question. How many Indians were killed during the skirmish or fight?

Answer. I could not state.

Question. Were any prisoners taken? If so, state what was done with them.

Answer. I saw two squaws and three pappooses taken prisoners. The squaws and two pappooses were sent to Fort Lyon; the other pappoose was left at our first camp this side of Sand creek.

Question. Were there any others taken prisoners by Colonel Chivington's command?

Answer. I did not see any others taken prisoners myself.

Question. State if anything was done to the Indians after they had been killed.

(John M. Chivington most respectfully objects to the question for the following reasons: that the witness has stated that he had related all that occurred, &c.; that the question is leading, suggesting to the witness that something had been done to the Indians; that there is no evidence to show that they were touched, &c.

Objections sustained by the commission.)

Question. Was anything done to the Indians after they had been killed?

Answer. They were scalped; skulls broken in in several instances; I saw several of the third regiment cut off their fingers to get the rings off of them; I saw Major Sayre scalp a dead Indian; the scalp had a long tail of silver hanging to it; I believe that is all.

Commission adjourned until 9 a. m. Monday, April 3, 1865.

333

THIRTY-NINTH DAY.

APRIL 3, 1865.

Commission met pursuant to adjournment.  Present, all members and recorder.
Proceedings of Saturday, April 1, 1865, read and approved.

Direct examination of Sergeant Lucian Palmer, company C, veteran battalion
first Colorado cavalry, by the commission, continued:

Question. At what time was the scalping done, during or after the fight?
Answer. All I saw done was done the day after the fight.
Question. Were any of the officers present during the time you saw the
scalping?
(John M. Chivington most respectfully objects to the question for the follow-
ing reason: that the question is leading and suggests the answer required.
Objection overruled by the commission.)
Answer. Major Sayre, of the third regiment, was present, and about eight or
ten privates.
Question. Did he give any orders or attempt to prevent the scalping of the
dead?
(John M. Chivington most respectfully objects to the question for the following reasons: that the question is leading, and suggests the answer required;
that there is no evidence before the court that there were any orders given in
regard to it, and that if they had given any orders, it has not been shown that
the orders were legal and should have been obeyed.
Objection sustained by the commission.)
Question. Were any orders given to the command previous to or during the
fight?
Answer. I don't recollect of hearing any orders.
Question. Was anything done after the fight? If so, state what was done.
Answer. We laid in camp on Sand creek; on the 30th of November the
lodges were burnt; also their saddles and lodge-poles. We camped in Sand
creek, twelve miles from the battle-ground, the night of the 1st of December.
Question. State where the command first camped after the fight on the 29th.
Answer. They camped on the ground that the Indians had their lodges on.
Question. How far from the camp was the scalping done?
Answer. Half a mile, all the way from camp as far up as that.

Direct examination of Sergeant Lucian Palmer by the commission closed.

Cross-examination of Sergeant Lucian Palmer by J. M. Chivington:

Question. Could the command have killed the Indian warriors at Sand creek
without killing squaws and children, and were they not all fighting together
against the troops, so that had the troops attempted to take the squaws prisoners they would have been shot by the Indian warriors?
Answer. I think if the fight had been properly managed it would have been
an easy matter to take the squaws and children prisoners without being shot by
the warriors, from the fact that our forces were far superior to theirs.
Question. You say that Colonel Chivington ordered your battery to take
another position, &c.; why do you state in the conclusion of your testimony
that you heard no orders given previous to or during the fight?
Answer. I don't know unless I looked at it in a different light from the way
the question was asked of me.
Question. What are your means of knowledge that the pappoose was left in
your first camp, this side of Sand creek, as you have stated.
Answer. I saw it left there.
Question. Did not the squaws you had with you refuse to have anything to
do with it, refusing to take care of the pappoose, &c.
Answer. They took care of it the first day after we left Sand creek; they

334

had it in bed with them the night we stopped this side of Sand creek; they left it themselves, as no one else had anything to do with it to my knowledge.

Question. Did you see any person besides the ones you have mentioned scalping or mutilating Indians? and are you positive that the person you saw scalping the Indian mentioned was Major Sayre, of the third regiment, or that he was an officer at all?

Answer. Those I have mentioned are the only ones I saw scalping and mutilating the Indians, only from the fact that the party he had with him called him Major Sayre, and he was pointed out to me by officers of the first regiment as Major Sayre of the third regiment.

Cross-examination of Sergeant Lucian Palmer by J. M. Chivington closed.

Re-examination of Sergeant Lucian Palmer. No questions asked.

AMOS D. JAMES called on by the commission to give evidence.

The oath being administered according to law, he (James) testified as follow:
Question. What is your full name and occupation?

Answer. Amos D. James; occupation a soldier, company C, veteran battalion first Colorado cavalry.

Question. How long have you been a soldier?

Answer. Between three and four years, since September, 1861.

Question. Where were you during the latter part of November, 1864?

Answer. I was at this post, and on a campaign; I left this post the 29th of November on a campaign; on the afternoon of the 30th I arrived at the camp on the battle-ground; when I arrived at camp it was in the afternoon, and I saw nothing that day of importance. The morning we left the battle-ground I rode over the field; I saw in riding over the field a man (a sergeant of the 3d) dismount from his horse and cut the ear from the body of an Indian, and the scalp from the head of another. I saw a number of children killed; I suppose they were shot, they had bullet holes in them; one child had been cut with some instrument across the side. I saw another that both ears had been cut off. That is all I have to say, only there was an officer in company with the man that scalped the Indian.

Question. Who was the officer you saw with the man that scalped the Indian?
Answer. I don't know his name.

Question. How far from the camp of the command was the scalping and mutilating done?

Answer. What I saw I should think was between a quarter and a half a mile.

Question. How many dead Indians did you see in riding over the field?

(John M. Chivington most respectfully objects to the question for the following reasons: that there is no evidence that the witness rode all over the field, which has to be shown first, in order to inquire what he saw on the entire field. Objection not sustained by the commission).

Answer. I could not say how many I saw; I did not count all; I counted one hundred or a little over.

Question. How many of those you saw were warriors?
Answer. I could not say.

Question. How many children did you see that were killed?
Answer. I couldn't tell how many.

Question. Did anything of an unusual character happen in camp on Sand creek the morning after you arrived there?

Answer. What I have already stated I saw in the morning.

Commission adjourned until 1½ p. m. this day.

*One and half p. m.*—Commission met pursuant to adjournment. Present, all members and recorder.

Ex. Doc. 26——10

Direct examination of Amos D. James, a soldier, company C, veteran battalion first Colorado cavalry, closed.

Cross-examination of Amos D. James, by J. M. Chivington :

Question. You say that you saw at Sand creek a sergeant cut off an ear of an Indian, and the scalp of another ; were there any persons near these parties except yourself, and what part of the field did this occur ?

Answer. There was quite a number present. There was a lieutenant along. It occurred between a quarter and a half a mile above the camp, towards the lower part of the field.

Cross-examination of Amos D. James, a soldier, company C, veteran battalion first Colorado cavalry, closed.

Re-examination of Amos D. James, a soldier, veteran battalion first Colorado cavalry :

No question asked.

W. P. MINTON called in by commission to give evidence. The oath being administered according to law, he (Minton) testified as follows :

Question. What is your full name and occupation ?

Answer. William P. Minton; my occupation has been a soldier.

Question. What was your rank in the army, and when were you mustered out of the service ?

Answer. I was a second lieutenant. I was mustered out of the service February 4, 1865.

Question. Where had you been on duty previous to your muster out of the service ?

Answer. At Fort Lyon.

Question. How long have you been on duty at Fort Lyon ?

Answer. Since the 10th of September, 1864.

Question. Were there any councils with the Indians at Fort Lyon, while you were on duty at said post ?

Answer. Yes ; several of them.

Question. Were you present at any or all of them ? If so, state what transpired.

Answer. I was present at one council. There was an understanding made with the Indians that they were to go to camp at Sand creek, and were to be considered under the protection of the post. They were to give any information that might be useful to the commanding officer of the post, such as hostile Indians approaching the post or anything of that kind, and the commanding officer guaranteed to them that they could stay there without being molested, until he got some further news from the commander of the department as to what course he should take in regard to them. I don't know of anything more of importance that transpired at it.

Question. Who were present at that council ?

Answer. Major Scott Anthony, Major Wynkoop, Captain Soule, Lieutenant Cramer, Lieutenant Phillips. I think there were more there, but I do not remember their names. Major Colley, Indian agent, was there; Colonel Bent's son, Bob Bent. Of the Indians, Black Kettle was there, and Left Hand. That is about as far as my acquaintance went with the Indians.

Question. Where were you during the latter part of November, 1864 ?

Answer. At Fort Lyon.

Question. Did anything unusual transpire at Fort Lyon about that time ? If so, state what it was.

Answer. Yes ; Colonel Chivington's command came in one day.

Question. Did you see Colonel Chivington at that time, and have a conversation with him in reference to the Indians ?

(John M. Chivington most respectfully objects to the question for the following reasons : That it is leading and suggests the answer required. There is no evidence yet that the witness had any conversation with Colonel Chivington, and asking questions upon presumption that the witness has had conversations with Colonel Chivington in regard to Indians, &c., is irregular and improper. Objection sustained by the commissioner.)

Question. Did you have any conversation with any officer of that command in reference to the Indians ?

Answer. I heard a conversation between some of the officers of that command and officers of this post. I did not have any conversation with them myself in regard to the Indians.

Question. State who those officers were.

Answer. The officers belonging to this post were Captain Cook, Lieutenant Cossitt and myself, also Major Colley ; Colonel Chivington was there; a gentleman by the name of Maynard was also there. I don't recollect any others particularly. The conversation was general.

Question. State what was said during that conversation.

Answer. Some of the parties were endeavoring to press upon Colonel Chivington the injustice of going to attack that camp on Sand creek, and explaining to him the particular circumstances in which the officers of this post and the Indians were situated. Colonel Chivington was walking the room in a very excitable manner, and he wound up the conversation by saying, D——n any man who is in sympathy with an Indian.

Direct examination of W. P. Minton, by the commission, closed.

Cross-examination of W. P. Minton, by J. M. Chivington:

Question. What tribes did the Indians represent who had the council at Fort Lyon, and at which the understanding was they should encamp on Sand creek ?

Answer. Cheyennes and some Arapahoes.

Question. In what language was the conversation between the officers and the Indians carried on at the council of which you have spoken ?

Answer. I don't know what language was used. There was an interpreter there. The officers spoke in English to the interpreter, and he speaking some language I did not understand to the Indians.

Question. Then your only means of knowledge that an agreement made between the officers and the Indians as you have stated was from the interpreter, was it not ?

Answer. I spoke to another person whose name was Prowers, who was present; he stated that the agreement was as I stated, as well as the interpreter.

Question. Is what you have stated all your means of knowledge that an agreement was made between the officers and Indians, as you have stated ?

Answer. Yes.

Question. Will you state the interpreter's name in full, as well as Prowers's in full ?

Answer. The interpreter's name is John Smith ; John Prowers was the name of the other.

Question. You state that the agreement between the officers and Indians was that the Indians should go into camp on Sand creek. Will you state where on Sand creek the Indians were to go particularly, according to your understanding of the agreement ?

Answer. I did not understand at that time where Sand creek was, or anything about it.

Question. Did you understand that there was any agreement that the Indians should go to any particular place on Sand creek, how far from the fort, &c.?

Answer. Yes; there appeared to be an understanding that they knew where they were to camp ; I did not know where it was or how far from the fort.

Question. You state the agreement between the officers and the Indians was that the Indians should be under the protection of the post. Please explain what was understood by this protection of the Indians, &c., as you understood it; and whether the Indians were to be fed, &c.; and if attacked, whether they were to be protected by the troops.

Answer. That there should be no hostile parties sent against them; there was no agreement made to feed them; I did not understand that they were to be protected by the troops if attacked; there was nothing of that kind thought of.

Question. Who called this council of which you have been speaking, and who was in command of Fort Lyon at the time the council was held?

Answer. I don't know who called it; Major Scott Anthony was in command of the post. I heard the officers invited to go up to the commissary, to a council, by Major Anthony.

Commission adjourned until 9 a. m. to-morrow, April 4, 1865.

FORTIETH DAY.

APRIL 4, 1865.

Commission met pursuant to adjournment. Present, all members and recorder.

Proceedings of yesterday read and approved.

Cross-examination of William P. Minton by J. M. Chivington continued:

Question. Will you state the time, as near as you are able, that this council was held, of which you have been speaking?

Answer. I can't tell the exact date; it was some time about the middle of November, 1864, or about two weeks before the attack on the Indians at Sand creek.

Question. At that time had you seen Field Orders No. 2, issued from headquarters department of Kansas by Major General Curtis, commanding, relating to the treatment of Indians by post commanders, &c.?

Answer. I don't know as I had; I saw it a few days after Major Anthony took command of Fort Lyon; I don't recollect of seeing it before that time; Major Anthony brought the first copy I saw.

Question. How many days after Major Anthony assumed command of Fort Lyon did you see Field Orders No. 2, department of Kansas? and did you see it before the council of which you have spoken?

Answer. I could not say how many days it was; I don't recollect whether I saw it before the council or not.

Question. What is your means of knowledge that Major Anthony brought copies of Field Orders No. 2, department of Kansas, to Fort Lyon, as you have stated?

Answer. I saw them after he brought them, and heard him say he brought them; I ought to know what he brought, I was adjutant at that time.

Question. You say that at the council between the officers at Fort Lyon and the Indians, it was agreed that the Indians should give the officers at Fort Lyon information of the approach of any hostile band of Indians, &c. What hostile tribes were named?

Answer. Sioux.

Question. Were any other tribes of hostile Indians named besides the Sioux?

Answer. Kiowas are all I recollect of having been named besides the Sioux.

Question. Was all you have stated in regard to the council, as you have stated as coming from or being agreed to by the Indians, told to you by John Powers or related by John Smith, interpreter, as you have stated; and is John Powers or John Smith, interpreter, your only means of knowledge of what the Indians stated they would do?

338

Answer. Through those two gentlemen was the only means of my knowledge of what the Indians had said.

Question. Can you name the persons who endeavored to impress upon Colonel Chivington the injustice of attacking the Indians' camp on Sand creek ? If yes, state them to the court.

Answer. Most all the parties that were present; I could not name the parties.

Question. Did Major Colley, Indian agent, or Major Anthony, take any part in the conversation to which you have alluded, as occurring between officers at Fort Lyon and Colonel Chivington, when the said officers attempted to impress upon Colonel Chivington's mind the injustice of attacking the Indians' camp on Sand creek ? If yes, state what they said.

Answer. I could not say whether either of them did or not, I did not notice.

Question. You state that you cannot relate any of the conversation that occurred between the officers at Fort Lyon and Colonel Chivington, except what Colonel Chivington said; can you state anything else that Colonel Chivington said in the conversation to which you have alluded, besides that which you have related ?

Answer. I did not hear anything else that I thought worth remembering.

Cross-examination of William P. Minton by J. M. Chivington closed.

Re-examination of William P. Minton. No questions asked.

Corporal JAMES ADAMS called in by the commission to give evidence. The oath being administered according to law, he (Adams) testified as follows:

Question. Your full name and occupation ?

Answer. James J. Adams; occupation a soldier, company C, veteran battalion first Colorado cavalry.

Question. How long have you been a soldier ?

Answer. Three years the 22d of last February.

Question. Where were you during the latter part of November, 1864 ?

Answer. At Fort Lyon, I believe.

Question. Did anything of an unusual character happen at Fort Lyon during the latter part of November, 1864 ? If so, state what it was.

Answer. I think it was about that time the third regiment came down here, and went out to Sand creek, and had a fight with the Indians there. I don't remember the dates exactly.

Question. Were you present at that fight with the Indians ?

Answer. Yes.

Question. State what you saw there?

Answer. We left here in the night, I should judge about 8 or 9 o'clock, travelled all night and came in sight of their stock on the prairie just about daylight. We went on a short distance further and came in sight of the village; when we got down to where we could get a good view of the village the command broke out so as to surround the village; our company at the time was acting as artillery; we had two pieces along, with mules attached to them ; we were left behind in the run; our mules could not keep up with the pieces; finally we got to the village with our artillery. The cavalry were around on the different hills firing at the Indians; the Indians had left the village and taken to the banks of the creek ; they got under the banks of the creek, I suppose, to keep out of the road as much as possible, within fifty yards or thereabouts. We were ordered to take a position with our guns; we were ordered to shell the Indians out from under the banks above the village. We fired a few rounds from there, and then we were ordered to change our position, and take a position further up the creek ; took position further up the creek ; used up all the ammunition we had, and then had to draw off; we left here with only sixteen rounds to the gun ; the ammunition wagon was back with the train. Stood around awhile, and then were ordered into camp. I believe that is about all of importance that day, except there was an alarm about 9 or 10 o'clock that night by the guard.

Question. State where you went into camp, and how long you remained there.

Answer. We went into camp right in the upper end of the Indian village; we remained there two nights and one day.

Commission adjourned until 1½ p. m. this day.

*One and a half p. m.*—Commission met pursuant to adjournment. Present, all members and recorder.

Direct examination of Corporal James J. Adams by the commission continued:

Question. What became of the Indians attacked on Sand creek by Colonel Chivington's command?

Answer. I believe that the most of them were killed, by what I could see; I believe some of them got away before we got there with our outfit.

Question. How many were killed?

Answer. I could not say; I saw a great many women and children that were killed.

Question. Was anything done to the Indians after they had been killed?

Answer. Scalped, I believe; I did not see any but what were scalped.

Question. By whom and at what time was the scalping done?

Answer. I suppose most of the scalping was done on the day of the fight. I saw some scalping done on the day after. I believe there was some done by officers of the third regiment, and men likewise.

Question. Give the names of those you saw scalping the dead Indians?

Answer. There was one person that they called Major. I suppose he belonged to the third regiment; he did not belong to the first. There was another officer there—I do not remember his rank—they called Richmond. No other officers that I remember of. There were some privates engaged in scalping, likewise, in the same party. I saw some men cutting the fingers off of dead Indians to get the rings off.

Question. Were any other officers than those you have mentioned present during the scalping and mutilation of the Indians?

Answer. I did not notice any.

Question. How far was this scalping you have mentioned done from the camp of Colonel Chivington's command?

Answer. I should judge it was about a mile and a quarter, or a mile and a half.

Question. How near the camp lay those Indians you saw, that had been scalped?

Answer. I saw some Indians lying right in the camp.

Question. Were any orders given to the command? If so, state what those orders were.

(John M. Chivington most respectfully objects to question, for the following reasons: That the witness has said that he stated all the orders, &c.; that it is improper and irregular to draw by piecemeal evidence from a witness introduced by the prosecution, after the witness has been requested by the court to tell, and has told, all he said he knew in regard to the matter.

Objections overruled by the commission.)

Answer. I don't recollect of hearing any orders at that time.

Question. Was anything done to prevent scalping and mutilating the Indians?

(John M. Chivington most respectfully objects to the question, for the following reasons: That it has not yet been shown by the witness that he knew what was or was not done, and that the court in asking the question is presuming a position which has not been proven, and is irregular. That the question is leading, and may be answered in the affirmative or negative. That the witness being introduced by the court, and supposed to incline toward the prosecution, such questions are illegal and irregular.

Objections sustained by the commission.)

340

Question. Were any prisoners taken at Sand creek by Colonel Chivington's command ?

Answer. I don't know. There was one person there, a half Indian, (John Smith's son,) whom I don't know whether he was taken prisoner or gave himself up ; likewise two squaws.

Question. What was done with these prisoners by the command ?

Answer. They were stopping there in the encampment, in a lodge with John Smith, and the two women were sent from there to Fort Lyon. After we broke camp there John Smith's son was shot there in the lodge.

Question. Do you know how John Smith's son was shot ? If so, state what you know about it.

Answer. I don't know anything about that part of it, as I was not present at the time ; I was not at the time within fifty yards of the lodge.

Direct examination of Corporal James J. Adams, company C, veteran battalion first Colorado cavalry, by the commission, closed.

Cross-examination of Corporal James J. Adams, by J. M. Chivington :

Question. You state that most of the Indians attacked by Colonel Chivington were killed ; what is your means of knowledge for this statement? and why do you think some got away ?

Answer. I simply state that some got away, because I saw some on the hill after the fight was over, in the afternoon. The most of the Indians I saw were dead—the largest portion of them. I saw a great many more dead ones than I did live ones.

Question. Is what you have stated your only means of knowledge for your statement that the most of the Indians attacked by Colonel Chivington were killed, and that some of the Indians got away ?

Answer. Yes, I believe it is. I had but very little chance of seeing the Indians before the fight commenced, as we came in behind the command on account of our mules having given out.

Question. You state that you saw a great many women and children killed ; did you see them at the time they were killed, and where did these women and children lie ? Please state particularly.

Answer. I think the most of them I saw were after they were killed, before we got up there ; they were lying under the bank, I should judge from a quarter to a half a mile above the village. There were some dead women lying in the camp ; in the upper part of the camp there was one or two men lying, one of them within twenty yards of the edge of camp ; the other one was lying out about one hundred yards from camp, on a sand bank in the bed of the creek.

Question. You say you did not see any Indians that were not scalped ; how many Indians did you see, and where did they lie ? Please state particularly.

Answer. I could not tell how many I saw ; I did not count them ; I noticed that in places they were lying pretty thick ; one place in particular. They were lying under the bank on the bed of the creek, right at the foot of the bank. I should judge those were all about a quarter of a mile up the creek, above the village.

Question. When did you see these Indians—during or after the fight ?

Answer. The morning after the fight.

Question. Do we understand that you state positively that all the Indians you saw were scalped, and that the Indians you saw mutilated were really scalped ; might they not have been so mutilated by dogs, wolves, or other animals ?

Answer. I don't hardly think that dogs or wolves would chaw the scalp off and leave the body alone, although such a thing might be. I believe that all the Indians I saw were scalped, or in the act of being scalped.

Question. You state there were officers scalping ; one they called Major, and one they called Richmond. Were these parties together when you saw them scalping Indians, and how many were in the party, and how far were they from camp, and how many scalps did the party obtain ?

Answer. Those officers were together; I couldn't tell exactly how many soldiers there were in the party besides those two officers. I should judge they were somewhere in the neighborhood of a mile and a quarter and a mile and a half from camp. I could not say how many scalps the party obtained.

Question. Did not the men who were cutting the fingers off the dead Indians for rings tell you that they were simply obtaining trophies, to preserve as reminiscences, to bequeath to their children, of the glorious field of Sand creek ?

Answer. No, sir.

Question You say that you saw some scalped Indians lying right in camp; state particularly what part of the camp those Indians were lying, and at what time they were scalped, during the fight or after it.

Answer. Those Indians I saw were right in the camp, or lay within twenty feet of the hospital tent, and another not over forty feet. I could not tell whether they were scalped before or after the fight. They were scalped when I first saw them, when we made camp.

Cross-examination of Corporal James J. Adams by J. M. Chivington closed.

Re-examination of Corporal James J. Adams:

No questions asked.

Commission adjourned until 9 a. m. to-morrow, April 5, 1865.

### FORTY-FIRST DAY.

APRIL 5, 1865.

Commission met pursuant to adjournment. Present, all members and recorder.

On account of the inclemency of the weather, and the witness being unable to attend, the commission adjourned until 9 a. m. to-morrow, April 6, 1865.

### FORTY-SECOND DAY.

APRIL 6, 1865.

Commission met pursuant to adjournment. Present, all members and recorder.

Proceedings of the fourth and fifth days of April read and approved.

Lieutenant C. M. COSSITT, veteran battalion first Colorado cavalry, called in by the commission to give evidence. The oath being administered, he (Cossit) testified as follows :

Question. What is your full name and occupation ?

Answer. Chauncy M. Cossitt, lieutenant United States army, acting assistant quartermaster, and acting commissary of subsistence at this post, (Fort Lyon.)

Question. How long have you been on duty at Fort Lyon?

Answer. Since May 1, 1864.

Question. Have you, since you have been on duty at Fort Lyon, attended any councils held by the military with the Indians ? If so, state when, and what occurred there.

Answer. I have never been present at any council, except a few minutes—not long enough to give any particulars in regard to the proceedings.

Question. Did anything unusual occur at Fort Lyon during the latter part of November, 1864 ? If so, state what it was.

Answer. There was an arrival of troops from up the country, (Denver or vicinity.) They were under the command of Colonel Chivington. They afterwards went out to fight the Indians. On the 28th of November, 1864, Colonel Chivington and his command (a portion of the first and third regiments) started for Sand creek, as they informed me, to fight the Indians.

Question. Did Colonel Chivington receive any re-enforcements and supplies at this post? If so, state what they were.

342

Answer. He received re-enforcements of Major Anthony and his command. I could not give the number of troops that accompanied him. I can't give you the amount of supplies he got without referring to my books. I believe there were twenty thousand rations of commissary stores drawn. I could not approximate the amount of forage they drew without referring to my books. The forage was drawn in bulk.

Question. Did you have any conversation with any officer, or officers, of Colonel Chivington's command in reference to the Indians? If so, state who were present, and what was said.

Answer. Had a conversation in my room with Colonel Chivington, Lieutenant Minton, Major Colley, Indian agent, and several others; I don't remember the names of the balance; I think Captain Cook was there, but not sure. Colonel Chivington was denouncing Major Wynkoop's previous course; Lieutenant Minton and myself were upholding him, (Major Wynkoop.) I stated to the colonel how we were situated here in regard to the Indians, and that the Indian interpreter, a soldier, and a citizen, were there in the Indian camp by permission of Major Anthony, and said all I could to prevent the command going out there to the Indians; told him Major Anthony had an Indian employed, who was supposed to be there in the Indian camp, employed as a peace messenger. The colonel concluded the conversation by damning anybody in sympathy with Indians. This, of course, was previous to the battle.

Question. Was that conversation, to which you have referred, the only one you had with Colonel Chivington previous to the fight?

Answer. It was the only one that related to Indians particularly. When he first came in, I had a conversation with him in relation to forage and whiskey.

Question. Do you know how large a train, and the number of animals, Colonel Chivington had in his command? If so, give the number.

Answer. I do not exactly. When he first came in he told his brigade quartermaster that he had better draw forage for fourteen hundred head; whether he included his transportation stock I do not know; I tried to find out how many head of stock he had there, and neither of his quartermasters could tell me; he had three quartermasters.

Question. Give the names of the three quartermasters.

Answer. J. S. Maynard, brigade quartermaster; he signed himself captain first cavalry of Colorado. D. B. Elliott, first lieutenant and regimental quartermaster of the third regiment. Lieutenant Olney, battalion quartermaster, first cavalry of Colorado.

Question. Did you have any conversation with either of these officers in reference to their quartermaster business? If so, state what was said.

Answer. I had a conversation with Elliott; he said they had got to have a fight in order to get even on their stores; that is all worth mentioning.

Question. Did the command again return to this post? If so, state what was done.

Answer. They returned again to this post, drew more forage, received their captured stock and went on up the river towards Denver.

Question. Did you receive any captured stock? If so, state the amount.

Answer. I received three hundred and twenty-seven head of ponies and mules; they were here two or three days before they were turned over to me.

Question. From whom did you receive this captured stock, and what was done with it?

Answer. I received it from Lieutenant Antobe, third regiment, and turned it over to Captain Johnson, of the third regiment.

Question. Was all the captured stock brought in to the post received by you?

Answer. It was not. I made a rough count of them as they came in. I made four hundred and fifty. They were herded here by Lieutenant Antobe for several days; I should judge about three or four days.

Question. By whom was the captured stock brought into the post?
Answer. By Lieutenant Antobe and a portion of his command.
Question. What disposition did Lieutenant Antobe make of this stock?
Answer. He mounted a portion of his command—I think about thirty men; I do not know what he did with the balance. Some of Antobe's men run off a portion of the stock. Lieutenant Hewitt, third regiment, caught them and recovered sixty-six head. Those sixty-six head were not turned over to me. Lieutenant Hewitt said that he recovered it on the Purgatory.
Question. At what time and from what direction did Lieutenant Hewitt arrive at this post with the captured stock?
Answer. I don't think I can give you the date; he came from above—up the Arkansas.
Question. Did Lieutenant Hewitt arrive here after Colonel Chivington's command?
Answer. Yes.
Question. Was forage drawn for the captured stock? If so, state in what quantity.
Answer. It was drawn for the time I had charge of it, fourteen pounds of hay per day to each animal; no corn; also for those that Hewitt brought down.
Question. Was all the captured stock remaining at Fort Lyon delivered to Captain Johnson?
(J. M. Chivington most respectfully objects to the question, for the following reasons: That the question is leading and can be answered by a negative or an affirmative; that there is no evidence before the court that any particular person received the stock at Fort Lyon; and interrogating the witness upon presumptions that Captain Johnson or any other person received all or part of the stock, is irregular and improper.
Objection sustained by the commission.)
Question. Why did you turn over the stock to Captain Johnson, third regiment?
(J. M. Chivington most respectfully objects to the question, for the following reasons: That it is not competent for the court to inquire into the reasons that prompted the action of a witness who has been introduced by the court on behalf of the prosecution, and who has stated, that he performed certain acts which he has stated to the court. This kind of examination is more particularly in the province of the defence or cross-examination.
Objection overruled by the commission.)
Answer. I turned it over by a verbal order of Major Anthony, post commander.
Question. Did Captain Johnson receipt to you for the stock?
(J. M. Chivington most respectfully objects to the question, for the following reason: That the question is leading, suggesting the answer required, and may be answered by a negative or an affirmative.
Objection sustained by the commission.)
Question. Did you receive from Captain Johnson anything to show that you had turned over the stock to him? If so, state what it was.
Answer. I received my memorandum receipt which I had given for the stock.
Question. Was any action taken by any party to obtain all the captured stock at Fort Lyon? If so, state what was done.
(John M. Chivington most respectfully objects to the question, for the following reasons: That the question is leading, and may be answered by a negative or an affirmative, and suggests the answer required; that it is incompetent for this court to inquire whether there was any action taken by any person or not, as it has not been shown that any neglect has been manifested by any person, and the conduct of every officer in this district is not, as we understand it, under

the administration or official scrutiny of the court; and if the court will decide on this objection that fact, we would be willing to waive all objections we have to the question, in order to bring under investigation acts of certain parties whom we will be compelled in all probability to prosecute for taking stock, &c.)

Commission adjourned until 1½ this p. m.

*One and a half p. m.*—Commission met pursuant to adjournment. Present, all members and recorder.

Objection of J. M. Chivington to last question before adjournment overruled by the commission. The commission asks this question for the purpose of ascertaining what became of the captured stock, and what measures were taken by the officers to protect it for the benefit of the government, and not for the purpose of implicating or of prosecuting any officer to obtain the facts; and in overruling the objection of John M. Chivington, it does it for the purpose of obtaining the information desired and without reference to any particular officer or officers.

Direct examination of Lieutenant Chauncey M. Cossitt by the commission continued:

Answer. Captain Johnson, who was provost marshal, ordered his men to search about the post for captured stock, which they did.

Question. What was done with the stock captured by Captain Johnson?

(John M. Chivington most respectfully objects to the question for the following reasons: That there is no evidence before the court to show that the witness knew what became of the stock, or was in such a position that he could learn what became of it; therefore it is improper for the court to inquire of the witness regarding facts which they can only presume the witness knows, without first introducing evidence of his knowledge of such facts, in order to lay the foundation for such evidence as the court by their interrogatory seek to introduce.

Objection overruled by the commission.)

Answer. His men drove it away up the river.

Question. What quantity of forage did you issue to Colonel Chivington's command on his return to Fort Lyon?

Answer. I can't tell without referring to my books. It was issued in bulk.

Question. Can you furnish an exact statement of the amount issued both before and after the fight on Sand creek?

Answer. Yes. Before the fight I transferred fifty-four thousand two hundred and sixty-four pounds of corn; nineteen thousand one hundred and three pounds of hay. After the battle forty-two thousand three hundred and fifty-nine pounds of corn; one hundred and thirteen thousand six hundred and twenty-six pounds of hay. All receipted for by J. S. Maynard. That did not include the Fort Lyon battalion. They receipted for theirs separately.

Question. Did you see Colonel Chivington's command on its return from Sand creek?

Answer. I did.

Question. State its condition, when you saw it, in reference to the number of horses, men mounted, or on foot.

(John M. Chivington most respectfully objects to the question, for the following reasons: That the court has not shown that the witness has had any opportunity to learn the condition, &c., of the command, or that the witness knew anything of the command sufficient to give even an ordinary opinion. That the question for these reasons is irregular and improper, and it is not competent for the court, as we have insisted in many instances during this investigation, to presume a certain fact, and upon presumption inquire of the witness in regard to other facts.

Objection not sustained by the commission.)

Answer. As far as I was able to judge there was no material increase or de-

345

crease in the number of stock. There were more men mounted on ponies when they came back than when they went out.

Question. Did you have any conversation with any officer of Colonel Chivington's command on its return from Sand creek in reference to that affair? If so, state with whom, and what was said.

(J. M. Chivington most respectfully objects to the question, for the following reasons: That it is improper to introduce as evidence statements of officers or others in relation to matters that occurred at Sand creek or any other place; if the court wishes testimony in regard to the Sand creek affair the only testimony competent to prove any particular fact is that which should be obtained from an officer present at Sand creek, and he could only offer testimony of facts that came under his own observation. We have no objection to the witness stating what he knows of his own knowledge, but not what others state, not speaking under the binding obligations of an oath.

Objections overruled by the commission.)

Answer. I had but a few minutes' conversation with any one after their return, except with Major Anthony, and those that remained here afterwards. I don't remember enough about the conversations to repeat them.

Direct examination of Lieutenant C. M. Cossitt by the commission closed.

Cross-examination of Lieutenant C. M. Cossitt by J. M. Chivington:

Question. You state you had a conversation with Colonel Chivington in regard to- the Indians, &c., and Major Colley, Indian agent, was present. Did Major Colley engage in that conversation of which you have spoken; and if so, what did he say?

Answer. He did engage in the conversation; he upheld Major Wynkoop's course; stated that the Cheyennes had been misunderstood, misrepresented, and ill-treated by Captain Parmeter and others.

Question. Did you ever hear Major Colley say that the Indians on Sand creek ought to be punished, &c., and state that he (Colley) was in favor of punishing them?

Answer. No.

Question. Can you give the names of any other persons who were present when you had the conversation with Colonel Chivington to which you have referred? If yes, state the names as near as you can, the time of the day and the month this conversation occurred, and in what part of Fort Lyon.

Answer. There were other persons in the room, but I cannot state positively who they were. As I said before, I think Captain Cook was there; also Evander Light. My impression is that there were others in the room, but I can't name them. The conversation occurred, I think, on the 28th of November, 1864, and about 9 o'clock in the evening. It may have been earlier in the evening. It was in my office.

Question. You state that you had a conversation with Lieutenant Elliot in regard to his business, and that he stated he had to have a fight to get even, &c.; was not this said in a jesting manner, and is not such talk often innocently engaged in by quartermasters or officers on duty as such?

Answer. I don't think he said it in a jesting manner; he seemed very anxious about the affair; he said he was horribly mixed up. I don't know but such talk is occasionally engaged in by quartermasters or officers acting as such.

Question. Was not Lieutenant Elliot laughing when he made the remark—they had to have a fight to get even, &c., and was he not in the habit of talking in a very loose manner, more in jest than in earnest?

Answer. I don't think he was laughing, and I am not well enough acquainted with him to know what his habits of conversation are. He did not appear in a laughing humor.

Question. You state that when the captured stock was brought in you made

346

a rough count of them, and made four hundred and fifty ponies, mules, &c.; might you not have been mistaken, and there have been less than that number brought in?

Answer. Yes. I said I made a rough count, but there would be apt to be more than less, when they were running past as I counted them. I think it was an under-estimate. I think it would exceed that number.

Question. Will you state about what you think the real number of ponies, mules, &c., was, and how it exceeded the number you made on what you call a rough count?

Answer. I did not say they exceeded that number; I said it would be apt to, as I counted them as they were driven past me.

Commission adjourned until 9 a. m. to-morrow, April 7, 1865.

### FORTY-THIRD DAY.

APRIL 7, 1865.

Commission met pursuant to adjournment. Present, all members and recorder. Proceedings of yesterday read and approved.

Cross-examination of Lieutenant C. M. Cossitt by J. M. Chivington continued:

Question. Who was present when you had the conversation with Lieutenant Elliott, as you have stated, when he said they would have a fight in order to get even?

Answer. J. S. Maynard, and several others. It was in the commissary building at Fort Lyon; it was on the 29th of November, 1864, after the command had gone out to Sand creek. I don't remember the time of day.

Question. You state that Lieutenant Autobee's men ran off some of the captured stock. What is your means of knowledge that Lieutenant Autobee's men ran off the stock as you have stated?

Answer. Their own acknowledgment (I think that the man that made it was a sergeant) and Lieutenant Hewitt's statement.

Question. Is what Lieutenant Hewitt and others told you the only means of knowledge you have of the capturing of the sixty-six head of stock, and the running of it off by Lieutenant Autobee's men?

Answer. It is.

Question. What is your means of knowledge that sixty-six head of stock were recovered by Lieutenant Hewitt, as you have stated?

Answer. I saw the stock; heard Lieutenant Hewitt's statement of the affair, and the acknowledgment of the men that drove it off.

Question. You state that fourteen pounds of hay were issued for the captured stock, &c. Do you know whether the stock received this fourteen pounds of hay, and whether your men issued the hay according to your direction?

Answer. I do. I saw it issued. I was short of help, and had to help do it myself.

Question. Did not Captain Johnson have a great deal of trouble in obtaining the captured stock at Fort Lyon?

Answer. He had no trouble with that portion I turned over to him. His men were some time in looking up the stock.

Question. Did you see Colonel Chivington's command when it started from Fort Lyon after Indians?

Answer. I did not see it at the time of its departure; I saw it a short time before.

Question. How long before its departure did you see it?

Answer. About two hours.

Question. Where was the command of Colonel Chivington when you saw it, before its departure after Indians, and were the men mounted?

Answer. In camp near Fort Lyon. The men were not mounted.

347

Question. How many times did you see Colonel Chivington's command, mounted or dismounted, before the fight?

Answer. Twice.

Question. How near Colonel Chivington's command were you the first time you saw it?

Answer. About two hundred yards, as it passed in column.

Question. Did you see the entire command, or were you not engaged in other duties some of the time, while it was passing?

Answer. I saw the entire command except stragglers—all they had in their column.

Question. The last time you saw Colonel Chivington's command, was it light? You say you saw it two hours before its departure after Indians.

Answer. Yes.

Question. Is what you have stated your only means of knowledge that more men of Colonel Chivington's command, after the fight with the Indians, on their return to Fort Lyon, were mounted on ponies than when they started from Fort Lyon?

Answer. It is.

Question. Did you have, or if you had, did you improve your opportunities for learning how many ponies there were in Colonel Chivington's command before it started from Fort Lyon after Indians?

Answer. The only opportunities I had was good eye-sight and a fair position, which I improved.

Question. Your answers appear to show a great deal of hilarity on your part. Will you please state whether we are to understand all that you state in regard to this serious subject is to be taken in the same jocular manner?

(Objection to the question by Lieutenant Colonel S. F. Tappan, president of commission.

It does not, or has not appeared to the undersigned that the witness has shown any great degree of hilarity in answering interrogations, as intimated by the last question. A little pleasantry has been occasionally indulged in, when the question appeared a little ambiguous, but as soon as sufficiently explained, in a manner to be understood, and in many instances changed by the attorney for John M. Chivington, they have been answered directly and promptly by the witness, and therefore I object to the question.

SAM. F. TAPPAN,
*President of Commission.*

Objection sustained by the commission.)

Cross-examination of First Lieutenant C. M. Cossitt, by J. M. Chivington, closed.

Re-examination of First Lieutenant C. M. Cossitt:
No questions asked.

Commission adjourned until 1½ p. m. this day.

*One and a half p. m.*—Commission met pursuant to adjournment. Present, all members and recorder.

Commission adjourned until 9 a. m. to-morrow.

### FORTY-FOURTH DAY.

APRIL 8, 1865.

Commission met pursuant to adjournment. Present, all members and recorder.

Proceedings of yesterday read and approved.

Documents, marked in red letters F, G, and H, (being Major Wynkoop's reports,) read to the commission, and adopted as a part of the record.

Commission adjourned at Fort Lyon, Colorado Territory, this day, to meet again at Denver, Colorado Territory, on the 17th instant, or as soon thereafter as practicable.

### FORTY-FIFTH DAY.
DENVER, C. T., *April* 20, 1865.

*Two p. m.*—Commission met pursuant to adjournment. Present, all members and recorder.
Proceedings of the forty-fourth day (April 8, 1865) read and approved. The commission, not being ready to examine witnesses this afternoon, adjourned until 9 a. m. to-morrow, April 21, 1865.

### FORTY-SIXTH DAY.
APRIL 21, 1865.

Commission met pursuant to adjournment. Present, all members and recorder.
Proceedings of yesterday read and approved.
Commission adjourned until 2 p. m. this day.

*Two p. m.*—Commission met pursuant to adjournment. Present, all members and recorder.
Commission adjourned until 9 a. m. to-morrow, April 22, 1865.

### FORTY-SEVENTH DAY.
APRIL 22, 1865.

Commission met pursuant to adjournment. Present, all members and recorder.
Proceedings of yesterday read and approved.
Commission adjourned until 2 p. m. this day.

*Two p. m.*—Commission met pursuant to adjournment. Present, all members and recorder.
Commission adjourned until 9 a. m. Monday, April 24, 1865.

### FORTY-EIGHTH DAY.
APRIL 24, 1865.

Commission met pursuant to adjournment. Present, all members and recorder.
Proceedings of Saturday, April 22, read and approved.
Commission adjourned until 2 p. m. this day.

*Two p. m.*—Commission met pursuant to adjournment. Present, all members and recorder.
Captain Silas S. Soule, veteran battalion first Colorado cavalry, having (while in the performance of his duty as provost marshal) been assassinated in the streets of this city, the commission, in respect to the memory of the deceased, adjourned until 9 a. m. to-morrow, April 25, 1865.

### FORTY-NINTH DAY.
APRIL 25, 1865.

Commission met pursuant to adjournment. Present, all members and recorder.
Proceedings of yesterday read and approved.
The following communication received and read to commission :

DENVER, C. T., *April* 25, 1865.

*To the President and members of military commission, &c. :*
I would most respectfully notify the court that I will file objections to the admission of reports, affidavits, &c., relating to Major Wynkoop's expedition to the Smoky Hill, &c.

J. M. CHIVINGTON,
*Late Colonel First Colorado Cavalry.*

Captain C. L. GORTON, assistant quartermaster, called in by the commission to give evidence.

The oath being administered according to law, he (Captain Gorton) testified as follows :

Question. Your full name and rank in the army ?

Answer. Cyrus L. Gorton, assistant quartermaster United States volunteers. On duty as assistant quartermaster at Denver.

Question. How long have you been on duty in Denver ?

Answer. Since the middle of last September.

Question. Whom did you relieve as quartermaster at Denver ?

Answer. Captain Lenden Mullen, assistant quartermaster United States volunteers.

Question. Did you receive from him any public property ? If so, state what it was.

Answer. I received some clothing, camp and garrison equipage, and quartermaster stores.

Question. How many public horses did you receive from him ? Were they branded, and what disposition did you make of them ?

(John M. Chivington most respectfully objects to the question for the following reasons : That that portion of question referring to the branding of the horses is irrelevant, and not pertinent to the subject-matter of the investigation.

Objection sustained by the commission.)

Question. Have any mounted troops been equipped by you since you have been on duty in Denver ? If so, state who they were.

Answer. The first, second, and third regiments were partially equipped by me.

Question. What did you furnish the third regiment ?

Answer. I furnished them with clothing, camp and garrison equipage, and quartermaster stores.

Question. Did you furnish them any horses ? If so, state the number, and to whom delivered.

Answer. I did furnish them horses. To First Lieutenant D. P. Elliot, regimental quartermaster, three hundred and thirty-six horses ; Captain W. H. Morgan, company C, four horses ; Captain F. G. Cree, company H, three horses ; First Lieutenant J. A. Fry, company F, ten horses.

Question. Of whom did you procure the horses furnished the third regiment ?

Answer. Some I purchased, and part I received from Captain Mullen.

Question. How many did you receive from Captain Mullen ?

Answer. Two hundred and thirty ; some of them were unserviceable.

Question. State the condition of those horses you received from Captain Mullen and turned over to the third regiment ?

Answer. Those turned over to the third regiment were issued as serviceable.

Question. At what time did you turn over the horses to the third regiment ?

Answer. In the months of September, October, November, and December, 1864; but three were turned over in December.

Question. How long after these horses were turned over by you did the third regiment remain in the public service ?

Answer. The regiment was mustered out in December, 1864, I believe.

Question. State the condition of the horses purchased and turned over by you to the third regiment ?

Answer. They were mostly very good horses. The horses were inspected and received by the colonel first, the lieutenant colonel second, and afterwards by the major, of the third regiment.

Question. Give the names of the officers who inspected these horses ?

Answer. Colonel George L. Shoup, Lieutenant Colonel L. L. Bowen, and Major W. F. Wilder.

Question. Were these officers appointed to inspect horses? If so, by whom.

Answer. They were appointed by Colonel Chivington, commanding district. I asked that some officer be appointed to inspect them, because the purchase was entirely irregular, and I had no authority from the Cavalry Bureau to purchase these horses.

Question. Did you purchase the horses by contract, or in open market?

Answer. In open market.

Question. When you turned over these horses to the third regiment were they, or were they not, branded or otherwise marked so as to be known as government horses?

(John M. Chivington most respectfully objects to the question, for the following reasons : That the question is leading, and can be answered by a negative or an affirmative; that the fact of their (the horses) being branded at the time Captain Gorton turned them over to the third regiment is immaterial to the issue; that the irregularity of interrogating a witness in regard to his duties, their correct performance, &c., is novel, to say the least. We object to the court interrogating witnesses introduced by themselves in such a manner that a negative answer will make the witness liable for neglect of duty, and so framing their questions that the witness is always instructed what answer is required.

Objection sustained by the commision.)

Question. What disposition was made of the horses on the muster out of the third regiment?

Answer. I cannot say what disposition was made of all of them.

Commission adjourned until 2 p. m. this day.

*Two p. m.*—Commission met pursuant to adjournment. Present, all members and recorder.

The members of the commission having been requested to assist in making arrangements for the funeral of the late lamented Silas S. Soule, commission adjourned until Thursday morning, April 27, 1865, at 9 o'clock.

FIFTIETH DAY.

APRIL 27, 1865.

Commission met pursuant to adjournment. Present, all members and recorder.

Proceedings of yesterday read and approved.

Direct examination of Captain C. L. Gorton, assistant quartermaster United States volunteers, by the commision, continued :

Question. How many of the horses you received from Captain Mullen were unserviceable?

(J. M. Chivington most respectfully objects to the question for the following reasons : That it has not been shown that any of the unserviceable horses received from Captain Mullen, if any were received, were turned over to officers of the third regiment, or any other regiment, and that the question is therefore irrelevant, and not pertinent to the subject-matter of the investigation ; that all quartermasters have more or less unserviceable horses, &c., in their possession, and that it is competent for this court to inquire only in regard to stock used by the late officers of the third regiment, or others who were on duty in this district, giving it the most liberal interpretation the court has placed upon these orders heretofore. That the question is leading, and for that reason, also, is improper.

Objection overruled by the commission.)

Answer. One hundred and ten.

Question. State what you know concerning the disposition made of the horses of the third regiment, or any portion of them.

(John M. Chivington most respectfully objects to the question for the follow-

Ex. Doc. 26——11

ing reasons: That the witness has stated all he knew on that point; that it has not been shown that the witness knew what disposition was made of the horses, and is therefore improper; that the question is leading, and therefore improper. Objection overruled by the commission.)

Answer. A portion of them were turned over to me.

Question. How many, and by whom were they turned over to you?

(John M. Chivington most respectfully objects to the question for the following reasons: The witness has stated all he knew in regard to the number of horses turned over, &c., and it is therefore irrelevant and improper; that the question is leading and should not be proposed by the party introducing the witness; that the question is improper for the reason that, according to the orders by which the court should be guided, the question does not pertain to the subject-matter of this investigation.

Commission rooms were cleared for private discussion.

Rooms again opened.

Objection overruled by the commission.)

Answer. I received from Lieutenant Elliot, regimental quartermaster, four hundred and sixty-five horses; from Lieutenant Colonel Bowen, one horse; from Colonel Shoup, one horse; from Captain Nichols, one horse; from Captain Talbot, four horses; from Captain Phillips, one horse; from Captain Cree, one horse; from Captain McDonald, two horses; from Captain Morgan, four horses; from Lieutenant Fry, twenty-four horses; from Lieutenant De La Mar, eighteen horses; from Lieutenant Elliot, regimental quartermaster, ninety-five captured ponies. That is all, I believe.

Question. Did you receive any other property than that mentioned, reported as captured from the Indians?

Answer. I did not from any member of the third regiment.

Question. Did you from any other person? If so, state what it was, and from whom received.

Answer. I did, from government detectives, ponies and two small mules. I cannot tell exactly how many ponies now.

Question. Can you furnish this commission with a statement of the number of ponies so received?

Answer. I can, by referring to my accounts.

Commission adjourned until 2½ o'clock p. m. this day.

*Two and a half o'clock p. m.*—Commission met pursuant to adjournment. Present, all the members and the recorder.

The following communication was received and read to the commission:

*To the president and members of the military commission sitting in Denver, C. T.:*

I would most respectfully represent that one Clark Dunn, late a lieutenant in the first cavalry of Colorado, is a material witness for me in my defence, and that the said Clark Dunn is about to leave this Territory for the States, and that I would most respectfully request this commission to take the evidence of the said Dunn this afternoon, that we may not entirely lose it. Said Dunn is to leave in to-morrow morning's coach.

Yours respectfully,
                    J. M. CHIVINGTON,
               *Late Colonel First Cavalry of Colorado.*

DENVER, C. T., *April* 27, 1865.

Commission decided to postpone the further examination of Captain Gorton upon the application of J. M. Chivington, and proceeded to take the deposition of Lieutenant Clark Dunn, a witness for the said Chivington, to be made a part of the proceedings of this commission.

352

Commission adjourned at 5½ o'clock p. m., to meet again to-morrow April 28, 1865, at 9 o'clock a. m.

### FIFTY-FIRST DAY.

APRIL 28, 1865.

Commission met pursuant to adjournment. Present, all the members and the recorder.

Commission adjourned until 2 o'clock p. m. this day.

*Two o'clock p. m.*—Commission met pursuant to adjournment. Present, all the members and the recorder.

Proceedings of yesterday were read and approved.

Direct examination of Captain C. L. Gorton by the commission continued :

Question. How many ponies did you receive from government detectives ?

Answer. Ninety-three.

Direct examination of Captain C. L. Gorton, assistant quartermaster, by the commission, closed.

Cross-examination of C. L. Gorton, assistant quartermaster, by J. M. Chivington:

Question. You state that one hundred and ten of the horses received from Captain Mullen, assistant quartermaster, were unserviceable ; what are your means of knowledge ?

Answer. By my own observation, and they were so transferred by Captain Mullen.

Cross-examination of Captain C. L. Gorton, assistant quartermaster United States volunteers, by J. M. Chivington, closed.

Re-examination of Captain C. L. Gorton, United States volunteers.

No questions asked.

The following objection of J. M. Chivington to the admission of the reports, affidavits, &c., of Major E. W. Wynkoop, as part of the record, received and read to commission :

The following described affidavits and reports having been introduced as evidence before the commission convened in pursuance of Special Order No. 23, headquarters district of Colorado, dated Denver, Colorado Territory, February 1, 1865, of which Lieutenant Colonel S. F. Tappan, veteran battalion first Colorado cavalry, is president, to wit :

Report of Major Wynkoop, first cavalry of Colorado, to his excellency John Evans, governor Colorado Territory, dated September 18, 1864, signed by Major Wynkoop;

Report of Major Wynkoop, first cavalry of Colorado, commanding Fort Lyon, to the commander of the department of Kansas, dated October 8, 1864, signed by Wynkoop, &c.;

Report or letter to Colonel Ford, commanding district upper Arkansas, dated January 15, 1865 signed by Wynkoop, &c.;

Affidavit of John Smith, United States Indian interpreter, dated January 15, 1865, signed by John Smith ;

Affidavit of Captain R. A. Hill, first New Mexico volunteer infantry, dated January 16, 1865, signed by Captain Hill ;

Affidavit of Lieutenant James D. Cannon, first New Mexico volunteer infantry, dated January 16, 1865 ;

Affidavit of second Lieutenant W. P. Minton, first New Mexico volunteer infantry, and Lieutenant C. M. Cossitt, first Colorado cavalry, dated January 16, 1865 ;

Affidavit of private David Louderback, first cavalry of Colorado, and R. W. Clark, citizen, dated January 16, 1865, signed by D. H. Louderback and R. W. Clark;

Affidavit of Samuel G. Colley, United States Indian agent, dated January 27, 1865, signed by S. G. Colley;

I would most respectfully object to their introduction as evidence, for the following reasons:

That the reports and report or letter of Major Wynkoop, of the first cavalry of Colorado, are ex parte and irregular, not being such evidence as could be introduced before any properly constituted court to establish any fact whatever. That Major Wynkoop, first cavalry of Colorado, testified before this commission after the reports and letter were made, and related to the court all his knowledge of the subject-matter of these reports and letter or report, and that is the only evidence the commission can legally receive.

That the affidavits of R. W. Clark, a citizen, John Smith, Indian interpreter, S. G. Colley, Indian agent, and Captain Hill, first New Mexico volunteers infantry, are ex parte and illegal, and should not be received as evidence, being a violation of that rule of law guaranteed by the Constitution, "that the accused shall be allowed to meet his accuser face to face." That by the introduction of affidavits as evidence I am deprived of my right of cross-examination, which is the only protection I have against the malicious perjurer and the designing villain.

That during the sitting of this commission at Fort Lyon, Colorado Territory, Captain Hill, first New Mexico infantry, was at Fort Lyon, and his evidence, if deemed material, could have been taken by this commission.

That the affidavits of James D. Cannon, lieutenant first New Mexico volunteer infantry, the affidavit of Lieutenant W. P. Minton, first New Mexico volunteer infantry, Lieutenant C. M. Cossitt, first cavalry of Colorado, and the affidavits of private David Louderback, first cavalry of Colorado, are ex parte and illegal, and not such evidence as should be received to prove any fact in issue on a trial before a legally constituted tribunal.

That all the parties appeared at this commission were sworn, and testified all they knew in regard to the subject-matter of these affidavits; that this is the best evidence, and that affidavits should not be introduced as evidence under any circumstances to prove a fact in issue, but particularly after the party seeking to introduce such affidavits have introduced the parties themselves, and obtained all their evidence in relation to the subject-matter of the investigation.

Rooms cleared for private discussion.

Commission adjourned until 9 a. m. to-morrow, April 29, 1865.

FIFTY-SECOND DAY.

APRIL 29, 1865.

Commission met pursuant to adjournment. Present, all members and recorder. Commission adjourned until 2 p. m. this day.

*Two p. m.*—Commission met pursuant to adjournment. Present, all members and recorder.

To enable the members of the commission to examine district records, to obtain documents necessary in the investigation of late Indian difficulties, &c., the commission adjourned until Monday 9 a. m., May 1, 1865.

FIFTY-THIRD DAY.

MAY 1, 1865.

Commission met pursuant to adjournment. Present, all members and recorder. Proceedings of fifty-second day, April 29, 1865, read, amended as follows, and approved: In both the forenoon and afternoon proceedings to read, Present, a majority of the commission.

354

The following copies of official documents received, read, and ordered to be made a part of the record:

[General Field Order No. 1.]

HEADQUARTERS DISTRICT OF COLORADO,
*Camp Fillmore, near Booneville, November 23, 1864.*

The following are announced as on the staff of the colonel commanding, during the campaign against the Indians: Dr. T. J. Leas, surgeon-in-chief of volunteers, aide-de-camp; Major J. Downing, first cavalry of Colorado, inspector; Captain J. S. Maynard, first cavalry of Colorado, acting assistant adjutant general and acting assistant quartermaster; Captain J. I. Johnson, third cavalry of Colorado, provost marshal; Lieutenant J. S. Boyd, third cavalry of Colorado, acting assistant commissary of subsistence; Captain A. J. Gill, Colorado militia, volunteer aide-de-camp.

By order of J. M. Chivington, colonel first cavalry of Colorado, commanding first Indian expedition:

J. S. MAYNARD,
*Acting Assistant Adjutant General.*

HEADQUARTERS DISTRICT OF THE PLAINS,
*Denver, Colorado Territory, April 28, 1865.*

Official copy:

GEO. F. PRICE,
*Acting Assistant Adjutant General, District of the Plains.*

---

[General Field Order No. 2.]

HEADQUARTERS DISTRICT OF COLORADO,
*Camp in Field, near Fort Lyon, November 28, 1864.*

I. Hereafter, no officer will be allowed to leave his command without the consent of the colonel commanding, and no soldier without a written pass from his company commander, approved by the commander of his battalion.

II. No fires will be allowed to burn after dark, unless specially directed from these headquarters.

III. Any person giving the Indians information of the movements of troops will be deemed a spy and shot to death.

By order of J. M. Chivington, colonel first cavalry of Colorado, commanding first Indian expedition:

J. S. MAYNARD,
*Acting Assistant Adjutant General.*

HEADQUARTERS DISTRICT OF THE PLAINS,
*Denver, Colorado, April 28, 1865.*

Official:

GEO. F. PRICE,
*Acting Assistant Adjutant General.*

---

HEADQUARTERS DISTRICT OF COLORADO, IN THE FIELD,
*Cheyenne country, South Bend Big Sandy, November 29, 1864.*

Major General S. R. CURTIS, *Department of Kansas, Fort Leavenworth:*

In the last ten days my command has marched three hundred miles, one hundred of which the snow was two feet deep. After a march of forty miles last night, I at daylight this morning attacked Cheyenne villages of one hundred and thirty lodges, from nine to ten hundred warriors strong, killed chiefs Black Kettle,

White Antelope, Knock Kno, and Little Robe, and between four and five hundred other Indians, and captured many ponies and mules. Our loss nine killed, thirty-eight wounded. All did nobly. Think I will catch some more of them. Eighty miles on Smoky Hill, found white man's scalp, not more than three days' old, in one of the lodges.

J. M. CHIVINGTON,
*Colonel Comd'g District of Colorado, and first Indian Expedition.*

HEADQUARTERS DISTRICT OF THE PLAINS,
*Denver, Colorado Territory, April 28, 1865.*

Official copy:

GEO. F. PRICE,
*Acting Assistant Adjutant General, District of the Plains.*

----

HEADQUARTERS DISTRICT OF COLORADO,
*Denver, December 16, 1854.*

GENERAL: I have the honor to transmit the following report of operations of the Indian expedition under my command, of which brief-notice was given you by my telegram of November 29:

Having ascertained that the hostile Indians had proceeded south from the Platte, and were almost within striking distance of Fort Lyon, I ordered Colonel George L. Shoup, third regiment of Colorado volunteer cavalry, (100-days service,) to proceed with the mounted men of his regiment in that direction. On November 20th I left Denver, and at Booneville, Colorado Territory, on the 24th of November, joined and took command in person of the expedition, which had been increased by battalion first cavalry of Colorado, consisting of detachments of companies C, E, and H. I proceeded with the utmost caution down the Arkansas river, and on the morning of the 28th instant arrived at Fort Lyon, to the surprise of the garrison of that post. On the same evening I resumed my march, being joined by Scott J. Anthony, first cavalry of Colorado, with one hundred and twenty-five men of said regiment, consisting of detachments of companies D, G, and K, with two howitzers.

\* \* \* \* \* \*

It may perhaps be unnecessary for me to state that I captured no prisoners; between five and six hundred Indians were left dead upon the field. About five hundred and fifty ponies, mules, and horses were captured and all their lodges were destroyed, the contents of which have served to supply the command with an abundance of trophies, comprising the paraphernalia of Indian warfare and life. My loss was eight killed on the field and forty (40) wounded, of which two have since died. \* \* \* Of the effects of the punishment sustained by the Indians you will be the judge. Their chiefs, Black Kettle, White Antelope, One-Eye, Knock Kno, and Little Robe, were numbered with the killed and their bands almost annihilated.

I am, general, very respectfully, your obedient servant,

J. M. CHIVINGTON,
*Colonel First Cavalry of Colorado, Comd'g District of Colorado.*

Major General S. R. CURTIS,
*Commanding Department of Kansas, Fort Leavenworth, Ks.*

HEADQUARTERS DISTRICT OF THE PLAINS,
*Denver, Colorado, May 1, 1865.*

A true copy:

GEO. F. PRICE,
*Acting Assistant Adjutant General.*

## SAND CREEK MASSACRE.

[By telegraph.]

HEADQUARTERS DISTRICT OF COLORADO,
*Denver, December 7,* 1864.

Governor JOHN EVANS,
*Care National Hotel, Washington, D. C.*

Had fight with Cheyennes about forty miles north of Fort Lyon. I lost nine killed and thirty-eight wounded; killed five hundred Indians; destroyed one hundred and thirty lodges; took five hundred mules and ponies; marched three hundred miles in ten days—snow two feet deep for one hundred miles—and still after them.

J. M. CHIVINGTON,
*Colonel Comd'g District of Colorado and First Indian Expedition.*

HEADQUARTERS DISTRICT OF THE PLAINS,
*Denver, Colorado, April* 30, 1865.

A true copy:

GEO. J. PRICE, *A. A. A. G.*

---

The following are copies of reports of John Evans, governor of Colorado Territory, to the Commissioner of Indian Affairs, Washington, D. C., 1864, in relation to Indian difficulties in Colorado Territory:

[Extract.]

COLORADO SUPERINTENDENCY OF INDIAN AFFAIRS,
*Denver, C. T., October* 15, 1864.

SIR: In compliance with the regulations of the Department of the Interior I have the honor of making the following report:

\*   \*   \*   \*   \*   \*   \*

While a general Indian war was inevitable, it was dictated by sound policy, justice, and humanity that those Indians who were friendly, and disposed to remain so, should not fall victims to the impossibility of soldiers discriminating between them and the hostile, upon whom they must to do any good, inflict the most severe chastisement. Having procured the consent of the department to collect the friendly Indians of the plains at places of safety, by a telegraphic despatch reading as follows: "Act according to your best judgment with regard to friendly Indians, but do not exceed the appropriations"—I issued a proclamation, and sent it by special messengers and through every practicable channel of communication, to all the tribes of the plains.

The following is a copy of the proclamation:

COLORADO SUPERINTENDENCY OF INDIAN AFFAIRS,
*Denver, June* 27, 1864.

*To the friendly Indians of the plains:*

Agents, interpreters, and traders will inform the friendly Indians of the plains that some members of their tribes have gone to war with the white people.

They steal stock and run it off, hoping to escape detection and punishment. In some instances they have attacked and killed soldiers and murdered peaceable citizens. At this the great father is angry, and will certainly hunt them out, and punish them. But he does not want to injure those who remain friendly to the whites. He desires to protect and take care of them. For this purpose I direct that all friendly Indians keep away from those who are at war, and go to places of safety.

357

Friendly Arapahoes and Cheyennes belonging on the Arkansas river will go to Major Colly, United States Indian agent at Fort Lyon, who will give them provisions and show them a place of safety.

Friendly Kiowas and Comanches will go to Fort Larned, where they will be cared for in the same way.

Friendly Sioux go to their agent at Fort Laramie for directions.

Friendly Arapahoes and Cheyennes of the Upper Platte will go to Camp Collins, on the Cache la Poudre, where they will be assigned a place of safety, and provisions will be given them.

The object of this is to prevent friendly Indians from being killed through mistake; none but those who intend to be friendly with the whites must come to these places. The families of those who have gone to war with the whites must be kept away from among the friendly Indians.

The war on hostile Indians will be continued until they are all effectually subdued.

JOHN EVANS,
*Governor of Colorado Territory and Superintendent of Indian Affairs.*

\* \* \* \* \* \* \*

As I learned that Major Wynkoop, who was in command of Fort Lyon, had gone on an expedition to the Indian camp at the Bunch of Timbers, I directed agent Colley to await the result. Upon the major's return to Fort Lyon from this expedition, he reported the result of his visit to the Indians, a copy of which, marked R, is forwarded herewith.

As proposed in his report, the major brought the chiefs and headmen to Denver, and I held an interview with them on September 28, in the presence of Colonel Chivington, commanding the district of Colorado; Colonel Shoup, of the third Colorado cavalry; Major Wynkoop, and a number of the military officers; John Smith, the interpreter; agent Whitely, and a number of citizens.

They were earnest in their desire for peace, and offered to secure the assent of their bands to lay down their arms, or to join the whites in the war against the other tribes of the plains. They stated that the Kiowas, Comanches, Apaches, and fourteen different bands of the Sioux, including the Yanktonais and other bands from Minnesota, and all of those of the northern plains, were among the strong forces on the war path; that the Sioux were very hostile and determined against the whites. They stated that the chiefs of their bands had been opposed to the war, but they had been overpowered by the influence of their young men.

\* \* \* \* \* \* \*

I advised them to make immediate application to the military authorities for and to accept the terms of peace they might be able to obtain, and left them in the hands of Major Wynkoop, who took them back to Fort Lyon. I have since learned that about four hundred of their tribes have surrendered and are now at Fort Lyon.

JOHN EVANS,
*Governor of Colorado Territory, and ex officio*
*Superintendent of Indian Affairs.*

\* \* \* \* \* \* \*

COLORADO SUPERINTENDENCY OF INDIAN AFFAIRS.
*Denver, July* 12, 1864.

SIR : I enclose for your instruction copy of letter received from the Department of the Interior.

While a literal compliance with the suggestion that the Indians should be collected about the Buffalo range may be impracticable on account of the presence of hostile Indians, yet so far as possible you will act in compliance therewith, and avoid any great outlay on their account. I send by Colonel Chivington three thousand dollars on account of Cheyenne and Arapahoe treaty stipulations, with which to provide means to feed those tribes, as they come in on my request.

You will be careful to keep a separate account of the money expended for each tribe.

Your obedient servant,

JOHN EVANS,
*Governor and Superintendent Indian Affairs.*

Major S. G. COLLEY,
*United States Indian Agent, Fort Lyon, Colorado Territory.*

---

FORT LYON, COLORADO TERRITORY,
*Sunday, September* 4, 1864.

DEAR SIR : Two Cheyenne Indians and one squaw have just arrived at this post. They report that nearly all of the Arapahoes, most of the Cheyennes, and two large bands of Ogallala and Brule Sioux are encamped near the Bunch of Timbers, some eighty to one hundred miles northeast of this place ; that they have sent runners to the Comanches, Apaches, Kiowas, and Sioux, requesting them to make peace with the whites. They brought a letter purporting to be signed by Black Kettle and other chiefs, a copy of which is here enclosed. They say the letter was written by George Bent, a half-breed son of W. W. Bent, late United States Indian agent for this agency. They also state that the Indians have seven prisoners ; one says four women and three children ; the other states three women and four children.

Major Wynkoop has put these Indians in the guard house, and requested that they be well treated, in order that he may be able to rescue the white prisoners from the Indians.

Very respectfully, your obediant servant,

S. G. COLLEY,
*United States Indian Agent, Upper Arkansas.*

Hon. JOHN EVANS,
*Superintendent Indian Affairs.*

---

CHEYENNE VILLAGE, *August* 29, 1864.

SIR : We received a letter from Bent, wishing us to make peace. We held a council in regard to it ; all came to the conclusion to make peace with you, providing you make peace with the Kiowas, Comanches, Arapahoes, Apaches, and Sioux. We are going to send a messenger to the Kiowas and to the other nations about our going to make peace with you. We heard that you have some prisoners at Denver ; we have some prisoners of yours which we are willing to give up, providing you give up yours. There are three war parties out yet, and two of Arapahoes ; they have been out some time and expected in soon. When we held this council there were a few Arapahoes and Sioux present. We want true news from you in return. (That is a letter.)

BLACK KETTLE and other Chiefs.

Major COLLEY.

Commission adjourned until 2 p. m.

*Two p. m.*—Commission met pursuant to adjournment. Present, all members and recorder.

The objection filed by J. M. Chivington against the receipt as evidence of the reports of Major Wynkoop, with accompanying affidavits, is overruled by the commission, on the grounds that the said reports and affidavit were made officially by Major Wynkoop, and are consequently a matter of record in the office of the Departments of War and Interior. Major Colley, Indian agent, John Smith, and R. H. Clark, are out of the Territory; their appearance before this commission cannot be procured. Those affidavits of these persons as evidence, and the report of Major Wynkoop, is the only evidence we can get from these parties, and therefore they are made a portion of this record.

DENVER, C. T., May 1, 1865.

GENTLEMEN: We would most respectfully request your honorable court to adjourn till next Thursday, for the following reasons:

1. That not knowing what we had to defend till the close of the testimony on behalf of the government, we wish time to arrange our testimony and give the names of the witnesses to the court to be summoned, that we may require to explain, notify, and deny the testimony offered against us by the government.

2. That the time we ask, for the purpose of properly arranging our testimony, we think, will be a sufficient economy of time to amply repay the court in granting it, reducing the time and labor required for our defence one-half.

3. That the testimony taken on behalf of the government will, as the court can clearly see, require at least the time we ask to properly examine.

Respectfully, yours,

J. M. CHIVINGTON,<br>
Late Colonel First Cavalry of Colorado.

The PRESIDENT AND MEMBERS
*of the Military Commission convened at*
*Denver, C. T., in pursuance of Special Order*
*No. 23, District Headquarters, Colorado, &c.*

Commission adjourned until to-morrow at 9 o'clock a. m., May 2, 1865.

FIFTY-FOURTH DAY.

MAY 2, 1865.

Commission met pursuant to adjournment. Present, all members and recorder.

Proceedings of yesterday read and approved.

The following official copy of telegram having been omitted in the proceedings of yesterday, is here inserted, and is as follows:

[By telegraph.]

HEADQUARTERS DISTRICT OF COLORADO,<br>
Denver, August 18, 1864.

Major CHARLOTT, *C. S., A. A. G., Fort Leavenworth, Dep't of Kansas:*

Have honor to report that Indians all around us; all troops out after guerillas; six (6) of these caught and killed. Hundred-days regiment will fill up in ten days, perhaps. Utes are threatening; have proclaimed martial law, and am preparing for defence as fast as I can. Have large numbers of negroes here; can easily raise a company for hundred days—most likely two or three; can I do it? Needed immediately for defence against Indians.

J. M. CHIVINGTON,<br>
Colonel Commanding District.

360

HEADQUARTERS DISTRICT OF THE PLAINS,
*Denver, Colorado, April 30, 1865.*

A true copy:

GEO. F. PRICE, *A. A. A. G.*

The request of J. M. Chivington is granted, and the commission adjourned until Thursday, May 4, 1865, at 9 o'clock a. m.

### FIFTY-FIFTH DAY.

MAY 4, 1865.

Commission met pursuant to adjournment. Present, all members and recorder.

Proceedings of yesterday read and approved.

The following copies of official documents presented by J. M. Chivington to become a part of the record, as a portion of his defence in the matter of investigation:

[General Field Order No. 2.]

HEADQUARTERS DEPARTMENT OF KANSAS,
*In the field, Fort Larned, July* 31, 1864.

I. At all military posts or stations west of the Kansas and Nebraska settlements in this department, stockades or abattis enclosures must be made for the troops and stock, and animals must be kept in such enclosures at night, and never herded during the day without distant and careful pickets, who can give warning of approaching enemies in time to preserve the stock from surprise.

II. Indians and their allies, or associates, will not be allowed within the forts except blindfolded, and then they must be kept totally ignorant of the character and number of our forces. Neglect of this military concealment will be followed by the most severe and summary punishment.

Commanders of forts and stations will furnish scouts according to their best judgments, keeping in view the safety of their own posts, the stage or public property to be guarded and the preservation of the horses. These precautions must not be relaxed without permission of the commander of the department, and all officers, of whatever grade, will report promptly to the nearest and most available assistance, and to district and department headquarters any patent neglect of this order, or any palpable danger to a command.

The industry and skill displayed by Lieutenant Ellsworth and the troops under his command, in the erection of a block-house and other protection for his troops and animals, at Smoky Hill crossing, deserve special commendation, while the negligence exhibited elsewhere, especially at this post, while under its former commander, is deprecated and denounced.

By command of Major General S. R. Curtis:

JOHN WILLIAMS,
*Assistant Adjutant General.*

---

[Pacific Telegraph Company.]

FORT LEAVENWORTH, *April* 8, 1864.

*To Colonel J. M. Chivington:*

I hear that Indians have committed depredations on or near Platte river. Do not let district lines prevent pursuing and punishing them. Give Colonel Collins and General Mitchell your full co-operation, and any information you can. You can furlough veterans, but give them government transportation.

S. R. CURTIS, *Major General.*

A true copy:

CHARLES WHEELER.
*First Lieut. and A. A. A. General, Dist. of Colorado.*

[Pacific Telegraph Company.]

FORT LEAVENWORTH, *May* 30, 1864.

*To Colonel Chivington:*

Some four hundred (400) Cheyennes attacked Lieutenant Clayton on Smoky Hill. After several hours' fight the Indians fled, leaving twenty-eight (28) killed. Our loss four (4) killed and three (3) wounded. Look out for Cheyennes everywhere. Especially instruct the troops in upper Arkansas.

S. R. CURTIS, *Major General.*

Official copy :

CHARLES WHEELER,
*First Lieut. and A. A. A. General, Dist. of Colorado.*

---

[Pacific Telegraph Company.]

FORT LEAVENWORTH, *June* 3, 1864.

*To Colonel Chivington, care Governor Evans, Denver:*

Send out force to crush the Indians that are in open hostility, as requested by Governor Evans.

S. R. CURTIS, *Major General.*

Official copy :

CHARLES WHEELER,
*First Lieut. and A. A. A. General, Dist. of Colorado.*

---

[Pacific Telegraph Company.]

FORT LEAVENWORTH, *June* 7, 1864.

*To Colonel Chivington:*

What troops have moved, and where are they ? What can you send forward ? The sending of supplies, as well as Indian troubles, makes it important to know. The Indians are very troublesome between Fort Lyon and the Kansas settlements.

S. R. CURTIS, *Major General.*

Official copy :

CHARLES WHEELER,
*First Lieut. and A. A. A. General, Dist. of Colorado.*

---

[Pacific Telegraph Company.]

FORT KEARNEY, *August* 8, 1864.

*To Colonel Chivington:*

Nine (9) men killed to-day about two miles east of Plum creek; two (2) women and four (4) children supposed to be taken prisoners—Mrs. Smith supposed to be one of them. Indians attacked three trains, destroyed one and killed all the men in the train.

H. RUHL, *Captain, Commanding.*

Official copy :

CHARLES WHEELER,
*First Lieut. and A. A. A. General, Dist. of Colorado.*

362

[Pacific Telegraph Company.]

HEADQUARTERS IN THE FIELD, VIA PLUM CREEK.

*To Colonel Chivington:*

I am near hundredth meridian, and near Kansas line, South Republican. Indian signs, but show no great force. Scouting all directions. Have about seven hundred, (700.) Co-operate if you can west from junction and south of Allyn's bluffs.

Official ·copy :

S. R. CURTIS, *Major General.*

CHARLES WHEELER,
*First Lieut. and A. A. A. General, Dist. of Colorado.*

---

[Pacific Telegraph Company.]

FORT LEAVENWORTH, *September* 28, 1864.

*To Colonel Chivington :*

I shall require the bad Indians delivered up; restoration of equal numbers of stock; also hostages to secure. I want no peace till the Indians suffer more. Left-Hand is said to be a good chief of the Arapahoes, but Big Mouth is a rascal. I fear the agent of the Interior Department will be ready to make presents too soon. It is better to chastise before giving anything but a little tobacco to talk over. No peace must be made without my directions.

S. R. CURTIS, *Major General.*

Official copy:

CHARLES WHEELER,
*First Lieut and A. A. A. General, Dist. of Colorado.*

---

[Pacific Telegraph Company.]

FORT LEAVENWORTH, ——— 30, 1864.

*To Colonel Chivington:*

Some four hundred (400) Cheyennes attacked the Yanctons on Smoky Hill; after several hours' fight the Yanctons fled, leaving twenty-eight killed; our loss four (4) killed and three (3) wounded. Look out for Cheyennes everywhere, and especially instruct the troops on the Upper Arkansas.

S. R. CURTIS, *Major General.*

Official copy:

CHARLES WHEELER,
*First Lieut.·and A. A. A. General, Dist. of Colorado.*

---

[Pacific Telegraph Company.]

FORT LEAVENWORTH, *October* 3, 1864.

*To Colonel Chivington :*

Better not detain company K, because it is small and broken down. We need every man in the line, and must not offer inducements to depletion. General Blunt deserves and must be consulted.

S. R. CURTIS, *Major General.*

A true copy:

CHARLES WHEELER,
*First Lieut. and A. A. A. General, Dist. of Colorado.*

363

PACIFIC TELEGRAPH COMPANY,
*Fort Leavenworth, October 7, 1864.*

General Blunt came on camps of Indians near head of Pawnee, September 25, 1864, three or four thousand strong, routed and pursued them several days. Nine Indians killed. Our loss two (2) killed and seven (7) wounded. The Indians went towards head of Smoky. These are probably the same Indians Colonel Wynkoop reports, erroneously and unfortunately, out of his command.

S. R. CURTIS, *Major General.*

Official copy:

CHARLES WHEELER,
*First Lieut., and A. A. A. General, Dist. of Colorado.*

Colonel CHIVINGTON.

Commission adjourned until 3 p. m. this day.

*Two p. m.*—Commission met pursuant to adjournment. Present, all members and recorder.

Copies of official documents presented by J. M. Chivington continued :

DEPARTMENT OF THE INTERIOR,
*Office of Indian Affairs, March 24, 1865.*

SIR : I have the honor to acknowledge the receipt of your communication of February 28, 1865, requesting me to forward "a certified copy of the report of the proceedings of the council held by Governor Evans, superintendent of Indian affairs in Colorado, with the Cheyenne and Arapahoe Indian chiefs, held at Camp Weld, Colorado Territory on or about the 27th September, 1864," and in reply have to state that there is nothing in the files of this office which purports to be a report of said proceedings. All that appears is printed upon page 220 of the annual report of this office for 1864, in Governor Evans's annual report, and I herewith transmit a copy of that portion of the report.

Very respectfully, your obedient servant,

W. P. DOLE, *Commissioner.*

Captain GEORGE H. STILWELL,
*Recorder Military Commission, Denver, C. T.*

" As proposed in this report the major (Wynkoop) brought the chiefs and headmen to Denver, and I held an interview with them on September 28, in presence of Colonel Chivington, commanding the district of Colorado; Colonel Shoup, of third Colorado cavalry; Major Wynkoop, and a number of military officers; John Smith, the intrepreter, Agent Whiteley, and a number of citizens. They were earnest in their desires for peace, and offered to secure the assent of their bands to lay down their arms, or to join the whites in the war against the other tribes of the plains. They stated that the Kiowas, Comanches, Apaches, and fourteen different bands of the Sioux, including the Yanktonais and other bands from Minnesota, and all of those of the northern plains, were among the strong forces on the war path ; that the Sioux are very hostile and determined against the whites. They stated that the chiefs of their bands had been opposed to the war, but they had been overpowered by the influence of their young men."

" After collecting all the information I could from them as to the parties who had committed the murders and drepredations during the spring and summer, and hearing their propositions for peace, I admonished them of their failure to meet me in council last autumn, and of their neglect to respect my proclamation directing the friendly Indians to repair to their agencies; that they had joined the alliance for war, and had committed the most horrible murders, and destroyed immense amounts of property, for which they offered no atonement or repara tion, and that I had by that proclamation turned them over to the military authorities, with whom they must make their terms of peace, as it might embarrass the military authorities who were in pursuit of their hostile allies."

"I advised them to make immediate application to the military authorities for and to accept the terms of peace they might obtain, and left them in the hands of Major Wynkoop, who took them back to Fort Lyon."

The depositions of Colonel George L. Shoup, Mr. Gill, and Clark Dunn, late lieutenant veteran battalion first Colorado cavalry, presented by J. M. Chivington as a portion of his defence.

They are as follows:

Personally appeared this the 3d day of February, 1865, before me, Samuel F. Tappan, lieutenant colonel veteran battalion first Colorado cavalry, George L. Shoup, late colonel third Colorado cavalry, who, being first duly sworn according to law, deposeth and saith:

Question. What is your name and former rank in the army?
Answer. George L. Shoup, formerly first lieutenant first Colorado cavalry; more recently colonel of third Colorado cavalry.

Question. When were you appointed colonel?
Answer. September 21, 1864.

Question. When did you assume command?
Answer. September 21, 1864.

Question. How many men and horses at that time?
Answer. About one thousand and forty enlisted men; I think between three hundred and fifty and four hundred horses at that time.

Question. How many men enlisted after you took command?
Answer. About twenty-five.

Question. How many horses were furnished afterwards by quartermaster?
Answer. About four hundred.

Question. What disposition was made of the regiment after you resumed command?

Answer. When I assumed command the regiment was stationed as follows: Six companies at Camp Evans, near Denver, commanded by Major Wilder; one company at Fort Lupton, about thirty miles below Denver, commanded by Captain Morgan, (an artillery company;) one company at Junction, about one hundred miles below Denver, commanded by Lieutenant Fry; one company at Valley Station, about one hundred and fifty miles below Denver, commanded by Captain Nichols; one company in the Fountain-qui-bouit, divided in detachments between Colorado City and Pueblo, commanded by Captain Call; one company on the Arkansas river, five miles below Pueblo, commanded by Captain Baxter. Companies at Camp Evans marched for Bijou basin, by order of district commander, on or about the 14th of October, under my command; company from Latham marched for the same place, on or about the 16th of October, under command of Major Sayre; company on Fountain-qui-bouit marched for same place on or about the 20th of October; two companies marched from Bijou basin on or about the 25th of October, to relieve the companies stationed at Junction and Valley Station. On or about the 25th of October I left Bijou basin, leaving Major Sayre in command, and came to Denver, for the purpose of concentrating the companies of my regiment then on the Platte river, thence to rejoin that portion of the regiment on Bijou basin. Heavy snows prevented a concentration of these troops at Bijou basin. The troops on the Platte were, in consequence, concentrating at Denver, and on or about the 12th of November I left Denver for Fort Lyon, with companies C, D, and F of my regiment and company H of the first Colorado cavalry, and on or about the 18th of November joined Major Sayre at Boonville with that portion of the regiment which had been left at Bijou basin, (he having been ordered to precede me,) consisting of companies A, B, and E, and I and M. On or about the 20th Captain Baxter joined the command with company G, and the day following Colonel John M. Chivington, commander of the district of Colorado, arrived and assumed command of the column, I still commanding my regiment. On or about the 22d the column, consisting of my regiment and a battalion of the first, marched from Boonville towards Fort Lyon, and reached Fort Lyon on the 28th, and went into camp. On the evening of the 28th I received orders from the colonel commanding to prepare three days' cooked rations, and be ready and march at eight o'clock the same evening. At eight o'clock the column marched in the following order: the first regiment on the right, my regiment on the left. I had under my immediate command between five hundred and fifty and six hundred men mounted. My transportation was left at Fort Lyon. The column marched all night in a northerly direction. About daylight the next morning came in sight of an Indian village. Colonel Chivington and myself being about three-fourths of a mile in advance of the column, it was determined to make an immediate attack. Lieutenant Wilson, commanding a battalion of the first, was ordered to cut off the ponies of the Indians at the northeast of the village. By order of Colonel Chivington I was ordered to send men to the southwest of the village, to cut off the ponies in that direction, and then to immediately engage the Indians.

Question. Did Colonel Chivington make any remarks to the troops, in your hearing?
Answer. He did not.
Question. Did you approach the camp of the Indians in line of battle with your men mounted, or dismounted?
Answer. Kept my men in column of fours till I arrived at the village, when I formed them in line of battle, and to the left of a battalion of the first, commanded by Lieutenant Wilson, my men mounted.
Question. At what distance was your command from the village when you commenced fire upon it?
Answer. I did not allow my men to fire when I formed my first line; the battalion on my right was firing. I wheeled my men into column of fours and marched to the rear of the battalion on my right, to the right of that battalion, to obtain a better position. I marched up Sand creek some distance, following the Indians who were retreating up the creek. When opposite the main body of Indians, wheeled my men into line, dismounted, and opened fire.
Question. Did you know what band of Indians it was at the time of the attack?
Answer. I heard while at Fort Lyon that Left Hand, of the Arapahoes, and Black Kettle, of the Cheyennes, were at the village.
Question. Did you, at any time prior to the attack, hear Colonel Chivington say that he was going to attack Black Kettle's band?
Answer. I did not.
Question. How long did the fight last?
Answer. The fighting did not entirely cease until about three o'clock in the afternoon.
Question. Did you camp with your regiment near the battle ground?
Answer. We camped on ground occupied by the Indians before the battle.
Question. What was done with the Indians and other property?
Answer. The lodges were burned. The ponies, numbering, as I was told, five hundred and four, were placed in charge of the provost marshal. A few remained in the hands of the troops.
Question. What were the casualties of your regiment?
Answer. Ten killed, one missing, about forty wounded.
Question. In your opinion how many Indians were killed?
Answer. From my own observation I should say about three hundred.
Question. Were they men, or women and children?
Answer. Some of each.

Question. Did you witness any scalping or other mutilation of the dead by your command ?

Answer. I saw one or two men who were in the act of scalping, but I am not positive.

Question. Were any prisoners taken, to your knowledge ?

Answer. Several persons were saved during the engagement and brought into camp.

Question. Was Jack Smith among them ?

Answer. He was.

Question. Do you know what became of Jack Smith ?

Answer. He was killed by some person unknown to me. I heard the report of the revolver, went out to the lodge, found Smith shot, and could not ascertain who had done it.

Question. What did you hear Colonel Chivington say in reference to prisoners or persons brought into camp ?

Answer. I heard him say we must not allow John Smith and family, father of Jack Smith, to be harmed ; that he did not intend to take any Indians prisoners. He said he would allow the half-breed Bent to return to his father.

Question. How long after the fight closed was Jack Smith shot ?

Answer. The next day, between 10 a. m. and 2 p. m.

Question. Where did you then march ?

Answer. Followed down Sand creek to the Arkansas river, where we arrived about dark of 2d of December ; broke camp about 10 o'clock same evening, marched about forty miles down to the Arkansas river that night, hoping to surprise Little Raven's band of Indians, but found, on arriving at their camp, that they had left. Command went into camp. I took a detachment of my regiment, went out to ascertain, if possible, the direction taken by the Indians. When in the vicinity of the village found trails going in all directions, the most of which concentrated on the plains about eight miles distant, and then went into an easterly direction. I followed them till near dark, and returned that night. Next morning command went down the river in two columns, Colonel Chivington commanding column on north side ; I, the column on the south side. That evening at dark camped opposite Colonel Chivington's command. I left my command, crossed the river, ascertained that Colonel Chivington, with a small detachment, had continued on the trail, and had not yet returned. Colonel Chivington returned about 10 o'clock, and ordered commands on both sides of the river to be ready to march in about an hour, as he had discovered Indians. I crossed the river at once. In about an hour the column moved down the river. Just before daylight we arrived at the place where Colonel Chivington had discovered the Indians. The column halted, a reconnoissance made, but it was found that the Indians had left. As soon as light enough to find their trail, we followed them, they taking a northeasterly direction ; but finding our horses so jaded, twenty-five or thirty having given out in the last five or six miles, the colonel commanding held a consultation with his officers. They decided that it was impracticable to pursue the Indians further, as most of the horses would give out before water could be reached. The column returned to the Arkansas river, and from thence back to Denver. I was mustered out of the service as colonel of the third Colorado cavalry, on the 28th of December, 1864. My regiment enlisted for one hundred days from the 17th of September, 1864.

Question. Were you present in council with some Indian chiefs in Denver, some time last summer or fall ?

Answer. I was.

Question. Who were present—whites and Indians?

Answer. Governor Evans, Colonel Chivington, Captain S. M. Robbins, Major Wynkoop, Major Whiteley, Amos Steck, J. Bright Smith, Nelson Sargent,

Ex. Doc. 26——12

Captain John Wanless, Black Kettle, White Antelope, and five or six other Indians, and John Smith and Sam Ashcroft, interpreters.

Question. Did the Indians express a desire for peace with the whites?

Answer. Yes.

Question. Upon what terms did they desire peace?

Answer. That they have protection and supplies while the war was carried on against hostile Indians.

Question. Was peace guaranteed to them on any terms?

Answer. They were told by Colonel Chivington that if they would come in and surrender themselves, he would then tell them what to do.

Question. What did the governor tell them?

Answer. That as they had violated all treaties they would have to treat with the military authorities, to whom he had given up all authority.

Question. Did Colonel Chivington tell them that he would guarantee them peace only on condition that they would come into the post and lay down their arms?

Answer. Colonel Chivington did not guarantee them peace upon any terms, but if they would come into the post, surrender themselves, and lay down their arms, he would tell them what to do.

Question. Did the Indians say that they would do so?

Answer. They said they would go back to their people, tell them and advise them to do so.

Question. You made an official report of the Sand creek engagement to the colonel commanding the district?

Answer. I did.

Question by J. M. C. How many horse equipments had you for your regiment on the 21st of September?

Answer. I think about two hundred.

Question. What was the reason the companies were sent from Bijou basin to relieve the companies at Junction and Valley stations?

Answer. The companies at Junction and Valley stations being mounted, and those relieving them being dismounted.

Question. Were a complete number of horses and horse equipments to mount your regiment ever obtained?

Answer. There were not.

Question. How long was it after the last horse equipments reached Denver for your regiment from Leavenworth, before you received orders and marched your command to the field?

Answer. The next day.

Question. Did or did not the chiefs, in their interview with Governor Evans, say that they had wanted peace all the time during the last spring and summer?

Answer. They said that they always wanted peace, but had been unable to control their young men.

Question. Did you have any conversation with Major Colley, Indian agent for the Arapahoe and Cheyennes of the Upper Arkansas, respecting the disposition of the Indians and the policy that ought to be pursued towards them? If so, state what he said.

Answer. I had an interview with Major Colley, on the evening of the 28th of November, in which he stated to me that these Indians had violated their treaty; that there were a few Indians that he would not like to see punished, but as long as they affiliated with the hostile Indians we could not discriminate; that no treaty could be made that would be lasting till they were all severely chastised; he also told me where these Indians were camped.

Question. State what you heard Major Scott J. Anthony say in reference to these Indians on the 28th of November last.

SAND CREEK MASSACRE.

Answer. He said he would have fought these Indians before if he had had a force strong enough to do so, and left a sufficient garrison at Fort Lyon, he being at the time in command of Fort Lyon.

GEO. L. SHOUP.

Sworn and subscribed to before me at Denver this 3d day of February, 1865.

SAM. F. TAPPAN,
*Lieut. Col. Veteran Batt. First Colorado Cavalry.*

Personally appeared this 3d day of February, 1865, before me, Samuel F. Tappan, lieutenant colonel of veteran battalion first Colorado cavalry, Captain A. J. Gill, of Denver, Colorado, who being duly sworn according to law, deposeth and saith, being called by Colonel Chivington:

Question. Your full name and rank?

Answer. Andrew J. Gill, captain of territorial militia.

Question. Were you connected with the column that moved from Denver to Fort Lyon, and which afterwards engaged with the Indians at Sand creek?

Answer. I joined it at Booneville.

Question. Were you connected with it in an official capacity?

Answer. I was a volunteer aid on the staff of the colonel commanding.

Question. Did you furnish the command with hay?

Answer. I furnished some hay at different points.

Question. At what places?

Answer. At Spring Bottom, and at points where contracts had not been let.

Question. How much hay did you furnish the command?

Answer. Have no recollection.

Question. Did you furnish the command with corn?

Answer. I did with a part, but not all they used.

Question. Who receipted to you for the corn and hay, Lieutenant Elliot or Captain Maynard?

[Answer not given.]

Question. Did you furnish corn and hay in bulk?

Answer. I did.

Question. Was any officer in the service of the United States interested with you as a partner, furnishing the column with forage?

Answer. No one interested.

Question. Did you accompany the column after it left Boonville on its march to Sand creek?

Answer. I did.

Question. Were you at Sand creek at the time of the engagement with the Indians?

Answer. I was.

Question. From your own observation, what is your opinion of the number of Indians killed?

Answer. I supposed at the time that there were about five hundred killed.

Question. How many lodges dou you suppose there were?

Answer. Rising one hundred.

Question. Did you hear Colonel Chivington make a speech to his men just before the attack?

Answer. I did.

Question. What was it?

Answer. Now, boys, I sha'n't say who you shall kill, but remember our murdered women and children.

Question. Did he give any order?

Answer. He then ordered the troops to strip off their overcoats.

Question. Did you witness any scalping or mutilation of the dead?

369

Answer. I saw one soldier scalp an Indian.

Question. Did you hear any officer trying to prevent soldiers from scalping the dead?

Answer. I heard the colonel say afterwards "that I wouldn't do any scalping;" this to me privately, but I heard no orders given to prevent scalping.

Question. Do you know anything of the death of Jack Smith?

Answer. I know nothing of it. While in camp near Fort Lyon I heard Major Scott J. Anthony, commanding Fort Lyon, say that he should have attacked the Indians before this if he had sufficient force, and was glad Colonel Chivington had come. Also heard Major Colley, Indian agent, say that the Indians were hard to manage, and the only thing to do any good was to chastise them severely.

A. J. GILL.

Sworn and subscribed to before me.

SAMUEL F. TAPPAN.
*Lieut. Col. Vet. Batt. First Colorado Cavalry.*

———

DENVER, C. T., *April* 27, 1865.

CLARK DUNN, late lieutenant veteran battalion first Colorado cavalry, introduced by J. M. Chivington to give evidence.

The oath being administered according to law, he (Dunn) testified as follows:

By J. M. CHIVINGTON.

Question. What is your name, and what has been your occupation for the past three years?

Answer. Clark Dunn; a soldier in the United States army for the last three years. I was mustered out of the service as an officer the 22d day of March, 1865.

Question. What position did you occupy in the army?

Answer. I was a private soldier, a sergeant, a second and first lieutenant. Was mustered out as a first lieutenant.

Question. Do you know anything of the origin and history of the Indian difficulties in this Territory and Kansas? State what you know of your own knowledge.

Answer. On the 12th day of April, 1864, I was stationed at Camp Santono, Colorado Territory. On the morning of that day I was ordered out by Captain Sanborn, then in command of camp, with forty men of companies C and H, first Colorado cavalry, in pursuit of a party of Indians, who, it was said, had stolen stock, and driven people from their ranches on Bijou creek. It was also reported that they had torn down portions of the telegraph wire. I left Camp Sanborn about nine o'clock that day with a man by the name of Ripey; I think he was the man that had reported about the Indians, and said that they had stock that belonged to him. Shortly after leaving Sanborn I divided my command, and sent half of them direct to Bijou ranch, on Bijou creek. I went with the balance of the command down the Platte to the junction. Hearing nothing of the Indians, I then went in the direction of the Bijou ranch, on Bijou creek, in order to meet the balance of my command. I joined them about 2 p. m. Shortly afterwards I discovered the trail of the Indians. They were going north towards the Platte river. I followed their trail to within about three miles of the river. I discovered a smoke to the right of the trail and about three or four miles further down the Platte; there the course of the trail would intercept the river. Thinking that the Indians had, perhaps, changed the course of their trail between that point and the river, I again divided my command, sending half of them in the direction of the smoke, and I followed the trail with the balance. When I got to the brink of the river I discovered a party of about thirty Indians crossing the river about one mile below me. There was also another small party of Indians, in advance of those, driving stock. The party of Indians with the stock were across the river. When I discovered them I crossed the river at that point. In crossing the river I stopped to water my horses, as they had been a long time without water. Mr. Ripey and one of my men crossed in advance. They came back and met me as I was getting across Mr. Ripey stated that it was his stock, and the soldier stated the Indians were going to fight, as they were drawn up in line, and loading their rifles. When I got across the river into open ground where I could see the Indians, the party that I had seen crossing the river had halted, and were drawn up in line on the bank of the river. My orders from Captain Sanborn were to recapture the stock taken by them, disarm the Indians, and bring them prisoners to Camp Sanborn. The party of Indians that were driving the stock were driving it very rapidly towards the bluffs when I came in sight of them again, after crossing the river. I started then in pursuit of the party of Indians with the stock, intending to get the stock first. The party of Indians on the banks of the river started in the direction of the stock at the same time, when I halted my command, and wheeled into line towards the Indians. The Indians also formed in line. They were then about five hundred yards from me down the Platte. I then detailed four men to go with Mr. Ripey in pursuit of the stock, with instructions to get the stock if they could and bring it back without making a fight I then rode out about one hundred and fifty (150) yards in front of my command and requested that one or two of the Indians come out that I might talk with them. They paid no attention, but marched forward in line to where I was, with their bows strung. My men called to me to come back, that the Indians would kill me; I returned to my command, as the Indians came up to me. The Indians came up to my command with me. I found that my men had their revolvers drawn. I ordered them to return them and dismount, and endeavor to take the arms from the Indians. As soon as they were dismounted the Indians fired upon us. I immediately ordered my men to fire on them in return and mount. We had an engagement there; it must have lasted between half and three quarters of an hour. I had four men wounded, and killed quite a number of the Indians. I saw four fall from their horses at the first fire. I could not tell the exact number of Indians, because they packed their dead Indians away as fast as they were killed. While the engagement was going on, Mr. Ripey, with the men I had detailed to go along with him, had returned. The party of Indians with the stock, to the number of fifteen or twenty, also joined the Indians, who were fighting me. I finally succeeded in driving the Indians back about half or three quarters of a mile, to a bluff. I then ordered my command to load their revolvers, which were empty, when I again started in pursuit of the Indians, the balance of my command having joined me. I pursued them about sixteen miles; night coming on, and it having commenced storming, I abandoned the pursuit and returned to Camp Sanborn, a distance of about twenty miles. The Indians were armed with bows and arrows, rifles, revolvers, and horse-pistols. My men were armed with cavalry sabres and Whitney revolvers, navy size, and of a very inferior quality. I started on the trail again the next day, with Geary as guide, but it having stormed that night and snowed the next day we were unable to follow their trail. I afterwards made repeated scouts after them for that and other depredations, but did not find them.

Question. Were you at Fort Lyon on the 28th day of November, 1864, and did you hear any conversation that occurred between Major Anthony, commanding, and Colonel Chivington? If so, state it and all you heard Anthony say in regard to Indians.

Answer. I was at Fort Lyon on November 28, 1864; I don't recollect that I heard any conversation between Major Anthony and Colonel Chivington in regard to Indians; I talked to Major Anthony a number of times in regard to it.

He told me that those Indians that were encamped on Sand creek were hostile, and not under protection of the troops at that post; that he would have gone out there himself and killed them, if he had had a sufficient number of troops under his command. He stated this before the fight at Sand creek, and after it. The first conversation I had with him, when we arrived at Fort Lyon on that day, (the 28th of November,) he said that he was d——d glad we had come, and the only thing that he was surprised at was that we had not come long before, knowing how he was situated.

Question. Did you hear any conversation that occurred between Colonel Chivington and a citizen by the name of Combs, on or about the 25th of November, 1864, at Spring Bottom, on the Arkansas river, while the command under Colonel Chivington was en route for Fort Lyon? If yes, state what that conversation was.

Answer. I heard a conversation there between Colonel Chivington and a man by the name of Combs, but I don't recollect what the conversation was well enough to state the conversation in full. He (Combs) stated that at the time Major Anthony came to Fort Lyon and assumed command, he (Anthony) did not approve of Major Wynkoop's proceedings, and ordered the Indians out of the post. He also ordered the Indians to give up their arms. The Indians gave up some bows and arrows, a few broken rifles and pistols, with which Anthony was not satisfied, and ordered them to leave the vicinity of the post. He also ordered the guard stationed around the post to fire on the Indians if they came towards the post; and that the guard had fired on them frequently before the Indians left their camp below the post; and that after the Indians had moved to Sand creek parties of warriors had visited the post and demanded rations, which were refused, and they were daily expecting the post to be attacked. He stated that at one time (I think it was while Wynkoop was in command of Fort Lyon) a party of Cheyenne Indians came into the camp of the Indians below Fort Lyon, and stated that a large war party of Utes were near by. The chief of the Arapahoes and Cheyennes immediately made application for protection, and two companies of cavalry were ordered down to the camp to protect them, but it did not prove to be Utes, and so they did not have any fight. He stated that previous to Anthony's coming there, the Indians in large numbers were continually at the post, in the officers' quarters, and that the officers gave them whiskey, and that the Indians rode government horses and mules, and carried government arms with them.

Direct examination of Clark Dunn, late lieutenant veteran battalion first Colorado cavalry, by J. M. Chivington, closed.

Cross-examination of Clark Dunn, late lieutenant, &c., by the commission:

Question. Did you have any acquaintance with Mr. Ripey prior to your scout after Indians?

Answer. No, I did not.

Question. What evidence had you that Mr. Ripey's stock had been stolen by Indians?

Answer. I was under Captain Sanborn's orders; he sent Ripey with me, and said he would know the stock and the Indians, and he owned part of it himself; and when we met the Indians he (Ripey) stated that there was his stock, and they were the Indians that had taken it from him.

Question. How far were you and your command from the Indians at the time they fired upon you?

Answer. About eight or ten feet.

Question. In your conversation with Major Anthony did not he (Anthony) tell you that the Indians had sent him a challenge to come out and fight them, and that he (Anthony) was anxious to do so?

Answer. I don't think he did; he stated he was anxious to go out after them, but, in reference to the challenge, I don't recollect of his saying anything about it.

Question. Was not Major Anthony's conversation with you in reference to the hostile Indians of the Sioux encamped on a branch of the Smoky Hill, north of Fort Lyon?

Answer. I had conversation with Major Anthony in reference to those Indians. The conversation I have already related had no reference to the Sioux at all.

Question. What conversation did you have with him in reference to the Sioux?

Answer. He told me that they had sent him a challenge to come out and fight them; that he would not go there with less than a thousand men.

Cross-examination of Clark Dunn, late lieutenant, &c., by the commission, closed.

Re-examination of Clark Dunn, late lieutenant, &c.:
No questions asked.

Commission adjourned until 9 a. m. to-morrow, May 5, 1865.

FIFTY-SIXTH DAY.

MAY 5, 1865.

Commission met pursuant to adjournment. Present, all members and recorder. Proceedings of yesterday read and approved.

The following deposition was presented by J. M. Chivington, as a portion of his defence:

PLANTERS' HOUSE, DENVER, C. T.,
*April 7, 1865.*

GENERAL: Will you be kind enough to have the deposition of Mr. Meyer taken at 2 o'clock p. m.? My reason for the request is, Mr. Hallat, my counsel, is employed in suit this a. m. before probate court.

Very respectfully,

J. M. CHIVINGTON,
*Late Colonel First Colorado Cavalry.*

Brigadier General CONNOR,
*Commanding District of the Plains.*

The general commanding district of the plains directs that the within request be complied with, and J. M. Chivington, late colonel first Colorado cavalry' be notified of hour and meeting.

GEO. F. PRICE,
*Acting Assistant Adjutant General.*

Respectfully referred to Captain Anderson for his guidance. Notify Colonel Chivington of the hour and place.

T. M., *Colonel.*

———

DENVER, COLORADO TERRITORY,
*Office of A. C. M., April 7, 1865.*

DEAR SIR: I have the honor respectfully to inform you that I have been directed to notify you that, in compliance with your request to Brigadier General Connor, commanding district of the plains, the deposition of Mr. Meyer will be taken before me, at my office, at 2½ o'clock this p. m.

Very respectfully, your obedient servant,

JNO. C. ANDERSON,
*Capt. Vet. Batt., 1st Col. Cav., A. C. M., and Judge Advocate.*

J. M. CHIVINGTON,
*Late Colonel First Colorado Cavalry.*

HEADQUARTERS DISTRICT OF COLORADO,
*Denver, April 7, 1865.*

CAPTAIN: Colonel J. M. Chivington, late of the first regiment Colorado cavalry, having made application to Brigadier General Connor, commanding district of the plains, to have the evidence of one L. Meyer taken, regarding the Sand creek affair, in the absence of the military commission now investigating the matter at Fort Lyon, you will, in obedience to instructions received from General Connor, take the affidavit of Meyer on the subject, in presence of Colonel Chivington, and forward the same, properly attested, to these headquarters to-day.

Respectfully, your obedient servant,

T. MOONLIGHT,
*Colonel Eleventh Kansas Cavalry, Commanding.*

Captain JOHN C. ANDERSON,
*Judge Advocate, Denver, Colorado Territory.*

Pursuant to the foregoing authorities directing me, as judge advocate of the district of Colorado, district of the plains, to take the deposition of one L. Meyer, with reference to his knowledge of facts connected with the Sand creek affair, in accordance with directions by me received, and proper notification to the parties being given that the deposition of L. Meyer would be taken before me, at my office, at 2½ o'clock p. m. of April 7, 1865, J. M. Chivington, late colonel first Colorado cavalry, duly appeared by counsel at the hour and place above mentioned, and presented Mr. L. Meyer, who, being by me first duly sworn, testified and deposed as follows, viz:

1st question, direct examination, by J. M. Chivington's counsel. State your name, age, occupation, and place of residence.

Answer. Lipman Meyer; age, thirty-four years; freighter; place of residence, Leavenworth.

2d question, by counsel. Where were you on or about the 1st day of December, 1864, and what were you then engaged in?

Answer. I was on the Arkansas, about thirty miles east of Fort Lyon. I was on my way with a train going to New Mexico.

3d question, by J. M. Chivington's counsel. Do you know a captain by the name of Silas S. Soule?

Answer. I know an officer by the name of Soule. I have heard him styled captain.

4th question, by J. M. Chivington's counsel. Did you see Captain Soule at the time you came on the Arkansas, and was he then in command of a detachment of troops? If so, how many men had he under his command, and upon what duty were they ordered, and were you with that command; did you accompany them?

Answer. I did see Captain Soule when I was on the Arkansas. He was in command of troops, to the best of my knowledge; I believe he had twenty men. I heard them say they were ordered to go and see after my train. I accompanied the command.

5th question. Where was your train at that time?

Answer. It was on the Aubrey route, about thirty miles south of the Arkansas river.

6th question. Did Captain Soule start with his command for your train?

Answer. He started about the 2d or 3d day of December.

7th question. Were you with the command?

Answer. I was with the command.

8th question. At what hour did Captain Soule with his command start for your train?

Answer. I suppose it was between 10 and 11 o'clock in the forenoon of the 2d or 3d day of December.

9th question. How far did the command go south of the Arkansas river?

Answer. I cannot give the exact distance; but I suppose, judging from the time we were going, we might have gone fifteen miles.

10th question. Did you see any Indians during the trip?

Answer. I did not?

11th question. Did the command go to your train?

Answer. They did not.

12th question. At what hour did Captain Soule's command return to place of starting?

Answer. The following day, in the morning, by 6 or 7 o'clock.

13th question. At what hour did the command arrive at the Arkansas?

Answer. We commenced to return to the Arkansas on the night of the same day. I cannot give the hour; between 7 and 8 o'clock, I suppose.

14th question. Was Captain Soule with the command all this time?

Answer. He was.

15th question. Why did not Captain Soule proceed to the train?

Answer. He gave me his reasons; he had no provisions along, and he saw a fire in the direction where I suppose my train was, and was afraid to go there.

16th question. Did you hear the report that Captain Soule made to Colonel Chivington, on his return from this expedition?

Answer. I heard Captain Soule making a statement to Colonel Chivington.

17th question. State as nearly as you can what that report or statement was.

Answer. He said that he had seen two Indian camps, and was from a half mile to a mile from them, and supposed the Indians numbered from three to five hundred, and heard the dogs bark.

18th question. When was this report made?

Answer. It was made on the 4th or 5th of December.

19th question. Did you see any Indian camps on the expedition?

Answer. I did not see any Indians.

20th question. Did you see any fires?

Answer. I did see fires.

21st question. At what time?

Answer. I saw it in day-light; the smoke from 2 o'clock in the day until 12 o'clock at night.

22d question. How far from you and the command did the fire appear to be?

Answer. One fire I judged to be fifteen miles distant, and one fire I would suppose was a mile or a mile and a half distant.

23d question. Did you see anything more than the smoke of the fire?

Answer. I did not.

24th question. Did Captain Soule send any one forward to ascertain whether the smoke arose from a camp-fire of emigrants or of Indians?

Answer. He did not. I insisted on his going, but he refused to do so.

25th question. Did he at the time say that he saw Indians?

Answer. He said he supposed they must be Indians?

26th question. In what condition was Captain Soule on this expedition; intoxicated, or not?

Answer. I should judge him to be drunk—judging from his actions.

27th question. In what condition was he when this command went into camp that night at the Arkansas?

Answer. He was drunk.

28th question. State did Colonel Chivington and his command pass the camp of Captain Soule that night, on their way down the Arkansas.

Answer. I did not see them; but I understand they did.

29th question. State what you know about Captain Soule's belief that his camp was attacked by Indians that night, and what occurred in connection therewith.

Answer. At about two o'clock a. m., about the fourth or fifth of December, while we were in camp, we heard a great noise, indicating that Indians were moving up or down the road. The sentinel, or whoever was on guard, gave the alarm of Indians, and everybody was waked up. Captain Soule remained sleeping. The sergeant tried to wake him up, but he delayed and detained the company about half an hour before he got awake or rational. When he got awake he did not know which was up or down the river. His programme was to go up the river, to the camp where we started from, but he was unable to tell which was up or down, and I and the sergeant insisted upon his going with us. We knew the road to the camp where we started from, and he insisted on his way of going, but his company refused to follow him, and stated they never would go out with him any more on a scout. Finally he went the way we wanted him to go—up the river, as we proposed.

30th question. Did you have any blankets upon that trip, and in whose possession or keeping were they?

Answer. I had blankets—two pair, and they were stolen from me.

31st question. By whom do you think they were taken?

Answer. I have reason to believe that either they were taken by Captain Soule or Lieutenant Cannon.

Cross-examined by judge advocate:

1st question. You say you are by occupation a freighter. State under what circumstances you became acquainted with Captain Soule.

Answer. I met Captain Soule in the command of Colonel Chivington on or about the 1st or 2d of December, 1864.

2d question. Was Captain Soule in command of troops at this time?

Answer. He was in command of troops.

3d question. How many men had he under his command?

Answer. To the best of my belief, there were about twenty men.

4th question. Where was Colonel Chivington's command at the time you became acquainted with Captain Soule?

Answer. He was at a place near Camp Wynkoop, about sixty miles from Fort Lyon.

5th question. How long did you remain at Camp Wynkoop?

Answer. I remained near Camp Wynkoop one night.

6th question. Was your train near Camp Wynkoop?

Answer. My train, I suppose, at that time was from thirty to forty miles from Camp Wynkoop.

7th question. Did you accompany Colonel Chivington's command?

Answer. I did.

8th question. How long were you with his command on the march?

Answer. I was with his command on the march between five and seven days. Not less than five nor more than seven days.

9th question. Was Captain Soule's command with Colonel Chivington's on the 4th day of December?

Answer. It was, to the best of my belief.

10th question.. State upon what expedition and for what purpose Captain Soule and his command were sent away from Colonel Chivington's command.

Answer. Captain Soule told me that Colonel Chivington sent him out to see after my train, which was upon the Aubrey route on the way to New Mexico.

11th question. Did Captain Soule tell you this while in Colonel Chivington's camp?

Answer. He told me this while on the road from the camp.

12th question. How far from Colonel Chivington's camp was it when he told you the object of his expedition?

Answer. I would suppose within three miles of the camp.

13th question. Did you accompany the expedition with the consent of Captain Soule before he left camp?

Answer. I did not ask him before he left camp. I merely followed. Colonel Chivington told me that the command was going, and if I wanted to go, I could do so.

14th question. Did you see Captain Soule drink any spirituous or intoxicating liquor when upon that expedition?

Answer. I did, sir.

15th question. How do you know it to have been spirituous or intoxicating?

Answer. He offered it to me, and I drank with him.

16th question. Did he drink frequently?

Answer. He did.

17th question. Did he offer it to you frequently?

Answer. He did.

18th question. Did you not drink upon such occasions with him?

Answer. I did.

19th question. Did you at any time refuse to drink with him?

Answer. I did.

20th question. How near your train did the expedition go?

Answer. I can only say indefinitely; I suppose we went within twenty miles of it.

21st question. How many days were you out upon that expedition? I mean the time between when you started, until your return to place of starting?

Answer. I should say it was from eighteen to twenty hours.

22d question. At the time of an alarm in camp, did you see Captain Soule asleep, and know that it was difficult to arouse him?

Answer. I did, sir; I saw him asleep and tried to wake him up myself.

23d question. Did you advise his men not to follow him when he wished to go down the river, and tell them that Captain Soule was wrong?

Answer. I did not exercise any influence over his men. I told the sergeant or corporal, in the hearing of the men, that the other way, up the river, was the way we wanted to go.

24th question. Did you repeat this remark more than once?

Answer. I could not say whether I did or not.

25th question. Did you express to the men any dislike you felt for Captain Soule?

Answer. I did not.

26th question. Did you ever say to Captain Soule or Lieutenant Cannon, you thought he or they had stolen your blankets?

Answer. I made that assertion to Lieutenant Cannon through a letter, after hearing from Colonel Schoup that Dr. Leas, being in my company when my blankets were taken, had said that he heard Lieutenant Cannon making his brags that he knew what became of my blankets, and knew who had taken them. I have never accused him of taking the blankets.

Cross-examination, by judge advocate, here closed.

Direct examination by the counsel resumed:

1st question. How often and how much did you drink when you were upon that expedition with Captain Soule?

Answer. I drank twice, and very little.

LIPMAN MEYER.

Sworn and subscribed to before me this 7th day of April, A. D. 1865.

JOHN C. ANDERSON,
*Captain Veteran Battalion First Colorado Cavalry,*
*Assistant Commissary of Musters, and Judge Advocate.*

Witness: ALFRED SAYRE.

I, Jno. C. Anderson, captain veteran battalion first Colorado cavalry, judge advocate, Territory of Colorado, district of the plains, do certify on honor, that, previous to the commencement of the examination of Mr. L. Meyer, he, the said L. Meyer, was duly sworn by me to testify to the truth and nothing but the truth, so far as he should be interrogated.

The foregoing deposition was taken in my office, in the city of Denver, county of Arapahoe, Territory of Colorado, on the 7th day of April. A. D. 1865; and that after said deposition was taken by me as aforesaid, the interrogatories and answers thereto, as written down, were read over to the said witness, and that thereupon the same was signed and sworn to by the said deponent, L. Meyer, before me, the oath being administered by me, at the place and on the day and year last aforesaid.

JOHN C. ANDERSON,
*Captain Veteran Battalion First Colorado Cavalry,*
*A. C. M., and Judge Advocate.*

[Indorsements on the above paper.]

DENVER, COLORADO TERRITORY, *April 7, 1865.*

Evidence of Lipman Meyer, concerning the Sand creek affair, taken in absence of the military commission, by Captain John C. Anderson, veteran battalion first Colorado cavalry, judge advocate, district of Colorado, on the 7th day of April, 1865.

HEADQUARTERS DISTRICT OF COLORADO,
*Denver, April 8, 1865.*

Respectfully forwarded to Brigadier General Connor, commanding district of the plains.

T. MOONLIGHT.
*Colonel Eleventh Cavalry, Commanding.*

HEADQUARTERS DISTRICT OF THE PLAINS,
*Denver, April 10, 1865.*

Respectfully forwarded to Captain George H. Stilwell, veteran battalion first Colorado cavalry, recorder of military commission.

By command:

GEORGE F. PRICE,
*Acting Assistant Adjutant General.*

I object to receiving, as evidence, the deposition of L. Meyer, for the following reasons:

1st. The order of Colonel Moonlight, district commander, directing Captain Anderson to take deposition of L. Meyer, instructs him to have the evidence of one L. Meyer taken regarding the Sand creek affair, to which the deposition has no reference, but refers to a scout made afterwards, and therefore is not relevant to the matter of this investigation.

2d. It is evident that this witness has been introduced to testify that Captain Soule, on that scout, "was afraid, got drunk, and stole blankets;" also that he refused to send men in advance, when he, Meyer, insisted upon his doing so—to push recklessly into the heart of the Indian country, when his (Soule's) command was so small as hardly to justify his leaving camp, and, under circumstances requiring the greatest caution, would have been criminal, and his failing to do so is no evidence that he (Soule) was afraid.

3d. Because it is evident that this deposition has been taken for the purpose of blackening the character of Captain Soule, to accuse him of drunkenness, theft, and neglect of duty—this officer, who, since he was introduced before this commission as a witness, has been assassinated, twice before attempted, often threatened, and at last successful in his being instantly killed.

4th. The said Captain Soule has been known to the undersigned for several years, and there is not in my opinion any reason to suspect him of being guilty of the charges alleged against him in the deposition of L. Meyer.

5th. For the reason that Captain Soule having been introduced before this commission to testify in regard to the Sand creek affair, has been made subject to threats and assaults against his life, and as appears from annexed statement of Captain Price, who had a conversation with the deceased in reference to the affair of Sand creek, that Captain Soule had reason to believe that his assassination had been determined on, and that attempts would be made to blacken his character after his death, on account of certain evidence given by him, the said Captain Soule, before this commission;

"During the latter part of March, 1865, Captain Silas S. Soule and myself were riding in a buggy from Denver, Colorado Territory, to Central City, Colorado Territory. In a conversation had on that occasion, he referred to the affair at Sand creek, Colorado Territory, and the nature of his testimony about it; that he fully expected to be killed on account of that testimony ; that he was also fully satisfied, after they had killed him, his character would be assailed, and an attempt made to destroy his testimony before a certain commission instructed to take testimony concerning the said Sand creek affair.

"I testified the above in substance before a certain coroner's jury held in this town over the body of Captain Silas S. Soule, who was assassinated in the streets of Denver on the night of April 23, 1865.

"GEORGE F. PRICE,
" *Captain Second California Cavalry, Denver City, C. T.,*
" *District Inspector and A. A. A. General.*
" MAY 3, 1865."

Therefore I object to receive as evidence the deposition of the said L. Meyer.

SAMUEL F. TAPPAN,
*Lieut. Colonel Vet. Batt., First Colorado Cavalry,*
*President Military Commission.*

The following protest was filed by J. M. Chivington:

*To the president and members of the military commission convened as per Special Orders No. 23, headquarters district of Colorado:*

I protest against the objections made by Lieutenant Colonel S. F. Tappan, president of said commission—

1st. That the action of the president of this commission in going inside of the record in making his objections, by relating conversations, &c., related by others, is, to say the least, manifesting an interest in the disposition of this case that does not accord with the presumption we must entertain of his impartial feelings in regard to the matter.

2d. That the evidence of Mr. Meyer, a person who was with Captain Soule, and who testified in compliance with orders, &c., from the general commanding, was given before Captain Soule's death, and to Captain Soule's knowledge, while they, Soule and Meyer, were both in Denver; that the intimations thrown out by the president of this commission in regard to the death of Captain Soule, calling it "an assassination," when it is well known that Captain Soule was killed by one Squires, a soldier of the second Colorado cavalry, which Squires admitted before he made his escape, is, to say the least, not becoming the dignity of one holding the position of president of a tribunal such as this commission is supposed to be, and appears to me more like malice than a desire to fairly object to the question. Hoping such is not the case,

I remain, respectfully,

J. M. CHIVINGTON.

Commission rooms were cleared for discussion. Commission adjourned until 2 p. m. this day.

*Two p. m.*—Commission met pursuant to adjournment. Present, all members and recorder.

(The objection of Lieutenant Colonel Samuel F. Tappan, president of the commission, relative to deposition of one L. Meyer, sustained by the commission.)

T. G. CREE, late captain third Colorado cavalry, introduced by J. M. Chivington, to give evidence. The oath being administered according to law, he (Cree) testified as follows:

Question. What is your name, and what position have you occupied in the army for the last three years? State particularly.

Answer. Theodore G. Cree. I have been in the army part of the time as an officer, both in the States and Colorado Territory. Very near three years ago I went into the army as second lieutenant after the battle of Vicksburg, promoted to captain in the 23d Iowa infantry. On the 27th of August, 1863, I resigned on account of ill health, and came to this country. In the latter part of July, (I think it was,) 1864, upon the request of Governor Evans, of Colorado, I raised a company for the third Colorado cavalry. I held the position of captain until mustered out on account of expiration of time of service.

Question. Did you have any conversation with Major Anthony, commanding Fort Lyon, or other officers, in regard to the propriety of attacking the Indians at Sand creek, either before or after the battle of Sand creek? If so, state what that conversation was.

Answer. I had a conversation with Major Anthony after the battle of Sand creek, at the last camp down the Arkansas, I think about one hundred miles below Fort Lyon. Colonel Chivington was talking of moving back, and not pursuing the Indians; and further, I was talking with Major Anthony in his tent about the propriety of going back, and he said that he was very much opposed to it, and said he should do all he could to prevent it. He said that we had done a good thing, and he believed in following it up; that he knew about where their camp was or where they made their headquarters, and he thought we could catch them. That is about all the conversation I had with him in regard to that matter.

Question. Do you remember anything else Major Anthony said in regard to the Indians at Sand creek? If so, state it.

Answer. I don't recollect anything else he said; I did not pay much attention to what he said at the time; I thought he was about two-thirds tight.

Question. On your return toward Denver, and while at Colonel Bent's ranch, at the mouth of the Purgatory, did you have a conversation with any officer in regard to Colonel Chivington; and if so, what was that conversation, and who was the officer or officers?

Answer. I had a conversation there with Lieutenant Cramer in regard to Colonel Chivington and officers of the third. I don't recollect all the conversation that occurred there. I recollect of his saying that all that Colonel Chivington was working for was a brigadier general's commission, and that he did not care how many lives he lost in getting it so that he got it; and that we (meaning himself and I don't know who else) were going to crush him if we could. He said he thought they could make a massacre out of the Sand creek affair and crush him. I asked him what Colonel Chivington had done to him to make him hate him so. He said that he did not know that he had done anything. He said he would like to see the Indians killed just as much as we would. He said that they had got their play in on Chivington and they were going to play it. Then I told him that there was no use of our discussing that question, as we would only make enemies of ourselves, and I thought it was best for us not to say anything more about it. The rest of our talk was not in connection with this affair.

Question. Did you have any conversation with Cramer in regard to the guerillas that were killed?

380

(Question objected to by Lieutenant Colonel Tappan, president of the commission, on the ground of its being leading.

Objection sustained by the commission.)

Question. Did you have any conversation with Cramer in regard to guerillas? If so, what was the conversation? State particularly.

Answer. I had some conversation with him in regard to guerillas. They were known by the name of Reynolds's party. He wanted to know what my orders were in relation to them. I told him my orders were to take them to Captain Gray's camp on the Arkansas and to turn them over to him, and he was to take them to Fort Lyon. Then he wanted to know what was done with them; I told him that they died for the want of breath; he said that was another murder of Colonel Chivington's. I asked him how he knew; he said he did not know for certain, but he thought it was done to enable him to get his brigadier's straps. I told him he was badly mistaken; that I took that all on myself. He said that he did not like to dispute my word, but that he could not think otherwise but what it was orders from Chivington. I told him I could not help what he thought; that is about all that was said in reference to them. He said he hoped they were in heaven; I said I hoped so too, as I thought they would be better off there than in this country.

Question. Did you, at any time during that conversation with Cramer, state that the guerillas were killed by Chivington's orders?

Answer. I did not.

Question. Upon your arrival at Colonel Bent's with your detachment, did you take command of all the troops at that place? If so, state what you did.

Answer. I took command of the troops that were there as soon as I arrived. I gave Lieutenant Cramer an order to report at Fort Lyon in his own district the next morning. I also gave the lieutenant commanding detachment of third regiment orders to report to his command at Bent's old fort.

Question. Did Lieutenant Cramer obey the order you gave him?

Answer. I suppose he did. He left there the next morning the same time I left.

Question. Did Lieutenant Cramer make any remarks to you concerning the order you gave him?

Answer. No.

Direct examination of T. G. Cree by J. M. Chivington closed.

Cross-examination of T. G. Cree, by the commission:

Question. What was the date of your muster into the service as captain third Colorado cavalry, and the date of your muster out?

Answer. Mustered in, I think, the 20th of August, 1864. Mustered out the 28th of December, (I think it was,) 1864.

Question. Who were present at Colonel Bent's during the conversation you had with Lieutenant Cramer?

Answer. Colonel Bent. He was there part of the time, and a part of the time we were alone. Part of the time Lieutenant Graham was present.

Question. How many of Reynolds's party were you ordered to take to Camp Fillmore?

Answer. Five, I believe.

Question. Where and from whom did you receive these prisoners?

(J. M. Chivington objects to the question, for the reason that the court has no right to cross-examine in relation to new matter not called out in the examination in chief.

Objection sustained by the commission.)

Question. What did you tell Lieutenant Cramer you had done with these prisoners?

Answer. I did not tell him I had done anything with them.

Question. In what manner, and by what authority, did you assume command of all the troops at Colonel Bent's?

Answer. I assumed command by order of Colonel Shoup, commanding the troops on their way up to Denver.

Question. Did Lieutenant Cramer report to you for orders?

Answer. He did not.

Question. Did Lieutenant Cramer say the Indians at Sand creek were under the protection of the government, as a reason for his denouncing the fight as, a murder or massacre?

(J. M. Chivington objects to the question, on the ground that it is new matter, not called on the examination in chief, and therefore illegal.

Objection sustained by the commission.)

Question. What did you tell Lieutenant Cramer you took all on yourself?

Answer. In regard to disposing of those "guerillas."

Question. Did you refer to the killing of them?

(J. M. Chivington objects to the question, for the reason that the witness has not stated anything in regard to the killing of the guerillas, therefore this is new matter and illegal.

Objection sustained by the commission.)

Question. In your conversation with Lieutenant Cramer, who did you refer to as having died for the want of breath?

Answer. I referred to James Reynolds and his guerilla party.

Cross-examination of T. G. Cree by the commission closed.

Re-examination:

No questions asked.

Commission adjourned until 8½ a. m. to morrow, May 6, 1865.

### FIFTY-SEVENTH DAY.

MAY 6, 1865.

Commission met pursuant to adjournment. Present, all members and recorder. Proceedings of yesterday read and approved.

S. P. ASHCRAFT introduced by J. M. Chivington to give evidence. The oath being administered according to law, he (Ashcraft) testified as follows:

Question. What is your full name, and how long have you lived in what is now known as Colorado Territory, and how long have you been acquainted with the Indians of the plains?

Answer. Samuel Plummer Ashcraft; I have been in Colorado Territory since 1857; I have known the Indians of the plains since 1847.

Question. What have been your means of knowledge of the Indians of the plains? State particularly.

Answer. I have been with them and traded with them; as for the Sioux Indians, I expect I understand them about as well as any person in the country. The Cheyennes, I expect I understand their ways and actions as well as the Sioux, but I do not speak their language as well.

Question. Do you know whether or not the Cheyenne and Sioux Indians have been at war with the whites? If yes, please state your first knowledge of it—particularly, as well as you know, of their hostile acts.

Answer. Yes, I know they were at war with the whites, and more than that, I know that they commenced the war with the whites. In the first part of this war, some sixteen or eighteen Cheyennes came from some place on the headwaters of Beaver creek, and came into Frémont's Orchard; a day or two, I think, before they came in, they took some horses and mules from a man, who came in and reported the fact to Captain Sanborn. Captain Sanborn sent out Lieutenant Dunn with a squad of men—I don't know how many, I

382

think fifteen Under what orders Lieutenant Dunn was, I do not know. After Lieutenant Dunn found these Indians near Frémont's Orchard, on the north side of the South Platte, he went to them and ordered them to give up their arms; his men dismounted to take their arms. They gave up one gun and a single barrelled pistol. The Indians then turned and fired. I suppose they fired three or four shots before the soldiers fired; one of their men that died was shot before the soldiers fired. They had a fight there, which lasted probably an hour and a half. Lieutenant Dunn had two men killed, and four wounded. The Indians had two of their number wounded, none killed.

Question. Did you hear any rumors of hostility from the Indians toward the whites before this?

Answer. Yes; the winter before. All winter I heard it from the Indians three or four different times.

Question. State what you heard from the Indians.

Answer. The Sioux told me that the Cheyennes had been talking of war with the whites all winter. They said that they (the Cheyennes) were going to war against the whites on the road in the spring; that they were going to clean out all the ranchmen that were on the road. (They came mighty near telling the truth, too.)

Question. What is your means of knowledge of the facts concerning the fight Lieutenant Dunn had with the Indians near Frémont's Orchard; did you see the fight, or only hear of it through others?

Answer. I only heard of it through others.

Question. Do you know of any acts of hostility perpetrated by the Indians upon the whites; if yes, please state what those acts were, and what Indians perpetrated them?

Answer. I know that they killed men and drove off stock. They drove off some of my stock and killed one of my men, the next after they had the fight with Lieutenant Dunn.

Direct examination of Samuel P. Ashcraft by J. M. Chivington closed.

Cross-examination of Samuel P. Ashcraft by the commission:

Question. Where do you at present reside?

Answer. I live about fifty miles below here on the Platte. I also have a ranch one hundred miles below here on the Platte. I live there part of the time.

Question. When did the Sioux Indians come into what is now known as Colorado Territory?

Answer. I don't recollect. Before '47 they were in this country.

Question. Are you acquainted with all the Cheyennes?

Answer. I am acquainted with all the different bands of Cheyennes.

Question. Into how many bands were the Cheyennes divided?

Answer. Four bands of them.

Question. Of what band were those Indians who had the fight with Lieutenant Dunn?

Answer. They were a part of Black Kettle's band.

Question. Were they what is known as Dog soldiers?

Answer. They were not. The Dog soldiers are Bull Bear's band.

Question. How many horses and mules did these Indians steal before crossing into Frémont's Orchard?

Answer. I am not positive of more than two.

Question. Where is Beaver creek—head-waters of it?

Answer. It heads under the divide between the Platte and Arkansas, and empties into the Platte. The head of it is about eighty-five miles southeast from here.

Ex. Doc. 26——13

Question. What is your means of knowledge that the Cheyennes stole a horse and a mule before reaching Frémont's Orchard?

Answer. They acknowledged it. They said that they had found them, and the man they were taken from said they stole them.

Question. What did the Indians do with the horse and mule?

Answer. One of them the soldiers got, the other they kept.

Question. Was the taking of this horse and mule the commencement of the Indian difficulties?

Answer. I do not think it was. They claimed that the whites were beating them out of their land. They were dissatisfied with the Boone treaty. I think this treaty was in the spring of 1861.

Question. Was the taking of this horse the first hostile act of the Indians against the whites?

Answer. Yes.

Question. Was this considered by the people an act of war, or the commencement of war by the Indians against the whites?

(John M. Chivington most respectfully objects to the question for the reason that the opinion of Mr. Ashcraft is not proper; that the court has commenced the examination of the witness on new matter, and that the witness has stated the knowledge he has of the facts is from others.

Objection sustained by the commission.)

Question. What bands of the Cheyennes were referred to by the Sioux as intending to make war upon the whites?

Answer. All of them. They were all then in the village.

Question. Is what you have stated your only means of information that the Cheyennes intended to make war upon the whites?

Answer. Yes. My information came through the Indians.

Cross-examination of Samuel P. Ashcraft by the commission closed.

Re-examination of Samuel P. Ashcraft:

By J. M. CHIVINGTON:

Question. What is your means of knowledge of the fight between Lieutenant Dunn and the Indians, and the stealing of horse and mule or horses and mules; is it from others, or did you see these things?

Answer. Only from the Indians and the whites.

Re-examination of Samuel P. Ashcraft closed.

Commission adjourned until 2 p. m. this day.

*Two p. m.*—Commission met pursuant to adjournment. Present, all members and recorder.

STEPHEN DECATUR introduced by J. M. Chivington to give evidence. The oath being administered according to law, he (Decatur) testified as follows:

Question. What is your full name, and are you acquainted with the habits and customs of Indians. If yes, state how long you have been acquainted, and what your means of knowledge were?

Answer. Stephen Decatur. I lived among the Indians nearly seven years.

Question. Where were you on the 29th day of November, 1864? Have you been in the army?

Answer. I was at Sand creek. I served in the Mexican war, and also in the one hundred day regiment of Colorado, (third regiment of Colorado cavalry.)

Question. Please state particularly what occurred at Sand creek of your own knowledge only.

Answer. We came in sight of the village about daylight, or a little after. I think it was about sunrise, or a little after, when our company was ordered to halt in the bed of the creek, by Colonel Chivington, and strip for the fight. We then moved up a short distance and unlimbered, (I belonged to Captain

384

Morgan's company, C, artillery,) and commenced throwing shell. I was not with the company all the time, for the reason that Lieutenant Colonel Bowen had requested me to act as his battalion adjutant. This firing took place near the upper end of the village; after firing a few rounds the company was ordered forward, and we took a position about three-quarters of a mile above the village; at which place, and near there, I remained the principal part of the day. I saw one man lying dead, partially under his horse, in the village. I saw a number of wounded passing up to the ambulances. I saw one fellow with a squaw prisoner and a child. He asked what he should do with them. I told him to take them up to headquarters. To sum it all up in brief, that was my fourth battle, and I never saw harder fighting on both sides in my life. The next day after the battle I went over the battle-ground, in the capacity of clerk, for Lieutenant Colonel Bowen, and counted four hundred and fifty dead Indian warriors. I will here explain that a question was raised in camp what chiefs were killed. Lieutenant Colonel Bowen took an escort of troops and went over the field. John Smith was taken along to recognize the chiefs and the principal warriors that were killed, I acting as clerk, and I took pleasure in going, as the evening before, while the village was being burned, (which was not all completely destroyed when I came back to camp, which was in the Indian village,) I saw that which made me feel as though I should have liked to have spent a little more time fighting As I was going out to get some of the lodge-poles for wood, I saw some of the men opening bundles or bales. I saw them take therefrom a number of white persons' scalps—men's, women's, and children's; some daguerreotypes, ladies' wearing apparel and white children's, and saw part of a lady's toilet and one box of rouge, also a box containing a powder puff. I saw one scalp of a white woman in particular that I want to describe to you. It had been taken entirely off the head; the head had been skinned, taking all the hair; the scalp had been tanned to preserve it; the hair was auburn and hung in ringlets; it was very long hair. There were two holes in the scalp in front, for the purpose of tying it on their heads when they appeared in the scalp dance. Seeing all these things made me anxious to go over the battle-ground and see how many we had killed. I saw, comparatively speaking, a small number of women killed. They were in the rifle-pits. (The most of them where it would have been impossible to have avoided killing them if we had been ever so much disposed to save them.) After going over the main battle-ground we returned to the village, and I did all I could to destroy their effects. That is, in brief, what I saw on the 29th and 30th of last November at Sand creek. There is one matter that occurs to me just at this moment: Just after our artillery had ceased firing, I saw an acquaintance in the bed of the creek, and I told him he was in a dangerous place, and asked him what he was going to do, and, (I thought I would have a little fun on my own hook) he said there was an Indian in a hole under the bank that could talk English, (this was in reply to me,) and I started to go to him; just as I got near the edge of the bank he hallooed out to me not to come down there, for the Indian would shoot me; as I turned on my heel to go away from the bank, I heard a voice under the bank say, "Come on, you God damn white sons of bitches, and kill me if you are a brave man."

Question. Were the scalps you speak of the scalps of white men, women, and children?

Answer. Yes, they were.

Question. Had the Indians prepared any rifle-pits, or other means of defence, on your arrival at the village on Sand creek, on the 29th day of November, 1864?

Answer. They must have done it, as there were holes longer and deeper than they could have dug after we attacked them in the morning. That is my honest opinion.

Question. Describe these rifle-pits, how they were constructed, and where dug.

Answer. They were dug under the banks, and in the bed of the creek, and, in fact, all over, where there was a little mound or bunch of grass or weeds favorable for concealment. They were dug with hoes or shovels large enough for a man to operate in, from three to four feet wide, some six feet long and longer. That is my recollection of it now. I did not measure them. I thought at the time that they must have been dug, for the reason that at the first camp from the battle-field I found some of the same kind of pits, where they (the Indians) had camped quite recently before.

Question. Were you at the village when the attack was first made by the troops on the Indians?

Answer. I was not quite in the village; I saw it.

Direct examination of Stephen Decatur, by J. M. Chivington, closed.

Cross-examination of Stephen Decatur, by the commission:

Question. Where do you reside?

Answer. In Denver.

Question. What position did you hold in the third regiment?

Answer. Commissary sergeant of company C.

Question. You say you counted four hundred and fifty dead Indian warriors. Where did you find these dead Indians?

Answer. Scattered promiscuously over the battle-ground.

Question. How large was the battle-ground?

Answer. It was pretty extensive. We, I should think, went up the creek about three miles, as near as I could judge from the time we rode.

Question. Did you ride all over the battle-ground?

Answer. There was one portion of the battle-ground that I did not go on. John Smith had recognized Black Kettle, Little Robe, and White Antelope, and the near approach of night caused the lieutenant colonel to return to camp.

Question. Who accompanied you?

Answer. Lieutenant Colonel Bowen, in command, and Lieutenant De La Mar, in command of the escort, and John Smith, who I understand was the Indian interpreter at Fort Lyon, whom we found in the village trading with the Indians.

Question. At what time did you start out to ride over the battle-field to count the dead?

Answer. My impression now is that it was between two and three o'clock in the afternoon of the 30th of November, 1864.

Question. At what time did you return to camp?

Answer. Not a great while before night; about time to eat a little, and fix my bed, before it was dark.

Question. Was it during this ride you saw the four hundred and fifty dead Indian warriors?

Answer. Yes, the ride on the 30th, I said.

Question. Who did the counting of the dead for the party?

Answer. I counted on my own hook, for my own satisfaction.

Question. On which side of the creek did you see the dead Indians?

Answer. I saw them on both sides, and in the bed of the creek.

Question. Did you ride up one side of the creek and down the other?

Answer. Our route took us up angling across from one bank to the other, and coming back we returned on the east side of the bank nearly all the way on the prairie. I do not know that my knowledge of the points of the compass is right, but we returned on the side next to Lort Fyon.

Question. How many did you see on the east side of the creek?

Answer. I did not keep an account of their exact whereabouts. I did not expect to be called upon at any time to give any testimony in regard to it before a military commission.

Question. Were there any dead Indians on the east side of the creek?

Answer. If the east side is next to Fort Lyon, there were.

Question. How many, or what proportion of the whole number, did you see on the east side of the creek?

Answer. On what I call the east side, on the prairie, *i. e.*, out of the bed of the creek, there was only a small proportion of the four hundred and fifty.

Question. How many or what proportion of the whole number did you see on the west side of the creek?

Answer. I cannot say, as I did not think at the time of remembering their whereabouts or their particular position on the battle-field.

Question. Did you see any dead Indians in the bed of the creek?

Answer. Yes, plenty of them.

Question. How many did you see in the bed of the creek?

Answer. I don't recollect what proportion were in the bed of the creek, but the most of the whole number I saw were in the bed of the creek.

Question. How far above the village did you see the dead Indians?

Answer. I commenced counting at the village and about three miles or thereabouts up the creek, and counted on my return those that lay upon the prairie.

Question. Did the Indians appear as having been disturbed after they were killed?

(J. M. Chivington most respectfully objects to the question for the following reasons : That the question is in relation to new matter which was not called out by the examination in chief; that it is therefore illegal and improper. The witness, in his examination in chief, did not state, nor was he asked, anything about the Indians, whether they were disturbed or not.)

Commission rooms were cleared for deliberation.

Commission adjourned until 9 a. m. Monday, May 8, 1865.

### FIFTY-EIGHTH DAY.

MAY 8, 1865.

Commission met pursuant to adjournment. Present, all members and recorder.
Proceedings of yesterday read and approved.

The objection of J. M. Chivington not having been decided, the commission rooms were cleared for deliberation.

Commission rooms again opened and the following decision of the commission announced, viz:

The objection of J. M. Chivington to question before adjournment, Saturday, May 6, 1865, not sustained by the commission.

The following request was filed by J. M. Chivington :

*To the president and members of the military commission convened in pursuance of Special Orders No. 23, headquarters district Colorado, &c. :*

We would most respectfully request of the commission that they would have the following persons summoned immediately, to testify to the subject-matter of this investigation.

Jay J. Johnson, Central City ; D. H. Nichols, Boulder ; Hal. Sayre, Central City ; C. C. Hawley, Central City ; Dr. James Bell, Idaho ; David Ripley, Boulder ; Alexander F. Safely, company C, veteran battalion first Colorado cavalry.

J. M. CHIVINGTON.

MAY 8, 1865.

Cross-examination of Stephen Decatur by the commission, continued:

Answer to last question before adjournment, Saturday, May 6, 1865. They did appear to have been disturbed, some of them, not all.

Question. What Indians have you lived among for nearly seven years.

Answer. The Omahas, Ottoes and Missourias, Pawnees, Poncas, Santee, Sioux, and Yancton Sioux; I resided at Bellevue, Nebraska Territory, I became intimately acquinted with the Omaha language, and well enough acquainted with the language of all the rest to trade with them.

Question. What acquaintance have you with the Cheyennes and Arapahoes of the Upper Arkansas agency?

Answer. No personal acquaintance with them, only at Sand creek.

Question. You say Sand creek was your fourth battle, name the other three?

Answer. Battle of Brazito, Sacramento, about eleven or fifteen miles north of the city of Chihuahua, and in the State of Chihuahua. The next was an Indian fight which occurred at a ranch about fifteen or twenty miles north of the city of Paras. It was with the White Lipans or Comanches. I have seen the White Lipans or Comanches scalp their own men to prevent their scalps from being taken by the whites.

Question. You say your name is Stephen Decatur; are you a descendant of the celebrated commodore of that name?

Answer. I am distantly connected.

Question. How do you know the scalps you saw were those of white men, women, and children?

Answer. By the color and fineness of their hair; I never saw an Indian with auburn hair in my life.

Question. How do you know the wearing apparel you saw in Black Kettle's camp was that of white women and children?

Answer. I know the habits and customs of the Indians, especially the wild Indians of the plains, well enough to know their prejudices against the wearing apparel of the whites. I know that they had no person among them well skilled enough to make the dresses I saw there.

Question. Are not the Cheyennes an exception to that rule? Have they not for years employed white women to make dresses for their women and children, and received dress goods from their agent?

Answer. I don't know what has been given to them by their agents.

Question. Were not the tanned scalps you speak of as being auburn of a dull rusty color, very coarse in texture, and formerly of a dark color, but faded by age?

Answer. No.

Question. What became of that scalp?

Answer. I do not know.

Question. Have you seen it since the time you speak of?

Answer. No. I heard that it was in town, and heard that it was in Boulder district somewhere, but I have not seen it.

Question. How near did you ride to the four hundred and fifty dead Indian warriors, on the 30th of November last?

Answer. Near enough to count them and be positive.

Question. Did you keep a tally of the dead Indians as you passed them?

Answer. Every time I counted a hundred I dotted them down on my thumb-nail. I will here state that the reason I was so particular in counting is this: I was at the house of Mrs. Hungate only a few days before she was murdered, and I became attached to her and her babes, and I wished her friends to know how many of the bloody villains we had killed.

Question. Did you see the bodies of Black Kettle, White Antelope, Little Robe, and other chiefs as you rode over the field?

388

Answer. I did, if John Smith told the truth. He pointed out what he said were the bodies of White Antelope, Black Kettle, and Little Robe.

Question. Did you or your party scalp or mutilate these dead Indians?

(John M. Chivington most respectfully objects to the question, for the following reasons: That, like the question in relation to the white women employed by the savages, and the dress-goods issued to the Indians, it is irrelevant and improper; that it is examining on new matter, which is improper on a cross-examination, and to which we would have objected when the inquiry was made in regard to the white women employed by the savages, but we thought the question so ridiculous to a person at all acquainted with the Indians that we did not object, though if that led to the present question, we claim not to have lost any right that we may have to object to the present question.)

Commission adjourned until 2 p. m. this day.

*Two p. m.*—Commission met pursuant to adjournment. Present, all the members and recorder.

The objection of J. M. Chivington before adjournment this a. m. overruled by the commission.

Answer. So far as I am concerned, I do not think I am a competent witness to exculpate or criminate myself. So far as any gentleman of the party is concerned, I saw no mutilating or scalping by any of them.

Question. Have you now, or have you had since the 29th of November, 1864, in your possession, as trophies of Sand creek, ears brought here to present to any person?

(John M. Chivington most respectfully objects to the question, for the following reasons: That the question relates to new matter and is therefore improper, having no right in a cross-examination to inquire into anything except that which was called out by the defence.

Objection sustained by the commission.)

Question. What were the depth, location, and number of the holes you saw at Sand creek, and call rifle-pits?

Answer. There were a great many of them, I did not count the number; they were deep enough for men to lie down and conceal themselves, and load their guns in; some of them I should think were deeper than three feet. They were under the banks and in every possible place where any degree of concealment could be afforded in the bed of the creek. They were all in the bed of the creek. I saw none on the high prairie. They were above the village.

Question. What is the character of the soil in Sand creek where you saw the holes or rifle-pits?

Answer. Sandy, with strata of hard baked gravel.

Question. You say you saw some similar holes at a former and abandoned camp of Indians; state how many of these holes you saw, and if these holes are not common in the Cheyenne camps, constructed for domestic purposes?

Answer. In all Indian villages in which I have been, they usually dug holes for the purpose of cooking meat. Those holes are dug in the village, in the confines of the village, near the lodges. They do not go a mile or a half mile from camp; but these holes I saw were not for cooking purposes, unless they cooked on a larger scale than any Indians I ever saw or knew.

Question. What became of the scalps you saw in the camp, and who saw them besides yourself?

Answer. They were in the possession of various ones; I saw some of them a number of times in the road. I would know the men if I saw them, but I do not know their names; I can find out, I think, if the court desires it.

Question. Have you ever gone by any other name than that of Stephen Decatur?

(J. M. Chivington most respectfully objects to the question, for the following reasons: That the question is insulting to the witness, and the court, instead of putting such questions, should protect the witness from them; that the question is irrelevant and improper, not pertaining to the subject-matter of this investigation, upon which the court has recently decided that such evidence is improper; that the witness has been introduced to testify in regard to Sand creek and not regarding his own private matters; that it is immaterial to this court whether the witness goes by one name or another. Though the Indians might have called him by another name than Decatur, the custom is a common one, known to all white men in this Territory, when coming in contact with Indians.

Commission rooms were cleared for discussion.

Commission rooms opened.

Objection of J. M. Chivington overruled by the commission.)

Answer. Not among white men; it is customary among Indians to give their traders an Indian name.

Question. Did the Indians, or others, ever call you by the name of Bross?

Answer. No.

Cross-examination of Stephen Decatur by the commission closed.

Re-examination of Stephen Decatur.

By J. M. CHIVINGTON:

Question. You stated you wished to make an amendment to your testimony; you will please do it now.

Answer. I said this morning that a great deal had been said about a white flag—about the Indians sending out a white flag, a flag of truce. I saw none.

Question. Was there anything occurred, or any conversation had by any person, in regard to a white flag? If so, please state what that was particularly.

Answer. I never had any conversation with any one, only a short time since, and that was with Captain McCannon, and what I saw charged in the paper, "that we had fired on the Indians after they had exhibited a white flag." I don't recollect of having any conversation with any one about it, except Captain McCannon.

Question. If there had been a white flag shown by the Indians, would you have seen it?

Answer. Yes, I think I would.

Re-examination of Stephen Decatur closed.

Commission adjourned until 9 a. m. to-morrow, May 9, 1865.

FIFTY-NINTH DAY.

MAY 9, 1865.

Commission met pursuant to adjournment. Present, all members and recorder. Proceedings of yesterday read and approved.

HENRY H. HEWITT introduced by J. M. Chivington to give evidence. The oath being administered according to law, he (Hewitt) testified as follows:

Question. What has been your occupation during the past eight months? If in the army, what position did you occupy, &c.?

Answer. On the 17th day of September, 1864, I was mustered into the service as second lieutenant, company I, third Colorado cavalry, (one-hundred-days men,) and served in that capacity for the period of one hundred days.

Question. In your official capacity did you or not receive any ponies, &c., said to be captured at the battle of Sand creek? If so, state the particulars.

Answer. I did. While in command of a detachment of the third Colorado cavalry, en route to Fort Lyon, on or about the 5th day of December, 1864, while camping at Boone's ranch, I received information that one Duncan McKeith, and some Mexicans of Lieutenant Antobe's detachment, had run off some ponies and mules while the fight was progressing at Sand creek. Thinking it my duty to inquire into the matter, I took a detachment of men and proceeded across the Arkansas river to Charles Antobe's ranch, and surrounded the corral to prevent the escape of men and stock, if there concealed. I went into the corral and found Duncan McKeith in a room adjoining the corral, who informed me that he had driven off between sixty and seventy head of ponies and mules while the battle was progressing at Sand creek; that he did this by order of Lieutenant Antobe, and that Lieutenant Antobe said to him that both Colonels Chivington and Shoup knew that the stock was driven off, and raised no objection to it. I took Duncan McKeith and four Mexicans (names not now recollected) in charge, and seized between sixty and seventy head of ponies and mules, and drove them across the Arkansas river to Boone's ranche, where I placed them under guard. On the following morning I started with the ponies and mules and Mexicans, with Duncan McKeith, for Fort Lyon, where I arrived on the 8th or 9th of December, 1864; on arriving at Fort Lyon, I found from general conversation with officers and soldiers at the fort that the ponies and mules had been stolen while the battle of Sand creek was progressing; also, that another herd had been driven over on the Cimaron, towards New Mexico. Colonel Chivington arrived at Fort Lyon from pursuit of the Indians, after the battle of Sand creek, (as I was informed by different persons,) the second night after my arrival at Fort Lyon. I reported to Colonel Chivington my action in seizing the ponies, mules, and men in charge. His reply was, "You have done perfectly right; I am glad you did it; the men had no authority from myself or Colonel Shoup to drive the stock off when they did. Lieutenant Antobe was instructed to drive the captured stock to Fort Lyon." I turned in the stock which I took at Antobe's ranch, except four or five head that were re-stolen, and two head that gave out on the road, to Lieutenant C. M. Cossitt, acting quartermaster at Fort Lyon, taking his receipt therefor. That, I think, comprises all I can say on that question. I will say this: Colonel Chivington said to me, "that it was a scandal, that while the troops were fighting the Indians, some scoundrels should shrink to plunder," or words to that effect. Colonel Chivington ordered me (verbally) to report with my detachment to Colonel Shoup, in command of third Colorado cavalry, which I did the day following.

Direct examination of Henry H. Hewitt by J. M. Chivington closed.

Cross-examination of Henry H. Hewitt, by the commission:

Question. Were the parties you have mentioned as driving off or stealing the stock a portion of Colonel Chivington's command?

Answer. They were; so they informed me.

Question. Did Colonels Chivington or Shoup ever place these parties under arrest, and bring them to punishment for their acts?

Answer. I do not know.

Question. Were these ponies and mules included in the number reported captured from the Indians, by Colonel Chivington?

Answer. I cannot say, from my own knowledge; I was not present at the battle of Sand creek.

Question. Did Lieutenant Cossitt give you a memorandum receipt for the ponies?

Answer. He did, for the ponies and mules.

Question. Did you take this stock up on your returns as government property, and account for it as turned over to Lieutenant Cossitt?

Answer. I made a report to Colonel Shoup of the stock, but not to the Quartermaster General, from the fact that I did not consider (never having receipted for the stock) that I was required to make a report to the Quartermaster General. I merely took Lieutenant Cossitt's memorandum receipt for my own protection.

I also made a report in writing to Lieutenant Charles Wheeler, acting assistant adjutant general of the district of Colorado.

Cross-examination of Henry H. Hewitt by the commission closed.

Re-examination of Henry H. Hewitt:

No questions asked.

The following copy of request and affidavit filed by J. M. Chivington:

*To the president and members of the military commission convened at Denver, Colorado Territory, in pursuance of Special Orders No. 23, headquarters District of Colorado, &c.:*

GENTLEMEN : We would most respectfully request that you summon and cause to appear before your honorable court, without fail, one Alexander Safely, company C, veteran battalion first Colorado cavalry, to testify to all he knows concerning the marches of the troops under command of Colonel J. M. Chivington, first Colorado cavalry, and the battle of Sand creek, fought November 29, 1864, said Safely being an important witness in the investigation of said marches and battle, as will more fully appear by accompanying affidavit.

Most respectfully,

JOHN M. CHIVINGTON,
*Late Colonel First Colorado Cavalry.*

John M. Chivington, late colonel first Colorado cavalry, being first duly sworn, deposes and says that one Alexander F. Safely, company C, veteran battalion first Colorado cavalry, is material witness in his behalf to show certain facts connected with the marches and battle of Sand creek, before the military commission now convened in Denver, Colorado Territory, in pursuance of Special Orders No. 23, headquarters district of Colorado, &c.; that the said facts, or all of them, cannot be shown by any other person that I know of at present, and that without the said Alexander F. Safely he would lose very reliable evidence which would materially affect his acts in the eyes of the government; and further deponent saith not.

J. M. CHIVINGTON.

Subscribed and sworn to before me this 9th day of May, 1865.

[SEAL.]

——— ———,
*Notary Public.*

The recorder is hereby ordered to summon the witnesses as requested by J. M. Chivington.

By order of the commission.

Commission adjourned until 2 o'clock this p. m.

*Two p. m.*—Commission met, pursuant to adjournment. Present, all members and recorder.

Dr. CALEB S. BIRDSAL introduced by J. M. Chivington to give evidence. The oath being administered according to law, he (Burdsal) testified as follows:

Question. Did you occupy a position in the third regiment Colorado cavalry? If so, what was it, and were you at the battle of Sand creek, fought November 29, 1864?

Answer. I was first assistant surgeon, and I was at the battle of Sand creek.

Question. Did you see any captured or pressed property for any purpose? If yes, please state all the particulars concerning its final disposition, &c.

Answer. On the afternoon of the 29th (after the battle) I went to Colonel Chivington and Colonel Shoup; told them that I was going to take some buffalo robes for the wounded from John Smith's (Indian interpreter and trader) wagon; that I had no blankets to cover the wounded. I detailed three or four men to go with me, and when I arrived there the larger amount of soldiers there (there were a great number of soldiers there) pitched in and got a large number of robes at the same time. I suppose that they thought every man was helping himself. I can't tell the number I got, as I never counted them, but I should think in the neighborhood of forty. That same evening Colonel Shoup requested me to return John Smith some of the robes to sleep on. I returned five or six, I think. Of the balance of the robes, a portion was stolen from the sick out of the lodges, some were claimed by others on the grounds that they had left them for the use of the wounded, the balance were given to the wounded soldiers.

Question. Did you have any conversation with any parties at Fort Lyon in relation to captured property? If yes, please state who the parties were and what the conversation was.

Answer. I think I had a conversation once with Major Anthony, first cavalry of Colorado, and Dr. Leas, assistant surgeon on the staff. The major asked me what had become of those robes I took from John Smith; that John Smith had lost one hundred and fifteen robes, and the government would have to pay twenty dollars apiece for them. Dr. Leas asked me the same question, and wanted to know what had become of two hundred robes I took, and that government would have to pay twenty dollars apiece for them if they were not returned. I remarked wherever they could find any of John Smith's robes to go and take them, as I had other business to attend to.

Question. Did you see any white scalps at Sand creek? if yes, please state the particulars in regard to them.

Answer. I think it was about three or four o'clock p. m., November 29, the day of the battle, I was in the lodge dressing the wounded; some man came to the opening of the lodge and hallooed to me to look at five or six scalps he had in his hand. I should judge, from a casual look, that they were the scalps of white persons.

Question. Did you see all the wounded of Colonel Chivington's command? if yes, please state whether, in your professional opinion, any of them were wounded by their own comrades.

Answer. Yes, I saw all the wounded; my impression is two or three were wounded by their own comrades; I judge from the size and cavity of the bullet wounds.

Question. Do you know what arms the Indians had, and whether they had not arms in their possession, and used on the field November 29, 1864, capable of inflicting wounds whose cavities would be as large and deep as any in possession of the troops?

Answer. I am not capable of answering that, as I did not examine particularly their guns; I was busy, and was not away from the lodge over ten steps.

Direct examination of Dr. Caleb S. Burdsal by J. M. Chivington closed.

Cross-examination of Dr. Caleb S. Burdsal by the commission:

Question. Have you any other reasons than those you have stated for believing some of the wounded were shot by their comrades instead of by the Indians? if so, what those reasons were.

Answer. The large majority of those that were wounded with balls were wounded in the upper part of the body; two were wounded in the calf of the leg, and one in the knee; the cavities were much larger than those shot in the upper part of the body. These are the grounds of my opinion. My impression is that two of the men were under that impression themselves.

Question. Did any of the command exhibit any other scalps than those you have mentioned at the time or afterwards?

(John M. Chivington most respectfully objects to the question for the following reasons: That it is examining in relation to new matter, which is illegal and improper; that if the court will confine its questions to the inquiry in regard to white scalps we have no objection, but the question in its general form is too hard.

Objection overruled by the commission.)

Answer. I saw scalps in the hands of several after returning from the battle.

Question. Did you ever see an Indian scalp? if so, state what is the difference between it and a white scalp?

(John M. Chivington most respectfully objects to the question for the following reasons: That no inquiry has been made in relation to the difference between white and Indian scalps; that it is new matter; therefore illegal and improper; that the professional opinion of Dr. Burdsal, as an expert, has been asked in regard to wounds, not in regard to scalps.

Objection sustained by the commission.)

Question. What reason have you for saying the scalps you saw in the lodge were those of white persons?

Answer. I judge by the color of the hair.

Question. What was the color of those you saw in the lodge?

Answer. I think there were some white, some sandy brown. I don't think there were any that were very black.

Question. Did not these scalps present the appearance of having faded and changed from their original color by age?

Answer. I think not. My impression is that one or two of them were not more than ten days off of the head.

Question. From what indications do you determine the time not to have been over ten days?

Answer. The skin and flesh attached to the hair appeared to be yet quite moist.

Question. Did you examine these scalps closely?

Answer. Yes; my attention was called to that by others, to decide whether they were fresh or not.

Question. How many wounded were under your charge at Sand creek?

Answer. Thirty-eight. Three of the wounded, after their wounds were dressed, continued with the command down the Arkansas.

Cross-examination of Dr. Caleb Burdsal by the commission closed.

Re-examination: No questions asked.

Commission adjourned until 9 a. m. to-morrow, May 10, 1865.

### SIXTIETH DAY.

MAY 10, 1865.

Commission met pursuant to adjournment. Present, all members and recorder.

Proceedings of yesterday read and approved. Commission adjourned until two o'clock p. m. this day.

*Two o'clock p. m.*—Commission met pursuant to adjournment. Present, a majority of the commission. Adjourned until nine o'clock a. m. to-morrow, May 11, 1865.

### SIXTY-FIRST DAY.

MAY 11, 1865.

Commission met pursuant to adjournment. Present, all members and recorder. Proceedings of yesterday read and approved.

B. N. FORBES introduced by J. M. Chivington to give evidence. The oath being administered according to law, he (Forbes) testified as follows:

Question. What is your name, and have you been a soldier? If yes, state what regiment and company you served in.

Answer. B. N. Forbes; served in company D, first cavalry of Colorado.

Question. Were you with Major Wynkoop, commanding Fort Lyon, when he made an expedition to the Smoky Hill, about September, 1864, and recovered some white prisoners? If yes, state all that occurred, of your own knowledge, on that expedition.

Answer. .Yes, I was with that expedition. I think it was about the middle of September, 1864. When we came in sight of the Indians Major Wynkoop halted our command, and sent the chief we had with us, (One-Eye, I think,) as messenger to the Indians. After he (the Indian) returned, the major turned off to the left about a mile and encamped for the night; next morning resumed the march. After travelling four miles, I should judge, we came in sight of the Indians drawn up in line of battle. The major halted the command; there was a short consultation held between the chief and the major, (it was with Black-Kettle, I believe,) after which the command went on and the Indians fell in rear; travelled that way nearly eight miles and camped. Then there was a consultation held between Major Wynkoop and the Indian chiefs. I do not know what was done in that consultation, I not understanding the Indian language.

Question. How long did you remain in the camp where the consultation was held, and did the Indians come into your camp? State particularly all that occurred in this camp.

Answer. We remained there, I should judge, about six hours. The Indians came into camp, quite a number of them—probably five Indians to one white man. They (the Indians) were armed and equipped. They took some of our provisions out of the wagons, forcibly.

Question. How did the Indians behave toward the troops, as regards peace or war? State particularly.

Answer. They were pretty saucy for friendly Indians. A few that could talk English used pretty hard words. Looking at us, (the troops,) they would say, "Damn you." They kept the troops guarded. If a man would get up to leave his place, two or three Indians would follow him. Whether this was done by the Indians so as to have the best of the men, I don't know. They had their bows strung and their arrows in their hands. They also surrounded the cannon, quite a number of them. Lieutenant Hardin went to Black Kettle and got him to talk to them, (the Indians;) they dispersed. They then commenced saddling up their ponies and striking off, after setting fire to the grass to the windward of the camp. We then broke camp and went back about ten or fifteen miles, and camped for the night.

Question. How was your camp in which these things occurred arranged for defence? Describe it particularly.

Answer. We were camped in an elbow or bend of the creek. The creek encircled us on three sides, about two hundred yards from the centre of our camp. The camp was arranged very poorly for defence, I think, on account of the creek furnishing a very good ambuscade for the Indians.

Question. How was the ground on the other side of the creek that encircled your camp? Was it clear, or covered with brush; and how was it situated to conceal an enemy? Describe it particularly.

Answer. It was covered with a thick undergrowth, the banks being pretty high on both sides, sloping off gradually to the creek. It would be very favorable for concealment of an enemy.

Question. Were any orders given by Major Wynkoop to keep the Indians out of camp? If yea, were the troops able to enforce these orders in the position they occupied? State only what you know of your own knowledge.

Answer. I was sergeant of the guard that day, and did not receive any orders from any one—Major Wynkoop or the officer of the day—in relation to keeping the Indians out of camp.

Question. What occurred in the camp to which you moved after the consultation, and which you state was ten or fifteen miles distant, as regards the troops and Major Wynkoop in relation to the orders?

Answer. We remained there for two nights and one day. Some of the Indians that were with us left us in the afternoon of the first day. It aroused some excitement in the minds of the troops. There was strong talk among the troops of breaking camp and returning to Fort Lyon without orders from the officers. They (the men) sent for Major Wynkoop; they told him that they did not have the confidence in the Indians that he had. He talked to the men and explained to them what the Indians had promised, and the excitement died away, and they (the troops) concluded to wait for orders.

Question. Were there any other motives that prompted the men in telling Major Wynkoop that they would go back to Fort Lyon? If yes, state them particularly.

Answer. There was some talk that there was more whiskey aboard than was really necessary. Some said that they had full confidence in Major Wynkoop when sober, but that they did not like to trust themselves with him among the Indians when he had been drinking.

Question. When the Indians fell in rear of you, as you have stated, after Wynkoop's consultation with Black Kettle, how near did the Indians keep to Major Wynkoop's command, and did the Indians threaten the command? State particularly.

Answer. They kept within one hundred and fifty to two hundred yards of us; they kept up their war song continually. I do not know whether the Indians threatened the command or not.

Direct examination of B. N. Forbes by J. M. Chivington closed.

Cross-examination of B. N. Forbes by the commission:

Question. Are you still in the service? If not, when were you discharged, and where is your residence?

Answer. I was discharged the 30th of November, 1864; my residence has been in Denver most of the time since I have been discharged.

Question. Were any of Major Wynkoop's command killed, fired upon, or assaulted in any manner by the Indians?

Answer. There were none of the command fired upon, none killed, only assaulted by words.

Question. You say you do not understand the Indian language; then how do you know they assaulted with words?

Answer. Some of them spoke a little English, as I told you at the time; some of them used pretty hard words.

Question. Where were the chiefs of the Indians at the time the cannon was surrounded, and where were the officers of Major Wynkoop's command at that time?

Answer. The chiefs were in their council lodge, and the officers were mostly there, all but Lieutenant Hardin and Lieutenant Phillips; I believe Lieutenant Hardin was officer of the day.

Question. How deep was the creek upon which the command camped?

Answer. About belly deep to our horses, where we watered opposite to the camp.

Question. Did any of the Indians conceal themselves in the brush on the creek, to attack Major Wynkoop's command?

(J. M. Chivington most respectfully objects to the question, for the following reasons: That the cross-examination of the witness in regard to the new matter is improper, no questions being put on the examination in chief of the concealment of Indians anywhere; if the court wants such evidence, they can obtain it legally only by making the witness their own.

Objection sustained by the commission.)

Question. You say the troops while in camp manifested a spirit of mutiny in declaring they would disobey their officers, and return to Fort Lyon; was it anything more than idle talk?' Did any leave the camp? If so, how many and who were they?

Answer. There were none left the camp.

Question. You say the excitement died away after Major Wynkoop left the command; after that, was there any more talk of leaving camp, and did any one leave?

Answer. There was none left, and there was no talk that amounted to anything after that—only idle talk.

Question. How do you know that it was a war song the Indians kept up as they followed in rear of Major Wynkoop's command?

Answer. It was a song that I heard once before when engaged with the Indians.

Question. Were you present at the council between Major Wynkoop and the Indians?

Answer. No.

Cross-examination of B. N. Forbes, by the commission closed.

Re-examination of B. N. Forbes. No questions asked.

Commission adjourned until 2 p. m. this day.

*Two p. m.*—Commission met pursuant to adjournment. Present, all members and recorder.

PRESLEY TALBOT introduced by J. M. Chivington to give evidence. The oath being administered according to law, he (Talbot) testified as follows:

Question. What is your name? Were you in the third regiment Colorado cavalry? If yes, what position did you hold? And were you at the battle of Sand creek? If yes, state what occurred there. State particularly what you know of your own knowledge.

Answer. My name is Presley Talbot. I was in the third regiment Colorado cavalry, and held the position as captain of company M. I was at the battle of Sand creek; I was ordered to go into the fight by Colonel Chivington; ordered to cross Sand creek to the right side of the bank. There I received so very galling a fire from the Indians under the bank and from ditches dug out just above the bank that I ordered my company to advance, to prepare to dismount and fight on foot. At the command to fight on foot I was shot, with a ball about fifty to the pound, from the rifle of a chief known by the name of One-Eye. When shot—was shot in right side—dragged my right leg from horse, eased myself as well as I could, and fell; laid on right side; had a soldier to place blankets under right leg so as to ease pain from wound. Indians, twenty-five or thirty in number, (bucks) made charge, were repulsed, some of my men clubbing their guns on account of guns refusing to discharge, and forced Indians to seek shelter under the banks, and in holes dug out for concealment. Firing ceased for not more than five minutes; one Indian, which proved to be Big Head, who as a signal showed buffalo robe to the height of a person, as the means of drawing the fire from the soldiers, so that they would empty their guns, and then would give a whoop and rise *en masse* and fire arrows, shot muskets, and squirrel rifles. I commanded my troops to be guarded, hold their fire, and be very particular what they fired at, and to be sure it was an Indian. There was a lull in hostilities for a few minutes. The Indians *en masse*, at least thirty in number, made a charge, which was repulsed by eight of company M; being wounded, I was then taken from the field to the hospital lodge designated by the commander. I furthermore state that the Indians were hostile, and acted with desperation and bravery; that Colonel John M. Chivington, commanding, acted with discretion and bravery. Furthermore, that there were at least thirty Indians killed by company M, assisted by two men of the first regiment Colorado cavalry, within seventy-five feet of where the company fought.

Question. Did you, before or after the battle of Sand creek, have any conversation with Major Anthony, commanding Fort Lyon, Major Colley, Indian agent, or John Smith, Indian interpreter, in relation to the battle of Sand creek? If yes, state particularly what that conversation was.

Answer. I had a conversation before the battle of Sand creek, with Major Anthony, in company with Captain Soule, deceased, Lieutenant Richmond, of the third regiment. He (Anthony) expressed himself gratified that we had come to make an attack on the Indians; said that he would have attacked them before this time if he had had force enough at his command. Had several consultations with Major Colley, Indian agent, and John Smith, Indian interpreter; stated that they had considerable sympathy for me, being wounded; would give me all the attention and assistance in their power, but they would do anything to damn Colonel John M. Chivington, or Major Downing; that they had lost at least six thousand dollars each by the Sand creek fight; that they had one hundred and five robes and two white ponies bought at the time of attack, independent of the goods which they had on the battle-ground, which they never had recovered, but would make the general government pay for the same, and damn old Chivington eventually. Furthermore, John Smith had a bill made out against the government—showed me the same—for government indebtedness to him, sworn and subscribed to by one David Louderback, stating that he would go to Washington city and would present the same, and that he had friends who would help him get it. Smith and Colley both told me that they were equally interested in the trade with the Indians.

Question. Did you hear Major Colly, Indian agent, and John Smith, Indian interpreter, say that they would swear to anything to ruin Colonel Chivington? If so, state particularly what that conversation was.

I object to the question being asked the witness, for the reason that it is leading; has no reference to the matter of this investigation, and after the witness has given the conversation he had with these parties in reference to Sand creek and the Indians.

SAMUEL F. TAPPAN,
*Lieut. Col. Veteran Battalion First Colorado Cavalry,*
*President of Commission.*

Objection sustained by the commission.

Question. In the conversation you stated you had with Major Colley and John Smith, in which they stated they would do anything to damn Colonel Chivington, did they say they would do anything else?

I object to the question, for the reason that it has no reference to the subject-matter of this investigation, and after the witness has given the conversation of Major Colley and John Smith in reference to Sand creek and the Indians, and whatever threats (if any were made) these parties may have made against Colonel Chivington or any other person is not a proper subject of this investigation.

SAMUEL F. TAPPAN,
*President of Commission.*

John M. Chivington would most respectfully explain that Major Colley and John Smith having testified before the "Committee on the Conduct of the War," and as we are informed the evidence taken by this commission is to be considered by that committee, we consider it our right by this witness to show what these men, Colley and Smith, have threatened to do, that we may defend ourselves against the testimony of these men, and therefore we consider the testimony relevant and proper, and most respectfully insist that this commission allow the question to be put, and receive the evidence.

J. M. CHIVINGTON.

I have no information that the evidence taken by this commission is to go before the "Committe on the Conduct of the War," but, on the contrary, I understand that a committee of the two houses of Congress are now on their way to this Territory to investigate this affair of Sand creek, to present to the "Committee on the Conduct of the War."

This commission was ordered to investigate all matters relating to the Indians and Sand creek. Private threats and quarrels growing out of that or any other affair is not, in my opinion, a legitimate and proper matter of record by this commission.

SAMUEL F. TAPPAN,
*Lieut. Col. Veteran Battalion First Colorado Cavalry,*
*President of Commission .*

(Objection sustained by commission.)

Question. State any other conversation that you had with Major Colley and John Smith, if you remember any, pertaining to matters connected with Sand creek.

Answer. I heard a portion of a letter read in the adjoining room, in which I lay wounded, in which I recognized the voices of Smith, Colley, and Olmsted, the purport of which was denouncing Colonel Chivington and the Sand creek fight, addressed to the superintendent of Indian affairs, Washington city. I also heard Smith boastingly in my presence state that the eastern papers would be filled with letters from that post, (Fort Lyon,) denouncing the same, and that Colonel Chivington had murdered his boy, and that he would be avenged by using every effort with the department possible. Furthermore he said, with tears in his eyes, that he was a bad boy and deserved punishment, but it was hard for a father to endure it. He furthermore stated that he had tried to influence his boy to quit committing depredations. I asked him why he could not prevail on him to do so. He said that it was inherited, not from him, but from the Indian blood. I furthermore asked him why he did not deserve death. He stated that he did deserve death, and burst into a flood of tears. Colley and Smith stated to me in person that they would go to Washington and represent the Sand creek battle as nothing more than a massacre; and Smith said that he would realize twenty-five thousand dollars from his losses.

Commission adjourned until 9 a. m. to-morrow, May 12, 1865.

SIXTY-SECOND DAY.

MAY 12, 1865.

Commission met pursuant to adjournment. Present, all members and recorder.
Proceedings of yesterday read and approved.

Direct examination of Presley Talbot by J. M. Chivington continued :

Question. Have you stated all the conversation you had between Smith and Colley, pertaining to the Sand creek affair ?
Answer. I think I have.

John M. Chivington then, after the witness had in answer to the above question stated that he had related all the conversation which he heard between Colley and Smith in reference to Sand creek, and after he had given the conversation between himself and these men upon that subject, repeated by asking the question if the witness "had stated all the conversation he had with Colley and Smith pertaining to Colonel Chivington, as regards the Sand creek affair."

Ex. Doc. 26——14

Question ruled out by a majority of commission on the grounds that it was improper, the commission having decided that private threats and quarrels growing out of that (Sand creek) or any other matter was not a legitimate and proper matter of record by this commission, and that it was not proper to cumber the record with improper and irrelevant questions.

Question. You stated near the close of your examination that you wished to make some amendment or explanation. What was that amendment?

I object to the question, for the reason that the evidence given by the witness has been read to the witness, and he has stated that it was all correct.

SAMUEL F. TAPPAN,

*Lieut. Col. Veteran Battalion First Colorado Cavalry,*
*President of Commission.*

Commission rooms were cleared for discussion. Commission adjourned until 2 p. m. this day.

*Two p. m*—Commission met pursuant to adjournment. Present, all members and recorder.

The objection to the last question of J. M. Chivington sustained by the commission.

Direct examination of Presley Talbot by J. M. Chivington continued :

Question. Are you acquainted with David H. Louderback, private first cavalry of Colorado?

I object to the question because it is irrelevant to the subject-matter of this investigation, is leading, can be answered by a yes or no, and to ascertain the acquaintance of the witness is not the business of this commission.

SAM. F. TAPPAN,

*Lieut. Col. Veteran Battalion First Colorado Cavalry,*
*President of Commission.*

J. M. Chivington would most respectfully state, in explanation to the question proposed, that our object in asking it is to lay the foundation for impeaching Louderback, which we assert we can do ; and if the court will grant us what interpretation of the law tells us is our right, we will do it.

Room cleared for deliberation.

Commission adjourned until 9 a. m. to-morrow, May 13, 1865.

SIXTY-THIRD DAY.

MAY 13, 1865.

Commission met pursuant to adjournment. Present, all members and recorder.

The room was cleared for discussion. The question under discussion at adjournment yesterday resumed.

Commission adjourned until 2 p. m. this day.

*Two p. m.*—Commission met pursuant to adjournment. Present, all members and recorder.

Proceedings of yesterday read and approved.

The question of John M. Chivington, late colonel first cavalry of Colorado, was objected to on account of its irrelevancy to the subject-matter of this investigation, and to prevent the evidence from branching off into a variety of collateral issues perfectly immaterial to the matter this commission has been ordered to investigate.

After the question was objected to, J. M. Chivington stated the object of the question was, to lay the foundation for impeaching Louderback. The only way to impeach the credit of a witness by the testimony of others is—

400

First. By disproving the facts stated by him, by other testimony.
Second. By general evidence of reputation.
Third. By proof of self-contradiction.

If J. M. Chivington intends to impeach the credit of the said Louderback, by disproving his testimony by other evidence, showing a different state of facts than those given by Louderback, this can be done, if done at all, without reference to witness's personal acquaintance with Louderback, or to make any reference to him (Louderback) whatever, which makes the question asked by J. M. Chivington irrelevant and consequently improper.

If by general evidence of reputation, the examination in chief must be confined to the general reputation of Louderback; to adduce evidence as to that, not to particular facts, and not the witness's personal acquaintance with the said Louderback, but to his knowledge of the reputation only of the said Louderback: for these reasons the question as to the witness's personal acquaintance is immaterial, and for that reason improper.

If by proving self-contradiction—that the witness had made verbal statements outside differing from what he has testified to before this commission, J. M. Chivington having failed to prepare the way for its admission by cross-examining the witness (Louderback) as to the supposed contradictory statements, and giving him an opportunity of denying or explaining such statements, &c., it is now too late, and inadmissible as evidence. For these reasons the objection is sustained by the commission.

Commission adjourned until 9 a. m., Monday, May 15, 1865.

### SIXTY-FOURTH DAY.

MAY 15, 1865.

Commission met pursuant to adjournment. Present, all members and recorder.
Proceedings of yesterday read and approved.
Owing to absence of witness the commission adjourned until 2 p. m. this day.

*Two p. m.*—Commission met pursuant to adjournment. Present, all members and recorder.

Owing to absence of witness the commission adjourned until 9 a. m. to-morrow, May 16, 1865.

### SIXTY-FIFTH DAY.

MAY 16, 1865.

Commission met pursuant to adjournment. Present, all members and recorder.
Proceedings of yesterday read and approved.
Owing to the illness of Presley Talbot, a witness introduced by J. M. Chivington, his further examination is postponed.

HARRY RICHMOND introduced by J. M. Chivington to give evidence. The oath being administered according to law, he (Richmond) testified as follows:

By J. M. CHIVINGTON:

Question. What is your name? Have you been in the army? If so, state in what corps, and what position you occupied.
Answer. Name, Harry Richmond; position, second lieutenant company B, third Colorado cavalry.
Question. Were you on the expedition against the Indians, under command of Colonel John M. Chivington, which resulted in the battle of Sand creek, near Fort Lyon?
Answer. I was.
Question. Did you at any time before or after the battle of Sand creek have any conversation with Major Anthony, first cavalry of Colorado, commanding

401

Fort Lyon, in relation to the battle of Sand creek and the Indians? If yes, state the conversation particularly.

Answer. I met Major Anthony as the command was between Fort Lyon and the commissary building. On shaking hands with me, and in reply to "Where are the Indians?" asked by me, he said, "I am damned glad you have come; I have got them over here about twenty-five miles until I could send to Denver for assistance." This was before the battle of Sand creek. At another time he asserted that he should have attacked them himself if he had had sufficient force. That is about all the remarks I heard him make concerning the battle or the Indians, that I remember of. I never heard Anthony express himself except exultingly over the battle of Sand creek or the arrival of troops to give battle.

Direct examination of Harry Richmond by J. M. Chivington closed.

Cross-examination of Harry Richmond by the commission:

Question. Did Major Anthony, in his conversation with you, refer to the Indians on the Smoky Hill, or on Sand creek?

Answer. Without specially referring to either, I thought he meant both. The indication of his finger was the same direction as that we marched to go for the Sand creek Indians.

Question. In what direction did you march, to reach the Indians on Sand creek, from Fort Lyon?

Answer. I could not answer that question as regards the points of the compass. I should judge we marched in a line directly from the Arkansas river, our road forming a right angle with the river. It was dark when we left Fort Lyon.

Question. Where is your present residence?

Answer. Denver, Colorado Territory. Post office address, box 93.

Cross-examination of Harry Richmond by the commission closed.

Re-examination: No questions asked.

Commission adjourned until 2 p. m. this day.

*Two p. m.*—Commission met pursuant to adjournment. Present, all members and recorder.

SIMEON WHITELEY introduced by J. M. Chivington to give evidence. The oath being administered according to law, he (Whiteley) testified as follows:

### By J. M. CHIVINGTON:

Question. What is your name, residence, and do you hold any official position under the government of the United States? If yes, state what that official position is.

Answer. Simeon Whiteley; residence in this city. I at present hold the office of United States Indian agent of the Grand River and Uintah bands of Utah Indians.

Question. Were you at a council held at Camp Weld, near Denver, Colorado Territory, in September, 1864, between Governor Evans and chiefs of the Cheyenne and Arapahoe nations, and can you state what occurred there? If yes, please state it particularly, and who was present.

Answer. I was present at the council and acted as clerk at the time. I made a verbatim report of the proceedings there had, which I can give to this commission if desired. In this report referred to, I have the names of the prominent individuals present.

Question. Please state the report verbatim, and under what circumstances, and in what manner you took that report?

Answer. Governor Evans has been in the habit of having me make copies of

SAND CREEK MASSACRE.

the proceedings of all councils, when my other duties would permit. I made this report of the proceedings of the council at Camp Weld at his request. He (the governor) warned me before I commenced that upon the result of this council very likely depended a continuance of the Indian war on the plains, and it was important that the minutes should be full and complete. I frequently, while taking these notes, had to stop the interpreter as well as the governor, so that I could get every word down. I think I was successful in doing it.

The following is the report:

CAMP WELD, DENVER,
*Wednesday, September* 28, 1864.

Present—Governor John Evans; Colonel Chivington, commanding district of Colorado; Colonel George L. Shoup, third Colorado volunteer cavalry; Major E. Wynkoop, Colorado first; S. Whiteley, United States Indian agent; Black Kettle, leading Cheyenne chief; White Antelope, chief central Cheyenne band; Bull Bear, leader of Dog soldiers (Cheyenne;) Neva, sub Arapahoe chief, who was in Washington; Bosse, sub Arapahoe chief; Heaps-of-Buffalo, Arapahoe chief; No-ta-nee, Arapahoe chief; the Arapahoes are all relatives of Left Hand, chief of the Arapahoes, and are sent by him in his stead; John Smith, interpreter to Upper Arkansas agency; and many other citizens and officers.

His excellency Governor Evans asked the Indians what they had to say.

BLACK KETTLE then said: On sight of your circular of June 27, 1864, I took hold of the matter, and have now come to talk to you about it. I told Mr. Bent, who brought it, that I accepted it, but that it would take some time to get all my people together, many of my young men being absent; and I have done everything in my power since then to keep peace with the whites. As soon as I could get my people all together we held a council and got a half-breed who was with us to write a letter to inform Major Wynkoop, or other military officer nearest us, of our intention to comply with the terms of the circular. Major Wynkoop was kind enough to receive the letter, and visited us in camp, to whom we delivered four white prisoners—one other, Mrs. Snyder, having killed herself. There are two women and one child yet in our camp, whom we will deliver up as soon as we can get them in. These are their names: Laura Roper, aged sixteen or seventeen years; Ambrose Asher, aged seven or eight years; Daniel Marble, aged seven or eight years; Isabel Ubanks, aged four or five years. The prisoners still with us, are Mrs. Ubanks and babe, and a Mrs. Morton, who was taken on the Platte. Mrs. Snyder is the name of the woman who hung herself. The boys were taken between Fort Kearney and the Blue. I followed Major Wynkoop to Fort Lyon, and Major Wynkoop proposed that we come up to see you. We have come with our eyes shut, following his handful of men, like coming through the fire. All we ask is that we may have peace with the whites; we want to hold you by the hand. You are our father; we have been travelling through a cloud; the sky has been dark ever since the war began. These braves who are with me are all willing to do what I say. We want to take good tidings home to our people, that they may sleep in peace. I want you to give all the chiefs of the soldiers here to understand that we are for peace, and that we have made peace, that we may not be mistaken by them for enemies. I have not come here with a little wolf's bark, but have come to talk plain with you. We must live near the buffalo or starve. When we came here we came free, without any apprehension, to see you, and when I go home and tell my people that I have taken your hand and the hands of all the chiefs here in Denver, they will feel well, and so will all the different tribes of Indians on the plains, after we have eaten and drunk with them.

Governor EVANS replied: I am sorry you did not respond to my appeal at once; you have gone into an alliance with the Sioux, who were at war with

403

us; you have done a great deal of damage, have stolen stock, and now have possession of it. However much a few individuals may have tried to keep the peace, as a nation you have gone to war; while we have been spending thousands of dollars in opening farms for you, and making preparations to feed, protect, and make you comfortable, you have joined our enemies and gone to war. Hearing last fall that you were dissatisfied, the Great Father at Washington sent me out on the plains to talk with you and make it all right. I sent messengers out to tell you that I had presents and would make you a feast; but you sent word to me that you did not want anything to do with me, and to the Great Father at Washington that you could get along without him. Bull Bear wanted to come in to see me at the head of the Republican, but his people held a council and would not let him come.

BLACK KETTLE. That is true.

Governor EVANS, (resuming.) I was under the necessity, after all the trouble and expense I was at, of returning home without seeing them. Instead of this, your people went away and smoked the "war pipe" with our enemies.

BLACK KETTLE. I don't know who could have told you this.

Governor EVANS. No matter who said this, but your conduct has proved to my satisfaction that such was the case.

SEVERAL INDIANS. This is a mistake; we have made no alliance with the Sioux or any one else.

Governor EVANS explained that smoking the "war pipe" was a figurative term, but their conduct had been such as to show they had an understanding with other tribes.

SEVERAL INDIANS. We acknowledge that our actions have given you reason to believe this.

Governor EVANS. So far as making a treaty now is concerned, we are in no condition to do it; your young men are on the war path, my soldiers are preparing for the fight. You so far have had the advantage, but the time is near at hand when the plains will swarm with United States soldiers. I understand that these men who have come to see me now have been opposed to the war all the time, but that their people have controlled them, and they could not help themselves. Is this so?

ALL THE INDIANS. It has been so.

Governor EVANS. The fact that they have not been able to prevent their people from going to war in the past spring, when there was plenty of grass and game, makes me believe that they will not be able to make a peace which will last longer than until winter is past.

WHITE ANTELOPE. I will answer that, after a time.

Governor EVANS. The time when you can make war best is in the summer time; the time when I can make war best is in the winter. You so far have had the advantage; my time is fast coming. I have learned that you understand that as the whites are at war among themselves, you think you can now drive the whites from this country, but this reliance is false. The Great Father at Washington has men enough to drive all the Indians off the plains, and whip the rebels at the same time. Now, the war with the whites is nearly through, and the Great Father will not know what to do with all his soldiers, except to send them after the Indians on the plains. My proposition to the friendly Indians has gone out. I shall be glad to have them all come in under it. I have no new proposition to make. Another reason that I am not in condition to make a treaty is, that war is begun, and the power to make a treaty of peace has passed from me to the great war chief. My advice to you is to turn on the side of the government, and show by your acts that friendly disposition you profess to me. It is utterly out of the question for you to be at peace with us while living with our enemies and being on friendly terms with them.

404

Inquiry was made by one Indian, what was meant by being on the side of the government. Explanation being made, all gave assent, saying, "All right."

Governor EVANS. The only way you can show this friendship is by making some arrangement with the soldiers to help them.

BLACK KETTLE. We will return with Major Wynkoop to Fort Lyon; we will then proceed to our village and take back to my young men every word you say. I cannot answer for all of them, but think there will be but little difficulty in getting them to assent to help the soldiers.

Major WYNKOOP to Black Kettle. Did not the Dog soldiers agree, when I had my council with you, to do whatever you said, after you had been here?

BLACK KETTLE. Yes.

Governor EVANS explained that if the Indians did not keep with the United States soldiers, or have an arrangement with them, they would be all treated as enemies. You understand, if you are at peace with us, it is necessary to keep away from our enemies; but I hand you over to the military, one of the chiefs of whom is here to-day, and can speak for himself if he chooses.

WHITE ANTELOPE. I understand every word you have said, and will hold on to it. I will give you an answer directly. The Cheyennes, all of them, have their ears open this way, and they will hear what you say. I am proud to have seen the chief of all the whites in this country. I will tell my people. Ever since I went to Washington and received this medal, I have called all white men as my brothers, but other Indians have since been to Washington and got medals, and now the soldiers do not shake hands, but seek to kill me. What do you mean by us fighting your enemies? Who are they?

Governor EVANS. All Indians who are fighting us.

WHITE ANTELOPE. How can we be protected from the soldiers on the plains?

Governor EVANS. You must make that arrangement with the military chief.

WHITE ANTELOPE. I fear these new soldiers who have gone out may kill some of my people while I am here.

Governor EVANS. There is great danger of it.

WHITE ANTELOPE. When we sent our letter to Major Wynkoop, it was like going through a strong fire, or blast, for Major Wynkoop's men to come to our camp; it was the same for us to come to see you. We have our doubts whether the Indians south of the Arkansas, or those north of the Platte, will do as you say. A large number of Sioux have crossed the Platte in the vicinity of the Junction, into our country. When Major Wynkoop came, we proposed to make peace. He said he had no power to make peace, except to bring us here and return us safe.

Governor EVANS, again. Whatever peace you make must be with the soldiers, and not with me. Are the Apaches at war with the whites?

WHITE ANTELOPE. Yes; and the Comanches and Kiowas, as well; also a tribe of Indians from Texas whose name we do not know. There are thirteen different bands of Sioux who have crossed the Platte, and are in alliance with the others named.

Governor EVANS. How many warriors with the Apaches, Kiowas, and Comanches?

WHITE ANTELOPE. A good many; don't know.

Governor EVANS. How many of the Sioux?

WHITE ANTELOPE. Don't know, but many more than the southern tribes.

Governor EVANS. Who committed the depredations on the trains near the Junction, about the first of August?

WHITE ANTELOPE. Do not know; did not know any was committed; have taken you by the hand, and will tell the truth, keeping back nothing.

Governor EVANS. Who committed the murder of the Hunsgate family, on Burning creek?

405

NEVA. The Arapahoes, a party of the northern band who were passing north; it was Medicine Man, or Roman Nose, and three others.

Agent WHITELEY. That cannot be true; I am satisfied, from the time he left a certain camp for the north, that it was not this party of four persons.

Governor EVANS. Where is Roman Nose now?

NEVA. You ought to know better than me; you have been nearer to him.

Governor EVANS. Who killed a man and boy at the head of Cherry creek, four weeks ago?

NEVA (after consultation,) Kiowas and Comanches.

Governor EVANS. Who stole soldiers' horses and mules from Jimmie's camp, twenty-seven days ago?

NEVA. Fourteen Cheyennes and Arapahoes together.

Governor EVANS. What were their names?

NEVA. Powder-face and Whirlwind, who are now in our camp, were the leaders.

Colonel SHOUP. I counted twenty Indians on that occasion.

Governor EVANS. Who stole Charley Antobe's horses?

NEVA. Raven's son.

Governor EVANS. Who took the stock from Frémont's Orchard, and had the first battle with the soldiers this spring, north of there?

WHITE ANTELOPE. Before answering this question, I would like for you to know that this was the beginning of the war, and I should like to know what it was for—a soldier fired first.

Governor EVANS. The Indians had stolen about forty horses; the soldiers went to recover them, and the Indians fired a volley into their ranks.

WHITE ANTELOPE. This is all a mistake; they were coming down the Bijou, and found one horse and one mule. They returned one horse, before they got to Geary's, to a man; then went to Geary's, expecting to turn the other one over to some one. They then heard that the soldiers and the Indians were fighting somewhere down the Platte; they then took a fright, and all fled.

Governor EVANS. Who were the Indians who had the fight?

WHITE ANTELOPE. They were headed by Fool Badger's son, a young man, one of the greatest of the Cheyenne warriors, who was wounded, and, though still alive, he will never recover.

NEVA. I want to say something. It makes me feel bad to be talking about these things, and opening old sores.

Governor EVANS. Let him speak.

NEVA. Mr. Smith has known me ever since I was a child; has he ever known me commit depredations on the whites? I went to Washington last year, receiving good counsel; I hold on to it. I am determined always to keep peace with the whites. Now, when I shake hands with them they seem to pull away. I came here to seek peace, and nothing else.

Governor EVANS. We feel that you have, by your stealing and murdering, done us great damage. You come here and say you will tell us all, and that is what I am trying to get.

NEVA. The Comanches, Kiowas, and Sioux have done much more injury than we have. We will tell you what we know, but cannot answer for others.

Governor EVANS. I suppose you acknowledge the depredations on the Little Blue, as you have the prisoners there taken in your possession?

WHITE ANTELOPE. We (the Cheyennes) took two prisoners west of Fort Kearney, and destroyed the trains.

Governor EVANS. Who committed depredations at Cottonwood?

WHITE ANTELOPE. The Sioux; what band I do not know.

Governor EVANS. What are the Sioux going to do next?

BULL BEAR. Their intention is to clear out all this country. They are angry, and will do all the damage to the whites they can. I am with you and the troops to fight all those who have no ears to listen to what you say. Who are they? Show them to me—I am young. I have never harmed a white man. I am pushing for something good. I am always going to be friendly with the whites; they can do me good.

Governor EVANS. Where are those Sioux?

BULL BEAR. Down on the Republican, where it opens out.

Governor EVANS. Do you know that they intend to attack the trains this week?

BULL BEAR. Yes; about one-half of all the Missouri river Sioux and Yanktons who were driven from Minnesota are those who have crossed the Platte. I am young, and can fight. I have given my word to fight with the whites. My brother, Lean Bear, died in trying to keep peace with the whites. I am willing to die in the same way, and expect to do so.

NEVA. I know the value of the presents which we receive from Washington; we cannot live without them. That is why I try so hard to keep peace with the whites.

Governor EVANS. I cannot say anything about these things now.

NEVA. I can speak for all the Arapahoes under Left Hand. Raven has sent no one here to speak for him. Raven has fought whites.

Governor EVANS. Are there any whites among your people?

NEVA. There are none except Keith, who is now in the store at Fort Larned.

Colonel CHIVINGTON. I am not a big war chief, but all the soldiers in this country are at my command. My rule of fighting white men or Indians is, to fight them until they lay down their arms and submit to military authority. You are nearer Major Wynkoop than any one else, and you can go to him when you get ready to do that.

The council then adjourned.

Direct examination of Simeon Whiteley, United States Indian agent, by J. M. Chivington, closed.

Cross-examination of Simeon Whiteley, United States Indian agent, by the commission:

Question. You say that explanations were made as to what it was to be, on the side of the government, to which the Indians gave assent; state particularly what that explanation was.

Answer. I don't recollect the exact language that was used. If I should attempt to give the explanation, it would, probably, be mostly according to my own ideas, and not what was really said, or the words used. It is my recollection of what was said, that they must obey the requirements of the military officers, to render them such assistance as they could, by giving information, acting as scouts, &c. I don't know that any of those particular terms were used, but this is the general idea of the explanation.

Question. Was the assent of the Indians an expression of their willingness to comply with the terms proposed?

Answer. Yes.

Question. What reply did the Indians make to the remark of Colonel Shoup, that he counted twenty Indians in the attack on Jimmie's camp?

Answer. None.

Question. What reply did the Indians make to your remark in council, that they were mistaken as to who killed the Hunsgate family?

Answer. None whatever. I don't know whether they heard my remark. I do not recollect whether it was interpreted to them. I addressed it more particularly to Governor Evans. I knew it was a lie.

Question. State how you know it was a lie.

Answer. From my knowledge of the time when Medicine Man was in this part of the country, I know that he had not been in this section of the country since the preceding September.

Question. State particularly your knowledge of Medicine Man and Roman Nose, where they were at the time the Hunsgate family were killed.

Answer. About that time I received word from the camp of the northern band of Arapahoes that Roman Nose was dead. Subsequently I received word that Medicine Man was fighting the Snakes in Montana Territory, and was off on the war path, beyond Powder river, about the time of the murder of the Hunsgate family. After the council adjourned I told what I knew of Medicine Man's locality to Governor Evans and Colonel Chivington.

Question. Have you stated your only means of knowing that Medicine Man was absent and Roman Nose dead?

Answer. I can explain that in saying that I have, in addition to other duties, had charge of a portion of this northern band of Arapahoes; that I have sent and received messages from Medicine Man at various times since the 1st of July last. He is now reported to me as being near the Medicine Bow mountains. I have talked with a good many Indians of his band. Two weeks ago yesterday I had a council with Black Bear, one of his leading chiefs, who has just come in from the northern country, and I have not a shadow of doubt of the falsity of Neva's statement.

Cross-examination of Simeon Whiteley, United States Indian agent, by the commission, closed.

Re-examination of Simeon Whiteley, United States Indian agent, by J. M. Chivington:

Question. Who gave the Indians the explanations you have stated were given in regard to their being on the side of the government?

Answer. Governor Evans.

Re-examination of Simeon Whiteley, United States Indian agent, closed.

Commission adjourned until 9 a. m. to-morrow, May 17, 1865.

### SIXTY-SIXTH DAY.

MAY 17, 1865.

Commission met pursuant to adjournment. Present, all members and recorder.

On account of the non-appearance of the witnesses, the commission adjourned until 2 p. m. this day.

*Two p. m.*—Commission met pursuant to adjournment. Present, all members and recorder.

Proceedings of yesterday read and approved.

Owing to the non-appearance of witnesses, the commission adjourned until 9 a. m. to-morrow, May 18, 1865.

### SIXTY-SEVENTH DAY.

MAY 18, 1865.

Commission met pursuant to adjournment. Present, all members and recorder.

Proceedings of yesterday read and approved.

Direct examination of Presley Talbot by J. M. Chivington continued:

No question asked.

Cross-examination of Presley Talbot by the commission.

Question. Where is your residence?

Answer. Denver City, Colorado Territory.

Cross-examination of Presley Talbot by the commission closed.

Re-examination of Presley Talbot:

No questions asked.

# SAND CREEK MASSACRE.

*To the president and members of the military commission convened at Denver, Colorado Territory, in pursuance of Special Orders No, 23, headquarters district of Colorado, &c.:*

We would most respectfully request your honorable court to allow us to introduce Major Simeon Whiteley on new matter, to wit, to prove a conversation that he (Whiteley) had with Major Anthony, formerly first cavalry of Colorado, and commanding Fort Lyon, Colorado Territory, November 28, 1864, in relation to the hostility of the Indians killed at Sand creek. We wish to prove by Major Whiteley that Anthony stated to Whiteley that the Indians at Sand creek killed by Chivington were hostile; that he had fired on them repeatedly before the "battle of Sand creek;" that he entertained serious apprehensions for the safety of Fort Lyon on account of these Indians; and that he represented these facts to Colonel Chivington and urged him to attack and kill the Indians.

J. M. CHIVINGTON.

MAY 18, 1865.

This commission, in its investigation of the affairs of Sand creek, in order to ascertain all the facts and the exact relations existing between the Indians and the military authorities, have allowed evidence to be introduced as to statements made by Major Anthony while in command at Fort Lyon and in the public service as an officer. Therefore, in the opinion of this commission, evidence as to what Major Anthony may have said since leaving the public service and the country, in reference to the Indians and Sand creek, (and since this commission and a committee of Congress have been ordered to investigate the affair of Sand creek,) is merely accumulative, irrelevant, and improper; and for these reasons the request of J. M. Chivington cannot be complied with.

Commission adjourned until 2 p. m. this day.

*Two p. m.*—Commission met pursuant to adjournment. Present, a majority of the commission.

On account of the non-appearance of witnesses, the commission adjourned until 9 a. m. to-morrow, May 19, 1865.

## SIXTY-EIGHTH DAY.

MAY 19, 1865.

Commission met pursuant to adjournment. Present, all members and recorder. Proceedings of yesterday read and approved.

ALEXANDER F. SAFELY introduced by J. M. Chivington to give evidence. The oath being administered according to law, he (Safely) testified as follows:

Question. What is your name, and have you been a soldier? If yes, state how long, to what corps did you belong, and what position did you occupy in the army.

Answer. Alexander F. Safely; I have been a soldier three years and a half; belonged to first cavalry of Colorado; I was a private.

Question. Were you on the expedition made by Colonel Chivington and command, which resulted in the battle of Sand creek last November? If yes, what duty were you on during that expedition?

Answer. I was on the expedition with Colonel Chivington and command, which resulted in the battle of Sand creek, and acted as a scout during that campaign.

Question. Were you with Colonel Chivington on the 28th of November last, when he entered Fort Lyon? If yes, please state particularly who Colonel Chivington spoke with on the road into Fort Lyon from your camp, and how long Colonel Chivington halted at any time before he reached Fort Lyon.

Answer. I was with Colonel Chivington on the 28th of November last, and rode into Fort Lyon with him; he did not stop to talk with any one on the road, that I saw. He met Captain Soule's command about eight miles from Fort Lyon, and he spoke to the boys as he was riding by, saying, "How are you, boys?" That is the only time I heard him speak to anybody, unless those that were riding along with him.

Question. Did you see Captain Soule when he spoke to the boys; and did Colonel Chivington halt when he spoke to the boys?

Answer. Colonel Chivington did not halt; Captain Soule's command were watering their horses at the time Colonel Chivington rode by; he (Chivington) merely said "How are you, boys?"

Question. Did you hear any conversation between Colonel Chivington and Major Anthony, commanding Fort Lyon, in regard to Indians, either before or after the battle of Sand creek? If yes, state what that conversation was particularly.

Answer. I did hear a conversation between Colonel Chivington and Major Anthony, both before and after the battle of Sand creek; and it was in regard to Indians. Major Anthony stated to Colonel Chivington, in my presence, that when he took command of Fort Lyon, or shortly after that, he made a demand on the Indians to give up all their arms; he (Anthony) said that the Indians agreed to do so, and that instead of turning in arms that were of any use to the Indians, they turned in some boys' bows, and some double-barrelled shot-guns, and one Hawkins's rifle, which had no lock on it. He said that he considered that they were sincere about it, and gave them back their arms, and ordered them out of the post; that if they came back again he would open his artillery upon them. He said that they removed from there, and were then somewhere on Sand creek. He said that he was glad that we had come down there, as the Indians had sent him word that if he wanted to fight he could get as big a one as he wanted by coming out there to Sand creek. Indeed (he said) he was becoming alarmed that they would come in to the post and give him a fight. He said that he and every man he commanded would go with Colonel Chivington's command. That is about all I can think of that he said before the battle. The day after the battle I heard Major Anthony say that this would put a stop to the Indian war; that he considered that it was the biggest Indian fight that ever was recorded. I heard him ask Colonel Chivington's permission to proceed to Fort Lyon with the dead and wounded, and that he would overtake the command with the balance of the troops that had arrived there since we left. That is about all.

Question. Did you witness the commencement of the battle of Sand creek? If yes, please describe it particularly; who fired the first shot and how it commenced.

Answer. I witnessed the commencement of the battle of Sand creek, being the first man on the ground. Lieutenant Wilson brought his battalion on the left of the village, while company H, of the first cavalry of Colorado, came up in line directly in front on the right of the village, where I then was. While Lieutenant Wilson was coming up, I saw a man's horse running away with him, which I afterwards learned was George Pierce, of F company. His horse carried him through the lower end of the village, and suddenly I saw him and his horse fall together. Shortly afterwards I saw him (Pierce) get up on his feet and run a short distance, stopped and turned around, when I saw the smoke rise from an Indian gun, and also saw George Pierce drop. At that time Wilson's battalion commenced firing, and at the same time company H, of the first, commenced firing. Before company H had taken their position, there were three Indians who had left the village and advanced to meet us. There was a company of the third regiment directly behind company H, and these three Indians, who were firing bows and arrows, shot over company H and

410

took effect in the company of the third, directly behind company H. One of the Indians was killed right there. The next Indian that came out of the village from the side we were on was White Antelope. He came running directly towards company H; he had a pistol in his left hand, and a bow with some arrows in his right. He got within about fifty yards of the company; he commenced shooting his pistol, still in his left hand. There were a good many shots fired at him from off the horses, but the horses were jumping around so, that the men could hardly manage them, there being a company in rear firing. One of the men, who was considerably excited, asked " if no one could hit that Indian?" I told him if he would hold my horse, I would try and see if I could not get him. He did so; I got off and fired at the Indian, the ball taking effect in the groin. He turned then and ran back towards the village, and Billy Henderson, of H company, shot the Indian through the head when he was about the middle of the creek. That was the commencement of the fight, as near as I can recollect.

Question. Did you at any time see any white flag in the village of the Indians, or held by any of the Indians near the village?

Answer. I did not.

Question. Was your position such that you would have seen a white flag, if any had been exhibited by the Indians?—you have stated that you was the first man on the ground.

Answer. It was.

Question. Did you hear, at any time, a conversation between Major Colley, Indian agent, and Colonel Chivington in regard to the Indians?

Answer. Before the battle I did not know Major Colley by sight, and cannot think of anything he said and be positive about it.

Direct examination of Alexander F. Safely by J. M. Chivington closed.

Cross-examination of Alexander F Safely by the commission:

Question. When Major Anthony referred to certain Indians as sending him word " to come out and fight, or they would attack him in the post," did he refer to the Sioux on the Smoky Hill, or the Cheyennes on Sand creek?

Answer. He referred to the Cheyennes and Arapahoes on Sand creek.

Question. Did you hear Colonel Chivington tell Major Anthony that the hostile Indians had moved south from the Platte and were to attack Fort Lyon?

Answer. No.

Question. What are your means of knowledge that Major Anthony referred to the Cheyennes and Arapahoes instead of the Sioux?

Answer. Because I heard him say, in the course of the conversation, they were Cheyennes and Arapahoes.

Question. In the conversation between Major Anthony and Colonel Chivington, what did Colonel Chivington say in reference to the Indians?

Answer. He did not have much to say about it. He said that he would start for them that night and march all night. Major Anthony did pretty much all the talking.

Question. What portion of Colonel Chivington's command was the first to reach the Indian camp on Sand creek?

Answer. Lieutenant Wilson's battalion on the left, and company H of the first regiment came up on the right of the village. About the same time a company of the third regiment came up in rear of company H—immediately afterwards.

Question. How long after you saw the horse running towards the Indian village did Lieutenant Wilson's command reach his position to the right of the village?

Answer. He reached his position at the end of the village about the time

411

Pierce was shot. It was about a moment difference of time from the time Pierce was shot to the time Lieutenant Wilson opened fire.

Question. From what portion of the column did this horse start?

Answer. I could not say; when I saw him he was at full speed and ahead of the column.

Question. You say that White Antelope came out of the Indian village and attacked company H. How do you know it was White Antelope?

Answer. Because I have seen him before. I know him by sight.

Question. How far from the Indian village was company H when you fired at White Antelope?

Answer. About one hundred yards.

Question. Was White Antelope between company H and the village, and was he alone?

Answer. He was between company H and the village, and he was alone.

Question. You say your position was such as to enable you to see all that transpired in the Indian village. How large a tract of ground did the village cover?

Answer. I do not know exactly. It was about a quarter of a mile long, I should judge.

Cross-examination of Alexander F. Safely by the commission closed.

Re-examination of Alexander F. Safely. No questions asked.

Commission adjourned until 2 p. m. this day.

*Two p. m.*—Commission met pursuant to adjournment. Present, a majority of the commission.

The witnesses summoned not having arrived, the commission adjourned until 9 a. m. to-morrow, May 20, 1865.

SIXTY-NINTH DAY.

MAY 20, 1865.

Commission met pursuant to adjournment. Present, all members and recorder.

Proceedings of yesterday read, amended as follows, and approved :

On page 816, answer to first question, insert " I saw Captain Soule at the time."

Witnesses not having reported, commission adjourned until 2 p. m. this day.

*Two. p. m.*—Commission met pursuant to adjournment. Present, a majority of the commission.

Witnesses not having reported, commission adjourned until 9 a. m. Monday, May 22, 1865.

SEVENTIETH DAY.

MAY 22, 1865.

Commission met pursuant to adjournment. Present, a majority of the commission.

Witnesses not having reported, commission adjourned until 2 p. m. this day.

*Two p. m.*—Commission met pursuant to adjournment. Present, a majority of the commission.

The witnesses not having reported, commission adjourned until 9 a. m. to-morrow, May 23, 1865.

SEVENTY-FIRST DAY.

MAY 23, 1865.

Commission met pursuant to adjournment. Present, a majority of the commission.

Proceedings of yesterday read and approved.

Witnesses not having reported, commission adjourned until 2 p. m. this day.

*Two p. m.*—Commission met pursuant to adjournment. Present, all members and recorder.

T. P. BELL introduced by J. M. Chivington to give evidence.

The oath being administered according to law, he (Bell) testified as follows :

Question. What is your full name, where do you reside, and were you at the battle of Sand creek, fought November 29, 1864.

Answer. Thaddeus P. Bell ; reside in Lake Gulch, Gilpin county, Colorado Territory ; post office address, Central City, Colorado Territory. I was at the battle of Sand creek, fought November 29, 1864.

Question. Did you see any white scalps in the Indian village at Sand creek ? If yes, please describe them particularly.

Answer. I saw a good many white scalps there. The number, I have not any idea how many. There were some that looked old, as if they might have been taken a considerable time ; others not so long, and one that was quite fresh, not over from five to eight days old at furthest. I did not notice them particularly enough at the time to give a more minute description. The fresh scalp was from a red haired man.

Direct examination of Thaddeus P. Bell by J. M. Chivington closed.

Cross-examination of Thaddeus P. Bell by commission :

Question. Was there a soldier of Colonel Chivington's command killed and scalped by the Indians at the commencement of the fight at Sand creek ?

Answer. I cannot say whether he was scalped or not, but there was one killed. The first man I saw killed was one of Colonel Chivington's command. There was one man scalped, but that was later in the day.

Question. Was not the fresh scalp you saw taken on the day of the fight by the Indians ?

Answer. It was not.

Question. State how you know it was not.

Answer. I saw the scalp before the fight had been going on any length of time ; before there had been any wounded or dead brought in off the field, and at a place where there had been none either wounded or killed on either side ; and further, by the appearance of the scalp itself. It was lying in or near the door of one of the Indian lodges ; it looked like it might have been recently dropped there.

Question. What was done with this scalp?

Answer. I do not know what was done with it.

Question. Have you seen any of the scalps you saw at Sand creek since?

Answer. I have not seen any of the white scalps except one; I saw one since.

Question. Where did you see it, and in whose possession was it?

Answer. I saw it between where we leave the Arkansas river and cross to the Fountain-qui-bouit. It was in possession of a man whose name I believe is Rhoades, one of the third regiment.

Question. How long after the fight commenced did you see these scalps you speak of?

Answer. I suppose the fight had been going on probably an hour; it might have been more or it might have been less.

Question. State particularly from what you determine the age of a scalp.

Answer. If the scalp had been taken that day the capillary vessels would have yet been bleeding, which they were not, but the scalp was yet soft and green.

Cross-examination of Thaddeus P. Bell by the commission closed.

Re-examination of Dr. Thaddeus P. Bell. No questions asked.

Commission adjourned until 9 a. m. to-morrow, May 24, 1865.

413

MAY 24, 1865.

Commission met pursuant to adjournment. Present, all members and recorder. Proceedings of yesterday read and approved.

JAY J. JOHNSON introduced by J. M. Chivington to give evidence. The oath being administered according to law, he (Johnson) testified as follows:

Question. What is your full name; have you been in the United States military service? If yes. state how long, and what position you occupied. Where do you now reside?

Answer. Jay J. Johnson; I have been in the United States military service from the 10th of September, 1861, to the 28th day of December, 1864; I was an enlisted man up to the 16th of August, 1864; I acted as adjutant third Colorado cavalry from that time to the 28th of September, 1864, I think, when I was mustered in as captain of company E of same regiment, and served as captain until mustered out.

Question. Was you with Colonel Chivington's command when he (Chivington) made an expedition against the Indians, which resulted in the battle of Sand creek, November 29, 1864? If yes, what position did you occupy, and what duty was assigned for your performance before and after the battle?

Answer. I was with the command from the time that Colonel Chivington came up to Boonville until it returned to Denver, and acted as provost marshal of the expedition during that time. I reside in Central City, Gilpin county, Colorado Territory.

Question. What orders did you receive as provost marshal, in relation to captured property, from Colonel Chivington, commanding? Please state particularly.

Answer. My orders from Colonel Chivington, at the time I received the appointment, were to take charge of all captured property, and see that it was turned over to the quartermaster.

Question. Did you receive any other orders from Colonel Chivington in regard to captured property, at any other time? State particularly the orders, times, and places.

Answer. I did receive other orders the night before Colonel Chivington left the command on the Arkansas. He then ordered me, "when I got to Fort Lyon, to take my company and take charge of the stock captured from the Indians there, and drive it to Denver and turn it in to the assistant quartermaster."

Direct examination of Jay J. Johnson, late captain third Colorado cavalry, by J. M. Chivington closed.

Cross-examination of Jay J. Johnson, late captain, &c., by the commission:

Question. Did you obey the order of Colonel Chivington by turning over the captured property to the quartermaster?

(John M. Chivington most respectfully objects to the question, for the following reasons: That the question relates to new matter, and that it is therefore irregular and improper. We have examined the witness only in relation to what orders Colonel Chivington gave him—not what he did in the performance of his duty as provost marshal. We simply have asked what he was told to do by Colonel Chivington when acting officially. That it is not competent for the court to ask the witness questions which will criminate him if answered in the affirmative, and if answered in the negative will relate to new matter not called out by the defendant, Chivington, in the examination in chief of the witness.

Objection sustained by the commission.)

Question. Did you ever report to Colonel Chivington how you had executed his order in reference to the captured stock?

(J. M. Chivington objects to the question, for the same reasons expressed in the last objection filed by him.

Objection sustained by the commission.)

Question. Did you receive a verbal or written order from Colonel Chivington in reference to the captured stock?

Answer. The first order I refer to was a verbal order. I was regularly detailed as provost marshal from district headquarters, in the field; but my instructions at that time were verbal. My instructions from Colonel Chivington the night before he left the command on the Arkansas were verbal; but just before I got into the post of Fort Lyon I received the same instructions, written, from the Adjutant General.

Question. Were those instructions, in writing, in reference to the taking and disposition you should make of the captured stock?

Answer. The instructions in writing were the same as the verbal instructions from Colonel Chivington.

Cross-examination of Jay J. Johnson by the commission closed.

Re-examination of Jay J. Johnson, late captain, &c.:
No questions asked.

Commission adjourned until 2 p. m. this day.

*Two p. m.*—Commission met pursuant to adjournment. Present, all members and recorder.

W. H. VALENTINE introduced by J. M. Chivington to give evidence. The oath being administered according to law, he (Valentine) testified as follows:

Question. What is your full name? Where do you reside? Have you been a soldier? If yes, how long; in what corps did you serve; what position did you occupy in the military service of the United States, and where have you been stationed?

Answer. William H. Valentine; reside in Denver at present. I have been a soldier two years and six months; served in the first cavalry of Colorado; position, veterinary surgeon; have been stationed at Fort Lyon, on the Arkansas.

Question. Were you at Fort Lyon on or about October last, when Major Wynkoop returned from Denver with the Indians Black Kettle, &c.? If yes, did you have any conversation with any of them or hear any of them talk after Major Wynkoop returned from Denver? Please state such conversation, if you had any.

Answer. I was at Fort Lyon when Major Wynkoop returned from Denver with Black Kettle and other Indians. All the conversation I had at that time was with Left Hand. He was the only one I could talk with. I pointed out two or three Indians that stood on the parade-ground, and asked him if those were the ones that killed the soldier and blacksmith beyond Spring Bottom. He said, "they are the Indians."

Question. Did you ever hear the Indians that you pointed out to Left Hand say anything about the killing of the blacksmith and soldiers? State particularly.

Answer. I never heard those Indians say anything about it in language that I could understand. They told me in signs and motions. I made a motion to them if they were the Indians that killed the soldiers and the blacksmith; they gave me to understand, by motions, that they were.

Question. Did the Indians have government stock in their possession at this time? State particularly.

Answer. They had eight head of mules; the soldiers that were killed had them formerly—four in a wagon and four in an ambulance.

Question. How did you know that they belonged to the government; who

Ex. Doc. 26——15

was in command of the post at this time, and did the commanding officer of the post at this time attempt to take, or did he at any time take these mules from the Indians.?

Answer. I know four of the mules were sent from the quartermaster's corral to Denver with an officer; I forget who it was. Major Wynkoop was in command of the post at this time. I don't think he did take or attempt to take these mules himself from the Indians.

Question. Who succeeded Major Wynkoop in command of Fort Lyon, and how did the guard, while he was in command of Fort Lyon, treat the Indians? State what you saw.

Answer. Major Anthony succeeded Major Wynkoop in command of Fort Lyon. While Major Anthony was in command I saw one of the guard fire on the Indians.

Question. What were the Indians trying to do when the guard fired on them; and what reason did the guard give for firing on them?

Answer. They were trying to come into the post. The guard gave as their reason for firing on them that they were ordered to do so by Major Anthony.

Question. Where was Major Anthony when the guard fired upon the Indians, as you have stated?

Answer. I think that he was in front of his own office, or near there.

Question. What remark did he, Major Anthony, make in regard to the guard firing upon the Indians?

Answer. I don't know as he made any just at that time. Some few hours afterwards he was laughing at the idea of seeing the Indians run. He said that they had annoyed him enough, and that was the only way to get rid of them, or words to that effect.

Direct examination of W. H. Valentine by J. M. Chivington closed.

Cross-examination of W. H. Valentine by the commission:

Question. Are you familiar with the signs and motions used by Indians in conversation?

Answer. I understand some of it.

Question. Are you sure the Indians you accused of killing the soldiers understood your signs and motions?

Answer. I was pretty sure they did. That was what brought the conversation and motions about. They were in my office at the time, and I drove them out.

Question. Of what tribe were these Indians you speak of?

Answer. John Smith, Indian interpreter, said that they were Arapahoes and Cheyennes.

Question. Were the mules you speak of brought into the post by the Indians?

Answer. Yes, they were. They were on the opposite side of the river from the post—eight head of them—and were annoying us all the time. It was an impossible thing to keep them out of the quartermaster's herd. There was an order issued by Wynkoop not to meddle with those mules until after the difficulty with the Indians was settled.

Question. Did the Indians take the mules away from the post when they left?

Answer. No; five of them were turned over to Major Anthony, by the Indians.

Question. Were not the guard instructed to discharge their pieces, and give the alarm of Indians, when seen to approach the post?

Answer. Their orders were to fire either over or at them, or close to them, to frighten them. They were to shoot in the direction of the Indians, to drive them out of the post.

416

Question. Did the guard fire upon all Indians who approched the post after Major Anthony took command ?

Answer. Only this one time that I ever saw the guard fired on the Indians.

Question. Did the guard kill or wound any of the Indians they fired upon ?

Answer. Not any.

Question. Did you see any Indians in the post after you saw the guard fire upon them ?

Answer. I saw Left Hand afterwards. He was the only one I saw for about ten days, I think.

Question. Could Left Hand talk to you in English ?

Answer. Yes.

Question. Did Major Anthony, after the Indians had left the post, meet them in council, or have any talk with them, outside the post ?

(John M. Chivington most respectfully objects to the question, for the following reasons : That the question is calling out new matter, which cannot be done in a cross-examination. We have not inquired in regard to any council that Major Anthony might have had with them—only what the guard did when Major Anthony was in command of the post.

Objection sustained by the commission.)

Cross-examination of W. H. Valentine by the commission closed.

Re-examination of W. H. Valentine : No questions asked.

Commission adjourned until 9 a. m. to-morrow, May 25, 1865.

SEVENTY-THIRD DAY.

MAY 25, 1865.

Committee met pursuant to adjournment. Present, a majority of the commission.

Proceedings of yesterday read and approved.

J. M. Chivington gave notice that he did not wish to introduce any more witnesses on the defence.

Therefore the defence is hereby closed.

Captain E. A. Jacobs, acting as president of the commission. announced that the commission stood adjourned until 9 a. m. Saturday, May 27, 1865. No vote taken. Which action I respectfully protest against.

GEORGE H STILWELL,
*Captain Company F, Veteran Battalion,*
*First Colorado Cavalry, Recorder.*

DENVER, *May* 25, 1865.

I was absent this morning on the reading of the journal, and find that a majority of the commission having assembled, read and approved of the journal of yesterday, and adjourned until Saturday, 9 o'clock. I have caused the journal to be read to me by the clerk, find it correct, and therefore add my approval to the same, and also to the adjournment until Saturday morning, 9 o'clock.

SAMUEL F. TAPPAN,
*Lieut. Col. Veteran Battalion First Colorado Cavalry,*
*President of the Commission.*

SEVENTY-FOURTH DAY.

MAY 27, 1865.

Commission met pursuant to adjournment. Present, a majority of the commission.

Recorder being absent, commission adjourned until 2 p. m. this day.

*Two p. m.*—Commission met pursuant to adjournment. Present, a majority of the commission.

Commission adjourned until 9 a. m. Monday, May 29, 1865.

417

SAND CREEK MASSACRE.

SEVENTY-FIFTH DAY.
MAY 29, 1865.

Commission met pursuant to adjournment. Present, all members and recorder.
Proceedings of Saturday, May 27, 1865, read and approved.

I move that a careful synopsis of the evidence, as taken by the commission, be made in an index form, or what may more properly be called an index, giving all the facts as testified to by the witnesses, the pages upon which they can be found, and appended to these proceedings.

SAMUEL F. TAPPAN,
*Lieut. Col. Veteran Battalion First Colorado Cavalry.*

The motion was not sustained by a majority of the commission.
Commission adjourned until 2 p. m. this day.

*Two p. m.*—Commission met pursuant to adjournment. Present, all members and recorder.

To enable the recorder to complete certain papers the commission adjourn until 9 a. m. to-morrow, May 30, 1865; J. M. Chivington having been notified that no more evidence would be received or introduced by this commission.

SEVENTY-SIXTH DAY.
MAY 30, 1865.

Commission met pursuant to adjournment. Present, all members and recorder.
Proceedings of yesterday read and approved.

The journal of Saturday, May 27th, instant, amended so as to read " that the journal of the 25th instant was read and approved."

The recorder was instructed by the commission to examine the record, to carefully unite it by a tape, and seal it in such a manner as to keep it together, and certify to its being properly arranged, previous to its being signed by the commission.

" I certify that I have, in compliance with the foregoing order, carefully examined the record, and to the best of my knowledge it is properly arranged.

"GEORGE H. STILWELL,
" *Captain Veteran Battalion, First Colorado Cavalry, Recorder.*"

SAMUEL F. TAPPAN,
*Lieut. Colonel Veteran Battalion First Colorado Cavalry,
President Military Commission.*

E. A. JACOBS,
*Captain Vet an Battalion First Colorado Cavalry.
Member Military Commission.*

GEORGE H. STILWELL,
*Captain Veteran Battalion First Colorado Cavalry,
Recorder Military Commission.*

The commission, having no further business before it, adjourned *sine die.*

SAMUEL F. TAPPAN,
*Lieut. Colonel Veteran Battalion First Colorado Cavalry,
President of the Commission.*

GEORGE H. STILWELL,
*Captain Veteran Battalion First Colorado Cavalry,
Recorder of the Commission.*

ADJUTANT GENERAL'S OFFICE,
*Washington, February 12, 1867.*

Official copy :

E. D. TOWNSEND,
*Assistant Adjutant General.*

418